THE LOEB CLASSICAL LIBRARY

FOUNDED BY JAMES LOEB

EDITED BY

G. P. GOOLD

JOSEPHUS

LCL 490

JOSEPHUS

JEWISH ANTIQUITIES
BOOKS IV–VI

WITH AN ENGLISH TRANSLATION BY

H. ST. J. THACKERAY
AND RALPH MARCUS

HARVARD UNIVERSITY PRESS
CAMBRIDGE, MASSACHUSETTS
LONDON, ENGLAND

Book IV first published 1930; Books V–VI, 1934
Reprinted seven times
Jewish Antiquities bound in nine volumes beginning 1998

LOEB CLASSICAL LIBRARY® is a registered trademark
of the President and Fellows of Harvard College

ISBN 0-674-99539-2

Printed in Great Britain by St Edmundsbury Press Ltd,
Bury St Edmunds, Suffolk, on acid-free paper.
Bound by Hunter & Foulis Ltd, Edinburgh, Scotland.

CONTENTS

PREFACE

WHEN Dr. Thackeray died early in the summer of 1930, he had sent to press the text and translation of *Antiquities* Book V. and a portion of Book VI. (to § 140, with explanatory notes extending to § 60). The present writer has slightly revised this part, and has supplied a text and annotated translation of the rest of Book VI. and of Books VII. and VIII. No one realizes more fully than the writer himself how difficult it is to come up to the standard of excellence set by Dr. Thackeray in his skilful translation of the works of Josephus included in the earlier volumes of this series. An attempt has been made to adhere to the spirit of his rendering, but some changes in style have been made, chiefly in the direction of a less formal and a more modern idiom. In undertaking to continue the edition the writer has greatly profited by being able to consult a roughly drafted translation of Books VI.– VIII., of which Dr. Thackeray's widow has been kind enough to make a fair copy, and by having before him several notebooks containing Dr. Thackeray's studies of Josephus's style, his use of Greek authors and other useful material, which Mrs. Thackeray has generously placed at his disposal. The writer has also had the great advantage of using the MS. of Dr. Thackeray's *Index Verborum*, on the basis of which he was preparing his Greek Lexicon to

PREFACE

Josephus, published under the auspices of the Kohut Foundation of the Jewish Institute of Religion. The first fascicle of this Lexicon appeared some time after Dr. Thackeray's death, and a second fascicle, completed by the writer, is expected to appear shortly.

Beside the earlier versions of the *Antiquities* made by Hudson, Weill and Whiston-Shilleto, two recent works have been consulted in preparing the latter part of this volume; these are *Agada und Exegese bei Flavius Josephus* by Salomo Rappaport, Vienna, 1930, and *Legends of the Jews* by Louis Ginzberg (six volumes), Philadelphia, 1909–1928 (abbr. Ginzberg in the footnotes); the latter is an invaluable collection of rabbinic material illustrating the amplification of scriptural narratives and furnishing many instructive parallels to Josephus's treatment of his biblical text. The writer has, in addition, independently examined the text of the Targum (the Aramaic translation of the Bible, used in the early synagogue) and the mediaeval Hebrew commentaries reprinted in the Rabbinic Bible. For the identification of many of the Biblical place-names the writer is indebted to the researches of Professor W. F. Albright and other scholars, whose results have appeared in the *Bulletin of the American Schools of Oriental Research*.

With regard to the Greek text, the writer, like Dr. Thackeray, has attempted to furnish a critical edition on the basis of the apparatus in Niese's *editio maior*, not (as some reviewers of the earlier volumes by Dr. Thackeray have described it) an edition based solely on Niese's text. Whether the text here given is as satisfactory as the excellent

PREFACE

ones furnished by Niese and by Naber in the Teubner series must be left to the critics to decide. The problems of Josephus's text in these books are very complex, partly because of the twofold MS. tradition, partly because of the use made by the author of a Greek version of Scripture, and the corrections made by Christian copyists in the interest of conformity to the biblical text known to them, and partly because of the apparent revisions made by Josephus's Greek assistants. These difficulties are illustrated by the inconsistent spelling of biblical names of persons and places in the same MS. and the variants in the two families of MSS. No editor may reasonably hope to have established, in every case, the forms used by Josephus himself.

The writer has been similarly inconsistent in his rendering of these biblical names. The most commonly known names, such as Hebron, Absalom, etc., are given in the form familiar to English readers, whether or not they accurately reproduce the Greek spelling of Josephus's text; where the name is not quite so well known and where the Greek form differs only slightly from that found in the Authorized Version of Scripture, it is rendered approximately, *e.g.* Abisai (for Abisaios ; bibl. Abishai), Achab (for Achabos ; bibl. Ahab) ; in all other cases the hellenized form is simply transliterated, *e.g.* Jebosthos (bibl. Ish-bosheth), Adrazaros (bibl. Hadadezer).

For a discussion of Josephus's use of the Hebrew original of Scripture and of the Greek version known as the Septuagint (abbr. LXX in the footnotes), the reader may consult Dr. Thackeray's *Josephus, the Man and the Historian* (Stroock Lectures at the Jewish Institute of Religion), N.Y., 1929, Lecture IV. It

PREFACE

will be seen from the discussion there and from the explanatory notes in this volume that Josephus's text often agrees with that group of LXX MSS. which represent the so-called Lucianic recension (abbr. Luc. in the footnotes), made at the end of the third century A.D. It is, therefore, evident that this recension is based on a text which existed as early as the time of Josephus. To Dr. Thackeray's comments on Josephus's agreement with the Targum in certain passages against the Hebrew and Greek texts of Scripture, and to the examples of such agreement adduced by Mez (*Die Bibel des Josephus*) and Rappaport, the present writer has added in the footnotes what he ventures to believe are new instances of Josephus's use of an Aramaic translation of Scripture practically identical with the traditional Targum of Jonathan, which has usually been supposed to date from a period almost a century later than Josephus.

R. M.

JEWISH ANTIQUITIES

ΒΙΒΛΙΟΝ Δ

(i. 1.) Ἑβραίους δ' ὁ κατὰ τὴν ἐρημίαν βίος
ἀηδὴς καὶ χαλεπὸς ὢν ἐπόνει[1] καὶ κωλύοντος τοῦ
θεοῦ τῶν Χαναναίων πεῖραν λαμβάνειν· οὐ γὰρ
ἠξίουν τοῖς Μωυσέος πειθαρχοῦντες λόγοις ἠρεμεῖν,
ἀλλὰ καὶ δίχα τῆς παρ' ἐκείνου προθυμίας κρατήσειν αὐτοὶ τῶν πολεμίων νομίζοντες κατηγόρουν
μὲν αὐτοῦ καὶ πραγματεύεσθαι μένειν αὐτοὺς
ἀπόρους ὑπενόουν, ἵν' ἀεὶ τῆς ἐξ αὐτοῦ βοηθείας
2 δέωνται, πολεμεῖν δὲ τοῖς Χαναναίοις ὡρμήκεσαν
λέγοντες τὸν θεὸν οὐχὶ Μωυσεῖ χαριζόμενον
ἐπικουρεῖν αὐτοῖς, ἀλλὰ καὶ κοινῇ κηδόμενον
αὐτῶν τοῦ ἔθνους διὰ τοὺς προγόνους ὧν ἐπ-
ετρόπευσε καὶ διὰ τὴν αὐτῶν ἀρετὴν πρότερόν
τε παρασχεῖν τὴν ἐλευθερίαν καὶ νῦν βουλομένοις
3 πονεῖν ἀεὶ παρέσεσθαι σύμμαχον· εἶναί τε καὶ
καθ' αὐτοὺς ἱκανοὶ κρατεῖν τῶν ἐθνῶν ἔφασκον,
κἂν ἀπαλλοτριοῦν αὐτῶν Μωυσῆς ἐθελήσῃ τὸν
θεόν· ὅλως τε συμφέρειν αὐτοῖς τὸ αὐτοκράτορσιν
εἶναι, καὶ μὴ χαίροντας ἐπὶ τῷ τῆς παρ' Αἰγυπτίων
ἐξελθεῖν ὕβρεως Μωυσῆν τύραννον ἀνέχεσθαι καὶ
ζῆν πρὸς τὴν τούτου βούλησιν ἐξαπατωμένους,
4 ὅτι μόνῳ τὸ θεῖον αὐτῷ προδηλοῖ περὶ τῶν ἡμε-

---

[1] ἐπίεξε PLS[2]: ἐποίει Ernesti.

2

BOOK IV

(i. 1) The Hebrews, however, found life in the The Hebrews decide to fight the Canaanites in defiance of Moses. Numb. xiv. 40. desert so unpleasant and hard that it drove them, notwithstanding the prohibition of God, to make an assault on the Canaanites. For they refused to remain inactive in obedience to the words of Moses, and, imagining that even without his support they could by themselves defeat their enemies, they proceeded to accuse and suspect him of scheming to keep them without resources, in order that they might always stand in need of his aid. They were accordingly bent on war with the Canaanites, declaring that it was from no favour for Moses that God succoured them, but because in general He had a care for their race out of regard for their ancestors whom He had taken under His protection. It was thanks to them and to their own valour that He had in the past given them their liberty, and now, would they but exert themselves, He would be ever at their side as their ally. They further asserted that they were strong enough by themselves to defeat these nations, even should Moses desire to alienate God from them. Besides, it was wholly to their advantage to be their own masters, and not, while rejoicing in their deliverance from Egyptian insolence, to tolerate a tyrant in Moses and to live in accordance with his will—" deluded into believing that to him alone does

3

τέρων κατὰ τὴν πρὸς αὐτὸν εὔνοιαν, ὡς οὐχ ἁπάντων ἐκ τῆς Ἀβράμου γενεᾶς ὄντων, ἀλλ᾽ αἴτιον
ἕνα τοῦτον[1] τοῦ θεοῦ παρεσχηκότος εἰς τὸ πάντ᾽
αὐτὸν εἰδέναι τὰ μέλλοντα παρ᾽ αὐτοῦ μανθάνοντα·
5 δόξειν τε συνετοὺς εἶναι, εἰ τῆς ἀλαζονείας αὐτοῦ
καταγνόντες καὶ τῷ θεῷ πιστεύσαντες κτήσασθαι
γῆν ἣν αὐτοῖς ὑπέσχηται θελήσουσιν, ἀλλὰ μὴ
τῷ διὰ τὴν αἰτίαν ταύτην ἐπ᾽ ὀνόματι τοῦ θεοῦ
6 κωλύοντι προσσχοῖεν. τὴν ἀπορίαν οὖν λογιζόμενοι καὶ τὴν ἐρημίαν, ὑφ᾽ ἧς ἔτι ταύτην αὐτοῖς
χείρω συνέβαινεν εἶναι δοκεῖν, ἐπὶ τὴν πρὸς τοὺς
Χαναναίους μάχην ἦσαν ὡρμημένοι, τὸν θεὸν
προστησάμενοι στρατηγὸν ἀλλ᾽ οὐχὶ τὴν παρὰ
τοῦ νομοθέτου συνεργίαν περιμένοντες.
7 (2) Ὡς[2] οὖν ταῦτ᾽ ἄμεινον αὐτοῖς ἕξειν ἔκριναν
καὶ τοῖς πολεμίοις ἐπῆλθον, οἱ μὲν οὐ καταπλαγέντες αὐτῶν τὴν ἔφοδον οὐδὲ τὴν πληθὺν
γενναίως αὐτοὺς ἐδέξαντο, τῶν δὲ Ἑβραίων
ἀποθνήσκουσί τε πολλοὶ καὶ τὸ λοιπὸν στράτευμα
τῆς φάλαγγος αὐτῶν διαλυθείσης ἀκόσμως διω-
8 κόμενον εἰς τὴν παρεμβολὴν συνέφυγε, καὶ τῷ
παρ᾽ ἐλπίδας δυστυχῆσαι[3] παντάπασιν ἀθυμοῦν
οὐδὲν ἔτι χρηστὸν προσεδόκα, λογιζόμενον ὅτι
καὶ ταῦτα κατὰ μῆνιν θεοῦ πάθοιεν προεξορμή-
σαντες ἐπὶ τὸν πόλεμον τῆς ἐκείνου[4] βουλήσεως.
9 (3) Μωυσῆς δὲ τοὺς μὲν οἰκείους ὁρῶν ὑπὸ τῆς
ἥττης καταπεπληγότας, φοβούμενος δὲ μὴ θαρ-
σήσαντες ἐπὶ τῇ νίκῃ οἱ πολέμιοι καὶ μειζόνων
ὀρεχθέντες ἐπ᾽ αὐτοὺς ἔλθοιεν, ἔγνω δεῖν τὴν
στρατιὰν ἀπαγαγεῖν πορρωτέρω τῶν Χαναναίων

---

[1] SP : τούτων rell.   [2] ἕως OL Lat.
[3] ἀτυχῆσαι RO.   [4] + δίχα SPL (Lat. ?).

4

the Deity reveal our destiny from goodwill towards him, as though we were not all of the stock of Abraham, but God had made this one man responsible for knowing all the future, as taught by Him." They would (they said) show themselves sensible if, scorning the arrogance of Moses and in reliance upon God, they were to determine to win this land which He had promised them, without heeding the man who, under this pretext, would, in the name of God, prevent them. And so, reflecting on their distress and on this desert, which made it appear yet worse, they were all eager for battle with the Canaanites, claiming God as their leader and without waiting for any concurrence on the part of their legislator.

(2) Having then decided that this course would be the better for them, they marched against their foes. These, undaunted by their onset or numbers, received them valiantly ; of the Hebrews, many perished and the rest of the army, their line once broken, fled, pursued by the enemy, in disorder to the camp ; and, utterly despondent at this unexpected reverse, they looked for no more good hereafter, concluding that they owed this disaster also to the wrath of God, having rushed precipitately into battle without His assent. *Their defeat. Numb. xiv. 44.*

(3) But Moses, seeing his people downhearted at this defeat and fearing that the enemy, emboldened by their victory and ambitious of greater achievements, would march upon them, decided that he ought to lead his army further from the Canaanites *Moses leads them off into the desert.*

5

10 εἰς τὴν ἔρημον. καὶ τοῦ πλήθους ἐπιτρέψαντος
ἑαυτὸ πάλιν ἐκείνῳ, συνῆκε γὰρ δίχα τῆς αὐτοῦ
προνοίας οὐ δυνησόμενον ἐρρῶσθαι τοῖς πράγμασιν,
ἀναστήσας τὸ στράτευμα προῆλθεν εἰς τὴν ἔρημον,
ἐνταῦθα νομίζων ἡσυχάσειν αὐτοὺς καὶ μὴ πρότερον
τοῖς Χαναναίοις εἰς χεῖρας ἥξειν πρὶν ἢ παρὰ
τοῦ θεοῦ τὸν εἰς τοῦτο καιρὸν λάβωσιν.

11   (ii. 1) Ὅπερ δὲ τοῖς μεγάλοις συμβαίνει στρατο-
πέδοις καὶ μάλιστα παρὰ τὰς κακοπραγίας δυσ-
άρκτοις εἶναι καὶ δυσπειθέσι, τοῦτο καὶ τοῖς
Ἰουδαίοις συνέπεσεν· ἑξήκοντα γὰρ ὄντες μυριάδες
καὶ διὰ τὸ πλῆθος ἴσως ἂν μηδ' ἐν ἀγαθοῖς ὑπο-
ταγέντες τοῖς κρείττοσι, τότε μᾶλλον ὑπὸ τῆς
ἀπορίας καὶ συμφορᾶς ἐξηγανάκτουν καὶ πρὸς
12 ἀλλήλους καὶ πρὸς τὸν ἡγεμόνα. στάσις οὖν
αὐτοὺς οἵαν¹ ἴσμεν οὔτε παρ' Ἕλλησιν οὔτε παρὰ
βαρβάροις γενομένην κατέλαβεν, ὑφ' ἧς ἅπαντας
ἀπολέσθαι κινδυνεύσαντας² ἔσωσε Μωυσῆς, οὐ
μνησικακῶν ὅτι παρ' ὀλίγον ἦλθε καταλευσθεὶς
13 ὑπ' αὐτῶν ἀποθανεῖν. οὐδ' ὁ θεὸς δὲ ἠμέλησε
τοῦ μηδὲν αὐτοὺς παθεῖν τῶν δεινῶν, ἀλλὰ καίπερ
εἰς τὸν νομοθέτην αὐτῶν ἐξυβρισάντων καὶ τὰς
ἐντολάς, ἃς αὐτὸς διὰ Μωυσέος αὐτοῖς ἐπέστειλεν,
ἐρρύσατο τῶν ἐκ τοῦ στασιάζειν αὐτοῖς ἂν γενομένων δεινῶν, εἰ μὴ προενόησε. τήν τε οὖν
στάσιν καὶ ὅσα μετὰ ταύτην³ Μωυσῆς ἐπο-

---

¹ + οὐκ SPL.
² ed. pr.: ἀπολείπεσθαι κινδ. ἢ ἀπολέσθαι codd.
³ μετ' αὐτὴν RO.

ᵃ In Numb. xiv. 25 it is God who instructs Moses to turn
back into the wilderness " by the way to the Red Sea "

out into the desert.[a] So, the people having once
more committed themselves to him—for they understood that without his vigilance they could never
prosper in their affairs—he called up the army and
advanced into the desert, thinking that there they
would be tranquil and would not come to grips with
the Canaanites before the opportunity for so doing
should be granted them by God.

(ii. 1) However, just as large armies,[b] especially in
reverses, are wont to become ungovernable and in-
subordinate, even so it fell out with the Jews. These
sixty myriads of men, who, by reason of their numbers, might perchance even in prosperity not have
submitted to their superiors, now so much the more,
under the stress of want and calamity, became en-
raged both with each other and with their leader.
Thus it was that a sedition, for which we know of no
parallel whether among Greeks or barbarians, broke
out among them ; this sedition brought them all into
peril of destruction, from which they were saved by
Moses, who bore them no malice for having come near
to being stoned to death at their hands. Nor did
God himself suffer them altogether to escape a dreadful disaster, but, notwithstanding that they had
outraged their lawgiver and the commandments
which He himself through Moses had enjoined upon
them, He delivered them from those dire con-
sequences which would have ensued from their
sedition but for Moses' watchful care. This sedition,
along with the measures thereafter taken by Moses,

The great
sedition

(*i.e.* towards its eastern arm, the Gulf of Akabah) ; the
abortive attack on the Canaanites follows later.
    [b] An echo of Thuc. vii. 80 οἷον φιλεῖ καὶ πᾶσι στρατοπέδοις
μάλιστα δὲ τοῖς μεγίστοις ; with the adjectives following *cf.*
B.J. ii. 92 τό τε δύσαρκτον καὶ τὸ δυσπειθές.

λιτεύσατο διηγήσομαι προδιελθὼν τὴν αἰτίαν
ἀφ᾽ ἧς ἐγένετο.

14 (2) Κορῆς τις Ἑβραίων ἐν τοῖς μάλιστα καὶ
γένει καὶ πλούτῳ διαφέρων ἱκανὸς δ᾽ εἰπεῖν καὶ
δήμοις ὁμιλεῖν πιθανώτατος, ὁρῶν ἐν ὑπερβαλλούσῃ
τιμῇ τὸν Μωυσῆν καθεστῶτα χαλεπῶς εἶχεν
ὑπὸ φθόνου, καὶ γὰρ φυλέτης ὢν ἐτύγχανεν αὐτοῦ
καὶ συγγενής, ἀχθόμενος ὅτι ταύτης τῆς δόξης
δικαιότερον ἂν τῷ¹ πλουτεῖν ἐκείνου μᾶλλον μὴ
15 χείρων ὢν κατὰ γένος αὐτὸς ἀπέλαυε. παρά τε
τοῖς Λευίταις, φυλέται δ᾽ ἦσαν, καὶ μάλιστα παρὰ
τοῖς συγγενέσι κατεβόα, δεινὸν εἶναι λέγων Μωυσῆν
δόξαν αὑτῷ θηρώμενον κατασκευάσαι καὶ κακουρ-
γοῦντα κτήσασθαι ταύτην ἐπὶ προφάσει τοῦ θεοῦ
περιορᾶν, παρὰ τοὺς νόμους μὲν τἀδελφῷ τὴν
ἱερωσύνην Ἀαρῶνι δόντα, μὴ τῷ κοινῷ δόγματι
16 τοῦ πλήθους ἀλλ᾽ αὑτοῦ ψηφισαμένου, τυράννων²
δὲ τρόπῳ καταχαριζομένου τὰς τιμὰς οἷς ἂν
ἐθελήσῃ· χαλεπώτερον ⟨τ᾽⟩³ ἤδη τυγχάνειν τοῦ
βιάζεσθαι τὸ λεληθότως ἐξυβρίζειν, ὅτι μὴ μόνον
ἄκοντας ἀλλὰ μηδὲ συνιέντας τῆς ἐπιβουλῆς τὴν

¹ ἂν τῷ Dindorf: αὐτῷ codd.
² Niese: τυράννῳ or τυράννου codd.
³ A τε, which the mss. insert before λεληθότως, has perhaps
been misplaced.

ᵃ Gr. Κορῆς; Heb. Ḳoraḥ (= " baldness "), lxx. Κόρε.
ᵇ Tradition enlarges upon the wealth of Korah, which it
attributes to his discovery of treasures buried by Joseph in
Egypt (see *Jewish Encyclopaedia*). Psalm xlix. (a psalm
attributed to " the sons of Korah," his degenerate descendants), and in particular *v.* 17 (16), " Be not thou afraid when
one is made rich," is interpreted by the Midrash as referring
to Korah and his company.

8

I shall now recount, having first related the occasion out of which it arose.

(2) Korah,[a] one of the most eminent of the Hebrews by reason both of his birth and of his riches,[b] a capable speaker and very effective in addressing a crowd, seeing Moses established in the highest honours, was sorely envious; for he was of the same tribe and indeed his kinsman,[c] and was aggrieved at the thought that he had a greater right to enjoy all this glory himself, as being richer than Moses without being his inferior in birth. So he proceeded to denounce him among the Levites, who were his tribesmen, and especially among his kinsmen, declaring that it was monstrous to look on at Moses hunting round to create glory for himself and mischievously working to attain this in the pretended name of God. In defiance of the laws he had (he said) given the priesthood to his brother Aaron, not by the common decree of the people but by his own vote, and in despotic fashion was bestowing the honours upon whom he would.[d] Graver than open violence was now this clandestine form of outrage, because not only were those whom it robbed of power unwilling victims but even un-

Korah's jealousy: his harangue to his fellow Levites. Numb. xvi. 1.

[c] His first cousin. The pedigree (Ex. vi. 16, 18; Numb. xvi. 1) was:

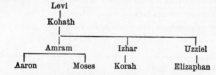

[d] According to tradition Korah's main grievance was that the office of " prince " of the Kohathites had been bestowed upon Elizaphan, who belonged to a branch of the family younger than his own (Numb. iii. 30: see pedigree above).

17 ἰσχὺν ἀφαιρεῖται· ὅστις γὰρ αὑτῷ σύνοιδεν ὄντι
λαβεῖν ἀξίῳ πείθει τυγχάνειν αὐτὸν καὶ ταῦτα¹
βιάσασθαι μὴ θρασυνόμενος, οἷς δὲ ἄπορον ἐκ
τοῦ δικαίου τιμᾶσθαι βίαν μὲν ἀγαθοὶ βουλόμενοι
δοκεῖν οὐ προσφέρουσι, τέχνῃ δ᾽ εἶναι κακουργοῦσι
18 δυνατοί. συμφέρειν δὲ τῷ πλήθει τοὺς τοιούτους
ἔτι λανθάνειν οἰομένους κολάζειν καὶ μὴ παρελθεῖν
εἰς δύναμιν ἐάσαντας φανεροὺς ἔχειν πολεμίους.
‘‘ τίνα γὰρ καὶ λόγον ἀποδοῦναι δυνάμενος Μωυσῆς
Ἀαρῶνι καὶ τοῖς υἱέσιν αὐτοῦ τὴν ἱερωσύνην
19 παρέδωκεν; εἰ μὲν γὰρ ἐκ τῆς Λευίτιδος φυλῆς
τὴν τιμὴν ὁ θεός τινι παρασχεῖν ἔκρινεν, ἐγὼ
ταύτης δικαιότερος τυγχάνειν, γένει μὲν ὁ αὐτὸς
ὢν Μωυσεῖ, πλούτῳ δὲ καὶ ἡλικίᾳ διαφέρων· εἰ
δὲ τῇ πρεσβυτάτῃ τῶν φυλῶν, εἰκότως ἂν ἡ
Ῥουβήλου τὴν τιμὴν ἔχοι λαμβανόντων αὐτὴν
Δαθάμου καὶ Ἀβιράμου καὶ Φαλαοῦ· πρεσβύτατοι
γὰρ οὗτοι τῶν ταύτην τὴν φυλὴν νεμομένων
καὶ δυνατοὶ χρημάτων περιουσίᾳ.’’
20 (3) Ἐβούλετο μὲν οὖν ταῦτα λέγων ὁ Κορῆς
τοῦ κοινοῦ προνοεῖσθαι δοκεῖν, ἔργῳ δὲ εἰς ἑαυτὸν
ἐπραγματεύετο τὴν παρὰ τοῦ πλήθους τιμὴν
μεταστῆσαι. καὶ ὁ μὲν ταῦτα κακοήθως μετ᾽
21 εὐπρεπείας πρὸς τοὺς φυλέτας ἔλεγε. προϊόντος
δ᾽ εἰς τοὺς πλείονας κατ᾽ ὀλίγον τοῦ λόγου
καὶ τῶν ἀκροωμένων προστιθεμένων ταῖς κατὰ

¹ τότε RO.

---

^a Reuben (see i. 304 note).
^b Gr. Dathames (most mss.) : Bibl. Dathan.
^c Pallu (lxx Φαλλούς) is mentioned as the second son of
Reuben in Ex. vi. 14. But the name Phalaus here probably
comes rather from the historian's text of Numb. xvi. 1 ; that

aware of the plot. For one who is conscious of meriting promotion seeks to obtain it by persuasion, and that without venturing to resort to force ; but those who are incapable of obtaining honours by just means, while doubtless they refrain from violence, because they wish to be taken for honest people, scheme by wicked artifice to attain to power. It was expedient for the people, he continued, to punish such persons, while yet they believed themselves undetected, instead of allowing them to advance to power and having them for open enemies. " What reason, pray, could Moses give for having conferred the priesthood upon Aaron and his sons ? If God has decided to award this honour to one of the tribe of Levi, *I* have more right to receive it, being by birth on a level with Moses, in wealth and years his superior. If, on the other hand, it is meant for the oldest of the tribes, naturally that of Rubel *a* should have this dignity, to be held by Datham,*b* Abiram, and Phalaus *c* ; for they are the eldest of the members of that tribe, and powerful through abundance of possessions."

(3) Now by these words Korah wished it to appear that he was concerned for the public welfare ; in reality, he was but scheming to have the dignity transferred by the people to himself. Thus with specious malice did he address the members of his tribe ; his words then spreading gradually among the crowd and those who listened to them crediting *d*

Spread of the rebellion.

verse in its traditional form (which is thought to be corrupt) mentions along with Dathan and Abiram " On the son of Peleth " (LXX Φαλέθ).

d Or " assenting to " (in *A.* vi. 287 προστίθεσθαι is a synonym for πιστεύειν) ; not, I think, as earlier translators take it, " adding to," " improving upon."

11

Ἀαρῶνος διαβολαῖς ἀναπίμπλαται τούτων ἅπας ὁ
στρατός. ἦσαν δὲ οἱ συντεταγμένοι τῷ Κορῇ
πεντήκοντα καὶ διακόσιοι τῶν πρώτων ἄνδρες
σπεύδοντες ἀφελέσθαι τὴν ἱερωσύνην τὸν Μωυσέος
22 ἀδελφὸν καὶ τοῦτον αὐτὸν ἀτιμοῦν. ἀνηρέθιστο
δὲ καὶ τὸ πλῆθος καὶ βάλλειν τὸν Μωυσῆν ὡρμήκεσαν, εἴς τε ἐκκλησίαν ἀκόσμως μετὰ θορύβου
καὶ ταραχῆς συνελέγοντο, καὶ πρὸ τῆς σκηνῆς
τοῦ θεοῦ στάντες[1] ἐβόων διώκειν[2] τὸν τύραννον
καὶ τῆς ἀπ' αὐτοῦ δουλείας ἀπηλλάχθαι τὸ πλῆθος,
τῇ τοῦ θεοῦ προφάσει βίαια προστάγματα κελεύ-
23 οντος· τὸν γὰρ θεόν, εἴπερ αὐτὸς ἦν ὁ τὸν ἱερασόμενον[3] ἐκλεγόμενος, τὸν ἄξιον ἂν εἰς τὴν τιμὴν
παραγαγεῖν,[4] οὐχὶ τοῖς πολλῶν ὑποδεεστέροις
ταύτην φέροντα προσνεῖμαι, κρίνοντά τε παρασχεῖν
Ἀαρῶνι ταύτην ἐπὶ τῷ πλήθει ποιήσασθαι τὴν
δόσιν, ἀλλ' οὐκ ἐπὶ τἀδελφῷ καταλιπεῖν.
24 (4) Μωυσῆς δὲ τὴν Κορέου διαβολὴν ἐκ πολλοῦ
προειδὼς καὶ τὸν λαὸν παροξυνόμενον ἰδὼν οὐκ
ἔδεισεν, ἀλλὰ θαρρῶν οἷς περὶ τῶν πραγμάτων
καλῶς ἐβουλεύετο καὶ τὸν ἀδελφὸν εἰδὼς κατὰ τὴν
τοῦ θεοῦ προαίρεσιν τῆς ἱερωσύνης τυχεῖν, ἀλλ' οὐ
25 κατὰ τὴν αὐτοῦ χάριν, ἧκεν εἰς τὴν ἐκκλησίαν. καὶ
πρὸς μὲν τὸ πλῆθος οὐδένα ἐποιήσατο λόγον,
πρὸς δὲ τὸν Κορῇ βοῶν ἐφ' ὅσον ἐδύνατο,
δεξιὸς ὢν καὶ κατὰ τἄλλα καὶ πλήθεσιν ὁμιλεῖν

---

[1] πάντες ROM Lat.
[2] M ed. pr.: ἥκειν rell. (exeat Lat.).
[3] ἱερωσόμενον codd. (and so § 28).
[4] Niese: παράγειν codd.

---

[a] Traditional detail, not in Scripture.

these calumnies upon Aaron, the whole army was soon pervaded with them. Korah's confederates were two hundred and fifty of the leading men, burning to deprive the brother of Moses of the priesthood and to dishonour Moses himself. But the multitude was equally excited and bent on stoning [a] Moses ; and, trooping to assembly in disorderly wise with tumult and uproar, they stood before the tabernacle of God and shouted : " Away with [b] the tyrant and let the people be rid of their bondage to one who, in the pretended name of God, imposes his despotic orders. For God, had it been He who selected him that is to be priest, would have installed the most deserving in this office and would not have conferred and settled it [c] upon persons inferior to many of us ; and, had He decided to grant it to Aaron, He would have committed the presentation of it to the people, instead of leaving it to his brother."

(4) But Moses, though he had long since known of the calumnies of Korah and seen the people's growing exasperation, yet was not afraid ; no, with the assurance of having taken counsel for affairs aright, and knowing that his brother had obtained the priesthood through God's deliberate choice and not through any favouritism of his own, he came to the assembly. To the multitude he addressed no word, but turning to Korah and shouting with all his might —he who, with all his other talents, was so gifted in

Numb.
xvi. 2.

Moses
addresses
the
assembly.
Cf. ib. 4-11

[b] Literally " pursue " or " prosecute " ; most MSS. have " let the tyrant come (forth)."

[c] The rendering " would not have consented (literally " endured ") to settle it " (so Hudson and Weill) seems hardly justifiable : φέρειν in that sense takes a participle, not an infinitive. Cf. φέρων ἔδωκα below, § 26.

εὐφυής, "ἐμοί," φησίν, "ὦ Κορῆ, καὶ σὺ καὶ
τούτων ἕκαστος," ἀπεδήλου δὲ τοὺς πεντήκοντα καὶ
διακοσίους ἄνδρας, "τιμῆς ἄξιοι δοκεῖτε, καὶ τὸν
ὅμιλον δὲ πάντα τῆς ὁμοίας οὐκ ἀποστερῶ τιμῆς,
κἂν ὑστερῶσιν ὧν ὑμῖν ἐκ πλούτου καὶ τῆς ἄλλης
26 ἀξιώσεως ὑπάρχει. καὶ νῦν Ἀαρῶνι τὴν ἱερωσύνην
οὐκ ἐπειδὴ πλούτῳ προεῖχε, σὺ γὰρ καὶ ἀμφοτέρους
ἡμᾶς μεγέθει χρημάτων ὑπερβάλλεις, οὐ μὴν
οὐδ' εὐγενείᾳ, κοινὸν γὰρ ἡμῖν τοῦτ' ἐποίησεν ὁ
θεὸς τὸν αὐτὸν δοὺς προπάτορα, οὐδὲ διὰ φιλ-
αδελφίαν ὃ δικαίως ἂν ἕτερος εἶχε τοῦτο φέρων
27 ἔδωκα τἀδελφῷ· καὶ γὰρ εἰ μὴ φροντίζων τοῦ
θεοῦ καὶ τῶν νόμων τὴν τιμὴν ἐχαριζόμην, οὐκ
ἂν ἐμαυτῷ παρεὶς δοῦναι παρέσχον ἑτέρῳ, συγ-
γενέστερος ὢν ἐμαυτῷ τἀδελφοῦ καὶ πρὸς ἐμαυτὸν
οἰκειότερον ἢ πρὸς ἐκεῖνον διακείμενος· καὶ γὰρ
οὐδὲ¹ συνετὸν ἦν τοῖς κινδύνοις ἐμαυτὸν ὑποτιθέντα
τοῖς ἐκ τοῦ παρανομεῖν ἄλλῳ τὴν διὰ τούτου²
28 εὐδαιμονίαν χαρίζεσθαι. ἀλλ' ἐγώ τε κρείττων
ἢ κακουργεῖν, ὅ τε θεὸς οὐκ ἂν περιεῖδεν ἑαυτὸν
καταφρονούμενον οὐδ' ὑμᾶς ἀγνοοῦντας ὅ τι να
ποιοῦντες αὐτῷ χαρίζεσθε, ἀλλ' αὐτὸς ἐπιλεξάμενος
τὸν ἱερασόμενον αὐτῷ τῆς κατὰ τοῦτ' αἰτίας ἡμᾶς
29 ἠλευθέρωσεν. οὐ μὴν ἐξ ἐμῆς χάριτος λαβὼν³
⟨Ἀαρὼν⟩⁴ ἀλλὰ μὴ κατὰ κρίσιν θεοῦ, κατατίθησιν αὐτὴν εἰς μέσον ἐπιδικάσιμον τοῖς βουλο-

¹ Dindorf: οὔτε codd.   ² ΜΕ: τοῦτ' rell.
³ ed. pr.: λαβεῖν codd.   ⁴ ex Lat.: om. codd.

ᵃ Weill aptly compares the words of Moses in Num. xi. 29
(in the episode of Eldad and Medad, not reported by
Josephus). " Would God that all the LORD's people were
prophets ! "

14

moving a crowd—" To my mind, Korah," said he,
" not thou alone but each of these men "—indicating
the two hundred and fifty—" appears worthy of
promotion ; nay, this whole concourse I would not
deprive of the like honour *a* even though they lack
what ye derive from wealth and other distinctions.
And now, if Aaron has been presented with the
priesthood, it is not because he was pre-eminent in
wealth, for thou surpassest even the twain of us in
magnitude of possessions ; nor yet for nobility of
birth, for God has made us equal in this respect by
giving us the same forefather *b* ; nor was it from
fraternal love that I conferred an honour, which
justly another should have had, upon my brother.
For even had I disregarded God and the laws in
giving away this dignity, I should never have passed
over myself and bestowed it upon another, seeing
that I am a nearer kinsman to myself than is my
brother and more closely attached to my person than
to his ! Nay, it would not even have been sensible
to expose myself to the risks of an unlawful act only
to present to another the resultant benefits. No ; I
on my side am above malpractices, while God would
not have brooked such outrage to Himself nor left
you ignorant what ye should do to win His favour.
But since He himself has chosen him that is to serve
as His priest, He has freed us *c* from all responsibility
in this regard.

" However, Aaron, though far from having received
his office through my favour and not by the judgement
of God, now lays it down as an open prize to be sued

b Their common grandfather, Kohath.
c Or " me " (as often).

μένοις, οὐκ ἐκ τοῦ προκριθεὶς ἤδη τυχεῖν αὐτῆς
ἀξιῶν ἐπιτραπῆναι καὶ τὸ¹ νῦν αὐτῷ² περὶ αὐτῆς
30 σπουδάσαι, προτιμῶν ⟨δὲ⟩³ τοῦ τὸ γέρας ἔχειν
τὸ μὴ στασιάζοντας ὑμᾶς ὁρᾶν καίτοι κατὰ τὴν
ὑμετέραν γνώμην αὐτοῦ τυγχάνων· ὃ γὰρ ἔδωκεν
ὁ θεὸς οὐχ ἡμάρτομεν τοῦτο καὶ βουλομένων ὑμῶν
31 λαβεῖν νομίζοντες.⁴ ἦν δὲ καὶ τὸ μὴ προσέσθαι
παρέχοντος ἐκείνου τὴν τιμὴν ἀσεβές, καὶ πάλιν
ἀξιοῦν γ᾽⁵ ἔχειν εἰς ἅπαντα χρόνον μὴ τὴν ἀσφάλειαν
τὴν ἐπ᾽ αὐτῇ βεβαιοῦντος ἡμῖν τοῦ θεοῦ παντάπασιν ἀλόγιστον. κρινεῖ τοίνυν πάλιν αὐτός,
τίνας βούλεται τὰς ὑπὲρ ὑμῶν⁶ αὐτῷ θυσίας
32 ἐπιτελεῖν καὶ προεστάναι τῆς εὐσεβείας· ἄτοπον
γὰρ Κορῆν ἐφιέμενον τῆς τιμῆς τὴν ἐξουσίαν
τοῦ τίνι παράσχῃ ταύτην ἀφελέσθαι τὸν θεόν.
τῆς οὖν στάσεως καὶ τῆς διὰ τοῦτο ταραχῆς
παύσασθε, πρωῒ δὲ ὅσοι τῆς ἱερωσύνης ἀντιποιεῖσθε
κομίζων ἕκαστος θυμιατήριον οἴκοθεν σὺν θυμιά-
33 μασι καὶ πυρὶ πάριτε. καὶ σὺ δέ, Κορῆ, παρα-
χώρησον τὴν κρίσιν τῷ θεῷ καὶ τὴν ἐπὶ τούτοις
αὐτοῦ μένε ψηφοφορίαν, ἀλλὰ μὴ σαυτὸν ποίει
τοῦ θεοῦ κρείττονα, παραγίνου δὲ κριθησόμενος
οὕτως περὶ τοῦ γέρως. ἀνεμέσητον δ᾽ οἶμαι καὶ
Ἀαρῶνα προσδέξασθαι συγκριθησόμενον, γένους
μὲν ὄντα τοῦ αὐτοῦ μηδὲν δὲ μεμφθῆναι τοῖς παρὰ
34 τὴν ἱερωσύνην πεπραγμένοις δυνάμενον. θυμιά-

---

¹ SP: τοῦ or τοῦτο rell.
² Text RO: + συγχωρηθῆναι rell.
³ ins. Niese.
⁴ καὶ μὴ βουλ. ὑμῶν λαμβάνοντες RO.
⁵ ἀξιοῦντ᾽ (ἀξιοῦντα) codd.
⁶ ἡμῶν SP.

ᵃ Or " now again " ; but Weill is doubtless right in render-

for by any who will. He makes no claim on the ground of his previous selection and present tenure of it to be allowed on this occasion also to compete for it ; but rather than keep this privilege he would prefer to see no dissension among you, notwithstanding that he holds it in virtue of your own decision; for that which God gave, we were not wrong in supposing that he received with your goodwill also. Nay, to have refused this honour when proffered by Him would have been impious ; as, on the other hand,[a] to claim to keep it for ever without having the assured possession of it guaranteed to us by God, would be utterly unreasonable. He, then, it is who shall decide anew, whom He would have to offer Him the sacrifices on your behalf and to preside over the rites of worship ; for it were monstrous that Korah, in coveting this honour, should deprive God of the power of deciding to whom He would accord it.

"Cease ye then from this sedition and the turbulence arising therefrom, and at daybreak let all claimants for the priesthood bring each a censer from his home, with incense and fire, and come hither. And do thou too, Korah, leave the judgement to God, await the casting of His vote thereon and make not thyself superior to God, but come to stand thy trial even so concerning this prize. Nor can it, I imagine, cause offence, that Aaron too should be admitted as a competitor, he who is of the same family and beyond all reproach for his actions during his tenure of the priesthood. Ye will then burn your

Numb. xvi. 6, 16.

ing " en revanche," though the temporal sense occurs just below. It is a Sophoclean use (*El.* 371), and the marks of the " Sophoclean " assistant (see Introduction) are evident in this speech.

σετε¹ οὖν συνελθόντες ἐν φανερῷ παντὶ τῷ λαῷ,
καὶ θυμιωμένων ὑμῶν οὗπερ ἂν τὴν θυσίαν ἡδίω
κρίνειεν ὁ θεός, οὗτος ὑμῖν ἱερεὺς κεχειροτονήσεται,
τῆς ἐπὶ τἀδελφῷ διαβολῆς ὡς κεχαρισμένου
⟨ἐμοῦ⟩² τὴν τιμὴν αὐτῷ ῥυόμενος."

35   (iii. 1) Ταῦτα Μωυσέος εἰπόντος παύεται καὶ
τῆς ταραχῆς τὸ πλῆθος καὶ τῆς εἰς Μωυσῆν
ὑποψίας, ἐπένευσαν³ δὲ τοῖς εἰρημένοις· καὶ γὰρ
ἦν καὶ ἐδόκει χρηστὰ τῷ λαῷ. τότε μὲν οὖν
διαλύουσι τὸν σύλλογον, τῇ δ' ἐπιούσῃ συνῆλθον
εἰς τὴν ἐκκλησίαν παρατευξόμενοι τῇ θυσίᾳ καὶ
τῇ δι' αὐτῆς κρίσει τῶν περὶ τῆς ἱερωσύνης
36   ἀγωνιζομένων. συνέβαινε δ' εἶναι θορυβώδη τὴν
ἐκκλησίαν μετεώρου τοῦ πλήθους ὄντος ἐπ' ἐλπίδι
τῶν ἐσομένων, καὶ τῶν μὲν εἰς ἡδονὴν λαμβανόντων
εἰ Μωυσῆς ἐλεγχθείη κακουργῶν, τῶν δὲ φρονίμων
εἰ πραγμάτων ἀπαλλαγείησαν καὶ ταραχῆς· ἐδεδίεσαν γὰρ μὴ τῆς στάσεως προϊούσης ἀφανισθῇ
37   μᾶλλον αὐτοῖς ὁ κόσμος τῆς καταστάσεως· ὁ
δὲ πᾶς ὅμιλος φύσει χαίρων τῷ καταβοᾶν τῶν
ἐν τέλει καὶ πρὸς ὅ τις εἴποι πρὸς τοῦτο τὴν
γνώμην τρέπων ἐθορύβει. πέμψας δὲ καὶ Μωυσῆς
πρὸς Ἀβίραμον καὶ Δαθάμην ὑπηρέτας ἐκέλευσεν
ἥκειν κατὰ τὰ συγκείμενα καὶ περιμένειν τὴν
38   ἱερουργίαν. ὡς δ' οὔτε ὑπακούσεσθαι τοῖς ἀγγέλοις
ἔφασαν καὶ Μωυσῆν οὐ περιόψεσθαι κατὰ τοῦ
λαοῦ παντὸς ἐκ κακουργίας αὐξανόμενον, ἀκούσας
τὰ παρ' αὐτῶν ὁ Μωυσῆς ἀκολουθεῖν αὐτῷ τοὺς

---

¹ O : θυμιάσατε rell.   ² ex Lat. ins. Niese.
            ³ RO : ἐπῄνεσαν rell.

incense, on assembling here, in the sight of all the people ; and, on your offering your incense, whosesoever sacrifice God shall judge to be most acceptable, he shall be your elected priest, thereby clearing me of the charge of having through favour bestowed this dignity upon a brother."

(iii. 1) After this speech of Moses, the multitude ceased their turbulence and their suspicions of him, and assented to his proposals, which indeed were, as they were thought, excellent for the people.   So for the time they dissolved the meeting, but on the morrow they gathered to the assembly to assist at the sacrifice and at the judgement to be passed thereby upon the competitors for the priesthood. It proved indeed a tumultuous assembly, the multitude being all agog in expectation of the issue : some would have taken pleasure in seeing Moses convicted of a crime, others of the sager sort in being delivered from troubles and turbulence, for they feared, if sedition gained ground, a further obliteration of the ordered beauty of their constitution ; while the general mass, with its innate delight in decrying those in authority and its opinion swayed by what anyone said, was in a ferment.   Moses sent attendants also to Abiram and Datham,[a] bidding them come, as had been agreed, and await the issue of the sacred ceremony.   But, since they informed the messengers that they would neither obey nor suffer Moses to wax great at the expense of the whole community by nefarious means, Moses, on hearing their reply, requested his chief councillors[b] to accompany him and

Fresh meeting of the assembly.
Numb. xvi. 18.

Moses confronts Dathan and Abiram.
Ib. 12.

xvi. 25.

---

    [a] Bibl. Dathan (§ 19).
    [b] " The elders of Israel " (Numbers).

προβούλους ἀξιώσας ἀπῄει πρὸς τοὺς περὶ Δαθάμην,
οὐχ ἡγούμενος εἶναι δεινὸν βαδίζειν πρὸς τοὺς ὑπερ-
ηφανήσαντας· οἱ δ' οὐδὲν ἀντειπόντες ἠκολούθουν.
39 οἱ δὲ περὶ Δαθάμην πυθόμενοι τὸν Μωυσῆν μετὰ
τῶν ἀξιολόγων τῆς πληθύος πρὸς αὐτοὺς παρα-
γινόμενον προελθόντες γυναιξὶν ἅμα καὶ τέκνοις
πρὸ τῶν σκηνῶν ἀπέβλεπον, τί καὶ μέλλοι ποιεῖν
ὁ Μωυσῆς· ἔτι τε θεράποντες ἦσαν περὶ αὐτούς,
ὡς εἰ βίαν τινὰ προσφέροι Μωυσῆς ἀμυνούμενοι.
40 (2) Ὁ δὲ πλησίον γενόμενος τὰς χεῖρας εἰς
τὸν οὐρανὸν ἀνασχὼν γεγωνότερον ἐκβοήσας,
ὡς ἀκουστὸν πάσῃ τῇ πληθύι γενέσθαι, " δέσποτα,"
φησί, " τῶν ἐπ' οὐρανοῦ τε καὶ γῆς καὶ θαλάσσης·
σὺ γὰρ ἐμοὶ τῶν ὑπ' ἐμοῦ πεπραγμένων μάρτυς
ἀξιολογώτατος, ὡς γνώμῃ τε σῇ γίνεται τὰ πάντα
καὶ δρωμένοις[1] μηχανὴν ἐξεπόρισας οἶκτον ἐν
πᾶσι δεινοῖς Ἑβραίων ποιησάμενος· ἐλθέ μοι
41 τούτων ἀκροατὴς τῶν λόγων, σὲ γὰρ οὔτε πρατ-
τόμενον οὔτε νοηθὲν λανθάνει, ὥστ' οὐδὲ φθονήσεις
μοι τῆς ἀληθείας τὴν τούτων ἀχαριστίαν ἐπίπροσθεν θέμενος. τὰ μὲν οὖν πρεσβύτερα τῆς
ἐμῆς γενέσεως αὐτὸς οἶσθ' ἀκριβέστερον, οὐκ
ἀκοῇ μαθὼν ὄψει δὲ τότ' αὐτοῖς παρὼν γινομένοις,
ἃ δὲ ἐπὶ τούτοις καίπερ ἐπιστάμενοι σαφῶς ἀδίκως
42 ὑπονοοῦσι, τούτων μοι γενοῦ μάρτυς. ἐγὼ βίον
ἀπράγμονα καταστησάμενος ἀνδραγαθίᾳ μὲν ἐμῇ
σῇ δὲ βουλῇ, καὶ τοῦτον Ῥαγουήλου μοι τοῦ

---

[1] δεομένοις Niese : ἀπορουμένοις Naber : emendation needless.

---

[a] So, not (as earlier translators) "deeming it dangerous":
cf. B.J. iv. 393 δεινὸν ἡγουμένων ὑποτετάχθαι τὸ πρὶν ἰσοτίμῳ.
[b] The Arabic version of Numbers adds a similar phrase,
"ut viderent quid futurum esset" (trans. Walton, Polyglot).

went off to the faction of Datham, not scorning *a* to go
to these insolent rebels ; and the councillors followed
him without demur.   Datham's company, on learning
that Moses was coming to them, attended by the
chief notables of the people, came forth with their
wives and children before their tents to see what
Moses proposed to do.*b*   Moreover they had their
servants *c* around them to defend them, should Moses
resort to any act of violence.

(2) But he, on approaching them, raised his hands
to heaven and, in stentorian tones, so as to be heard
by all the throng, said : " Lord of all that is in heaven
and earth and sea, since thou for my actions art the
witness most worthy of belief, how that all things
have been done in accordance with thy will and how
for their performance thou didst devise a way, taking
pity on the Hebrews in all adversities, come and
lend thine ear to my words.   For from thee no deed
nor thought is hid ; thou wilt not then grudge me
the revelation of the truth, preferring above it the
ingratitude of these men.   Truly, the events anterior
to my birth thou knowest best thyself, not through
hearing of the ear, but through seeing them pass at
the time in thy presence ; but of the events thereafter, which, though they know them well, these men
so unjustly suspect, of them be thou my witness.   I,
who had secured for myself a life of ease, through
my prowess *d* and at thy will, thanks too to what

Appeal of
Moses for
the inter-
vention of
God. *Cf.*
Numb. xvi.
15, 28.

---

c This is J.'s rendering of the Hebrew *taph* "(their) *little
ones*" in Num. xvi. 27 : LXX ἀποσκευή (" chattels "),
Targum of Onkelos " their families," Vulgate " omnique
frequentia."

d ἀπράγμονα . . . ἀνδραγαθίᾳ : an echo of Thuc. ii. 63
ἀπραγμοσύνῃ ἀνδραγαθίζεται.

21

πενθεροῦ καταλιπόντος, ἀφεὶς τὴν ἐκείνων ἀπόλαυσιν τῶν ἀγαθῶν ἐμαυτὸν ἐπέδωκα ταῖς ὑπὲρ
τούτων ταλαιπωρίαις. καὶ πρότερον μὲν ὑπὲρ
τῆς ἐλευθερίας αὐτῶν, νῦν δ' ὑπὲρ τῆς σωτηρίας
μεγάλους ὑπέστην πόνους καὶ παντὶ δεινῷ τοὐμὸν
43 ἀντιτάξας πρόθυμον. νῦν οὖν ἐπεὶ κακουργεῖν
ὑποπτεύομαι παρ' ἀνδράσιν, οἷς ἐκ τῶν ἐμῶν
καμάτων ὑπάρχει[1] τὸ περιεῖναι, εἰκότως ἂν αὐτός,
ὁ τὸ πῦρ ἐκεῖνό μοι φήνας κατὰ τὸ Σιναῖον καὶ
τῆς σαυτοῦ φωνῆς ἀκροατὴν τότε καταστήσας
καὶ θεατὴν τεράτων ὅσα μοι παρέσχεν ἰδεῖν ἐκεῖνος
ὁ τόπος ποιήσας, ὁ κελεύσας ἐπ' Αἰγύπτου
σταλῆναι καὶ τὴν σὴν γνώμην τούτοις ἐμφανίσαι,
44 ὁ τὴν Αἰγυπτίων εὐδαιμονίαν σείσας καὶ τῆς ὑπ'
αὐτοῖς[2] δουλείας δρασμὸν ἡμῖν παρασχὼν καὶ
μικροτέραν ἐμοῦ τὴν Φαραώθου ποιήσας ἡγεμονίαν,
ὁ γῆν ἡμῖν ἀμαθῶς ἔχουσι τῶν ὁδῶν ποιήσας τὸ
πέλαγος καὶ τὴν ἀνακεκομμένην θάλασσαν τοῖς
Αἰγυπτίων ἐπικυμήνας ὀλέθροις, ὁ γυμνοῖς οὖσι
45 τὴν ἐξ ὅπλων ἀσφάλειαν χαρισάμενος, ὁ ποτίμους
ἡμῖν διεφθαρμένας πηγὰς ῥεῦσαι παρασκευάσας
καὶ τελέως ἀποροῦσιν ἐκ πετρῶν ἐλθεῖν ἡμῖν
ποτὸν μηχανησάμενος, ὁ τῶν γήθεν ἀπορουμένους
εἰς τροφὴν διασώσας τοῖς ἀπὸ θαλάσσης, ὁ καὶ
ἀπ' οὐρανοῦ τροφὴν καταπέμψας οὐ πρότερον
ἱστορηθεῖσαν, ὁ νόμων ἡμῖν ἐπίνοιαν ὑποθέμενος
46 καὶ διάταξιν πολιτείας· ἐλθέ, δέσποτα τῶν ὅλων,
δικαστής μου καὶ μάρτυς ἀδωροδόκητος, ὡς οὔτε
δωρεὰν ἐγὼ παρ' Ἑβραίων τινὸς κατὰ τοῦ δικαίου

---

[1] ὑπῆρχε RO.   [2] αὐτοὺς RO.

Raguel my father-in-law left me,[a] abandoning the enjoyment of those good things, devoted myself to tribulations on behalf of this people. At first for their liberty, and now for their salvation, great are the toils that I have undergone, opposing to every peril all the ardour of my soul. Now therefore, when I am suspected of knavery by men who owe it to my exertions that they are yet alive, well mayest thou thyself—thou who didst show me that fire on Sinai and didst cause me then to listen to thy voice and to behold all those prodigies which I was permitted by that place to see ; thou who badest me make speed to Egypt and reveal thy will to this people ; who didst shake the prosperity of the Egyptians and grant us escape from the yoke of their bondage, humbling beneath me the dominion of Pharaoh ; who, when we knew not whither to go, didst change the deep into dry land and, when the sea had been beaten back, broughtest up its surging billows to the Egyptians' destruction ; who to our naked army gavest arms for their protection ; who didst cause sweet water to flow for us from polluted springs and in the depth of our distress find means to bring us drink from the rocks [b] ; who when the fruits of earth failed us preservedst us with sustenance from the sea,[c] aye and from heaven didst send down meat unheard of aforetime [d] ; thou who didst put into our minds a scheme of laws and an ordered constitution—O come, Lord of the universe, to judge my cause and to attest, as witness incorruptible, that neither have I accepted a present from a single Hebrew to pervert justice, ^{Numb.} ^{xvi. 15.}

---

^a *Ant.* ii. 263 ; or " which Raguel . . . too left me free to enjoy."

^b iii. 35.   ^c Quails, iii. 25.   ^d Manna, iii. 26.

προσηκάμην οὔτε πλούτῳ κατέκρινα πενίαν νικᾶν
δυναμένην οὔτε ἐπὶ βλάβῃ τοῦ κοινοῦ πολιτευσά-
μενος εἰς ἀλλοτριωτάτας τῶν ἐμῶν ἐπιτηδευμάτων
ἐπινοίας πάρειμι, ὡς οὐχὶ σοῦ κελεύσαντος Ἀαρῶνι
47 δοὺς τὴν ἱερωσύνην ἀλλὰ κατ' ἐμὴν χάριν. παρά-
στησον δὲ καὶ νῦν, ὅτι πάντα σῇ προνοίᾳ διοικεῖται
καὶ μηδὲν αὐτομάτως ἀλλὰ κατὰ βούλησιν βρα-
βευόμενον τὴν σὴν εἰς τέλος ἔρχεται, ὅτι δὲ
φροντίζεις τῶν Ἑβραίους ὀνησόντων, μετελθὼν
Ἀβίραμον καὶ Δαθάμην, οἵ σου καταδικάζουσιν
ἀναισθησίαν ὡς ὑπ' ἐμῆς τέχνης νικωμένου.
48 ποιήσεις δὲ φανερὰν τὴν ἐπ' αὐτοῖς δίκην οὕτως
μεμηνότων κατὰ τῆς σῆς δόξης, μὴ κοινῶς ἐκ
τοῦ ζῆν αὐτοὺς μεταστήσας μηδ' ὡς ἀποθανόντας
κατ' ἀνθρώπινον ἐξεληλυθότας τοῦ βίου φανέν-
τας νόμον, ἀλλὰ χάνοι περὶ αὐτοὺς ἅμα τῇ γενεᾷ
49 καὶ τοῖς ὑπάρχουσιν ἣν πατοῦσι γῆν· τοῦτο γὰρ
σῆς ἐπίδειξις ἂν ἰσχύος ἅπασι γένοιτο καὶ διδασκαλία σωφροσύνης δέει τοῦ[1] ταῦτα πείσεσθαι
περὶ σοῦ δοξάζοντας οὐχ ὅσια· εὑρεθείην γὰρ ἂν
οὕτως ἀγαθὸς ὑπηρέτης ὧν σὺ προστάσσεις.
50 εἰ δ' ἀληθεῖς πεποίηνται τὰς κατ' ἐμοῦ διαβολάς,
τοὺς μὲν ἀπαθεῖς ἀπὸ παντὸς φυλάξειας[2] κακοῦ,
ὃν δ' ἐπηρασάμην ὄλεθρον αὐτοῖς τοῦτον ποιήσειας[3]
ἐμόν· καὶ δίκην εἰσπραξάμενος παρὰ τοῦ τὸν σὸν
ἀδικῆσαι θελήσαντος λαὸν τοῦ λοιποῦ βραβεύων
ὁμόνοιαν καὶ εἰρήνην σῷζε τὴν πληθὺν ἑπομένην
τοῖς σοῖς προστάγμασιν, ἀπαθῆ τηρῶν αὐτὴν καὶ

---

[1] δέει τοῦ Holwerda : δὲ εἰς τοὺς codd.
[2] φυλάξεις ROM.   [3] ποιήσεις RO.

---

[a] Moses here *suggests* the earthquake to God (in Scripture

24

nor in the interest of wealth condemned poverty that
deserved to win, nor, acting to the detriment of the
public weal, have allowed thoughts so wholly alien
to my conduct to enter my mind, as to give the
priesthood to Aaron not by thy command but through
my favouritism. Prove now once again that all is
directed by thy providence, that nothing befalls
fortuitously, but that it is thy will that overrules and
brings everything to its end ; prove that thou carest
for those who would benefit the Hebrews, by pursuing with vengeance Abiram and Datham, who
accuse thee of such insensibility as to have been
defeated by artifice of mine. Aye and thou wilt
make manifest thy judgement upon them, these mad Numb.
xvi. 29 f.
assailants of thy majesty, by removing them in no
common manner out of existence : let it not appear
that in perishing they quitted life according to the
law of humanity : nay, let there open to engulf them,
them and their families and their belongings, the very
ground they tread ! *a* *That* would be for all an
exhibition of thy might and a lesson in sobriety,
through fear of suffering the like fate for impious
imaginations concerning thee ; for thus should I be
proved a faithful minister of thy behests. But, if the
accusations which they have made against me be
true, then mayest thou keep these men free from all
harm, and that destruction which I have imprecated
on them bring thou upon me. And, having exacted
justice from him that would have wronged thy people,
henceforward, awarding harmony and peace, save
thou this multitude that followeth thy commandments, preserving them unscathed and exempt from

his words are addressed to the people), as at the Red Sea he
had suggested three alternative expedients (ii. 337).

ἀκοινώνητον τῆς τῶν ἡμαρτηκότων κολάσεως· σὺ
γὰρ αὐτὸς οἶσθα, ὡς οὐ δίκαιον ὑπὲρ τῆς ἐκείνων
κακίας κοινῇ πάντας Ἰσραηλίτας τιμωρίαν ἐκ-
τίνειν.[1]"

51   (3) Ταῦτ᾽ εἰπόντος καὶ δακρύοντος σείεται μὲν
αἰφνίδιον ἡ γῆ, σάλου δ᾽ ἐπ᾽[2] αὐτῆς κινηθέντος
ὥσπερ ἐξ ἀνέμου βίας σαλευομένου κύματος πᾶς
μὲν ἔδεισεν ὁ λαός, πατάγου δὲ καὶ σκληροῦ
ῥαγέντος ἤχου κατὰ τὰς ἐκείνων σκηνὰς συνίζησεν
ἡ γῆ καὶ πάνθ᾽ ὅσα φίλα τούτοις ἦν ὑπήνεγκεν
52 εἰς αὑτήν. ἠφανισμένων δ᾽ οὕτως, ὡς μηδὲ
φθῆναι[3] τινας γνῶναι, συνῄει τε πάλιν τῆς γῆς
τὸ περὶ ἐκείνοις κεχηνὸς καὶ καθίστατο, ὡς μηδ᾽
εἰ πάθοι τι τῶν προειρημένων φανερὸν εἶναι τοῖς
ὁρῶσι. καὶ οἱ μὲν οὕτως ἀπώλοντο ἐπίδειξις
53 τοῦ θεοῦ τῆς ἰσχύος γενόμενοι· ὀδύραιτο δ᾽ ἄν
τις οὐ μόνον τῆς συμφορᾶς αὐτοὺς καὶ καθ᾽ αὑτὴν
οὔσης ἀξίας οἴκτου, ἀλλ᾽ ὅτι καὶ τοιαῦτα παθόντων
ἐφήσθησαν οἱ συγγενεῖς· τῶν γὰρ συντεταγμένων
ἐκλαθόμενοι πρὸς τὴν ὄψιν τοῦ συμβεβηκότος
ἐβεβαίουν τὴν κρίσιν, καὶ νομίζοντες ὡς ἀλιτηρίους
ἀπολωλέναι τοὺς περὶ Δαθάμην οὐδ᾽ ἐλυποῦντο.

54   (4) Μωυσῆς δ᾽ ἐκάλει τοὺς περὶ τῆς ἱερωσύνης
ἁμιλλωμένους διὰ τὴν τῶν ἱερέων δοκιμασίαν,
ἵν᾽ οὐ προσδέξεται τὴν θυσίαν ὁ θεὸς ἥδιον ἐκεῖνος[4]

---

[1] ἐκτιννύναι M.   [2] RO : ἀπ᾽ rell.
[3] Cocceii : ὀφθῆναι or φανῆναι codd.   [4] om. RO.

---

[a] Or possibly (neuter) " their confederacy," the compact
between the two parties. Critics have long recognized that
in the Biblical narrative two distinct stories have been welded
together : (1) a revolt against the civil authority of Moses,

the punishment of them that have sinned. For thou thyself knowest that it were not just that for their iniquity all Israel together should pay the penalty."

(3) So spake he, weeping withal, when suddenly the earth shook, a tremor moved over its surface as when a wave is tossed by the violence of the wind, and all the people were afraid ; then a crash and a burst of booming sound, and over against the tents of those men the earth subsided and swept all that was precious to them down into its bosom. The victims being obliterated so swiftly that some were even unaware of their fate, the ground that had opened around them closed up again and settled down, so that there was nothing to show the onlookers that it had actually suffered any such convulsion. Thus they perished, furnishing an exhibition of God's mighty power. Yet one might commiserate them, not only for a catastrophe by itself alone meriting compassion, but because moreover their kinsfolk rejoiced over their awful fate. For, oblivious of their confederates,[a] at the sight of what had befallen they ratified the sentence, and, judging that Datham and his followers had perished as miscreants, they refrained even from grief.[b]

(4) But [c] Moses summoned the rival claimants for the priesthood to proceed to the scrutiny for that office, to the end that he whose sacrifice should be received with most favour by God should be declared

Marginal notes: Dathan's company engulfed by earthquake. Numb. xvi. 31.

Korah's company consumed by celestial fire. *Ib.* 2, 18.

led by Dathan and Abiram, (2) a revolt of representatives of the whole people, led by Korah, against the Levites.

[b] Addition to Scripture.

[c] Peculiarities in this section, noted below, indicate the reappearance of the " Thucydidean " assistant (see Introduction). There is some lack of coherence with what has preceded.

27

ᾗ[1] κεχειροτονημένος. συνελθόντων δὲ πεντήκοντα
καὶ διακοσίων ἀνδρῶν, οἳ καὶ διὰ πατέρων ἀρετὴν
ἐτιμῶντο παρὰ τῷ λαῷ καὶ διὰ τὴν αὐτῶν, ᾗ
κἀκείνους ὑπερεβάλλοντο, προῆλθον καὶ Ἀαρὼν
καὶ Κορῆς, καὶ πρὸ τῆς σκηνῆς πάντες καθήγνισαν
ἐπὶ τοῖς θυμιατηρίοις ὁπόσα κομίζοντες ἔτυχον.
55 ἐξέλαμψε δὲ πῦρ τοσοῦτον ὅσον οὔτε[2] χειροποίητον
ἱστόρησέ τις οὔτε γῆθεν ἀναδοθὲν κατὰ ὑποδρομὴν
καύματος οὔτε κατὰ βίαν πνευμάτων ὕλης πρὸς
αὐτὴν[3] παρατριβείσης αὐτομάτως ἐξεκρούσθη, ἀλλ᾽
ὁποῖον ⟨ἂν⟩[4] θεοῦ κελεύσαντος ἀφθείη λαμπρὸν καὶ
56 φλογωδέστατον· ὑφ᾽ οὗ πάντες, οἵ τε διακόσιοι
καὶ πεντήκοντα καὶ Κορῆς, ἄξαντος ἐπ᾽ αὐτοὺς
ἐφθάρησαν, ὡς καὶ τὰ σώματα αὐτῶν ἀφανῆ
γεγονέναι. περισώζεται δὲ μόνος Ἀαρὼν μηδὲν
ὑπὸ τοῦ πυρὸς βλαβεὶς τῷ τὸν θεὸν εἶναι τὸν
57 οὓς ἔδει καίειν ἀπεσταλκότα. Μωυσῆς δὲ τούτων
ἀπολομένων βουλόμενος τὴν τιμωρίαν αὐτῶν
μνήμῃ παραδοθῆναι καὶ τοὺς αὖθις ἐσομένους
αὐτὴν μαθεῖν, ἐκέλευσεν Ἐλεάζαρον τὸν Ἀαρῶνος

---

[1] ML: εἴη rell.   [2] Dindorf: οὐδὲ codd.
[3] Bekker: αὐτὸ codd.   [4] ins. Bekker.

---

[a] There is no indication that they have already been mentioned (§ 21).

[b] " Princes of the congregation, called to the assembly (LXX σύνκλητοι βουλῆς), men of renown," Numb. xvi. 2.

[c] In the conflate Biblical narrative Korah appears to share the fate of Dathan and Abiram (xvi. 27, and expressly in xxvi. 10). In Josephus he is burnt with the 250. The nature of his end was in fact the subject of Rabbinic controversy (Talmud, *Sanhedrin*, 110a, quoted by Weill).

[d] The use of ὁπόσος for ὅσος is a distinctive mark of the

elected. Then assembled two hundred and fifty men,[a] held in high esteem by the people alike for the merits of their ancestors and for their own, in which they even surpassed their sires [b]; Aaron and Korah [c] advanced likewise, and the whole company in front of the tabernacle burnt incense on all those censers which [d] they had brought with them. And suddenly there blazed forth a fire, the like of which had never in the record of history been made by the hand of man, nor was ever ejected from the earth through subterranean current of heat, nor yet spontaneously broke out in the woods from the violence of the wind and mutual attrition,[e] but such a flame as might be kindled at the bidding of God, brilliant and of the fiercest heat. Beneath this blaze, which leapt out upon them, all those two hundred and fifty, along with Korah, were consumed, insomuch that all trace of their bodies disappeared. Aaron alone survived, in no wise injured by the fire, because it was God who had sent it to burn up those whose burning was requisite. Moreover Moses, after the destruction of these men, wishing their penalty to be commemorated and future generations to learn thereof, ordered Eleazar, the son of Aaron, to deposit

Numb. xvi. 35.

xvi. 36 (xvii. 1 Heb.).

" Thucydidean " assistant responsible for *Ant.* xvii - xix ; there are 100 instances of it in those books and only four, including this one, elsewhere.

[e] A description based on, and intended to outdo, that of the Plataean bonfire in Thuc. ii. 77 : " A flame arose of which the like had never before been made by the hand of man ; I am not speaking of fires in the mountains, when the woods have spontaneously blazed up from the action of the wind and mutual attrition " (Jowett). With this is combined an apparent allusion to the great eruption of Vesuvius which in A.D. 79 buried Pompeii and Herculaneum, and which is expressly mentioned in *A.* xx. 144.

JOSEPHUS

υἱὸν τὰ θυμιατήρια αὐτῶν παρὰ τὸν χάλκεον
58 καταθέσθαι βωμόν, ὡς ἂν ὑπόμνησις εἴη τοῖς
αὖθις ὧν ἔπαθον [καὶ]¹ ὅτι τὴν ἰσχὺν τοῦ θεοῦ
νομίσειαν ἀπατᾶσθαι δύνασθαι. καὶ Ἀαρὼν μὲν
οὐκέτι τῇ Μωυσέος χάριτι τὴν ἀρχιερωσύνην
ἔχειν δοκῶν, ἀλλὰ τῇ τοῦ θεοῦ κρίσει φανερᾷ
γενομένῃ, μετὰ τῶν υἱῶν ἤδη βεβαίως ἀπέλαυε
τῆς τιμῆς.
59 (iv. 1.) Τὴν μέντοι στάσιν οὐδ' οὕτως συνέβη
παύσασθαι, πολλῷ δὲ μᾶλλον αὔξειν καὶ φύεσθαι
χαλεπωτέραν· ἐλάμβανε δὲ² τῆς ἐπὶ τὸ χεῖρον
προκοπῆς αἰτίαν, ὑφ' ἧς οὐδέποτε λήξειν τὸ
60 δεινὸν ἦν εἰκὸς ἀλλ' εἰς χρόνον παραμενεῖν. οἱ
γὰρ ἄνθρωποι πεπιστευκότες ἤδη μηδὲν γίνεσθαι
δίχα τῆς τοῦ θεοῦ προνοίας οὐκ ἐβούλοντο ταῦτα
χωρὶς τῆς εἰς Μωυσῆν χάριτος τοῦ θεοῦ πεπρᾶχθαι,
κατηγόρουν δ' αὐτοῦ τὴν ὀργὴν τοῦ θεοῦ γενέσθαι³
τοσαύτην οὐχ οὕτω διὰ τὴν τῶν κολασθέντων
61 ἀδικίαν, ὡς Μωυσέος πραγματευσαμένου· καὶ τοὺς
μὲν διεφθάρθαι μηδὲν ἐξαμαρτόντας ἢ ὅτι περὶ
τὴν τοῦ θεοῦ θρησκείαν ἐσπουδάκεσαν, τὸν δὲ
τοιούτων⁴ ἀνδρῶν ὀλέθρῳ καὶ πάντων ἀρίστων
ἐζημιωκότα τὸν λαὸν πρὸς τῷ μηδεμίαν ὑποσχεῖν
δίκην ἔτι καὶ τὴν ἱερωσύνην ἀναμφίλεκτον τἀδελφῷ
62 παρασχεῖν· οὐδένα γὰρ ἔτι αὐτῆς ἄλλον ἀντι-
ποιήσεσθαι⁵ καὶ τοὺς πρώτους ὁρῶντα κακῶς
ἀπολωλότας. ἔτι γε μὴν καὶ παρὰ τῶν οἰκείων

---

¹ om. Lat.
² om. δὲ RO : χαλεπωτέραν ⟨τ'⟩ ἐλάμβανε Niese.
³ Bekker : γίνεσθαι codd.   ⁴ τοσούτων Niese.
⁵ ἀντιποιήσασθαι codd.

ᵃ " Let them be made beaten plates for a covering (lxx

30

their censers beside the brazen altar,[a] as a reminder to posterity of the fate which had befallen them for imagining that it was possible for deceit to be practised on the power of God. And Aaron, being no longer believed to owe his high-priesthood to the favour of Moses, but to the judgement of God thus clearly manifested, had now, along with his sons, the assured enjoyment of this dignity.

(iv. 1) Not even so, however, was the sedition brought to an end, nay it assumed far larger proportions and grew more grievous ; indeed it found an occasion for proceeding from bad to worse such that the trouble seemed likely never to cease but to become chronic. For those people, though convinced at length that nothing befell without God's providence, yet refused to believe that His favour for Moses had played no part in what had passed ; and they now laid it to his charge that the severity of God's wrath was due not so much to the iniquity of those who had been punished as to the machinations of Moses. The victims, so they said, had perished for no other crime save the zeal that they had displayed for God's worship ; while he who had chastised [b] the people by the destruction of such worthies, the noblest of them all, besides undergoing no punishment, had further conferred on his brother undisputed possession of the priesthood ; since none else would hereafter claim it, seeing that the very first to do so had come to a miserable end. Furthermore, the relatives of the victims made constant

Continuance of sedition.

Numb. xvi. 41 (xvii. 6 Heb.).

περίθεμα) of the altar." Numb. xvi. 38. For περίθεμα Josephus perhaps read παράθεμα : the two words appear as variant readings in Ex. xxxviii. 24 LXX, in a similar connexion.

[b] Literally " mulcted," with the collateral idea of " crippled."

τοῖς διεφθαρμένοις δέησις ἐγένετο πολλὴ τοῦ
πλήθους μειῶσαί τι τῆς Μωυσέος μεγαλαυχίας·
ἀσφαλὲς γὰρ αὐτοῖς τοῦτ᾽ εἶναι.

63 (2) Μωυσῆς δέ, καὶ γὰρ ἐκ πολλοῦ συνιστάμενον
ἠκροᾶτο τὸν θόρυβον, δείσας μή τι νεωτερίσωσι
πάλιν καὶ γένηταί τι μέγα καὶ χαλεπόν, συνήγαγε
τὸ πλῆθος εἰς ἐκκλησίαν [καὶ]¹ περὶ μὲν ὧν ἠκροᾶτο
εἰς ἀπολογίαν οὐ καθιστάμενος, ἵνα μὴ παροξύνῃ
τὸ πλῆθος, αὐτὸ δὲ μόνον τοῖς φυλάρχοις προειπὼν κομίζειν τὰ τῶν φυλῶν ὀνόματα βακτηρίαις
64 ἐπιγεγραμμένα· λήψεσθαι γὰρ ἐκεῖνον τὴν ἱερωσύνην, οὗπερ ἂν ὁ θεὸς ἐπισημήνῃ τῇ βακτηρίᾳ.
δόξαν οὖν κομίζουσιν οἵ τε ἄλλοι καὶ Ἀαρὼν
ἐπιγράψας Λευΐτην² ἐν τῇ βακτηρίᾳ, καὶ ταύτας
Μωυσῆς ἐν τῇ σκηνῇ τοῦ θεοῦ κατατίθησι. τῇ
δὲ ἐπιούσῃ προεκόμισε τὰς βακτηρίας· γνώριμοι
δ᾽ ἦσαν κατασημναμένων αὐτὰς τῶν τε ἀνδρῶν
65 οἵπερ ἐκόμιζον καὶ τοῦ πλήθους. καὶ τὰς μὲν
ἄλλας ἐφ᾽ οὗπερ αὐτὰς σχήματος Μωυσῆς παρ-
έλαβεν ἐπὶ τούτου μεμενηκυίας ἔβλεπον, ἐκ δὲ
τῆς Ἀαρῶνος βλαστούς τε καὶ κλάδους ἀναφύντας
ἑώρων καὶ καρπὸν ὡραῖον, ἀμύγδαλα δ᾽ ἦν, ἐκ
τοιούτου ξύλου τῆς βακτηρίας κατεσκευασμένης.
66 ἐκπλαγέντες δ᾽ ἐπὶ τῷ παραλόγῳ τῆς θέας, εἰ
καί τισι διὰ μίσους ἦν ὁ Μωυσῆς καὶ Ἀαρών,
ἀφέντες τοῦτο θαυμάζειν ἤρξαντο τὴν τοῦ θεοῦ
περὶ αὐτῶν κρίσιν καὶ τὸ λοιπὸν ἐπευφημοῦντες
τοῖς δεδογμένοις τῷ θεῷ συνεχώρουν Ἀαρῶνι

---

¹ om. edd.   ² Λευΐτιν Niese.

petition to the people to abate somewhat of Moses' arrogance, as this would make for their security.

(2) But[a] Moses, who long since had given ear to the troubles brewing, dreading some fresh revolution with some grave and grievous result, convened the people in assembly ; where, without embarking on any defence concerning the complaints which had come to his ears, for fear of exasperating the people, he merely directed the tribal chiefs to bring with them staves with the names of their tribes inscribed thereon, adding that the priesthood should be awarded to him upon whose staff God should set his mark. This being approved, they all brought them, including Aaron, who had inscribed " Levite "[b] upon his staff, and Moses laid them up in the tabernacle of God. On the morrow he produced the staves, which were clearly recognizable, having been marked both by the men who had brought them and by the people. All the rest were then seen to have remained in the state in which they were when Moses received them ; but from that of Aaron shoots and twigs had sprouted, so they beheld, and ripe fruit, to wit almonds, for it was of the wood of that tree that his staff was formed. Amazed at this extraordinary spectacle, any who bore malice against Moses and Aaron now renounced it and began to marvel at God's sentence concerning them ; and henceforth, applauding the divine decrees, they

The budding of Aaron's rod quells the rebels. Numb. xvii. 1 (16 Heb.).

---

[a] Josephus omits the incident of the plague, causing the death of 14,700 persons, occasioned by these further murmurings (Numb. xvi. 41-50).
[b] Or (with Niese's text) " (tribe) of Levi " ; according to Numb. xvii. 3 it was Aaron's name that was inscribed on the staff.

καλῶς ἔχειν τὴν ἀρχιερωσύνην. καὶ ὁ μὲν τρὶς
αὐτὸν τοῦ θεοῦ χειροτονήσαντος βεβαίως εἶχε
τὴν τιμήν, ἡ δὲ τῶν Ἑβραίων στάσις πολὺν
ἀκμάσασα χρόνον τοῦτον ἐπαύθη τὸν τρόπον.

67   (3) Μωυσῆς δ', ἐπεὶ πολέμου καὶ στρατείας ἡ
τῶν Λευιτῶν ἀφεῖτο φυλὴ θεραπεύσουσα[1] τὸν
θεόν, ἵνα μὴ δι' ἀπορίαν μηδὲ ζήτησιν τῶν εἰς
τὸν βίον ἀναγκαίων ἀμελοῖεν τοῦ ἱεροῦ, κατὰ
βούλησιν τοῦ θεοῦ τὴν Χαναναίαν κτησαμένους
τοὺς Ἑβραίους ἐκέλευε κατανεῖμαι τοῖς Λευίταις
ὀκτὼ καὶ τεσσαράκοντα πόλεις ἀγαθὰς καὶ καλὰς
τῆς τε πρὸ αὐτῶν γῆς περιγράψαντας εἰς δισχιλίους
68 πήχεις ἀπὸ τῶν τειχῶν αὐτοῖς ἀνεῖναι. πρὸς
τούτοις δὲ καὶ τὸν λαὸν διέταξε[2] τῶν ἐπετείων
καρπῶν δεκάτην αὐτοῖς τε τοῖς Λευίταις καὶ
ἱερεῦσι τελεῖν. καὶ ἃ μὲν ἡ φυλὴ παρὰ τοῦ πλήθους
λαμβάνει ταῦτ' ἐστίν· ἀναγκαῖον δ' ἡγησάμην ἃ
τοῖς ἱερεῦσιν ἴδια[3] παρὰ πάντων γίνεται δηλῶσαι.

69   (4) Τῶν μὲν τεσσαράκοντα καὶ ὀκτὼ πόλεων
τρισκαίδεκα παραχωρῆσαι τοὺς Λευίτας αὐτοῖς
προσέταξε καὶ τῆς δεκάτης, ἧς παρὰ τοῦ λαοῦ
κατ' ἔτος λαμβάνουσι, δεκάτην αὐτοῖς ἀπομερίζειν.
70 ἔτι δὲ ἀπαρχὰς τὸν λαὸν δίκαιον τῷ θεῷ πάντων
τῶν ἐκ τῆς γῆς φυομένων καρπῶν ἐπιφέρειν, καὶ

---

[1] ex Lat. Bernard: θεραπεύουσα codd.
[2] Niese: ἐξέταξε (ἐξέταζε RO) codd.   [3] ἰδίᾳ O (Niese).

[a] Or, perhaps, " conceded Aaron's honourable right to
the priesthood."
[b] The " Sophoclean " assistant, like his favourite poet,
has a partiality for the lucky number (see Introduction).
Here probably he breaks off and in the following sections
Josephus the priest seems to take up the pen himself.

allowed Aaron to hold the priesthood with honour.[a] So he, having thrice[b] been elected by God, was now firmly established in his office, and the sedition of the Hebrews, so long rampant, was thus terminated.

(3) Now, since the tribe of Levi had been exempted from war and military service to devote itself to the service of God, Moses, from fear that through indigence and the quest of the necessaries of life they should neglect the temple,[c] commanded the Hebrews, when by the will of God they should have conquered Canaan, to assign to the Levites forty-eight cities, goodly and fair, and of the land without these cities to mark off and make over to them a portion extending to two thousand[d] cubits from the ramparts. Furthermore he ordained that the people should pay a tithe of the annual produce of the ground to the Levites along with the priests.[e] That is what this tribe receives from the community; but I think it necessary to explain what contributions are made by all to the priests for themselves alone.

(4) In the first place, of those forty-eight cities he enjoined the Levites to cede thirteen to the priests,[f] and of the tithe which they annually received from the people to deduct a tithe for them. Moreover, the people are required to offer to God first-fruits of all the produce of the soil, and again of those quad-

Marginal notes: Levitical cities and tithes. Numb. xviii. 2. xxxv. 1. xviii. 21. The priests dues. Ib. 26. Ib. 12 f. Ib. 15.

[c] *i.e.* of after times; or perhaps " the sacred ministry " (Weill).

[d] So LXX, Numb. xxxv. 4; Hebrew, " a thousand," which is difficult to reconcile with the next verse.

[e] See further, §§ 205, 240 ff.

[f] Not in the Pentateuch; but see Josh. xxi. 4-19, where the thirteen cities given to the priests are enumerated.

τῶν τετραπόδων δὲ τῶν εἰς τὰς θυσίας νενομισμένων τὸ γεννηθὲν πρῶτον, ἂν ἄρσεν ᾖ, καταθῦσαι
παρασχεῖν τοῖς ἱερεῦσιν, ὥστε αὐτοὺς πανοικὶ
71 σιτεῖσθαι ἐν τῇ ἱερᾷ πόλει. τῶν δ' οὐ νενομισμένων
ἐσθίειν παρ' αὐτοῖς κατὰ τοὺς πατρίους νόμους
τοὺς δεσπότας [τῶν τικτομένων]¹ σίκλον καὶ ἥμισυ
αὐτοῖς ἀναφέρειν, ἀνθρώπου δὲ πρωτοτόκου πέντε
σίκλους, εἶναι δὲ ἀπαρχὰς αὐτοῖς καὶ τῆς τῶν
προβάτων κουρᾶς, τούς τε πέττοντας τὸν σῖτον
καὶ ἀρτοποιουμένους τῶν πεμμάτων αὐτοῖς τινα
72 χορηγεῖν. ὅσοι δ' ἂν αὐτοὺς καθιερῶσιν εὐχὴν
πεποιημένοι, ναζιραῖοι δὲ οὗτοι καλοῦνται, κο-
μῶντες καὶ οἶνον οὐ προσφερόμενοι, τούτους δὲ
ὅταν τὰς τρίχας ἀφιερῶσιν ἐπὶ θυσίᾳ τε δρῶσι
73 τὰς κουρὰς νέμεσθαι πρὸς τοὺς ἱερέας. καὶ οἱ
κορβᾶν αὐτοὺς ὀνομάσαντες τῷ θεῷ, δῶρον δὲ
τοῦτο σημαίνει κατὰ Ἑλλήνων γλῶτταν, βουλομένους ἀφίεσθαι τῆς λειτουργίας τοῖς ἱερεῦσι
καταβάλλειν ἀργύριον, γυναῖκα μὲν τριάκοντα
σίκλους ἄνδρα δὲ πεντήκοντα. ὅσοι δὲ ἂν ἐν-
δεέστερα τῶν ὡρισμένων ἔχωσι χρημάτων² τοῖς
ἱερεῦσιν ἐξεῖναι περὶ τούτων ὡς βούλονται δο-
74 κιμάσαι. εἶναι δὲ καὶ τοῖς κατ' οἶκον θύουσιν
εὐωχίας ἔνεκα τῆς αὐτῶν ἀλλὰ μὴ θρησκείας
ἀνάγκην κομίζειν τοῖς ἱερεῦσιν ἔνυστρόν τε καὶ

---

¹ om. RO. ² χρήματα Bekker.

ᵃ To be erected hereafter (§ 200).

ᵇ So generally " the firstling of unclean beasts shalt thou
redeem " (Numb. xviii. 15) ; early tradition (see Weill)
limited this to " the firstling of an ass " (Ex. xxxiv. 20).

ᶜ Amount not in Scripture, but has Rabbinical authority
(Weill).

rupeds which the law sanctions as sacrifices they are
to present the firstborn, if a male, to the priests for
sacrifice, to be consumed by them with their families
in the holy city.[a]   In the case of creatures[b] which
they are forbidden to eat in compliance with their
ancestral laws, the owners thereof must pay to the
priests a shekel and a half,[c] and for the firstborn of
man five shekels.[d]   To them too fall first-fruits of
the shearing of the sheep ; and when the corn is
baked and made into bread, some of these cakes
must be supplied to them. All who consecrate
themselves in fulfilment of a vow—Nazirites as they
are called, people who grow long hair and abstain
from wine—these too, when they dedicate their hair
and offer it in sacrifice assign their shorn locks to
the priests.[e]   Again, those who describe themselves
as " Corban "[f] to God—meaning what Greeks would
call " a gift "—when desirous to be relieved of this
obligation must pay down to the priests a fixed sum,
amounting for a woman to thirty shekels, for a man
to fifty[g] ; for those whose means are insufficient to
pay the appointed sum, the priests are at liberty to
decide as they choose. Furthermore, any persons
slaughtering animals at their homes for their own
good cheer and not for the ritual are bound to bring
to the priests the maw, the breast, and the right

Numb.
xviii. 16.
Deut.

xviii. 4.
Numb.
xv. 20 f.

Ib. vi. 2.

Lev. xxvii.
1-8.

Deut. xviii.
3 with
Lev. vii.
31 ff.
Cf. Numb.
xviii. 18.

---

[a] In Numbers this sum applies to the firstborn of unclean
beasts also.

[e] According to Numb. vi. 18 the Nazirite throws his hair
on to the sacrificial fire.

[f] *korbān*, an " offering," " oblation " ; translated, as
here, by δῶρον in Mark vii. 11, by Josephus again in *Ap.*
i. 167 (where it denotes an oath) by δῶρον θεοῦ.

[g] Special terms for minors and superannuated (Lev. xxvii.
5-7) are here omitted.

χελύνιον καὶ τὸν δεξιὸν βραχίονα τοῦ θύματος.
καὶ τοῖς μὲν ἱερεῦσι Μωυσῆς τοσαύτην, πάρεξ
ὧν ὑπὲρ ἁμαρτημάτων θύων ὁ λαὸς δίδωσιν
αὐτοῖς, ὡς ἐν τῇ πρὸ ταύτης βίβλῳ δεδηλώκαμεν,
75 εὐπορίαν ἐπενόησε. πάντων δὲ τῶν τοῖς ἱερεῦσι
τελουμένων κοινωνεῖν διέταξε καὶ τοὺς οἰκέτας
καὶ θυγατέρας καὶ γυναῖκας ἔξω τῶν ὑπὲρ ἁμαρτημάτων ἐπιφερομένων θυσιῶν· ταύτας γὰρ ἐν
τῷ ἱερῷ μόνοι δαπανῶσιν οἱ ἄρρενες τῶν ἱερέων
αὐθημερόν.

76 (5) Ὡς δὲ ταῦτα μετὰ τὴν στάσιν Μωυσῆς
διέταξεν, ἄρας μετὰ πάσης τῆς στρατιᾶς ἐπὶ τοὺς
τῆς Ἰδουμαίας ὅρους ἦλθε καὶ πρέσβεις πρὸς τὸν
βασιλέα τῶν Ἰδουμαίων πέμψας ἠξίου δίοδον
αὐτῷ παρασχεῖν, πίστεις ἃς αὐτὸς ἐθέλοι λαβεῖν
ὑπὲρ τοῦ μηδὲν ἀδικηθήσεσθαι δώσειν ὁμολογῶν,
ἀγοράν τε τῷ στρατῷ χορηγῆσαι κἂν¹ τιμὴν τοῦ
77 ὕδατος αὐτοὺς κελεύσειε² καταβαλεῖν. ὁ δ' οἷς
ἐπρεσβεύσατο Μωυσῆς οὐκ ἀρεσκόμενος οὐδὲ
συγχωρῶν τὴν δίοδον ἔνοπλον τὴν στρατιὰν
ἀγαγὼν προαπήντα τῷ Μωυσεῖ, κωλύσων αὐτοὺς
εἰ τολμήσειαν βίᾳ περαιοῦσθαι. καὶ Μωυσῆς,
ἄρχειν γὰρ μάχης οὐ συνεβούλευσεν ὁ θεὸς χρω-
μένῳ, τὴν δύναμιν ὑπανῆγε διὰ τῆς ἐρήμου
ἐκπεριών.

¹ ed. pr.: καὶ codd.   ² ML: κελεῦσαι RO, εἰ κελεύσειε SP.

ᵃ Or " shoulder " ; Greek " arm."
ᵇ The Law contains two contradictory statements concerning the portions of the victim assigned to the priests *at the
ordinary sacrifices* : (1) Deut. xviii. 3 naming " the shoulder,
the two cheeks and the maw " (*i.e.* the fourth stomach of
ruminants), and (2) Lev. vii. 31 f. naming " the breast " and

leg *a* of the victim.*b* Such is the ample provision
designed by Moses for the priests, beside what is
given them by the people from their sin-offerings,
as we have mentioned in the preceding book.*c*
Moreover, in all these dues payable to the priests, he
ordained that their servants, daughters, and wives
should also participate, with the exception of the
sacrifices offered for sins : these are for the males
only of the priestly families, being consumed by them
in the temple on the selfsame day.

Cf. Numb.
xviii. 11.

Cf. Lev. vi.
26 (19),
Numb.
xviii. 10.

(5) When Moses had drawn up these regulations
after the sedition, he set out with his whole army and
came to the frontiers of Idumaea ; then, sending
envoys to the king of the Idumaeans, he requested
him to grant him passage, promising to give whatever
guarantees he might desire to ensure himself against
injury, asking him to open a market for his army,
and even undertaking to pay a price for water should
he order them to do so.*d* But the king was ill pleased
with this message of Moses, refused him passage,
and led forth his armed troops to encounter Moses
and check these people should they essay to cross
his territory by force. And Moses, since upon his
inquiry God did not counsel him to open battle,
withdrew his forces to pursue a circuitous route
through the desert.

The king of
Edom
refuses
passage
through his
realm.
Ib. xx. 14.

"the right thigh" (leg). The two passages doubtless represent regulations in force at different periods. But to
remove the discrepancy Jewish tradition interpreted the
Deuteronomy passage as referring not to the sacrifices but
to animals slaughtered at home ; so Philo, *De spec. leg.* i. 3
§ 147 ἀπὸ τῶν ἔξω τοῦ βωμοῦ θυομένων ἕνεκα κρεωφαγίας,
and Mishnah, *Ḥullin* 10. 1 (quoted by Driver *in loc.*).
Josephus presents a mixture of the two lists.

c iii. 230-232, etc.   *d* Text a little uncertain.

78 (6) Τότε δὴ καὶ τὴν ἀδελφὴν αὐτοῦ Μαριάμμην
τελευτὴ τοῦ βίου καταλαμβάνει τεσσαρακοστὸν
ἔτος πεπληρωκυῖαν ἀφ' οὗ τὴν Αἴγυπτον κατέλιπε
μηνὸς δὲ Ξανθικοῦ νουμηνίᾳ κατὰ σελήνην.
θάπτουσι δ' αὐτὴν δημοσίᾳ πολυτελῶς ὑπέρ τινος
ὄρους, ὃ καλοῦσι Σείν, καὶ πενθήσαντα ἐπὶ τριάκοντα ἡμέρας τὸν λαὸν ἐκάθηρε Μωυσῆς τούτῳ
79 τῷ τρόπῳ· μόσχον θήλειαν, ἀρότρου μὲν καὶ γε-
ωργίας ἄπειρον ὁλόκληρον δέ, ξανθὴν πᾶσαν,
μικρὸν ἄπωθεν τοῦ στρατοπέδου προαγαγὼν εἰς
χωρίον καθαρώτατον ὁ ἀρχιερεὺς ἔθυέ τε καὶ τοῦ
αἵματος ἑπτάκις ἔρραινε τῷ δακτύλῳ ἀντικρὺ
80 τῆς σκηνῆς τοῦ θεοῦ. ἔπειτα καιομένης ὡς εἶχεν
ὅλης τῆς δαμάλιδος σὺν τῇ δορᾷ καὶ τοῖς ἐντὸς
ξύλον κέδρινον εἰς μέσον ἐμβάλλουσι τὸ πῦρ καὶ
ὕσσωπον καὶ φοινικτὸν ἔριον· συναγαγὼν δ' αὐτῆς
ἅπασαν τὴν τέφραν ἁγνὸς ἀνὴρ κατατίθησιν εἰς
81 χωρίον καθαρώτατον. τοὺς οὖν ἀπὸ νεκροῦ με-
μιασμένους, τῆς τέφρας ὀλίγον εἰς πηγὴν ἐνιέντες
καὶ ὕσσωπον βαπτίσαντές [τε καὶ τῆς τέφρας
ταύτης εἰς πηγήν],[1] ἔρραινον τρίτῃ τε καὶ ἑβδόμῃ
τῶν ἡμερῶν καὶ καθαροὶ τὸ λοιπὸν ἦσαν. τοῦτο
δὲ καὶ κατελθοῦσιν εἰς τὰς κληρουχίας προσέταξε,
ποιεῖν.

[1] om. Bekker.

---

[a] *Alias* on the 1st of Nisan (*A.* i. 81). Numbers (xx. 1)
mentions " the first month," but neither the year nor the
day ; other Jewish authorities, *e.g.* the Palestinian Targum,
name the 10th of Nisan.

[b] Numbers mentions " the *wilderness* of Zin," and Kadesh,
situated within it, as the burial-place of Miriam. The reading
" mountain " for " wilderness " occurs in one Egyptian
(Bohairic) version made from the lxx, but there it is
probably due to a confusion, found in that and other
authorities, between " Sin " and " Sinai."

(6) And now it was that death overtook his sister Mariamme, who had completed her fortieth year since she left Egypt, on the new moon, by lunar reckoning, of the month Xanthicus.[a] They buried her at the public expense in state on a mountain which they call Sin[b]; and when the people had mourned for her thirty days, they were purified by Moses on this wise.[c] A heifer, yet ignorant of the plough and of husbandry, without blemish and entirely red, was conducted by the high priest a little way outside the camp to a place of spotless purity,[d] where he sacrificed it and sprinkled with his finger drops of its blood seven times in the direction of the tabernacle of God. Next, the heifer was burnt whole, just as it was, including its skin and entrails, and into the midst of the blaze they cast cedar-wood and hyssop and crimson[e] wool. Its ashes were then all collected by a holy[f] man, who deposited them in a place of spotless purity. When, therefore, any had been polluted by contact with a corpse, they put a little of these ashes in running water, dipped hyssop into the stream, and sprinkled such persons therewith on the third and on the seventh day, and thenceforth they were clean. This ceremony Moses charged them to continue when they had entered upon their allotted territories.

Death of Miriam. Institution of ceremony of the Red Heifer. Numb. xx. 1.

Ib. xix. 1.

Ib. xix. 11 f., 18 f.

[c] In Scripture the law of the Red Heifer (relating to pollution from contact with a corpse) immediately *precedes* the death of Miriam, but without any express connexion with it; tradition has traced a connexion between the contiguous chapters, Numb. xix and xx.

[d] This phrase on its first occurrence (see § 80) is not in the Hebrew, but the LXX has εἰς τόπον καθαρόν (Numb. xix. 3).

[e] Or " red " : Bibl. " scarlet."

[f] *i.e.* ceremonially clean.

82 (7) Μετὰ δὲ τὴν ἐπὶ τῷ πένθει τῆς ἀδελφῆς
τοῦ στρατηγοῦ κάθαρσιν τοιαύτην γενομένην ἀπῆγε
τὴν δύναμιν διὰ τῆς ἐρήμου, καὶ τῆς Ἀραβίας
ἐλθὼν εἰς χωρίον, ὃ μητρόπολιν αὐτῶν Ἄραβες
νενομίκασι, πρότερον μὲν Ἄρκην[1] λεγομένην
83 Πέτραν δὲ νῦν ὀνομαζομένην, ἐνταῦθα ὑψηλοῦ
περιέχοντος ὄρους αὐτὸ ἀναβὰς Ἀαρὼν ἐπ' αὐτό,
Μωυσέος αὐτῷ δεδηλωκότος ὅτι μέλλοι τελευτᾶν,
ἅπαντος τοῦ στρατεύματος ὁρῶντος, κατάντες
γὰρ ἦν τὸ χωρίον, ἀποδύεται τὴν ἀρχιερατικὴν
στολὴν καὶ παραδοὺς αὐτὴν Ἐλεαζάρῳ τῷ παιδί,
πρὸς ὃν διὰ τὴν ἡλικίαν ἡ ἀρχιερωσύνη παραγίνεται, θνήσκει τοῦ πλήθους εἰς αὐτὸν ἀφ-
84 ορῶντος, τῷ μὲν αὐτῷ τελευτήσας ἔτει, ᾧ καὶ
τὴν ἀδελφὴν ἀπέβαλε, βιοὺς δὲ ἔτη τὰ πάντα
τρία πρὸς τοῖς εἴκοσι καὶ ἑκατόν. ἀποθνήσκει
δὲ κατὰ σελήνην νουμηνίᾳ μηνὸς ὄντος τοῦ παρὰ
μὲν Ἀθηναίοις Ἑκατομβαιῶνος καλουμένου Λώου
δὲ παρὰ Μακεδόσι⟨ν⟩, Ἀββὰ[2] δὲ παρ' Ἑβραίοις.
85 (v. 1) Πένθος δὲ ἐπ' αὐτῷ τοῦ λαοῦ τριακον-
θήμερον ἄγοντος, ἐπεὶ τοῦτ' ἐλώφησεν, ἀναλαβὼν
ἐκεῖθεν Μωυσῆς τὸν στρατὸν παρῆν ἐπὶ τὸν
ποταμὸν Ἀρνῶνα, ὃς ἐκ τῶν τῆς Ἀραβίας ὀρῶν
ὡρμημένος[3] καὶ διὰ πάσης ἐρήμου ῥέων εἰς τὴν

---

[1] Ἀρκὲμ Eus.: Ἀρεκέμην Bernard.
[2] Bernard: σαβ(β)ὰ, σαβὰr (sebath Lat.) codd.
[3] RO: ὁρμώμενος rell.

---

a Not mentioned in Numbers, which, however, names the
mountain which Aaron ascended, viz. Mount Hor. Since
later on (§ 161) Josephus identifies Petra with Ῥεκέμη, deriving that name from its king Rekem, probably Ἄρκην is
here corrupt and we should read Ἀρεκέμην. When Josephus
wrote, Petra was the capital of the powerful Nabataean kingdom.

(7) After a purification held in such wise in consequence of the mourning for the sister of their chief, he led his forces away through the desert and came to a place in Arabia which the Arabs have deemed their metropolis, formerly called Arce,[a] to-day named Petra. There Aaron ascended a lofty mountain range that encloses the spot, Moses having revealed to him that he was about to die, and, in the sight of the whole army—for the ground was steep—he divested himself of his high priestly robes and, after delivering them to Eleazar his son, upon whom by right of age the high priesthood descended, he died with the eyes of the multitude upon him. He ended his days in the same year in which he had lost his sister, having lived in all one hundred and twenty-three years. He died on the opening day, by lunar reckoning, of the month called by the Athenians Hecatombaeon, by the Macedonians Lous, and by the Hebrews Abba.[b]

(v. 1) For thirty days [c] the people mourned for him, and, when this mourning was ended, Moses, marching his army thence, arrived at the river Arnon, which, springing from the mountains of Arabia and traversing an absolute desert, plunges into the lake Asphal-

Death of Aaron. Numb. xx. 22.

Ib. xxxiii. 38.

Sihon, king of the Amorites, refuses passage. Ib. xxi. 13.

---

[b] Aram. *abba*, Hebr. *ab*, the fifth month of the Hebrew year (*c.* July-August): " Aaron . . . died in the fortieth year [after the exodus] . . . in the fifth month, on the first day of the month " (Numb. *l.c.*). " Abba " is, however, an emendation ; and it is possible that the ms. reading σαβάτ (Lat. *sebath*) should stand, and that Josephus followed another tradition, dating the event six months later, on the 1st of *Shebat*.

[c] Numb. xx. 29. Josephus here omits (1) the victory at Hormah (incorporated perhaps in the victory over Sihon described below), and (2) the story of the brazen serpent.

Ἀσφαλτῖτιν λίμνην ἐκδίδωσιν ὁρίζων τήν τε
Μωαβῖτιν καὶ Ἀμορῖτιν. γῇ δ᾽ αὕτη καρποφόρος
καὶ πλῆθος ἀνθρώπων[1] τοῖς παρ᾽ αὐτῆς ἀγαθοῖς
86 ἱκανὴ τρέφειν. πρὸς οὖν Σιχῶνα τὸν βασιλεύοντα
τῆς χώρας ταύτης ἀπέστειλε Μωυσῆς τῷ στρατῷ
δίοδον αἰτῶν ἐφ᾽ αἷς ἂν θελήσειε πίστεσιν, ὥστε
μηδὲν ἀδικηθῆναι μήτε τὴν γῆν μήτε τοὺς ἐνοικοῦντας, ὧν Σιχὼν ἐκράτει, τοῖς τε κατὰ τὴν
ἀγορὰν χρῆσθαι πρὸς τὸ ἐκείνων λυσιτελές, εἰ
καὶ τὸ ὕδωρ αὐτοῖς πιπράσκειν ἐθέλοιεν. Σιχὼν
δ᾽ ἀρνούμενος ὁπλίζει τὸν οἰκεῖον στρατὸν καὶ
τοὺς Ἑβραίους διαβαίνειν τὸν Ἀρνῶνα κωλύειν
ἑτοιμότατος ἦν.

87 (2) Μωυσῆς δὲ ὁρῶν πολεμίως αὐτοῖς τὸν
Ἀμοραῖον διακείμενον οὔτε περιφρονούμενος
ἀνέχεσθαι δεῖν ἔγνω καὶ τοὺς Ἑβραίους τῆς
ἀπραξίας καὶ τῆς δι᾽ αὐτὴν ἀπορίας, ὑφ᾽ ἧς
στασιάσαι τε πρότερον αὐτοῖς συνέπεσε καὶ τότε
δυσκόλως εἶχον, ἀπαλλάξαι διαγνοὺς ἤρετο τὸν
88 θεόν, εἰ πολεμεῖν αὐτῷ δίδωσι. τοῦ δὲ θεοῦ καὶ
νίκην ἀποσημήναντος[2] αὐτὸς θαρσαλέως εἶχε πρὸς
τὸν ἀγῶνα καὶ τοὺς στρατιώτας παρώρμα, νῦν
αὐτοὺς ἀξιῶν τῆς τοῦ πολεμεῖν ἡδονῆς ἀπολαύειν,
ὅτ᾽ αὐτῇ συγχωρεῖ χρῆσθαι τὸ θεῖον. οἱ δ᾽ ἧς
ἐπόθουν ἐξουσίας λαβόμενοι καὶ τὰς πανοπλίας
89 ἀναλαβόντες εὐθέως ἐχώρουν εἰς τὸ ἔργον. ὁ
δὲ Ἀμοραῖος οὐκέτ᾽ ἦν ἐπιόντων ὅμοιος αὑτῷ,
ἀλλ᾽ αὐτός τε κατεπλάγη τοὺς Ἑβραίους καὶ ἡ
δύναμις αὐτοῦ παρέχουσα θᾶττον αὐτὴν εὔψυχον
εἶναι δοκεῖν τότ᾽ ἀπηλέγχθη πεφοβημένη. τὴν

---

[1] + ἴσον OML. [2] ἐπισημήναντος RO.

titis,[a] forming the boundary between the Moabite
and Amorite countries. The latter region is fertile
and capable of supporting with its riches an host of
men. Moses accordingly sent an embassy to Sihon, Numb.
the sovereign of this country, soliciting passage for xxi. 21.
his army upon such guarantees as he might choose
to impose, so as to ensure that no injury should be
done either to the land or to its inhabitants, whom
Sihon governed, and offering to purchase provisions
to the advantage of the Amorites, including even
water, should they choose to sell it to them. But
Sihon refused, armed his troops, and was fully prepared to stop the Hebrews from crossing the Arnon.

(2) Moses, seeing this hostile attitude of the Defeat
Amorite, determined that he ought not to brook this of the
affront, and, since he withal resolved to deliver the and con-
Hebrews from that inactivity and consequent in- their
digence, which had produced their previous mutiny country.
and their present discontent, he inquired of God Ib. 24.
whether He authorized him to fight. When, therefore, God even betokened victory, he was himself
encouraged for the contest and roused the ardour
of his soldiers, urging them now to gratify their
lust of battle, now when they had the sanction of the
Deity to indulge it. And they, having won that
concession for which they craved, put all their armour
on and proceeded straight into action. The Amorite,
faced by their advance, was a different man, himself
viewing the Hebrews with dismay, while his army,
which had of late [b] made such a show of spirit, now
proved positively afraid. Thus, without waiting to

[a] The " Bituminous " lake = the Dead Sea.

[b] For $\theta\hat{a}\tau\tau o\nu = \pi\rho\acute{o}\tau\epsilon\rho o\nu$ cf. A. v. 171 (and so frequently
$\tau\acute{a}\chi\iota o\nu$, A. i. 98, etc.); but the word here may connote " too
hastily."

45

πρώτην οὖν σύνοδον οὐχ ὑπομείναντες ἀντιστῆναι
καὶ δέξασθαι τοὺς Ἑβραίους τρέπονται, τοῦτο
ἑαυτοῖς σωτηρίαν ὑπολαβόντες ἢ τὸ μάχεσθαι
90 παρέξειν· ἐθάρρουν γὰρ ταῖς πόλεσιν οὔσαις
ὀχυραῖς. παρ' ὧν οὐδὲν αὐτοῖς ὄφελος ἦν εἰς
ταύτας συνδιωχθεῖσιν· Ἑβραῖοι γὰρ ὡς ἐνδόντας
αὐτοὺς εὐθὺς εἶδον, ἐνέκειντο καὶ παραλύσαντες
91 αὐτῶν τὸν κόσμον εἰς φόβον κατέστησαν. καὶ
οἱ μὲν ἀπορραγέντες ἔφευγον ἐπὶ τῶν πόλεων, οἱ
δὲ πρὸς τὴν δίωξιν οὐκ ἔκαμνον, ἀλλ' οἷς προ-
πεπονήκεσαν προσεπιταλαιπωρῆσαι προσθέμενοι,[1]
καὶ σφενδονᾶν τε ἄριστοι τυγχάνοντες καὶ πᾶσι
τοῖς ἐκηβόλοις δεξιοὶ χρῆσθαι, καὶ διὰ τὴν ὅπλισιν
οὖσαν εὐσταλῆ κοῦφοι πρὸς τὸ διώκειν ὄντες
μετέθεον τοὺς πολεμίους καὶ τοὺς πορρωτάτω
συλληφθῆναι γεγονότας ταῖς σφενδόναις καὶ τοῖς
92 τοξεύμασι κατελάμβανον. φόνος τε οὖν γίνεται
πολὺς καὶ τραύμασιν ἐπόνουν οἱ διαφεύγοντες,
ἔκαμνον δὲ[2] ἐπὶ δίψει μᾶλλον ἤ τινι τῶν πολεμικῶν·
καὶ γὰρ ὥρα θέρους ἦν· καὶ ἐπιθυμίᾳ τοῦ πιεῖν
ἐπὶ ποταμὸν τοὺς πλείους καταραχθέντας, καὶ
ὅσον συνεστραμμένον ἔφευγε, περιστάντες ἔβαλλον
καὶ πάντας αὐτοὺς ἀκοντίζοντες ἅμα καὶ τοξεύοντες
93 διέφθειραν. ἀποθνήσκει δ' αὐτῶν καὶ Σιχὼν ὁ
βασιλεύς. Ἑβραῖοι δὲ νεκροὺς ἐσκύλευον καὶ
λείαν ἔλαβον καὶ πολλὴν ἀφθονίαν τῶν ἐκ τῆς
γῆς εἶχον μεστῆς ἔτι τῶν καρπῶν ὑπαρχούσης,

---

[1] προθέμενοι (Bekker, Niese) is a needless emendation.
[2] τε RO.

---

[a] Triple alliteration in the Greek. If the "Sophoclean"
assistant is here at work, he had warrant for this in his model,

withstand the first shock and receive the Hebrews, they turned their backs, deeming that flight would afford them better safety than a fight ; for they relied on their cities with strong fortifications. These, however, profited them naught when they were pursued thither. For the Hebrews, on seeing them at once give way, pressed hard upon them and, throwing their ranks into disorder, reduced them to panic. So, breaking from the ranks, they fled for the cities ; while the others showed no slackness for the pursuit, but, crowning their previous pains with perseverance,[a] being at once excellent slingers and experts in the use of all long-range missiles, and withal through their light equipment [b] swift to pursue, they were on their enemies' heels, while those who were now much too far to be captured they reached with their slings and arrows. So there was great carnage and the fugitives suffered sorely from wounds. But they succumbed more to thirst than to any engines of war ; for it was the height of summer, and in their craving for drink the greater number, indeed all who had kept together in the rout, dashed down into a river, where their pursuers, surrounding and pelting them at once with javelins and arrows, destroyed them all.[c] Sihon their king was among the slain. The Hebrews then rifled the corpses and took the spoil, obtaining also abundance of the produce of the land, which was still laden with

e.g. Soph. *O.C.* 589 κεῖνοι κομίζειν κεῖσε, 804 f. φύσας φανεῖ φρένας, 1140 τεκνοῖσι τερφθεὶς τοῖσδε.

[b] After Thuc. iii. 22 εὐσταλεῖς τῇ ὁπλίσει.

[c] This spirited scene is drawn from the famous account of the retreat of the Athenians from Syracuse, the river being the Sicilian Assinaros (Thuc. vii. 83 f.) ; while the phrase ὅσον συνεστραμμένον recalls Plataea (*ib.* ii. 4) ! Here clearly the " Thucydidean " assistant lends his aid.

94 καὶ διεξῄει πᾶσαν¹ ἀδεῶς τὸ στράτευμα προνομῇ
χρώμενον, ἁλισκομένων καὶ τῶν πόλεων· οὐδὲν
γὰρ παρὰ τούτων ἦν ἐμπόδιον τοῦ μαχίμου παντὸς
ἀπολωλότος. Ἀμοραίους μὲν οὖν τοιοῦτο πάθος
κατέλαβεν οὔτε φρονῆσαι δεινοὺς οὔτε ἀγαθοὺς
κατὰ τὸ ἔργον γεγονότας, Ἑβραῖοι δὲ τὴν ἐκείνων
95 παρελάμβανον. ἔστι δὲ χωρίον, ὃ τριῶν μεταξὺ
ποταμῶν κείμενον ὅμοιόν τι νήσῳ τὴν φύσιν
ὑπάρχει, τοῦ μὲν Ἀρνῶνος ἀπὸ μεσημβρίας ὁρί-
ζοντος αὐτό, Ἰοβάκου δὲ τὴν ἀρκτῷαν αὐτοῦ
πλευρὰν περιγράφοντος, ὃς εἰς τὸν Ἰόρδανον
ποταμὸν ἐκβάλλων ἐκείνῳ καὶ τοῦ ὀνόματος²
μεταδίδωσι· τὰ μέντοι γε πρὸς τῇ δύσει τοῦ χωρίου
περίεισιν αὐτὴν Ἰόρδανος.

96 (3) Οὕτως οὖν ἐχόντων τῶν πραγμάτων ἐπι-
τίθεται τοῖς Ἰσραηλίταις Ὤγης ὁ τῆς Γαλαδηνῆς
καὶ Γαυλανίτιδος βασιλεὺς στρατὸν ἄγων, καὶ
σπεύδων μὲν ὡς ἐπὶ συμμαχίαν τὴν Σιχῶνος,
φίλου τυγχάνοντος, εὑρὼν δὲ ἐκεῖνον ἤδη προ-
απολωλότα καὶ οὕτως ἔγνω τοῖς Ἑβραίοις εἰς
μάχην ἐλθεῖν περιέσεσθαί τε νομίζων καὶ τῆς
97 ἀρετῆς αὐτῶν διάπειραν βουλόμενος λαβεῖν· δι-
αμαρτὼν δὲ τῆς ἐλπίδος αὐτός τε ἀποθνήσκει
κατὰ τὴν μάχην καὶ σύμπας ὁ στρατὸς αὐτοῦ
διαφθείρεται. Μωυσῆς δὲ τὸν ποταμὸν Ἰόβακον
περαιωσάμενος διεξῄει τῆς Ὤγου βασιλείας τάς
τε πόλεις καταστρεφόμενος καὶ κτείνων πάντας
τοὺς ἐνοικοῦντας, οἳ καὶ πλούτῳ διέφερον πάντων

---

¹ Bekker: πᾶσιν codd.   ² νάματος Naber.

ᵃ Bibl. Jabbok (Ἰαβόκ).
ᵇ Cf. i. 177, where Josephus seems to imply that the Jordan derived its second syllable from " Dan, one of its two

the crops and was, without fear of molestation, traversed in every direction by the troops for foraging purposes ; the cities too were captured, for these presented no obstacle now that all combatants had perished. Such was the catastrophe that overtook the Amorites, who had shown neither skill in counsel nor valour in action ; and the Hebrews took possession of their land. It is a region situated between three rivers, which give it something of the nature of an island : the Arnon forming its southern boundary, its northern flank being circumscribed by the Jobak,[a] which pours into the river Jordan and gives that stream a portion of its name,[b] while the western area of the district is compassed by the Jordan.

(3) Such was the position of affairs when there came to attack the Israelites Og, the king of Galadene and Gaulanitis,[c] at the head of an army, and hastening, as he believed, to the support of his friend Sihon ; yet, though he found that he had already perished, he none the less resolved to give battle to the Hebrews, confident of success and fain to make trial of their valour. But, disappointed in this hope, he met his own end in the battle and his whole army was annihilated. Moses then, crossing the river Jobak, overran the realm of Og, subduing the cities and killing all the inhabitants, who surpassed in riches all the occupants of those inland parts, thanks

Defeat of Og. Numb. xxi. 33 : Deut. iii. 1.

sources " : here he suggests that it owes the first syllable (or rather the first two letters) to its tributary the Jo-bak as he calls it. According to the widely accepted etymology, Jordan means " the descender."

[c] Bibl. " king of Bashan " ; Josephus substitutes names of his own day, which do not exactly correspond to the ancient Bashan. Gilead (Galadene) was a distinct district to the south of it.

49

τῶν ἐκείνῃ ἠπειρωτῶν δι' ἀρετὴν γῆς καὶ πλῆθος
98 χρημάτων. Ὤγης δὲ μέγεθός τε καὶ κάλλος
ἦν οἷον ὀλίγοις¹ σφόδρα, ἦν δὲ καὶ κατὰ χεῖρα
γενναῖος ἀνήρ, ὡς ἴσα τὰ τῶν ἔργων εἶναι τοῖς
τοῦ μεγέθους καὶ τῆς εὐπρεπείας πλεονεκτήμασι.
τὴν δ' ἰσχὺν αὐτοῦ καὶ τὸ μέγεθος ἐτεκμηριώσαντο
κλίνην αὐτοῦ λαβόντες ἐν Ῥαβαθᾶ πόλει τῶν
βασιλείων τῆς Ἀμμανίτιδος, τῇ μὲν κατασκευῇ
σιδηρέαν,² τεσσάρων δὲ πηχῶν τὸ εὖρος, μήκει
99 δὲ τοῦ διπλασίονος ἑνὶ πήχει μείζονα. τούτου
τοίνυν πταίσαντος οὐκ εἰς τὸ παρὸν μόνον τοῖς
Ἑβραίοις ἐπέδωκε τὰ πράγματα, ἀλλὰ καὶ πρὸς
τὸ μέλλον ἀγαθῶν αὐτοῖς αἴτιος ἀποθανὼν ὑπῆρξε·
καὶ γὰρ πόλεις ἑξήκοντα λαμπρῶς πάνυ τετει-
χισμένας ὑποτελεῖς ἐκείνῳ παρέλαβον καὶ λείαν
πολλὴν ἰδίᾳ τε καὶ δημοσίᾳ πάντες εὐπόρησαν.
100 (vi. 1) Μωυσῆς μὲν οὖν στρατοπεδεύει κατ-
αγαγὼν³ τὴν δύναμιν ἐπὶ τῷ Ἰορδάνῳ κατὰ τὸ
μέγα πεδίον Ἱεριχοῦντος ἀντικρύ, πόλις δ' ἐστὶν
εὐδαίμων αὕτη φοίνικάς τε φέρειν ἀγαθὴ καὶ
βάλσαμον νεμομένη. ἤρχοντο δὲ φρονεῖν ἐφ'
ἑαυτοῖς μέγα Ἰσραηλῖται καὶ τὴν πρὸς τοὺς
101 πολέμους ἐπιθυμίαν ὑπερέτεινον. καὶ Μωυσῆς
ὀλίγων ἡμερῶν θύσας χαριστήρια πρῶτον τῷ
θεῷ καὶ τὸν λαὸν εὐωχήσας μέρος τι τῶν ὁπλιτῶν
ἐξέπεμψε δῃῶσον τὴν Μαδιανιτῶν γῆν καὶ τὰς
πατρίδας αὐτῶν ἐκπολιορκῆσον. τοῦ δ' ἐκπο-
λεμηθῆναι πρὸς αὐτοὺς αἰτίαν ἔλαβε τοιαύτην.
102 (2) Βάλακος ὁ τῶν Μωαβιτῶν βασιλεὺς φιλίας
αὐτῷ πατρῴας οὔσης καὶ συμμαχίας πρὸς Μα-

¹ οἷος ὀλίγοι RO.   ² σιδηρέην codd.
³ Niese: καὶ ἀγαγὼν codd.

to the excellence of the soil and an abundance of commodities. Og himself had a stature and beauty such as few could boast; he was withal a man of a doughty arm, so that his exploits were on a par with his superior gifts of height and a handsome presence. Of his strength and stature they had evidence on capturing his bedstead in Rabatha,[a] the capital of the Ammonite country : this was constructed of iron and was four cubits broad and double as much, with a cubit over, in length. With this giant's fall not merely was there an instant amelioration in the Hebrews' fortunes, but for the future too his death proved a source of benefits [b] ; for withal they captured sixty cities, magnificently fortified, that had owned his sway, and, individually and collectively, all reaped an ample booty. Deut. iii. 11.

Ib. 4 f.

(vi. 1) So Moses led his forces down towards the Jordan and encamped on the great plain [c] over against Jericho; this is a prosperous city, prolific of palm-trees and a nursery of balsam. The Israelites were now beginning to have a high opinion of themselves and becoming intensely keen in their ardour for battle. And Moses, after spending a few days first in sacrificing thank-offerings to God, and then in feasting the people, sent out a division of his troops to ravage the land of the Madianites [d] and to carry their cities by storm. For hostilities against this people, however, he had received provocation on this wise. The camp opposite Jericho.
Numb. xxii. 1.

(2) Balak, the king of the Moabites, who was linked by an ancestral amity and alliance to the Embassy of Balak to the Midianites and Balaam.
Ib. 2.

---

[a] Bibl. " Rabbah," Aramaic " Rabbath."
[b] Cf. iii. 56.
[c] The *Ghōr* (=" Rift ") or Jordan valley, *B.J.* iv. 455.
[d] So Josephus throughout: Bibl. Midian(ites), LXX Μαδιάμ.

διανίτας, ἐπεὶ τοὺς Ἰσραηλίτας τοσοῦτον φυο-
μένους ἑώρα καὶ περὶ τῶν αὑτοῦ πραγμάτων
λίαν εὐλαβεῖτο, καὶ γὰρ οὐδὲ πέπυστο γῆν ἄλλην
⟨οὐ⟩[1] πολυπραγμονεῖν τοὺς Ἑβραίους ἀπηγορευ-
κότος τοῦ θεοῦ κτησαμένους τὴν Χαναναίων,[2]
θᾶττον ἢ φρονιμώτερον ἐγχειρεῖν ἔγνω τοῖς
103 λόγοις.[3] καὶ πολεμεῖν μὲν ἐπὶ ταῖς εὐπραγίαις
θρασυτέροις τε[4] ὑπὸ τῆς κακοπραγίας κατ-
ειλημμένοις οὐκ ἔκρινε, κωλῦσαι δ᾽ εἰ δύναιτο
γενέσθαι μεγάλους λογιζόμενος πρεσβεῦσαι πρὸς
104 Μαδιανίτας ὑπὲρ αὑτῶν. οἱ δέ, ἦν γάρ τις ἀπὸ
Εὐφράτου Βάλαμος μάντις ἄριστος τῶν τότε καὶ
πρὸς αὐτοὺς ἐπιτηδείως ἔχων, πέμπουσι μετὰ
τῶν Βαλάκου πρέσβεων ἄνδρας τῶν παρ᾽ αὐτοῖς
ἀξιολόγων παρακαλέσοντας τὸν μάντιν ἐλθεῖν,
ὅπως ἂν ἐπ᾽ ἐξωλείᾳ τῶν Ἰσραηλιτῶν ἀρὰς
105 ποιήσηται. παραγενομένους δὲ τοὺς πρέσβεις
δέχεται ξενίᾳ φιλοφρόνως καὶ δειπνίσας ἀνέκρινε
τὴν τοῦ θεοῦ διάνοιαν, τίς αὕτη ἐστὶν ἐφ᾽ οἷς
Μαδιανῖται παρακαλοῦσι. τοῦ δ᾽ ἐμποδὼν στάντος ἀφικνεῖται πρὸς τοὺς πρέσβεις, προθυμίαν
μὲν καὶ σπουδὴν τὴν ἰδίαν ἐμφανίζων αὐτοῖς εἰς
ἃ δέονται τυχεῖν, τὸν δὲ θεὸν ἀντιλέγειν αὐτοῦ
τῇ προαιρέσει δηλῶν, ὃς αὐτὸν ἐπὶ τοσοῦτον κλέος
δι᾽ ἀλήθειαν καὶ τὴν ταύτης πρόρρησιν ἀγάγοι·
106 τὸν γὰρ στρατόν, ᾧ καταρασόμενον αὐτὸν ἐλθεῖν
παρακαλοῦσι, δι᾽ εὐνοίας εἶναι τῷ θεῷ· συν-

[1] ἄλλω (sic) R : ἄλλην rell. [2] + καὶ ed. pr. (Lat.).
[3] τοῖς ὅλοις Herwerden. [4] Text doubtful.

[a] " to try an assault of a verbal nature " (i.e. through
imprecations), or possibly " to essay parley (with his friends)."
52

Madianites, on seeing the Israelites growing so great, became gravely concerned for his own interests. For he had not learned that the Hebrews were not for interfering with other countries, God having forbidden them so to do, upon their conquest of the land of Canaan, and with more haste than discretion he resolved to essay what words could do.[a] To fight with men fresh from success and who were found to be only the more emboldened by reverse was not to his mind ; but with intent to check their aggrandizement, if he could, he decided to send an embassy to the Madianites concerning them. And these, forasmuch as there was a certain Balaam hailing from the Euphrates,[b] the best diviner of his day and on friendly terms with them, sent, along with the ambassadors of Balak, some of their own notables to entreat the seer to come and deliver curses for the extermination of the Israelites. When these envoys arrived Balaam received them with cordial hospitality and, after giving them supper, inquired of God what was His mind touching this invitation of the Madianites. Meeting with opposition from Him, he returned to the envoys and, making plain to them his own readiness and zeal to comply with their request,[c] he explained that God gainsaid his purpose, even that God who had brought him to his high renown for truth's sake and for the prediction thereof. For (he continued) that army, which they invited him to come and curse, was in favour with

There is no need to alter λόγοις : the phrase recurs in *B.J.* vii. 340 ἐνεχείρει λόγοις " essayed a flight of oratory."

[b] In Numb. xxii. 5 Balak sends messengers to Balaam " to Pethor which is by the river," *i.e.* (as Josephus and the Targum interpret) the Euphrates.

[c] So the Midrash (Weill).

ἐβούλευέ τε διὰ ταύτην τὴν αἰτίαν χωρεῖν παρ᾽
αὐτοὺς τὴν ἔχθραν τὴν πρὸς τοὺς Ἰσραηλίτας
καταλυσαμένους. καὶ τοὺς μὲν πρέσβεις ταῦτ᾽
εἰπὼν ἀπέλυσε.

107 (3) Μαδιανῖται δὲ Βαλάκου σφόδρα ἐγκειμένου
καὶ δέησιν λιπαρὰν προσφέροντος πάλιν πέμπουσι
πρὸς τὸν Βάλαμον. κἀκεῖνος βουλόμενος χαρίζεσθαί τι τοῖς ἀνδράσιν ἀνήρετο τὸν θεόν, ὁ
δὲ καὶ τῆς πείρας δυσχεράνας κελεύει μηδὲν
ἀντιλέγειν τοῖς πρέσβεσιν. ὁ δ᾽ οὐχ ὑπολαβὼν
ἀπάτῃ ταῦτα τὸν θεὸν κεκελευκέναι συναπήει
108 τοῖς πρέσβεσι. κατὰ δὲ τὴν ὁδὸν ἀγγέλου θείου
προσβαλόντος αὐτῷ κατά τι στενὸν χωρίον περι-
ειλημμένον αἱμασιαῖς διπλαῖς ἡ ὄνος, ἐφ᾽ ἧς
ὁ Βάλαμος ὠχεῖτο, συνεῖσα τοῦ θείου πνεύματος
ὑπαντῶντος ἀπέκλινε τὸν Βάλαμον πρὸς τὸν
ἕτερον τῶν τριγχῶν ἀναισθήτως ἔχουσα τῶν
πληγῶν, ἃς ὁ Βάλαμος ἐπέφερεν αὐτῇ κακοπαθῶν
109 τῇ θλίψει τῇ πρὸς τὸν τριγχόν. ὡς δ᾽ ἐγκειμένου
τοῦ ἀγγέλου ἡ ὄνος τυπτομένη ὤκλασε, κατὰ
βούλησιν θεοῦ φωνὴν ἀνθρωπίνην ἀφεῖσα[1] κατεμέμφετο τὸν Βάλαμον ὡς ἄδικον ἐπὶ ταῖς
πρότερον διακονίαις μηδὲν ἔχοντα ἐγκαλεῖν αὐτῇ
πληγὰς ἐπιφέρειν, μὴ συνιεὶς ὅτι νῦν κατὰ θεοῦ
προαίρεσιν οἷς αὐτὸς ἔσπευσεν ὑπηρετεῖν εἴργεται.
110 ταραττομένου δὲ αὐτοῦ διὰ τὴν τῆς ὄνου φωνὴν
ἀνθρωπίνην οὖσαν ἐπιφανεὶς καὶ ὁ ἄγγελος ἐναργὴς
ἐνεκάλει τῶν πληγῶν, ὡς οὐχὶ τοῦ κτήνους ὄντος
αἰτίου, τὴν δὲ ὁδὸν αὐτοῦ διακωλύοντος παρὰ
111 γνώμην τοῦ θεοῦ γενομένην. καταδείσας δ᾽ ὁ

---

[1] RO: λαβοῦσα rell.

[a] Or " breath," " afflatus."

God ; he therefore counselled them to depart to their people and renounce that hatred which they bore to the Israelites. Having spoken thus he took leave of the embassy.

(3) But the Madianites, at the urgent instance and persistent entreaties of Balak, sent once again to Balaam. And he, fain to give these men some gratification, consulted God anew ; whereat God, indignant that he should even tempt Him thus, bade him in no wise to gainsay the envoys. So he, not dreaming that it was to delude him that God had given this order, set off with the envoys. But on the road an angel of God confronted him in a narrow place, enclosed by stone walls on either side, and the ass whereon Balaam rode, conscious of the divine spirit *a* approaching her, turning aside thrust Balaam against one of these fences, insensible to the blows with which the seer belaboured her, in his pain at being crushed against the wall. But when, on the angel's nearer approach, the ass sank down beneath the blows, she, so God willed, broke out in *b* human speech and reproached Balaam for the injustice wherewith, though he had no cause to complain of her past ministries, he thus belaboured her, failing to understand that to-day it was God's purpose that debarred her from serving him on the mission whereon he sped. Then, while he was aghast at hearing his ass thus speak with human voice, the angel himself appeared in visible form and reproached him for his blows, in that the beast was not to blame : it was he himself, he said, who was obstructing a journey undertaken in defiance of the will of God. Terrified,

Second embassy : Balaam's journey and his ass. Numb xxii. 15.

b Or, according to another reading, " received," " was given."

Βάλαμος οἷός τε ἦν ἀναστρέφειν, ἀλλ᾽ ὁ θεὸς αὐτὸν
χωρεῖν τὴν προκειμένην παρώρμησε προστάξας
ὅ τι περ ἂν αὐτὸς κατὰ νοῦν αὐτῷ ποιήσειε τοῦτο
σημαίνειν.

112 (4) Καὶ ὁ μὲν ταῦτα τοῦ θεοῦ κελεύσαντος
ἥκει πρὸς Βάλακον. δεξαμένου δὲ αὐτὸν τοῦ
βασιλέως ἐκπρεπῶς ἠξίου προαχθεὶς ἐπί τι τῶν
ὀρῶν σκέψασθαι, πῶς τὸ τῶν Ἑβραίων ἔχοι
στρατόπεδον. Βάλακος δ᾽ αὐτὸς ἀφικνεῖται τὸν
μάντιν σὺν βασιλικῇ θεραπείᾳ φιλοτίμως ἀγόμενος
εἰς ὄρος, ὅπερ ὑπὲρ κεφαλῆς αὐτῶν ἔκειτο τοῦ
113 στρατοπέδου σταδίους ἀπέχον ἑξήκοντα. κατιδὼν
δ᾽ αὐτοὺς ἐκεῖνος βωμούς τε ἐκέλευσεν ἑπτὰ
δείμασθαι τὸν βασιλέα καὶ τοσούτους ταύρους
καὶ κριοὺς παραστῆσαι· ὑπουργήσαντος δὲ διὰ
ταχέων τοῦ βασιλέως ὁλοκαυτεῖ τυθέντας, ὡς
114 ⟨τ᾽ ἄ⟩τροπον¹ εἶδε σημαινομένην, "ὁ λεώς,"
φησίν, "οὗτος εὐδαίμων, ᾧ ὁ θεὸς δίδωσι μυρίων
κτῆσιν ἀγαθῶν καὶ σύμμαχον εἰς ἅπαντα καὶ
ἡγεμόνα τὴν ἑαυτοῦ πρόνοιαν ἐπένευσεν. ὡς
οὐδέν ἐστιν ἀνθρώπειον² γένος, οὗ μὴ κατ᾽ ἀρετὴν
καὶ ζήλωσιν ἐπιτηδευμάτων ἀρίστων καὶ καθαρῶν
πονηρίας ὑμεῖς ἀμείνους κριθήσεσθε καὶ παισὶ
βελτίοσιν αὐτῶν ταῦτα καταλείψετε, θεοῦ μόνους
ὑμᾶς ἀνθρώπους³ ἐφορῶντος καὶ ὅθεν ἂν γένοισθε
πάντων εὐδαιμονέστεροι τῶν ὑπὸ τὸν ἥλιον
115 ἐκπορίζοντος. γῆν τε οὖν ἐφ᾽ ἣν ὑμᾶς αὐτὸς
ἔστειλε καθέξετε δουλεύσουσαν⁴ αἰεὶ παισὶν ὑμε-

---

¹ conj. : τρόπον RO, τροπὴν rell.
² ἀνθρώπινον RO.   ³ ἀνθρώπων Niese.
⁴ ex Lat. : δουλεύουσαν codd.

ᵃ Distance unspecified in Scripture.

Balaam was prepared to turn back ; God, however, exhorted him to pursue his intended way, while enjoining upon him to announce just whatsoever He himself should put into his heart.

(4) Charged with these behests from God he came to Balak. After a magnificent reception from the king, he desired to be conducted to one of the mountains, to inspect the disposition of the Hebrews' camp. Balak thereupon went himself, escorting the seer with all the honours of a royal retinue to a mountain lying over their heads and sixty furlongs distant from the camp.[a] Having seen the Hebrews beneath, he bade the king to have seven altars built and as many bulls and rams brought forward. The king having promptly ministered to his wishes, he burnt the slaughtered victims whole ; and when he saw the indications of inflexible Fate,[b] " Happy," said he, " is this people, to whom God grants possession of blessings untold and has vouchsafed as their perpetual ally and guide His own providence. For there is not a race on earth which ye shall not, through your virtue and your passion for pursuits most noble and pure of crime, be accounted to excel, and to children yet better than yourselves shall ye bequeath this heritage, God having regard for none among men but you and lavishing on you the means whereby ye may become the happiest of all peoples beneath the sun. That land, then, to which He himself hath sent you, ye shall surely occupy : it

Balaam predicts Israel's future greatness.
Numb. xxii. 35.

Ib. xxiii. 1.

---

[b] My conjecture ἄτροπον (Atropos, the divinity of inflexible fate) yields the required sense and accounts for both readings of the MSS. ; first the ἄ was dropped, and then the feminine part. σημαινομένην caused the conversion of τρόπον into τροπήν (which Weill adopts, rendering " comme il y vit le signe d'une fuite ").

τέροις, καὶ τοῦ περὶ αὐτῶν κλέους ἐμπλησθήσεται
πᾶσα ἡ γῆ καὶ θάλασσα, ἀρκέσετε δὲ τῷ κόσμῳ
παρασχεῖν ἑκάστῃ γῇ τῶν ἀφ᾽ ὑμετέρου γένους
116 οἰκήτορας. θαυμάζετε οὖν, ὦ μακάριος[1] στρατός,
ὅτι τοσοῦτος ἐξ ἑνὸς πατρὸς γεγόνατε;[2] ἀλλὰ
τὸν νῦν ὑμῶν ὀλίγον ἡ Χαναναίων χωρήσει γῆ,
τὴν δ᾽ οἰκουμένην οἰκητήριον δι᾽ αἰῶνος ἴστε
προκειμένην ὑμῖν, καὶ τὸ πλῆθος ὑμῶν ἔν τε
νήσοις καὶ κατ᾽ ἤπειρον βιοτεύσετε ὅσον ἐστὶν
οὐδ᾽ ἀστέρων ἀριθμὸς ἐν οὐρανῷ. τοσούτοις δὲ
οὖσιν οὐκ ἀπαγορεύσει τὸ θεῖον ἀφθονίαν μὲν
παντοίων ἀγαθῶν ἐν εἰρήνῃ χορηγοῦν, νίκην δὲ
117 καὶ κράτος ἐν πολέμῳ. παῖδας ἐχθρῶν ἔρως
τοῦ πρὸς ὑμᾶς πολέμου λάβοι καὶ θρασυνθεῖεν
ὥστε εἰς ὅπλα καὶ τὰς ὑμετέρας χεῖρας ἐλθεῖν·
οὐ γὰρ ἂν ὑποστρέψειέ τις νικηφόρος οὐδ᾽ ὥστε
παῖδας εὐφρᾶναι καὶ γυναῖκας. τοσοῦτον ὑμῖν
ἀνδρείας τὸ περιὸν ἐκ θεοῦ προνοίας ἀνήρτηται,[3] ᾧ
καὶ τὰ περιττὰ μειοῦν ἰσχὺς καὶ τὰ λείποντα
διδόναι.''

118 (5) Καὶ ὁ μὲν τοιαῦτ᾽ ἐπεθείαζεν οὐκ ὢν ἐν
ἑαυτῷ τῷ δὲ θείῳ πνεύματι πρὸς αὐτὰ νενικημένος.
τοῦ δὲ Βαλάκου δυσχεραίνοντος καὶ παραβαίνειν
αὐτὸν τὰς συνθήκας ἐφ᾽ αἷς αὐτὸν ἀντὶ μεγάλων
λάβοι δωρεῶν παρὰ τῶν συμμάχων ἐπικαλοῦντος,
ἐλθόντα γὰρ ἐπὶ κατάρᾳ τῶν πολεμίων ὑμνεῖν
αὐτοὺς ἐκείνους καὶ μακαριωτάτους ἀποφαίνειν
119 ἀνθρώπων, '' ὦ Βάλακε,'' φησί, '' περὶ τῶν ὅλων
λογίζῃ καὶ δοκεῖς ἐφ᾽ ἡμῖν εἶναί τι περὶ τῶν

---

[1] μακάριοι Niese.   [2] γεγόνατε. edd.
[3] Dindorf (Lat. prestabitur): ἀνῄρηται codd.

shall be subject for ever to your children, and with their fame shall all earth and sea be filled : aye and ye shall suffice for the world, to furnish every land with inhabitants sprung from your race. Marvel ye then, blessed army, that from a single sire ye have grown so great ? Nay, those numbers now are small and shall be contained by the land of Canaan ; but the habitable world, be sure, lies before you as an eternal habitation, and your multitudes shall find abode on islands and continent, more numerous even than the stars in heaven. Yet for all those mighty hosts the Deity shall not fail to supply abundance of blessings of every sort in peace-time, victory and mastery in war. Let the children of your foes be seized with a passion for battle against you, and be emboldened to take arms and to close with you in strife ; for not one shall return victorious or in such wise as to gladden the heart of child and wife.[a] With such superabundant valour have ye been invested by the providence of God, who has power alike to diminish what is in excess and to make good that which is lacking."

(5) Such was the inspired utterance of one who was no longer his own master but was overruled by the divine spirit to deliver it. But when Balak fumed and accused him of transgressing the covenant whereunder, in exchange for liberal gifts, he had obtained his services from his allies—having come, in fact, to curse his enemies, he was now belauding those very persons and pronouncing them the most blessed of men—" Balak," said he, " hast thou reflected on the whole matter and thinkest thou that

Balaam's defence to Balak and further predictions.
Numb. xxiii. 11.

---

[a] After Hom. *Il.* v. 688 εὐφρανέειν ἄλοχόν τε φίλην καὶ νήπιον υἱόν.

τοιούτων σιγᾶν ἢ λέγειν, ὅταν ἡμᾶς τὸ τοῦ θεοῦ
λάβῃ πνεῦμα; φωνὰς γὰρ ἃς βούλεται τοῦτο
120 καὶ λόγους οὐδὲν ἡμῶν εἰδότων ἀφίησιν. ἐγὼ
δὲ μέμνημαι μὲν ὄντε καὶ σὺ καὶ Μαδιανῖται
δεηθέντες ἐνταυθοῖ με προθύμως ἠγάγετε καὶ
δι' ἃ τὴν ἄφιξιν ἐποιησάμην, ἥν τέ μοι δι' εὐχῆς
121 μηδὲν ἀδικῆσαί σου τὴν ἐπιθυμίαν. κρείττων
δὲ ὁ θεὸς ὧν ἐγὼ χαρίζεσθαι διεγνώκειν· καὶ
παντελῶς ἀσθενεῖς οἱ προγινώσκειν περὶ τῶν
ἀνθρωπίνων[1] παρ' ἑαυτῶν ὑπολαμβάνοντες, ὡς μὴ
ταῦθ' ἅπερ ὑπαγορεύει τὸ θεῖον λέγειν, βιάζεσθαι
δὲ τὴν ἐκείνου βούλησιν· οὐδὲν γὰρ ἐν ἡμῖν ἔτι
122 φθάσαντος εἰσελθεῖν ἐκείνου ἡμέτερον. ἔγωγ' οὖν
τὸν στρατὸν τοῦτον οὔτ' ἐπαινέσαι προυθέμην
οὔτ' ἐφ' οἷς τὸ γένος αὐτῶν ὁ θεὸς ἀγαθοῖς
ἐμηχανήσατο διελθεῖν, ἀλλ' εὐμενὴς αὐτοῖς οὗτος
ὢν καὶ σπεύδων αὐτοῖς εὐδαίμονα βίον καὶ κλέος
αἰώνιον παρασχεῖν ἐμοὶ τοιούτων ἀπαγγελίαν
123 λόγων ὑπέθετο. νῦν δέ, χαρίζεσθαί τι[2] γὰρ αὐτῷ
σοὶ διὰ σπουδῆς ἐστί μοι καὶ Μαδιανίταις, ὧν
ἀπώσασθαί μοι τὴν ἀξίωσιν οὐκ εὐπρεπές, φέρε
βωμούς τε ἑτέρους αὖθις ἐγείρωμεν καὶ θυσίας
ταῖς πρὶν παραπλησίας ἐπιτελέσωμεν, εἰ πεῖσαι
τὸν θεὸν δυνηθείην ἐπιτρέψαι μοι τοὺς ἀνθρώπους
124 ἀραῖς ἐνδῆσαι." συγχωρήσαντος δὲ τοῦ Βαλάκου
δὶς μὲν τεθυκότι τὸ θεῖον οὐκ ἐπένευσε τὰς κατὰ
τῶν Ἰσραηλιτῶν ἀράς, [θύσας δὲ καὶ τρίτον ἄλλων
πάλιν ἀνασταθέντων βωμῶν οὐδὲ τότε μὲν κατ-

---

[1] ἀνθρωπείων ML.
[2] conj. Niese: τε RO: om. rell.

it rests with us at all to be silent or to speak on such
themes as these, when we are possessed by the spirit
of God ? For that spirit gives utterance to such
language and words as it will, whereof we are
all unconscious. For myself, I remember well what
both thou and the Madianites craved when ye
eagerly brought me hither and for what purpose I
have paid this visit, and it was my earnest prayer to
do no despite to thy desire. But God is mightier
than that determination of mine to do this favour ;
and wholly impotent are they who pretend to such
foreknowledge of human affairs, drawn from their own
breasts, as to refrain from speaking that which the
Deity suggests and to violate His will. For nothing
within us, once He has gained prior entry, is any
more our own. Thus, for my part, I neither intended
to extol this army nor to recount the blessings for
which God has designed their race ; it is He who, in
His gracious favour to them and His zeal to confer
on them a life of felicity and everlasting renown, has
put it into my heart to pronounce such words as these.
But now,[a] since it is my earnest desire to gratify Numb.
both thyself and the Madianites, to reject whose xxiii. 13.
request were unseemly, come, let us erect yet other
altars and offer sacrifices like unto the first, if perchance I may persuade God to suffer me to bind these
people under a curse." Balak consenting thereto,
twice did the seer offer sacrifice, but failed to obtain
the Deity's consent to imprecations upon the

---

[a] In Numbers it is Balak who proposes a second attempt.

JOSEPHUS

125 ἠράσατο τοῖς Ἰσραηλίταις,]¹ πεσὼν δ' ἐπὶ στόμα
πάθη προύλεγεν ὅσα τε βασιλεῦσιν ἔσται καὶ
ὅσα πόλεσι ταῖς ἀξιολογωτάταις, ὧν ἐνίαις οὐδ'
οἰκεῖσθαί πω² συνέβαινε τὴν ἀρχήν, ἅ τε καὶ
προϋπῆρξεν ἐν τοῖς ἔμπροσθεν χρόνοις γενόμενα
τοῖς ἀνθρώποις διὰ γῆς ἢ θαλάσσης εἰς μνήμην
τὴν ἐμήν. ἐξ ὧν ἁπάντων λαβόντων τέλος ὁποῖον
ἐκεῖνος προεῖπε τεκμήραιτ' ἄν τις, ὅ τι καὶ ἔσοιτο
πρὸς τὸ μέλλον.

126 (6) Βάλακος δὲ ἀγανακτήσας ἐπὶ τῷ μὴ κατ-
αράτους γενέσθαι τοὺς Ἰσραηλίτας ἀποπέμπει τὸν
Βάλαμον μηδεμιᾶς τιμῆς ἀξιώσας· ὁ δὲ ἀπιὼν
ἤδη κἀπὶ τῷ περαιοῦν τὸν Εὐφράτην γενόμενος
τόν τε Βάλακον μεταπεμψάμενος καὶ τοὺς ἄρχοντας

127 τῶν Μαδιανιτῶν " Βαλακέ," φησί, " καὶ Μαδιανιτῶν οἱ παρόντες, χρὴ γὰρ καὶ παρὰ βούλησιν
τοῦ θεοῦ χαρίσασθαι ὑμῖν, τὸ μὲν Ἑβραίων γένος
οὐκ ἂν ὄλεθρος παντελὴς καταλάβοι, οὔτ' ἐν
πολέμῳ οὔτ' ἐν λοιμῷ καὶ σπάνει τῶν ἀπὸ γῆς
καρπῶν, οὔτ'³ ἄλλη τις αἰτία παράλογος δια-

128 φθείρειεν. πρόνοια γάρ ἐστιν αὐτῶν τῷ θεῷ
σῴζειν ἀπὸ παντὸς κακοῦ καὶ μηδὲν ἐπ' αὐτοὺς
ἐᾶσαι τοιοῦτον πάθος ἐλθεῖν, ὑφ' οὗ κἂν ἀπόλοιντο
πάντες· συμπέσοι δ' ἂν αὐτοῖς ὀλίγα τε καὶ πρὸς
ὀλίγον, ὑφ' ὧν ταπεινοῦσθαι δοκοῦντες εἶτ' ἀν-
θήσουσιν ἐπὶ φόβῳ τῶν ἐπαγαγόντων αὐτοῖς τὰς

---

¹ hab. SP: ins. post στόμα L: om. rell. Doubtless a
gloss.
² Dindorf: πως codd.   ³ οὐδ' Niese.

62

Israelites.[a] Instead, falling upon his face, he foretold what calamities were to come for kings and
what for cities of the highest celebrity (of which
some had not yet so much as been inhabited at all),
along with other events which have already befallen
men in bygone ages, by land or sea, down to times
within my memory. And from all these prophecies
having received the fulfilment which he predicted
one may infer what the future also has in store.[b]

(6) Balak, furious because the Israelites had not
been cursed, dismissed Balaam, dignifying him with
no reward. But he, when already departing and on
the point of crossing the Euphrates, sent for Balak
and the princes of Madian and said : " Balak and
ye men of Madian here present—since it behoves
me despite God's will to gratify you—doubtless this
race of Hebrews will never be overwhelmed by utter
destruction, neither through war, nor through pestilence and dearth of the fruits of the earth, neither
shall any other unlooked-for cause exterminate it.
For God is watching over them to preserve them
from all ill and to suffer no such calamity to come
upon them as would destroy them all. Yet misfortunes may well befall them of little moment and
for a little while, whereby they will appear to be
abased, though only thereafter to flourish once more
to the terror of those who inflicted these injuries

Balaam's
parting
advice.

---

[a] Some mss. insert the gloss : " He sacrificed also a third
time, other altars being again erected : yet even then he
pronounced no imprecation on the Israelites " (cf. Numb.
xxiii. 30). The glossator has not observed that δίς, with the
sacrifice already narrated, brings up the number to three :
he has apparently interpreted δίς as δεύτερον.

[b] Cf. a rather similar mysterious reference to the fulfilment
of the prophecies of Daniel in A. x. 210.

JOSEPHUS

129 βλάβας. ὑμεῖς δ᾽ εἰ νίκην τινὰ πρὸς βραχὺν
καιρὸν κατ᾽ αὐτῶν κερδᾶναι ποθεῖτε, τύχοιτ᾽ ἂν
αὐτῆς ταῦτα ποιήσαντες· τῶν θυγατέρων τὰς
μάλιστα εὐπρεπεῖς καὶ βιάσασθαι καὶ νικῆσαι
τὴν τῶν ὁρώντων σωφροσύνην ἱκανὰς διὰ τὸ
κάλλος ἀσκήσαντες τὴν εὐμορφίαν αὐτῶν ἐπὶ τὸ
μᾶλλον εὐπρεπὲς πέμψατε πλησίον ἐσομένας τοῦ
ἐκείνων στρατοπέδου, καὶ δεομένοις συνεῖναι τοῖς
130 νεανίαις αὐτῶν προστάξατε. ἐπειδὰν δὲ κεχει-
ρωμένους ὁρῶσι ταῖς ἐπιθυμίαις, καταλιπέτωσαν
καὶ παρακαλούντων μένειν μὴ πρότερον ἐπι-
νευέτωσαν, πρὶν ἂν πείσωσιν αὐτοὺς ἀφέντας
τοὺς πατρίους νόμους καὶ τὸν τούτους αὐτοῖς
θέμενον τιμᾶν θεὸν τοὺς Μαδιανιτῶν καὶ Μωαβιτῶν
σέβωσιν· οὕτως γὰρ αὐτοῖς τὸν θεὸν ὀργισθή-
σεσθαι." καὶ ὁ μὲν τοῦθ᾽ ὑποθέμενος αὐτοῖς
ᾤχετο.

131 (7) Τῶν δὲ Μαδιανιτῶν πεμψάντων τὰς θυγατέρας κατὰ τὴν ἐκείνου παραίνεσιν οἱ τῶν
Ἑβραίων ἁλίσκονται νέοι τῆς εὐπρεπείας αὐτῶν
καὶ παραγενόμενοι εἰς λόγους αὐταῖς παρεκάλουν
μὴ φθονεῖν αὐτοῖς τῆς τοῦ κάλλους αὐτῶν ἀπολαύσεως μηδὲ τῆς τοῦ πλησιάζειν συνηθείας· αἱ
δ᾽ ἀσμένως δεξάμεναι τοὺς λόγους συνῆσαν
132 αὐτοῖς. ἐνδησάμεναι δ᾽ αὐτοὺς τῷ πρὸς αὐτὰς
ἔρωτι καὶ τῆς ἐπιθυμίας ἀκμαζούσης περὶ ἀπαλλαγὴν ἐγίνοντο. τοὺς δ᾽ ἀθυμία δεινὴ[1] πρὸς

¹ πολλὴ RO.

ᵃ Cf. Is. lvii. 17 LXX δι᾽ ἁμαρτίαν βραχύ τι ἐλύπησα αὐτόν
and the concluding portion of the Ep. of Baruch (end of
1st cent. A.D.), beginning ὁ ἐπαγαγὼν ὑμῖν τὰ κακά (iv. 29).
ᵇ This suggestion is foreign to the older (" J ") narrative
64

upon them.[a] Ye then, if ye yearn to gain some short-
lived victory over them, may attain that end by acting
on this wise. Take of your daughters those who are
comeliest and most capable of constraining and
conquering the chastity of their beholders by reason
of their beauty, deck out their charms to add to their
comeliness, send them to the neighbourhood of the
Hebrews' camp, and charge them to company with
their young men when they sue their favours. Then,
when they shall see these youths overmastered by
their passions, let them quit them and, on their
entreating them to stay, let them not consent or
ever they have induced their lovers to renounce the
laws of their fathers and the God to whom they
owe them, and to worship the gods of the Madianites
and Moabites. For thus will God be moved to
indignation against them." And, having propounded
to them this scheme, he went his way.[b]

(7) Thereupon the Madianites having sent their
daughters in accordance with his advice, the Hebrew
youths were captivated by their charms and, falling
into parley with them, besought them not to deny
them the enjoyment of their beauty or the intimacy
of intercourse ; and they, gladly accepting their suit,
consorted with them. Then, having enchained
them with love towards themselves, at the moment
when their passion was at its height, they made
ready to go. The young men were in the depths

Seduction
of the
Hebrew
youth by
the
Midianite
women.
Cf. Numb.
xxv. 1.

in Numbers, but is alluded to in the later (" Priestly ")
document : " Behold these (women) caused the children of
Israel, *through the counsel of Balaam*, to commit trespass "
(Numb. xxxi. 16). Jewish Midrash (see Weill) enlarged
upon this and even traced a reference to the story in Numb.
xxiv. 14 " I will advertise (or rather " counsel ") thee what
this people shall do."

JOSEPHUS

τὴν ἀναχώρησιν τῶν γυναικῶν κατέλαβε καὶ
λιπαροῦντες ἐνέκειντο, μὴ σφᾶς καταλιπεῖν, ἀλλὰ
γαμετὰς αὐτῶν ἐσομένας αὐτόθι μένειν καὶ δε-
σποίνας ἀποδειχθησομένας πάντων ὧν ὑπῆρχεν
133 αὐτοῖς. ταῦτα δὲ ὀμνύντες ἔλεγον καὶ θεὸν
μεσίτην ὧν ὑπισχνοῦντο ποιούμενοι, δακρύοντές
τε καὶ πανταχόθεν αὐτοὺς ἐλεεινοὺς ταῖς γυναιξὶ
κατασκευάζοντες εἶναι. αἱ δ᾽ ὡς δεδουλωμένους
αὐτοὺς κατενόησαν καὶ τελέως ὑπὸ τῆς συνηθείας
ἐχομένους, ἤρξαντο πρὸς αὐτοὺς λέγειν·
134 (8) " Ἡμῖν, ὦ κράτιστοι νέων, οἶκοί τέ εἰσι
πατρῷοι καὶ κτῆσις ἀγαθῶν ἄφθονος καὶ ἡ παρὰ
τῶν γονέων καὶ τῶν οἰκείων εὔνοια καὶ στοργή,
καὶ κατ᾽ οὐδενὸς τούτων πόρον[1] ἐνθάδ᾽ ἥκουσαι
ἡμεῖς εἰς ὁμιλίαν ἥκομεν, οὐδ᾽ ἐμπορευσόμεναι
τὴν ὥραν τοῦ σώματος προσηκάμεθα τὴν ὑμετέραν
ἀξίωσιν, ἀλλ᾽ ἄνδρας ἀγαθοὺς καὶ δικαίους ὑπο-
λαβοῦσαι τοιούτοις ὑμᾶς τιμῆσαι ξενίοις δεομένους
135 ἐπείσθημεν. καὶ νῦν, ἐπεὶ φατε πρὸς ἡμᾶς
φιλοστόργως ἔχειν καὶ λυπεῖσθαι[2] μελλουσῶν ἀναχωρεῖν, οὐδ᾽ αὐταὶ τὴν δέησιν ὑμῶν ἀποστρε-
φόμεθα, πίστιν δ᾽ εὐνοίας λαβοῦσαι τὴν μόνην
ἡμῖν ἀξιόλογον νομισθεῖσαν ἀγαπήσομεν τὸν μεθ᾽
136 ὑμῶν βίον ὡς γαμεταὶ διανύσαι. δέος γάρ, μὴ
καὶ κόρον τῆς ἡμετέρας ὁμιλίας λαβόντες ἔπειθ᾽
ὑβρίσητε καὶ ἀτίμους ἀποπέμψητε πρὸς τοὺς
γονεῖς"· συγγινώσκειν τε ταῦτα φυλαττομέναις
ἠξίουν. τῶν δὲ ἦν βούλονται πίστιν δώσειν

---

[1] ἀπορροῦσαι SP Lat. (-ούσαις L): ? lege ἀπορίαν.
[2] RO Lat.: λυπεῖσθε rell.

---

[a] The model for this speech and for the episode as a whole
66

of despondency at the women's departure : they pressed and implored them not to abandon them, but to stay where they were, to be their brides and to be installed as mistresses of all that they possessed. This they affirmed with oaths, invoking God as arbiter of their promises, and by their tears and by every means seeking to render themselves an object of the women's compassion. And these, when they perceived them to be enslaved and completely holden by their society, began to address them thus :

(8)[a] " We, most excellent young men, have our paternal houses, goods in abundance, and the bene- Conditions imposed by them. volence and affection of our parents and kinsfolk. It was not in quest of [b] any of those things that we came hither to consort with you, nor with intent to traffic with the flower of our persons that we accepted your suit ; nay, it was because we took you for honest and just men that we were induced to honour your petition with such hospitable welcome. And now, since ye say that ye have so tender an affection for us and are grieved at our approaching departure, we do not—for our part—reject your request ; but, on receiving from you the only pledge of goodwill which we can account of worth, we shall be content to end our lives with you as your wedded wives. For it is to be feared that, becoming sated with our society, ye may then do us outrage and send us back dishonoured to our parents "—and they begged to be excused for protecting themselves against *that*. The youths thereupon promising to

was furnished by the similar story of the Scythians and the Amazons in Herodotus iv. 111 ff. (esp. the speeches in 114, beginning Ἡμῖν εἰσὶ μὲν τοκέες εἰσὶ δὲ κτήσεις).

[b] Or, with another reading, " for lack of."

ὁμολογούντων καὶ πρὸς [τὸ]¹ μηδὲν ἀντιλεγόντων
137 ὑπὸ τοῦ πρὸς αὐτὰς πάθους, "ἐπεὶ ταῦτα ὑμῖν,"
ἔφασαν, "δέδοκται, τοῖς δ' ἔθεσι καὶ τῷ βίῳ πρὸς
ἅπαντας ἀλλοτριώτατα χρῆσθε, ὡς καὶ τὰς τροφὰς
ὑμῖν ἰδιοτρόπους εἶναι καὶ τὰ ποτὰ μὴ κοινὰ τοῖς
ἄλλοις, ἀνάγκη βουλομένους ἡμῖν συνοικεῖν καὶ
θεοὺς τοὺς ἡμετέρους σέβειν, καὶ οὐκ ἂν ἄλλο
γένοιτο τεκμήριον ἧς ἔχειν τε νῦν φατε πρὸς ἡμᾶς
εὐνοίας καὶ τῆς ἐσομένης ἢ τὸ τοὺς αὐτοὺς ἡμῖν
138 θεοὺς προσκυνεῖν. μέμψαιτο δ' ἂν οὐδείς, εἰ γῆς εἰς
ἣν ἀφῖχθε τοὺς ἰδίους αὐτῆς θεοὺς προστρέπῃσθε,²
καὶ ταῦτα τῶν μὲν ἡμετέρων κοινῶν ὄντων πρὸς
ἅπαντας, τοῦ δ' ὑμετέρου πρὸς μηδένα τοιούτου
τυγχάνοντος." δεῖν οὖν αὐτοῖς ἔλεγον ἢ ταὐτὰ
πᾶσιν ἡγητέον ἢ ζητεῖν ἄλλην οἰκουμένην, ἐν ᾗ
βιώσονται μόνοι κατὰ τοὺς ἰδίους νόμους.
139   (9) Οἱ δ' ὑπὸ τοῦ πρὸς αὐτὰς ἔρωτος κάλλιστα
λέγεσθαι ταῦτα ὑπολαβόντες καὶ παραδόντες αὑτοὺς εἰς ἃ προεκαλοῦντο παρέβησαν τὰ πάτρια,
θεούς τε πλείονας εἶναι νομίσαντες καὶ θύειν
αὐτοῖς κατὰ νόμον τὸν ἐπιχώριον τοῖς καθιδρυσα-
μένοις προθέμενοι ξενικοῖς τε βρώμασιν ἔχαιρον
καὶ πάντ' εἰς ἡδονὴν τῶν γυναικῶν ἐπὶ τοὐναντίον
οἷς ὁ νόμος αὐτῶν ἐκέλευε ποιοῦντες διετέλουν,
140 ὡς διὰ παντὸς ἤδη τοῦ στρατοῦ τὴν παρανομίαν
χωρεῖν τῶν νέων καὶ στάσιν αὐτοῖς πολὺ χείρω
τῆς προτέρας ἐμπεσεῖν καὶ κίνδυνον παντελοῦς
τῶν ἰδίων ἐθισμῶν ἀπωλείας. ἅπαξ γὰρ τὸ νέον

---

¹ RO: om. rell.   ² S¹: προτρέποισθε rell.

give whatever pledge they chose and gainsaying
them in nothing, such was their passion for them,
" Seeing then," said the maidens, " that ye agree
to these conditions, and that ye have customs and
a mode of life wholly alien to all mankind, insomuch
that your food is of a peculiar sort and your drink
is distinct from that of other men, it behoves you,
if ye would live with us, also to revere our gods ;
no other proof can there be of that affection which
ye declare that ye now have for us and of its continuance in future, save that ye worship the same gods
as we. Nor can any man reproach you for venerating
the special gods of the country whereto ye are
come, above all when our gods are common to all
mankind, while yours has no other worshipper." They
must therefore (they added) either fall in with the
beliefs of all men or look for another world, where they
could live alone in accordance with their peculiar laws.

(9) So these youths, dominated by their love for The
the damsels, regarding their speech as excellent corruption
and surrendering to their proposal, transgressed spreads.
the laws of their fathers. Accepting the belief Numb.
in a plurality of gods and determining to sacrifice xxv. 2.
to them in accordance with the established rites
of the people of the country,[a] they revelled in strange
meats and, to please these women, ceased not to
do everything contrary to that which their Law
ordained ; with the result that the whole army was
soon permeated by this lawlessness of the youth
and a sedition far graver than the last descended
upon them, with a danger of complete ruin of their
own institutions. For the youth, once having tasted

---

[a] Lit. " according to the law native to those who had
established " (" it " ; or " them," i.e. the gods).

γευσάμενον ξενικῶν ἐθισμῶν ἀπλήστως ἐνεφορεῖτο,
καὶ εἴ τινες τῶν πρώτων ἀνδρῶν διὰ πατέρων
ἀρετὰς ἐπιφανεῖς ἦσαν συνδιεφθείροντο.

141 (10) Καὶ Ζαμβρίας ὁ τῆς Σεμεωνίδος ἡγούμενος
φυλῆς Χοσβίᾳ, συνὼν Μαδιανίτιδι Σούρου[1] θυγατρὶ
τῶν ἐκείνῃ δυναστεύοντος ἀνδρός, κελευσθεὶς
ὑπὸ τῆς γυναικὸς πρὸ τῶν Μωυσεῖ δοχθέντων τὸ
142 πρὸς ἡδονὴν αὐτῇ γενησόμενον ἐθεράπευεν.[2] ἐν
τούτοις δ᾽ ὄντων τῶν πραγμάτων δείσας Μωυσῆς,
μὴ γένηταί τι χεῖρον, συναγαγὼν εἰς ἐκκλησίαν
τὸν λαὸν οὐδενὸς μὲν κατηγόρει πρὸς ὄνομα, μὴ
βουλόμενος εἰς ἀπόνοιαν περιστῆσαι τοὺς ἐκ τοῦ
143 λανθάνειν μετανοῆσαι δυναμένους, ἔλεγε δ᾽ ὡς
οὐκ ἄξια δρῷεν οὔθ᾽ αὑτῶν οὔτε πατέρων τὴν
ἡδονὴν προτιμήσαντες τοῦ θεοῦ καὶ τοῦ κατὰ
τοῦτον βιοῦν,[3] προσήκειν δ᾽ ἕως[4] ἔτι καὶ καλῶς
αὐτοῖς[5] ἔχοι μεταβαλέσθαι, τὴν ἀνδρείαν ὑπο-
λαμβάνουσιν οὐκ ἐν τῷ βιάζεσθαι τοὺς νόμους
144 ἀλλ᾽ ἐν τῷ μὴ εἴκειν ταῖς ἐπιθυμίαις εἶναι. πρὸς
τούτοις δ᾽ οὐδ᾽ εὔλογον ἔφασκε σωφρονήσαντας
αὐτοὺς ἐπὶ τῆς ἐρήμου νῦν ἐν τοῖς ἀγαθοῖς ὄντας
παροινεῖν, μηδὲ τὰ κτηθέντα ὑπὸ τῆς ἐνδείας δι᾽
εὐπορίαν αὐτῶν ἀπολέσθαι. καὶ ὁ μὲν ταῦτα
λέγων ἐπειρᾶτο τοὺς νέους ἐπανορθοῦν καὶ εἰς
μετάνοιαν ἄγειν ὧν ἔπραττον.

[1] Bernard: Οὔρου codd.
[2] RO : + οὔτε θύων τὰ πάτρια καὶ γάμον ἡγμένος ἀλλόφυλον
rell.
[3] βίου RO.   [4] Niese (Lat. dum): ὡς codd.
[5] αὐτοῖς ἂν (or ἂν αὐτοῖς) codd.

---

[a] Bibl. Zimri (lxx Ζαμβρεί).
[b] Gr. " Semeon."
[c] Bibl. Cozbi (Χασβεί).   [d] Bibl. Zur (Σούρ).

of foreign customs, became insatiably intoxicated with them ; and some even of the leading men, persons conspicuous through the virtues of their ancestors, succumbed to the contagion. Numb. xxv. 4.

(10) Among others Zambrias,[a] the chief of the tribe of Simeon,[b] who was consorting with Chosbia[c] the Madianite, daughter of Sur,[d] a local prince, at the bidding of this woman, in preference to the decrees of Moses, devoted himself to the cult that would be to her liking.[e] Such was the state of things when Moses,[f] fearing lest worse should befall, convened the people in assembly ; he accused no one by name, not wishing to reduce to desperation any who under cover of obscurity might be brought to repentance, but he said that they were acting in a manner neither worthy of themselves nor of their fathers in preferring voluptuousness to God and to a God-fearing life, and that it beseemed them, while it was yet well with them,[g] to amend their ways, reckoning that courage consisted not in violating the laws but in resisting their passions. He added that neither was it reasonable, after their sobriety in the desert, to relapse now, in their prosperity, into drunken riot, and to lose through affluence what they had won by penury. By this speech he endeavoured to correct the youthful offenders and to bring them to repent of their actions. Apostasy of Zambrias : remonstrance of Moses. *Ib.* 14 f.

[e] Most mss. add " by ceasing to sacrifice according to the laws of his fathers and by contracting a foreign marriage " (perhaps a gloss).

[f] This speech and that of Zambrias which follows have no warrant in Scripture.

[g] Or, according to another reading, " in order that it might yet be well with them."

145 (11) Ἀναστὰς δὲ μετ' αὐτὸν Ζαμβρίας " ἀλλὰ
σὺ μέν," εἶπεν, " ὦ Μωυσῆ, χρῶ νόμοις οἷς αὐτὸς
ἐσπούδακας ἐκ τῆς τούτων εὐηθείας[1] τὸ βέβαιον
αὐτοῖς παρεσχημένος· ἐπεὶ μὴ τοῦτον αὐτῶν
ἐχόντων τὸν τρόπον πολλάκις ἂν ἤδη κεκολασμένος
146 ἔγνως ἂν οὐκ εὐπαραλογίστους Ἑβραίους. ἐμὲ
δ' οὐκ ἂν ἀκόλουθον οἷς σὺ προστάσσεις τυραννικῶς
λάβοις· οὐ γὰρ ἄλλο τι μέχρι νῦν ἢ προσχήματι
νόμων καὶ τοῦ θεοῦ δουλείαν μὲν ἡμῖν ἀρχὴν δὲ
σαυτῷ κακουργεῖς, ἀφαιρούμενος ἡμᾶς τὸ ἡδὺ
καὶ τὸ κατὰ τὸν βίον αὐτεξούσιον, ὃ τῶν ἐλευθέρων
147 ἐστὶ καὶ δεσπότην οὐκ ἐχόντων. χαλεπώτερος
δ' ἂν οὕτως Αἰγυπτίων Ἑβραίοις γένοιο τιμωρεῖν
ἀξιῶν κατὰ τοὺς νόμους τὴν ἑκάστου πρὸς τὸ
κεχαρισμένον αὐτῷ βούλησιν. πολὺ δ' ἂν δικαιότερον αὐτὸς τιμωρίαν ὑπομένοις τὰ παρ'
ἑκάστοις ὁμολογούμενα καλῶς ἔχειν ἀφανίσαι
προῃρημένος καὶ κατὰ τῆς ἁπάντων δόξης ἰσχυρὰν
148 τὴν σεαυτοῦ κατεσκευακὼς ἀτοπίαν· ἐγὼ δ' ἂν
στεροίμην εἰκότως ὧν πράττω νῦν, εἰ[2] κρίνας
ἀγαθὰ ταῦτ' ἔπειτα περὶ αὐτῶν ὁμολογεῖν ἐν
τούτοις[3] ὀκνήσαιμι. γύναιόν τε ξενικόν, ὡς φής,
ἦγμαι· παρ' ἐμαυτοῦ γὰρ ἀκούσῃ τὰς ἐμὰς πράξεις
ὡς παρὰ ἐλευθέρου, καὶ γὰρ οὐδὲ λαθεῖν προεθέμην·
149 θύω τε θεοῖς οἷς θύειν μοι νομίζεται δίκαιον
ἡγούμενος παρὰ πολλῶν ἐμαυτῷ πραγματεύεσθαι
τὴν ἀλήθειαν, καὶ οὐχ ὥσπερ ἐν τυραννίδι ζῆν
τὴν ὅλην ἐξ ἑνὸς ἐλπίδα τοῦ βίου παντὸς ἀνηρτη-

---

[1] SPE: συνηθείας rell.
[2] νῦν, εἰ edd.: νυνὶ codd.   [3] + οὐκ codd.

(11) But after him rose up Zambrias and said : " Nay, do *thou*, Moses, keep these laws on which thou hast bestowed thy pains, having secured confirmation for them only through these men's simplicity ; for, were they not men of that character, thou wouldest often ere now have learnt through chastisement that Hebrews are not duped so easily. But *me* thou shalt not get to follow thy tyrannical orders ; for thou hast done nought else until now save by wicked artifice, under the pretext of ' laws ' and ' God,' to contrive servitude for us and sovereignty for thyself, robbing us of life's sweets and of that liberty of action,[a] which belongs to free men who own no master. By such means thou wouldest prove more oppressive to the Hebrews than were the Egyptians, in claiming to punish in the name of these laws the intention of each individual to please himself. Nay, far rather is it thyself who deservest punishment, for having purposed to abolish things which all the world has unanimously admitted to be excellent and for having set up, over against universal opinion, thine own extravagances. For myself, fairly might I be debarred from my present course of action, if, after deciding that it was right, I were then to shrink from confessing it before this assembly. I have married, as thou sayest, a foreign wife,—aye, from mine own lips shalt thou hear of my doings, as from a free man, and indeed I had no intention of concealment—aye, and I sacrifice to gods to whom I hold sacrifice to be due, deeming it right to get at the truth for myself from many persons, and not to live as under a tyranny, hanging all my hopes for

---

[a] The modern word " self-determination " closely corresponds to the Greek.

κότα· χαρείη τ' ἂν οὐδεὶς κυριώτερον αὐτὸν περὶ
ὧν πράξαιμι γνώμης τῆς ἐμῆς ἀποφαινόμενος."

150 (12) Τοῦ δὲ Ζαμβρίου ταῦτα περὶ ὧν αὐτός τε
ἠδίκει καὶ τῶν ἄλλων τινὲς εἰπόντος ὁ μὲν λαὸς
ἡσύχαζε φόβῳ τε τοῦ μέλλοντος καὶ τὸν νομοθέτην δὲ ὁρῶν μὴ περαιτέρω τὴν ἀπόνοιαν αὐτοῦ
προαγαγεῖν ἐκ τῆς ἄντικρυς διαμάχης θελή-
151 σαντα· περιίστατο γάρ, μὴ πολλοὶ τῆς τῶν λόγων
ἀσελγείας αὐτοῦ μιμηταὶ γενόμενοι ταράξωσι τὸ
πλῆθος. καὶ διαλύεται μὲν ἐπὶ τούτοις ὁ σύλλογος·
προεληλύθει δ' ἂν ἐπὶ πλεῖον ἡ τοῦ κακοῦ πεῖρα
μὴ φθάσαντος Ζαμβρία τελευτῆσαι ἐκ τοιαύτης
152 αἰτίας. Φινεὲς ἀνὴρ τά τε ἄλλα τῶν νεωτέρων
κρείττων καὶ τοῦ πατρὸς ἀξιώματι τοὺς ἡλικιώτας
ὑπερέχων, Ἐλεαζάρου γὰρ τοῦ ἀρχιερέως [υἱὸς]
ἦν [Μωυσέως δὲ ἀδελφοῦ παιδὸς υἱός],[1] περιαλγήσας
τοῖς πεπραγμένοις ὑπὸ τοῦ Ζαμβρίου, καὶ πρὶν
ἰσχυροτέραν γενέσθαι τὴν ὕβριν ὑπὸ τῆς ἀδείας
ἔργῳ τὴν δίκην αὐτὸν εἰσπράξασθαι διαγνοὺς
καὶ κωλῦσαι διαβῆναι τὴν παρανομίαν εἰς πλείονας
153 τῶν ἀρξαμένων οὐ κολαζομένων, τόλμῃ δὲ καὶ
ψυχῆς καὶ σώματος ἀνδρείᾳ τοσοῦτον προύχων,
ὡς μὴ πρότερον εἴ τινι συσταίη τῶν δεινῶν
ἀπαλλάττεσθαι, πρὶν ἢ καταγωνίσασθαι καὶ νίκην
τὴν ἐπ' αὐτῷ λαβεῖν, ἐπὶ τὴν τοῦ Ζαμβρίου σκηνὴν
παραγενόμενος αὐτόν τε παίων τῇ ῥομφαίᾳ καὶ
154 τὴν Χοσβίαν ἀπέκτεινεν. οἱ δὲ νέοι πάντες, οἷς
ἀρετῆς ἀντιποίησις ἦν καὶ τοῦ φιλοκαλεῖν, μιμηταὶ

---

[1] ROE om. words in brackets.

[a] Bibl. Phinehas (LXX Φεινεές).
[b] Some MSS. omit these words.
[c] A variation on the writer's favourite Thucydidean
phrase οἱ ἀρετῆς τι μεταποιούμενοι (ii. 51); while the follow-

my whole life upon one. And woe be to any man
who declares himself to have more mastery over my
actions than my own will ! "

(12) After this speech of Zambrias concerning the
crimes which he and some of the others had committed, the people held their peace, in terror of what
might come and because they saw that the lawgiver
was unwilling further to provoke the fellow's frenzy
by direct controversy. He feared, in fact, that his
wanton language might find many imitators to foment
disorder among the crowd. Accordingly the meeting
was thereon dissolved ; and this wicked assault
might have gone to further lengths, had not Zambrias
promptly come to his end under the following circumstances. Phinees,[a] a man superior in every way to
the rest of the youth besides being exalted above
his fellows by his father's rank—for he was son of
Eleazar the high-priest [and grandson of the brother
of Moses] [b]—being deeply distressed at the deeds
of Zambrias, determined, before his insolence gained
strength through impunity, to take the law into his
own hands and to prevent the iniquity from spreading
further afield, should its authors escape chastisement.
Gifted moreover with an intrepidity of soul and a
courage of body so pre-eminent that when engaged
in any hazardous contest he never left it until he had
conquered and come off victorious, Phinees repaired
to the tent of Zambrias and smote him with his
broadsword, along with Chosbia, and killed them.
Thereupon all the young men who aspired to make
a display of heroism [c] and of a love of honour,

He is slain
by Phinees :
punishment
of the
sinners.

Numb.
xxv. 7.

Ib. 8.

ing φιλοκαλεῖν (lit. " to love beauty ") recalls another famous
phrase in Thuc. ii. 40. According to Numb. xxv. 5, " Moses
said unto the judges (LXX ταῖς φυλαῖς) of Israel, Slay ye
every one his men," etc.

γενόμενοι τῆς Φινεέσσου τόλμης ἀνήρουν τοὺς
ἐπὶ τοῖς ὁμοίοις Ζαμβρίᾳ τὴν αἰτίαν εἰληφότας.
ἀπόλλυνται μὲν οὖν καὶ ὑπὸ τῆς τούτων ἀνδρα-
155 γαθίας πολλοὶ τῶν παρανομησάντων, ἐφθάρησαν δὲ
πάντες καὶ λοιμῷ, ταύτην ἐνσκήψαντος αὐτοῖς τοῦ
θεοῦ τὴν νόσον, ὅσοι τε συγγενεῖς ὄντες κωλύειν
δέον ἐξώτρυνον αὐτοὺς ἐπὶ ταῦτα συναδικεῖν[1]
τῷ θεῷ δοκοῦντες ἀπέθνησκον.[2] ἀπόλλυνται μὲν
οὖν ἐκ τῶν τάξεων ἄνδρες οὐκ ἐλάττους τετρα
κισχιλίων καὶ μυρίων.[3]

156 (13) Ὑπὸ δὲ ταύτης παροξυνθεὶς τῆς αἰτίας
Μωυσῆς ἐπὶ τὸν Μαδιανιτῶν ὄλεθρον τὴν στρατιὰν
ἐξέπεμπε, περὶ ὧν τῆς ἐπ’ αὐτοὺς ἐξόδου μετὰ
μικρὸν ἀπαγγελοῦμεν, προδιηγησάμενοι πρῶτον
ὃ παρελίπομεν, δίκαιον γὰρ ἐπὶ τούτου τὴν τοῦ
νομοθέτου γνώμην μὴ παρελθεῖν ἀνεγκωμίαστον.
157 τὸν γὰρ Βάλαμον παραληφθέντα ὑπὸ τῶν Μαδιανιτῶν, ὅπως ἐπαράσηται τοῖς Ἑβραίοις, καὶ
τοῦτο μὲν οὐ δυνηθέντα θείᾳ προνοίᾳ, γνώμην δὲ
ὑποθέμενον, ᾗ χρησαμένων τῶν πολεμίων ὀλίγου
τὸ τῶν Ἑβραίων πλῆθος διεφθάρη τοῖς ἐπιτηδεύμασι νοσησάντων δή τινων περὶ ταῦτα, μεγάλως
158 ἐτίμησεν ἀναγράψας αὐτοῦ τὰς μαντείας, καὶ
παρὸν αὐτῷ σφετερίσασθαι τὴν ἐπ’ αὐτοῖς δόξαν καὶ ἐξιδιώσασθαι μηδενὸς ἂν γενομένου
μάρτυρος τοῦ διελέγχοντος, ἐκείνῳ τὴν μαρτυρίαν
ἀπέδωκε[4] καὶ τῆς ἐπ’ αὐτῷ μνήμης ἠξίωσε. καὶ

---

[1] SP Exc.: ἀδικεῖν rell.   [2] συναπέθνησκον Bekker.
[3] καὶ μυρίων] δισμυρίων L.   [4] ἔδωκε RO.

imitating the daring deed of Phinees, slew those who were found guilty of the same crimes as Zambrias. Thus, through their valiancy, perished many of the transgressors ; all (the rest) were destroyed by a pestilence, God having launched this malady upon them ; *Ibid.* while such of their relatives as, instead of restraining them, instigated them to those crimes were accounted by God their accomplices and died likewise. Thus there perished from the ranks no less than fourteen *Ib.* xxv. 9. thousand men.[a]

(13) That was the reason why Moses was provoked to send that army to destroy the Madianites.[b] Of its campaign against them we shall speak anon, after a preliminary word on a point which we omitted ; for it is right that in this particular the judgement of the lawgiver should not be left without its meed of praise. This Balaam, in fact, who had been summoned by the Madianites to curse the Hebrews and who, though prevented from so doing by divine providence, had yet suggested a plan which, being adopted by the enemy, well-nigh led to a demoralization of the whole Hebrew community and actually infected the morals of some—this was the man to whom Moses did the high honour of recording his prophecies ; and though it was open to him to appropriate and take the credit for them himself, as there would have been no witness to convict him, he has given Balaam this testimony and deigned to perpetuate his memory.[c]

The candour of Moses in recording the prophecies of Balaam.

---

[a] Numb. " twenty and four thousand " (as one MS. reads here).   [b] § 101.

[c] *Cf.* the eulogy of Moses for similar candour in the case of Jethro, *A.* iii. 74. From the Talmudic passage, *Baba Bathra* 14b, " Moses wrote his own book and the section (*Parashah*) about Balaam," Weill infers that the prophecies of Balaam once formed a separate treatise.

ταῦτα μὲν ὡς ἂν αὐτοῖς τισι δοκῇ οὕτω σκο-
πείτωσαν.

159 (vii. 1) Μωυσῆς δὲ ὑπὲρ ὧν καὶ προεῖπον ἐπὶ
τὴν Μαδιανιτῶν γῆν ἔπεμψεν στρατιὰν τοὺς
πάντας εἰς δισχιλίους καὶ μυρίους, ἐξ ἑκάστης
φυλῆς τὸν ἴσον ἀριθμὸν ἐπιλεξάμενος, στρατηγὸν
δ' αὐτῶν ἀπέδειξε Φινεές, οὗ μικρῷ πρότερον
ἐμνήσθημεν φυλάξαντος τοῖς Ἑβραίοις τοὺς νόμους
καὶ τὸν παρανομοῦντα τούτους Ζαμβρίαν τιμωρη-
160 σαμένου. Μαδιανῖται δὲ προπυθόμενοι τὸν στρατὸν ἐπὶ σφᾶς ἐλαύνοντα καὶ ὅσον οὐδέπω παρ-
εσόμενον ἠθροίζοντό τε καὶ τὰς εἰσβολὰς τῆς
χώρας, ᾗ προσεδέχοντο τοὺς πολεμίους, ἀσφα-
161 λισάμενοι περιέμενον αὐτούς. ἐλθόντων δὲ καὶ
συμβολῆς γενομένης πίπτει τῶν Μαδιανιτῶν πλῆθος
ἀσυλλόγιστον καὶ ἀριθμοῦ κρεῖττον οἵ τε βασιλεῖς
αὐτῶν ἅπαντες· πέντε δὲ ἦσαν, Ὠχός τε καὶ
Σούρης ἔτι δὲ Ῥοβέης καὶ Οὔρης,[1] πέμπτος δὲ
Ῥέκεμος, οὗ πόλις ἐπώνυμος τὸ πᾶν ἀξίωμα τῆς
Ἀράβων ἔχουσα γῆς καὶ μέχρι νῦν ὑπὸ παντὸς
τοῦ Ἀραβίου τοῦ κτίσαντος βασιλέως τὸ ὄνομα
Ῥεκέμης καλεῖται, Πέτρα παρ' Ἕλλησι λεγομένη.
162 τραπέντων δὲ τῶν πολεμίων οἱ Ἑβραῖοι διήρπασαν αὐτῶν τὴν χώραν καὶ πολλὴν λείαν λαβόντες
καὶ τοὺς οἰκήτορας γυναιξὶν ἅμα διαφθείραντες
μόνας τὰς παρθένους κατέλιπον, τοῦτο Μωυσέος

---

[1] RO (Lat.): Οὔβης rell.

On this narrative readers are free to think what they please.[a]

(vii. 1) So Moses, for the reasons which I have already stated, sent to the land of the Madianites an army of twelve thousand men in all, selecting an equal number from each tribe ; for their general he appointed Phinees who, as we mentioned just now,[b] had preserved to the Hebrews their laws and punished Zambrias for transgressing them. The Madianites, forewarned that the army was marching upon them and might at any moment arrive, mustered their troops and, having fortified the passes into the country which they expected the enemy to take, awaited their appearance. They came and an engagement ensued, in which there fell of the Madianites a multitude incalculable and past numbering, including all their kings. Of these there were five : Ochus and Sures, Robees and Ures, and, the fifth, Rekem[c] ; the city which bears his name ranks highest in the land of the Arabs and to this day is called by the whole Arabian nation, after the name of its royal founder, Rekeme[d] : it is the Petra of the Greeks. Upon the rout of the enemy, the Hebrews pillaged their country, captured abundance of booty, and put the inhabitants with their wives to death, leaving only the unmarried women, such

Defeat of the Madianites. Numb. xxxi. 1 (xxv. 16).

Ib. xxxi. 8 (Josh. xiii. 21).

Ib. 18.

---

[a] This recurrent formula (see i. 108) must here, at the close of chap. vi, refer to the story of Balaam as a whole and in particular to the miraculous element in it, such as the speaking of the ass.   [b] § 152.

[c] Bibl. Evi (Εὐείν) : Zur (Σούρ) : Reba (Ῥοβόκ : in Josh. Ῥοβέ) : Hur (Οὔρ) : Rekem (Ῥοκόμ). Josephus omits the last half of the verse in Numbers : " Balaam also the son of Beor they slew with the sword."

[d] Cf. § 82 (note), where the name appears in the mss. as Ἄρκη.

163 Φινέει κελεύσαντος. ὃς ἧκεν ἄγων τὸν στρατὸν
ἀπαθῆ καὶ λείαν ἄφθονον, βόας μὲν γὰρ δισχιλίους
καὶ πεντακισμυρίους, οἷς δὲ πεντακισχιλίας πρὸς
μυριάσιν ἑπτὰ καὶ ἑξήκοντα, ὄνους δὲ ἑξακισμυρίας
χρυσοῦ δὲ καὶ ἀργύρου ἄπειρόν τι πλῆθος κατα-
σκευῆς, ᾗ κατ᾽ οἶκον ἐχρῶντο· ὑπὸ γὰρ εὐδαιμονίας καὶ ἁβροδίαιτοι σφόδρα ἐτύγχανον. ἤχ-
θησαν δὲ καὶ αἱ παρθένοι περὶ δισχιλίας καὶ
164 τρισμυρίας. Μωυσῆς δὲ μερίσας τὴν λείαν τῆς
μὲν ἑτέρας τὸ πεντηκοστὸν Ἐλεαζάρῳ δίδωσι
καὶ τοῖς ἱερεῦσι, Λευίταις δὲ τῆς ἑτέρας τὸ πεντηκοστὸν μέρος, τὴν δὲ λοιπὴν νέμει τῷ λαῷ.
καὶ διῆγον τὸ λοιπὸν εὐδαιμόνως, ἀφθονίας μὲν
ἀγαθῶν αὐτοῖς ὑπ᾽ ἀρετῆς γεγενημένης, ὑπὸ
μηδενὸς δὲ σκυθρωποῦ ταύτης ἀπολαύειν ἐμ-
ποδιζόμενοι.[1]

165 (2) Μωυσῆς δὲ γηραιὸς ἤδη τυγχάνων διάδοχον
ἑαυτοῦ Ἰησοῦν καθίστησιν ἐπί τε ταῖς προφητείαις
καὶ στρατηγὸν εἴ που δεήσειε γενησόμενον, κελεύσαντος καὶ τοῦ θεοῦ τούτῳ τὴν προστασίαν
ἐπιτρέψαι τῶν πραγμάτων. ὁ δὲ Ἰησοῦς πᾶσαν
ἐπεπαίδευτο τὴν περὶ τοὺς νόμους παιδείαν καὶ
τὸ θεῖον Μωυσέος ἐκδιδάξαντος.

166 (3) Κἂν τούτῳ δύο φυλαὶ Γαδίς[2] τε καὶ Ῥου-

[1] ἐμποδιζομένοις codd.   [2] Μ : Γάδου rell.

---

a The virgins, who have not taken part in the previous
seduction of the Israelites, are to be preserved (" keep alive
for yourselves "), presumably in the expectation of their
conversion to Judaism.
b Bibl. (Heb. and LXX) 72,000.
c Bibl. (both texts) 61,000.
d So both Biblical texts ; the qualifying word " about "
possibly indicates acquaintance with a variant reading.
80

being the orders of Moses to Phinees.[a] That officer returned with his army unscathed and booty in abundance, to wit 52,000 [b] oxen, 675,000 sheep, 60,000 [c] asses, and an unlimited quantity of articles of gold and silver for domestic use ; for prosperity had rendered these people very luxurious. They brought also the unmarried women, numbering about 32,000.[d] Moses, having divided the spoils into two portions, gave a fiftieth of the first half to Eleazar and the priests, a fiftieth of the other half to the Levites, and the rest he distributed among the people.[e] So they lived thenceforth in felicity, with this abundance of goods which their valour had brought them, and with no tragic incidents to thwart their enjoyment of it.

Numb.
xxxi. 32 f.

Ib. 27-30.

(2) Moses, already advanced in years, now appointed Joshua [f] to succeed him both in his prophetical functions and as commander-in-chief, whensoever the need should arise, under orders from God himself to entrust the direction of affairs to him. Joshua had already received a thorough training in the laws and in divine lore under the tuition of Moses.

Moses
appoints
Joshua
as his
successor.
Ib. xxvii. 18.

(3) And now also the two tribes of Gad and of

The Amorite
land
assigned
to the two
and a half
tribes.
Ib. xxxii. 1.

---

[e] The account in Numbers is more precise. There is first an equal division of the booty between combatants and non-combatants. Then, before it is distributed to individuals, a tax is deducted for religious purposes : from the portion of the combatants one *five hundredth* (not, as in Josephus, one fiftieth) is set apart for the priests, and from the portion of the non-combatants one fiftieth is set apart for the Levites. The Levites thus receive ten times as much as the priests. Josephus, who, as a priest, is concerned for priestly privileges (§ 68), equalizes the shares, not, however, without authority ; the reading " 50 " for " 500 " is found in a small group of LXX mss. in Numb. xxxi. 28.

[f] Gr. " Jesus," here and throughout.

81

βήλου καὶ τῆς Μανασσίτιδος ἡμίσεια, πλήθει
τετραπόδων εὐδαιμονοῦντες καὶ τοῖς ἄλλοις ἅπασι,
κοινολογησάμενοι παρεκάλουν τὸν Μωυσῆν ἐξαίρετον
αὐτοῖς τὴν Ἀμορῖτιν παρασχεῖν δορίκτητον οὖσαν·
167 ἀγαθὴν γὰρ εἶναι βοσκήματα τρέφειν. ὁ δ᾽
ὑπολαβὼν αὐτοὺς δείσαντας τὴν πρὸς Χαναναίους
μάχην πρόφασιν εὐπρεπῆ τὴν τῶν βοσκημάτων
ἐπιμέλειαν εὑρῆσθαι κακίστους τε ἀπεκάλει καὶ
δειλίας εὐσχήμονα[1] πρόφασιν ἐπινοήσαντας αὐτοὺς
μὲν βούλεσθαι τρυφᾶν ἀπόνως διάγοντας, πάντων
τεταλαιπωρηκότων ὑπὲρ τοῦ κτήσασθαι τὴν αἰ-
168 τουμένην ὑπ᾽ αὐτῶν γῆν, μὴ θέλειν δὲ συναραμένους τῶν ἐπιλοίπων ἀγώνων γῆν ἣν διαβᾶσιν
αὐτοῖς τὸν Ἰόρδανον ὁ θεὸς παραδώσειν ὑπέσχηται
ταύτην λαβεῖν καταστρεψαμένους οὓς ἐκεῖνος
169 ἀπέδειξεν ἡμῖν πολεμίους. οἱ δ᾽ ὁρῶντες ὀργιζόμενον αὐτὸν καὶ δικαίως ἠρεθίσθαι πρὸς τὴν
ἀξίωσιν αὐτῶν ὑπολαβόντες ἀπελογοῦντο μὴ διὰ
φόβον κινδύνων μηδὲ διὰ· τὴν πρὸς τὸ πονεῖν
170 μαλακίαν πεποιῆσθαι τὴν αἴτησιν, ἀλλ᾽ ὅπως τὴν
λείαν ἐν ἐπιτηδείοις καταλιπόντες εὔζωνοι πρὸς
τοὺς ἀγῶνας καὶ τὰς μάχας χωρεῖν δύναιντο,
ἑτοίμους τε ἔλεγον ἑαυτοὺς κτίσαντας πόλεις εἰς
φυλακὴν τέκνων καὶ γυναικῶν καὶ κτήσεως αὐτοῦ
171 διδόντος συναπιέναι[2] τῷ στρατῷ. καὶ Μωυσῆς
ἀρεσθεὶς τῷ λόγῳ καλέσας Ἐλεάζαρον τὸν
ἀρχιερέα καὶ Ἰησοῦν καὶ τοὺς ἐν τέλει πάντας
συνεχώρει τὴν Ἀμορῖτιν αὐτοῖς ἐπὶ τῷ συμμαχῆσαι τοῖς συγγενέσιν, ἕως ἂν καταστήσωνται

---

[1] ed. pr.: ἀσχήμονα codd.   [2] συναπεῖναι codd.

[a] Reuben (i. 304).

Rubel[a] and half the tribe of Manasseh, being blest
with an abundance of cattle and all sorts of other
possessions, after conferring together besought Moses
exceptionally[b] to award them the Amorite land that
their arms had won, since it was excellent for the
pasturage of flocks. But he, supposing that it was
fear of the contest with the Canaanites which had
led them to discover this specious pretext of the
tending of their flocks, denounced them as arrant
knaves, who had devised this plausible excuse for
their cowardice, because they wished to live themselves in luxury and ease—though all had toiled to
win this land for which they craved—and were loath
to take their part in the remaining struggles and to
occupy the land which God had promised to deliver
to them after crossing the Jordan and after subduing
those whom He had designated as their enemies.
The tribes, seeing his anger and conceiving that he
had just cause for being provoked at their request,
replied in self-defence that it was through no fear of
perils or slackness for toil that they had made their
petition ; no, it was that, by leaving their booty on
suitable ground, they might march the more briskly
to the struggles and combats ; and they professed
themselves ready, once they had built cities for the
protection of their children, their wives, and their
chattels, with his consent, to set off with the army.
Moses, being satisfied with this statement, thereupon Numb.
summoned Eleazar the high-priest and Joshua and xxxii. 28.
all those in authority and conceded the Amorite land
to these tribes, on condition of their fighting along
with their brethren until the general settlement.   So

[b] *i.e.* independently and in advance of the general allotment of territory.

τὰ πάντα. λαβόντες οὖν ἐπὶ τούτοις τὴν χώραν
καὶ κτίσαντες πόλεις καρτερὰς τέκνα [τε] καὶ
γυναῖκας καὶ τἆλλα ὅσα συμπεριάγειν μέλλουσιν
αὐτοῖς ἂν ἦν ἐμπόδια τοῦ πονεῖν ἀπέθεντο εἰς
αὐτάς.

172   (4) Οἰκοδομεῖ δὲ καὶ Μωυσῆς τὰς δέκα πόλεις
τὰς εἰς τὸν ἀριθμὸν τῶν ὀκτὼ καὶ τεσσαράκοντα
γενησομένας, ὧν τρεῖς ἀπέδειξε τοῖς ἐπ' ἀκουσίῳ
φόνῳ φευξομένοις, καὶ χρόνον ἔταξεν εἶναι τῆς
φυγῆς τὸν αὐτὸν τῷ ἀρχιερεῖ, ἐφ' οὗ δράσας τις
τὸν φόνον ἔφυγε· μεθ' ὃν συνεχώρει τελευτήσαντα
κάθοδον, ἐχόντων ἐξουσίαν τῶν τοῦ πεφονευμένου
συγγενῶν κτείνειν, εἰ λάβοιεν ἔξω τῶν ὅρων τῆς
πόλεως εἰς ἣν ἔφυγε τὸν πεφονευκότα· ἑτέρῳ δὲ
173   οὐκ ἐπετέτραπτο. αἱ δὲ πόλεις αἱ πρὸς τὰς
φυγὰς ἀποδεδειγμέναι ἦσαν αἵδε· Βόσορα[1] μὲν
ἐπὶ τοῖς ὁρίοις τῆς Ἀραβίας, Ἀρίμανον δὲ τῆς
Γαλαδηνῶν γῆς, καὶ Γαυλανὰν δ' ἐν τῇ Βατανίδι.
κτησαμένων δ' αὐτῶν καὶ τὴν Χαναναίων γῆν
τρεῖς ἕτεραι πόλεις ἔμελλον ἀνατεθήσεσθαι τῶν
Λευίτιδων πόλεων τοῖς φυγάσιν εἰς κατοικισμὸν
Μωυσέος ἐπιστείλαντος.

174   (5) Μωυσῆς δὲ προσελθόντων αὐτῷ τῶν πρώτων
τῆς Μανασσίτιδος φυλῆς καὶ δηλούντων μὲν ὡς
τεθνήκοι τις τῶν φυλετῶν ἐπίσημος ἀνὴρ Σωλο-
φάντης ὄνομα, παῖδας μὲν οὐ καταλιπὼν ἄρσενας
θυγατέρας δέ τοι,[2] καὶ πυθομένων εἰ τούτων ὁ

---

[1] Βωσάρα RO.   [2] δέ τοι RO : μέντοι rell.

---

   [a] i.e. the proportionate number (4 for each tribe, hence
10 for the 2½ trans-Jordanic tribes) of the 48 cities assigned
to the priests and Levites (§§ 67-69).

84

having received the territory on these conditions and
founded cities with strong defences, they deposited
there children and wives and everything which, had
they been required to carry it about with them,
would have been an impediment to their labours.

(4) Moses himself too built the ten cities that were
to be reckoned among the number of the forty-eight.[a]
Of these he appointed three for persons to flee to
after involuntary manslaughter, and he ordained that
the term of their exile should be the lifetime of the
high-priest in office when the manslayer fled. Upon
the death of the high-priest he permitted him to
return ; the relatives of the slain had moreover the
right to kill the slayer, if they caught him without
the bounds of the city whither he had fled, but this
permission was given to no one else. The cities
appointed as refuges were these : Bosora[b] on the
confines of Arabia, Ariman in the land of Galadene,[c]
and Gaulana in Batanaea.[d] But when they had
conquered also the land of Canaan, three more of
the Levitical cities were to be dedicated as havens
for fugitives, by the injunction of Moses.

(5) Moses was now approached by the head men
of the tribe of Manasseh, who informed him that a
certain notable member of their tribe, by name
Solophantes,[e] had died, leaving no male issue though
there were daughters ; and on their inquiring whether

The cities of refuge. Deut. iv. 41 ff.: Numb. xxxv. 9 ff.

Ib. 25 ff.

Deut. iv. 43 (Josh. xx. 8).

Regulation concerning heritage. Numb. xxxvi. 1 (xxvii. 1).

[b] Bibl. " Bezer (Βοσόρ) in the wilderness, in the table-
land " ; unidentified.

[c] Bibl. " Ramoth in Gilead " ; elsewhere called by
Josephus Ἀραμαθά or Ῥαμάθη, Ant. viii. 398 etc. ; commonly
identified with es-Salṭ.

[d] Bibl. " Golan (Γαυλών) in Bashan " : unidentified. It
gave its name to the province of Gaulanitis often mentioned
in Josephus, and was " a very large village " in the time of
Eusebius.   [e] Bibl. Zelophehad (Σαλπαάδ).

175 κλῆρος ἔσοιτο, φησίν, εἰ μὲν μέλλουσί τινι συνοικεῖν τῶν φυλετῶν, μετὰ τοῦ κλήρου πρὸς αὐτοὺς
ἀπιέναι, εἰ δ' ἐξ ἄλλης γαμοῖντό τισι φυλῆς, τὸν
κλῆρον ἐν τῇ πατρῴᾳ φυλῇ καταλιπεῖν. καὶ τότε
μένειν ἑκάστου τὸν κλῆρον ἐν τῇ φυλῇ διετάξατο.

176 (viii. 1) Τῶν δὲ τεσσαράκοντα ἐτῶν παρὰ τριάκοντα ἡμέρας συμπεπληρωμένων Μωυσῆς ἐκκλησίαν ἐπὶ τῷ Ἰορδάνῳ συναγαγών, ὅπου νῦν
πόλις ἐστὶν Ἀβίλη, φοινικόφυτον δ' ἐστὶ τὸ
χωρίον, συνελθόντος τοῦ λαοῦ παντὸς λέγει
τοιάδε·

177 (2) "Ἄνδρες συστρατιῶται καὶ τῆς μακρᾶς
κοινωνοὶ ταλαιπωρίας, ἐπεὶ τῷ θεῷ δοκοῦν ἤδη
καὶ τῷ γήρᾳ χρόνον ἐτῶν εἴκοσι καὶ ἑκατὸν
ἠνυσμένον δεῖ με τοῦ ζῆν ἀπελθεῖν καὶ τῶν πέρα
τοῦ Ἰορδάνου πραχθησομένων οὐ μέλλω βοηθὸς
ὑμῖν ἔσεσθαι καὶ σύμμαχος, κωλυόμενος ὑπὸ τοῦ
178 θεοῦ, δίκαιον ἡγησάμην μηδὲ νῦν ἐγκαταλιπεῖν
τοὐμὸν ὑπὲρ τῆς ὑμετέρας εὐδαιμονίας πρόθυμον,
ἀλλ' ἀίδιόν τε ὑμῖν πραγματεύσασθαι τὴν τῶν
ἀγαθῶν ἀπόλαυσιν, καὶ μνήμην ἐμαυτῷ γενομένων
179 ὑμῶν ἐν ἀφθονίᾳ τῶν κρειττόνων. φέρε οὖν
ὑποθέμενος ὃν τρόπον ὑμεῖς τ' ἂν εὐδαιμονήσαιτε[1]
καὶ παισὶ τοῖς αὐτῶν καταλίποιτε κτῆσιν ἀγαθῶν

[1] Dindorf: εὐδαιμονήσητε codd.

---

[a] According to the Talmud (quoted by Weill) this law
had only temporary validity.

[b] Abel-shittim (lxx Βελσά etc.) " by Jordan . . . in the
plains of Moab " is mentioned in Numb. xxxiii. 49 as the
last station in the itinerary of the wilderness wanderings ;
Josephus calls it indifferently Abile, Abele (v. 4) and Abila

the inheritance should pass to these, he replied that, if they proposed to unite themselves to persons of their tribe, they should carry the inheritance with them to their husbands, but if they were married into another tribe, the inheritance should be left in their father's tribe. Then it was that he ordained that each man's heritage should remain in his tribe.[a]

(viii. 1) When the forty years had, save for thirty days, now run their course, Moses called together an assembly nigh to the Jordan, where to-day stands the city of Abile[b] in a region thickly planted with palm-trees, and addressed to a congregation of the whole people the following words :

(2) " Comrades in arms and partners in this long tribulation, seeing that now, by God's decree and at the call of age, having completed a span of one hundred and twenty years, I must quit this life, and that in those coming actions beyond the Jordan I am not to be your helper and fellow-combatant, being prohibited by God, I have deemed it right even now not to renounce my zeal for your welfare, but to labour to secure for you the everlasting enjoyment of your good things and for myself an abiding memorial when ye shall be endowed with a store of blessings yet better. Come then, let me first propound the means whereby ye may yourselves attain bliss and may bequeath to your children the possession of blessings for all eternity,

Assembly at Abile near Jordan. Deut. i. 1, 3.

Moses exhorts the people before his death. *Ib.* xxxi. 2.

(*B.J.* iv. 438), and tells us elsewhere (v. 4) that it was 60 stades (*c.* 7 miles) distant from the Jordan. It is the modern *Khurbet el-Keffrein,* situate at about the same distance (N.E.) from the Dead Sea. It is not mentioned in an array of names in Deut. i. 1, which attempts to define the precise spot at which the final discourses of Moses were delivered.

ἀίδιον [παραθέμενος][1] οὕτως ἀπέλθω τοῦ βίου.
πιστεύεσθαι δὲ ἄξιός εἰμι διά τε τὰς πρότερον
ὑπὲρ ὑμῶν φιλοτιμίας καὶ διὰ τὸ τὰς ψυχὰς ἐπὶ
τελευτῇ γιγνομένας μετ᾽ ἀρετῆς πάσης ὁμιλεῖν.[a]

180   " Ὦ παῖδες Ἰσραήλου, μία πᾶσιν ἀνθρώποις ἀγαθῶν κτήσεως αἰτία ὁ θεὸς εὐμενής· μόνος γὰρ οὗτος
δοῦναί τε ταῦτα τοῖς ἀξίοις καὶ ἀφελέσθαι τῶν
ἁμαρτανόντων εἰς αὐτὸν ἱκανός, ᾧ παρέχοντες
ἑαυτοὺς οἵους αὐτός τε βούλεται κἀγὼ τὴν διάνοιαν
αὐτοῦ σαφῶς ἐξεπιστάμενος παραινῶ, οὐκ ἂν
ὄντες μακαριστοὶ καὶ ζηλωτοὶ πᾶσιν [ἀτυχήσαιτέ
ποτ᾽ ἤ][2] παύσαισθε, ἀλλ᾽ ὧν τε νῦν ὑμῖν ἐστιν
ἀγαθῶν ἡ κτῆσις βεβαία μενεῖ τῶν τε ἀπόντων
181 ταχεῖαν ἕξετε τὴν παρουσίαν. μόνον οἷς ὁ θεὸς
ὑμᾶς ἕπεσθαι βούλεται, τούτοις πειθαρχεῖτε, καὶ
μήτε νομίμων τῶν παρόντων ἄλλην προτιμήσητε
διάταξιν μήτ᾽ εὐσεβείας ἧς νῦν περὶ τὸν θεὸν
ἔχετε[3] καταφρονήσαντες εἰς ἄλλον μεταστήσησθε
τρόπον. ταῦτα δὲ πράττοντες ἀλκιμώτατοι μάχας
διενεγκεῖν ἁπάντων ἔσεσθε καὶ μηδενὶ τῶν ἐχθρῶν
182 εὐάλωτοι· θεοῦ γὰρ παρόντος ὑμῖν βοηθοῦ πάντων
περιφρονεῖν εὔλογον. τῆς δ᾽ ἀρετῆς ἔπαθλα ὑμῖν
μεγάλα κεῖται πρὸς ἅπαντα τὸν βίον κτησαμένοις[4]·
αὕτη γε τὸ[5] πρῶτον ἀγαθῶν τὸ πρέσβιστόν ἐστιν,
ἔπειτα καὶ τὴν τῶν ἄλλων χαρίζεται περιουσίαν,

[1] om. Bekker: ἀίδιον παραθέμενος om. Lat.
[2] om. Dindorf: text uncertain: ἀτυχήσητέ (or -σετέ) . . .
παύσησθε (-εσθε) codd.
[3] ed. pr. (Lat. geritis): ἔχοντες codd.
[4] κτησομένοις conj. Niese.
[5] γέ τοι conj. Niese.

[a] ὁμιλεῖν, " speak," " converse " (with others), not

and so depart from life. Aye and I deserve your confidence, alike by reason of those jealous efforts on your behalf in the past, and because souls when on the verge of the end deliver themselves with perfect integrity.[a]

"O children of Israel, there is for all mankind but one source of felicity—a gracious God : He alone has power to give these good things to those who merit them and to take them from those who sin against Him ; will ye but show yourselves in His sight such as He would have you, aye and such as I, who know His mind right well, exhort you to be, then will ye never cease to be blessed and envied of all men ; nay, your possession of those good things which ye have already will rest assured, and those yet absent will soon be present in your hands. Only obey those precepts[b] which God would have you follow, prefer not above your present statutes any other code, nor, spurning that pious worship of God which now is yours, desert it for another fashion. Act ye but thus and ye will be the doughtiest of all to sustain the fight nor lightly conquered by any of your foes ; for with God at your side to succour you ye may well despise them all. And for such virtue great are the rewards set before you, to be won for all your life[c] : she herself, to begin with, is the choicest of treasures, and then she bestows abundance of the rest, so

Deut. *passim.*

"consort," "are in touch with every virtue" : cf. *Vita* 258 μετὰ πάσης ἀρετῆς πεπολίτευμαι.

[b] The Greek might be either neuter (" what ") or masc. (" whom ") ; but he comes to the question of subordination to rulers later, § 186.

[c] Not, I think, as earlier translators take it, " if ye possess (or " preserve ") it (*i.e.* virtue) for all your life."

183 ὡς καὶ πρὸς ἀλλήλους ὑμῖν χρωμένοις αὐτῇ
μακαριστὸν ποιῆσαι τὸν βίον καὶ τῶν ἀλλοφύλων
πλέον δοξαζομένους ἀδήριτον καὶ παρὰ τοῖς αὖθις
τὴν εὔκλειαν ὑμῖν ὑπάρξαι. τούτων δ' ἂν ἐφικέσθαι
δυνηθείητε, εἰ τῶν νόμων οὓς ὑπαγορεύσαντός μοι
τοῦ θεοῦ συνεταξάμην κατήκοοι καὶ φύλακες
γένοισθε καὶ μελετῷητε τὴν σύνεσιν αὐτῶν.
184 ἄπειμι δ' αὐτὸς χαίρων ἐπὶ τοῖς ὑμετέροις ἀγαθοῖς
παρατιθέμενος ὑμᾶς νόμων τε σωφροσύνῃ[1] καὶ
κόσμῳ τῆς πολιτείας καὶ ταῖς τῶν στρατηγῶν
ἀρεταῖς, οἳ πρόνοιαν ἕξουσιν ὑμῶν τοῦ συμ-
185 φέροντος. θεός τε ὁ μέχρι νῦν ἡγεμονεύσας ὑμῶν,[2]
καθ' οὗ βούλησιν κἀγὼ χρήσιμος ὑμῖν ἐγενόμην,
οὐ μέχρι τοῦ δεῦρο στήσει τὴν αὐτοῦ πρόνοιαν,
ἀλλ' ἐφ' ὅσον αὐτοὶ βούλεσθε χρόνον τοῦτον ἔχειν
προστάτην ἐν τοῖς τῆς ἀρετῆς ἐπιτηδεύμασι
μένοντες, ἐπὶ τοσοῦτον αὐτοῦ χρήσεσθε τῇ προ-
186 μηθείᾳ. γνώμας τε ὑμῖν εἰσηγήσονται τὰς ἀρί-
στας, αἷς ἑπόμενοι τὴν εὐδαιμονίαν ἕξετε, ὁ ἀρχιερεὺς Ἐλεάζαρος καὶ Ἰησοῦς ἥ τε γερουσία καὶ
τὰ τέλη τῶν φυλῶν, ὧν ἀκροᾶσθε μὴ χαλεπῶς,
γινώσκοντες ὅτι πάντες οἱ ἄρχεσθαι καλῶς εἰδότες
καὶ ἄρχειν εἴσονται παρελθόντες εἰς ἐξουσίαν
187 αὐτοῦ, τήν τ' ἐλευθερίαν ἡγεῖσθε μὴ τὸ προσ-
αγανακτεῖν οἷς ἂν ὑμᾶς οἱ ἡγεμόνες πράττειν
ἀξιῶσι· νῦν μὲν γὰρ ἐν τῷ τοὺς εὐεργέτας ὑβρίζειν
ἐν τούτῳ τὴν παρρησίαν τίθεσθε, ὃ δὴ τοῦ λοιποῦ
188 φυλαττομένοις ὑμῖν ἄμεινον ἕξει τὰ πράγματα· μηδὲ
τὴν ἴσην ἐπὶ τούτοις ὀργήν ποτε λαμβάνετε, ᾗ
κατ' ἐμοῦ πολλάκις ἐτολμήσατε χρῆσθαι· γινώ-

---

[1] Niese: νόμῳ τε σωφροσύνης codd.   [2] ἡμῖν RO.

that, will you but practise her among yourselves, she will make your life blissful, render you more glorious than foreign races, and assure you an uncontested renown with future generations. And these blessings might ye attain, would ye but hearken to and observe those laws which, at the dictation of God, I have drawn up, and muse on their inward meaning.

"I am leaving you myself, rejoicing in your happiness, committing you to the sober guidance of the laws, to the ordered scheme of the constitution, and to the virtues of those chiefs who will take thought for your interests. And God, who heretofore has governed you, and by whose will I too have been of service to you, will not at this point set a term to His providence, but so long as ye yourselves desire to have His protection, by continuing in the paths of virtue, so long will ye enjoy His watchful care. Moreover the best of counsels, by following which ye will attain felicity, will be put before you by Eleazar the high-priest and Joshua, as also by the council of elders and the magistrates of the tribes ; to whom give ear ungrudgingly, recognizing that all who know well how to obey will know also how to rule, should they reach the authority of office. And think not that liberty lies in resenting what your rulers require you to do. For now indeed it is in naught but insulting your benefactors that ye reckon freedom of speech to consist ; whereof henceforth if ye beware, things will go better with you. Never display towards these rulers the like of that wrath which ye have oft-times dared to vent on me ; for ye know that my life has more often

σκετε γάρ, ὡς πλεονάκις ἐκινδύνευσα ὑφ' ὑμῶν
189 ἀποθανεῖν ἢ ὑπὸ τῶν πολεμίων. ταῦτα δ' οὐκ
ὀνειδίζειν[1] ὑμᾶς προεθέμην, οὐ γὰρ ἐπ' ἐξόδῳ τοῦ
ζῆν δυσχεραίνοντας καταλιπεῖν ἠξίουν εἰς τὴν
ἀνάμνησιν φέρων μηδὲ παρ' ὃν ἔπασχον αὐτὰ
καιρὸν ἐν ὀργῇ γενόμενος, ἀλλ' ὥστε τοῦ σωφρο-
νήσειν[2] ὑμᾶς εἰς τὸ μέλλον κατ' αὐτό γε τοῦτο
τἀσφαλὲς[3] εἶναι, καὶ μηδὲν εἰς τοὺς προεστηκότας
ἐξυβρίσαι διὰ πλοῦτον, ὃς ὑμῖν πολὺς διαβᾶσι τὸν
Ἰόρδανον καὶ τὴν Χαναναίαν κτησαμένοις περι-
190 στήσεται. ἐπεὶ προαχθέντες εἰς καταφρόνησιν ὑπ'
αὐτοῦ καὶ τῆς ἀρετῆς ὀλιγωρίαν ἀπολεῖτε καὶ τὴν
εὔνοιαν τὴν παρὰ τοῦ θεοῦ, ποιήσαντες δὲ τοῦτον
ἐχθρὸν τήν τε γῆν, ἣν κτήσεσθε, κρατηθέντες
ὅπλοις ὑπὸ τῶν αὖθις ἀφαιρεθήσεσθε μετὰ μεγίστων
ὀνειδῶν καὶ σκεδασθέντες διὰ τῆς οἰκουμένης πᾶσαν
ἐμπλήσετε καὶ γῆν καὶ θάλασσαν τῆς αὑτῶν δου-
191 λείας. ἔσται δ' ὑμῖν τούτων πεῖραν λαμβάνουσιν
ἀνωφελὴς ἡ μετάνοια καὶ ἡ τῶν οὐ φυλαχθέντων
νόμων ἀνάμνησις. ὅθεν εἰ βούλοισθε τούτους ὑμῖν
μένειν, τῶν πολεμίων μηδέν' ἂν ὑπολείποισθε[4]
κρατήσαντες αὐτῶν, ἀλλ' ἀπολλύναι πάντας κρί-
ναιτε[5] συμφέρειν, ἵνα μὴ ζώντων παραγευσάμενοι
τῆς ἐκείνων ἐπιτηδεύσεως διαφθείρητε τὴν πάτριον
192 πολιτείαν. ἔτι δὲ καὶ βωμοὺς καὶ ἄλση καὶ νεὼς
ὁπόσους ἂν ἔχοιεν κατερείπειν παραινῶ καὶ
δαπανᾶν πυρὶ τὸ γένος αὐτῶν καὶ τὴν μνήμην·
βεβαία γὰρ ἂν οὕτως ὑμῖν μόνον ὑπάρξειεν ἡ τῶν

---

[1] ὀνειδίζων P[2] (Lat. ?).   [2] σωφρονίσειν L.
[3] τοῦτ‹ο τ›ἀσφαλὲς conj.: τοῦτ' (τοῦτο SP) ἀσφαλὲς (ἀσφαλεῖς
SPL) codd.
[4] Niese: μηδένα ὑπολείπησθε codd.   [5] Niese: κρίνατε codd.
92

been imperilled by you than by the enemy. I say this with no intent to reproach you—at my exit from life I should be loath to leave you aggrieved by recalling these things to mind, I who even at the moment when I underwent them refrained from wrath—but rather that ye may learn moderation for the future (and) that it is just in this thing that the path of safety lies,[a] and to prevent you from breaking out into any violence against those set over you, by reason of that wealth which will come to you in abundance when ye have crossed the Jordan and conquered Canaan. For, should ye be carried away by it into a contempt and disdain for virtue, ye will lose even that favour which ye have found of God ; and, having made Him your enemy, ye will forfeit that land, which ye are to win, beaten in arms and deprived of it by future generations with the grossest ignominy, and, dispersed throughout the habitable world, ye will fill every land and sea with your servitude. And when ye undergo these trials, all unavailing will be repentance and recollection of those laws which ye have failed to keep. Deut.
iv. 26 ff

"Wherefore, if ye would have those laws remain to you, ye will leave not one of your enemies alive after defeating them, but will deem it expedient to destroy them all, lest, should they live, ye having had but a taste of any of their ways should corrupt the constitution of your fathers. Furthermore, I exhort you to demolish all such altars, groves, and temples as they may have, and to consume with fire their race and their memory ; for thus only can ye have firmly en- Ib. xii. 2 f.

[a] Text uncertain.

193 οἰκείων ἀγαθῶν ἀσφάλεια. ἵνα δὲ μὴ δι᾽ ἀμαθίαν
τοῦ κρείττονος ἡ φύσις ὑμῶν πρὸς τὸ χεῖρον
ἀπονεύσῃ, συνέθηκα ὑμῖν καὶ νόμους ὑπαγορεύσαντός μοι τοῦ θεοῦ καὶ πολιτείαν, ἧς τὸν κόσμον
φυλάξαντες πάντων ἂν εὐδαιμονέστατοι κριθείητε."
194 (3) Ταῦτα εἰπὼν δίδωσιν αὐτοῖς ἐν βιβλίῳ τοὺς
νόμους καὶ τὴν διάταξιν τῆς πολιτείας ἀναγεγραμ-
μένην. οἱ δὲ ἐδάκρυόν τε καὶ πολλὴν ἐπιζήτησιν
ἐποιοῦντο τοῦ στρατηγοῦ μεμνημένοι τε ὧν
κινδυνεύσειε καὶ προθυμηθείη τῆς περὶ αὐτῶν
σωτηρίας καὶ δυσελπιστοῦντες περὶ τῶν μελλόντων ὡς οὐκ ἐσομένης ἄλλης ἀρχῆς τοιαύτης,
ἧττόν τε τοῦ θεοῦ προνοησομένου διὰ τὸ Μωυσῆν
195 εἶναι τὸν παρακαλοῦντα. ὧν τε ἐπὶ τῆς ἐρήμου
μετ᾽ ὀργῆς ὁμιλήσειαν αὐτῷ μετανοοῦντες ἤλγουν,
ὡς ἅπαντα τὸν λαὸν εἰς δάκρυα προπεσόντα
κρεῖττον καὶ τῆς ἐκ λόγου παρηγορίας τὸ ἐπ
αὐτῷ[1] ποιῆσαι πάθος. Μωυσῆς δ᾽ αὐτοὺς παρ-
ηγόρει, καὶ τοῦ δακρύων αὐτὸν ἄξιον ὑπολαμβάνειν
ἀπάγων αὐτοὺς χρῆσθαι τῇ πολιτείᾳ παρεκάλει.
καὶ τότε μὲν οὕτω διελύθησαν.

196 (4) Βούλομαι δὲ τὴν πολιτείαν πρότερον εἰπὼν τῷ
τε Μωυσέος ἀξιώματι τῆς ἀρετῆς ἀναλογοῦσαν
καὶ μαθεῖν παρέξων δι᾽ αὐτῆς τοῖς ἐντευξομένοις,
οἷα τὰ καθ᾽ ἡμᾶς ἀρχῆθεν ἦν, [οὕτως][2] ἐπὶ τὴν
τῶν ἄλλων τραπέσθαι διήγησιν. γέγραπται δὲ
πάνθ᾽ ὡς ἐκεῖνος κατέλιπεν οὐδὲν ἡμῶν ἐπὶ
καλλωπισμῷ προσθέντων οὐδ᾽ ὅ τι μὴ κατα-

---

[1] Niese: ἐπ᾽ αὐτὸν (or ὑπ᾽ αὐτῶν) codd.   [2] om. RO.

sured to you the security of your own privileges. But, for fear lest through ignorance of the better way your nature should incline you to the worse, I have compiled for you, at the dictation of God, a code of laws and a constitution ; keep but its ordered harmony and ye will be accounted the most fortunate of all men."

(3) Having spoken thus, he presented them with these laws and this constitution recorded in a book. But they were in tears and displaying deep regret for their general, alike remembering the risks which he had run and all that ardent zeal of his for their salvation, and despondent concerning the future, in the belief that they would never more have such a ruler and that God would be less mindful of them, since it was Moses who had ever been the intercessor. And of all those angry speeches to him in the desert they now repented with grief, insomuch that the whole people plunged into tears and displayed for him an emotion too strong for words to console. Yet Moses consoled them and, diverting their minds from the thought that he merited their tears, exhorted them to put their constitution into practice. And thus on that occasion they parted. *Moses delivers his book to the Hebrews : their deep emotion ; cf. Deut. xxxi. 9.*

(4) But here I am fain first to describe this constitution, consonant as it was with the reputation of the virtue of Moses, and withal to enable my readers thereby to learn what was the nature of our laws from the first, and then to revert to the rest of the narrative. All is here written as he left it : nothing have we added for the sake of embellishment, nothing which *Observations on the following summary of the Law.*

197 λέλοιπε Μωυσῆς. νενεωτέρισται δ' ἡμῖν τὸ κατὰ
γένος ἕκαστα τάξαι· σποράδην γὰρ ὑπ' ἐκείνου
κατελείφθη γραφέντα καὶ ὡς ἕκαστόν τι παρὰ τοῦ
θεοῦ πύθοιτο. ⟨δ⟩[1] τούτου χάριν ἀναγκαῖον ἡγησάμην προδιαστείλασθαι, μὴ καί τις ἡμῖν παρὰ
τῶν ὁμοφύλων ἐντυγχανόντων τῇ γραφῇ μέμψις
198 ὡς διημαρτηκόσι γένηται. ἔχει δὲ οὕτως ἡ
διάταξις ἡμῶν τῶν νόμων τῶν ἀνηκόντων εἰς τὴν
πολιτείαν. οὓς δὲ κοινοὺς ἡμῖν καὶ πρὸς ἀλλήλους
κατέλιπε τούτους ὑπερεθέμην εἰς τὴν περὶ ἐθῶν
καὶ αἰτιῶν ἀπόδοσιν, ἣν συλλαμβανομένου τοῦ
θεοῦ μετὰ ταύτην ἡμῖν τὴν πραγματείαν συν-
τάξασθαι πρόκειται.

199 (5) " Ἐπειδὰν τὴν Χαναναίων γῆν κτησάμενοι
καὶ σχολὴν ἐπὶ[2] χρήσει τῶν ἀγαθῶν ἔχοντες
πόλεις[3] τὸ λοιπὸν ἤδη κτίζειν προαιρῆσθε, ταῦτα
ποιοῦντες τῷ θεῷ φίλα πράξετε[4] καὶ τὴν εὐδαι-
200 μονίαν βεβαίαν ἕξετε· ἱερὰ πόλις ἔστω μία τῆς
Χαναναίων γῆς ἐν τῷ καλλίστῳ καὶ δι' ἀρετὴν
ἐπιφανεῖ, ἣν ἂν ὁ θεὸς ἑαυτῷ διὰ προφητείας
ἐξέληται,[5] καὶ νεὼς εἷς ἐν ταύτῃ ἔστω, καὶ βωμὸς
εἷς ἐκ λίθων μὴ κατειργασμένων ἀλλὰ λογάδην
συγκειμένων, οἳ κονιάματι χρισθέντες εὐπρεπεῖς

---

[1] ins. Niese. [2] ἐν RO. [3] +τε codd.
[4] Bekker: πράττετε codd.
[5] ME: ἕληται RO: ἐκλέξηται rell.

---

[a] This statement, like similar assertions of the author
(A. i. 17, x. 218), cannot be taken at its face value. He has,
in fact, inserted several regulations which, if based on tradition, are yet unknown to the Mosaic Law: he has also
omitted some relevant topics (noted by Weill), though indeed
he does not claim to be exhaustive.

96

has not been bequeathed by Moses.*a* Our one inno-
vation has been to classify the several subjects ; for
he left what he wrote in a scattered condition, just as
he received each several instruction from God.*b* I
have thought it necessary to make this preliminary
observation, lest perchance any of my countrymen
who read this work should reproach me at all for
having gone astray. Here then is the code of those
laws of ours which touch our political constitution.
As for those which he has left to us in common concerning our mutual relations,*c* these I have reserved
for that treatise on " Customs and Causes," which,
God helping, it is our intention to compose after the
present work.*d*

(5) " Whensoever, having conquered the land of THE MOSAIC
Canaan and being at leisure to enjoy those bounties, CODE.
ye shall determine from that time forward to found city, the
cities, this is what ye should do that your actions may the altar.
be pleasing to God and your felicity assured :

" Let there be one holy city in that place in the land Deut. xii. 5.
of Canaan that is fairest and most famous for its excellence, a city which God shall choose for himself by
prophetic oracle. And let there be one temple therein, and one altar of stones, not worked but picked out Ex. xx. 25.
and put together,*e* and which, coated with plaster, will

b Weill compares the opinion expressed by a 2nd century
Rabbi, to the effect that the Law was given to Moses " roll
by roll," not *en bloc* (*Giṭṭin* 60a) ; just as Mahomet claims
to have received the Qur'an.
c The exact distinction intended is not evident.
d See i. 25 note.
e The phrase comes from Thuc. iv. 4 λογάδην δὲ φέροντες
λίθους καὶ ξυνετίθεσαν ὡς ἕκαστόν τι ξυμβαίνοι, " brought stones
which they picked out and put them together as they
happened to fit " (Jowett).

201 τ' ἄν¹ εἶεν καὶ καθάριοι πρὸς τὴν θέαν. ἡ δ' ἐπὶ
τοῦτον πρόσβασις ἔστω μὴ διὰ βαθμίδων, ἀλλὰ
προσχώσεως αὐτῷ καταπρανοῦς γενομένης. ἐν
ἑτέρᾳ δὲ πόλει μήτε βωμὸς μήτε νεὼς ἔστω· θεὸς
γὰρ εἷς καὶ τὸ Ἑβραίων γένος ἕν.

202 (6) " Ὁ δὲ βλασφημήσας θεὸν καταλευσθεὶς
κρεμάσθω δι' ἡμέρας καὶ ἀτίμως καὶ ἀφανῶς
θαπτέσθω.

203 (7) " Συνερχέσθωσαν δὲ εἰς ἣν ⟨ἄν⟩² ἀποφήνωσι
πόλιν τὸν νεὼν τρὶς τοῦ ἔτους οἱ ἐκ τῶν περάτων
τῆς γῆς, ἧς ἂν Ἑβραῖοι κρατῶσιν, ὅπως τῷ θεῷ
τῶν μὲν ὑπηργμένων εὐχαριστῶσι καὶ περὶ τῶν
εἰς τὸ μέλλον παρακαλῶσι καὶ συνιόντες ἀλλήλοις

204 καὶ συνευωχούμενοι προσφιλεῖς ὦσι· καλὸν γὰρ
εἶναι μὴ ἀγνοεῖν ἀλλήλους ὁμοφύλους τε ὄντας
καὶ τῶν αὐτῶν κοινωνοῦντας ἐπιτηδευμάτων,
τοῦτο δὲ ἐκ μὲν τῆς τοιαύτης³ ἐπιμιξίας αὐτοῖς
ὑπάρξειν, τῇ τε ὄψει καὶ τῇ ὁμιλίᾳ μνήμην αὐτῶν
ἐντιθέντας· ἀνεπιμίκτους γὰρ ἀλλήλοις μένοντας
ἀλλοτριωτάτους αὐτοῖς νομισθήσεσθαι.

205 (8) " Ἔστω δὲ καὶ δεκάτη τῶν καρπῶν ἐξαίρεσις
ὑμῖν χωρὶς ἧς διέταξα⁴ τοῖς ἱερεῦσι καὶ Λευίταις
δεδόσθαι, ἣ πιπρασκέσθω μὲν ἐπὶ τῶν πατρίδων,
εἰς δὲ τὰς εὐωχίας ὑπηρετείτω καὶ τὰς θυσίας

¹ τ' ἂν Niese : τε codd.
² ins. Niese.
³ T. Reinach : αὐτῆς codd.
⁴ SPL : διετάξατε (-ετάξατο) rell.

ᵃ Cf. Ap. ii. 193 εἰς ναὸς ἑνὸς θεοῦ.
ᵇ The penalty of stoning only is prescribed by Leviticus
l.c.; Deuteronomy requires the body of any malefactor,
who, after execution, has been exposed on a tree, to be buried
before nightfall. In practice the double penalty of stoning

be seemly and neat to look upon; and let the ap- Ex. xx. 26.
proach to this altar be not by steps but by a sloping
embankment. In no other city let there be either
altar or temple; for God is one and the Hebrew race
is one.[a]

(6) "Let him that blasphemeth God be stoned, Blasphemy.
Lev. xxiv.
16 : cf. Deut.
xxi. 22 f.
then hung for a day, and buried ignominiously and in
obscurity.[b]

(7) "Let them assemble in that city in which they The three
annual
pilgrim
festivals.
xvi. 16.
shall establish the temple, three times in the year,
from the ends of the land which the Hebrews shall
conquer, in order to render thanks to God for benefits
received, to intercede for future mercies, and to
promote by thus meeting and feasting together
feelings of mutual affection. For it is good that they
should not be ignorant of one another, being members of the same race and partners in the same
institutions; and this end will be attained by such
intercourse, when through sight and speech they
recall those ties to mind,[c] whereas if they remain
without ever coming into contact they will be regarded by each other as absolute strangers.

(8) "Let a tithe of the fruits be set apart by you, Tithe of
fruits.
Ib. xiv. 22 ff.
beside that which I appointed[d] to be given to the
priests and Levites: let it be sold at its native place,
but let the proceeds serve for the repasts and the

and exposure seems to have been confined to the blasphemer.
So far Josephus follows tradition, but in adding the words
" for a day (long) " he departs from the practice described
in the Mishnah (see M. Weill's note).

[c] Lit. " putting in (instilling) a memory of them " (*i.e.*
of their common race and common institutions). Others,
taking αὐτῶν as αὑτῶν, render " sui recordationem efficiunt "
(Hudson), " se souviendront d'eux-mêmes " (Weill). The
motives here mentioned do not appear in Scripture.

[d] § 68; some mss. read " ye appointed."

99

τὰς ἐν τῇ ἱερᾷ πόλει· δίκαιον γὰρ εἶναι τῶν ἐκ τῆς γῆς ἀναδιδομένων, ἣν ὁ θεὸς αὐτοῖς κτήσασθαι παρέσχεν, ἐπὶ τιμῇ τοῦ δεδωκότος ἀπολαύειν.

206 (9) '' Ἐκ μισθοῦ γυναικὸς ἡταιρημένης θυσίας μὴ τελεῖν· ἥδεσθαι γὰρ μηδενὶ τῶν ἀφ' ὕβρεως τὸ θεῖον, χείρων[1] δ' οὐκ ἂν εἴη τῆς ἐπὶ τοῖς σώμασιν αἰσχύνης· ὁμοίως μηδ' ἂν ἐπ' ὀχεύσει κυνὸς ἤτοι θηρευτικοῦ ἢ ποιμνίοις φύλακος λάβῃ[2] τις μισθόν, ἐκ τούτου θύειν τῷ θεῷ.

207 (10) '' Βλασφημείτω δὲ μηδεὶς θεοὺς οὓς πόλεις ἄλλαι νομίζουσι· μηδὲ συλᾶν ἱερὰ ξενικά, μηδ' ἂν ἐπωνομασμένον ᾖ τινι θεῷ κειμήλιον λαμβάνειν.

208 (11) '' Μηδεὶς δ' ἐξ ὑμῶν κλωστὴν ἐξ ἐρίου καὶ λίνου στολὴν φορείτω· τοῖς γὰρ ἱερεῦσι μόνοις ταύτην ἀποδεδεῖχθαι.

209 (12) '' Συνελθόντος δὲ τοῦ πλήθους εἰς τὴν ἱερὰν πόλιν ἐπὶ ταῖς θυσίαις δι' ἐτῶν ἑπτά, τῆς σκηνοπηγίας ἑορτῆς ἐνστάσης, ὁ ἀρχιερεὺς ἐπὶ βήματος

---

[1] edd.: χείρω codd.   [2] Dindorf: λάβοι codd.

---

[a] Josephus, in common with tradition (*Sifre* 96a, quoted by Weill), generalizes a rule which in Scripture applies only to a special case : " if the way be too long for thee . . . then shalt thou turn it into money," Deut. xiv. 24 f.

[b] To " the hire of a whore " Deut. adds " the wages of a dog " (lxx ἄλλαγμα κυνός), *i.e.* of the *kadesh* or temple prostitute ; this technical use of " dog " is found in inscriptions. " In the impure worships of antiquity, it was not uncommon for the gains of prostitution to be dedicated to a deity " (Driver). Like Josephus, the Mishnah (see Weill) takes the word " dog " literally, but interprets the phrase

100

sacrifices to be held in the holy city.[a] For it is right that the produce of that land, which God has enabled men to win, should be enjoyed to the honour of the giver.

(9) "From the hire of a prostitute let no sacrifices be paid ; for the Deity has pleasure in naught that proceeds from outrage, and no shame could be worse than the degradation of the body. Likewise, if one has received payment for the mating of a dog, whether hound of the chase or guardian of the flocks,[b] he must not use thereof to sacrifice to God.

(10) "Let none blaspheme the gods which other cities revere,[c] nor rob foreign temples, nor take treasure that has been dedicated in the name of any god.[d]

(11) "Let none of you wear raiment woven of wool and linen ; for that is reserved for the priests alone.[e]

(12) "When the multitude hath assembled in the holy city for the sacrifices, every seven years at the season of the feast of tabernacles, let the high

Wages that may not be expended on sacrifices. Deut. xxiii. 18.

Foreign cults. Ex. xxii. 28 (27) LXX. : Deut. vii. 25.

Forbidden raiment. Ib. xxii. 11.

Septennial reading of the Laws. Ib. xxxi. 10.

to refer to a proposed exchange of a dog for a pure animal, such as a lamb, for sacrifice.

[c] Ex. *l.c.* "Thou shalt not revile *Elohim*," meaning, according to Palestinian tradition, "the judges." Here Josephus follows Alexandrian exegesis : the LXX translated the plural *Elohim* by θεούς, and so Philo (*Vita Mos.* ii. 26, § 205, *De spec. leg.* i. 7, § 53). Cf. *Ap.* ii. 237, where the same reason for the injunction is given as in Philo, viz. the hallowing of the word "God."

[d] Deut. *l.c.* "The graven images of their gods shall ye burn with fire : thou shalt not covet the silver or the gold that is on them, nor take it unto thee . . ." Scripture emphasizes the destruction of such things ; Josephus is concerned to show that the Jews are not sacrilegious.

[e] Reason not given in Scripture : the Mishnah merely states that the priests wore such garments (*Kil'aim* ix. 1, Weill).

ὑψηλοῦ σταθείς, ἀφ'[1] οὗ γένοιτ' ⟨ἂν⟩[2] ἐξάκουστος,
ἀναγινωσκέτω τοὺς νόμους ἅπασι, καὶ μήτε γυνὴ
μήτε παῖδες εἰργέσθωσαν τοῦ ἀκούειν, ἀλλὰ μηδὲ[3]
210 οἱ δοῦλοι· καλὸν γὰρ ταῖς ψυχαῖς ἐγγραφέντας
καὶ τῇ μνήμῃ φυλαχθῆναι μηδέποτε ἐξαλειφθῆναι
δυναμένους. οὕτως γὰρ οὐδὲ[4] ἁμαρτήσονται μὴ
δυνάμενοι λέγειν ἄγνοιαν τῶν ἐν τοῖς νόμοις
διωρισμένων, οἵ τε νόμοι πολλὴν πρὸς ἁμαρτάνοντας
ἕξουσι παρρησίαν, ὡς προλεγόντων αὐτοῖς ἃ πεί-
σονται καὶ ταῖς ψυχαῖς ἐγγραψάντων διὰ τῆς
211 ἀκοῆς ἃ κελεύουσιν, ὥστ' εἶναι διὰ παντὸς ἔνδον
αὐτοῖς τὴν προαίρεσιν αὐτῶν, ἧς ὀλιγωρήσαντες
ἠδίκησαν καὶ τῆς ζημίας αὐτοῖς αἴτιοι γεγόνασι.
μανθανέτωσαν δὲ καὶ οἱ παῖδες πρῶτον τοὺς
νόμους, μάθημα κάλλιστον καὶ τῆς εὐδαιμονίας
αἴτιον.

212 (13) '' Δὶς δ' ἑκάστης ἡμέρας ἀρχομένης τε αὐτῆς
καὶ ὁπότε πρὸς ὕπνον ὥρα τρέπεσθαι μαρτυρεῖν
τῷ θεῷ τὰς δωρεάς, ἃς ἀπαλλαγεῖσιν αὐτοῖς ἐκ
τῆς Αἰγυπτίων γῆς παρέσχε, δικαίας οὔσης φύσει
τῆς εὐχαριστίας καὶ γενομένης ἐπ' ἀμοιβῇ μὲν
τῶν ἤδη γεγονότων ἐπὶ δὲ προτροπῇ τῶν ἐσομένων·
213 ἐπιγράφειν δὲ καὶ τοῖς θυρώμασιν αὐτῶν τὰ

---

[1] ex Lat. (unde) Niese: ἐφ᾽ codd.
[2] ins. Niese: γένοιτο codd.
[3] edd.: μήτε codd.   [4] οὐδὲν RO.

---

[a] The reader is not clearly defined in Scripture : Deut.
xxxi. 11 (after mention of priests and elders) '' thou shalt
read,'' LXX '' ye shall read,'' Samaritan Pent. (G. A. Smith *in
loc.*) '' he '' or '' one shall read.'' The Mishnah, *Sotah* vii. 8,
states that it was customary to read a selection of passages
from Deut., and that the reader on one occasion was king
Agrippa (whether Agrippa I. or II. does not appear). On the
102

priest,[a] standing upon a raised platform from which
he may be heard, recite the laws [b] to the whole
assembly ; and let neither woman nor child be
excluded from this audience, nay nor yet the slaves.
For it is good that these laws should be so graven on
their hearts and stored in the memory that they can
never be effaced. Thus will they be kept from sin,
being unable to plead ignorance of what the laws
enact ; while the laws will speak with great authority
to sinners, in that they forewarn them what they will
have to suffer and will have so graven on their hearts
through the hearing that which they command, that
they will for ever carry within their breasts the
principles of the code : which if they disdain they
are guilty, and will have brought their penalty upon
themselves. Let your children also begin by learn- Deut. xi. 19
ing the laws, most beautiful of lessons and a source
of felicity.[c]

(13) "Twice each day,[d] at the dawn thereof and Daily
when the hour comes for turning to repose, let all prayers; symbols
acknowledge before God the bounties which He has on house and person.
bestowed on them through their deliverance from the
land of Egypt : thanksgiving is a natural duty, and
is rendered alike in gratitude for past mercies and
to incline the giver to others yet to come. They shall
inscribe also on their doors the greatest of the Ib. vi. 8 f., xi. 18, 20.

apparent inconsistency between Josephus and the Mishnah
as to the reader, and the various explanations offered, reference
must be made to M. Weill's note.
    [b] Deut. " this law " ; the Mishnah specifies passages
drawn from eleven chapters of that book.
    [c] Cf. Ap. ii. 204.
    [d] Not specified in Scripture : tradition attributed to Moses
an ordinance to pray thrice daily, including a midday prayer,
Moore, Judaism, ii. 218, 220.

μέγιστα ὧν εὐεργέτησεν αὐτοὺς ὁ θεὸς ἔν τε
βραχίοσιν ἕκαστον διαφαίνειν, ὅσα τε τὴν ἰσχὺν
ἀποσημαίνειν δύναται τοῦ θεοῦ καὶ τὴν πρὸς
αὐτοὺς εὔνοιαν φέρειν ἐγγεγραμμένα ἐπὶ τῆς
κεφαλῆς καὶ τοῦ βραχίονος, ὡς περίβλεπτον
πανταχόθεν τὸ περὶ αὐτοὺς πρόθυμον τοῦ θεοῦ.

214 (14) '' 'Αρχέτωσαν δὲ καθ' ἑκάστην πόλιν ἄνδρες
ἑπτὰ οἱ καὶ τὴν ἀρετὴν καὶ τὴν περὶ τὸ δίκαιον
σπουδὴν προησκηκότες· ἑκάστῃ δὲ ἀρχῇ δύο
ἄνδρες ὑπηρέται διδόσθωσαν ἐκ τῆς τῶν Λευιτῶν
215 φυλῆς. ἔστωσαν δὲ καὶ οἱ δικάζειν λαχόντες ταῖς
πόλεσιν ἐν ἁπάσῃ τιμῇ, ὡς μήτε βλασφημεῖν
ἐκείνων παρόντων μήτε θρασύνεσθαί τισιν ἐξεῖναι,
τῆς πρὸς τοὺς ἐν ἀξιώματι τῶν ἀνθρώπων αἰδοῦς
αὐτῶν εὐλαβεστέρους, ὥστε τοῦ θεοῦ μὴ κατα-
216 φρονεῖν, ἀπεργαζομένης. οἱ δὲ δικασταὶ ἀποφήνασθαι κύριοι περὶ τοῦ δόξαντος αὐτοῖς ἔστωσαν,
πλὴν εἰ μή τι χρήματα λαβόντας τις αὐτοὺς ἐπὶ
διαφθορᾷ τοῦ δικαίου ἐνδείξαιτ'[1] ἢ ἄλλην τινὰ
αἰτίαν προφέροι, καθ' ἣν οὐ καλῶς ἐλέγχει αὐτοὺς
ἀποφηναμένους· οὔτε γὰρ κέρδει χαριζομένους
οὔτ' ἀξιώματι προσῆκε φανερὰς ποιεῖσθαι τὰς

---

[1] Dindorf: ἐνδείξηται (-εται) codd.

---

a Or " and they shall display each (of them) on their
arms " : the double mention of the arm, here and below,
suggests a glossed text.

b Mezuzah (" door-post ") was the name given to a small
metal cylinder enclosing a parchment, inscribed with Deut.
vi. 4-9 and xi. 13-21, and affixed to the right-hand door-post
of Jewish houses ; tephillin, the N.T. " phylacteries "
(φυλακτήρια), were scrolls similarly inscribed, enclosed in

benefits which they have received from God and
each shall display them on his arms [a] ; and all that
can show forth the power of God and His goodwill
towards them, let them bear a record thereof written
on the head and on the arm, so that men may see
on every side the loving care with which God sur-
rounds them.[b]

(14) " As rulers let each city have seven men long
exercised in virtue and in the pursuit of justice ; and
to each magistracy let there be assigned two subordinate officers of the tribe of Levi.[c] Let those to whom
it shall fall to administer justice in the cities be held
in all honour, none being permitted to be abusive or
insolent in their presence ; for a respect for human
dignitaries will make men too reverential to be ever
contemptuous of God. Let the judges have power
to pronounce what sentence they think fit, always
provided that no one denounce them for having
received a bribe to pervert justice or bring forward
some other charge to convict them of not having
pronounced aright ; for they must be influenced
neither by lucre nor by rank in declaring judgement,

*Administra-
tion of
justice.
Deut.
xvi. 18.*

cases, and bound on the forehead and left arm at certain
hours of prayer.
  [c] Deut. says merely " Judges and officers shalt thou make
thee in all thy gates," specifying no numbers. In mentioning
civic bodies of seven magistrates and two assistants Josephus is
attributing to Moses the practice with which he was familiar :
how much older it may have been is uncertain. He himself
instituted in Galilee " seven individuals in each city to adjudi-
cate upon petty disputes " (*B.J.* ii. 571), perhaps, as Schürer
thinks, merely enforcing an older custom. The Talmud
has one reference to " the seven leading men of the town "
(*Megillah* 26a) ; Josephus mentions " the seven judges "
again in § 287. Of the two assistants we hear nowhere else,
but *cf.* Deut. xxi. 5 for Levites acting in such a capacity.

105

κρίσεις, ἀλλὰ τὸ δίκαιον ἐπάνω πάντων τιθεμένους.
217 ὁ γὰρ θεὸς ἂν οὕτως δόξειε καταφρονεῖσθαι καὶ
ἀσθενέστερος ἐκείνων οἷς ἄν τις κατὰ φόβον
ἰσχύος προσνέμοι τὴν ψῆφον κεκρίσθαι· τοῦ θεοῦ
γὰρ ἰσχύς ἐστι τὸ δίκαιον. ὃ τοῖς[1] ἐν ἀξιώματι
τυγχάνουσι καταχαριζόμενός τις ἐκείνους τοῦ θεοῦ
218 δυνατωτέρους ποιεῖ. ἂν δ' οἱ δικασταὶ μὴ νοῶσι
περὶ τῶν ἐπ' αὐτοῖς[2] παρατεταγμένων ἀποφήνασθαι,
συμβαίνει δὲ πολλὰ τοιαῦτα τοῖς ἀνθρώποις,
ἀκέραιον[3] ἀναπεμπέτωσαν τὴν δίκην εἰς τὴν ἱερὰν
πόλιν, καὶ συνελθόντες ὅ τε ἀρχιερεὺς καὶ ὁ
προφήτης καὶ ἡ γερουσία τὸ δοκοῦν ἀποφαινέ-
σθωσαν.

219 (15) " Εἷς δὲ μὴ πιστευέσθω μάρτυς, ἀλλὰ τρεῖς
ἢ τὸ τελευταῖον δύο, ὧν τὴν μαρτυρίαν ἀληθῆ
ποιήσει τὰ προβεβιωμένα. γυναικῶν δὲ μὴ ἔστω
μαρτυρία διὰ κουφότητα καὶ θράσος τοῦ γένους
αὐτῶν· μαρτυρείτωσαν δὲ μηδὲ[4] δοῦλοι διὰ τὴν
τῆς ψυχῆς ἀγένειαν, οὓς ἢ διὰ κέρδος εἰκὸς ἢ διὰ
φόβον μὴ τἀληθῆ μαρτυρῆσαι. ἂν δέ τις ψευδο-
μαρτυρήσας πιστευθῇ, πασχέτω ταῦτ' ἐλεγχθεὶς
ὅσα ὁ καταμαρτυρηθεὶς πάσχειν ἔμελλεν.

220 (16) " Ἂν δὲ πραχθέντος φόνου ἔν τινι χώρᾳ μὴ
εὑρίσκηται ὁ δράσας μηδ'[4] ὑπονοῆταί τις ὡς διὰ
μῖσος ἀπεκτονηκώς, ζητείτωσαν μὲν αὐτὸν μετὰ
πολλῆς σπουδῆς μήνυτρα προθέμενοι· μηδενὸς δὲ
μηνύοντος αἱ ἀρχαὶ τῶν πόλεων τῶν πλησίον τῇ
χώρᾳ, ἐν ᾗ ὁ φόνος ἐπράχθη, καὶ ἡ γερουσία

---

[1] δ τοῖς RO: τοῖς οὖν rell.   [2] αὐτοὺς RO.
[3] om. RO.   [4] Dindorf: μήτε (μήθ') codd.

---

* Deut. xvii. 9 names as the high court " the priests (of
the tribe of Levi) and the judge that shall be in those days."

but must set justice above all. Else God would appear to be contemned and accounted weaker than those to whom, from fear of their strength, the judge accords his vote. For God's strength is justice ; and one who gives this away out of favour to persons of rank makes them more powerful than God. But if the judges see not how to pronounce upon the matters set before them—and with men such things oft befall—let them send up the case entire to the holy city and let the high priest and the prophet and the council of elders ^a meet and pronounce as they think fit. Deut. xvii. 8.

(15) " Put not trust in a single witness, but let there be three or at the least two, whose evidence shall be accredited by their past lives. From women let no evidence be accepted,^b because of the levity and temerity of their sex ; neither let slaves bear witness ^b because of the baseness of their soul, since whether from cupidity or fear it is like that they will not attest the truth. If anyone be believed to have borne false witness, let him on conviction suffer the penalty which would have been incurred by him against whom he hath borne witness. Witnesses. *Ib.* 6, xix. 15. *Ib.* 16 ff.

(16) " If a murder hath been done in any place and the doer thereof be not found nor is anyone suspected of having killed the victim from hatred, let them make diligent search for the culprit, offering rewards for information ^c ; but if no informer appear, let the magistrates of the towns adjacent to the spot where the murder was done, along with the The undetected murderer. *Ib.* xxi. 1.

The " senate " in Josephus recalls the Sanhedrin of later days : *cf.* the provincial council of seventy set up by himself in Galilee for the trial of major cases, *B.J.* ii. 570 f.

^b Traditional ruling : not in Scripture.

^c Detail not in Scripture.

συνελθόντες μετρείτωσαν ἀπὸ τοῦ τόπου ὅπου
221 κεῖται ὁ νεκρὸς τὴν χώραν. ᾗ δ᾽ ἂν ᾖ πλησιαιτάτη
πόλις, οἱ ἐν αὐτῇ δημόσιοι πριάμενοι δάμαλιν καὶ
κομίσαντες εἰς φάραγγα καὶ ἀνεπιτήδειον ἀρότῳ[1]
καὶ φυτοῖς χωρίον τοὺς τένοντας κοψάτωσαν τῆς
222 βοός, καὶ χέρνιβας ἑλόμενοι ὑπὲρ κεφαλῆς τῆς
βοὸς οἱ ἱερεῖς καὶ οἱ Λευῖται καὶ ἡ γερουσία τῆς
πόλεως ἐκείνης καθαρὰς ἀναβοησάτωσαν τὰς χεῖρας ἔχειν ἀπὸ τοῦ φόνου καὶ μήτε δρᾶσαι μήτε
δρωμένῳ παρατυχεῖν, ἐπικαλεῖσθαι δὲ ἵλεω τὸν
θεὸν καὶ μηκέτι τοιοῦτον δεινὸν συμβῆναι τῇ γῇ
πάθος.

223 (17) '' Ἀριστοκρατία μὲν οὖν κράτιστον καὶ ὁ
κατ᾽ αὐτὴν βίος, καὶ μὴ λάβῃ[2] πόθος ὑμᾶς ἄλλης
πολιτείας, ἀλλὰ ταύτην στέργοιτε καὶ τοὺς νόμους
ἔχοντες δεσπότας κατ᾽ αὐτοὺς ἕκαστα πράττετε·
ἀρκεῖ γὰρ ὁ θεὸς ἡγεμὼν εἶναι. βασιλέως δ᾽ εἰ
γένοιτο ἔρως ὑμῖν, ἔστω μὲν οὗτος ὁμόφυλος,
πρόνοια δ᾽ αὐτῷ δικαιοσύνης καὶ τῆς ἄλλης
224 ἀρετῆς διὰ παντὸς ἔστω. παραχωροίη δὲ οὗτος
τοῖς μὲν νόμοις καὶ τῷ θεῷ τὰ πλείονα τοῦ φρονεῖν,
πρασσέτω δὲ μηδὲν δίχα τοῦ ἀρχιερέως καὶ τῆς
τῶν γερουσιαστῶν γνώμης, γάμοις τε μὴ πολλοῖς
χρώμενος μηδὲ πλῆθος διώκων χρημάτων μηδ᾽
ἵππων, ὧν αὐτῷ παραγενομένων ὑπερήφανος ἂν
τῶν νόμων ἔσοιτο. κωλυέσθω δ᾽, εἰ τούτων τι

---

[1] Niese: ἀρότρῳ codd. [2] λάβοι ROM.

---

[a] Deut. " a valley with (ever) running water."
[b] The text seems sound ; M. Weill would alter it, rendering " Qu'il confie aux lois et à Dieu les desseins les plus
importants."

council of elders, assemble and measure the ground from the place where the body lies. And whichever town is the nearest, let the public officers thereof purchase a heifer and, conducting it to a ravine,[a] to a spot unfitted for ploughing or plantation, let them cut the sinews of the creature's neck; then, after washing their hands in holy water over the head of the animal, let the priests, the Levites, and the council of that city proclaim that their hands are pure of this murder, that they neither did it nor saw it done, and that they implore God to be gracious and that so dire a calamity may no more befall the land.

(17) " Aristocracy, with the life that is lived thereunder, is indeed the best: let no craving possess you for another polity, but be content with this, having the laws for your masters and governing all your actions by them; for God sufficeth for your ruler. But should ye become enamoured of a king, let him be of your own race and let him have a perpetual care for justice and virtue in every other form. Let him concede to the laws and to God the possession of superior wisdom,[b] and let him do nothing without the high priest and the counsel of his senators[c]; let him not indulge in many wives nor in the pursuit of abundance of riches or of horses, through the attainment of which things he might become disdainful of the laws. Should he set his heart on any of these things, let him be restrained

[c] M. Weill quotes the Talmud (*Sanhedrin* 20b), to the effect that the king must consult his tribunal of seventy-one members before engaging in an " optional " or " aggressive " war (*i.e.* with others than the Amalekites or the nations of Canaan).

διὰ σπουδῆς ἔχοι, γίγνεσθαι τοῦ συμφέροντος
ὑμῖν δυνατώτερος.

225 (18) "Ὅρους γῆς μὴ ἐξέστω κινεῖν μήτε οἰκείας
μήτ' ἀλλοτρίας πρὸς οὕς ἐστιν ὑμῖν εἰρήνη,
φυλαττέσθω δ' ὥσπερ θεοῦ ψῆφον βεβαίαν¹ εἰς
αἰῶνα κειμένην ἀναιρεῖν, ὡς πολέμων ἐντεῦθεν
καὶ στάσεων γινομένων ἐκ τοῦ πλεονεκτοῦντας
προσωτέρω χωρεῖν βούλεσθαι τῶν ὅρων· μὴ γὰρ
μακρὰν εἶναι τοῦ καὶ τοὺς νόμους ὑπερβαίνειν τοὺς
τὸν ὅρον μετακινοῦντας.

226 (19) "Γῆν ὁ φυτεύσας, πρὸ ἐτῶν τεσσάρων ἂν
καρπὸν προβάλῃ τὰ φυτά, μήτε τῷ θεῷ ἀπαρχὰς
ἐντεῦθεν ἀποφερέτω μήτ' αὐτὸς χρήσθω· οὐ γὰρ
κατὰ καιρὸν τοῦτον ὑπ' αὐτῶν ἐνεχθῆναι, βιασα-
μένης δὲ τῆς φύσεως ἀώρως μήτε τῷ θεῷ ἁρμόζειν
227 μήτ' αὐτῷ τῷ δεσπότῃ χρῆσθαι. τῷ δὲ τετάρτῳ
τρυγάτω πᾶν τὸ γενόμενον, τότε γὰρ ὥριον εἶναι,
καὶ συναγαγὼν εἰς τὴν ἱερὰν πόλιν κομιζέτω, καὶ
σὺν τῇ δεκάτῃ τοῦ ἄλλου καρποῦ μετὰ τῶν φίλων
εὐωχούμενος ἀναλισκέτω καὶ μετ' ὀρφανῶν καὶ
χηρευουσῶν γυναικῶν. πέμπτου δὲ ἔτους κύριος
ἔστω τὰ φυτὰ καρποῦσθαι.

228 (20) "Τὴν ἀμπέλοις κατάφυτον γῆν μὴ σπείρειν·
ἀρκεῖσθαι² γὰρ αὐτὴν τρέφειν τοῦτο τὸ φυτὸν καὶ
τῶν ἐξ ἀρότρου πόνων ἀπηλλάχθαι. βουσὶν ἀροῦν
τὴν γῆν, καὶ μηδὲν τῶν ἑτέρων ζῴων σὺν αὐτοῖς³

---

¹ RO: βέβαιον rell.   ² RO: ἀρκεῖ rell.
³ σὺν αὐτοῖς om. RO.

ᵃ Literally "God's pebble": the ψῆφος was the pebble
used in voting, to which the boundary-stone is here compared
as recording God's decision.

110

from becoming more powerful than is expedient for your welfare.

(18) " Let it not be permitted to displace boundary-marks, whether of your own land or of the land of others with whom ye are at peace; beware of uprooting as it were a stone by God's decree [a] laid firm for eternity. For thence come wars and seditions, even from that desire of the covetous to overstep their boundaries. In truth, they are not far from transgressing the laws to boot who displace a boundary.

Non-removal of landmarks. Deut. xix. 14 (xxvii. 17).

(19) " When a man planteth a piece of land, if the plants produce fruit before the fourth year, let him neither cull thereof first-fruits for God nor enjoy it himself; for this fruit has not been borne by them in season,[b] and what nature has forced untimely is befitting neither for God nor for the use of the owner himself.[c] But in the fourth year let him reap all the produce, for then is it seasonable, and having gathered it in let him take it to the holy city and there expend it, along with the tithe of his other fruits, in feasting with his friends, as also with orphans and widows.[d] In the fifth year he shall be at liberty to enjoy the fruits of his planting.

Fruits of the fourth year. Lev. xix. 23.

(20) " Land that is planted with vines is not to be sown; for it sufficeth that it rear this plant and be exempt from the labours of the plough. Use oxen to plough the ground and put no other animal

Prohibition of unnatural " mixing." Deut. xxii. 9 f.: Lev. xix. 19.

[b] I take τοῦτον to refer to καρπόν, not (as other translators) with κατὰ καιρόν.

[c] Motive not given in Scripture.

[d] Traditional practice: Lev. merely states that the fruit of the fourth year " shall be holy, for giving praise unto the Lord."

111

JOSEPHUS

ὑπὸ ζεύγλην ἄγοντας, ἀλλὰ κατ᾽ οἰκεῖα γένη
κἀκείνοις ποιεῖσθαι τὸν ἄροτον.[1] εἶναι δὲ καθαρὰ
τὰ σπέρματα καὶ ἀνεπίμικτα, καὶ μὴ σύνδυο καὶ
τρία σπείρειν· οὐ γὰρ τῇ τῶν ἀνομοίων κοινωνίᾳ
229 χαίρειν τὴν φύσιν. μηδὲ κτήνεσιν ἐπάγειν ὅσα
μὴ συγγενῆ· δέος γὰρ ἐκ τούτου μὴ διαβῇ καὶ
μέχρι τῶν ἀνθρωπείων ἡ πρὸς τὸ ὁμόφυλον
ἀτιμία τὴν ἀρχὴν ἀπὸ τῶν περὶ τὰ μικρὰ καὶ τὰ
230 φαῦλα πρότερον λαβοῦσα. δεῖ δὲ μηδὲν εἶναι
τοιοῦτον συγκεχωρημένον, ἐξ οὗ κατὰ μίμησιν
παρατροπή τις τῶν κατὰ τὴν πολιτείαν ἔσοιτο,
ἀλλ᾽ ὡς οὐδὲ περὶ τῶν τυχόντων †ἀμελήσεται[2]
τοῖς νόμοις εἰδόσι προνοεῖσθαι τοῦ κατ᾽ αὐτοὺς
ἀμέμπτου.
231 (21) '' Ἀμῶντας δὲ καὶ συναιροῦντας τὰ θέρη μὴ
καλαμᾶσθαι, καταλιπεῖν δέ τινα καὶ τῶν δραγ-
μάτων τοῖς βίου σπανίζουσιν ἕρμαιον εἶναι[3] πρὸς
διατροφήν· ὁμοίως δὲ καὶ τῆς τρύγης ἀπολιπεῖν
τὰς ἐπιφυλλίδας τοῖς πένησι καὶ τῶν ἐλαιώνων[4]
παρεῖναί τι τοῦ καρποῦ πρὸς συλλογὴν τοῖς ἐξ
232 ἰδίων οὐκ ἔχουσι μεταλαβεῖν· οὐ τοσαύτη γὰρ ἂν
ἐκ τῆς ἐπ᾽ ἀκριβὲς αὐτῶν συλλογῆς εὐπορία τοῖς
δεσπόταις γένοιτο, ὅση χάρις ἐκ τῶν δεομένων
ἔλθοι, τό τε θεῖον τὴν γῆν προθυμοτέραν εἰς τὴν
ἐκτροφὴν τῶν καρπῶν ἀπεργάσεται μὴ τοῦ καθ᾽
αὑτοὺς προνοουμένων ⟨μόνον⟩[5] λυσιτελοῦς, ἀλλὰ
καὶ τῆς τῶν ἄλλων διατροφῆς λόγον ἐχόντων.

---

[1] edd.: ἄροτρον codd.
[2] conj.: ἀμελεῖται, ἀμεληταὶ (sic), or ἠμέληται codd.
[3] + καὶ εὕρεμα ROM: + τούτοις rell.
[4] ROM: ἐλαιῶν rell.
[5] ins. ex Lat. Niese.

112

with them beneath the yoke ; nay, these too should
be paired according to their own kinds for the labours
of the field.[a] Let your seeds too be pure and
without mixture, and sow not two or three kinds
together ; for nature delighteth not in the con-
junction of things dissimilar. Neither shall ye
mate beasts that are not of kindred nature ; for
it is to be feared that from this custom a disregard
for the law of the breed may pass over even into the
practices of humanity, having owed its origin to
the treatment of petty and insignificant objects.
Nothing, in short, must be permitted that is calcu-
lated to lead, through imitation, to some perversion
of the principles of the constitution ; nay, even
trivial matters must not be neglected by the laws,[b]
which should know how to guard themselves against
all reproach.

(21) " When reaping and gathering in the crops
ye shall not glean, but shall even leave some of the
sheaves[c] for the destitute, to come as a godsend
for their sustenance ; likewise at the vintage leave
the little bunches for the poor, and pass over somewhat of the fruit of the olive-yards to be gathered
by those who have none of their own whereof to
partake. For that minute care in garnering will
not bring the owners wealth so great as the gratitude which would so come to them from the needy ;
the Deity, too, will render the earth more eager
to foster its fruits for those who look not only to
their own interests but also have regard to the

Rights of
the poor :
the beasts
and the
wayfarers
to share in
the harvest.
Deut.
xxiv. 19 :
Lev.
xix. 9.

---

[a] Additional detail, not in Scripture.
[b] Text doubtful. The construction δεῖ . . . ὡς with fut.
ind. has the support of Sophocles (δεῖ σ' ὅπως δείξεις), whose
style was imitated by the assistant of Josephus.
[c] Or " handfuls."

233 μηδὲ βοῶν ὁπότε τρίβοιεν τοὺς στάχυας ἀποδεῖν
τὰ στόματα ἐπὶ τῆς ἅλωος· οὐ γὰρ εἶναι δίκαιον
εἴργειν τοὺς συνειργασμένους τοῦ καρποῦ καὶ περὶ
234 τὴν γένεσιν αὐτοῦ πονήσαντας. μηδὲ ὀπώρας
ἀκμαζούσης κωλύειν ἅπτεσθαι τοὺς ὁδῷ βαδί-
ζοντας, ἀλλ᾽ ὡς ἐξ οἰκείων αὐτοῖς ἐπιτρέπειν
ἐμπίπλασθαι, κἂν ἐγχώριοι τυγχάνωσι κἂν ξένοι,
χαίροντας ἐπὶ τῷ παρέχειν αὐτοῖς τῶν ὡραίων
μεταλαμβάνειν· ἀποφέρεσθαι¹ δ᾽ αὐτοῖς μηδὲν
235 ἐξέστω. μηδὲ τρυγῶντες ὧν ἂν εἰς τὰς ληνοὺς
κομίζωσιν εἰργέτωσαν τοὺς ὑπαντιάζοντας ἐπ-
εσθίειν· ἄδικον γὰρ ἀγαθῶν, ἃ κατὰ βούλησιν θεοῦ
παρῆλθεν εἰς τὸν βίον, φθονεῖν τοῖς ἐπιθυμοῦσιν
αὐτῶν μεταλαμβάνειν, τῆς ὥρας ἐν ἀκμῇ τε οὔσης
236 καὶ σπευδούσης ἀπελθεῖν· ὡς τῷ θεῷ κεχαρισμένον
ἂν εἴη, κἂν ὑπ᾽ αἰσχύνης τινὰς ὀκνοῦντας ἅψασθαι
λαβεῖν παρακαλοῖεν,² ὄντας μὲν Ἰσραηλίτας ὡς
κοινωνοὺς καὶ δεσπότας διὰ τὴν συγγένειαν,
ἀφιγμένους δ᾽ ἀλλαχόθεν ἀνθρώπους ξενίων τυχεῖν
ἀξιοῦντας ὧν ὁ θεὸς καθ᾽ ὥραν αὐτοῖς παρέσχεν.
237 ἀναλώματα γὰρ οὐχ ἡγητέον ὅσα τις κατὰ χρη-
στότητα παρίησιν ἀνθρώποις λαμβάνειν, τοῦ θεοῦ
τὴν ἀφθονίαν τῶν ἀγαθῶν χορηγοῦντος οὐκ ἐπὶ τῷ
καρποῦσθαι μόνοις, ἀλλὰ καὶ τῷ τοῖς ἄλλοις μετα-
διδόναι φιλοτίμως, καὶ βουλομένου³ τῷ τρόπῳ
τούτῳ τὴν ἰδίαν περὶ τὸν Ἰσραηλιτῶν λαὸν εὔνοιαν
καὶ τὴν χορηγίαν τῆς εὐδαιμονίας καὶ τοῖς ἄλλοις
ἐμφανίζεσθαι, ἐκ πολλοῦ τοῦ περιόντος αὐτοῖς
238 κἀκείνοις μεταδιδόντων. ὁ δὲ παρὰ ταῦτα ποιήσας

¹ SP: ἐπιφέρεσθαι rell.
² Dindorf: παρακαλῶεν codd.: -καλῶσιν Niese.
³ L ed. pr.: βουλόμενος rell.

114

support of others. Neither muzzle ye the oxen Deut.
xxv. 4. when they crush the ears of corn on the thresh-ing-floor; for it is not just to exclude from the fruit your fellow-labourers who have toiled to produce it. Nor yet, when autumn fruits are at their prime, Ib. xxiii. 25. must ye forbid wayfarers to touch them, but let them take their fill, as if they were their own, be they natives or strangers, rejoicing at thus affording them a share in the fruits of the season; but let it not be permitted to them to carry any of them away. Neither let the vintagers hinder such as they meet from eating of that which they are carrying to the wine-vats; for it were unjust to grudge the good things which by God's will have come into the world to such as long for a share in them, when the season is at its prime and so swiftly to pass. Nay, it would be acceptable to God that one should even invite to take thereof any who, through modesty, should hesitate to touch them —be they Israelites, as partners and owners, in virtue of their kinship, be they come from another country, entreating them to accept, as guests, of these gifts which God has granted them in season. For one must not account as expenditure that which out of liberality one lets men take; since God bestows this abundance of good things not for our enjoyment alone, but that we may also share them generously with others, and He is desirous that by these means the special favour that He bears to the people of Israel and the bounty of His gifts may be manifested to others also, when out of all that superabundance of ours they too receive their share from us. But let him who acts contrary to

πληγὰς μιᾷ λειπούσας τεσσαράκοντα τῷ δημοσίῳ
σκύτει λαβὼν τιμωρίαν ταύτην αἰσχίστην ἐλεύθερος ὑπομενέτω, ὅτι τῷ κέρδει δουλεύσας ὕβρισε
239 τὸ ἀξίωμα· καλῶς γὰρ ὑμῖν ἔχει πεπειραμένοις ἐν
Αἰγύπτῳ συμφορῶν καὶ κατὰ τὴν ἐρημίαν πρόνοιαν
τῶν ἐν τοῖς ὁμοίοις ὑπαρχόντων ποιεῖσθαι, καὶ
τυχόντας εὐπορίας ἐξ ἐλέου καὶ προνοίας τοῦ θεοῦ
τὴν αὐτὴν ταύτην ἐξ ὁμοίου πάθους ἀπομερίζειν
τοῖς δεομένοις.
240 (22) ''Ταῖς δὲ δεκάταις ταῖς δυσίν, ἃς ἔτους
ἑκάστου προεῖπον τελεῖν, τὴν μὲν τοῖς Λευίταις,
τὴν δ' ἑτέραν πρὸς τὰς εὐωχίας, τρίτην πρὸς
αὐταῖς κατὰ τὸ ἔτος[1] τρίτον συμφέρειν εἰς δια-
νέμησιν τῶν σπανιζόντων γυναιξί τε χήραις καὶ
241 παισὶν ὀρφανοῖς· τῶν δ' ὡραίων ὅ τι καὶ πρῶτον
ἑκάστῳ τύχῃ γενόμενον εἰς τὸ ἱερὸν κομιζέτωσαν,
καὶ τὸν θεὸν ὑπὲρ τῆς ἐνεγκαμένης αὐτὸ γῆς ἣν
αὐτοῖς κτήσασθαι παρέσχεν εὐλογήσαντες, θυσίας
ἃς ὁ νόμος αὐτοῖς ἐπιφέρειν κελεύει ἐπιτελέσαντες
τούτων τὰ προτέλεια τοῖς ἱερεῦσι διδότωσαν.
242 ἐπειδὰν δὲ ταῦτά τις ποιήσας καὶ πάντων τὰς
δεκάτας ἅμα ταῖς εἰς τοὺς Λευίτας καὶ τὰς εὐωχίας[2]
ἀπενηνοχὼς ἀπιέναι μέλλῃ πρὸς αὐτὸν οἴκαδε,
στὰς ἀντικρὺ τοῦ τεμενίσματος εὐχαριστησάτω

---

[1] κατ' ἔτος Dindorf.   [2] + ταῖς ἀπαρχαῖς MSPL.

---

[a] As Reinach remarks, the verses in Deut. about scourging,
though interposed between the precepts with which Josephus
has been dealing, are really of much more general applica-
tion. Throughout this paragraph Josephus is concerned to
extol Jewish charity in the eyes of pagan readers ; but it
was indeed a thing of which he might justly be proud (see
the excellent chapter in G. F. Moore, *Judaism*, ii. p. 162).
[b] The forty stripes allowed by the Law were by tradition

these precepts [a] receive forty stripes save one [b] Penalty of scourging. Deut. xxv. 3. from the public lash, undergoing, free man as he is, this most disgraceful penalty, because through slavery to lucre he has outraged his dignity. For it beseems you, after your experience of afflictions in Egypt and in the desert, to take thought for those who are in like case, and, after receiving such store of blessings through the mercy and providence of God, of that same store and from kindred feelings to impart to those in need.

(22) " In addition to the two tithes which I have Triennial tithe for widows and orphans. Ib. xiv. 28, xxvi. 12. already directed you [c] to pay each year, the one for the Levites and the other for the banquets, ye should devote a third [d] every third year to the distribution of such things as are lacking to widowed women and orphan children. The very first of the ripe fruits which shall fall to each man's lot are to be brought to the temple, where, after blessing God for the land which has borne them and which He has enabled them to win, and after performing the sacrifices which the law commands them to offer, let them present the first-fruits thereof to the priests. And when any man, after having done all Ceremony after offering tithes. Cf. ib. xxvi. 3 ff. this and having offered tithes of all, along with those [e] for the Levites and for the banquets, is about to depart to his own home, let him stand right opposite the sacred precincts and render

reduced to thirty-nine, doubtless for fear of a miscount, *Makkoth* iii. 10 ff. ; *cf.* 2 Cor. xi. 24.   [e] §§ 68, 205.

    [d] This " third " or " poor " tithe was, according to one tradition, not an *additional* tithe, as Josephus interprets it, but only a particular use to which the " second " or " festival " tithe was put every third year (see Weill's note). The two conflicting Greek texts of Tobit i. 6 ff. illustrate the current variety of interpretation ; Josephus does not stand alone.

    [e] Text a little uncertain.

μὲν τῷ θεῷ, ὅτι τῆς ἀπ' Αἰγυπτίων αὐτοὺς ὕβρεως
ἀπαλλάξας γῆν αὐτοῖς ἀγαθὴν καὶ πολλὴν ἔδωκε
καρποῦσθαι, μαρτυράμενος δὲ ὡς τάς τε δεκάτας[1]
243 κατὰ τοὺς Μωυσέος τελέσειε νόμους αἰτησάσθω
τὸν θεὸν εὐμενῆ καὶ ἵλεων αὐτῷ διὰ παντὸς εἶναι
καὶ κοινῇ πᾶσιν Ἑβραίοις διαμένειν, φυλάττοντα
μὲν ἃ δέδωκεν αὐτοῖς ἀγαθὰ προσκτήσασθαι[2] δὲ
ὅσα δύναται χαρίζεσθαι.

244 (23) " Γαμείτωναν δὲ ἐν ὥρᾳ γάμου γενόμενοι
παρθένους ἐλευθέρας γονέων ἀγαθῶν, ὁ δὲ μὴ μέλ-
λων ἄγεσθαι παρθένον μὴ ζευγνύσθω συνοικοῦσαν
ἄλλῳ νοθεύσας μηδὲ λυπῶν[3] τὸν πρότερον αὐτῆς
ἄνδρα· δούλας δὲ μὴ γαμεῖσθαι τοῖς ἐλευθέροις,
μηδ' ἂν ὑπ' ἔρωτος πρὸς τοῦτό τινες ἐκβιάζωνται,
κρατεῖν δὲ τῆς ἐπιθυμίας τὸ εὐπρεπὲς καὶ τοῖς
245 ἀξιώμασι πρόσφορον· ἔτι[4] μηδὲ ἡταιρημένης εἶναι
γάμον, ἧς δι' ὕβριν τοῦ σώματος τὰς ἐπὶ τῷ γάμῳ
θυσίας ὁ θεὸς οὐκ ἂν προσοῖτο. γένοιτο γὰρ ἂν
οὕτω τῶν παίδων τὰ φρονήματα ἐλευθέρια καὶ
πρὸς ἀρετὴν ὄρθια, εἰ μὴ τύχοιεν ἐκ γάμων φύντες
αἰσχρῶν μηδ' ἐξ ἐπιθυμίας οὐκ ἐλευθερίας συν-
246 ελθόντων· εἴ τις ὡς παρθένον μνηστευσάμενος
ἔπειτα μὴ τοιαύτην εὕροι, δίκην λαχὼν αὐτὸς μὲν
κατηγορείτω χρώμενος εἰς ἀπόδειξιν οἷς ἂν ἔχῃ
τεκμηρίοις, ἀπολογείσθω δὲ ὁ τῆς κόρης πατὴρ

----

[1] + καὶ τἆλλα E.
[2] προσκτήσαντα ex Lat. (et addat) Bernard.
[3] λιποῦσαν O[2] (Reinach).   [4] + δὲ SPL.

----

[a] One authority adds " and all else."
[b] Cf. the shorter summary of marriage laws in Ap. ii.
199 ff.

thanks to God for having delivered his race from the
insolence of the Egyptians and given them a good
land and spacious to enjoy the fruits thereof; then,
after attesting that he has paid the tithes [a] in accordance with the laws of Moses, let him ask God ever to
be favourable and gracious to himself and to continue such favour towards all Hebrews in common,
preserving to them the good things that He had given
them and adding thereto all else that He could bestow.

(23) " Let [b] your young men, on reaching the age   Marriage
of wedlock, marry virgins, freeborn and of honest   laws.
parents. He that will not espouse a virgin must
not unite himself to a woman living with another   Deut.
man, corrupting her or wronging [c] her former hus-   xxii. 22 :
band. Female slaves must not be taken in marriage   Lev. xxi. 7.
by free men, however strongly some may be constrained thereto by love : such passion must be
mastered by regard for decorum and the proprieties
of rank. Again, there must be no marriage with   Lev.
a prostitute,[d] since by reason of the abuse of her
body God could not accept her nuptial sacrifices.[e]
For so only can your children have spirits that are
liberal and uprightly set towards virtue, if they are
not the issue of dishonourable marriages or of a
union resulting from ignoble [f] passion.

" If a man, having betrothed a bride in the belief   Deut.
that she is a virgin, thereafter find that she is not   xxii. 13.
so, let him bring a suit and make his own accusation,
relying upon what evidence he may have to prove
it ; and let the damsel's defence be undertaken by

[a] Lit. " grieving ": but we should probably read λιπούσαν,
" nor let him marry one that has left her former husband."
[d] In Scripture this prohibition applies only to the priests ;
and so Josephus elsewhere interprets it, iii. 276.
[e] § 206.   [f] Gr. " illiberal," *i.e.* a passion for a slave.

ἢ ἀδελφὸς ἢ ὃς ἂν μετὰ τούτους ἐγγυτέρω δοκῇ
247 τοῦ γένους. καὶ κριθεῖσα μὲν ἡ κόρη μὴ ἀδικεῖν
συνοικείτω τῷ κατηγορήσαντι μηδεμίαν ἐξουσίαν
ἔχοντος ἐκείνου ἀποπέμπεσθαι αὐτήν, πλὴν εἰ μὴ
μεγάλας αἰτίας αὐτῷ παράσχοι καὶ πρὸς ἃς οὐδ᾽[1]
248 ἀντειπεῖν δυνηθείη. τοῦ δὲ τολμηρῶς καὶ προ-
πετῶς ἐπενεγκεῖν αἰτίαν καὶ διαβολὴν πρόστιμον
ἐκτινύτω, πληγὰς τεσσαράκοντα μιᾷ λειπούσας
λαμβάνων, καὶ πεντήκοντα σίκλους ἀποτινύτω τῷ
πατρί. ἂν δ᾽ ἐξελέγξῃ τὴν παιδίσκην ἐφθαρμένην,
δημότις μὲν οὖσα τοῦ μὴ σωφρόνως προστῆναι
τῆς παρθενίας ἄχρι νομίμων γάμων καταλευέσθω,
249 ἂν δ᾽ ἐξ ἱερέων ᾖ γεγενημένη, καιέσθω ζῶσα. δύο
γυναικῶν οὐσῶν τινι, καὶ τῆς μὲν ἑτέρας ἐν τιμῇ
σφόδρα καὶ εὐνοίᾳ κειμένης ἢ δι᾽ ἔρωτα καὶ κάλλος
ἢ κατ᾽ ἄλλην αἰτίαν, τῆς δ᾽ ἑτέρας ἐν ἐλάττονι
μοίρᾳ τυγχανούσης, ἂν ὁ ἐκ τῆς ἀγαπωμένης παῖς
γενόμενος, νεώτερος ὢν τοῦ ἐκ τῆς ἑτέρας φύντος,
ἀξιοῖ διὰ τὴν πρὸς τὴν μητέρα τοῦ πατρὸς εὔνοιαν
τῶν πρεσβείων τυγχάνειν, ὥστε διπλοῦν τὸ μέρος
τῆς πατρῴας οὐσίας ἐκλαμβάνειν,[2] τοῦτο γὰρ ἐν
250 τοῖς νόμοις διεταξάμην, μὴ συγκεχωρήσθω· ἄδικον
γὰρ τὸν τῇ γενέσει πρεσβύτερον, ὅτι τὰ τῆς
μητρὸς αὐτῷ ἥττονα παρὰ τῇ διαθέσει τοῦ πατρός,
251 τῶν ὀφειλομένων αὐτῷ στερεῖσθαι. ὁ κόρην ἄλλῳ

---

[1] +⟨ἂν⟩ Naber. [2] RO: λαμβάνειν rell.

---

[a] Scripture mentions only the father (accompanied by the
mother) as counsel for the defence.

[b] Deut. xxii. 19 " an hundred (*shekels*) of silver " (LXX
ἑκατὸν σίκλους). The Hebrew names no coin; tradition,
supporting Josephus, names a coin equivalent to a half-
shekel (*Kethuboth* 45b, quoted by Weill).

her father or brother or whosoever, failing these, be considered her next of kin.[a] If the damsel be then declared innocent, let her continue to live with her accuser, who shall have no right to dismiss her, save only if she furnish him with grave and undeniable reasons for so doing. And for having rashly and precipitately brought a calumnious charge against her, let him undergo a double penalty, receiving forty stripes save one and paying fifty shekels[b] to the father. But should he prove that the young woman has been corrupted, then, if she be one of the people, for not having kept chaste guard over her virginity up to her lawful marriage, let her be stoned ; if she be of priestly parentage, let her be burnt alive.[c]

Deut. xxii. 18, xxv. 3.

"If a man have two wives, of whom the one is held in special honour and affection, be it for love and beauty, or for other cause, while the other has a lesser portion of his regard, should the son of the beloved one, being younger than the offspring of the other, claim, in virtue of his father's affection for his mother, the rights of the firstborn, to wit to receive a double portion of his father's substance— for that is what I have ordained in the laws[d]—let this claim be disallowed. For it were unjust that he that is elder by birth should, because his mother holds a lesser place in his father's affections, be deprived of that which is his due.

Ib. xxi. 15.

[c] This last clause has no authority in Scripture and is not strictly in accord with tradition (see Weill's note). Scripture mentions only the penalty of stoning for all alike.

[d] Only specified in this passage of Scripture (Deut. xxi. 17 ; cf. 2 K. ii. 9).

κατηγγυημένην φθείρας, εἰ μὲν πείσας καὶ πρὸς
τὴν φθορὰν συγκάταινον λαβών, ἀποθνησκέτω σὺν
αὐτῇ· πονηροὶ γὰρ ὁμοίως ἑκάτεροι, ὁ μὲν τὸ
αἴσχιστον πείσας ἑκουσίως ὑπομεῖναι καὶ προ-
τιμῆσαι τοῦτο τοῦ ἐλευθέρου γάμου τὴν κόρην,
ἡ δὲ παρασχεῖν ἑαυτὴν πεισθεῖσα δι᾽ ἡδονὴν[1] ἢ διὰ
252 κέρδος πρὸς τὴν ὕβριν· ἐὰν δέ που μόνη περιπεσὼν
βιάσηται μηδενὸς βοηθοῦ παρόντος, μόνος ἀποθνησκέτω. ὁ φθείρας παρθένον μήπω κατηγγυημένην αὐτὸς γαμείτω· ἢν δὲ τῷ πατρὶ τῆς
κόρης μὴ δόξῃ συνοικίζειν αὐτῷ, πεντήκοντα
253 σίκλους τιμὴν τῆς ὕβρεως καταβαλλέτω. γυναικὸς δὲ τῆς συνοικούσης βουλόμενος διαζευχ-
θῆναι καθ᾽ ἁσδηποτοῦν αἰτίας, πολλαὶ δ᾽ ἂν τοῖς
ἀνθρώποις τοιαῦται γίγνοιντο, γράμμασι μὲν περὶ
τοῦ μηδέποτε συνελθεῖν ἰσχυριζέσθω· λάβοι γὰρ
ἂν οὕτως ἐξουσίαν συνοικεῖν ἑτέρῳ, πρότερον γὰρ
οὐκ ἐφετέον· εἰ δὲ καὶ πρὸς ἐκεῖνον[2] κακωθείη ἢ[3]
τελευτήσαντος αὐτοῦ θελήσειε γαμεῖν ὁ πρότερος,
254 μὴ ἐξεῖναι αὐτῇ[4] ἐπανιέναι. τὴν ἄτεκνον, τἀνδρὸς
αὐτῇ τετελευτηκότος, ὁ ἀδελφὸς ἐκείνου γαμείτω

---

[1] ed. pr.: +ἰδίαν codd. [2] conj.: ἐκεῖνον codd.
[3] MLE: καὶ RO: om. SP. [4] RM: αὐτὴν rell.

---

[a] In Scripture the seducer is required to marry the girl
and to pay the customary " bride-price " to her father.
Josephus is in line with tradition, which required " compensation " to be paid only when no marriage took place
(references quoted by Weill).

[b] Deut. " if she find no favour in his eyes, because he hath
found in her some indecency " (lit. " the nakedness of a
thing "). This vague phrase gave rise to conflicting inter-
pretations : the school of Shammai (1st cent. B.C.) understanding by it unchastity, that of Hillel extending it to cover

"Should a man violate a damsel who is betrothed Deut.
xxii. 23.
to another, if he persuaded her and had obtained
her assent to the violation, let him die along with
her ; for both are guilty alike, he for having persuaded the damsel voluntarily to submit to the worst
disgrace and to prefer that to honest wedlock, she
for being persuaded to lend herself, for pleasure or
for lucre, to this outrage. But if he met her alone *Ib. 25.*
somewhere and forced her, when none was at hand
to aid, let him die alone. He that violateth a virgin *Ib. 28.*
who is not yet betrothed shall marry her himself ;
but if the father of the damsel be not minded to
give her away to him, he shall pay fifty shekels as
compensation for the outrage.*a*

"He who desires to be divorced from the wife who Divorce.
Ib. xxiv. 1.
is living with him for whatsoever cause *b*—and with
mortals many such may arise—must certify in
writing that he will have no further intercourse
with her ; for thus will the woman obtain the right
to consort with another, which thing ere then
must not be permitted. But if she be maltreated
by the other also or if upon his death her former
husband wishes to marry her, she shall not be allowed
to return to him.

"When a woman is left childless *c* on her husband's Levirate
marriage.
Ib. xxv. 5.
death, the husband's brother shall marry her, and

the most trivial causes. As Weill remarks, the latter view
seems to have prevailed, *cf. A.* xvi. 198, *Vita* 426 (the
historian's own divorce) : also the question of the Pharisees
as reported in Matt. xix. 3 " is it lawful to put away one's
wife *for every cause* ? " (κατὰ πᾶσαν αἰτίαν). with the saving
clause in the reply, μὴ ἐπὶ πορνείᾳ (v. 9), where the text
probably owes its form to its Jewish editor.

c Deut. " if one die and have no *son*." Josephus follows
tradition (*Baba Bathra* 109a, Weill) ; so LXX (σπέρμα) and
Matt. xxii. 24 with parallels (τέκνον, ἄτεκνος).

καὶ τὸν παῖδα τὸν γεν‹ησ›όμενον[1] τῷ τοῦ τεθνεῶ-
τος καλέσας ὀνόματι τρεφέτω τοῦ κλήρου διάδοχον·
τοῦτο γὰρ καὶ τοῖς δημοσίοις λυσιτελήσει γιγνό-
μενον τῶν οἴκων οὐκ ἐκλειπόντων καὶ τῶν χρημάτων τοῖς συγγενέσι μενόντων, καὶ ταῖς γυναιξὶ
κουφισμὸν οἴσει τῆς συμφορᾶς τοῖς ἔγγιστα τῶν
255 προτέρων ἀνδρῶν συνοικούσαις. ἐὰν δὲ μὴ βούληται γαμεῖν ὁ ἀδελφός, ἐπὶ τὴν γερουσίαν ἐλθοῦσα
ἡ γυνὴ μαρτυράσθω τοῦθ', ὅτι βουλομένην αὐτὴν
ἐπὶ τοῦ οἴκου μένειν καὶ τεκνοῦν ἐξ αὐτοῦ μὴ
προσδέχοιτο ὑβρίζων τὴν τοῦ τεθνηκότος ἀδελφοῦ
μνήμην. ἐρομένης δὲ τῆς γερουσίας, διὰ ποίαν
αἰτίαν ἀλλοτρίως ἔχοι πρὸς τὸν γάμον, ἄν τε
μικρὰν ἄν τε μείζω λέγῃ, πρὸς ταῦτα[2] ῥεπέτω·
256 ὑπολύσασα δ' αὐτὸν ἡ γυνὴ τἀδελφοῦ τὰ σάνδαλα
καὶ πτύσασα[3] αὐτοῦ εἰς τὸ πρόσωπον τούτων
αὐτὸν ἄξιον εἶναι παρ' αὐτῆς λεγέτω τυγχάνειν
ὑβρίσαντα τὴν τοῦ κατοιχομένου μνήμην. καὶ ὁ
μὲν ἐκ τῆς γερουσίας ἀπίτω τοῦτ' ἔχων ὄνειδος
πρὸς ἅπαντα τὸν βίον, ἡ δ' ᾧπερ ἂν βουληθῇ τινι
257 τῶν δεομένων γαμείσθω. ἂν δ' αἰχμάλωτόν τις
λάβῃ παρθένον ἄν τε καὶ γεγαμημένην, βουλομένῳ
συνοικεῖν μὴ πρότερον ἐξέστω εὐνῆς ἅψασθαι καὶ
κοινωνίας, πρὶν ἢ ξυραμένην αὐτὴν καὶ πένθιμον
σχῆμα ἀναλαβοῦσαν ἀποθρηνῆσαι συγγενεῖς καὶ
258 φίλους τοὺς ἀπολωλότας ἐν τῇ μάχῃ, ὅπως τὸ ἐπ'
αὐτοῖς κορέσασα λυπηρὸν ἔπειθ' οὕτως ἐπ' εὐωχίας
τράπηται καὶ γάμους· καλὸν γὰρ εἶναι καὶ δίκαιον

---

[1] γενόμενον (γεννώμενον) codd.
[2] Reinach: ταῦτα codd.   [3] πτύουσα ROM.

[a] Deut. draws no such distinction, "when thou . . . seest
among the captives a beautiful woman"; tradition, cited
124

shall call the child that shall be born by the name
of the deceased and rear him as heir to the estate ;
for this will at once be profitable to the public
welfare, houses not dying out and property remaining with the relatives, and it will moreover bring
the women an alleviation of their misfortune to
live with the nearest kinsman of their former husbands.   But if the brother be unwilling to marry
her, let the woman come before the council of
elders and testify that, while she desired to remain
in this family and to have children by him, he would
not accept her, thereby doing outrage to the memory
of his deceased brother.   And when the council
ask him for what reason he is opposed to the marriage,
be his alleged reason slight or serious, the result
shall be the same : the wife of his brother shall
loose his sandals and spit in his face and declare
that he merits this treatment from her for having
outraged the memory of the departed.   Then let
him quit the council of elders to carry this reproach
throughout his life, while she shall be free to marry
any suitor whom she will.

"Should a man have taken prisoner whether a virgin Deut.
or a woman who has already been married [a] and wish xxi. 10.
to live with her, let him not be permitted to approach
her couch and consort with her until such time as,
with shorn hair and in mourning apparel, she shall
have made lamentation for the kinsmen and friends
whom she has lost in the battle, in order that she
may satisfy her grief for them before turning to the
festivities and ceremonies of marriage.   For it is
honourable and just that, in taking her to bear him

by Weill, permitted marriage with a captive previously
married (sc. to a Gentile).

παιδοποιὸν παραλαμβάνοντα θεραπεύειν αὐτῆς τὸ
βουλητόν, ἀλλὰ μὴ τὴν ἰδίαν ἡδονὴν διώκοντα
259 μόνον τοῦ κατ᾽ αὐτὴν ἀμελεῖν κεχαρισμένου. τριάκοντα δ᾽ ἡμερῶν τῷ πένθει διελθουσῶν, αὐτάρκεις
γὰρ ἐπὶ τοῖς δακρύοις αὗται τῶν φιλτάτων ταῖς
φρονίμοις, τότε χωρεῖν ἐπὶ τὸν γάμον. εἰ δ᾽
ἐμπλησθεὶς τῆς ἐπιθυμίας ὑπερηφανεύσειεν αὐτὴν
γαμετὴν ἔχειν, μηκέτ᾽ ἐξουσίαν ἐχέτω καταδουλοῦν
αὐτήν, ἀλλ᾽ ὅπῃ βούλεται χωρεῖν ἄπιτω τοῦτο
ἐλεύθερον ἔχουσα.

260 (24) ""Οσοι δ᾽ ἂν τῶν νέων περιφρονῶσι τοὺς
γονεῖς καὶ τὴν τιμὴν αὐτοῖς μὴ νέμωσιν ἢ δι᾽
αἰσχύνην ἢ δι᾽ ἀσυνεσίαν¹ ἐξυβρίζοντες εἰς αὐτούς,
πρῶτον μὲν λόγοις αὐτοὺς νουθετείτωσαν οἱ
πατέρες, αὐτάρκεις γὰρ ἐφ᾽ υἱάσιν οὗτοι δικασταί,
261 συνελθεῖν μὲν ἀλλήλοις οὐχ ἡδονῆς ἕνεκα λέγοντες οὐδὲ τῆς τῶν χρημάτων αὐξήσεως κοινῶν
τῶν ἑκατέροις ὑπαρχόντων γενομένων, ἀλλ᾽ ὅπως
παίδων τύχωσιν, οἳ γηροκομήσουσιν αὐτοὺς καὶ
ὧν ἂν δέωνται παρ᾽ αὐτῶν ἕξουσι, "γενόμενόν
τέ σε² μετὰ χαρᾶς καὶ τοῦ τῷ θεῷ χάριν εἰδέναι
τὴν μεγίστην ἀράμενοι διὰ σπουδῆς ἀνεθρέψαμεν
μηδενὸς φειδὼ ποιούμενοι τοῦ καὶ δόξαντος εἰς
σωτηρίαν τὴν σὴν καὶ παιδείαν τῶν ἀρίστων
262 εἶναι χρησίμου. νῦν δέ, συγγνώμην γὰρ χρὴ³
νέμειν ἐφ᾽ ἁμαρτήμασι νέων, ἀπόχρη σοι ὅσα τῆς
εἰς ἡμᾶς τιμῆς ὠλιγώρησας, καὶ μεταβαλοῦ πρὸς

¹ ex Lat. (propter insipientiam): δι᾽ ἀσύνεσιν R: διὰ
σύνεσιν rell.
² τέ σε Niese: τε RO: δέ γε rell.
³ RO: δεῖ rell.

ᵃ i.e. smarting under some disgrace; such seems to be
126

children, he should respect her wishes, and that he should not, intent solely on his own pleasure, neglect what may be agreeable to her. But when thirty days for the mourning are past—for that period should suffice sensible women for tears for their dearest ones —then let him proceed to the nuptials. Should he, however, sated with his passion, disdain to keep her as his spouse, he shall have no right thenceforth to make her his slave ; let her go whither she will and have that liberty granted to her.

(24) "With regard to those youths who scorn their parents and pay them not the honour that is due, but whether by reason of disgrace[a] or through witlessness, break out insolently against them, first of all let the parents orally admonish them,[b] for they have the authority of judges over their sons. Let them tell them that they came together in matrimony not for pleasure's sake, nor to increase their fortunes by uniting their several properties in one, but that they might have children who should tend their old age and who should receive from them everything that they needed. 'And when thou wast born,' they shall proceed, ' it was with joy and deepest thankfulness to God that we raised thee up and devoted our utmost care to thine upbringing, sparing nothing that appeared profitable for thy welfare and training in all that was best. But now—since indulgence must be accorded to the errors of youth—have done with all that scorn of respect towards us and return to

Rebellious
children.
Deut
XXI. 18.

the meaning. The Biblical phrase is " a stubborn and rebellious son." For the Rabbinical treatment of the subject see the Mishnah, *Sanhedrin* viii. 1-5 (tr. H. Danby).

[b] Bibl. " chasten him," probably including corporal punishment. The Mishnah speaks of his being " warned in the presence of three witnesses and beaten " (*ibid.* viii. 4).

τὸ σωφρονέστερον, λογισάμενος καὶ τὸν θεὸν ἐπὶ
τοῖς εἰς πατέρας τολμωμένοις χαλεπῶς ἔχειν,
ὅτι καὶ αὐτὸς πατὴρ τοῦ παντὸς ἀνθρώπων γένους
ἐστὶ καὶ συνατιμοῦσθαι δοκεῖ τοῖς τὴν αὐτὴν αὐτῷ
προσηγορίαν ἔχουσιν οὐχ ὧν προσῆκεν αὐτοῖς
παρὰ τῶν παίδων τυγχανόντων, καὶ νόμος κολαστὴς
γίνεται τῶν τοιούτων ἀπαραίτητος, οὗ σὺ μὴ
263 πειραθείης." κἂν μὲν τούτοις θεραπεύηται τὸ
τῶν νέων αὔθαδες, ἀπαλλαττέσθωσαν τῶν ἐπὶ
τοῖς ἡγνοημένοις ὀνειδῶν· οὕτως γὰρ ἂν ὅ τε νομοθέτης ἀγαθὸς εἴη καὶ οἱ πατέρες εὐτυχεῖς οὐκ
ἐπιδόντες οὔτε υἱὸν κολαζόμενον οὔτε θυγατέρα.
264 ᾧ δ᾽[1] ἂν οἱ λόγοι καὶ ἡ παρ᾽ αὐτῶν διδασκαλία
τοῦ σωφρονεῖν τὸ μηδὲν εἶναι φανῶσιν, ἐχθροὺς
δ᾽ ἀσπόνδους αὐτῷ ποιῇ τοὺς νόμους τοῖς συνεχέσι
κατὰ τῶν γονέων τολμήμασι, προαχθεὶς ὑπ᾽
αὐτῶν τούτων ἔξω τῆς πόλεως τοῦ πλήθους
ἑπομένου καταλευέσθω καὶ μείνας δι᾽ ὅλης τῆς
ἡμέρας εἰς θέαν τὴν ἁπάντων θαπτέσθω νυκτός.
265 οὕτως δὲ καὶ οἱ ὁπωσοῦν ὑπὸ τῶν νόμων ἀν-
αιρεθῆναι κατακριθέντες. θαπτέσθωσαν δὲ καὶ οἱ
πολέμιοι καὶ νεκρὸς μηδὲ εἷς ἄμοιρος γῆς κείσθω
περαιτέρω τοῦ δικαίου τιμωρίαν ἐκτίνων.
266 (25) " Δανείζειν δ᾽ Ἑβραίων ἐπὶ τόκοις ἐξέστω
μηδενὶ μήτε βρωτὸν μήτε ποτόν· οὐ γὰρ δίκαιον
προσοδεύεσθαι τοῦ ὁμοφύλου τὰς τύχας, ἀλλὰ

---

[1] ᾧ δ᾽ Bekker ex Lat.: οὐδ᾽ (εἰ δ᾽ etc.) codd.

[a] In Scripture and in tradition (see Weill) the law applies
only to sons.
[b] According to the Mishnah, after trial by a court of
twenty-three judges, including the three witnesses previously
mentioned (Sanhedrin, loc. cit.).

saner ways, reflecting that God also is distressed at
acts of effrontery to a father, since He is himself
Father of the whole human race and regards himself
as a partner in the indignity done to those who bear
the same title as himself, when they obtain not from
their children that which is their due. And then
there is the Law—that chastiser of all such, and in-
exorable : never mayest thou make trial of that ! '
If, then, by such means the young men's contumacy
is cured, let them be spared further reproach for their
sins of ignorance ; for thus will be shown the good-
ness of the lawgiver, while the parents will be happy
in seeing neither son nor daughter [a] delivered to
punishment. But the youth with whom these words
and the lesson in sobriety conveyed by them appear
to pass for naught and who makes for himself im-
placable enemies of the laws by continuous defiance
of his parents, let him [b] be led forth by their own hands
without the city, followed by the multitude, and
stoned to death ; and, after remaining for the whole
day exposed to the general view, let him be buried
at night.[c] Thus shall it be too with all who howsoever
are condemned by the laws to be put to death. Let
burial be given even to your enemies ; and let not a
corpse be left without its portion of earth,[d] paying
more than its just penalty.

Burial of
criminals
and
enemies.
Deut.
xxi. 22.

(25) " Let it not be permitted to lend upon usury
to any Hebrew either meat or drink ; for it is not just
to draw a revenue from the misfortunes of a fellow-

Usury.
Ib. xxiii. 19
(20), etc.

---

[c] Cf. § 202 note.

[d] Such e.g. was the practice of Tobit (Tob. i. 18, ii. 8).
But the phrase " portionless (of earth) " is reminiscent of
Sophocles, the favourite poet of this assistant of Josephus :
cf. Ajax 1326 ταφῆς ἄμοιρον, Ant. 1071 (the later play,
turning on the burial of enemies, is doubtless in mind).

βοηθήσαντας ταῖς χρείαις αὐτοῦ κέρδος εἶναι
νομίζειν τήν τ' ἐκείνων εὐχαριστίαν καὶ τὴν ἀμοιβὴν
τὴν παρὰ τοῦ θεοῦ γενησομένην ἐπὶ τῇ χρηστότητι.

267 (26) " Οἱ δὲ λαβόντες εἴτε ἀργύρια εἴτε τινὰ τῶν
καρπῶν, ὑγρὸν ἢ ξηρόν, κατὰ νοῦν αὐτοῖς τῶν
παρὰ τοῦ θεοῦ χωρησάντων κομίζοντες μεθ'
ἡδονῆς ἀποδιδότωσαν τοῖς δοῦσιν ὥσπερ ἀποθέμενοι εἰς τὰ αὑτῶν καὶ πάλιν εἰ δεηθεῖεν ἕξοντες.

268 ἂν δὲ ἀναισχυντῶσι περὶ τὴν ἀπόδοσιν, μὴ περὶ
τὴν οἰκίαν βαδίσαντας ἐνεχυριάζειν πρὶν ἢ δίκη
περὶ τούτου γένηται· τὸ δ' ἐνέχυρον αἰτεῖν ἔξω
καὶ τὸν ὀφείλοντα κομίζειν δι' αὐτοῦ μηδὲν
ἀντιλέγοντα τῷ μετὰ νόμου βοηθείας ἐπ' αὐτὸν

269 ἥκοντι. κἂν μὲν εὔπορος ᾖ ὁ ἠνεχυρασμένος,
κατεχέτω τοῦτο μέχρι τῆς ἀποδόσεως ὁ δεδανεικώς,
ἂν δὲ πένης, ἀποτιθέτω πρὶν ἡλίου δυσμῶν, καὶ
μάλιστ' ἂν ἱμάτιον ᾖ τὸ ἐνέχυρον, ὅπως εἰς ὕπνον
ἔχῃ τοῦτο, φύσει τοῦ θεοῦ τοῖς πενομένοις ἔλεον

270 νέμοντος. μύλην δὲ καὶ τὰ περὶ ταύτην σκεύη
μὴ ἐξεῖναι λαμβάνειν ἐνέχυρον, ὅπως μὴ στερῶνται
καὶ τῶν πρὸς τὰ σιτία ὀργάνων μηδ' ὑπ' ἐνδείας
πάθωσί τι τῶν χειρόνων.

271 (27) " Ἐπ' ἀνθρώπου μὲν κλοπῇ θάνατος ἔστω
ζημία, ὁ δὲ χρυσὸν ἢ ἄργυρον ὑφελόμενος τὸ
διπλοῦν ἀποτινέτω. κτείνας δ' ἐπὶ τοῖς κατ'

ᵃ Exodus, Heb. text, (generally) " a man " : Deut. (more

130

countryman. Rather, in succouring his distress, ye should reckon as gain the gratitude of such persons and the recompense which God has in store for an act of generosity.

(26) "Those who have borrowed whether silver or produce of any kind, liquid or solid, if their affairs through God's grace proceed to their liking, shall bring back and with pleasure restore these loans to the lenders, as though they were laying them up with their own possessions and would have them again at need. But if they are shameless concerning restitution, one must not prowl about the house to seize a pledge before judgement has been given on the matter ; the pledge should be asked for at the door, and the debtor should bring it of himself, in no wise gainsaying his visitor who comes with the law to support him. If he from whom the pledge has been taken be well-to-do, the lender should retain possession of it until restitution be made ; but if he be poor, the lender should return it before sun-down, above all if the pledge consist of a cloak, that he may have it for his sleep, God by His nature according pity to the poor. But a mill and its accompanying utensils may not be taken in pledge, that folk be not deprived of the very means of preparing their food nor be reduced by want to the worst sufferings.

(27) "For the stealing of a person*a* the penalty shall be death ; the purloiner of gold or silver shall pay double the sum.*b* He that killeth another while en-

Loans and pledges.

Deut. xxiv. 10 f.

Ib. 12 f. (Ex. xxii. 26).

Ib. 6.

Theft. Ib. 7 : Ex. xxi. 16.

precisely) "any of his brethren of the children of Israel." The limitation of the death-penalty to the case of a free-born Israelite is emphasized in tradition (Weill).

b In Ex. xxii. 4 the "double" penalty applies to stolen *animals* found alive in the thief's hands : money is not mentioned

131

οἶκον κλεπτομένοις τις ἀθῷος ἔστω κἂν ᾖ[1] πρὸς
272 διορύγματι τειχίου. βόσκημα δὲ ὁ κλέψας τε-
τραπλῆν τὴν ζημίαν ἀποτινέτω πλὴν βοός, πεν-
ταπλῆν δ᾽ ὑπὲρ τούτου καταβαλλέτω. ὁ δὲ τὸ
ἐπιτίμιον ἄπορος διαλύσασθαι δοῦλος ἔστω τοῖς
καταδεδικασμένοις.[2]

273 (28) "Πραθεὶς δὲ ὁμοφύλῳ τις ἓξ ἔτη δουλευέτω,
τῷ δ᾽ ἑβδόμῳ ἐλεύθερος ἀφείσθω· ἐὰν δὲ τέκνων
αὐτῷ γενομένων ἐκ δούλης παρὰ τῷ πριαμένῳ
διὰ τὴν εὔνοιαν καὶ τὴν πρὸς τὰ οἰκεῖα φιλο-
στοργίαν βούληται δουλεύειν, ἐνιαυτοῦ ἐνστάντος
τοῦ ἰοβήλου, πεντηκοστὸς δὲ ἐνιαυτός ἐστιν,
ἐλευθερούσθω καὶ τὰ τέκνα καὶ τὴν γυναῖκα ἐλευ-
θέραν ἐπαγόμενος.

274 (29) "'Ἐὰν δέ τις ἢ χρυσίον ἢ ἀργύριον εὕρῃ
καθ᾽ ὁδόν, ἐπιζητήσας τὸν ἀπολωλεκότα καὶ κη-
ρύξας τὸν τόπον ἐν ᾧ εὗρεν ἀποδότω, τὴν ἐκ τῆς
ἑτέρου ζημίας ὠφέλειαν οὐκ ἀγαθὴν ὑπολαμβάνων.
ὁμοίως καὶ περὶ βοσκημάτων οἷς ἂν ἐντύχῃ τις
κατ᾽ ἐρημίαν πλανωμένοις· μὴ εὑρεθέντος [δὲ][3] τοῦ
κυρίου παραχρῆμα παρ᾽ αὑτῷ φυλαττέτω μαρτυράμενος τὸν θεὸν μὴ νοσφίζεσθαι ἀλλότρια.

---

[1] Bernard: εἱ codd.   [2] καταδικασαμένοις MPLE.
[3] ins. E: om. rell.

---

[a] *i.e.* had not got beyond the stage of digging through it.
Josephus omits the proviso added in Exodus, " If the sun be
risen upon him, there shall be bloodguiltiness," in other
words, as interpreted by Philo, εἰ δ᾽ ἥλιος ἀνάσχοι μηκέθ᾽
ὁμοίως αὐτοχειρίᾳ κτεινέσθω, πρὸς δὲ τοὺς ἄρχοντας καὶ δικαστὰς
ἀγέσθω (ii. 337 M., quoted by Weill, who adds another
fanciful interpretation).

[b] *i.e.* " an ox or a sheep " (Ex.): Josephus again omits
the Scriptural proviso " and kill it or sell it."

[c] In Ex., as the text stands, this refers only to the house-

gaged in burglary shall be innocent, even though the Ex. xxii. 2.
thief were yet but breaking through his wall.[a] He
that stealeth a head of cattle [b] shall pay fourfold as *Ib.* 1.
penalty, save in the case of an ox, for which he shall
be fined fivefold. He that hath not the means to de- *Ib.* 3.
fray the imposed amount shall become the slave of
those who have had him condemned.[c]

(28) " A Hebrew sold to another Hebrew shall serve Slavery and
him for six years : in the seventh let him go free.[d] emancipa-
tion.
But if, having had children by a slave woman at the *Ib.* xxi. 2 :
house of the master who bought him, he, out of love Deut. xv. 12.
and affection for his own,[e] desires to continue to serve
him, then on the coming of the year of jubilee—
which returns every fifty years—let him be liberated,
taking his children and wife, also free, along with
him.[f]

(29) " If anyone find gold or silver on the road, after Restitution
diligent search for the loser and public proclamation of lost
property.
of the place where he found it,[g] let him duly restore *Ib.* xxii. 1.
it, reckoning it dishonest to profit by another's loss.
Similarly in the case of beasts which one meets stray-
ing in a desert place ; but if the owner be not found
forthwith, let him keep them at his home, calling
God to witness that he has not appropriated the goods
of another.

breaker, but the verses have perhaps been displaced (Driver) :
the law as applied to housebreakers is found in *A.* xvi.
§ 3, of theft in general in Philo and Jewish *Halachah* (Weill).
    [d] And his wife, if he has one (Ex. xxi. 3).
    [e] The neut. (" his own " or " his home surroundings ")
includes his master, Ex. xxi. 5.
    [f] In Scripture the master bores the ear of the willing
servant, and he serves him " for ever " : the jubilee is not
mentioned here.
    [g] Detail not in Scripture, but attested by tradition (Weill).

275 (30) "Μὴ ἐξεῖναι δὲ παριέναι κτηνῶν τινι κακο-
παθούντων ὑπὸ χειμῶνος πεπτωκότων ἐν πηλῷ,
συνδιασώζειν δὲ καὶ τὸν πόνον οἰκεῖον ἡγησάμενον
βοηθεῖν.

276 (31) "Μηνύειν δὲ καὶ τὰς ὁδοὺς τοῖς ἀγνοοῦσι,
καὶ μὴ γέλωτα θηρωμένους αὐτοῖς ἐμποδίζειν
πλάνῃ τὴν ἑτέρου χρείαν.

(32) "Ὁμοίως μηδὲ βλασφημείτω τις τὸν ἄοπ-
τον[1] καὶ τὸν ἐνεόν.

277 (33) "Ἐν μάχῃ τις, ὅπου μὴ σίδηρος, πληγεὶς
παραχρῆμα μὲν ἀποθανὼν ἐκδικείσθω ταὐτὸν
παθόντος τοῦ πεπληχότος. ἂν δὲ κομισθεὶς παρ'
ἑαυτὸν καὶ νοσήσας ἐπὶ πλείονας ἡμέρας ἔπειτ'
ἀποθάνῃ, ἀθῷος ἔστω ὁ πλήξας, σωθέντος δὲ καὶ
πολλὰ δαπανήσαντος εἰς τὴν νοσηλείαν ἀποτινέτω
πάνθ' ὅσα παρὰ τὸν χρόνον τῆς κατακλίσεως
278 ἀνάλωσε καὶ ὅσα τοῖς ἰατροῖς ἔδωκεν. ὁ γυναῖκα
λακτίσας ἔγκυον, ἂν μὲν ἐξαμβλώσῃ ἡ γυνὴ
ζημιούσθω χρήμασιν ὑπὸ τῶν δικαστῶν ὡς παρὰ
τὸ διαφθαρὲν ἐν τῇ γαστρὶ μειώσας τὸ πλῆθος,
διδόσθω δὲ καὶ τῷ ἀνδρὶ τῆς γυναικὸς παρ' αὐτοῦ

---

[1] SP: ἀπόντα rell.: ἄοπον Bernard.

---

[a] Scripture speaks of " making the *blind* to wander out
of the way," " putting a stumbling-block before the blind."
Josephus, by generalizing the statement, seems to put into
the mouth of Moses a refutation of the scandalous precept
attributed to him in the historian's day, " non monstrare
vias eadem nisi sacra colenti " (Juv. *Sat.* xiv. 103).
[b] Text and meaning doubtful. For the first adjective
most mss. have the erroneous reading " the absent ": the
mss. followed in the text have a word which in its one occurrence elsewhere means " unseen " (not " unseeing "); a

(30) " It is not permissible to pass by unheeding, when a man's beasts of burden, buffeted by tempest, have fallen in the mire ; one must help to rescue them and lend aid as though one laboured for oneself. Assistance to beasts in distress. Deut. xxii. 4.

(31) " One must point out the road to those who are ignorant of it, and not, for the pleasure of laughing oneself, impede another's business by misleading him.^a Directions on the road. *Ib.* xxvii. 18 (Lev. xix. 14).

(32) " Similarly, let none revile the sightless or the dumb.^b Respect for blind and dumb.

(33) " In a fight without use of the blade,^c if one be stricken and die on the spot, he shall be avenged by a like fate for him that struck him. But if he be carried home and lie sick for several days before he dies, he that struck him shall go unpunished ; howbeit, if he recover and hath spent much on his doctoring, the other shall pay all that he hath expended during the time of his confinement to his couch and all that he hath given to the physicians.^d He that kicketh a woman with child, if the woman miscarry, shall be fined by the judges for having, by the destruction of the fruit of her womb, diminished the population, and a further sum shall be presented by *Cf.* Lev. xix. 14. Quarrels and bodily injuries. Ex. xxi. 18, 12, 21. *Ib.* 22.

similar word (ἄσπον) has been conjectured meaning " speechless." The passage in Leviticus mentions " deaf " and " blind."

^c Paraphrase of the Biblical " if men contend and one smiteth the other with a stone or with his fist."

^d Josephus here amalgamates two separate laws in Exodus : (1) *vv.* 18 f. relating to quarrels ; (2) *vv.* 20 f. relating to the beating of a slave by his master. The last clause corresponds to the Heb. " he shall pay for *shibtō* and shall cause him to be thoroughly healed " ; here *shibtō* may mean either " his sitting down " (from *yāshab*, as Josephus takes it) or " his cessation " *i.e.* " unemployment " (from *shābath*, as LXX takes it, translating by ἀργίας).

χρήματα· θνησκούσης δ' ἐκ τῆς πληγῆς καὶ αὐτὸς
ἀποθνησκέτω ψυχὴν ἀντὶ ψυχῆς καταθέσθαι δι-
καιοῦντος τοῦ νόμου.

279 (34) " Φάρμακον μήτε θανάσιμον μήτε τῶν εἰς
ἄλλας βλάβας πεποιημένων Ἰσραηλιτῶν ἐχέτω
μηδὲ εἷς· ἐὰν δὲ κεκτημένος φωραθῇ τεθνάτω,
τοῦτο πάσχων ὃ διέθηκεν ἂν ἐκείνους καθ' ὧν
τὸ φάρμακον ἦν παρεσκευασμένον.

280 (35) " ['Ο]¹ πηρώσας πασχέτω [τὰ ὅμοια]² στερού-
μενος οὗπερ ἄλλον ἐστέρησε, πλὴν εἰ μήτι χρήματα
λαβεῖν ἐθελήσειεν ὁ πεπηρωμένος, αὐτὸν τὸν πε-
πονθότα κύριον τοῦ νόμου ποιοῦντος τιμήσασθαι
τὸ συμβεβηκὸς αὐτῷ πάθος καὶ συγχωροῦντος,
εἰ μὴ βούλεται γενέσθαι πικρότερος.

281 (36) " Βοῦν τοῖς κέρασι πλήττοντα ὁ δεσπότης
ἀποσφαττέτω· εἰ δ' ἐφ' ἅλωος κτείνειέ τινα
πλήξας, αὐτὸς μὲν καταλευσθεὶς ἀποθνησκέτω
μηδ' εἰς τροφὴν εὔχρηστος εἶναι κατηξιωμένος,
ἐὰν δὲ καὶ ὁ δεσπότης ἐλέγχηται προειδὼς αὐτοῦ
τὴν φύσιν καὶ μὴ φυλαξάμενος, καὶ αὐτὸς
ἀποθνησκέτω ὡς αἴτιος τῷ ὑπὸ τοῦ βοὸς ἀνηρημένῳ
282 γεγενημένος. ἐὰν δὲ δοῦλον ἢ θεράπαιναν ἀπο-

¹ om. RO. ² om. R.

ᵃ Misunderstanding of Scripture, which (though the text
is uncertain) appears to contemplate one fine only payable
to the husband ; and so tradition (Weill).

ᵇ The traditional interpretation of the Heb. " if any mischief happen " ; lxx and Philo interpret otherwise.

ᶜ The nearest Biblical parallel to this section is Ex. xxii. 18,
" thou shalt not suffer a sorceress (lxx φαρμακούς) to live."
On that passage Philo ii. 315 ff. M. dilates on poison.

ᵈ i.e. ask an exorbitant sum. Scripture names no alternative to the talio, " eye for eye " etc. Josephus here
approximates to the ruling of the Pharisees who, in contrast

him to the woman's husband.[a] If she die of the blow,[b] he also shall die, the law claiming as its due the sacrifice of life for life.

(34) "Poison, whether deadly or of those designed for other injurious ends, let no Israelite possess ; if one be caught with it in his keeping, let him die, undergoing the fate that he would have inflicted on the intended victims of the drug.[c]

Poison forbidden.

(35) "He that maimeth a man shall undergo the like, being deprived of that limb whereof he deprived the other, unless indeed the maimed man be willing to accept money ; for the law empowers the victim himself to assess the damage that has befallen him and makes this concession, unless he would show himself too severe.[d]

Lex talionis.
Ex. xxi. 24 :
Lev. xxiv. 19.

(36) "An ox that goreth with its horns shall be slaughtered by its owner.[e] If on the threshing-floor it killeth any man by goring him, it shall itself be stoned to death and rejected as unfit even for consumption ; but if the owner himself be convicted of having known of its nature beforehand and taken no precautions,[f] he also shall die,[g] as answerable for the death of the beast's victim. If a slave or a maid-

The vicious ox.
Ex. xxi. 28.

to the Sadducees, substituted damages ; these, however, were fixed not by the injured individual, but by the competent tribunal (*Baba Kamma* 83b, with Weill's note).

Ib. 32.

[e] According to Scripture, only if it has caused a death. An ox with known vicious propensities must be " kept in " but need not be slaughtered. However, as Weill remarks, the statement of Josephus finds support in a saying attributed to R. Eliezer, " The best precaution is a knife " ; similarly LXX for " keep in " substitutes ἀφανίσῃ, " make away with (him)."

[f] Bibl. " hath not kept him (in)."

[g] Josephus ignores *v.* 30, which admits of a money compensation in lieu of death. According to Philo (ii. 323 M.), the court decides ὅ τι χρὴ παθεῖν ἢ ἀποτῖσαι.

κτείνῃ βοῦς, αὐτὸς μὲν καταλιθούσθω, τριάκοντα δὲ
σίκλους ὁ κύριος τοῦ βοὸς ἀποτινέτω τῷ δεσπότῃ
τοῦ ἀνῃρημένου. βοῦς δὲ ἐὰν οὕτως πληγεὶς
ἀποθάνῃ, πωλείσθωσαν καὶ ὁ τεθνεὼς καὶ ὁ πλήξας
καὶ τὴν τιμὴν τὴν ἀμφοτέρων οἱ δεσπόται αὐτῶν
διανεμέσθωσαν.

283   (37) " Οἱ φρέαρ ἢ λάκκον ὀρύξαντες ἐπιμελὲς
ποιείσθωσαν ὥστε σανίδων ἐπιβολαῖς ἔχειν κεκλει-
σμένα, οὐχ ὅπως τινὲς εἴργοιντο ὑδρείας, ἀλλ'
284 ἵνα μηδεὶς κίνδυνος ὡς ἐμπεσουμένοις ᾖ. οὗ δ'
ἂν εἰς ὄρυγμα τοιοῦτον μὴ κλειστὸν ἐμπεσὸν
βόσκημά τινος διαφθαρῇ, τὴν τιμὴν αὐτοῦ τῷ
δεσπότῃ καταβαλλέτω. περιβαλλέσθω δὲ καὶ τοῖς
στέγεσιν ἅπερ ὡς ἀντὶ τείχους ὄντα οὐκ ἐάσει
τινὰς ἀποκυλισθέντας ἀπολέσθαι.

285   (38) " Παρακαταθήκην δὲ ὥσπερ ἱερόν τι καὶ
θεῖον χρῆμα ὁ παραλαβὼν φυλακῆς ἀξιούτω, καὶ
μηδεὶς ἀποστερῆσαι θρασυνθείη τὸν πεπιστευκότα
μήτ' ἀνὴρ μήτε γυνή, μηδ' εἰ χρυσὸν ἄπειρον
μέλλοι κερδαίνειν, καταφρονῶν τῷ μηδένα εἶναι
286 τὸν ἐξελέγξοντα. καθόλου μὲν γὰρ τὸ συνειδὸς
ἐπιστάμενον τὸ αὐτοῦ προσῆκεν ἕκαστον εὖ
πράττειν, καὶ μάρτυρι ἀρκούμενος αὐτῷ πάντα
ποιείτω ἃ παρ' ἄλλων ἔπαινον αὐτῷ παρέξει,
μάλιστα δὲ τὸν θεόν, ὃν οὐδεὶς πονηρὸς ὢν λανθάνει.
287 εἰ δὲ μηδὲν ἐπίβουλον δρῶν ὁ πιστευθεὶς ἀπολέσειεν,

---

[a] In Scripture apparently only the live ox is sold : the dead
beast is literally " divided " between them.   Josephus omits
the special provisions of v. 36.

[b] i.e. at night, the roof being the usual sleeping-place in
the east ; Deut., more generally, speaks of a " fall."   It
has been suggested that Josephus, in uniting two laws (concerning wells and battlements) which are separated in

servant be killed by an ox, it shall be stoned, and
the owner of the ox shall pay thirty shekels to the
victim's master. If it be an ox that is killed by such Ex. xxi. 35.
a stroke, let them be sold, both the dead beast
and its assailant, and let their owners divide the
price of the pair between them.[a]

(37) "They that dig a well or a pit are to take care Safeguards
for wells
to keep them closed in by laying planks above, not and roofs.
to preclude any from drawing water, but to avoid Ib. 33.
all risk of falling into them. Should any man have a
cavity of such sort not closed, and another man's
beast fall into it and perish, he shall pay the price of
it to its owner. Let roofs also be surrounded by Deut. xxii. 8.
something in the nature of a wall, to prevent any
from rolling off [b] and being killed.

(38) "Let the receiver of a deposit [c] esteem it Deposits.
worthy of custody as of some sacred and divine Ex. xxii. 7.
object,[d] and let none venture to defraud him that
entrusted it to him, neither man nor woman, no not
though he might make gain of untold gold, in the
assurance of having none to convict him. For by all
means,[e] from the mere knowledge that he has of
his own conscience, ought everyone to act aright—
let him be content with that for witness and do all
that will bring him praise from others—but chiefly
from his knowledge of God, whose eye no criminal
escapes. But if, without any act of treachery, the Ib. 8, 11.
depositary lose the deposit, let him come before the

Scripture, is following the lead of Philo, who does the same
(ii. 324 M.).

[c] Cf. Ap. ii. 208, 216.

[d] Philo (ii. 341 M.) uses the same phrase, λαβὼν ὡς ἱερὸν
χρῆμα παρακαταθήκην (and a little above ἱερώτατον παρακατα-
θήκη).

[e] Or " to be sure " (καθόλου = Lat. omnino).

ἀφικόμενος ἐπὶ τοὺς ἑπτὰ κριτὰς ὀμνύτω τὸν
θεόν, ὅτι μηδέν¹ παρὰ τὴν αὐτοῦ βούλησιν ἀπόλοιτο
καὶ κακίαν, οὐδὲ χρησαμένου τινὶ μέρει αὐτῆς,
καὶ οὕτως ἀνεπαιτίατος ἀπίτω. χρησάμενος δὲ
κἂν ἐλαχίστῳ μέρει τῶν πεπιστευμένων, ἄν²
ἀπολέσας τύχῃ τὰ λοιπά, πάντα ἃ ἔλαβεν ἀπο-
288 δοῦναι κατεγνώσθω. ὁμοίως δὲ τῷ περὶ παρα-
καταθηκῶν κἂν μισθόν τις ἀποστερήσῃ τῶν ἐπὶ
σώμασι τοῖς αὐτῶν ἐργαζομένων, μεμισήσθω·
ὅθεν³ οὐκ ἀποστερητέον ἀνδρὸς πένητος μισθόν,
εἰδότας ὡς ἀντὶ γῆς καὶ τῶν ἄλλων κτημάτων ὁ
θεὸς αὐτῷ τοῦτον εἴη παρεσχηκώς· ἀλλὰ μηδὲ
ἀναβάλλεσθαι τὴν ἀπόδοσιν, ἀλλ' αὐθημερὸν ἐκ-
τίνειν ὡς οὐ βουλομένου τοῦ θεοῦ τῆς ἐξ ὧν πε-
πόνηκε χρήσεως ὑστερεῖν τὸν εἰργασμένον.⁴

289 (39) "Παῖδας ὑπὲρ ἀδικίας πατέρων μὴ κολάζειν,
ἀλλὰ διὰ τὴν ἐκείνων αὐτῶν ἀρετὴν οἴκτου μᾶλλον
ἀξιοῦν, ὅτι μοχθηρῶν ἐγένοντο πατέρων, ἢ μίσους
φύντας⁵ ἐκ φαύλων. οὐ μὴν οὐδὲ πατράσιν υἱῶν
ἁμαρτίαν λογιστέον, τῶν νέων πολλὰ παρὰ τὴν
ἡμετέραν διδασκαλίαν αὐτοῖς ἐπιτρεπόντων ὑπερ-
ηφανίᾳ τοῦ διδάσκεσθαι.

290 (40) "Γάλλους ἐκτρέπεσθαι καὶ σύνοδον φεύγειν
τὴν μετ' αὐτῶν ἀφελομένων αὐτοὺς τὸ ἄρρεν καὶ
τὸν τῆς παιδοποιίας καρπόν, ὃν ἀνθρώποις ἐπ'
αὐξήσει τοῦ γένους ἡμῖν ὁ θεὸς παρέσχεν, ἐλαύνειν

¹ MLE: μηδὲ rell.   ² RO: om. rell.
³ μεμνήσθω (M) ὅτι ed. pr.   ⁴ ἐργασάμενον RO.
⁵ ed. pr.: φύντες codd.

ᵃ Cf. § 214. Tradition (cited by Weill) mentions a tribunal
of three (or five) judges in such cases, not of seven.
140

seven judges [a] and swear by God that nothing had
been lost through his own intention or malice, and
that he had not appropriated any part of it to his
own use, and so let him depart exempt from blame.
But if he has used but the smallest portion of the
trust and happen to have lost the remainder,[b] he shall
be sentenced to restore all that he received. And
as with deposits, so if anyone withhold the wages
of those who labour with their bodies, let him be
execrated; since [c] one must not deprive a poor man
of his wages, knowing that this, instead of land and
other possessions, is the portion which God has
granted him. Nay, one must not even defer payment, but discharge it the selfsame day, for God
would not have the labourer kept waiting for the
enjoyment of the fruits of his toil.

Wages to be promptly paid. Deut. xxiv. 14.

(39) " Punish not children for the wrongdoing of
their fathers, but by reason of their own virtue
deem them deserving rather of pity for having been
born of depraved parents than of hatred for their
base lineage.[d] Nor yet must one impute to the
fathers the sin of the sons, for the young permit
themselves much that is contrary to our instruction
in their disdain of discipline.

Individual responsibility. Ib. xxiv. 16.

(40) " Shun eunuchs and flee all dealings with those
who have deprived themselves of their virility and of
those fruits of generation, which God has given to
men for the increase of our race; expel them even as

Banning of eunuchs, etc. Ib. xxiii. 1.

[b] I think τὰ λοιπά must be taken as dependent on ἀπολέσας,
not (as by Hudson and Weill) with πάντα. Josephus sum-
marizes without strictly following Scripture.
[c] Greek " whence " (" wherefore "). For " let him . . .
since " one text reads " let him remember that."
[d] Reinach, I think needlessly, suspects the text.

δὲ οὕτως ὡς ἐπὶ τέκνων σφαγῇ καὶ πρὸς τούτῳ[1]
291 ἀπολλύντας τὸ ἐκείνων αἴτιον· δῆλον γάρ, ὡς
τῆς ψυχῆς αὐτοῖς τεθηλυσμένης μετεκοσμήσαντο
πρὸς τοῦτο καὶ τὸ σῶμα. ὁμοίως δὲ καὶ πᾶν τὸ
νομιζόμενον τέρας τοῖς ὁρῶσι· μὴ ἐξεῖναι δὲ
ποιεῖν ἐκτομίας μήτε ἀνθρώπους μήτε τῶν ἄλλων
ζῴων.

292 (41) "Αὕτη μὲν οὖν ὑμῖν εἰρηνικὴ τῶν νόμων
κατὰ τὴν πολιτείαν διάταξις ἔστω· καὶ ὁ θεὸς
εὐμενὴς ἀστασίαστον αὐτῆς τὸν κόσμον παρέξεται,
γένοιτο δὲ χρόνος μηδὲ εἷς, ὃς καινίσει τι τούτων
293 καὶ πρὸς τὸ ἐναντίον μεταβαλεῖ. ἐπεὶ δὲ ἀνάγκη
τὸ ἀνθρώπειον καὶ εἰς ἀβουλήτους ἢ κατὰ προαίρεσιν ταραχὰς καὶ κινδύνους ἐμπεσεῖν, φέρε καὶ
περὶ τούτων βραχέα προσδιατάξωμεν, ὡς ἂν προ-
ειδότες ἃ χρὴ ποιεῖν ἐν τῇ χρείᾳ τῶν σωτηρίων
εὐπορῆτε καὶ μὴ τότε ἃ δεῖ ποιεῖν ἐπιζητοῦντες
ἀπαρασκεύαστοι τοῖς καιροῖς περιπέσητε.[2]

294 "Γῆν ὑμῖν ἣν ὁ θεὸς ἔδωκε πόνων καταφρονοῦσι
καὶ ψυχὰς πρὸς ἀρετὴν ἠσκημένοις ἀπόλεμον μὲν
νέμεσθαι παράσχοι τε[3] κεκτημένοις αὐτήν, μήτε
ἀλλοτρίων εἰς αὐτὴν ἐπὶ κακώσει στρατευσάντων
295 μήτε στάσεως ἐμφυλίου κατασχούσης ὑμᾶς, ὑφ'
ἧς τἀναντία πατράσι τοῖς ἑαυτῶν πράττοντες
ἀπολεῖτε τὰ ἐκείνοις νομισθέντα, χρώμενοί τε
νόμοις οὓς ἀγαθοὺς δοκιμάσας ὁ θεὸς παραδίδωσι
διατελοίητε· ἔργον δ' ὅ τι ἂν πολεμικὸν ἢ νῦν

---

[1] RO : πρὸ τούτων rell. : per hoc Lat.
[2] Bekker : παραπέσητε codd.   [3] τοῖς Dindorf.

---

[a] Another text reads " before them " *i.e.* " before the
infants' birth."
[b] *Cf.* iii. 287 for a similar transition from civil to military

infanticides who withal *a* have destroyed the means
of procreation. For plainly it is by reason of the
effeminacy of their soul that they have changed the
sex of their body also. And so with all that would be
deemed a monstrosity by the beholders. Ye shall
castrate neither man nor beast.

Cf. Lev.
xxii. 24 LXX.

(41) "Such then shall be for you in peace-time *b* the
legal constitution of your state ; and God in His
mercy will keep its shapely order unmarred by strife.
May there never come a time for amending aught
therein and establishing the contrary in its place !
Yet since humanity *c* must needs be plunged into
troubles and perils, be they involuntary or premedi-
tated, come let us append on these matters also some
brief ordinances, that, forewarned how ye must act,
ye may, in your need, be furnished with the means of
salvation, and not then go searching what ye ought
to do and plunge unprepared into those times of
crisis.

Provisions
for war and
prayers for
peace.

"This land which God hath given to you that are
contemptuous of fatigue and whose souls are schooled
to valour—may He grant you to occupy it in peace,
once ye have conquered it : may neither foreigner
invade it for its injury, nor civil strife o'ermaster you,
whereby ye shall be led to actions contrary to those
of your own fathers and destroy the institutions
which they established : and may ye continue to
observe laws which God has approved as good and
now delivers to you ! Yet whatever warfare it may
be yours to wage, be it now in your own time or here-

matters ; and as there, so here, in this " brief appendix "
(§ 293), the " Thucydidean " assistant appears to lend his
aid.

c τὸ ἀνθρώπειον, a Thucydidean phrase, characteristic of
A. xvii.-xix.

ὑφ᾽ ὑμῶν ἢ ὕστερον ἐπὶ παίδων ὑμετέρων γένηται
296 τοῦθ᾽ ὑπερόριον πραχθείη. μέλλοντας δὲ πολεμεῖν
πρεσβείαν καὶ κήρυκας πέμπειν παρὰ τοὺς ἑκουσίως
πολεμίους· πρὸ γὰρ τῶν ὅπλων καλὸν εἶναι χρῆσθαι
λόγοις πρὸς αὐτούς, δηλοῦντας ὅτι καὶ στρατιὰν
πολλὴν ἔχοντες καὶ ἵππους καὶ ὅπλα καὶ πρὸ
τούτων εὐμενῆ τὸν θεὸν καὶ σύμμαχον, ὅμως
ἀξιοῦτε μὴ ἀναγκάζεσθαι πολεμεῖν αὐτοῖς μηδὲ τὰ
ἐκείνων ἀφαιρουμένους ἀβούλητον αὐτοῖς κέρδος
297 προσλαμβάνειν. καὶ πειθομένων μὲν καλῶς ὑμᾶς
ἔχειν τὴν εἰρήνην φυλάττειν, εἰ δὲ φρονοῦντες
ἐφ᾽ ἑαυτοῖς ὡς ἰσχύι διαφέρουσιν ἀδικεῖν ἐθέλοιεν,
στρατὸν ἐπ᾽ αὐτοὺς ἀγάγετε,[1] στρατηγῷ μὲν
αὐτοκράτορι χρώμενοι τῷ θεῷ, ὑποστράτηγον
δὲ χειροτονήσαντες ἕνα τὸν ἀρετῇ προύχοντα·
πολυαρχία γὰρ πρὸς τῷ τοῖς ὀξέως τι πράττειν
ἀνάγκην ἔχουσιν ἐμπόδιον εἶναι καὶ βλάπτειν
298 πέφυκε τοὺς χρωμένους. στρατὸν δ᾽ ἄγειν καθαρὸν
ἐκ πάντων τῶν ῥώμῃ σωμάτων καὶ ψυχῆς εὐ-
τολμίᾳ διαφερόντων τὸ[2] δειλὸν ἀποκρίναντας,[a]μὴ
τοὺς πολεμίους παρὰ τὸ ἔργον τραπὲν εἰς φυγὴν
ὠφελήσῃ. τούς τε νεωστὶ δειμαμένους οἰκίας,
οἷς οὔπω χρόνος ἀπολαύσεως αὐτῶν ἐνιαύσιος,
καὶ φυτεύσαντας οὔπω δὲ καρπῶν μετεσχηκότας,
ἐᾶν κατὰ χώραν, καὶ τοὺς μνηστευσαμένους δὲ
καὶ νεωστὶ γεγαμηκότας, μὴ πόθῳ τούτων φει-
δόμενοι τοῦ ζῆν καὶ τηροῦντες αὑτοὺς εἰς τὴν τούτων ἀπόλαυσιν ἐθελοκακήσωσι [περὶ τὰς γυναῖκας].[4]

[1] ἀγάγοιτε RO.   [2] E: τὸ δὲ codd.
[3] M: ἀποκρίνοντας rell.   [4] om. Lat.

---

[a] στρατηγὸς αὐτοκράτωρ, after Thuc. vi. 72 τούς τε στρατη-
γοὺς καὶ ὀλίγους καὶ αὐτοκράτορας χρῆναι ἑλέσθαι.

after in the days of your children, may this action take place beyond your frontiers.

"When ye are on the verge of war, send an embassy with heralds to your aggressive enemy ; for, before taking arms, it is meet to parley with them and to represent that, though possessed of a large army, horses and munitions, and above all blest with God's gracious favour and support, nevertheless ye desire not to be constrained to make war on them and, in robbing them of what is theirs, to annex to yourselves unwanted profit. If, then, they yield to those representations, it behoves you to keep the peace ; but if, confident of their superior strength, they wish to do you wrong, lead out an army against them, taking God for your supreme commander[a] and electing as His lieutenant the one man who is pre-eminent for valour ; for divided control, besides being a hindrance to those for whom prompt action is imperative, is withal apt to injure those who practise it.[b] The army under him must be immaculate, made up of all who excel in vigour of body and hardihood of soul, after rejection of the cowardly, for fear lest they turn to flight during the action to the advantage of the enemy. Those too who have lately built themselves houses and have not yet had a year to enjoy them, with those who have planted and have not yet partaken of the fruits, must be left on the land, as also the betrothed and recently married, lest regret for these things should make them chary of their lives and, reserving themselves to enjoy them, they deliberately shirk danger.

Preliminaries before battle. Deut. xx. 10.

Ib. 1, 4.

Ib. 5-8 (xxiv. 5).

[b] After Thuc. *ibid.* μέγα δὲ βλάψαι καὶ τὸ πλῆθος τῶν στρατηγῶν καὶ τὴν πολυαρχίαν.

299 (42) "Στρατοπεδευσάμενοι δὲ προνοεῖσθε, μή τι
τῶν δυσχερεστέρων ἐργάσησθε. πολιορκοῦντας δὲ
καὶ ξύλων ἀπορουμένους εἰς ποίησιν μηχανημάτων
μὴ κείρειν τὴν γῆν ἥμερα δένδρα κόπτοντας ἀλλὰ
φείδεσθαι, λογιζομένους ἐπ' ὠφελείᾳ ταῦτα τῶν
ἀνθρώπων γεγονέναι, καὶ φωνῆς ἂν εὐπορήσαντα
δικαιολογήσασθαι πρὸς ὑμᾶς, ὡς οὐδὲν αἴτια τοῦ
πολέμου γεγονότα πάσχοι κακῶς παρὰ δίκην, εἰ
δύναμις αὐτοῖς ἦν καὶ μετοικήσαντα ἂν καὶ πρὸς
300 ἄλλην μεταβάντα γῆν. κρατήσαντες δὲ τῇ μάχῃ
τοὺς ἀντιταξαμένους κτείνατε, τοὺς δ' ἄλλους
εἰς τὸ τελεῖν ὑμῖν φόρους σώζετε πλὴν τοῦ Χαναναίων ἔθνους· τούτους γὰρ πανοικὶ χρῆναι
ἀφανίσαι.
301 (43) "Φυλάσσειν δὲ μάλιστα ἐν ταῖς μάχαις, ὡς
μήτε γυναῖκα ἀνδρικῇ σκευῇ χρῆσθαι μήτ' ἄνδρα
στολῇ γυναικείᾳ."

302 (44) Πολιτείαν μὲν οὖν τοιάνδε Μωυσῆς κατέλιπε,
νόμους δ' ἔτι πρότερον τεσσαρακοστῷ ἔτει γεγραμμένους παραδίδωσι, περὶ ὧν ἐν ἑτέρᾳ γραφῇ
λέξομεν. ταῖς δ' ἑξῆς ἡμέραις, συνεχὲς γὰρ
ἐξεκκλησίασεν, εὐλογίας αὐτοῖς δίδωσι καὶ κατάρας
ἐπὶ τοὺς μὴ κατὰ τοὺς νόμους ζησομένους ἀλλὰ
303 παραβησομένους τὰ ἐν αὐτοῖς διωρισμένα. ἔπειτα
ποίησιν ἑξάμετρον αὐτοῖς ἀνέγνω, ἣν καὶ κατα-

---

[a] The writer, while following Scripture, doubtless also has
in mind the practice of the Romans in the recent war:
B.J. v. 523, vi. 6 " sites formerly beautified with trees and
parks now reduced to an utter desert and stripped bare of
timber."

[b] Words not in Scripture, where the prohibition is doubtless

(42) "Once encamped, take heed to refrain from any of the more outrageous actions. When ye are engaged in a siege and lack timber for the construction of your engines, do not shear the ground by cutting down the cultivated trees[a]: nay, spare them, reflecting that they were created for the service of men and that, were they gifted with a voice, they would plead with you and say that they were in no way answerable for the war, that they were being maltreated unjustly and that, had they the power, they would have migrated and moved to another country. Having won the battle, slay those that have resisted you, but leave the rest alive to pay you tribute, save the race of the Canaanites : for them ye must exterminate wholesale.

Abstention from barbarities. Deut. xx. 19.

Ib. 13.

(43) "Beware, above all in battle,[b] that no woman assume the accoutrements of a man nor a man the apparel of a woman."

Costume of the sexes. *Ib.* xxii. 5.

(44) Such then is the constitution that Moses left ; he further delivered over those laws which he had written forty years before and of which we shall speak in another work.[c] On the following days—for assembly was held continuously—he gave them blessings, with curses upon such as should not live in accordance with the laws but should transgress the ordinances that were therein. Then he recited to them a poem in hexameter verse, which he has more-

Moses delivers the laws and other writings to the people. *Ib.* xxviii. (xxvii.).

Ib. xxxii. 1-43.

" directed against the simulated changes of sex which occurred in Canaanite and Syrian heathenism " (Driver). But Weill finds support for them in the opinion of R. Eliezer ben Jacob (1st cent. A.D.), who based upon this verse of Deut. the rule that a woman might not bear arms.

    [c] The projected " Customs and Causes " often mentioned ; see iii. 223.

λέλοιπεν ἐν βίβλῳ ἐν τῷ ἱερῷ πρόρρησιν περι-
έχουσαν τῶν ἐσομένων, καθ᾽ ἣν [καὶ] γέγονε [τὰ]
πάντα καὶ γίνεται, μηδὲν ἐκείνου διημαρτηκότος
304 τῆς ἀληθείας. ταῦτ᾽ οὖν τὰ βιβλία παραδίδωσι
τοῖς ἱερεῦσι καὶ τὴν κιβωτόν, εἰς ἣν καὶ τοὺς
δέκα λόγους γεγραμμένους ἐν δυσὶ πλαξὶ κατέθετο,
καὶ τὴν σκηνήν· τῷ τε λαῷ παρῄνεσε κρατήσαντι
τῆς γῆς καὶ ἱδρυθέντι μὴ λήθην λαβεῖν τῆς Ἀμαληκιτῶν ὕβρεως, ἀλλὰ στρατεύσαντας ἐπ᾽ αὐτοὺς
τιμωρίαν ἀπολαβεῖν ὧν ἐπὶ τῆς ἐρήμου τυγχάνον-
305 τας[1] ἐποίησαν κακῶς, ἐξελόντας δὲ τὴν Χαναναίων
γῆν καὶ πᾶσαν διαφθείραντας τὴν ἐν αὐτῇ πληθὺν
καθὰ πρέπει, τὸν βωμόν τε ἀναστῆσαι πρὸς ἥλιον
ἀνίσχοντα τετραμμένον οὐ πόρρω τῆς Σικίμων[2]
πόλεως [ἐμπεριάγειν][3] μεταξὺ δυοῖν ὁροῖν, Γαρι-
ζαίου[4] μὲν τοῦ ἐκ δεξιῶν κειμένου, τοῦ δ᾽ ἐκ
λαιῶν Βουλῆ[5] προσαγορευομένου, μερισθεῖσαν δὲ
τὴν στρατιὰν καθ᾽ ἓξ φυλὰς ἐπὶ τοῖν δυοῖν ὁροῖν

[1] ed. pr., Lat.: τυγχάνοντες codd.
[2] Σικιμίων RO.   [3] om. ed. pr., Lat.
[4] Γριζέου M: Γριζαίου Niese.
[5] Γιβάλου ed. pr.: Hebal Lat.

---

[a] Not, as in one ms. (followed by Hudson and Weill),
" in the holy book." Similar references to " writings
deposited in the temple " occur in *A*. iii. 38, v. 61 ; the
fact that these passages refer to lyrical portions of Scripture,
taken with the statement that this song of Moses, like that
other song at the Red Sea (*A*. ii. 346), was composed " in
hexameter verse," suggests that Josephus was acquainted
with a collection of chants, drawn from the Bible or from
elsewhere, and set to music for the use of the temple choir.
I may refer to my *Josephus the Man and the Historian*
(New York, 1929), pp. 90 f.

[b] *A*. iii. 39 ff. (esp. 60), Ex. xvii. 8-16. The passage in

over bequeathed in a book preserved in the temple,[a] containing a prediction of future events, in accordance with which all has come and is coming to pass, the seer having in no whit strayed from the truth. All these books he consigned to the priests, together with the ark, in which he had deposited the ten commandments written on two tables, and the tabernacle. He also exhorted the people, once they had conquered the country and were established therein, not to forget that insolence of the Amalekites, but to take the field against them and exact vengeance for the wrong which they had done them when they were in the desert.[b] Furthermore, when they had utterly vanquished the land of Canaan and destroyed its whole population, as was meet, they were to erect the altar pointing towards the rising sun,[c] not far from the city of Sikima[d] between two mountains, the Garizaean[e] on the right and that called " Counsel "[f] on the left ; and the army, divided into two portions of six tribes each, was to take up its station on these

Deut. xxxi.
9, 25.

Ib. xxv. 17.

Blessings
and curses
inscribed on
the altar.
Ib. xxvii. 4,
12 ff.

Deut. xxv., "Remember what Amalek did," was one of the earliest of the " lessons " from the Law to be read in Jewish worship.

[c] Direction not named in Scripture : the phrase " towards the sun-rising " seems to be taken from Herodotus (B.J. vii. 281 note).

[d] Shechem : some mss. read " the Sikimites." The word ἐμπεριάγειν (" to bring round ") which follows in the Greek mss., looks like a gloss on ἀναστῆσαι (" to erect "), or rather a correction of the assistant (B.J. v. 367, the only other instance known to the Lexicons), to indicate that the altar, inscribed by Moses (§ 308), was to be taken with them, and not, as in Scripture, to be erected ex tempore on the spot.

[e] Heb. Gerizim, LXX Γαριζείν.

[f] Heb. Ebal, LXX Γαιβάλ: Βουλή (" Counsel ") of Josephus is an instance of the frequent Hellenization of a Hebrew name ; the Heb. is perhaps connected with the god Bel.

ἀναστῆναι καὶ σὺν αὐτοῖς Λευίτας τε καὶ[1] ἱερέας.
306 καὶ πρώτους μὲν τοὺς ἐπὶ τῷ Γαριζεὶν[2] γενομένους
εὔχεσθαι τὰ κάλλιστα τοῖς περὶ τὴν θρησκείαν τοῦ
θεοῦ καὶ τὴν τῶν νόμων φυλακὴν σπουδάσασιν ὧν
τε Μωυσῆς εἶπε μὴ παρακροασαμένοις,[3] εὐφημεῖν
δὲ τὰς ἑτέρας, καὶ τούτων πάλιν εὐχομένων
307 τὰς προηγμένας ἐπαινεῖν. ἔπειτα κατὰ ταὐτὰ τοῖς
παραβησομένοις κατάρας τίθεσθαι ὑποφωνούσας
ἀλλήλαις ἐπὶ τῇ κυρώσει τῶν λεγομένων. ἀν-
έγραψε δὲ τὰς εὐλογίας καὶ τὰς κατάρας αὐτός,
ὡς μηδέποτε ἐκλιπεῖν τὴν μάθησιν αὐτῶν ὑπὸ
308 τοῦ χρόνου, ἃς δὴ καὶ τῷ βωμῷ τελευτῶν ἐν-
έγραψε κατὰ πλευρὰν ἑκατέραν, ᾗ καὶ στάντα φησὶ
τὸν λαὸν θῦσαί τε καὶ ὁλοκαυτῶσαι καὶ μετ' ἐκείνην
τὴν ἡμέραν οὐκ[4] ἐπενεγκεῖν ἱερεῖον ἕτερον, οὐ γὰρ
εἶναι νόμιμον. ταῦτ' οὖν Μωυσῆς διέταξε καὶ τὸ
Ἑβραίων ἔθνος ἀκόλουθα τούτοις ποιοῦν διατελεῖ.
309 (45) Τῇ δ' ὑστεραίᾳ τὸν λαὸν σὺν γυναιξὶν ἅμα
καὶ τέκνοις εἰς ἐκκλησίαν συναγαγών, ὡς παρεῖναι
καὶ τὰ ἀνδράποδα, ὅρκου τῶν νόμων αὐτοὺς
φυλακὴν ποιήσασθαι καὶ τῆς τοῦ θεοῦ διανοίας
ἀκριβεῖς λογιστὰς γινομένους ᾗ μηδὲν[5] αὐτοὺς
μήτε συγγενείᾳ χαριζομένους μήτε εἴκοντας φόβῳ
μήτε ἄλλην καθάπαξ αἰτίαν κυριωτέραν τῆς τῶν
νόμων φυλακῆς ὑπολαμβάνοντας παραβῆναι τού-

[1] RO: + τοὺς rell.   [2] Γρίζειν ROM.
[3] Holwerda: παρακρουσαμένοις (παρακουσ.) codd.
[4] + ἔτ' SPLE.
[5] ᾗ μηδὲν conj.: εἰ μηδὲν εἰς etc. codd.

[a] " And all the people shall say, Amen," Deut. xxvii. 26.
[b] In Scripture the people (not Moses) are to inscribe on the future altar, not the blessings and curses, but " all the words of this law " (xxvii. 3, 8).

two mountains, and with them Levites and priests.
And first those on Mount Garizin were to invoke the
best of blessings upon such as were zealous for the
worship of God and for the observance of the laws
and were not disobedient to the words of Moses, and
the other tribes were to express pious approval[a]; and
when these offered prayers in their turn, the first
party should signify their assent. Thereafter, in the
same order, they should imprecate curses upon future
transgressors, mutually responding in corroboration
of the pronouncements. These blessings and curses
he put on record himself, to the end that their lesson
might never be abolished by time, and indeed at the
last he inscribed them upon the altar,[b] on either side,
even where he said that the people were to stand[c]
and offer sacrifices and whole burnt-offerings, but
after that day they should offer no further victim
thereon,[d] that being unlawful. Such were the ordinances of Moses, and the Hebrew nation continues to
act in conformity therewith.

Cf. Deut.
xxvii. 8.

Ib. 6 f.
(Josh.
viii. 31).

(45) On the morrow, having called together the
people, women and children included, to an assembly
which even the slaves were required to attend, he
made them swear to observe the laws and that, taking
strict account[e] of the mind of God, they would verily
in no whit transgress them, neither through favouritism to kin, nor yielding to fear, nor in the belief that
any other motive whatsoever could be more imperative than the observance of the laws ; nay more, that

Oath of
allegiance
to the Law.
Cf. Deut.
xxix. 2 ff.

Ib. xiii. 6.

---

[c] Such seems to be the meaning, but the Greek is peculiar
and possibly corrupt.

[d] No such injunction in Scripture. " Josèphe est ici
plus loyaliste que la loi " (T. Reinach).

[e] Lit. " showing themselves strict accountants."

310 τους, ἀλλ᾽ ἄν τέ τις τῶν ἐξ αἵματος συγχεῖν καὶ
καταλύειν ἐπιχειρῇ τὴν κατ᾽ αὐτοὺς πολιτείαν ἄν
τε πόλις, ἀμύνειν αὐτοῖς καὶ κοινῇ καὶ κατ᾽ ἰδίαν,
καὶ κρατήσαντας μὲν ἐξ αὐτῶν ἀνασπᾶν θεμελίων
καὶ μηδὲ τὸ ἔδαφος τῶν ἀπονοηθέντων εἰ δυνατὸν
καταλιπεῖν, εἰ δ᾽ ἀσθενοῖεν λαβεῖν τὴν τιμωρίαν,
αὐτὸ τὸ μὴ κατὰ βούλησιν ἰδίαν ταῦτα γίνεσθαι
δεικνύναι. καὶ τὸ μὲν πλῆθος ὤμνυεν.

311 (46) Ἐδίδασκε δὲ αὐτούς, ὡς ἂν αἱ θυσίαι τῷ
θεῷ μᾶλλον κεχαρισμέναι γένοιντο καὶ ὅπως ἂν
οἱ στρατεύοντες ἐξίοιεν τεκμηρίῳ χρώμενοι τοῖς
λίθοις, ὡς καὶ πρότερον δεδήλωκα. προεφήτευσε
312 δὲ καὶ Ἰησοῦς Μωυσέος παρόντος. ἔπειτα πάνθ᾽
ὅσα ποιήσειεν[1] ὑπὲρ τῆς τοῦ λαοῦ σωτηρίας ἔν
τε πολέμοις καὶ κατ᾽ εἰρήνην νόμους τε συντιθεὶς
καὶ τὸν τῆς πολιτείας κόσμον συμπορίζων ἀνα-
λογιζόμενος προεῖπεν, ὡς δηλώσειεν αὐτῷ τὸ θεῖον,
ὅτι παραβάντες τὴν πρὸς αὐτὸν θρησκείαν πειρα-
313 θήσονται κακῶν, ὡς ὅπλων τε αὐτοῖς πολεμίων
πληρωθῆναι τὴν γῆν καὶ κατασκαφῆναι πόλεις καὶ
τὸν νεὼν καταπρησθῆναι καὶ πραθέντας δουλεύειν
ἀνδράσιν οὐδένα ληψομένοις οἶκτον ἐπὶ ταῖς συμ-
φοραῖς αὐτῶν, μετανοήσειν δ᾽ αὐτοὺς ἐπὶ μηδενὶ
314 χρησίμῳ ταῦτα πάσχοντας. "ὁ μέντοι θεὸς ὁ
κτίσας ὑμᾶς πόλεις τε πολίταις ὑμετέροις ἀποδώσει
καὶ τὸν ναόν· ἔσεσθαι δὲ τὴν τούτων ἀποβολὴν οὐχ
ἅπαξ ἀλλὰ πολλάκις."

315 (47) Παρορμήσας δὲ[2] τὸν Ἰησοῦν ἐπὶ τοὺς

---

[1] ποιήσειεν SP.   [2] οὖν RO.

should any person of their blood essay to confound and dissolve the constitution that was based on those laws, should any city do the like, they would rise in their defence, as a nation and as individuals, and, when victorious, would uproot that place from its very foundations, aye and leave not the very ground beneath those miscreants' feet, were that possible ; but should they be powerless to exact that punishment, they would at least demonstrate that these proceedings were contrary to their will.   And the people took the oath.

Deut. xiii. 12.

(46) He taught them, too, how their sacrifices might be made the more acceptable to God, and how the troops when taking the field should consult the oracular stones, as I have previously indicated.[a] Joshua also prophesied in the presence of Moses. Then, recounting all that he had done for the people's salvation in war and in peace, in compiling laws and in co-operating to procure for them an ordered constitution, Moses foretold, as revealed to him by the Divinity, that, if they transgressed His rites, they would experience afflictions of such sort that their land would be filled with the arms of enemies, their cities razed, their temple burnt ; that they would be sold into slavery to men who would take no pity on their misfortunes, and that their repentance would profit them naught amid those sufferings. " Howbeit," said he, " God who created you [b] will restore those cities to your citizens and the temple too ; yet will they be lost not once, but often."

Exhortation and warnings. Cf. Numb. xxviii. 1.

Deut. xxviii.

(47) Then, after exhorting Joshua to lead a cam-

---

[b] Reinach " qui a fondé votre empire " : the phrase θεὸς ὁ κτίσας recurs in B.J. iii. 379, v. 377.   This last sentence is the author's addition, without warrant in Scripture.

Χαναναίους στρατείαν[1] ἐξάγειν, ὡς τοῦ θεοῦ συν-
εργοῦντος οἷς ἂν ἐπιχειρήσειε, καὶ πᾶσαν ἐπ-
ευφημήσας τὴν πληθύν, "ἐπεί," φησί, "πρὸς τοὺς
ἡμετέρους ἄπειμι προγόνους καὶ θεὸς τήνδε μοι
τὴν ἡμέραν τῆς πρὸς ἐκείνους ἀφίξεως ὥρισε,
316 χάριν μὲν αὐτῷ ζῶν ἔτι καὶ παρὼν ὑμῖν ἔχειν
ὁμολογῶ προνοίας τε τῆς ὑπὲρ ὑμῶν, ἣν οὐχ ὑπὲρ
ἀπαλλαγῆς μόνον τῶν ὑμετέρων[2] ἐποιήσατο κακῶν,
ἀλλὰ καὶ δωρεᾶς τῶν κρειττόνων, ὅτι τε πονοῦντί
μοι καὶ κατὰ πᾶσαν ἐπίνοιαν[3] τῆς ἐπὶ τὸ βέλτιον
ὑμῶν μεταβολῆς φροντίδα λαμβάνοντι συνηγωνί-
σατο καὶ παρέσχεν ἐν ἅπασιν αὐτὸν ἡμῖν[4] εὐμενῆ.
317 μᾶλλον δ' αὐτὸς ἦν ὁ καὶ τὴν ἀφήγησιν αὐτῶν
διδοὺς καὶ τὰ τέλη χαριζόμενος, ὑποστρατήγῳ
χρώμενος ἐμοὶ καὶ ὑπηρέτῃ ὢν τὸν ἡμέτερον λαὸν
318 εὐεργετεῖν ἠθέλησεν. ἀνθ' ὧν προευλόγησα[5] τὴν
τοῦ θεοῦ δύναμιν, ᾧ μελήσει καὶ πρὸς τὸ μέλλον
ὑμῶν, ἀπαλλασσόμενος καλῶς ἔχειν ἡγησάμην,
αὐτός τε ταύτην ὀφειλομένην ἀμοιβὴν ἀποδιδοὺς
καὶ καταλείπων εἰς μνήμην ὑμῖν τὸ σέβειν τε καὶ
τιμᾶν προσήκειν τοῦτον ὑμῖν καὶ τοὺς νόμους,
πάντων ὧν τε παρέσχηκε καὶ μένων εὐμενὴς ἔτι
319 παρέξει δώρημα κάλλιστον, φυλάττειν· ὡς δεινὸς
μὲν ἐχθρὸς καὶ ἄνθρωπος νομοθέτης ὑβριζομένων
αὐτῷ τῶν νόμων καὶ μάτην κειμένων, θεοῦ δὲ
μὴ πειραθείητε χαλεπαίνοντος ὑπὲρ ἀμελουμένων
νόμων, οὓς αὐτὸς γεννήσας ὑμῖν ἔδωκε."
320 (48) Μωυσέος δὲ ταῦτα πρὸς τελευτῇ[6] τοῦ βίου
φήσαντος καὶ μετ' εὐλογίας ἑκάστῃ τῶν φυλῶν

---

[1] στρατιὰν MS.   [2] ex Lat. edd.: ἡμετέρων codd.
[3] ed. Genev.: ἐπινοοῦντι SP (omitting κατὰ): ἐπὶ νοῦν rell.
[4] ὑμῖν RO.

paign against the Canaanites, assured of God's co-operation in all his enterprises, and after addressing auspicious words to the whole assembly, " Seeing," said he, " that I am going to our forefathers and that this is the day that God hath appointed for my departure to them, while yet alive and among you I render thanks to Him, alike for the care which He has bestowed on you, not only in delivering you from your distress, but in presenting you with the best of boons, and then for that, while I was toiling and with utmost endeavour taking thought for the amelioration of your lot, He aided me in those struggles and showed Himself ever gracious towards me.[a] Nay rather it was He who both gave the lead in those endeavours and granted the gracious issues, employing me but as His subaltern and subordinate minister of the benefactions which He was fain to confer upon our people. Wherefore I thought it right, ere departing, to bless the power of God, who will still care for you for the time to come, myself rendering this return that is His due, and leaving in your memory the thought that it behoves you to revere and honour Him, and to *observe* His laws— that choicest boon of all that He has given you or, continuing to be gracious, will give you hereafter. For if even a human legislator is a formidable foe when his laws are outraged and laid down to none effect, then beware of experiencing the wrath of God for laws neglected—laws which He, the begetter of them, presented to you Himself."

(48) When Moses, at the close of life, had thus spoken, and, with benedictions, had prophesied to

Moses renders thanks to God: his last words. *Ib.* xxxi. 7.

Cf. Deut. xxxii.

The people's emotion. *Ib.* xxxiii. 1.

[a] Gr. " us " (sing. for plur., as often).

[5] προσευλογῆσαι SPL. [6] Niese: τελευτὴν codd.

προφητεύσαντος τὰ καὶ γενησόμενα[1] τὸ πλῆθος
εἰς δάκρυα προύπεσεν, ὡς καὶ τὰς γυναῖκας
στερνοτυπουμένας ἐμφανίζειν τὸ ἐπ' αὐτῷ τεθνη-
ξομένῳ πάθος. καὶ οἱ παῖδες δὲ θρηνοῦντες ἔτι
μᾶλλον, ὡς ἀσθενέστεροι κρατεῖν λύπης, ἐδήλουν
ὅτι τῆς ἀρετῆς αὐτοῦ καὶ μεγαλουργίας παρ' αὐτὴν
321 τὴν ἡλικίαν συνίεσαν. ἦν δὲ κατ' ἐπίνοιαν τοῖς τε
νέοις καὶ προηβηκόσιν[2] ἅμιλλα τῆς λύπης· οἱ μὲν
γὰρ εἰδότες οἵου στεροῖντο[3] κηδεμόνος περὶ τοῦ
μέλλοντος ἀπεθρήνουν, τοῖς δὲ καὶ περὶ τούτου τὸ
πένθος ἦν καὶ ὅτι μήπω καλῶς τῆς ἀρετῆς αὐτοῦ
322 γεγευμένοις ἀπολείπεσθαι συνέβαινεν αὐτοῦ. τὴν
δ' ὑπερβολὴν τῆς τοῦ πλήθους οἰμωγῆς καὶ τῶν
ὀδυρμῶν τεκμαίροιτο ἄν τις ἐκ τοῦ συμβάντος τῷ
νομοθέτῃ· καὶ γὰρ πεπεισμένος ἅπαντι τῷ χρόνῳ
μὴ δεῖν ἐπὶ μελλούσῃ τελευτῇ κατηφεῖν, ὡς κατὰ
βούλησιν αὐτὸ πάσχοντας θεοῦ καὶ φύσεως νόμῳ,
ἐπὶ τοῖς ὑπὸ τοῦ λαοῦ πραττομένοις ἐνικήθη δα-
323 κρῦσαι. πορευομένῳ δ' ἔνθεν οὗ ἔμελλεν ἀφανισθή-
σεσθαι πάντες εἵποντο δεδακρυμένοι, καὶ Μωυσῆς
τοὺς μὲν πόρρω τῇ χειρὶ κατασείων μένειν ἠρε-
μοῦντας ἐκέλευε, τοὺς[4] δ' ἔγγιον λόγοις παρεκάλει
μὴ ποιεῖν αὐτῷ δακρυτὴν τὴν ἀπαλλαγὴν ἑπο-
324 μένους. οἱ δὲ καὶ τοῦτ' αὐτῷ χαρίζεσθαι κρί-
νοντες, τὸ κατὰ βούλησιν ἀπελθεῖν αὐτῷ τὴν ἰδίαν
ἐφεῖναι, κατέχουσιν ἑαυτοὺς ἐν ἀλλήλοις δακρύοντες.
μόνη δ' ἡ γερουσία προύπεμψεν αὐτὸν καὶ ὁ
ἀρχιερεὺς Ἐλεάζαρος καὶ ὁ στρατηγὸς Ἰησοῦς.

[1] ex Lat.: γενόμενα codd.
[2] RO (+ ἡ): προβεβηκόσιν rell.
[3] ἐστέρηνται R: ἐστέρηντο O.
[4] τὸ RO.

^a According to another reading, " that in fact came to
pass."

each of the tribes the things that in fact were to come to pass,[a] the multitude burst into tears, while the women, too, with beating of the breast manifested their emotion at his approaching death. Aye, and the children, wailing yet more, in that they were too feeble to suppress their grief, displayed an understanding of his virtues and grand achievements even beyond their years. Yet in the thoughts of their hearts there was conflict between the grief of the young and of their seniors. For these, knowing of what a protector they were to be bereft, lamented for the future ; while those, beside that cause for grief, had the sorrow that, ere they had yet right well tasted of his worth, it was their lot to lose him. How extraordinary was this outburst of weeping and wailing of the multitude may be conjectured from what befell the lawgiver. For he, who had ever been persuaded that men should not despond as the end approached, because this fate befell them in accordance with the will of God and by a law of nature, was yet by this conduct of the people reduced to tears.

On his advancing thence toward the place where he was destined to disappear, they all followed him bathed in tears ; thereupon Moses, by a signal of his hand, bade those in the distance to remain still, while by word of mouth he exhorted those nearer to him not to make his passing a tearful one by following him. And they, deciding to gratify him in this also, to wit, to leave him to depart according to his own desire, held back, weeping with one another. Only the elders escorted him, with Eleazar the high priest, and Joshua the general. But when

The passing of Moses. Deut. xxxiv. 1.

325 ὡς δ' ἐπὶ τῷ ὄρει τῷ ᾿Αβαρεῖ καλουμένῳ ἐγένετο,
τοῦτο δὲ ὑψηλὸν ῾Ιεριχοῦντος¹ ἀντικρὺ κεῖται γῆν
ἀρίστην τῶν Χαναναίων καὶ πλείστην παρέχειν
τοῖς ἐπ' αὐτοῦ κατοπτεύειν, ἀπέπεμπε τὴν γερου-
326 σίαν. ἀσπαζομένου δὲ καὶ τὸν ᾿Ελεάζαρον αὐτοῦ
καὶ τὸν ᾿Ιησοῦν καὶ προσομιλοῦντος ἔτι, νέφους
αἰφνίδιον ὑπὲρ αὐτὸν στάντος ἀφανίζεται κατά
τινος φάραγγος. γέγραφε δ' αὐτὸν ἐν ταῖς ἱεραῖς
βίβλοις τεθνεῶτα, δείσας μὴ δι' ὑπερβολὴν τῆς
περὶ αὐτὸν ἀρετῆς πρὸς τὸ θεῖον αὐτὸν ἀναχωρῆσαι
τολμήσωσιν εἰπεῖν.

327 (49) ᾿Εβίωσε δὲ τὸν πάντα χρόνον ἐτῶν εἴκοσι
καὶ ἑκατόν, ὧν ἦρξε τὸ τρίτον μέρος ἑνὶ λεῖπον²
μηνί. ἐτελεύτησε δὲ τῷ ὑστάτῳ μηνὶ τοῦ ἔτους,
ὑπὸ μὲν Μακεδόνων Δύστρου καλουμένου ᾿Αδάρου
328 δ' ὑφ' ἡμῶν νουμηνίᾳ, συνέσει τε τοὺς πώποτ'
ἀνθρώπους ὑπερβαλὼν καὶ χρησάμενος ἄριστα τοῖς
νοηθεῖσιν, εἰπεῖν τε καὶ πλήθεσιν ὁμιλῆσαι κε-
χαρισμένος τά τε ἄλλα καὶ τῶν παθῶν αὐτοκράτωρ,
329 ὡς μηδὲ ἐνεῖναι τούτων τῇ ψυχῇ δοκεῖν αὐτοῦ καὶ
γινώσκειν μόνον αὐτῶν τὴν προσηγορίαν ἐκ τοῦ

---

¹ + κατ' SPL. ² Niese: λείποντι codd.

ᵃ Heb. Abarim, Deut. xxxii. 49: the name apparently
"applied to the range of mountains ' beyond ' (i.e. east of)
Jordan in which Nebo formed a particular ridge" (Driver).
Josephus ignores "mount Nebo" which is mentioned in
Deut. xxxiv. 1 as the precise spot.

ᵇ The Biblical account runs: "So Moses the servant of
the LORD died there in the land of Moab, according to the
word of the LORD. And He buried him in the ravine . . .
but no man knoweth of his sepulchre unto this day." The
account of Josephus seems to be reminiscent of the passing
of the two founders of the Roman race as described by
Dionysius of Halicarnassus: "But the body of Aeneas could
nowhere be found and some conjectured that he had been

he arrived on the mountain called Abaris *ᵃ*—a lofty
eminence situate over against Jericho and affording
to those on its summit a wide view beneath of the
best of the land of the Canaanites—he dismissed the
elders. And, while he bade farewell to Eleazar and
Joshua and was yet communing with them, a cloud
of a sudden descended upon him and he disappeared
in a ravine.*ᵇ* But he has written of himself in the
sacred books that he died,*ᶜ* for fear lest they should
venture to say that by reason of his surpassing virtue
he had gone back to the Deity.*ᵈ*

(49) He lived in all one hundred and twenty
years and was ruler for a third part of that time
bating one month. He departed in the last month
of the year, which the Macedonians call Dystros and
we Adar,*ᵉ* on the day of the new moon, having surpassed in understanding all men that ever lived and
put to noblest use the fruit of his reflections. In
speech and in addresses to a crowd he found favour
in every way, but chiefly through his thorough
command of his passions, which was such that he
seemed to have no place for them at all in his soul,
and only knew their names through seeing them in

Deut.
xxxiv. 5 f.

Encomium
of Moses.
Ib. 7.

translated to the gods " (*Ant. Rom.* i. 64. 4), and of Romulus,
" The more mythical writers say that as he was holding an
assembly (ἐκκλησιάζοντα) in the camp darkness descended
upon him from a clear sky and . . . he disappeared, and
they believe that he was caught up by his father Ares "
(*ib.* ii. 56. 2).
ᶜ Rabbis were divided on the question whether the last
eight verses of Deut. were written by Moses or by Joshua
(see Weill's note). The view of Josephus has the support of
R. Simeon.
ᵈ The same phrase in i. 85 (of Enoch), iii. 96 (of Moses).
ᵉ Feb.-March ; Rabbinic tradition named the 7th (not the
1st) of Adar (Weill).

παρ' ἄλλοις αὐτὰ βλέπειν μᾶλλον ἢ παρ' αὐτῷ.
καὶ στρατηγὸς μὲν ἐν ὀλίγοις, προφήτης δὲ οἷος
οὐκ ἄλλος, ὥσθ' ὅ τι ἂν φθέγξαιτο δοκεῖν αὐτοῦ
330 λέγοντος ἀκροᾶσθαι τοῦ θεοῦ. πενθεῖ μὲν οὖν
αὐτὸν ὁ λαὸς ἐφ' ἡμέρας τριάκοντα, λύπη δὲ οὐκ
ἄλλη κατέσχεν Ἑβραίους τοσαύτη τὸ μέγεθος,
331 ὅση τότε Μωυσέος ἀποθανόντος. ἐπόθουν δ'
αὐτὸν οὐχ οἱ πειραθέντες αὐτοῦ μόνον, ἀλλὰ
καὶ οἱ τοῖς νόμοις ἐντυγχάνοντες αὐτοῦ δεινὴν
ἐποιοῦντο τὴν ἐπιζήτησιν, τὸ περιὸν αὐτοῦ τῆς
ἀρετῆς ἐκ τούτων λογιζόμενοι. καὶ τὸ μὲν κατὰ
Μωυσῆν τέλος τοιοῦτον ἡμῖν δεδηλώσθω.

others rather than in himself. As general he had few to equal him, and as prophet none, insomuch that in all his utterances one seemed to hear the speech of God Himself. So the people mourned for him for thirty days, and never were Hebrews oppressed by grief so profound as that which filled them then on the death of Moses. Nor was he regretted only by those who had known him by experience, but the very readers of his laws have sadly felt his loss, deducing from these the superlative quality of his virtue. Such, then, be our description of the end of Moses.

ΙΟΥΔΑΪΚΗΣ ΑΡΧΑΙΟΛΟΓΙΑΣ

ΒΙΒΛΙΟΝ Ε

1 (i. 1) Μωυσέος δὲ τὸν προειρημένον τρόπον ἐξ
ἀνθρώπων ἀπογεγονότος Ἰησοῦς, ἁπάντων ἤδη
τῶν ἐπ᾽ αὐτῷ νενομισμένων τέλος ἐχόντων καὶ τοῦ
πένθους λελωφηκότος, παρήγγειλεν ἐπὶ στρατείαν
2 ἕτοιμον εἶναι τὸ πλῆθος, πέμπει τε κατασκόπους
εἰς Ἱεριχοῦντα τήν τε δύναμιν αὐτῶν καὶ τίνα
διάνοιαν ἔχουσιν αὐτοὶ γνωσομένους,[1] αὐτὸς δὲ
ἐξήταζε τὸν στρατὸν ὡς κατὰ καιρὸν διαβησόμενος
3 τὸν Ἰόρδανον. ἀνακαλεσάμενος δὲ τοὺς τῆς Ῥου-
βηλίδος φυλῆς ἄρχοντας καὶ τοὺς τῆς Γάδιδος καὶ
Μανασσήτιδος προεστῶτας, ἐξ ἡμισείας γὰρ καὶ
τῇδε τῇ φυλῇ τὴν Ἀμορίαν κατοικεῖν ἐπετέτραπτο
4 τῆς Χαναναίων γῆς ἕβδομον οὖσαν μέρος, ὑπεμί-
μνησκεν ἃ ὑπέσχοντο Μωυσεῖ, καὶ παρεκάλει
χαριζομένους τῇ τε ἐκείνου προνοίᾳ, μηδ᾽ ὅτε
ἀπέθνησκε περὶ αὐτοὺς καμούσῃ, τῷ τε κοινῇ
συμφέροντι παρέχειν αὐτοὺς εἰς τὰ παραγγελλόμενα
προθύμους. τῶν δ᾽ ἑπομένων ὁπλίταις πεντακισ-

---

[1] ex Lat.: γνωσόμενος codd.

162

JEWISH ANTIQUITIES

BOOK V

(i. 1) MOSES having in the aforesaid manner been
rapt away from men, Joshua, when all the customary
rites had now been accomplished in his honour and
the mourning had abated, directed the people to
make ready for a campaign. He also sent scouts to
Jericho to reconnoitre the strength and the disposition of the inhabitants, while he himself reviewed
his army, intending at the first opportunity to cross
the Jordan. Having, moreover, called up the princes
of the tribe of Rubel [a] and the chiefs of the tribes of
Gad and of Manasseh—for one half of this tribe too
had been permitted to settle in the Amorite country,
which forms a seventh part [b] of the land of Canaan
—he reminded them of their promises to Moses and
exhorted them, out of respect alike for that fore-
thought of his on their behalf which even in his dying
moments had never flagged, and for the common
weal, to respond to his orders with alacrity. These
duly following him, he with fifty thousand [c] men-

Joshua sends spies to Jericho and advances to the Jordan.
Jos. i. 10; ii. 1.

i. 12, 13.

---

[a] Reuben.

[b] The Amorites were one of the " seven nations " that
inhabited Canaan (Deut. vii. 1, Jos. iii. 10 ; cf. §§ 88 f. below).
From this apparently, as M. Weill suggests, Josephus infers
that they occupied a seventh part of the whole country.

[c] 40,000 according to Jos. iv. 13 (Heb. and LXX).

163

μυρίοις ἀπὸ τῆς Ἀβέλης[1] ἐπὶ τὸν Ἰόρδανον ἐξῄει
σταδίους ἑξήκοντα.

5 (2) Καὶ στρατοπεδεύσαντος εὐθὺς οἱ κατάσκοποι
παρῆσαν μηδὲν ἀγνοήσαντες τῶν παρὰ τοῖς
Χαναναίοις· λαθόντες[2] γὰρ τὸ πρῶτον ἅπασαν ἐπ'
ἀδείας αὐτῶν τὴν πόλιν κατενόησαν, τῶν τε τειχῶν
ὅσα καρτερὰ καὶ ὅσα μὴ τοῦτον ἔχει[3] τὸν τρόπον
αὐτοῖς ἀσφαλῶς καὶ τῶν πυλίδων αἳ πρὸς εἴσοδον
6 τῷ στρατοπέδῳ δι' ἀσθένειαν συνέφερον. ἠμέλουν
δὲ θεωμένων οἱ ἐντυγχάνοντες καθ' ἱστορίαν ξένοις
προσήκουσαν ἀκριβῶς ἕκαστα πολυπραγμονεῖν τῶν
ἐν τῇ πόλει νομίζοντες, ἀλλ' οὐχὶ διανοίᾳ πολεμίων.
7 ὡς δὲ γενομένης ὀψίας ὑποχωροῦσιν εἴς τι καταγώγιον τοῦ τείχους πλησίον, εἰς ὃ καὶ προήχθησαν
8 δειπνοποιησόμενοι[4] καὶ περὶ ἀπαλλαγῆς αὐτοῖς τὸ
λοιπὸν ἡ φροντὶς ἦν, μηνύονται τῷ βασιλεῖ περὶ
δεῖπνον ὄντι κατασκεψόμενοί τινες τὴν πόλιν ἀπὸ
τοῦ τῶν Ἑβραίων στρατοπέδου παρεῖναι καὶ
ὄντες ἐν τῷ τῆς Ῥαάβης καταγωγίῳ μετὰ πολλῆς
τῆς τοῦ λανθάνειν προνοίας ὑπάρχειν. ὁ δ' εὐθὺς
πέμψας πρὸς αὐτοὺς[5] ἐκέλευσεν ἀγαγεῖν συλλαβόντας, ἵνα βασανίσας μάθῃ, τί καὶ βουλόμενοι
9 παρεῖεν. ὡς δ' ἔγνω τὴν ἔφοδον αὐτῶν ἡ Ῥαάβη,
λίνου γὰρ ἀγκαλίδας ἐπὶ τοῦ τέγους[6] ἔψυχε, τοὺς
μὲν κατασκόπους εἰς ταύτας ἀποκρύπτει, τοῖς
δὲ πεμφθεῖσιν ὑπὸ τοῦ βασιλέως ἔλεγεν, ὡς ξένοι

---

[1] RO: Ἀβίλης etc. rell.
[2] codd. Lat.: ἐλθόντες E edd.   [3] ἔχοι SP.
[4] ex Lat.: -ποιησάμενοι codd.
[5] fort. αὐτὸν legendum.   [6] E: τείχους codd.

---

[a] Or Abile (bibl. Abel-shittim): A. iv. 176 note.

at-arms set out from Abele [a] and advanced sixty
stades towards the Jordan.

(2) Scarce had he pitched his camp when the The spies
scouts reappeared, in nothing ignorant of the con- Jos. ii. 1.
dition of the Canaanites. For, undetected at the
first, they had surveyed their entire city unmolested,
noting where the ramparts were strong and where
they offered a less secure protection to the inhabitants, and which of the gates through weakness
would facilitate entrance for the army. Those who
met them had disregarded their inspection, attributing to a curiosity natural to strangers this busy
study of every detail in the city, and in no wise to
any hostile intent. But when, at fall of even, they
retired to an inn [b] hard by the ramparts, to which
they had proceeded [c] for supper, and were now
only thinking of departure, word was brought to the
king as he supped that certain persons had come
from the camp of the Hebrews to spy upon the city
and were now in Rahab's inn, mightily anxious to
escape detection. And he straightway sent men
after them, with orders to arrest and bring them up,
that he might discover by torture to what intent
they were come. But when Rahab learnt of their
approach, being then engaged in drying some bundles
of flax upon the roof,[d] she concealed the spies therein,
and told the king's messengers that some unknown

---

[b] The Bible speaks of Rahab the "harlot" (Heb. *zonah*,
LXX πόρνη). Josephus follows the Palestinian interpretation
found in the Targum on Jos. ii. 1, where the noun is translated *pundeḳita* = Gr. πανδοκεύτρια or πανδόκισσα, "inn-keeper."
Cf. A. iii. 276 note.

[c] Or "been conducted" or "directed."

[d] Or, according to most MSS., "the wall." Jos. ii. 6 has
"the roof" (LXX δῶμα).

τινὲς[1] ἀγνῶτες ὀλίγῳ πρότερον ἢ δῦναι τὸν ἥλιον
παρ' αὐτῇ δειπνήσαντες ἀπαλλαγεῖεν, οὓς εἰ
φοβεροὶ τῇ πόλει δοκοῦσιν, ἢ κίνδυνον τῷ βασιλεῖ
φέροντες ἧκον, ἀπόνως εἶναι λαβεῖν διωχθέντας.
10 οἱ δέ, τῆς γυναικὸς οὕτως αὐτοὺς ὑπελθούσης,
οὐδένα ὑπονοήσαντες δόλον ἀπῆλθον οὐδ' ἐρευνή-
σαντες τὸ καταγώγιον. ἐπεὶ δ' ὁρμήσαντες καθ'
ἃς ἐνόμιζον αὐτοὺς μάλιστα τῶν ὁδῶν ἀπέρχεσθαι
καὶ κατὰ τὰς εἰς τὸν ποταμὸν φερούσας οὐδενὶ
γνωρίσματι περιετύγχανον, παύονται τοῦ πονεῖν.
11 τοῦ δὲ θορύβου σταλέντος ἡ Ῥαάβη καταγαγοῦσα
τοὺς ἄνδρας καὶ τὸν κίνδυνον εἰποῦσα, ὃν ὑπὲρ τῆς
αὐτῶν ὑπέλθοι σωτηρίας, ἁλοῦσαν γὰρ ἀποκρύπ-
τουσαν αὐτοὺς οὐκ ἂν διαφυγεῖν τὴν ἐκ τοῦ βασιλέως
τιμωρίαν, ἀλλὰ πανοικὶ αὐτὴν ἀπολέσθαι κακῶς,
12 παρακαλέσασα διὰ μνήμης ἔχειν, ὅταν ἐγκρατεῖς
τῆς Χαναναίων γῆς καταστάντες ἀμοιβὴν ἐκτῖσαι
δύνωνται τῆς ἄρτι σωτηρίας, χωρεῖν ἐκέλευεν ἐπὶ
τὰ οἰκεῖα ὁμόσαντας ἦ μὴν σώσειν αὐτὴν καὶ τὰ
αὐτῆς, ὅταν τὴν πόλιν ἑλόντες φθείρωσι πάντας
τοὺς ἐν αὐτῇ κατὰ ψήφισμα τὸ παρ' αὐτοῖς γενό-
μενον· ταῦτα γὰρ εἰδέναι σημείοις τοῖς ἐκ τοῦ θεοῦ
13 διδαχθεῖσαν. οἱ δὲ καὶ περὶ[2] τῶν παρόντων αὐτῇ
χάριν ἔχειν ὡμολόγουν καὶ περὶ τῶν αὖθις ὤμνυον
ἔργῳ τὴν ἀμοιβὴν ἀποδώσειν· ἡνίκα δ' ἂν αἴσθηται
μελλούσης ἁλίσκεσθαι τῆς πόλεως, συνεβούλευον
κτῆσίν τε τὴν αὐτῆς καὶ τοὺς οἰκείους ἅπαντας εἰς
τὸ καταγώγιον ἀποθεμένην ἐγκαθεῖρξαι, πρὸ τῶν

---

[1] P² edd.: τινὲς εἶεν rell. codd.   [2] om. M.

---

[a] Jos. ii. 9 f. speaks of Rahab's having heard that the
Israelites' God will again aid them as in the past. Perhaps

strangers had shortly before sundown supped with her and gone their way ; but, were it thought that the city had cause to fear them or were their coming fraught with peril to the king, they could be caught without difficulty if pursued. The messengers, thus cajoled by the woman and suspecting no guile, departed without even searching the inn ; but when, after speeding along the roads by which they thought it most likely that the men had fled, including all those leading to the river, they found no trace of them, they ceased to trouble themselves further. The tumult having subsided, Rahab brought the men down and, having told them of the risk which she had run for their salvation—for, had she been caught concealing them, she would not have escaped the vengeance of the king but she and all her house would have perished miserably—she besought them to bear this in mind when, once masters of the land of the Canaanites, they should be in a position to recompense her for their present salvation ; and she bade them depart to their own place, after swearing that they would verily save her and all that was hers when, on taking the city, they should destroy all its inhabitants, a. had been decreed by their people, for of this (she said) she knew through certain signs [a] which God had given her. In reply they expressed their gratitude to her for present favours and swore to repay her in future by recompense in act ; but they counselled her, when she should see that the city was on the point of being taken, to secure her chattels and all her household within the inn and to shut them in, and to extend

[a] σημεῖα here, as elsewhere in Josephus, means the " miracles " alluded to in the Scriptural passage.

JOSEPHUS

θυρῶν ἀνατείνασαν φοινικίδας, ὅπως εἰδὼς τὴν
οἰκίαν ὁ στρατηγὸς φυλάττηται κακῶς ποιεῖν·
14 " μηνύσομεν¹ γὰρ αὐτῷ," ἔφασαν, " διὰ τὸ σὸν
σώζεσθαι πρόθυμον. εἰ δέ τις ἐν τῇ μάχῃ πέσοι
τῶν σῶν, σύ τε οὐκ ἂν ἡμῖν ἐπενέγκοις αἰτίαν καὶ
τὸν θεὸν ὃν ὀμωμόκαμεν παραιτούμεθα μηδὲν ὡς
15 ἐπὶ παραβαίνουσι τοὺς ὅρκους δυσχερᾶναι." καὶ
οἱ μὲν ταῦτα συνθέμενοι ἐχώρουν διὰ τοῦ τείχους
καθιμήσαντες ἑαυτούς, καὶ διασωθέντες πρὸς τοὺς
οἰκείους ἐδήλωσαν ὅσα πράξαντες ἐπὶ τῆς πόλεως
ἧκον· Ἰησοῦς δὲ τῷ ἀρχιερεῖ Ἐλεαζάρῳ καὶ τῇ
γερουσίᾳ φράζει τὰ τοῖς σκοποῖς ὁμοθέντα πρὸς
τὴν Ῥαάβην· οἱ δ' ἐπεκύρουν τὸν ὅρκον.
16 (3) Δεδιότος δὲ τοῦ στρατοῦ² τὴν διάβασιν, μέγας
γὰρ ἦν ὁ ποταμὸς τῷ ῥεύματι καὶ οὔτε γεφύραις
πορευτός, οὐ γὰρ ἔζευκτο τὸ³ πρότερον, βουλομένους τε γεφυροῦν οὐχ ἕξειν σχολὴν παρὰ τῶν πολεμίων ὑπελάμβανον πορθμείων τε μὴ τυγχανόντων,
διαβατὸν αὐτοῖς ὁ θεὸς ἐπαγγέλλεται ποιήσειν τὸν
17 ποταμὸν μειώσας αὐτοῦ τὸ πλῆθος. καὶ δύο ἐπι-
ισχὼν ἡμέρας Ἰησοῦς διεβίβαζε τὸν στρατὸν καὶ
τὴν πληθὺν ἅπασαν τοιούτῳ τρόπῳ· προῆεσαν μὲν
οἱ ἱερεῖς τὴν κιβωτὸν ἔχοντες, ἔπειτα οἱ Λευῖται
τήν τε σκηνὴν καὶ τὰ πρὸς ὑπηρεσίαν ταῖς θυσίαις
σκεύη κομίζοντες, εἵποντο δὲ τοῖς Λευίταις κατὰ
φυλὰς ὁ πᾶς ὅμιλος μέσους ἔχων παῖδας καὶ γυναῖκας, δεδιὼς περὶ αὐτῶν μὴ βιασθεῖεν ὑπὸ τοῦ

¹ RO: μηνύσειν rell.
² SP: στρατηγοῦ rell.
³ RO: πω rell.

ᵃ Jos. ii. 18, " Thou shalt bind this line of scarlet thread
in the window which thou didst let us down by."
ᵇ Josephus, *more suo*, lessens the supernatural character
168

red flags before her doors,[a] in order that their general, recognizing the house, might refrain from doing it injury. "For," said they, "we shall report to him that it is to thy zeal that we owe our lives. But, should any of thy kinsmen fall in the battle, thou must not lay that to our charge, and we implore the God by whom we have sworn to be in no wise indignant at us, as though we had transgressed our oaths." So having made this compact, they departed, letting themselves down the wall by a rope and, when safely restored to their friends, they recounted their adventures in the city. Joshua thereupon reported to Eleazar the high priest and to the council of elders what the spies had sworn to Rahab; and they ratified the oath.

(3) Now since the army was afraid to cross the river, which had a strong current and could not be crossed by bridges—for it had not been spanned by any hitherto, and, should they wish to lay them now, the enemy would not, they imagined, afford them the leisure, and they had no ferry-boats—God promised to render the stream passable for them by diminishing its volume.[b] So Joshua, having waited two days,[c] proceeded to transport the army with the whole multitude in the following fashion. At the head went the priests bearing the ark, next the Levites carrying the tabernacle and the vessels for the ministry of the sacrifices, and, after the Levites, followed, tribe by tribe, the whole throng, with the children and women in the centre, for fear of their being swept away by the force of the current.

Crossing of the Jordan.

Jos. iii. 2.

of the miracle : the waters are not " wholly cut off " as in Joshua (iii. 13, 16).

c " After three days," Jos. iii. 2.

18 ῥεύματος. ὡς δὲ τοῖς ἱερεῦσι πρώτοις ἐμβᾶσι
πορευτὸς ἔδοξεν ὁ ποταμός, τοῦ μὲν βάθους
ἐπεσχημένου, τοῦ δὲ κάχληκος, τῷ μὴ πολὺν εἶναι
μηδ᾽ ὀξὺν τὸν ῥοῦν ὥσθ᾽ ὑποφέρειν αὐτὸν τῇ βίᾳ,
ἀντ᾽ ἐδάφους κειμένου, πάντες ἤδη θαρσαλέως
ἐπεραιοῦντο τὸν ποταμόν, οἷον αὐτὸν ὁ θεὸς
19 προεῖπε ποιήσειν τοιοῦτον κατανοοῦντες. ἔστησαν
δὲ ἐν μέσῳ οἱ ἱερεῖς ἕως οὗ διαβαίη τὸ πλῆθος
καὶ τἀσφαλοῦς ἁψάμενον τύχοι.¹ πάντων δὲ δια-
βάντων ἐξῄεσαν οἱ ἱερεῖς ἐλεύθερον ἀφέντες ἤδη
τὸ ῥεῦμα χωρεῖν κατὰ τὴν συνήθειαν. καὶ ὁ μὲν
ποταμὸς εὐθὺς ἐκβάντων αὐτὸν τῶν Ἑβραίων
ηὔξετο καὶ τὸ ἴδιον ἀπελάμβανε μέγεθος.
20 (4) Οἱ δὲ πεντήκοντα προελθόντες στάδια βάλ-
λονται στρατόπεδον ἀπὸ δέκα σταδίων τῆς Ἱεριχοῦντος, Ἰησοῦς δὲ τόν τε² βωμὸν ἐκ τῶν λίθων
ὧν ἕκαστος ἀνείλετο τῶν φυλάρχων ἐκ τοῦ βυθοῦ
τοῦ προφήτου κελεύσαντος ἱδρυσάμενος, τεκμήριον
γενησόμενον τῆς ἀνακοπῆς τοῦ ῥεύματος, ἔθυεν
ἐπ᾽ αὐτοῦ τῷ θεῷ, καὶ τὴν φάσκα ἑώρταζον ἐν
21 ἐκείνῳ τῷ χωρίῳ, πάντων ὧν αὐτοῖς πρότερον
συνέβαινε σπανίζειν τότε ῥᾳδίως εὐποροῦντες· τόν
τε γὰρ σῖτον ἀκμάζοντα ἤδη τῶν Χαναναίων
ἐθέριζον καὶ τὰ λοιπὰ λείαν ἦγον· τότε γὰρ αὐτοὺς
καὶ ἡ τῆς μάννας ἐπελελοίπει τροφὴ χρησαμένους
ἐπὶ ἔτη τεσσαράκοντα.
22 (5) Ὡς δὲ ταῦτα ποιούντων τῶν Ἰσραηλιτῶν
οὐκ ἐπεξῄεσαν οἱ Χαναναῖοι τειχήρεις δ᾽ ἡσύχαζον,

¹ Dindorf: τύχῃ codd.   ² τε RO: om. τόν τε SPE (Lat.).

ᵃ Literally " touched safety ": the phrase recalls Thuc. ii.
22 πρὶν . . . τοῦ ἀσφαλοῦς ἀντιλάβοιντο (the escape from
Plataea).

170

When the priests, who were the first to enter, found the river fordable—the depth having diminished and the shingle, which the current was neither full nor rapid enough to force from under their feet, lying as a solid floor—all thereupon confidently traversed the stream, perceiving it to be even as God had foretold that He would make it. But the priests stood still in the midst until the multitude had crossed and reached the firm ground.[a] Then, when all had crossed, the priests emerged, leaving the stream free to resume its accustomed course. And the river, so soon as the Hebrews had quitted it, swelled and recovered its natural magnitude. iii. 17,
iv. 17 f.

(4) These, having advanced fifty stades, pitched their camp at a distance of ten stades [b] from Jericho. And Joshua, with the stones which each of the tribal leaders had, by the prophet's orders, taken up from the river-bed, erected that altar that was to serve as a token of the stoppage of the stream, and sacrificed thereon to God.[c] They also kept the feast of the Passover at that spot, being now readily and amply provided with all that they had lacked before ; for they reaped the corn of the Canaanites, now at its prime, and took any other booty they could. It was then too that the supply of manna ceased which had served them for forty years. Erection of
an altar and
celebration
of Passover.
Jos. iv. 1. v. 10.

(5) Since, notwithstanding these actions of the Israelites, the Canaanites did not sally out against them but remained motionless behind their walls, Encompass-
ing of the
walls of
Jericho.
Jos. vi. 1.

[b] These distances are unscriptural. The Gilgal of the camp (Jos. v. 10) is usually identified with a site more than ten stades distant (S.E.) from Jericho.

[c] Josephus here omits the renewal at Gilgal of the rite of circumcision which had been neglected in the wilderness (Jos. v. 2 ff.).

πολιορκεῖν αὐτοὺς Ἰησοῦς ἔγνω. καὶ τῇ πρώτῃ
τῆς ἑορτῆς ἡμέρᾳ τὴν κιβωτὸν οἱ ἱερεῖς φέροντες,
περὶ δ' αὐτὴν ἐν κύκλῳ μέρος τι τῶν ὁπλιτῶν
23 φυλάττον ἦν, ἄλλοι δὲ καὶ[1] προῄεσαν ἑπτὰ κέρασιν
αὐτῶν σαλπίζοντες παρεκάλουν τὸν στρατὸν εἰς
ἀλκήν, περιώδευόν τε τὸ τεῖχος ἑπομένης τῆς
γερουσίας, καὶ σαλπισάντων μόνον τῶν ἱερέων,
τούτου γὰρ οὐδὲν ἐποίησαν περισσότερον, ἀνέζευξαν
24 εἰς τὸ στρατόπεδον. καὶ τοῦτο ἐπὶ ἡμέρας ἓξ
ποιησάντων τῇ ἑβδόμῃ τὸ ὁπλιτικὸν Ἰησοῦς συναγαγὼν καὶ τὸν λαὸν ἅπαντα, τὴν ἅλωσιν αὐτοῖς
τῆς πόλεως εὐηγγελίζετο,[2] ὡς κατ' ἐκείνην τὴν
ἡμέραν αὐτοῖς τοῦ θεοῦ ταύτην παρέξοντος, αὐτομάτως καὶ δίχα τοῦ πόνου τοῦ σφετέρου τῶν τειχῶν
25 κατενεχθησομένων. κτείνειν μέντοι[3] πάνθ' ὁντιν-
οῦν εἰ λάβοιεν παρεκελεύετο καὶ μήτε κάμνοντας
ἀποστῆναι τοῦ φόνου τῶν πολεμίων, μήτ' ἐλέῳ
παραχωρήσαντας φείσασθαι[4] μήτε περὶ ἁρπαγὴν
26 γινομένους περιορᾶν φεύγοντας τοὺς ἐχθρούς· ἀλλὰ
τὰ μὲν ζῷα πάντα διαφθείρειν μηδὲν αὐτοὺς εἰς
ἰδίαν ὠφέλειαν λαμβάνοντας, ὅσα[5] δ' ἂν ἄργυρος ᾖ
καὶ χρυσός, ταῦτα ἐκέλευσε συγκομίζοντας ἀπαρχὴν
ἐξαίρετον τῶν κατωρθωμένων τῷ θεῷ τηρεῖν ἐκ
τῆς πρώτων ἁλισκομένης πόλεως εἰληφότας· σώζειν
δὲ μόνην Ῥαάβην καὶ τὴν γενεὰν αὐτῆς διὰ τοὺς
γενομένους πρὸς αὐτὴν τοῖς κατασκόποις ὅρκους.

---

[1] After Lat. (aliique sacerdotes): οἱ καὶ codd.
[2] RO: εὐηγγελίσατο rell.   [3] + γε SPL.
[4] SPL: om. rell.   [5] ὅσος RO: ὃς M.

---

[a] *i.e.* of the Passover just mentioned ; this date has no support in Scripture or, according to M. Weill, in tradition.

Joshua resolved to besiege them. And, on the first day of the feast,[a] the priests bearing the ark—which was surrounded by a party of armed men to protect it, while seven other priests marched in advance, sounding their horns—exhorted the army to valiance and made the circuit of the walls, followed by the council of elders. After merely those blasts from the priests—for beyond that they did nothing—they returned to the camp. For six days this was repeated, and on the seventh Joshua, having assembled the troops and all the people, announced to them the good news of the impending capture of the city, to wit that on that day God would deliver it to them and that, spontaneously and without effort on their part, the walls would collapse. Howbeit he charged them to slay all, whomsoever they caught, and neither through weariness, nor yielding to pity to desist from the slaughter of their enemies, nor yet while engaged in pillage to suffer the foe to escape. Nay, they were to destroy every living creature without taking aught to themselves for their private profit; but whatsoever there might be of silver or gold,[b] that he commanded them to amass and reserve for God as choice first-fruits of their success, won from the first captured city. They were to spare only Rahab and her family in virtue of the oaths which had been made to her by the spies.

Josephus has traced a connexion between the seven days of blowing of trumpets, mentioned in Scripture, and the duration of the feast. Perhaps, however, he has used a text which, like the LXX Jos. vi. 12, read " on the second day, Joshua rose early, and the priests bore the ark, etc.," and taken it to mean the day after the eve of Passover, or the first full day of the festival.

[b] Jos. vi. 19 adds " or brass or iron " ; *cf.* § 32.

27　(6) Ταῦτ᾽ εἰπὼν καὶ διατάξας τὸν στρατὸν προσ-
ῆγεν¹ ἐπὶ τὴν πόλιν· περιήεσαν δὲ πάλιν τὴν
πόλιν ἡγουμένης τῆς κιβωτοῦ καὶ τῶν ἱερέων τοῖς
κέρασιν ἐξοτρυνόντων τὴν δύναμιν πρὸς τὸ ἔργον.
καὶ περιελθόντων ἑπτάκις καὶ πρὸς ὀλίγον ἠρε-
μησάντων κατέπεσε τὸ τεῖχος μήτε μηχανῆς μήτε
ἄλλης βίας αὐτῷ προσενεχθείσης ὑπὸ τῶν Ἑβραίων.

28　(7) Οἱ δ᾽ εἰσελθόντες εἰς Ἱεριχοῦντα πάντας
ἔκτεινον, τῶν ἐν αὐτῇ πρὸς τὴν παράδοξον τοῦ
τείχους ἀνατροπὴν καταπεπληγότων καὶ τοῦ φρο-
νήματος αὐτοῖς πρὸς ἄμυναν ἀχρείου γεγονότος·
ἀνῃροῦντο δ᾽ οὖν ἐν ταῖς ὁδοῖς ἀποσφαττόμενοι
29　καὶ ἐν ταῖς οἰκίαις ἐπικαταλαμβανόμενοι. παρῃτεῖτο δ᾽ οὐδὲν αὐτούς, ἀλλὰ πάντες ἀπώλλυντο
ἄχρι γυναικῶν καὶ παιδίων, καὶ νεκρῶν ἡ πόλις
ἦν ἀνάπλεως καὶ διέφυγεν οὐδέν.　τὴν δὲ πόλιν
30　ἐνέπρησαν ἅπασαν καὶ τὴν χώραν.　καὶ τὴν
Ῥαάβην σὺν τοῖς οἰκείοις εἰς τὸ καταγώγιον συμ-
φυγοῦσαν ἔσωσαν οἱ κατάσκοποι, καὶ πρὸς αὐτὸν
Ἰησοῦς ἀχθείσῃ χάριν ἔχειν ὡμολόγει τῆς σωτηρίας
τῶν κατασκόπων καὶ μὴν² τῆς εὐεργεσίας ταύτης
ἔλεγεν ἐν ταῖς ἀμοιβαῖς οὐχ ἥττονα φανήσεσθαι.
δωρεῖται δ᾽ αὐτὴν εὐθὺς ἀγροῖς καὶ διὰ τιμῆς εἶχε
τῆς πάσης.

31　(8) Τῆς δὲ πόλεως εἰ καί τι παρέλθοι τὸ πῦρ
κατέσκαπτε καὶ κατὰ τῶν οἰκισόντων,³ εἴ τις
πορθηθεῖσαν ἀνεγείρειν ἐθελήσειεν, ἀρὰς ἔθετο,
ὅπως θεμελίους μὲν τειχῶν βαλλόμενος⁴ στερηθῇ
τοῦ πρώτου παιδός, τελειώσας δὲ τὸν νεώτατον
τῶν παίδων ἀποβάλῃ. τῆς δὲ ἀρᾶς τὸ θεῖον οὐκ

¹ προσήγαγεν RO.　　　　　² M : μηδὲν rell.
³ L : οἰκησόντων rell.　　　　⁴ βαλόμενος RO.

174

(6) Having spoken thus, he marshalled his army and led it towards the city. Again they compassed the city, the ark leading and the priests with the sounding of their horns inciting the troops to action. And when they had compassed it seven times and had halted for a while, the wall fell down, without either engine or force of any other kind having been applied to it by the Hebrews.

Fall of Jericho. Jos. vi. 15.

(7) And they, having entered Jericho, slew every soul, the inhabitants being dumbfounded at the miraculous overthrow of the ramparts and deprived of all effectual spirit for defence. At all events they perished, slaughtered in the streets or surprised in the houses. Nothing could exempt them ; all were destroyed down to the women and children, and the city was choked with corpses and nothing escaped. The city itself they burnt entire and the surrounding region. Rahab, who with her kinsfolk had all taken refuge in the inn, was saved by the spies ; and Joshua, on her being brought before him, acknowledged his gratitude to her for her protection of the spies and assured her that in recompensing her he would not be found to fall short of such a benefaction. Indeed he presented her with lands forthwith and showed her every consideration.

Massacre of the inhabitants, excepting Rahab. Jos. vi. 21.

(8) As for the city, whatever of it the fire had spared he demolished, and upon those who would settle there should any be fain to re-erect it from its ruins, he pronounced imprecations, that if he laid foundations of walls he should be bereft of his first-born and if he completed the walls he should lose the youngest of his sons. Nor was this curse un-

Destruction of the town and imprecation of Joshua. Jos. vi. 26.

175

ἠμέλησεν, ἀλλ' ἐν τοῖς ὑστέροις ἀπαγγελοῦμεν τὸ περὶ αὐτὴν πάθος γενόμενον.

32 (9) Ἄπειρον δέ τι πλῆθος ἐκ τῆς ἁλώσεως συναθροίζεται ἀργύρου τε καὶ χρυσοῦ καὶ προσέτι χαλκοῦ, μηδενὸς παραβάντος τὰ δεδογμένα μηδ' εἰς ἰδίαν ὠφέλειαν αὐτὰ διαρπασαμένων, ἀλλ' ἀποσχομένων ὡς ἤδη τῷ θεῷ καθιερωμένων. καὶ ταῦτα μὲν Ἰησοῦς τοῖς ἱερεῦσιν εἰς τοὺς θησαυροὺς παραδίδωσι καταθέσθαι. καὶ Ἱεριχοῦς μὲν τοῦτον ἀπώλετο τὸν τρόπον.

33 (10) Ἄχαρος δέ τις Ζεβεδαίου παῖς ὢν ἐκ τῆς Ἰούδα φυλῆς εὑρὼν χλαμύδα βασίλειον ἐκ χρυσοῦ μὲν πᾶσαν ὑφασμένην, μᾶζαν δὲ χρυσοῦ σταθμὸν ἕλκουσαν σίκλων διακοσίων καὶ δεινὸν ἡγησάμενος δ¹ κινδυνεύσας ηὕρατο κέρδος, τοῦτο τῆς ἰδίας χρείας ἀφελόμενος² δοῦναι φέρων τῷ θεῷ καὶ μὴ δεομένῳ, ὄρυγμα βαθὺ ποιήσας ἐν τῇ αὐτοῦ σκηνῇ κατώρυξεν εἰς τοῦτο, λήσειν³ νομίζων ὡς τοὺς συστρατιώτας οὕτως καὶ τὸν θεόν.

34 (11) Ἐκλήθη δὲ ὁ τόπος ἐν ᾧ στρατόπεδον ἐβάλετο Ἰησοῦς Γάλγαλα· σημαίνει δὲ τοῦτο ἐλευθέριον ὄνομα· διαβάντες γὰρ τὸν ποταμὸν ἐλευθέρους ἑαυτοὺς ἤδη ἀπό τε τῶν Αἰγυπτίων καὶ τῆς ἐν τῇ ἐρήμῳ ταλαιπωρίας ἐγίνωσκον.

---

¹ Ernesti: εἰ ὁ ML: εἰς ὁ RO.
² Niese suspects a lacuna after ἀφελόμενος.
³ ME: λήσεσθαι rell.

ᵃ In the reign of Ahab, 1 Kings xvi. 34. Josephus, however, in the sequel forgets to recount the incident; the verse which records it being apparently absent from the Greek Bible which he was then following (*A.* viii. 318 note).

ᵇ Heb. " Achan, son of Carmi, son of Zabdi " : the form Achar appears here in the lxx, as also in the Heb. in 1 Chron.

regarded by the Deity, but in the sequel we shall recount the calamity which it entailed.[a]

(9) An immense quantity of silver and gold, as also of brass, was amassed from the captured town, none having violated the decrees nor looted these things for his private profit : nay, they abstained therefrom as from objects already consecrated to God. And Joshua delivered them to the priests to lay up in the treasuries. Such, then, was the end of Jericho. Consecration of the booty to God.

(10) But a certain Achar, son of Zebedee,[b] of the tribe of Judah, having found a royal mantle all woven of gold and a mass of gold of the weight of two hundred shekels,[c] and thinking it cruel that he should deprive himself of the enjoyment of lucre, which he had won at his own peril, and bring and offer it to God, who had no need of it, dug a deep hole in his tent and buried his treasure therein, thinking to elude alike his comrades in arms and withal the eye of God. The sin of Achar. Jos. vii. 1.

(11) The place where Joshua had established his camp was called Galgala.[d] This name signifies "freedom"[e]; for, having crossed the river, they felt themselves henceforth free both from the Egyptians and from their miseries in the desert. Joshua at Gilgal. Jos. v. 9.

ii. 7. Moreover the etymological word-play in the Hebrew of Jos. vii. 25 presupposes the form Achar ('*Aḥar*).

[c] Heb. " a mantle of Shinar (*i.e.* Babylonia) and 200 shekels of silver and a wedge of gold of 50 shekels weight " (Jos. vii. 21).   [d] So LXX : Heb. Gilgal.

[e] One of the historian's " free " etymologies, but perhaps taken over from others (Weill quotes the translation ἐλευθερία in Theodoret i. p. 199). Scripture derives the name Gilgal from the verb *galal* (" to roll ") and adds the explanation " This day have I rolled away the reproach of Egypt from off you " (by the reinstitution of the practice of circumcision).

35 (12) Μετὰ δ' ὀλίγας ἡμέρας τῆς Ἱεριχοῦντος
συμφορᾶς πέμπει τρισχιλίους ὁπλίτας Ἰησοῦς εἰς[1]
Ναϊὰν[2] πόλιν ὑπὲρ τῆς Ἱεριχοῦντος κειμένην
αἱρήσοντας, οἳ συμβαλόντων αὐτοῖς τῶν Ναϊητῶν
τραπέντες ἀποβάλλουσιν ἄνδρας ἓξ καὶ τριάκοντα.
36 τοῦτ' ἀγγελθὲν τοῖς Ἰσραηλίταις λύπην τε μεγάλην
καὶ δεινὴν ἐποίησεν ἀθυμίαν, οὐ κατὰ τὸ οἰκεῖον
τῶν ἀπολωλότων, καίτοι γε πάντων ἀνδρῶν
ἀγαθῶν καὶ σπουδῆς ἀξίων διεφθαρμένων, ἀλλὰ
37 κατὰ ἀπόγνωσιν· πιστεύοντες γὰρ ἤδη τῆς γῆς
ἐγκρατεῖς εἶναι καὶ σῶον ἕξειν ἐν ταῖς μάχαις τὸν
στρατὸν οὕτως τοῦ θεοῦ προϋπεσχημένου, τε-
θαρρηκότας παραδόξως ἑώρων τοὺς πολεμίους·
καὶ σάκκους ἐπενδύντες ταῖς στολαῖς δι' ὅλης
ἡμέρας ἐν δακρύοις ἦσαν καὶ πένθει, τροφῆς οὐδεμίαν ἐπιζήτησιν ποιούμενοι, μειζόνως δὲ τὸ
συμβεβηκὸς εἶχον ἀχθόμενοι.
38 (13) Βλέπων δὲ οὕτως ὁ Ἰησοῦς τήν τε στρατιὰν
καταπεπληγυῖαν καὶ περὶ τῶν ὅλων πονηρὰν ἤδη
τὴν ἐλπίδα λαμβάνουσαν παρρησίαν λαμβάνει πρὸς
39 τὸν θεόν· '' ἡμεῖς '' γὰρ εἶπεν '' οὐχ ὑπ' αὐθαδείας
προήχθημεν ὥστε ταύτην ὑπάγεσθαι τοῖς ὅπλοις
τὴν γῆν, ἀλλὰ Μωυσέος τοῦ σοῦ δούλου πρὸς τοῦθ'
ἡμᾶς ἐξεγείραντος, ᾧ διὰ πολλῶν τεκμηρίων
ἐπηγγέλλου κτήσασθαι παρέξειν ἡμῖν τήνδε τὴν
γῆν καὶ τὸν στρατὸν ἡμῶν ἀεὶ τῶν πολεμίων
40 ποιήσειν τοῖς ὅπλοις κρείττονα. τινὰ μὲν οὖν κατὰ
τὰς ὑποσχέσεις ἡμῖν ἀπήντησε τὰς σάς, νῦν δὲ
παρὰ δόξαν ἐπταικότες καὶ τῆς δυνάμεώς τινας
ἀποβαλόντες ἐπὶ τούτοις ὡς οὐ βεβαίων τῶν παρὰ

---

[1] om. Ernesti.   [2] Ἀϊὰν E Lat.: v.l. Ἀν(ν)αν.

---

[a] Heb. Ai (Ἀἱ), lxx Γαί. The form Ναϊά has arisen out of

178

(12) A few days after the downfall of Jericho, Joshua sent three thousand men-at-arms to the city of Naia,[a] situated above Jericho, to capture it. These, being opposed by the Naietans, were routed and lost six-and-thirty men. The announcement of this news to the Israelites caused them great grief and dire despondency, not so much because of their kinship to the fallen, albeit they were all valiant and worthy men [b] who had perished, as from utter despair. For, believing themselves already masters of the country and that they would keep their army unscathed in the combats, even as God had promised heretofore, they now beheld their enemies unexpectedly emboldened. And so, putting sackcloth upon their apparel, they passed a whole day in tears and lamentation, without one thought for food, and in their vexation unduly magnified what had befallen.

(13) Seeing his army thus cast down and a prey to gloomy forebodings concerning the whole campaign, Joshua frankly appealed to God. " It was," he said, " from no confidence in ourselves that we were induced to subjugate this land by arms : nay, it was Moses, thy servant, who incited us thereto, he to whom by many tokens thou didst promise to vouchsafe to us to win this land, and ever to ensure to our army superiority in battle over our foes. And indeed some things have befallen in accordance with thy promises ; but now, having suffered unlooked-for defeat, having lost some of our force, we are distressed at these things, which make thy

'Aïá—attested by the Latin version and perhaps original—through duplication of the ν in the accusative—τὴν (Ν)αΐαν ; modern Greek supplies many parallels, e.g. Νίδα ="Ιδα.

[b] Amplification, for which there is Rabbinical authority (Weill).

σοῦ καὶ ὧν προεῖπε Μωυσῆς ἀχθόμεθα, καὶ χεῖρον
ἡ τῶν μελλόντων ἐλπὶς ἡμᾶς ἀνιᾷ τῇ πρώτῃ πείρᾳ
41 τοιαύτῃ συντυχόντας. ἀλλὰ σύ, δέσποτα, δύναμις
γάρ σοι τούτων ἴασιν εὑρεῖν, τό τε παρὸν ἡμῶν
λυπηρὸν νίκην παρασχόμενος καὶ τὸ περὶ τῶν
αὖθις δύσελπι διακείμενον οὕτως τῆς διανοίας
ἔξελε."
42 (14) Ταῦτα μὲν Ἰησοῦς ἐπὶ στόμα πεσὼν ἠρώτα
τὸν θεόν· χρηματίσαντος δὲ ἀνίστασθαι τοῦ θεοῦ
καὶ καθαίρειν τὸν στρατὸν μιάσματος ἐν αὐτῷ
γεγονότος κλοπῆς τε τῶν καθιερωμένων αὐτῷ
χρημάτων τετολμημένης, διὰ γὰρ ταῦτα τὴν νῦν
αὐτοῖς ἧτταν συμπεσεῖν, ἀναζητηθέντος δὲ τοῦ
δράσαντος καὶ κολασθέντος νίκην αὐτοῖς ἀεὶ περι-
έσεσθαι[1] τῶν πολεμίων, φράζει ταῦτα πρὸς τὸν
43 λαὸν Ἰησοῦς, καὶ καλέσας Ἐλεάζαρον τὸν ἀρχιερέα
καὶ τοὺς ἐν τέλει κατὰ φυλὴν ἐκλήρου. τούτου δὲ
τὸ τετολμημένον ἐκ τῆς Ἰούδα φυλῆς δηλοῦντος
κατὰ φατρίας πάλιν ταύτης προτίθησι τὸν κλῆρον.
τὸ δ' ἀληθὲς τοῦ κακουργήματος περὶ τὴν Ἀχάρου
44 συγγένειαν ηὑρίσκετο. κατ' ἄνδρα δὲ τῆς ἐξετά-
σεως γινομένης λαμβάνουσι τὸν Ἄχαρον· ὁ δ' οὐκ
ἔχων ἔξαρνος εἶναι, τοῦ θεοῦ δεινῶς αὐτὸν ἐκ-
περιελθόντος, ὡμολόγει τε τὴν κλοπὴν καὶ τὰ
φώρια παρῆγεν εἰς μέσον. καὶ οὗτος μὲν εὐθὺς
ἀναιρεθεὶς ἐν νυκτὶ ταφῆς ἀτίμου καὶ καταδίκῳ
πρεπούσης τυγχάνει.

_____
[1] conj. Niese: περισώζεσθαι RO: πορίζεσθαι rell.: proveniret
Lat.

_____
[a] Jos. vii. 25, " And all Israel stoned him with stones [and
they burned them with fire and (Targum ' after that they
had ') stoned them with stones]." The bracketed words,
absent from the lxx, are confused and the addition of later

promises and those predictions of Moses appear
unsure ; and yet more sorely are we pained at the
thought of what the future holds in store, having
met with such issue to our first assault. But do
thou, Lord, since thou hast power to find healing
for these ills, dispel our present affliction by vouch-
safing us victory and thus banish from our mind our
deep despondency concerning the future."

(14) Thus did Joshua, prostrated upon his face, ^{Discovery}
make petition to God. And the response came from ^{and death}
God, that he should arise and purge the army of the ^{of the}
pollution that had been wrought therein and of a ^{sinner Achar.}
daring theft of objects consecrated to Him, since ^{Jos. vii. 6, 10 ff.}
that was the cause of their recent defeat ; but were
the culprit sought out and punished, they would for
ever be assured of victory over their enemies. All
this Joshua repeated to the people and, summoning
Eleazar the high priest and the magistrates, he
proceeded to draw lots for the several tribes. And
when this revealed that the sacrilege issued from
the tribe of Judah, he again had lots drawn for its
several clans ; and the true story of the crime was
found to rest with the family of Achar. The inquiry
being pursued further man by man, they caught
Achar. And he, unable to make denial, being thus
shrewdly circumvented by God, avowed his theft
and produced the stolen goods before all. He was
straightway put to death and at nightfall was given
the ignominious burial proper to the condemned.[a]

editors. As M. Weill points out, Josephus doubtless adds
the burial, unrecorded in Scripture, to indicate that the
Mosaic law on stoning, which he has previously reported
(iv. 202), was exactly followed ; but he may already have
found here some addition in his Biblical text which he interpreted as an allusion to burial.

45 (15) Ἰησοῦς δὲ ἁγνίσας τὸν στρατὸν ἐξῆγεν ἐπὶ
τὴν Ναϊὰν αὐτούς[1] καὶ νυκτὸς τὰ περὶ τὴν πόλιν
ἐνέδραις προλοχίσας ὑπὸ τὸν ὄρθρον συμβάλλει
τοῖς πολεμίοις. τῶν δὲ μετὰ θάρσους[2] αὐτοῖς διὰ
τὴν προτέραν νίκην ἐπιόντων ὑποχωρεῖν προσποιη-
σάμενος ἕλκει τῷ τρόπῳ τούτῳ μακρὰν αὐτοὺς τῆς
πόλεως διώκειν οἰομένους καὶ ὡς ἐπὶ νίκῃ κατα-
46 φρονοῦντας. ἔπειτ' ἀναστρέψας τὴν δύναμιν κατὰ
πρόσωπον αὐτοῖς ποιεῖ, σημεῖά τε δοὺς ἃ πρὸς τοὺς
ἐν ταῖς ἐνέδραις συνετέτακτο κἀκείνους ἐπὶ τὴν
μάχην ἐξανίστησιν. οἱ δ' εἰσεπήδων εἰς τὴν πόλιν
τῶν ἔνδον περὶ τοῖς τείχεσιν ὄντων, ἐνίων δὲ καὶ
πρὸς θέαν τῶν ἔξω τὴν γνώμην περισπωμένων.
47 καὶ οἱ μὲν τὴν πόλιν ᾕρουν καὶ πάντας τοὺς ἐντυγ-
χάνοντας ἔκτεινον, Ἰησοῦς δὲ τοὺς προσελθόντας
εἰς χεῖρας βιασάμενος φυγεῖν τρέπεται, συνελαυνό-
μενοι δὲ ὡς εἰς ἀκέραιον τὴν πόλιν ἐπεὶ καὶ ταύτην
ἐχομένην[3] ἑώρων καὶ καταπιμπραμένην ὁμοῦ
γυναιξὶ καὶ τέκνοις κατέλαβον, διὰ τῶν ἀγρῶν
ἦσαν[4] σκεδασθέντες[5] ἀμύνειν αὐτοῖς ὑπὸ μονώσεως
48 οὐ δυνάμενοι. τοιαύτης δὲ τῆς συμφορᾶς τοὺς
Ναϊτιανοὺς καταλαβούσης, παίδων τε ὄχλος ἑάλω
καὶ γυναικῶν καὶ θεραπείας καὶ τῆς ἄλλης ἀπο-
σκευῆς ἄπειρόν τι πλῆθος, ἀγέλας τε βοσκημάτων
ἔλαβον οἱ Ἑβραῖοι καὶ χρήματα πολλά, καὶ γὰρ
πλούσιον ἦν τὸ χωρίον, καὶ ταῦτα πάντα τοῖς
στρατιώταις Ἰησοῦς διένειμεν ἐν Γαλγάλοις γενόμενος.
49 (16) Γαβαωνῖται δὲ κατοικοῦντες ἔγγιστα τοῖς

---

[1] ed. pr.: αὐτὸς codd.: om. E Lat.   [2] θράσους ME.
[3] οἰχομένην ROE.   [4] ἦεσαν M : ἦσαν SPL: om. rell.
[5] + καὶ ROE.

(15) Joshua, having purified his army, now led Conquest
of Naia.
Jos. viii. 3.
them out against Naia, and, after posting ambus-
cades during the night all about the town,[a] at daybreak joined battle with the enemy. And when
these advanced against them with an assurance begotten of their former victory, Joshua, feigning a
retreat, drew them in this way to a distance from
the town, they imagining themselves in pursuit of a beaten
foe and being disdainful of them in anticipation of
victory. Then, turning his forces about, he made
them face their pursuers and, giving the prearranged
signals to those in ambush, roused them also to the
fight. These flung themselves into the town, the
occupants of which were around the ramparts, some
wholly engrossed in watching their friends outside.[b]
So while they took the town and slew all whom
they encountered, Joshua broke the ranks of his
adversaries and forced them to flee. Driven in a
body to the town which they supposed to be intact,
when they saw that it too was taken and found that
it was in flames, along with their wives and children,
they scattered throughout the country, incapable
through their isolation of offering resistance. Such
being the fate that befell the Naietans, a crowd of
children, women and slaves was taken, beside an
immense mass of material. The Hebrews captured
moreover herds of cattle and money in abundance,
for the region was rich, and all this Joshua distributed to his soldiers, while he was at Galgala.

(16) Now the Gabaonites,[c] who lived quite close

---

[a] The Greek is modelled on Thuc. ii. 81.

[b] Amplification ; according to Jos. viii. 17 not a man had
been left in the town.

[c] So LXX (Γαβαών) : Heb. " Gibeon."

Ἱεροσολύμοις τά τε τοῖς Ἱεριχουντίοις συμβε-
βηκότα πάθη καὶ τὰ τοῖς Ναϊτίνοις ὁρῶντες καὶ
πρὸς σφᾶς μεταβήσεσθαι τὸ δεινὸν ὑπονοοῦντες,
Ἰησοῦν μὲν παρακαλεῖν οὐ διέγνωσαν· οὐδὲ[1] γὰρ
τεύξεσθαί τινος τῶν μετρίων ὑπελάμβανον ἐπ᾽
ὀλέθρῳ τοῦ Χαναναίων ἔθνους παντὸς πολεμοῦντος
50 αὐτούς· Κεφηρίτας δὲ καὶ Καριαθιαριμίτας γεί-
τονας ὄντας αὐτοῖς ἐπὶ συμμαχίαν παρεκάλουν,
οὐδ᾽ αὐτοὺς διαφεύξεσθαι τὸν κίνδυνον λέγοντες,
εἰ φθάσαιεν αὐτοὶ ληφθέντες ὑπὸ τῶν Ἰσραηλιτῶν,
συνασπίσαντας δὲ αὐτοῖς διέγνωσαν[2] διαδρᾶναι τὴν
51 δύναμιν αὐτῶν. προσδεξαμένων δὲ τοὺς λόγους
αὐτῶν πέμπουσι πρέσβεις πρὸς Ἰησοῦν φιλίαν
σπεισομένους οὓς μάλιστα τῶν πολιτῶν ἐδοκίμαζον
52 ἱκανοὺς πρᾶξαι τὰ συμφέροντα τῷ πλήθει. οἱ δὲ
ὁμολογεῖν αὐτοὺς Χαναναίους ἐπισφαλὲς ἡγούμενοι,
διαφεύξεσθαι·τὸν διὰ τοῦτο κίνδυνον ὑπολαμβάνοντες, εἰ λέγοιεν αὐτοὺς μὴ προσήκειν κατὰ μηδὲν
Χαναναίοις ἀλλὰ πορρωτάτω τούτων κατοικεῖν,
ἥκειν τε κατὰ πύστιν[3] τῆς ἀρετῆς αὐτοῦ πολλὴν
ἀνύσαντες ὁδὸν ἔφασκον καὶ τεκμήριον τοῦ λόγου
53 τούτου τὸ σχῆμα ὑπεδείκνυον· τὰς γὰρ ἐσθῆτας
καινὰς ὅτε ἐξῄεσαν οὔσας ὑπὸ τοῦ χρόνου τῆς
ὁδοιπορίας αὐτοῖς τετρῖφθαι· τρυχίνας γὰρ εἰς τὸ
ταῦτα πιστοῦσθαι πρὸς αὐτῶν ἐπίτηδες ἔλαβον.
54 στάντες οὖν εἰς μέσους ἔλεγον, ὡς πεμφθεῖεν ὑπὸ
τῶν Γαβαωνιτῶν καὶ τῶν περιοίκων πόλεων
πλεῖστον ἀπεχουσῶν τῆσδε τῆς γῆς ποιησόμενοι

---

[1] Dindorf: οὔτε codd.
[2] possent Lat.: hence I should read ἂν (διέγνωσαν may
have come into the text from § 49).
[3] Bekker: πίστιν codd.

to Jerusalem, seeing the disasters that had befallen
the inhabitants of Jericho and of Naia and suspecting
that they too would be visited by this dire fate, yet
resolved not to implore mercy of Joshua; for they
did not think to obtain any tolerable terms from a
belligerent whose aim was the extermination of the
whole race of the Canaanites. But they invited the
Kephêrites and the Kariathiarimites,[a] their neighbours, to make alliance with them, telling them that
neither would they escape this peril, should they
themselves have first been conquered by the Israelites, whereas if they united their arms with theirs
they might evade their violence.[b] These overtures
being accepted, the Gabaonites sent ambassadors to
Joshua to make a league of amity, choosing those of
their citizens whom they judged most capable of acting in the interests of the people. And these, deeming it hazardous to avow themselves Canaanites, and
thinking to escape the peril of so doing by asserting
that they had no connexion whatever with the
Canaanites but lived very far away from them, declared that it was the tidings of his valour which
had brought them thither, after accomplishing a
long journey, and in proof of this statement they
pointed to their apparel. Their garments, quite new
when they set out, had (they said) been worn out
by the length of their journey; for, to get them to
believe this story, they had purposely clothed themselves in rags. So, standing amidst the host, they
said that they had been sent by the Gabaonites
and the neighbouring cities, very remote from that

---

[a] Chephirah (LXX κεφειρά) and Kiriath-jearim (πόλεις Ἰαρείν)
are mentioned in Jos. ix. 18 as allied with Gibeon, along with
another city (Beeroth) ignored by Josephus.

[b] Text doubtful.

πρὸς αὐτοὺς φιλίαν ἐφ᾽ αἷς πάτριον αὐτοῖς ἐστι
συνθήκαις· μαθόντες γὰρ ἐκ θεοῦ χάριτος καὶ δωρεᾶς
τὴν Χαναναίων αὐτοῖς γῆν κτήσασθαι δεδόσθαι
τούτοις τ᾽ ἔλεγον ἤδεσθαι καὶ πολίτας ἀξιοῦν
55 αὐτῶν γενέσθαι. καὶ οἱ μὲν ταῦτα λέγοντες καὶ
ἐπιδεικνύντες τὰ τεκμήρια τῆς ὁδοιπορίας παρεκάλουν ἐπὶ συνθήκας καὶ φιλίαν τοὺς Ἑβραίους·
Ἰησοῦς δὲ πιστεύσας οἷς ἔλεγον, ὡς οὐκ εἰσὶ τοῦ
Χαναναίων ἔθνους, ποιεῖται πρὸς αὐτοὺς φιλίαν,
καὶ Ἐλεάζαρος ὁ ἀρχιερεὺς μετὰ τῆς γερουσίας
ὄμνυσιν ἕξειν τε φίλους καὶ συμμάχους καὶ μηδὲν
μοχλεύσεσθαι κατ᾽ αὐτῶν ἄδικον, τοῖς ὅρκοις
56 ἐπισυναινέσαντος τοῦ πλήθους. καὶ οἱ μὲν ὧν
ἤθελον τυχόντες ἐξ ἀπάτης ἀπήεσαν πρὸς αὐτούς.
Ἰησοῦς δὲ τῆς Χαναναίας στρατεύσας εἰς τὴν
ὑπώρειον καὶ μαθὼν οὐ πόρρω τῶν Ἱεροσολύμων
τοὺς Γαβαωνίτας κατῳκημένους καὶ τοῦ γένους
ὄντας τῶν Χαναναίων, μεταπεμψάμενος αὐτῶν
57 τοὺς ἐν τέλει τῆς ἀπάτης αὐτοῖς ἐνεκάλει. τῶν δ᾽
οὐκ ἄλλην ἀφορμὴν σωτηρίας ἔχειν ἢ ταύτην προ-
φασιζομένων καὶ διὰ τοῦτ᾽ ἐπ᾽ αὐτὴν ἐξ ἀνάγκης
καταφυγεῖν συγκαλεῖ τὸν ἀρχιερέα Ἐλεάζαρον καὶ
τὴν γερουσίαν, καὶ δημοσίους αὐτοὺς δικαιούντων
ποιεῖν ἐπὶ τῷ μὴ παραβῆναι τὸν ὅρκον ἀποδείκνυσιν[1]
εἶναι τοιούτους. καὶ οἱ μὲν τῆς καταλαβούσης
αὐτοὺς συμφορᾶς τοιαύτην φυλακὴν καὶ ἀσφάλειαν
εὕραντο.
58 (17) Τοῦ δὲ τῶν Ἱεροσολυμιτῶν βασιλέως χαλεπῶς φέροντος ἐπὶ τῷ μετατάξασθαι πρὸς τὸν

---

[1] ἀποδεικνύουσιν ROML.

---

[a] Or " engineer," " trump up " (literally " prise up ").

present land, to make alliance with them on such terms as were customary with their fathers ; for, having learnt that by the grace and bounty of God the land of the Canaanites had been granted them for their possession, they rejoiced thereat and craved to become their fellow-citizens. With these words, and withal displaying the tokens of their travel, they besought the Hebrews to make a covenant and league of amity with them. Thereupon Joshua, believing what they said, that they were not of the race of the Canaanites, made a league with them ; and Eleazar the high priest, along with the council of elders, swore to hold them as friends and allies and to contrive *a* no iniquity against them, and the people ratified the oaths. So the envoys, having attained their end by guile, returned to their own people ; but Joshua, having marched into the foothills of Canaan and learnt that the Gabaonites lived not far from Jerusalem and were of the stock of the Canaanites, sent for their magistrates and upbraided them for this fraud. When these alleged that they had no other means of salvation save that, and that they had therefore perforce had recourse to it, Joshua convoked the high priest Eleazar ·and the council ; and, acting upon their judgement that they should be made public slaves,*b* so as to avoid violation of the oath, he appointed them to those functions. Thus did these people, when confronted with calamity, find protection and security for themselves.

(17) But the king of the Jerusalemites,*c* indignant that the Gabaonites should have passed over to the

b "Hewers of wood and drawers of water for the congregation," Jos. ix. 27.
c Named Adonizedek, Jos. x. 1.

Ἰησοῦν τοὺς Γαβαωνίτας καὶ τοὺς τῶν πλησίον
ἐθνῶν παρακαλέσαντος βασιλέας συνάρασθαι τῷ
κατ' αὐτῶν πολέμῳ, ὡς τούτους τε εἶδον παρόντας
σὺν αὐτῷ, τέσσαρες δὲ ἦσαν, οἱ Γαβαωνῖται καὶ
στρατοπεδευσαμένους ἐπί τινι πηγῇ τῆς πόλεως
οὐκ ἄπωθεν παρασκευάζεσθαι πρὸς πολιορκίαν,
59 ἐπεκαλοῦντο σύμμαχον Ἰησοῦν· ἐν τούτοις γὰρ ἦν
αὐτοῖς τὰ πράγματα, ὡς ὑπὸ μὲν τούτων[1] ἀπολεῖ-
σθαι προσδοκᾶν, ὑπὸ δὲ τῶν ἐπ' ὀλέθρῳ τοῦ Χαναναίων γένους στρατευσάντων σωθήσεσθαι διὰ τὴν
60 γενομένην φιλίαν ὑπολαμβάνειν. καὶ Ἰησοῦς παν-
στρατιᾷ σπεύσας ἐπὶ τὴν βοήθειαν καὶ δι' ἡμέρας
καὶ νυκτὸς ἀνύσας ὄρθριος προσμίγνυσι τοῖς
πολεμίοις καὶ τραπεῖσιν εἵπετο διώκων διὰ χωρίων
ἐπικλινῶν, Βήθωρα καλεῖται. ἔνθα καὶ τὴν τοῦ
θεοῦ συνεργίαν ἔμαθεν ἐπισημήναντος αὐτοῦ βρονταῖς τε καὶ κεραυνῶν ἀφέσει καὶ χαλάζης καταφορᾷ
61 μείζονος τῆς συνήθους· ἔτι γε μὴν καὶ τὴν ἡμέραν
αὐξηθῆναι πλέον, ὡς ἂν μὴ καταλαβοῦσα νὺξ
ἐπίσχῃ τὸ τῶν Ἑβραίων πρόθυμον, συνέπεσεν,
ὥστε καὶ λαμβάνει τοὺς βασιλέας Ἰησοῦς ἔν τινι
κρυπτομένους σπηλαίῳ κατὰ Μακχίδα καὶ κολάζει
πάντας. ὅτι δὲ τὸ μῆκος τῆς ἡμέρας ἐπέδωκε τότε
καὶ τοῦ συνήθους ἐπλεόνασε, δηλοῦται διὰ τῶν
ἀνακειμένων ἐν τῷ ἱερῷ γραμμάτων.
62 (18) Κατεστραμμένων δ' οὕτως τῶν περὶ τοὺς
βασιλέας, οἳ τοὺς Γαβαωνίτας πολεμήσοντες ἐστράτευσαν, ἐπανῄει πάλιν τῆς Χαναναίας ἐπὶ τὴν

---

[1] M : τῶν τοιούτων RO : τῶν οἰκείων SPL (Lat. suis).

---

[a] Bibl. Beth-horon ; the pass was the scene of many later

side of Joshua, called upon the kings of the neighbouring nations to join him in a campaign against
them ; whereat the Gabaonites, having seen these
monarchs come with him, four in number, and en-
camp by a spring not far from their city, preparing
to besiege them, appealed to Joshua for aid. For
such was their case, that from their countrymen
they could await but destruction, while from those
who had taken the field for the extermination of the
Canaanite race they looked for salvation, thanks to
the alliance which had been concluded. Joshua,
with his whole army, sped to their assistance and,
marching all day and night, at early dawn fell upon
the foe, routed them and followed in pursuit down
the slopes of the region called Bēthōra.[a] There too
he was given to know of God's co-operation, manifested by thunder-claps, the discharge of thunder-
bolts and the descent of hail of more than ordinary
magnitude. Aye and moreover it befell that the
day was prolonged, to the end that night should
not overtake them and check the Hebrews' ardour ;
insomuch that Joshua both captured the kings, who
were hiding in a cave at Macchida,[b] and punished all
their host. That the length of the day was increased
on that occasion and surpassed the customary
measure, is attested by Scriptures that are laid up
in the temple.[c]

(18) Having thus overthrown that league of kings
who had set out to war against the Gabaonites,
Joshua remounted into the hill-country of Canaan ;

Defeat of
the league
of kings.
The
lengthened
day.
Jos. x. 1.

battles, notably of the rout of a Roman legion at the opening
of the Jewish War (B.J. ii. 546).

[b] Bibl. Makkedah (Maḳḳedah), LXX Μαχηδά, Jos. x. 10, 16:
perhaps el-Mughar (" the cavern ") S.W. of Ekron.

[c] Cf. iii. 38, iv. 303 with notes.

ὀρεινὴν Ἰησοῦς καὶ πολὺν τῶν ἐν αὐτῇ φόνον
ἐργασάμενος καὶ λείαν λαβὼν παρῆν εἰς τὸ ἐν
63 Γαλγάλοις στρατόπεδον. τοῦ δὲ περὶ τῆς τῶν
Ἑβραίων ἀρετῆς λόγου πολλοῦ φοιτῶντος εἰς τοὺς
περιοίκους κατάπληξις εἶχε τοὺς ἀκούοντας τὸ τῶν
ἀπολωλότων πλῆθος, καὶ στρατεύουσιν ἐπ' αὐτοὺς
οἱ περὶ Λίβανον ὄρος βασιλεῖς ὄντες Χαναναῖοι καὶ
οἱ ἐν τοῖς πεδίοις τῶν Χαναναίων Παλαιστίνους
προσλαβόντες στρατοπεδεύουσι[1] πρὸς Βηρώθῃ πόλει
Γαλιλαίας τῆς ἄνω Κεδέσης οὐ πόρρω· Γαλιλαίων
64 δ' ἐστὶ καὶ τοῦτο τὸ χωρίον. τοῦ δὲ στρατοῦ
παντὸς ὁπλιτῶν μὲν ἦσαν μυριάδες τριάκοντα,
μύριοι δ' ἱππεῖς καὶ ἅρματα δισμύρια. καταπλήττει δὲ τὸ πλῆθος τῶν πολεμίων αὐτόν τε
Ἰησοῦν καὶ τοὺς Ἰσραηλίτας καὶ πρὸς τὴν ἐλπίδα
τοῦ κρείττονος εὐλαβεστέρως εἶχον δι' ὑπερβολὴν
65 τοῦ δέους. τοῦ θεοῦ δ' ἐξονειδίσαντος αὐτοῖς τὸν
φόβον καὶ τί[2] πλέον τῆς παρ' αὐτοῦ βοηθείας
ποθοῦσιν, ὑποσχομένου τε νικήσειν τοὺς ἐχθροὺς
καὶ κελεύσαντος τούς τε ἵππους ἀχρήστους ποιῆσαι
καὶ τὰ ἅρματα πυρῶσαι, θαρσαλέος πρὸς τὰς ὑποσχέσεις τοῦ θεοῦ γενόμενος ἐξώρμησεν ἐπὶ τοὺς
66 πολεμίους, καὶ διὰ πέμπτης ἡμέρας ἐπ' αὐτοὺς
ἐλθὼν συνάπτει, καὶ καρτερὰ μάχη γίνεται καὶ
φόνος κρείττων πίστεως παρὰ τοῖς ἀκρωμένοις.
διώκων δ' ἐπὶ πλεῖστον ἐξῆλθε καὶ πᾶν τὸ στρά-

---

[1] veneruntque Lat.   [2] εἰ MSPL Lat.

[a] The Greek, here and throughout, has " Palestinians."
[b] Jos. xi. 5, " at the waters of Merom " (lxx Μαρρών), com-

there he made great carnage of the inhabitants and captured booty, and so returned to the camp at Galgala. The fame of the Hebrews' valour being now mightily noised abroad among the neighbouring peoples, consternation seized them on hearing of those multitudes of slain ; and there set off to war against them the kings of the region of Mount Libanus, who were Canaanites, and the Canaanites of the plains, joined by the Philistines,[a] and established their camp at Bērothe,[b] a city of upper Galilee, not far from Kedese,[c] another place within the Galilean area. Their entire army amounted to 300,000 men-at-arms, 10,000 horsemen, and 20,000 chariots.[d] This host of enemies dismayed both Joshua himself and the Israelites, and in the excess of their fear they scarce durst hope for success. But God rebuked them for their terror and for craving aught beyond His aid, promising them victory over their foes and bidding them put their horses out of action and to burn the chariots. Emboldened by these promises of God, Joshua set forth against the enemy, and on the fifth day [e] came upon them and engaged them : a fierce combat ensued and a carnage such that the tale of it would outrun belief. Advancing very far in pursuit, Joshua destroyed the

monly but incorrectly (G. A. Smith) identified with the small lake *Huleh*, north of the Lake of Tiberias. The site of the battle is unknown ; Josephus seems to identify it with one of the towns which he fortified during the war with Rome and which he calls elsewhere Mero(th) or Ameroth (*B.J.* ii. 573, iii. 39, *Vita* 188).

[c] Kedesh Naphtali, N.W. of the lake *Huleh*.

[d] The numbers are imaginary : Scripture speaks only of " much people, even as the sand that is upon the seashore in multitude, with horses and chariots very many."

[e] Amplification.

τευμα τῶν ἐχθρῶν πλὴν ὀλίγων διέφθειρε, καὶ οἱ
67 βασιλεῖς πάντες ἔπεσον, ὥστε τῶν ἀνθρώπων
ἐπιλελοιπότων πρὸς τὸ κτείνεσθαι τοὺς ἵππους
Ἰησοῦς αὐτῶν ἀνῄρει καὶ τὰ ἅρματα ἐνεπίμπρα,
τήν τε χώραν ἐπ' ἀδείας διεπορεύετο μηδενὸς
τολμῶντος εἰς μάχην ἐπεξελθεῖν, ἀλλὰ πολιορκίᾳ
τὰς πόλεις αἱρῶν καὶ πᾶν ὅ τι λάβοι φονεύων.
68 (19) Ἔτος δὲ πέμπτον ἤδη παρεληλύθει καὶ
Χαναναίων οὐκέτ' οὐδεὶς ὑπολέλειπτο πλὴν εἰ μή
τινες ὀχυρότητι τειχῶν διέφυγον. Ἰησοῦς δ' ἐκ
τῶν Γαλγάλων ἀναστρατοπεδεύσας εἰς τὴν ὄρειον[1]
ἱστᾷ τὴν ἱερὰν σκηνὴν κατὰ Σιλοῦν πόλιν, ἐπιτή-
δειον γὰρ ἐδόκει τὸ χωρίον διὰ κάλλος, ἕως οἰκο-
69 δομεῖν ναὸν αὐτοῖς τὰ πράγματα παράσχῃ.[2] καὶ
χωρήσας ἐντεῦθεν ἐπὶ Σικίμων σὺν ἅπαντι τῷ λαῷ
βωμόν τε ἵστησιν ὅπου προεῖπε Μωυσῆς καὶ
νείμας τὴν στρατιὰν ἐπὶ μὲν τῷ Γαριζεῖ ὄρει τὴν
ἡμίσειαν ἵστησιν, ἐπὶ δὲ τῷ Ἡβήλῳ[3] τὴν ἡμίσειαν,
ἐν ᾧ καὶ ὁ βωμός,[4] καὶ τὸ Λευιτικὸν καὶ τοὺς
70 ἱερέας. θύσαντες δὲ καὶ ἀρὰς ποιησάμενοι καὶ
ταύτας ἐπὶ τῷ βωμῷ γεγραμμένας καταλιπόντες
εἰς τὴν Σιλοῦν ἀνέζευξαν.

[1] ὀρεινήν SPE.
[2] παράσχοι Niese.　　　　[3] Γηβήλῳ ML.
[4] E: βωμός ἐστι (conj. ἔστη Niese) codd.

[a] Scripture makes no such exception: "they smote them
until they left them none remaining" (Jos. xi. 8).
[b] A calculation based apparently on Jos. xiv. 7 and 10,
where Caleb declares that he was 40 years old when sent
out as a spy and that he is now 85. Allowing 40 years for
the wanderings, this gives 5 years for the wars of Joshua.
Tradition, based on that same passage (together, it would

whole of the enemy's army, save for a few [a]—the kings all fell—in such wise that, when there were no more men to be killed, he slew their horses and burnt the chariots. He then overran the country unmolested, none daring to come out to give him battle; the cities too he captured by siege and massacred every creature that he caught.

(19) A fifth year had now passed away [b] and there was no longer any Canaanite left, save for such as had escaped through the solidity of their walls. So Joshua moved his camp up from Galgala into the hill country and set up the holy tabernacle at the city of Silo,[c] since that spot, by its beauty, seemed meet for it, until circumstances should permit them to build a temple. Proceeding thence to Sikima,[d] with all the people, he erected an altar at the spot foreordained by Moses,[e] and, dividing his army, posted one half of it on mount Garizin and the other half on Hēbēl,[f] whereon also stood the altar, along with the Levites and the priests. After sacrificing and pronouncing imprecations,[g] which they also left graven upon the altar, they returned to Silo.

Erection of the tabernacle at Shiloh and ceremonies at Sh'echem Jos. xviii. 1.

viii. 30 (LXX ix. 3).

seem, with Deut. ii. 14, which restricts the wanderings to 38 years) assigned 7 years to the conquest (Weill).

[c] Greek " Silous ": Heb. Shiloh, LXX Σηλώ.

[d] Bibl. Shechem, LXX Σίκιμα or Σύχεμ, mod. *Nablus*. Scripture places this episode earlier, immediately after the conquest of Ai—unnaturally, because northern Palestine had not then been conquered. Shechem is not mentioned in the Biblical account and there is reason to think that " in order to oppose Samaritan claims, the whole scene of the ceremony has (there) been transported from Shechem to Gilgal "(G. A. Cooke, *Camb. Bible*, on Jos. viii. 30).

[e] *A.* iv. 305.

[f] Bibl. Ebal, LXX Γαιβάλ : in *A.* iv. *l.c.* Βουλή.

[g] Prescribed in Deut. xxvii. ff. (*A.* iv. *l.c.*).

71 (20) Ἰησοῦς δ᾽ ἤδη γηραιὸς ὢν καὶ τὰς τῶν
Χαναναίων πόλεις ὁρῶν οὐκ εὐαλώτους ὑπό τε
τῆς τῶν χωρίων ἐν οἷς ἦσαν ὀχυρότητος καὶ τῆς
τῶν τειχῶν ἰσχύος, ἃ τῇ φυσικῇ τῶν πόλεων
πλεονεξίᾳ προσπεριβαλλόμενοι[1] προσεδόκων τοὺς
πολεμίους ἀφέξεσθαι πολιορκίας δι᾽ ἀπόγνωσιν τοῦ
72 λαβεῖν, καὶ γὰρ ἐπ᾽ ὀλέθρῳ τῷ ἑαυτῶν οἱ Χαναναῖοι
μαθόντες τοὺς Ἰσραηλίτας ποιησαμένους τὴν ἔξοδον
τὴν ἀπ᾽ Αἰγύπτου πρὸς τῷ τὰς πόλεις καρτερὰς
ποιεῖν ἐκεῖνον ἅπαντ᾽ ἦσαν τὸν χρόνον, συναγαγὼν
τὸν λαὸν εἰς τὴν Σιλοῦν ἐκκλησίαν παρήγγειλε.
73 καὶ σπουδῇ συνδραμόντων τά τε ἤδη κατωρθωμένα
καὶ τὰς γεγενημένας πράξεις, ὡς εἰσὶν ἄρισται καὶ
τοῦ θείου τοῦ παρασχόντος αὐτὰς ἄξιαι καὶ τῆς
ἀρετῆς τῶν νόμων οἷς κατακολουθοῦσιν ἔλεγε,
βασιλεῖς τε τριάκοντα καὶ ἕνα τολμήσαντας αὐτοῖς
εἰς χεῖρας ἐλθεῖν κεκρατῆσθαι δηλῶν, καὶ στρατιὰν
ὅση ποτὲ κατελπίσασα τῆς αὐτῶν δυνάμεως εἰς
μάχην συνῆψεν ἅπασαν διαφθαρεῖσαν, ὡς μηδὲ
74 γενεὰν αὐτοῖς ὑπολελεῖφθαι. τῶν δὲ πόλεων
ἐπειδήπερ αἱ μὲν ἑαλώκεσαν, πρὸς ἃς δὲ δεῖ
χρόνου καὶ μεγάλης πολιορκίας διὰ τὴν τῶν τειχῶν ὀχυρότητα καὶ τὴν ἐπὶ ταύτῃ τῶν οἰκητόρων
πεποίθησιν, ἠξίου τοὺς ἐκ τῆς περαίας τοῦ Ἰορδάνου συνεξορμήσαντας αὐτοῖς καὶ τῶν κινδύνων
συναραμένους ὄντας συγγενεῖς ἀπολύειν ἤδη πρὸς
τὰ οἰκεῖα, χάριν αὐτοῖς ὧν συνέκαμον ὁμο-
75 λογοῦντας, ἕνα τε κατὰ φυλὴν ἀρετῇ προύχειν
μαρτυρηθέντα πέμπειν, οἳ τὴν γῆν ἐκμετρησάμενοι

---

[1] προσεπιβαλλόμενοι ROE.

[a] Or perhaps " over-confident of (defeating) their forces."
[b] " Three men for each tribe," Jos. *l.c.*

(20) Joshua, being now old and seeing that the Joshua's
cities of the Canaanites were not lightly to be taken, address to the people
by reason both of the strength of the sites on which at Shiloh.
they stood and of the solidity of the walls with which Jos. xiii. 1.
the inhabitants had crowned the natural advantages
of their towns, reckoning that their enemies would
refrain from besieging what they despaired of capturing—for the Canaanites, since they heard that it
was for their destruction that the Israelites had made
their exodus from Egypt, had spent all that time in
fortifying their cities—Joshua, I say, called his xviii. 1.
people together to Silo and summoned an assembly.
Thither they sped with alacrity, and he spoke to
them of the successes already achieved and the
exploits accomplished, saying how fine they were
and worthy of the Deity who had vouchsafed them
and of the excellence of those laws which they were
following : he recalled how one and thirty kings who xii. 24.
had dared to close with them had been defeated,
and how that vast army which once, over-confident xi. 1 ff.
in its strength,[a] had joined battle with them, had
been entirely destroyed, insomuch that not one
family of theirs had survived. Of the cities too some
had been taken, but seeing that for the capture of
others there was need of time and great siege-works,
owing to the strength of their ramparts and the
confidence which this inspired in their inhabitants,
he deemed it right that those from beyond Jordan xxii. 1.
who had come to take part in their campaign and
had shared their dangers as kinsmen, should now
be dismissed to their homes with an expression of
thanks for their aid in the task. " Furthermore," xviii. 4.
said he, " we should send, one from each tribe,[b] men
of approved virtue, to measure out the land faith-

πιστῶς καὶ μηδὲν κακουργήσαντες[1] δηλώσουσιν
ἡμῖν ἀδόλως αὐτῆς τὸ μέγεθος.

76 (21) Καὶ Ἰησοῦς μὲν τούτους ποιησάμενος τοὺς
λόγους συγκάταινον ἔσχε τὸ πλῆθος καὶ ἄνδρας
τοὺς ἐκμετρησομένους τὴν χώραν αὐτῶν ἐξέπεμψε
παραδοὺς αὐτοῖς τινας γεωμετρίας ἐπιστήμονας,
οὓς τἀληθὲς οὐκ ἔμελλε λήσεσθαι διὰ τὴν τέχνην,
ἐντολὰς δοὺς ἀποτιμήσασθαι τῆς τε εὐδαίμονος ἰδίᾳ
77 τὸ μέτρον γῆς καὶ τῆς ἧσσον ἀγαθῆς. ἡ γὰρ
φύσις τῆς Χαναναίων γῆς τοιαύτη τίς ἐστιν, ὡς
ἴδοι τις ἂν πεδία μεγάλα καὶ καρποὺς φέρειν
ἱκανώτατα καὶ συγκρινόμενα μὲν ἑτέρᾳ γῇ πανευδαί-
μονα νομισθησόμενα, τοῖς δ' Ἰεριχουντίων χωρίοις
παραβαλλόμενα καὶ τοῖς Ἱεροσολυμιτῶν τὸ μηδὲν
78 ἀναφανησόμενα· καίτοι παντελῶς ὀλίγην αὐτῶν
εἶναι τὴν γῆν συμβέβηκε καὶ ταύτης ὀρεινὴν τὴν
πολλήν, ἀλλ' ὑπερβολὴν εἰς καρπῶν ἐκτροφήν τε
καὶ κάλλος οὐκ ἀπολέλοιπεν ἑτέρᾳ. καὶ διὰ τοῦτο
τιμητοὺς μᾶλλον ἢ μετρητοὺς τοὺς κλήρους εἶναι
δεῖν ὑπέλαβε, πολλάκις ἑνὸς πλέθρου κἂν χιλίων
79 ἀνταξίου γενομένου. οἱ δὲ ἄνδρες οἱ πεμφθέντες,
δέκα δὲ ἦσαν, περιοδεύσαντες καὶ τιμησάμενοι τὴν
γῆν ἐν ἑβδόμῳ μηνὶ παρῆσαν πρὸς αὐτὸν εἰς
Σιλοῦντα πόλιν, ἔνθα τὴν σκηνὴν ἑστάκεσαν.

[1] Niese: ἐκμετρησόμενοι . . . κακουργήσοντες codd.

---

[a] The representatives of the tribes (§ 75), excluding the
two (Reuben and Gad) for which complete provision had
already been made on the east of Jordan. In this account
of the division of the land Josephus departs from Scripture
and presents a simpler, possibly an older, narrative. In
Joshua, after a review of the allotment of land to the 2½ tribes
beyond Jordan (chap. xiii.), we are given a preliminary
allotment *at Gilgal* (xiv. 6) to Judah, Ephraim and the rest

196

fully and without fraudulence and honestly to report to us what are its dimensions."

(21) Having delivered this speech and won the assent of the people thereto, Joshua sent out men to measure the country, attaching to them certain expert surveyors, from whom by reason of their skill the truth would not be hid, instructions being given them to assess separately the extent of the favoured land and of that which was less fertile. For the nature of the land of Canaan is such that one may see plains, of great area, fully fitted for bearing crops, and which compared with another district might be deemed altogether blest, yet when set beside the regions of the people of Jericho and Jerusalem would appear as naught. Aye, though the territory of these folk happens to be quite diminutive and for the most part mountainous, yet for its extraordinary productiveness of crops and for beauty it yields to no other. And that was why Joshua held that the allotments should be fixed rather by valuation than by measurement, a single acre being often worth as much as a thousand. So the men who had been sent, ten [a] in number, having compassed the land and valued it, in the seventh month [b] returned to him to the city of Silo, where the tabernacle had been set up.

Mission of the measurers of the land. Jos. xviii. 8.

xviii. 9.

of Manasseh (xv.-xvii.); then from Shiloh emissaries are sent out (3 from each tribe or 21 in all) to measure out the land for the remaining *seven* tribes, and the allotment for these tribes follows (xviii.-xx.). In Josephus there is no preliminary allotment at Gilgal: the apportionment for the 9½ tribes all takes place at Shiloh.

[b] Not in Scripture, which instead has a reference to the " seven portions " into which the land was divided by the emissaries (see last note).

197

80 (22) Καὶ Ἰησοῦς Ἐλεάζαρόν τε καὶ τὴν γερουσίαν σὺν τοῖς φυλάρχοις παραλαβὼν νέμει ταῖς
ἐννέα φυλαῖς καὶ τῶν Μανασσητῶν τοῖς ἡμίσεσι,
κατὰ μέγεθος ἑκάστης τῶν φυλῶν τὴν μέτρησιν
81 ποιησάμενος. κληρώσαντος δὲ αὐτοῦ, ἡ μὲν Ἰούδα
λαχοῦσα πᾶσαν αἱρεῖται τὴν καθύπερθεν Ἰδουμαίαν
παρατείνουσαν μὲν ἄχρι τῶν Ἱεροσολύμων τὸ δ᾽
εὖρος ἕως τῆς Σοδομίτιδος λίμνης καθήκουσαν· ἐν
δὲ τῷ κλήρῳ τούτῳ πόλεις ἦσαν Ἀσκάλων καὶ
82 Γάζα. Σεμεωνὶς δέ, δευτέρα γὰρ ἦν, ἔλαχε τῆς
Ἰδουμαίας τὴν Αἰγύπτῳ τε καὶ τῇ Ἀραβίᾳ
πρόσορον οὖσαν. Βενιαμῖται δὲ τὴν ἀπὸ Ἰορδάνου
ποταμοῦ ἔλαχον ἄχρι θαλάσσης μὲν τὸ μῆκος, τὸ
δὲ πλάτος Ἱεροσολύμοις ὁριζομένην καὶ Βεθήλοις·
στενώτατος¹ δὲ ὁ κλῆρος οὗτος ἦν διὰ τὴν τῆς
γῆς ἀρετήν· Ἱεριχοῦντα γὰρ καὶ τὴν Ἱεροσο-
83 λυμιτῶν πόλιν ἔλαβον. ἡ δ᾽ Ἐφραίμου² φυλὴ τὴν
ἄχρι Γαζάρων ἀπὸ Ἰορδάνου ποταμοῦ μηκυνο-
μένην ἔλαχεν, εὐρεῖαν δὲ ὅσον ἀπὸ Βεθήλων εἰς
τὸ μέγα τελευτᾷ πεδίον, τῆς τε³ Μανασσήτιδος οἱ
ἡμίσεις ἀπὸ μὲν Ἰορδάνου μέχρι Δώρων πόλεως,
84 πλάτος δὲ ἐπὶ Βηθησάνων, ἣ νῦν Σκυθόπολις

¹ στενότατος codd.   ² Ἐφρὰν R.
³ δὲ Bernard (Lat. vers.).

ᵃ It is difficult to see what part the lot played in the matter
beyond determining the order of conferment of territories
already allocated in advance proportionate to the size of the
various tribes; there can have been no *choice* on the part
of the tribes. In rabbinical tradition the Urim and Thummim
are said to have been used for the purpose.

ᵇ "Length" and "breadth" in this description indicate
the longer and shorter dimensions of the lots, regardless of
their orientation.

ᶜ The lower end of the Dead Sea.

(22) Then Joshua, taking to him Eleazar and the council of elders, along with the tribal chiefs, distributed all between the nine tribes and the half-tribe of Manasseh, making his measurements proportional to the magnitude of each tribe. When, then, he had cast lots,[a] that of Judah obtained for its lot the whole of upper Idumaea, extending (in length) to Jerusalem and in breadth [b] reaching down to the lake of Sodom [c]; within this allotment were the cities of Ascalon and Gaza. That of Simeon, being the second, obtained the portion of Idumaea bordering on Egypt and Arabia. The Benjamites obtained the region which in length stretches from the river Jordan to the sea [d] and in breadth is bounded by Jerusalem and Bethel. This lot was the narrowest of all by reason of the excellence of the soil, for Jericho and the city of the Jerusalemites fell to their portion. The tribe of Ephraim obtained the land reaching in length from the river Jordan to Gazara [e] and in breadth from Bethel right up to the great plain.[f] The half-tribe of Manasseh had from the Jordan to the city of Dora [g] and in breadth as far as Bēthēsana,[h] now called Scythopolis. After

Marginal notes: Allotment of the land between the 9½ tribes. Jos. xviii. 10. — xv. 1. — xix. 1. — xviii. 11. — xvi. 5. — xvii. 1. — xix. 17.

[d] Jos. xviii. 12 " westward " (literally " sea-ward " ; LXX ἐπὶ τὴν θάλασσαν) ; the western border actually lay well inland.

[e] So Jos. xvi. 5 LXX (not in Heb. text). Gazara is the Greek form of the Heb. Gezer (Jos. *ib.* 10), now identified as *Tell Jezar*, some 18 miles N.W. of Jerusalem, on the Philistine border. [f] The plain of Esdraelon.

[g] Heb. Dor (LXX Δώρ), Jos. xvii. 11 ; a maritime town 16 miles S. of Carmel (mod. *Tanturah*).

[h] Heb. Beth-shean (LXX Βαιθσάν, mod. *Beisan*, midway between Mt. Gilboa and the Jordan ; of the real or supposed Scythian invasion which gave it its other name nothing is known.

καλεῖται, καὶ μετὰ τούτους Ἰσαχαρὶς Κάρμηλόν
τε τὸ ὄρος καὶ τὸν ποταμὸν τοῦ μήκους ποιησαμένη
τέρμονα,[1] τὸ δὲ Ἰταβύριον ὄρος τοῦ πλάτους.
Ζαβουλωνῖται δὲ τὴν μέχρι Γεηνσαρίδος, καθ-
ήκουσαν δὲ περὶ Κάρμηλον καὶ θάλασσαν ἔλαχον.
85 τὴν δὲ ἀπὸ τοῦ Καρμήλου κοιλάδα προσαγορευο-
μένην, διὰ τὸ καὶ τοιαύτην εἶναι, Ἀσηρῖται φέρον-
ται πᾶσαν τὴν ἐπὶ Σιδῶνος τετραμμένην· Ἄρκη
δὲ πόλις ὑπῆρχεν αὐτοῖς ἐν τῇ μερίδι ἡ καὶ
86 Ἐκδείπους. τὰ δὲ πρὸς τὰς ἀνατολὰς τετραμμένα
μέχρι Δαμασκοῦ πόλεως καὶ τῆς Γαλιλαίας τὰ
καθύπερθεν Νεφθαλῖται παρέλαβον ἕως τοῦ Λιβάνου
ὄρους καὶ τῶν τοῦ Ἰορδάνου πηγῶν, αἳ τὴν ὁρμὴν
ἐκ τοῦ ὄρους ἔχουσιν [ἐκ τοῦ καθήκοντος τοῖς
ὅροις κατὰ τὰ βόρεια πόλεως Ἄρκης παροικούσης].[2]
87 Δανῖται δὲ τῆς κοίλης ὅσα πρὸς δυόμενον τέτραπται
τὸν ἥλιον λαγχάνουσιν Ἀζώτῳ καὶ Δώροις ὁριζό-
μενοι, Ἰάμνειάν τε πᾶσαν καὶ Γίτταν ἀπ' Ἀκκα-
ρῶνος ἕως τοῦ ὄρους, ἐξ οὗ ἡ Ἰούδα ἤρκτο φυλή.
88 (23) Καὶ ἐξ μὲν ἔθνη τῶν υἱέων τοῦ Χαναναίου
φέροντα τὴν ἐπωνυμίαν διεῖλεν οὕτως Ἰησοῦς καὶ
τὴν γῆν ταῖς ἐννέα καὶ τῇ ἡμισείᾳ φυλαῖς ἔδωκε
89 νέμεσθαι· τὴν γὰρ Ἀμορῖτιν καὶ αὐτὴν οὕτως ἀφ'
ἑνὸς τῶν Χαναναίου παίδων καλουμένην Μωυσῆς
ἤδη προειληφὼς νενεμήκει ταῖς δυσὶ φυλαῖς καὶ
τῷ ἡμίσει· τοῦτο δὲ καὶ πρότερον δεδηλώκαμεν.[3]

---

[1] ML: τέρματα rell.   [2] om. Lat.
[3] Niese: δεδηλώκειμεν (-ώκει, -ώκειν) codd.

---

[a] Mount Tabor ; the town of that name is mentioned
among the borders of Issachar in Jos. xix. 22.
[b] The sea of Galilee.

these came Issachar, with mount Carmel and the river for its boundaries in length and mount Itabyrion *a* as limit of its breadth. They of Zabulon xix. 10 obtained the land which reaches to the (lake of) Genesar *b* and descends well-nigh to Carmel and the sea. The region beginning at Carmel, the Vale as xix. 24. it is called from its nature, was won by the men of Aser, all of it, that is to say, that faced towards Sidon ; to their portion fell the city of Arce, also called Ecdipus.*c* The territory to the eastward up xix. 32. to the city of Damascus, with upper Galilee, was occupied by the men of Nephthali, as far as mount Libanus and the sources of the Jordan, which spring from that mountain.*d* The Danites obtained those xix. 40. parts of the valley which face the setting sun with Azotus *e* and Dora for boundaries ; they had all Jamnia,*f* Gitta *g* (and) from Akkaron *h* to the mountain-range where the tribe of Judah began.

(23) Thus did Joshua divide six of the nations that Amoritis bore the names of the sons of Canaan and gave their unassigned land to the nine and a half tribes for their possession ; territory. for Amoritis, likewise so called after one of the children of Canaan, had already of yore been taken and apportioned by Moses to the two and a half tribes, as we have previously related.*i* But the

---

c Heb. Achzib (Jos. xix. 29), mod. *ez Zīb*, called Ecdippa, *B.J.* i. 257, on the coast midway between Carmel and Tyre.

d The mss. add some unintelligible words, omitted by the Latin version and perhaps a gloss : (?) " from the part where it descends to the boundary to the north of the adjacent city of Arce."

e Heb. Ashdod.

f Heb. Jabneel (Jos. xv. 11) or Jabneh, mod. *Yebnah*, another city in the Philistine plain.

g Gath.   *h* Ekron.   *i* iv. 166 ff.

τὰ δὲ περὶ Σιδῶνα καὶ ᾿Αρουκαίους καὶ ᾿Αμαθαίους
καὶ ᾿Αριδαίους¹ ἀδιακόσμητα ἦν.

90 (24) ᾿Ιησοῦς δέ, τοῦ γήρως ἐμποδίζοντος ἤδη
πράττειν ὅσα καὶ νοήσειε, τῶν τε μετ᾿ αὐτὸν τὴν
ἡγεμονίαν παραλαβόντων ἀμελῶς προστάντων τοῦ
κοινῇ συμφέροντος, παρήγγειλέ τε² φυλῇ ἑκάστῃ
τοῦ γένους τῶν Χαναναίων μηδὲν ὑπολιπεῖν ἐν τῇ
κατακεκληρωμένῃ γῇ· τὴν γὰρ ἀσφάλειαν αὐτοῖς
καὶ τὴν φυλακὴν τῶν πατρίων ἐθῶν ἐν μόνῳ τούτῳ
καὶ Μωυσῆν αὐτοῖς εἶναι προειπεῖν καὶ τοῦτ᾿ αὐ-
91 τὸς³ πεπεῖσθαι· καὶ τοῖς Λευίταις δὲ τὰς ὀκτὼ
καὶ τριάκοντα πόλεις ἀποδιδόναι· προειλήφεισαν
γὰρ ἤδη κατὰ τὴν ᾿Αμοραίαν τὰς δέκα. τούτων
τρεῖς ἀπονέμει τοῖς φυγάσιν οἰκεῖν ἐν αὐταῖς, πολλὴ
γὰρ ἦν πρόνοια τοῦ μηδὲν ὧν Μωυσῆς διέταξε
παραλιπεῖν, τῆς μὲν οὖν ᾿Ιούδα φυλῆς ῞Εβρωνα,
Σίκιμα δὲ τῆς ᾿Εφραίμ, τῆς Νεφθαλίτιδος δὲ
Κεδέσην· ἔστι δὲ τῆς καθύπερθεν Γαλιλαίας τοῦτο
92 τὸ χωρίον. νέμει δὲ καὶ τῆς λείας ὅσα ἦν ἔτι
λοιπά, πλείστη δ᾿ ἐγεγόνει, καὶ μεγάλους πλούτους
περιεβέβληντο καὶ κοινῇ πάντες καὶ κατ᾿ ἰδίαν
ἕκαστος χρυσοῦ τε καὶ ἀργύρου καὶ ἐσθήτων καὶ
τῆς ἄλλης ἐπισκευῆς ἕνεκα, τετραπόδων τε πλήθους
ὅσον οὐδὲ ἀριθμῷ μαθεῖν ἦν προσγενομένου.
93 (25) Μετὰ δὲ⁴ ταῦτα συναγαγὼν εἰς ἐκκλησίαν
τὸν στρατὸν τοῖς ὑπὲρ τὸν ᾿Ιόρδανον κατὰ τὴν
᾿Αμοραίαν ἱδρυμένοις, συνεστράτευον δ᾿ αὐτοῖς

¹ ᾿Αραδαίους conj. Niese.　　² om. τε Lat., ed. pr.
³ Naber: αὐτοὺς codd.　　⁴ ROE: δὴ rell.

ᵃ Cf. the list of the 11 sons of Canaan (Chananaeus)
previously given in A. i. 138 f., to which Josephus is here
referring. The countries of 7 of these have now been assigned:

regions about Sidon, with those of the Arucaeans, Amathaeans and Aridaeans, remained unassigned.[a]

(24) Joshua, now that age impeded him from carrying out his own designs and also because those who after him took over the command showed themselves careless guardians of the common weal, straitly charged each tribe to leave no remnant of the race of the Canaanites within their allotted territory, since their security and the maintenance of their ancestral institutions hung upon that alone : this Moses had already told them [b] and of this he was himself persuaded. They were also to render up to the Levites those eight and thirty cities—for these had already received the other ten in the Amorite country.[c] Of these cities, he assigned three for fugitives to dwell in—for he took strict care to neglect none of the ordinances of Moses— to wit Hebron belonging to the tribe of Judah— Sikima [d] to Ephraim and Kedese [e] to Nephthali, this last being a place in upper Galilee. He also distributed what yet remained of the spoils, of which there was a vast mass ; and all, collectively and individually, found themselves endowed with great riches, gold, silver, apparel and equipment of every kind, over and above such a multitude of cattle [f] as was past numbering.

(25) Thereafter, having collected his army in assembly, he addressed to those who had their settlement beyond Jordan in Amoraea—of whom 50,000

Margin notes:
Cities of Levites and of refuge : division of spoils. Jos. xxiii. 1.

xxi. 1.

xx. 1.

cf. xxii. 8.

Joshua's farewell address to the 2½ tribes. Jos. xxii. 1.

the 4 still outstanding are in Biblical nomenclature Zidon, Arkite, Hamathite and Arvadite (Gen. x. 15 ff.). Joshua (xiii. 2-6) also enumerates the unconquered territories, including that of the Philistines, not mentioned by Josephus.

[b] iv. 191 f.   [c] iv. 67, 172.   [d] Shechem.
[e] Kedesh.   [f] lit. " four-footed (beasts)."

πεντακισμύριοι ὁπλῖται, ἔλεξε τάδε· "ἐπεὶ ὁ θεός,[1]
πατὴρ καὶ δεσπότης τοῦ Ἑβραίων γένους, γῆν
τε κτήσασθαι ταύτην ἔδωκε καὶ κτηθεῖσαν εἰς
94 ἅπαν ἡμετέραν φυλάξειν ὑπέσχηται, συνεργίας δὲ
τῆς παρ' ὑμῶν κατ' ἐντολὴν τὴν ἐκείνου δεομένοις
ἑαυτοὺς εἰς ἅπαντα προθύμους ἐδώκατε, δίκαιον
ὑμᾶς μηδενὸς ἔτι δυσκόλου περιμένοντος ἀνα-
παύσεως ἤδη τυχεῖν φειδοῖ τῆς προθυμίας ὑμῶν,
ἵν' εἰ καὶ πάλιν δεήσειεν ἡμῖν αὐτῆς ἄοκνον ἔχωμεν
εἰς τὰ κατεπείξοντα καὶ μὴ τοῖς νῦν καμοῦσαν
95 αὖθις βραδυτέραν. χάριν τε οὖν ὑμῖν ὧν συνήρασθε
κινδύνων καὶ οὐχὶ νῦν μόνον ἀλλ' εἰς ἅπαν οὕτως
ἕξομεν, ὄντες ἀγαθοὶ μεμνῆσθαι τῶν φίλων καὶ
παρὰ τῇ διανοίᾳ κρατεῖν ὅσα παρ' αὐτῶν ἡμῖν
ὑπῆρξεν, ὅτι τε τὴν ἀπόλαυσιν τῶν ὑπαρχόντων
ὑμῖν ἀγαθῶν δι' ἡμᾶς ἀνεβάλεσθε καὶ πονήσαντες[2]
εἰς ἃ νῦν εὐνοίᾳ θεοῦ κατέστημεν ἔπειθ' οὕτως
96 ἐκρίνατε αὐτῶν μεταλαμβάνειν. γέγονε δὲ πρὸς
τοῖς ὑπάρχουσιν ἀγαθοῖς ἐκ τῶν σὺν ἡμῖν πόνων
πλοῦτος ἄφθονος, λείαν τε πολλὴν ἐπαξομένοις καὶ
χρυσὸν καὶ ἄργυρον, καὶ τὸ τούτων ἔτι πλεῖον, ἡ
παρ' ἡμῶν[3] εὔνοια καὶ πρὸς ὅ τι βουληθείητε κατ'
ἀμοιβὴν πρόθυμον. οὔτε γὰρ ὧν Μωυσῆς προεῖπεν
ἀπελείφθητε καταφρονήσαντες ἐξ ἀνθρώπων ἀπ-
ελθόντος οὔτ' ἔστιν οὐδὲν ἐφ' ᾧ μὴ χάριν ὑμῖν
97 οἴδαμεν. χαίροντας οὖν ὑμᾶς ἐπὶ τὰς κληρουχίας
ἀπολύομεν καὶ παρακαλοῦμεν μηδένα τῆς πρὸς
ἡμᾶς συγγενείας ὅρον ὑπολαμβάνειν, μηδ' ὅτι
μεταξὺ ποταμὸς οὗτός ἐστιν ἑτέρους ἡμᾶς νομίσητε

---

[1] θεὸς καὶ MSPL.   [2] ROL: συμπονήσαντες SP.
[3] MSPLE: παρ' ἡμῖν RO: vester Lat.

---

[a] i.e. in cattle.

men-at-arms had taken part in their campaign—
the following words : " Seeing that God, the Father
and Lord of the Hebrew race, has given us to win
this land and, being won, has promised to preserve
it to us for ever, and seeing that, when at His behest
we besought your assistance, ye offered your ready
services for all, it is but just, when no further arduous
task awaits us, that ye should now obtain repose,
husbanding your devotion, to the end that, should
we again have need of it, we may find it alert to
meet those future emergencies and not so worn by
the toils of to-day as to respond more sluggishly
hereafter. We therefore tender you our thanks for
having shared those perils with us, and not to-day
only but for ever shall we be grateful ; for we are
apt to remember our friends and to keep in mind
services which they have rendered to us, even how
for our sakes ye deferred the enjoyment of your
goodly possessions and resolved that, only after
toiling for the end whereto by the grace of God we
have now attained, would ye then at last partake of
them. Yet, to add to those goods that ye possess,
ye have by your labours with us won wealth in
abundance : ye will take with you rich booty,[a] gold
and silver and, what is more than all, our goodwill
and readiness to serve and requite you in whatsoever
ye may desire. For ye have in nowise shirked those
behests of Moses, nor disdained his authority now
that he has passed away, nor is there aught for which
we do not accord you gratitude. We therefore let
you joyfully depart to your heritages, and we entreat
you not to suppose that the kinship which unites us
owns any boundary, nor, because this river runs
between us, to regard us as strangers and not as

καὶ οὐχὶ Ἑβραίους. Ἀβράμου γὰρ ἅπαντές ἐσμεν
οἵ τ' ἐνθάδε κἀκεῖ κατοικοῦντες, θεός τε εἷς, ὃς
τούς τε ἡμετέρους προγόνους καὶ τοὺς ὑμῶν αὐτῶν
98 παρήγαγεν εἰς τὸν βίον· οὗ τῆς θρησκείας ἐπι-
μελεῖσθε καὶ πολιτείας, ἣν αὐτὸς διὰ Μωυσέος
διέταξε, φυλακὴν ἔχετε τὴν πᾶσαν, ὡς ἐμμενόντων
μὲν τούτοις καὶ τοῦ θεοῦ παρέξοντος εὔνουν εἶναι
καὶ σύμμαχον ἑαυτόν, ἐκτραπέντων δὲ εἰς ἑτέρων
ἐθνῶν μίμησιν ἀποστραφησομένου τὸ γένος ὑμῶν.''
99 ταῦτα εἰπὼν καὶ καθ' ἕνα τοὺς ἐν τέλει καὶ κοινῇ
τὸ πλῆθος αὐτῶν ἀσπασάμενος αὐτὸς μὲν ὑπέμεινε,
προύπεμπε δ' αὐτοὺς ὁ λαὸς οὐκ ἀδακρυτὶ καὶ
μόλις ἀλλήλων ἀπελύθησαν.
100 (26) Διαβᾶσα δὲ τὸν ποταμὸν ἥ τε Ῥουβηλὶς
φυλὴ καὶ Γαδὶς καὶ ὅσοι τῶν Μανασσητῶν αὐτοῖς
συνείποντο βωμὸν ὑπὲρ τῆς ὄχθης ἱδρύονται τοῦ
Ἰορδάνου, μνημεῖον τοῖς ἔπειτα γενησομένοις,[1]
σύμβολον[2] τῆς πρὸς τοὺς πέραν κατοικησομένους[3]
101 οἰκειότητος. ἀκούσαντες δὲ οἱ πέραν βωμὸν ἱδρύσ-
θαι τοὺς ἀπολυθέντας οὐ μεθ' ἧς ἐκεῖνοι γνώμης
ἀνέστησαν αὐτόν, ἀλλ' ἐπὶ νεωτερισμῷ καὶ ξενικῶν
εἰσαγωγῇ θεῶν, οὐκ ἤθελον ἀπιστεῖν, ἀλλὰ περὶ
τὴν θείαν[4] θρησκείαν τὴν διαβολὴν πιθανὴν νομίζοντες ἐν ὅπλοις ἦσαν, ὡς ἐπ' ἀμύνῃ τῶν τὸν
βωμὸν ἱδρυσαμένων περαιωσόμενοι τὸν ποταμὸν
καὶ κολάσοντες αὐτοὺς τῆς παρατροπῆς τῶν πατρίων
102 ἐθῶν. οὐ γὰρ ἐδόκει τὴν συγγένειαν αὐτοὺς λογί-
ζεσθαι καὶ τὸ ἀξίωμα τῶν τὴν αἰτίαν εἰληφότων,

---

[1] γενησόμενον Niese.
[2] σύμβολον before τῆς om. E Lat. (probably a gloss, cf.
§ 112).
[3] κατῳκημένους SPE.　　　　　　　[4] θείων RO.

Hebrews. For we are all of Abraham's stock, whether living here or there, and it is one God who brought our forefathers and yours into existence. To the worship of Him pay ye heed, and of that polity, which He Himself has instituted through Moses, observe ye every precept, in the assurance that, while ye remain faithful to these, God also will show Himself your gracious ally, but if ye turn aside to imitate other nations He will turn away from your race." Having thus spoken and bidden farewell, to the officers one by one, and to their whole company in general, he himself remained; but the people escorted them on their way not without tears, and hardly were they parted from one another.

(26) Having then crossed the river, the tribe of Rubel with that of Gad and all those of Manasseh who accompanied them erected an altar on the bank of the Jordan, as a memorial to future generations of their relationship to the inhabitants on the other side. But those beyond the river,[a] having heard tell that the migrants had erected an altar, not with the purpose which had led them to set it up, but with designs of sedition and the introduction of strange gods, were loth to distrust the report; nay, deeming this calumny concerning divine worship credible, they sprang to arms, with intent to cross the river and be avenged on those that had erected the altar and to punish them for this perversion of the rites of their fathers. For they held that they should take no account of their kinship or of the rank of those thus incriminated, but of the

xxii. 6.

They erect an altar beyond Jordan: embassy and expostulation of Phinees. Jos. xxii. 10.

---

[a] *i.e.* on the west; "beyond the river" from the point of view of those in trans-Jordania. In Scripture "beyond the river" invariably refers to the eastern side of the Jordan.

ἀλλὰ τὸ τοῦ θεοῦ βουλητὸν καὶ ᾧ τρόπῳ τιμώμενος
103 χαίρει. καὶ οἱ μὲν ἐστράτευσαν ὑπ' ὀργῆς, ἐπέσχε
δ' αὐτοὺς Ἰησοῦς καὶ ὁ ἀρχιερεὺς Ἐλεάζαρος καὶ
ἡ γερουσία λόγοις συμβουλεύοντες ἀπόπειραν
αὐτῶν τῆς γνώμης λαβεῖν πρῶτον, ἔπειτ' ἂν
κακοήθη μάθωσι τὴν διάνοιαν αὐτῶν τότε τοῖς
104 ὅπλοις χωρεῖν ἐπ' αὐτούς. πέμπουσιν οὖν πρε-
σβευτὰς πρὸς αὐτοὺς Φινεέσην τὸν υἱὸν Ἐλεαζάρου
καὶ δέκα σὺν αὐτῷ τῶν ἐν τιμῇ παρὰ τοῖς Ἑβραίοις
μαθησομένους, τί καὶ φρονήσαντες τὸν βωμὸν ἐπὶ
105 τῆς ὄχθης τοῦ ποταμοῦ διαβάντες ἔστησαν. ὡς
δὲ περαιωσαμένων καὶ πρὸς αὐτοὺς ἀφικομένων
ἐκκλησία συνελέγη, στὰς Φινεέσης μείζω μὲν
αὐτοὺς ἁμαρτεῖν ἔλεγεν ἢ ὥστε λόγοις ἐπιτιμη-
θέντας νενουθετῆσθαι πρὸς τὰ μέλλοντα· πλὴν οὐ
πρὸς τὸ μέγεθος τῆς παρανομίας ἀπιδόντας εὐθὺς
ἐφ' ὅπλα καὶ τὴν ἐκ χειρῶν τιμωρίαν ὁρμῆσαι,
πρὸς δὲ τὸ συγγενὲς καὶ τὸ τάχα καὶ λόγοις ἂν
σωφρονῆσαι σκοπήσαντας οὕτω ποιήσασθαι τὴν
106 πρεσβείαν, "ἵνα τὴν αἰτίαν μαθόντες ὑφ' ἧς
προήχθητε τὸν βωμὸν κατασκευάσαι μήτε προπετεῖς
δοκῶμεν ὅπλοις μετιόντες ὑμᾶς κατὰ λογισμὸν
ὅσιον ποιησαμένους τὸν βωμόν, καὶ[1] δικαίως
107 ἀμυνώμεθα τῆς διαβολῆς ἐλεγχθείσης ἀληθοῦς. οὐ
γὰρ ἐξιοῦμεν ὑμᾶς πείρᾳ τῆς τοῦ θεοῦ γνώμης
ἐντὸς γεγενημένους καὶ νόμων ὧν αὐτὸς ἡμῖν
δέδωκεν ἀκροατὰς ὑπάρχοντας, διαζευχθέντας ἡμῶν
καὶ παρόντας εἰς τὸν ἴδιον κλῆρον, ὃν κατὰ χάριν
τοῦ θεοῦ καὶ τῆς ἐκείνου περὶ ἡμᾶς[2] προνοίας

---

[1] ed. pr.: κατι (καὶ ἔτι, etc.) codd.
[2] ὑμᾶς edd.

will of God and the fashion in which He delights to
be honoured. So, moved by indignation, they prepared to take the field ; but Joshua and Eleazar
the high priest and the elders restrained them,
counselling them first to test their brethren's mind
by a parley, and, should they find their intent mis-
chievous, then and then only to proceed to hostilities.
They sent therefore ambassadors to them, Phinees, xxii. 18.
son of Eleazar, and with him ten others highly
esteemed among the Hebrews, to discover what they
could have meant by erecting that altar on the river-
bank after they had passed over. So, the embassy
having crossed the river and reached these people,
an assembly was convened, and Phinees arose and
said that their sin was too grave to be met by a
verbal reprimand and an admonition for the future ;
howbeit, they themselves had not wished to look at
the enormity of the crime so as to rush instantly to
arms and violent measures, but, looking rather to
their kinship and to the possibility that words might
suffice to bring them to reason, they had undertaken
this embassy. " We are here," said he, " in order
that, having learnt what reason induced you to
build this altar, we may on the one hand not be
deemed precipitate in bearing arms against you,
should ye have had some pious motive in erecting
it, and on the other that we may take righteous
vengeance, should the accusation prove true. For
we could not conceive that ye, with your experience
of instruction in the will of God, ye who had been
hearers of those laws which He Himself has given
us, once parted from us and entering on your own
heritage, which by the grace of God and His provi-
dential care for us has fallen to your lot, could have

ἐλάχετε, λήθην λαβεῖν αὐτοῦ καὶ τὴν σκηνὴν καὶ
τὴν κιβωτὸν καταλιπόντας καὶ βωμὸν ὃς ἡμῖν
πάτριος ξενικοὺς θεοὺς ἐπιφέρειν τοῖς Χαναναίων
108 κακοῖς προσκεχωρηκότας. ἀλλ' οὐδὲν ἀδικεῖν δό-
ξετε μετανοήσαντες καὶ μὴ περαιτέρω μανέντες,
νόμων δὲ πατρίων αἰδῶ καὶ μνήμην λαβόντες. ἂν
δ' ἐπιμένητε τοῖς ἡμαρτημένοις, οὐ περιστησόμεθα¹
τὸν ὑπὲρ τῶν νόμων πόνον, ἀλλὰ περαιωσάμενοι
τὸν Ἰόρδανον τούτοις βοηθήσομεν καὶ πρὸ αὐτῶν²
τῷ θεῷ, μηδὲν ὑμᾶς Χαναναίων διαφέρειν ὑπολαμβάνοντες ἀλλ' ὁμοίως ἐκείνοις διαφθείροντες.
109 μὴ γὰρ νομίσητε τῷ διαβεβηκέναι τὸν ποταμὸν καὶ
τῆς τοῦ θεοῦ δυνάμεως ἔξω γεγονέναι· πανταχοῦ
δ' ἐν τοῖς τούτου ἐστὲ καὶ ἀποδρᾶναι τὴν ἐξουσίαν
αὐτοῦ καὶ τὴν ἀπὸ ταύτης δίκην ἀδύνατον. εἰ δ'
οἴεσθε τὴν ἐνθάδε παρουσίαν ὑμῖν ἐμπόδιον εἶναι
τοῦ σωφρονεῖν, οὐδὲν κωλύει πάλιν τὴν γῆν ἡμᾶς³
110 ἀναδάσασθαι καὶ ταύτην ἀνεῖναι μηλόβοτον. ἀλλ'
εὖ ποιήσετε σωφρονήσαντες καὶ ἐπὶ νεαροῖς μετα-
τιθέμενοι τοῖς ἁμαρτήμασι. καὶ παρακαλοῦμεν
ὑμᾶς πρὸς παίδων καὶ γυναικῶν μὴ παρασχεῖν
ἡμῖν ἀνάγκην ἀμύνασθαι. ὡς οὖν τῆς ὑμετέρας
αὐτῶν σωτηρίας καὶ τῶν φιλτάτων ὑμῖν ἐν τῇδε
τῇ ἐκκλησίᾳ κειμένης οὕτω βουλεύεσθε, λόγοις
ἡττηθῆναι συμφέρειν ὑπολαμβάνοντες ἢ πεῖραν
ἔργων καὶ πολέμου περιμένειν."
111 (27) Τοσαῦτα τοῦ Φινεέσου διαλεχθέντος οἱ
προεστῶτες τῆς ἐκκλησίας καὶ τὸ πλῆθος αὐτὸ πᾶν
ἤρξαντο περὶ τῶν ἐγκεκλημένων αὐτοῖς ἀπολογεῖ-

---

¹ παραιτησόμεθα SPE.
² ante omnia Lat.: πρὸς (= προσέτι) αὐτῷ Hudson.
³ ὑμᾶς codd.

straightway forgotten Him and, abandoning the
tabernacle and the ark and the altar of our fathers,
introduced some strange gods and gone over to the
vices of the Canaanites. Howbeit ye shall be in no
wise held guilty, if ye repent and carry this madness no farther, but show that ye revere and are
mindful of the laws of your fathers. Should ye,
however, persist in your errors, we shall shun no
toil in defence of those laws, but, crossing the Jordan,
shall rally in support of them, aye and of God on
their behalf,[a] deeming you in no wise different from
the Canaanites but destroying you in like manner
with them. For think not that by crossing the river
ye have also passed beyond God's power : nay,
everywhere ye are within His domain and escape
from His authority and His vengeance is impossible.
But if ye regard your coming hither a hindrance to
sober living, there is nothing to prevent us [b] from
making a redistribution of the land and abandoning
this district to the grazing of sheep. Howbeit ye
will do well to return to sanity and to change your
ways while your sins are fresh. And we entreat you
in the name of your children and wives not to con-
strain us to resort to force. Let, then, the thought
that the salvation of your own selves and of them
that are dearest to you hangs upon this assembly
govern your deliberations, and reckon it more profitable to be defeated by words than to await the
trial of deeds and of war."

(27) After this discourse of Phinees, the presidents
of the assembly and the whole multitude themselves
began to disclaim the crimes wherewith they were

The tribes
protest
their
innocence.
Jos. xxii. 21.

---

[a] Text a little doubtful : perhaps " and, furthermore, of
God himself."   [b] The mss. have " you."

σθαι, καὶ μήτε συγγενείας τῆς πρὸς αὐτοὺς ἀπο-
στήσεσθαι¹ μήτε κατὰ νεωτερισμὸν ἀναστῆσαι τὸν
112 βωμὸν λέγειν, ἀλλὰ θεόν τε ἕνα γινώσκειν τὸν
Ἑβραίοις ἅπασι κοινὸν καὶ τὸν πρὸ τῆς σκηνῆς
βωμὸν χάλκεον, ᾧ τὰς θυσίας ποιήσειν· τὸν μέντοι
γε νῦν ἀνασταθέντα, δι' ὃν καὶ ὕποπτοι γεγόνασιν,
οὐ κατὰ θρησκείαν ἱδρῦσθαι, " σύμβολον δὲ ὅπως
εἴη καὶ τεκμήριον εἰς τὸν αἰῶνα τῆς πρὸς ὑμᾶς
οἰκειότητος καὶ ἀνάγκη τοῦ σωφρονεῖν καὶ τοῖς
πατρίοις ἐμμένειν, ἀλλ' οὐχὶ παραβάσεως ἀρχήν,
113 ὡς ὑπονοεῖτε. μάρτυς δ' ἡμῖν τοῦ ἐπὶ τοιαύτῃ τὸν
βωμὸν αἰτίᾳ κατασκευάσαι γένοιτο ὁ θεὸς ἀξιό-
χρεως, ὅθεν ἀμείνονα περὶ ἡμῶν ἔχοντες ὑπόληψιν
μηδὲν καταγινώσκετε τούτων, ἐφ' οἷς ἐξώλεις
εἶναι δίκαιοι πάντες ὅσοι τοῦ Ἁβράμου γένους
ὄντες νεωτέροις ἐπιχειροῦσιν ἔθεσι καὶ τοῦ συνήθους
τρόπου παρηλλαγμένοις."
114   (28) Ταῦτα εἰπόντας ἐπαινέσας ὁ Φινεέσης
παρῆν πρὸς Ἰησοῦν καὶ τὰ παρ' αὐτῶν ἀνήγγειλε
τῷ λαῷ. ὁ δὲ χαίρων, ὅτι μηδεμία στρατολογεῖν
αὐτοὺς ἀνάγκη μέλλει μηδ' εἰς αἷμα² καὶ πόλεμον
ἐξαγαγεῖν κατὰ ἀνδρῶν συγγενῶν, χαριστηρίους
115 ὑπὲρ τούτων τῷ θεῷ θυσίας ἐπιτελεῖ. καὶ διαλύσας
μετὰ ταῦτα τὸ πλῆθος εἰς τὰς ἰδίας κληρουχίας
Ἰησοῦς αὐτὸς ἐν Σικίμοις διῆγεν. ἔτει δ' ὕστερον
εἰκοστῷ ὑπέργηρως ὢν μεταπεμψάμενος τοὺς ἐπ'
ἀξιώματος μάλιστα τῶν πόλεων καὶ τὰς ἀρχὰς
καὶ τὴν γερουσίαν³ καὶ τοῦ πλήθους ὅσον ἦν ἐφικτὸν

¹ ἀποστήσασθαι Weill.   ² ὅπλα RO.
³ τὰς γερουσίας ML.

charged, saying that neither would they renounce [a] their kinship to their brethren, nor had they erected the altar with revolutionary intent : nay, they recognized but the one God, owned by all Hebrews alike, and the brazen altar before the tabernacle whereon the sacrifices should be offered. As for that which they had now set up and which had brought suspicion upon them, they had not erected it for worship : " nay," said they, " but as a symbol and token for eternity of our kinship with you, and an obligation to think soberly and to abide by the laws of our fathers, in no wise as a beginning of transgression, as ye suspect. And that such was our motive in building this altar be God our all-sufficient witness ! Wherefore, have a better opinion of us and cease to accuse us of any of those crimes, for which all would justly deserve to be extirpated who, being of the stock of Abraham, embark on new-fangled ways that are perversions of our customary practice."

(28) Phinees, having commended them for this speech, returned to Joshua and reported their answer to the people. And Joshua, rejoicing that there was to be no need to levy troops or to lead them to bloodshed and battle against kinsmen, offered sacrifices of thanksgiving to God for these mercies. Thereafter, having dismissed the multitude to their several provinces, Joshua himself abode at Sikima. Twenty years later,[b] in extreme old age, having sent for the chief notables of the cities, with their magistrates and elders, and assembled as many of the people as could be collected, he,

Jos. xxii. 30.

xxiv. 1.
Address of Joshua before his death.
Jos. xxiii., xxiv.

[a] Perhaps read, " had they renounced."
[b] Jos. xxiii. 1 " after many days."

αὐτῷ συναγαγών, ἐπεὶ παρῆσαν, τάς τε εὐεργεσίας
τοῦ θεοῦ ἁπάσας ἀνεμίμνησκεν αὐτούς, πολλαὶ δὲ
ἦσαν τοῖς ἐκ ταπεινοῦ σχήματος εἰς τοῦτο δόξης
116 καὶ περιουσίας προελθοῦσι, φυλάττειν τε τὴν τοῦ
θεοῦ προαίρεσιν οὕτως ἔχουσαν πρὸς αὐτοὺς παρεκάλει καὶ τῇ εὐσεβείᾳ[1] γε[2] μόνῃ φίλον αὐτοῖς
διαμενεῖν[3] τὸ θεῖον· αὐτῷ γὰρ καλῶς ἔχειν ἀπιέναι
μέλλοντι τοῦ ζῆν παραίνεσιν αὐτοῖς τοιαύτην καταλιπεῖν κἀκείνους ἠξίου διὰ μνήμης ποιήσασθαι τὴν
παρακέλευσιν.

117 (29) Καὶ ὁ μὲν τοσαῦτα πρὸς τοὺς παρόντας δια-
λεχθεὶς τελευτᾷ βιοὺς ἑκατὸν ἔτη καὶ δέκα, ὧν
Μωυσεῖ μὲν ἐπὶ διδασκαλίᾳ τῶν χρησίμων συν-
διέτριψε τεσσαράκοντα, στρατηγὸς δὲ μετὰ τὴν
118 ἐκείνου τελευτὴν γίνεται πέντε καὶ εἴκοσιν, ἀνὴρ
μήτε συνέσεως ὢν ἐνδεὴς μήτε τοῦ τὰ νοηθέντα
πρὸς τοὺς πολλοὺς σαφῶς ἐξενεγκεῖν ἄπειρος, ἀλλ᾽
ἐν ἀμφοτέροις ἄκρος, πρός τε τὰ ἔργα καὶ τοὺς
κινδύνους εὔψυχος καὶ μεγαλότολμος, πρυτανεῦσαί
τε τὰ κατὰ τὴν εἰρήνην δεξιώτατος καὶ πρὸς
119 ἅπαντα καιρὸν τὴν ἀρετὴν ἡρμοσμένος. θάπτεται
δὲ ἐν πόλει Θαμνᾶ τῆς Ἐφραίμου φυλῆς. θνήσκει
δὲ ὑπ᾽ αὐτὸν τὸν καιρὸν καὶ Ἐλεάζαρος ὁ ἀρχιερεὺς
Φινεέσῃ τῷ παιδὶ τὴν ἱερωσύνην καταλιπών, καὶ

---

[1] Text doubtful: for καὶ τῇ εὐσ. SP read τιμῇ πάσῃ
χρωμένους καὶ εὐσεβείᾳ.
[2] L: om. ROSP: ᾗ γε Niese.
[3] Niese: διαμένειν codd.

---

[a] Or perhaps " to observe God's will, so benevolent towards
them."

on their coming, recalled to them all the benefactions of God—and many had they been to folk
who from low estate had advanced to that pitch of
glory and affluence—and exhorted them to keep
God's goodwill unchanged towards them,[a] for by
piety [b] alone could they retain the friendship of the
Deity. It behoved him, he said, on the eve of
departure from life, to leave them such admonition,
and he besought them to bear his exhortation in
their memory.

(29) And so, after this address to the assembled
company, he died, having lived one hundred and ten
years ; of which he had passed forty in the company of Moses receiving profitable instruction, and
after his master's death had been commander-in-
chief for five-and-twenty.[c] A man [d] not wanting
either in intelligence or in skill to expound his ideas
to the multitude with lucidity, nay in both respects
supreme, in action and perils he was stout-hearted
and greatly daring, in peace-time a most dexterous
director of affairs, adapting himself admirably to
every occasion. He was buried in the city of Thamna [e]
of the tribe of Ephraim. About the same time died
also Eleazar the high priest, leaving the priesthood

Death of
Joshua and
of Eleazar.
Jos. xxiv.
29.

xxiv. 33.

---

[b] Text doubtful. Some mss. read "by showing Him
every honour and that piety," etc.

[c] The duration of Joshua's command is not stated in
Scripture. But, according to M. Weill, the figure here given
(25 years) is found also in the *Samaritan Chronicle*, while
Rabbinical tradition (*Seder Olam Rabba* xii.) extends the
period to 28 years.

[d] *Cf.* the previous brief character-sketch in *A.* iii. 49.

[e] Heb. Timnath-serah, identified by tradition with
Thamna (mod. *Tibneh*) in mount Ephraim and the seat of
a toparchy in Roman times (*B.J.* ii. 567, iii. 55).

μνημεῖον αὐτῷ καὶ τάφος ἐν Γαβαθᾶ πόλει τυγχάνει.

120 (ii. 1) Μετὰ δὲ τὴν τούτων τελευτὴν Φινεέσης προφητεύει κατὰ τὴν τοῦ θεοῦ βούλησιν ἐπ' ἐξωλείᾳ τοῦ Χαναναίων γένους τῇ Ἰούδα φυλῇ παρασχεῖν τὴν ἡγεμονίαν· καὶ γὰρ τῷ λαῷ διὰ σπουδῆς ἦν μαθεῖν τί καὶ τῷ θεῷ δοκεῖ. καὶ προσλαβοῦσα τὴν Σεμεωνίδα, ἐφ' ᾧτε ἐξαιρεθέντων τῶν ἐκείνης ὑποτελῶν καὶ τοὺς ἐν αὐτῇ τῇ κληρουχίᾳ τοῦτο ποιῶσιν * * *[1]

121 (2) Χαναναῖοι δ' ἀκμαζόντων αὐτοῖς κατ' ἐκεῖνον τὸν καιρὸν τῶν πραγμάτων στρατῷ μεγάλῳ κατὰ Ζεβέκην αὐτοὺς ὑπέμενον τῷ βασιλεῖ τῶν Ζεβεκηνῶν Ἀδωνιζεβέκῳ τὴν ἡγεμονίαν ἐπιτρέψαντες· τὸ δὲ ὄνομα τοῦτο σημαίνει Ζεβεκηνῶν κύριος· ἀδωνὶ γὰρ τῇ Ἑβραίων διαλέκτῳ κύριος γίνεται[2]· ἤλπιζόν τε κρατήσειν τῶν Ἰσραηλιτῶν διὰ τὸ

122 τεθνάναι Ἰησοῦν. συμμίξαντες δὲ αὐτοῖς Ἰσραηλῖται ταῖς δυσὶ φυλαῖς αἷς προεῖπον ἐμαχέσαντο λαμπρῶς καὶ κτείνουσι μὲν αὐτῶν ὑπὲρ μυρίους, τρεψάμενοι δὲ τὸ λοιπὸν καὶ διώκοντες αἱροῦσι τὸν Ἀδωνιζεβεκον, ὃς ἀκρωτηριασθεὶς ὑπ' αὐτῶν

123 φησιν, " ἀλλ' οὐκ εἰς τὸ πᾶν ἄρα λήσεσθαι θεὸν ἔμελλον, τάδε πεπονθὼς ἃ κατὰ δυοῖν καὶ ἑβδομή-

---

[1] Text of clause uncertain.   Niese indicates a lacuna: Dindorf instead alters καὶ προσλαβοῦσα above to προσλαβούσῃ.
[2] λέγεται E.

---

[a] Heb. " in Gibeah (or ' the hill ') of Phinehas his son " : in the MSS. of the LXX the name appears as Γαβαάθ, Γαβάθ, etc.: site unidentified.
[b] Lacuna in the Greek.

to his son Phinees; his monument and tomb are in the city of Gabatha.[a]

(ii. 1) Now after the death of these leaders, Phinees prophetically announced, in accordance with the will of God, that, for the extermination of the Canaanite race, the tribe of Judah should be given the command; for the people were keenly desirous to learn what was God's good pleasure. So this tribe, having enlisted the aid of Simeon, on the condition that, once the Canaanites tributary to Judah had been destroyed, they would do the same to those within the lot of Simeon (advanced to battle).[b]

(2) But the Canaanites, who at that time were in a flourishing condition, awaited them with a large army at Zebekē,[c] having entrusted the command to the king of the Zebekēnians, Adonizebek[d]—this name signifies "lord of the Zebekēnians," for *adōni* in the speech of the Hebrews means "lord"—and they were hoping to defeat the Israelites, since Joshua was dead. However the Israelites of the two tribes which I mentioned, having joined battle with them, fought brilliantly, with the result that they slew of the enemy upwards of ten thousand, and having put the rest to rout pursued them and captured Adonizebek, who, with hands and feet mutilated by his captors, exclaimed: "Nay then I was not destined for ever to escape God's eye, having now suffered the fate which I scrupled not of yore

The tribe of Judah, with Simeon, takes the lead against the Canaanites. Jd. i. 1.

Defeat of Adonizebek and siege of Jerusalem. Jd. i. 4.

c Heb. "Bezek": site unidentified.

d Heb. Adoni-bezek. The form is suspected and it is thought by some critics that we have in this story in Judges another version of the defeat of Adoni-zedek, King of Jerusalem, narrated in Joshua x., where, however, LXX has Adoni-bezek as here.

κοντα βασιλέων πρᾶξαι πρότερον οὐκ ἐνετράπην.''
124 καὶ ζῶντα μὲν κομίζουσιν ἕως Ἱεροσολύμων,
τελευτήσαντα δὲ γῇ θάπτουσι. καὶ διεξῄεσαν
αἱροῦντες τὰς πόλεις, πλείστας τε λαβόντες ἐπο-
λιόρκουν Ἱεροσόλυμα· καὶ τὴν μὲν κάτω λαβόντες
σὺν χρόνῳ πάντας ἔκτεινον τοὺς ἐνοικοῦντας,
χαλεπὴ δ' ἦν ἡ καθύπερθεν αὐτοῖς αἱρεθῆναι τειχῶν
ὀχυρότητι καὶ φύσει τοῦ χωρίου.
125 (3) Ὅθεν μετεστρατοπέδευσαν εἰς Χεβρῶνα[1] καὶ
ταύτην ἑλόντες κτείνουσι πάντας· ὑπελείπετο δὲ
τῶν[2] γιγάντων ἔτι γένος, οἳ διὰ σωμάτων
μεγέθη καὶ μορφὰς οὐδὲν τοῖς ἄλλοις ἀνθρώποις
παραπλησίας παράδοξον ἦσαν θέαμα καὶ δεινὸν
ἄκουσμα. δείκνυται δὲ καὶ νῦν ἔτι τούτων ὀστᾶ
126 μηδὲν τοῖς ὑπὸ πύστιν[3] ἐρχομένοις ἐοικότα. καὶ
τοῦτο μὲν τοῖς Λευίταις ἐξαίρετον γέρας ἔδοσαν
μετὰ καὶ τῶν δισχιλίων πηχῶν, τὴν δὲ γῆν Χαλέβῳ
δωρεὰν ἔδοσαν κατὰ Μωυσέος ἐντολάς· οὗτος δ'
ἦν τῶν κατασκόπων εἷς ὧν ἔπεμψε Μωυσῆς εἰς
127 τὴν Χαναναίαν. διδόασι δὲ καὶ τοῖς Ἰοθόρου τοῦ
Μαδιανίτου ἀπογόνοις, Μωυσέος γὰρ ἦν γαμβρός,
γῆν ἵνα νέμοιντο· τὴν γὰρ πατρίδα καταλιπόντες
ἠκολουθήκεσαν[4] ἐκείνοις καὶ συνῆσαν αὐτοῖς ἐπὶ τῆς
ἐρήμου.
128 (4) Ἡ δὲ Ἰούδα φυλὴ καὶ Σεμεωνὶς τὰς μὲν
κατὰ τὴν ὀρεινὴν τῆς Χαναναίας πόλεις εἷλον, τῶν

---

[1] Νεβρῶνα RO. [2] RO : τὸ τῶν rell.
[3] Cocceii : πίστιν codd. [4] ML : ἠκολούθησαν rell.

---

[a] " 70 " according to Jd. i. 7, but some mss. of lxx read
" 72."
[b] The burial is not mentioned in Scripture.
[c] According to Jd. i. 8 the whole city was captured and
218

to inflict on two and seventy [a] kings." They brought him yet alive to Jerusalem, and at his death gave him sepulture.[b] Then they overran the district, taking the towns, and after capturing very many of them laid siege to Jerusalem. The lower town they mastered in time and slew all the inhabitants ; but the upper town proved too difficult to carry through the solidity of its walls and the nature of the site.[c]

(3) So they moved their camp to Hebron, took that town and massacred all therein. Howbeit there remained yet a race of giants,[d] who, by reason of their huge frames and figures in no wise like to the rest of mankind, were an amazing spectacle and a tale of terror to the ear. Their bones are shown to this day, bearing no resemblance to any that have come within men's ken. This town they gave to the Levites as a choice boon, along with the tract of two thousand cubits[e] ; but of the rest of the land they made, in accordance with the behests of Moses, a present to Caleb, who was one of the spies whom Moses had sent into Canaan. They gave also to the descendants of Jethro the Madianite, the father-in-law of Moses, territory for habitation ; for, quitting their native country, they had followed the Hebrews and companied with them in the wilderness.

(4) The tribes of Judah and Simeon also captured the cities in the hill-country of Canaan, and among

(marginal notes:) Capture of Hebron. Jd. i. 10. — i. 20. — i. 16.

destroyed—an incorrect statement contradicted by other passages of Scripture. The distinction drawn by Josephus between upper and lower town is an attempt to harmonize Jd. i. 8 with i. 21 and Jos. xv. 63.

[d] The " sons of Anak " driven out by Caleb, Jd. i. 20; for their stature *cf.* the description given by the spies in Numb. xiii. 33 (*A.* iii. 305).

[e] As prescribed by Moses, *A.* iv. 67

δ' ἐν τῷ πεδίῳ καὶ πρὸς θαλάσσῃ Ἀσκάλωνά τε
καὶ Ἄζωτον. διαφεύγει δ' αὐτοὺς Γάζα καὶ
Ἀκκάρων· πεδίων γὰρ ὄντων καὶ πολλῆς ἁρμάτων
εὐπορίας κακῶς ἐποίουν τοὺς ἐπελθόντας. καὶ
αἵδε μὲν αἱ φυλαὶ μεγάλως ἐκ τοῦ πολεμεῖν εὐ-
δαιμονήσασαι ἀνεχώρησαν εἰς τὰς ἑαυτῶν πόλεις
καὶ κατατίθενται τὰ ὅπλα.

129   (5) Βενιαμῖται δέ, τούτων γὰρ ἦν Ἱεροσόλυμα,
τοῖς οἰκήτορσιν αὐτῶν συνεχώρησαν φόρους τελεῖν.
καὶ οὕτως παυσάμενοι πάντες οἱ μὲν τοῦ κτείνειν
οἱ δὲ κινδυνεύειν ἐργάζεσθαι τὴν γῆν εὐσχόλουν.
τὸ δ' αὐτὸ καὶ αἱ λοιπαὶ φυλαὶ τὴν Βενιαμῖτιν
μιμησάμεναι ἐποίουν καὶ τοῖς τελουμένοις ἀρκού-
μενοι φόροις ἐπέτρεπον τοῖς Χαναναίοις ἀπολέμοις
εἶναι.

130   (6) Ἡ δ' Ἐφραίμου[1] πολιορκοῦσα Βήθηλα τέλος
οὐδὲν ἄξιον τοῦ χρόνου καὶ τῶν πόνων ηὕρισκε
τῆς πολιορκίας, οἱ δὲ καίπερ ἀχθόμενοι τῇ καθέδρᾳ
131   προσεκαρτέρουν. ἔπειτα συλλαβόντες τινὰ τῶν ἐν
τῇ πόλει προελθόντα[2] ἐπὶ κομιδῇ τῶν ἀναγκαίων
πίστεις ἔδοσαν αὐτῷ παραδόντι τὴν πόλιν σώσειν
αὐτόν τε καὶ τοὺς συγγενεῖς αὐτοῦ· κἀκεῖνος
ἐπὶ τούτοις ὤμνυε τὴν πόλιν αὐτοῖς ἐγχειριεῖν.[3]
καὶ ὁ μὲν οὕτως προδοὺς σῴζεται μετὰ τῶν
οἰκείων, οἱ δὲ ἀποκτείναντες ἅπαντας τοὺς ἐνοικοῦντας εἶχον τὴν πόλιν.

132   (7) Καὶ μετὰ ταῦτα πρὸς μὲν τοὺς πολεμίους
μαλακῶς εἶχον οἱ Ἰσραηλῖται, τῆς δὲ γῆς καὶ τῶν

---

[1] Ἐφρὰν RO.   [2] Niese: προσελθόντα codd.
[3] Dindorf: ἐγχειοεῖν codd.

those in the plain and on the sea-board, Ascalon and Azōtus. But Gaza and Akkarōn escaped them ; for, being situated in the plain and blest with an abundance of chariots, they sorely handled their assailants.[a] So these two tribes, greatly enriched by their warfare, retired to their own cities and laid down their arms.

Further conquests of the two tribes. Jd. i. 9, 17 ff.

(5) The Benjamites, within whose lot lay Jerusalem, permitted its inhabitants to pay them tribute ; and thus all reposing, these from slaughter and those from peril, were at leisure to till the soil. The other tribes, imitating that of Benjamin, did the same and, contenting themselves with the tributes paid to them, suffered the Canaanites to live in peace.

General peace with the Canaanites Jd. i. 21. i. 27 ff.

(6) The tribe of Ephraim, in besieging Bethel, could attain no result proportionate to the time and the toil expended upon the siege ; yet, for all their annoyance, they persevered in the blockade. Afterwards, having caught one of the inhabitants of the town who had gone out in search of provisions, they gave him their word that, if he would betray the city, they would spare the lives of him and his kin ; and he on these terms swore to deliver it into their hands. So he by such treason saved himself with his family, while they, having massacred all the inhabitants, occupied the town.

Capture of Bethel by Ephraim. Jd. i. 22.

(7) Thereafter the Israelites relaxed the struggle against their enemies and devoted themselves to

Peace leads to corruption Jd. ii. 11.

[a] Josephus here differs from both Biblical texts, presenting a sort of compromise between them. According to the Heb. (Jd. i. 18 f.) Judah took Gaza, Ashkelon and Ekron, but failed to drive out the inhabitants of the valley because of their chariots of iron (Ashdod or Azotus is not mentioned) : according to the LXX he could take neither Gaza, Ascalon, Akkaron, nor Azotus.

ταύτης ἔργων ἐπεμελοῦντο. τῶν δὲ κατὰ τὸν
πλοῦτον αὐτοῖς ἐπιδιδόντων ὑπὸ τρυφῆς καὶ ἡδονῆς
τοῦ κόσμου ὠλιγώρουν τῆς πολιτείας καὶ¹ τῶν
133 νόμων οὐκέτ' ἦσαν ἀκριβεῖς ἀκροαταί. παρ-
οξυνθὲν δ' ἐπὶ τούτοις τὸ θεῖον ἀναιρεῖ, πρῶτον μὲν
ὡς φείσαιντο παρὰ τὴν αὐτοῦ γνώμην τῶν Χαναναίων, ἔπειθ' ὡς ἐκεῖνοι χρήσοιντο² πολλῇ κατ'
134 αὐτῶν ὠμότητι καιροῦ λαβόμενοι. οἱ δὲ καὶ πρὸς
τὰ παρὰ τοῦ θεοῦ δυσθύμως εἶχον καὶ πρὸς τὸ
πολεμεῖν ἀηδῶς, πολλά τε παρὰ τῶν Χαναναίων
λαβόντες καὶ πρὸς τοὺς πόνους ἤδη διὰ τὴν τρυφὴν
135 ἐκλελυμένοι. καὶ συνέβαινεν ἤδη τὴν ἀριστοκρατίαν διεφθάρθαι, καὶ τὰς γερουσίας οὐκ ἀπ-
εδείκνυσαν οὐδ' ἀρχὴν ἄλλην οὐδεμίαν τῶν πρότερον
νενομισμένων, ἦσαν δὲ ἐν τοῖς ἀγροῖς ἡδονῇ τοῦ
κερδαίνειν προσδεδεμένοι. καὶ διὰ τὴν πολλὴν
ἄδειαν στάσις αὐτοὺς πάλιν καταλαμβάνει δεινὴ
καὶ προήχθησαν εἰς τὸ πολεμεῖν ἀλλήλοις ἐκ
τοιαύτης αἰτίας.

136   (8) Λευίτης ἀνὴρ τῶν δημοτικωτέρων τῆς
Ἐφραίμου³ κληρουχίας ὢν καὶ ἐν ἐκείνῃ κατοικῶν
ἄγεται γύναιον ἀπὸ Βηθλέμων, τῆς δὲ Ἰούδα
φυλῆς τοῦτ' ἔστι τὸ χωρίον. ἐρῶν δὲ σφόδρα
τῆς γυναικὸς καὶ τοῦ κάλλους αὐτῆς ἡττημένος
ἠτύχει τῶν παρ' ἐκείνης οὐχ ὁμοίων πειρώμενος.
137 ἀλλοτρίως δ' αὐτῆς ἐχούσης καὶ διὰ τοῦτο μᾶλλον

¹ τῆς πολ. καὶ trs. Niese: καὶ τῆς πολιτείας codd.
² Bekker: χρήσαιντο codd.   ³ v.ll. Ἐφρὰν, Ἐφράνου.

ᵃ The remarks on political corruption are an amplification
of Scripture.
ᵇ In Scripture this episode forms an appendix to the book
of Judges. Josephus has transposed it (along with another

the soil and to labours thereon. And as their riches increased, under the mastery of luxury and voluptuousness, they recked little of the order of their constitution and no longer hearkened diligently to its laws. Incensed thereat, the Deity warned them by oracle, first that they had acted contrary to His will in sparing the Canaanites, and next that those foes, seizing their occasion, would treat them with great ruthlessness. But the Israelites, while despondent at this message from God, were yet ill-disposed for warfare, for they had won much from the Canaanites and luxury had by now unnerved them for fatigues. Aye, even that aristocracy of theirs was now becoming corrupted : no more did they appoint councils of elders or any other of those magistracies beforetime ordained by law, but lived on their estates, enslaved to the pleasures of lucre.ª And so, by reason of this gross listlessness, grave discord again assailed them and they were launched into civil war through the following cause.

(8) ᵇ A Levite of the lower ranks, of the province of Ephraim and residing therein, married a woman of Bethlehem, a place belonging to the tribe of Judah. Being deeply enamoured of his wife and captivated by her beauty, he was unfortunate in meeting with no like return from her. And, whereas she held herself aloof and he thereby only became

Jd. ii. 14.

The Levite of Ephraim and the outrage on his wife. Jd. xix. 1.

appendix) to an earlier date, to the period before the judges : perhaps, as has been suggested, to allow time for the tribe of Benjamin to recover itself before it furnished the nation with its first king. " It is incredible," writes Dr. G. F. Moore (*Int. Crit. Comm.* p. 405), " that the tribe of Benjamin was almost exterminated only a generation or two before the time of Saul ; but the events related in these chapters probably fall in a much earlier period . . ."

223

ἐκκαιομένου τῷ πάθει μέμψεις συνεχεῖς αὐτοῖς
ἐγίνοντο, καὶ τέλος ἡ γυνὴ πρὸς αὐτὰς βαρυνομένη
καταλιποῦσα τὸν ἄνδρα πρὸς τοὺς γονεῖς παραγίνεται μηνὶ τετάρτῳ. χαλεπῶς δὲ φέρων ὁ ἀνὴρ
ἐπὶ τῷ ἔρωτι ἧκε πρὸς τοὺς πενθεροὺς καὶ δια-
λυσάμενος τὰς μέμψεις καταλλάττεται πρὸς αὐτήν.
138 καὶ τέτταρας μὲν ἡμέρας αὐτόθι[1] διαιτᾶται φιλο-
φρονουμένων αὐτὸν τῶν γονέων, τῇ δὲ πέμπτῃ
δόξαν ἀπιέναι πρὸς αὐτὸν περὶ δείλην ἔξεισι·
βράδιον γὰρ ἀπέλυον οἱ γονεῖς τὴν θυγατέρα καὶ
τῆς ἡμέρας τριβὴν ἐποιοῦντο. θεράπων δ' αὐτοῖς
εἷς εἵπετο καὶ ὄνος ἦν αὐτοῖς, ἐφ' ἧς ὠχεῖτο τὸ
139 γύναιον. γενομένων δ' αὐτῶν κατὰ Ἱεροσόλυμα,
σταδίους δ' ἐληλύθεσαν ἤδη τριάκοντα, συνεβού-
λευεν ὁ θεράπων καταχθῆναί που, μὴ καί τι τῆς
νυκτὸς αὐτοὺς ὁδεύοντας καταλάβῃ δύσκολον καὶ
ταῦτα οὐδὲ πόρρω πολεμίων ὄντας, τοῦ καιροῦ
πολλάκις ἐπισφαλῆ καὶ ὕποπτα ποιοῦντος καὶ τὰ
140 φίλα. τῷ δ' οὐκ ἤρεσεν ἡ γνώμη παρ' ἀλλοφύλοις
ἀνδράσι ξενοῦσθαι, Χαναναίων γὰρ ἦν ἡ πόλις,
ἀλλὰ προελθόντας εἴκοσι στάδια εἰς οἰκείαν ἠξίου
κατάγεσθαι πόλιν, καὶ κρατήσας τῇ γνώμῃ παρῆν
εἰς Γάβαν φυλῆς τῆς Βενιαμίτιδος ἤδη[2] ὀψίας
141 οὔσης. καὶ μηδενὸς ἐπὶ ξενίαν τῶν κατὰ τὴν
ἀγορὰν αὐτὸν παρακαλοῦντος πρεσβύτης ἐξ ἀγροῦ
κατιὼν τῆς μὲν Ἐφραιμίτιδος φυλῆς ὢν ἐν δὲ τῇ
Γάβῃ διαιτώμενος συντυγχάνων αὐτῷ, τίς τε ὢν

[1] SPL: πρὸς αὐτόθι ROM: προσαυτόθι Niese.
[2] + δὲ SPE.

---

[a] A misreading of Scripture. In Jd. xix. 2 the woman
returns to her father's house " and was there the space of
four months."

the more ardent in his passion, quarrels were continually arising between them, and at last the woman, utterly weary of them, left her husband and in the fourth month [a] rejoined her parents. But her husband, in sore affliction through love of her, visited her parents, redressed her grievances and was reconciled to her. For four days more he abode there, kindly treated by her parents, but on the fifth, having resolved to return to his home, he set off towards evening ; for the parents were loth to part with their daughter and let the day slip away. A single servant accompanied them, and they had an ass on which the woman rode. Now when they were come over against Jerusalem, having already gone thirty furlongs, [b] the servant counselled them to lodge somewhere, lest, journeying by night, some misadventure should befall them, above all when they were not far from foes, that hour oft rendering perilous and suspect even the offices of friends. The Levite, however, misliked the thought of seeking shelter with aliens—for the city was in Canaanite hands [c]—preferring rather to proceed twenty furlongs further and to lodge in a town of the Hebrews ; and, his counsel prevailing, he arrived at Gaba, [d] in the tribe of Benjamin, when evening had now fallen. No one in the market-place offering him hospitality, an old man returning from the fields, who though of the tribe of Ephraim was residing in Gaba, fell in with him and asked who he was and why he was

[b] Gr. " stades " (about ⅛ mile). Bethlehem is 5 miles S. of Jerusalem : elsewhere the distance is reckoned as only " 20 stades " (A. vii. 312). [c] Cf. § 124 (note).
[d] Heb. Gibeah, usually identified with Tell el-Ful, c. 4 miles N. of Jerusalem ; in B.J. v. 51 described as " Gabath Saul . . . about 30 stades from Jerusalem."

ἤρετο καὶ δι᾽ ἃς αἰτίας στελλόμενος σκότους ἤδη
142 τὰ πρὸς τὸ δεῖπνον αὐτῷ λαμβάνοι. ὁ δὲ Λευίτης
μὲν ἔφησεν εἶναι, γύναιον δὲ παρὰ τῶν γονέων
ἄγων πρὸς αὐτὸν ἀπιέναι,[1] τὴν δ᾽ οἴκησιν ἐδήλου
τυγχάνειν ἐν τῇ Ἐφραίμου κληρουχίᾳ. ὁ δὲ
πρεσβύτης καὶ διὰ συγγένειαν καὶ διὰ τὸ τὴν
αὐτὴν φυλὴν νέμειν καὶ διὰ τὴν συντυχίαν παρ᾽
143 αὐτὸν ξενισθησόμενον ἦγε. νεανίαι δέ τινες τῶν
Γαβαηνῶν ἐπὶ τῆς ἀγορᾶς τὸ γύναιον θεασάμενοι
καὶ τὴν εὐπρέπειαν θαυμάσαντες, ἐπεὶ παρὰ τῷ
πρεσβύτῃ κατηγμένην ἔμαθον καταφρονήσαντες τῆς
ἀσθενείας καὶ τῆς ὀλιγότητος ἧκον ἐπὶ τὰς θύρας.
τοῦ δὲ πρεσβύτου παρακαλοῦντος ἀπαλλάττεσθαι
καὶ μὴ προσφέρειν βίαν μηδὲ ὕβριν, ἠξίουν αὐτὸν
παρασχόντα τὴν ξένην πραγμάτων ἀπηλλάχθαι.
144 συγγενῆ δὲ[2] λέγοντος καὶ Λευίτην[3] τοῦ πρεσβύτου
καὶ δράσειν αὐτοὺς δεινὰ ὑφ᾽ ἡδονῆς εἰς τοὺς νόμους
ἐξαμαρτάνοντας ὠλιγώρουν τοῦ δικαίου καὶ κατ-
εγέλων, ἠπείλουν δὲ ἀποκτείνειν αὐτὸν ἐμποδίζοντα
145 ταῖς ἐπιθυμίαις αὐτῶν. εἰς δ᾽ ἀνάγκην περι-
ηγμένος καὶ μὴ βουλόμενος τοὺς ξένους περιιδεῖν
ὑβρισθέντας, τῆς ἑαυτοῦ θυγατρὸς αὐτοῖς παρεχώρει, πληρώσειν τε τὴν ἐπιθυμίαν αὐτοὺς λέγων
νομιμώτερον δίχα τῆς εἰς τοὺς ξένους ὕβρεως αὐτός
τε[4] μηδὲν ἀδικήσειν οὓς ὑπεδέξατο τούτῳ τῷ
146 τρόπῳ νομίζων. ὡς δ᾽ οὐδὲν τῆς σπουδῆς τῆς
ἐπὶ τὴν ξένην ἐνεδίδοσαν, ἀλλ᾽ ἐνέκειντο ταύτην
παραλαβεῖν ἀξιοῦντες, ὁ μὲν ἱκέτευε μηδὲν τολμᾶν

---

[1] Dindorf: ἀπεῖναι codd.
[2] ὡς συγγενῆ δὲ RO : ὡς δὲ συγγενῆ τε rell.
[3] Λευίτιν E.
[4] Dindorf: δὲ codd.

setting off, when it was dark already, taking provisions for his supper. He replied that he was a *cf.* xix. 19.
Levite and that he was escorting his wife from her
parents back to his own home, informing him that
he had his abode in the province of Ephraim. Thereat the old man, because of their common stock, and
because they belonged to the same tribe and because
chance had thus brought them together, took him
as his guest to his own home. But some of the young xix. 22.
men of Gaba, who had seen the woman in the
market-place and admired her comeliness, when
they learnt that she lodged with the old man, scorning the feebleness of these few,[a] came to the doors ;
and when the old man bade them begone and not
to resort to violence and outrage, they required
him to hand over his woman guest if he wished to
avoid trouble. The old man replying that he [b] was
a kinsman and a Levite and that they would be
guilty of a dreadful crime in violating the laws at
the beck of pleasure, they recked little of righteousness, mocked at it, and threatened to kill him if
he thwarted their lusts. Driven to such a pass and
unwilling to suffer his guests to be abused, he offered
the men his own daughter, declaring that it would
be more legitimate for them thus to gratify their
lust than by doing violence to his guests, and for
his part thinking by this means to avoid wronging
those whom he had received. But they in no
wise abated their passion for the stranger, being
insistent in their demands to have her, and while
he was yet imploring them to perpetrate no iniquity,

[a] Gr. " their feebleness and fewness " (*cf. B.J.* iii. 317).
[b] *i.e.* the husband. One MS. reads " that she (the Levite's
wife) was a kinswoman " etc.

παράνομον, οἱ δ’ ἁρπασάμενοι καὶ προσθέμενοι
μᾶλλον τῷ βιαίῳ τῆς ἡδονῆς ἀπήγαγον πρὸς αὑτοὺς
τὴν γυναῖκα καὶ δι’ ὅλης νυκτὸς ἐμπλησθέντες τῆς
147 ὕβρεως ἀπέλυσαν περὶ ἀρχομένην ἡμέραν. ἡ δὲ
τεταλαιπωρημένη τοῖς συμβεβηκόσι παρῆν ἐπὶ τὴν
ξενίαν καὶ ὑπὸ λύπης ὧν. ἐπεπόνθει καὶ τοῦ μὴ
τολμᾶν ὑπ’ αἰσχύνης εἰς ὄψιν ἐλθεῖν τἀνδρί, τοῦτον
γὰρ μάλιστα τοῖς γεγενημένοις ἔχειν ἀνιάτως
148 ἐλογίζετο, καταπεσοῦσα τὴν ψυχὴν ἀφίησιν. ὁ δὲ
ἀνὴρ αὐτῆς οἰόμενος ὕπνῳ βαθεῖ κατεσχῆσθαι τὴν
γυναῖκα καὶ μηδὲν σκυθρωπὸν ὑφορώμενος ἀνεγείρειν ἐπειρᾶτο παραμυθήσασθαι διεγνωκώς, ὡς
οὐκ ἐξ ἑκουσίου γνώμης αὐτὴν παράσχοι τοῖς
καθυβρίσασιν, ἀλλ’ ἁρπασαμένων ἐπὶ τὴν ξενίαν
149 ἐλθόντων αὐτῶν.[1] ὡς δὲ τελευτήσασαν ἔμαθε,
σωφρονισθείς[2] πρὸς τὸ μέγεθος τῶν κακῶν ἐπιθέμενος τῷ κτήνει νεκρὰν τὴν γυναῖκα κομίζει
πρὸς αὑτόν, καὶ διελὼν αὐτὴν κατὰ μέλος εἰς μέρη
δώδεκα διέπεμψεν εἰς ἑκάστην φυλήν, ἐντειλάμενος
τοῖς κομίζουσι λέγειν τοὺς αἰτίους τῆς τελευτῆς
τῇ γυναικὶ καὶ τὴν παροινίαν τῆς φυλῆς.[3]
150 (9) Οἱ δ’ ὑπό τε τῆς ὄψεως καὶ τῆς ἀκοῆς τῶν
βεβιασμένων κακῶς διατεθέντες, πρότερον οὐδενὸς
τοιούτου πεῖραν εἰληφότες, ὑπ’ ὀργῆς ἀκράτου
καὶ δικαίας εἰς τὴν Σιλοῦν συλλεγέντες καὶ πρὸ
τῆς σκηνῆς ἀθροισθέντες εἰς ὅπλα χωρεῖν εὐθὺς
ὥρμηντο καὶ χρήσασθαι τοῖς Γαβαηνοῖς ὡς πολε-
151 μίοις. ἐπέσχε δ’ αὐτοὺς ἡ γερουσία πείσασα μὴ

---

[1] ἀλλ’ . . . αὐτῶν om. Lat.
[2] conj. (cf. § 256): σωφρόνως (σωφρονῶν SP) codd.
[3] τῆς φυλῆς R : ταῖς φυλαῖς rell.

they seized[a] the woman and, yielding still more to the force of their lust, carried her off to their homes and then, after sating their lewdness all night long, let her go towards the break of day. She, outworn with her woes, repaired to the house of her host, where, out of grief at what she had endured and not daring for shame to face her husband—since he above all, she deemed, would be inconsolable at her fate—she succumbed and gave up the ghost. But her husband, supposing his wife to be buried in deep sleep and suspecting nothing serious, tried to arouse her, with intent to console her by recalling how she had not voluntarily surrendered herself to her abusers, but that they had come to the lodging-house and carried her off. But when he found that she was dead, chastened before the enormity of the wrong, he laid the dead woman upon his beast, bore her to his home and then, dividing her limb by limb into twelve pieces, sent one to each tribe, enjoining the bearers to state who they were who had caused the death of his wife and to recount the debauchery of the tribe.[b]

(9) The Israelites, sorely moved by the spectacle and the tale of these deeds of violence, the like of which they had never known before, in intense and righteous wrath assembled at Silo[c] and, mustering before the tabernacle, were impatient to rush straight to arms and to treat these people of Gaba as enemies. But they were restrained by the elders, who urged

The Israelites vainly demand the surrender of the culprits. Jd. xx. 1.

---

[a] In Scripture, the Levite himself surrenders the woman.

[b] *Sc.* of Benjamin. " One to each tribe " is not in Scripture (" sent her throughout all the borders of Israel "); were that meant, one might expect the number to be eleven, Benjamin being excluded.

[c] In Scripture, the tribes assemble at Mizpah.

δεῖν ὀξέως οὕτως πρὸς τοὺς ὁμοφύλους ἐκφέρειν
πόλεμον πρὶν ἢ λόγοις διαλεχθῆναι περὶ τῶν ἐγ-
κλημάτων, τοῦ νόμου μηδ' ἐπὶ τοὺς ἀλλοτρίους ἐφ-
ιέντος δίχα πρεσβείας καὶ τοιαύτης πρὸς τὸ μετανοῆσαι πείρας τοὺς δόξαντας ἀδικεῖν στρατιὰν¹
152 ἀγαγεῖν· καλῶς οὖν ἔχειν τῷ νόμῳ πειθομένους
πρὸς τοὺς Γαβαηνοὺς ἐξαιτοῦντας τοὺς αἰτίους
ἐκπέμψαι καὶ παρεχομένων μὲν ἀρκεῖσθαι τῇ
τούτων κολάσει, καταφρονησάντων δὲ τότε τοῖς
153 ὅπλοις αὐτοὺς ἀμύνασθαι. πέμπουσιν οὖν πρὸς
τοὺς Γαβαηνοὺς κατηγοροῦντες τῶν νεανίσκων τὰ
περὶ τὴν γυναῖκα καὶ πρὸς τιμωρίαν αἰτοῦντες τοὺς
δράσαντας μὲν οὐ νόμιμα, γενομένους δὲ δικαίους
154 ἀντ' αὐτῶν ἐκείνων ἀποθανεῖν. οἱ δὲ Γαβαηνοὶ
οὔτε τοὺς νεανίσκους ἐξέδοσαν καὶ δεινὸν ἀλλοτρίοις
ὑπακούειν προστάγμασιν ἡγοῦντο πολέμου φόβῳ,
μηδενὸς ἀξιοῦντες εἶναι χείρους ἐν τοῖς ὅπλοις
μήτε διὰ πλῆθος μήτε δι' εὐψυχίαν. ἦσαν δὲ ἐν
παρασκευῇ μεγάλῃ μετὰ καὶ² τῶν ἄλλων φυλετῶν,
συναπενοήθησαν γὰρ αὐτοῖς ὡς ἀμυνούμενοι³
βιαζομένους.
155   (10) Ὡς δὲ τοιαῦτα τοῖς Ἰσραηλίταις τὰ παρὰ
τῶν Γαβαηνῶν ἀπηγγέλθη, ὅρκους ποιοῦνται
μηδένα σφῶν ἀνδρὶ Βενιαμίτῃ δώσειν πρὸς γάμον
θυγατέρα στρατεύσειν τε ἐπ' αὐτούς, μᾶλλον αὐτοῖς
δι' ὀργῆς ὄντες ἢ τοῖς Χαναναίοις⁴ τοὺς προγόνους

---

¹ στρατείαν ROSL.   ² μετὰ καὶ Dindorf: καὶ codd.
³ ex Lat. Niese: ἀμυνόμενοι codd.   ⁴ ed. pr.: +οἷς codd.

ᵃ Or, with other mss., " a campaign."
ᵇ This advice of the elders, not mentioned in Scripture,
is added to show that they conformed to the Mosaic law
(Deut. xx. 10 ; A. iv. 296).

that they ought not so hurriedly to make war on their brethren, ere they had parleyed with them concerning their grievances, the law not permitting them to lead an army *a* even against aliens without having sent an embassy and made other attempts of this nature to bring the supposed wrongdoers to repentance.*b* It therefore behoved them, in obedience to the law, to send envoys to the Gabaenians to demand the surrender of the culprits and, should they deliver them up, to be content with punishing these individuals ; but, should they flout this demand, then to retaliate on them by resort to arms. So they sent an embassy to Gaba to accuse the xx. 12. young men of the woman's fate and to require the surrender for punishment of those that had done thus lawlessly and who for those very deeds deserved to die.*c* But the people of Gaba refused to surrender the youths and scorned to bow to the behests of others through fear of war, holding themselves to be inferior in arms to none whether in numbers or valour. So they proceeded to make great preparations along with the rest of their tribe, who joined them in their desperate undertaking in the belief that they were repelling aggressors.

(10) Now when word was brought to the Israelites Civil war with the Benjamites defeat of Israel. of this response from the men of Gaba, they took an oath that not one among them would give his daughter to a man of Benjamin and that they would Jd. xxi. 1. march against them, being more indignant against them than were our forefathers, as we are told, xx. 17.

c Or perhaps (taking αὐτῶν ἐκείνων as masculines) " who deserved to die in lieu of their own people " : the balance of clauses (μὲν . . . δὲ . . .) favours this. The lawlessness of the deed warranted wholesale destruction, but at least the culprits should suffer.

156 ἡμῶν παρειλήφαμεν γενομένους. παραχρῆμά τε
ἐξῆγον ἐπ᾽ αὐτοὺς τὸ στρατόπεδον μυριάδας τεσ·
σαράκοντα ὁπλιτῶν· καὶ Βενιαμιτῶν τὸ ὁπλιτικὸι
ἦν ὑπὸ δισμυρίων καὶ πεντακισχιλίων καὶ ἑξακοσίων, ὧν ἦσαν εἰς πεντακοσίους ταῖς λαιαῖς
157 τῶν χειρῶν σφενδονᾶν ἄριστοι, ὥστε καὶ μάχης
πρὸς τῇ Γαβᾷ γενομένης τρέπουσι τοὺς Ἰσραηλίτας
οἱ Βενιαμῖται ἄνδρες τε πίπτουσιν ἐξ αὐτῶν εἰς
δισμυρίους καὶ δισχιλίους, ἐφθάρησαν δὲ ἴσως ἂν
καὶ πλείονες, εἰ μὴ νὺξ αὐτοὺς ἐπέσχε καὶ διέλυσε
158 μαχομένους. καὶ οἱ μὲν Βενιαμῖται χαίροντες ἀν-
εχώρουν εἰς τὴν πόλιν, οἱ δ᾽ Ἰσραηλῖται κατα-
πεπληγότες ὑπὸ τῆς ἥττης εἰς τὸ στρατόπεδον.
τῇ δ᾽ ἐπιούσῃ πάλιν συμβαλόντων οἱ Βενιαμῖται
κρατοῦσι καὶ θνήσκουσι τῶν Ἰσραηλιτῶν ὀκτα-
κισχίλιοι καὶ μύριοι, καὶ δείσαντες τὸν φόνον[1]
159 ἐξέλιπον τὸ στρατόπεδον. παραγενόμενοι δὲ εἰς
Βέθηλα πόλιν ἔγγιστα κειμένην καὶ νηστεύσαντες
κατὰ τὴν ὑστεραίαν τὸν θεὸν ἱκέτευον διὰ Φινεέσου
τοῦ ἀρχιερέως παύσασθαι τῆς ὀργῆς τῆς πρὸς
αὐτοὺς καὶ ταῖς δυσὶν αὐτῶν ἥτταις ἀρκεσθέντα
δοῦναι νίκην καὶ κράτος κατὰ τῶν πολεμίων. ὁ
δὲ θεὸς ἐπαγγέλλεται ταῦτα διὰ Φινεέσου προφητεύσαντος.
160 (11) Ποιήσαντες οὖν τὴν στρατιὰν δύο μέρη τὴν
μὲν ἡμίσειαν προλοχίζουσι νυκτὸς περὶ τὴν πόλιν,
οἱ δ᾽ ἡμίσεις συνέβαλον τοῖς Βενιαμίταις ὑπεχώρουν
τε ἐγκειμένων, καὶ ἐδίωκον οἱ Βενιαμῖται ⟨καὶ⟩

[1] om. L Lat.

---

[a] Heb. 26,000 Benjamites + 700 inhabitants of Gibeah:
LXX 25,000 (or 23,000) + 700. In Josephus the preposition

against the Canaanites. And forthwith they led ^{xx. 15 f.} out against them their host of 400,000 men-at-arms; the forces of the Benjamites numbered but some 25,600 [a] among whom were 500 [b] expert in using the sling with the left hand. And so, a battle ensuing near Gaba, the Benjamites routed the Israelites, and there fell of these 22,000 men; indeed perchance yet more would have perished, had not night checked them and parted the combatants. The Benjamites then withdrew, exultant, to the town, the Israelites, crest-fallen at their defeat, to their camp. On the morrow, when they renewed the attack, the Benjamites were again victorious: 18,000 of the Israelites perished, and daunted by this carnage they abandoned their encampment. Repairing to Bethel, the city nearest at hand,[c] and ^{xx. 26.} having fasted on the morrow, they besought God, through Phinees the high priest, to abate his anger against them and, content with their two defeats, to vouchsafe them victory and the mastery over their foes. And God promised them their petitions through the mouth of Phinees, His interpreter.

(11) So, dividing their army in two, they set half ^{Defeat of the Benjamites: reprisals of the Israelites. Jd. xx. 29.} in ambush around the town [d] under cover of night; the other half then engaged the Benjamites and before their onset retired. The Benjamites pursued

ὑπό, if genuine, seems to mean " about " and perhaps indicates acquaintance with variant readings in Scripture.

[b] Heb. (with some mss. of LXX) 700: other mss. of LXX omit the number.

[c] Bethel is some 8 miles N. of the traditional site of Gibeah (*Tell el-Ful*): Shiloh, the seat of the tabernacle (§ 150), lay considerably farther north.

[d] This battle scene, like others, recalls Thucydides: with προλοχίζειν περὶ τὴν πόλιν cf. Thuc. ii. 81, with πασσυδί (§ 161) viii. 1, with περιστάντες κατηκόντισαν (§ 162) vii. 84.

233

JOSEPHUS

τῶν Ἑβραίων ὑποφευγόντων ἠρέμα καὶ ἐπὶ πολὺ
θελόντων εἰς ἅπαν αὐτοὺς ἐξελθεῖν[1] ἀναχωροῦσιν
161 εἴποντο, ὡς καὶ τοὺς ἐν τῇ πόλει πρεσβύτας καὶ
νέους ὑπολειφθέντας δι' ἀσθένειαν συνεκδραμεῖν[2]
αὐτοῖς πασσυδὶ βουλομένους χειρώσασθαι τοὺς
πολεμίους. ὡς δὲ πολὺ τῆς πόλεως ἀπέσχον,
ἐπαύσαντο μὲν φεύγοντες οἱ Ἑβραῖοι, ἐπιστρα-
φέντες δ' ἵστανται πρὸς μάχην καὶ τοῖς ἐν ταῖς
ἐνέδραις οὖσι τὸ σημεῖον αἴρουσιν ὃ συνέκειτο.
162 οἱ δ' ἐξαναστάντες μετὰ βοῆς ἐπῄεσαν τοῖς πολεμίοις. οἱ δὲ ἅμα τε ἠπατημένους αὐτοὺς ᾔσθοντο
καὶ ἐν ἀμηχανίᾳ συνεστήκεσαν, καὶ εἴς τι κοῖλον
συνελαθέντας καὶ φαραγγῶδες χωρίον περιστάντες
κατηκόντισαν, ὥστε πάντας διαφθαρῆναι πλὴν
163 ἑξακοσίων. οὗτοι δὲ συστραφέντες καὶ πυκνώ-
σαντες ἑαυτοὺς καὶ διὰ μέσων ὠσάμενοι τῶν πολεμίων ἔφυγον ἐπὶ τὰ πλησίον ὄρη, καὶ κατασχόντες
ἱδρύθησαν. οἱ δ' ἄλλοι πάντες περὶ δισμυρίους
164 ὄντες καὶ πεντακισχιλίους ἀπέθανον. οἱ δ' Ἰσραηλῖται τήν τε Γάβαν ἐμπιπρᾶσι καὶ τὰς γυναῖκας
καὶ τῶν ἀρρένων τοὺς μὴ ἐν ἀκμῇ διεχρήσαντο,
τάς τε ἄλλας τῶν Βενιαμιτῶν πόλεις ταὐτὰ δρῶσιν·
οὕτως τε ἦσαν παρωξυμμένοι,[3] ὡς καὶ Ἰάβησον τῆς
Γαλαδίτιδος οὖσαν, ὅτι μὴ συμμαχήσειεν αὐτοῖς
κατὰ τῶν Βενιαμιτῶν, πέμψαντες μυρίους καὶ
165 δισχιλίους ἐκ τῶν τάξεων ἐκέλευσαν ἀνελεῖν. καὶ
φονεύουσι τὸ μάχιμον τῆς πόλεως οἱ πεμφθέντες
σὺν τέκνοις καὶ γυναιξὶ πλὴν τετρακοσίων παρ-
θένων. ἐπὶ τοσοῦτον ὑπ' ὀργῆς προήχθησαν, τῷ

---

[1] protrahere (? ἐξελεῖν) Lat., omisso ἐπὶ πολύ aut εἰς ἅπαν.
[2] ed. pr.: διεκδραμεῖν δι' ἀσθένειαν codd.
[3] παρωργισμένοι MSPL.

and, as the Hebrews fell back little by little to a
great distance, wishing them to come out *a* to a
man, they followed their retreating foe, in such wise
that even the old men and lads who had been left in
the town as incompetent sallied out also, eager as a
united body to crush the enemy. But when they
were now remote from the town, the Hebrews stayed
their flight and, turning, stood their ground for
battle, while they raised the concerted signal for
their friends in ambush ; and these, emerging with
a shout, fell upon the enemy. The Benjamites, from
the moment when they saw themselves entrapped,
were in a hopeless plight : driven into a rugged
hollow, they were there shot down by the darts of
the Hebrews who stood around them, with the result
that all perished save 600. These, rallying and
closing up their ranks, pushed through the enemy's
midst, fled for the neighbouring hills, and there, on
gaining them, established themselves ; all the rest,
in number about 25,000, perished. The Israelites xx. 46.
burnt Gaba and made away with the women and
males under age ; the other cities of the Benjamites
they treated in like manner. Moreover, so exasper- xxi. 8.
ated were they that, forasmuch as the town of Jabesh
in Gilead had not aided them in battle against the
Benjamites, they sent thither 12,000 men from their
ranks, with orders to destroy it. This detachment
massacred all of military age in the town, along with
the children and all the women save 400 who were unmarried. To such lengths did their rage carry them,

a Or, with the Latin, " wishing to draw them out."

κατὰ τὴν γυναῖκα πάθει προσλαβόντες καὶ τὸ κατὰ
τὴν ἀναίρεσιν τῶν ὁπλιτῶν.

166 (12) Μετάνοια δ' αὐτοὺς λαμβάνει τῆς τῶν
Βενιαμιτῶν συμφορᾶς καὶ νηστείαν ἐπ' αὐτοῖς προ-
έθεντο, καίτοι δίκαια παθεῖν αὐτοὺς ἀξιοῦντες εἰς
τοὺς νόμους ἐξαμαρτάνοντας, καὶ τοὺς διαφυγόντας
αὐτῶν ἑξακοσίους διὰ πρεσβυτέρων ἐκάλουν· καθ-
ίδρυντο γὰρ ὑπὲρ πέτρας τινὸς Ῥοᾶς καλουμένης
167 κατὰ τὴν ἔρημον. οἱ δὲ πρέσβεις ὡς οὐκ ἐκείνοις
τῆς συμφορᾶς μόνοις γεγενημένης ἀλλὰ καὶ αὐτοῖς τῶν συγγενῶν ἀπολωλότων ὀδυρόμενοι πρᾴως
ἔπειθον φέρειν καὶ συνελθεῖν εἰς ταὐτὸ καὶ μὴ
παντελῆ τῆς Βενιαμίτιδος φυλῆς ὄλεθρον τό γε ἐπ'
αὐτοῖς καταψηφίσασθαι. " συγχωροῦμεν δὲ ὑμῖν,"
ἔλεγον, " τὴν ἁπάσης τῆς φυλῆς γῆν καὶ λείαν
168 ὅσην ἂν ἄγειν δυνηθῆτε¹"· οἱ δὲ τῶν καθ' ἑαυτοὺς
θεοῦ ψήφῳ γεγονότων καὶ κατ' ἀδικίαν τὴν αὐτῶν
γνωσιμαχήσαντες κατῄεσαν εἰς τὴν πάτριον φυλὴν
πειθόμενοι τοῖς προκαλουμένοις. οἱ δ' Ἰσραηλῖται γυναῖκας αὐτοῖς τὰς τετρακοσίας ἔδοσαν
παρθένους τὰς Ἰαβίτιδας, περὶ δὲ τῶν διακοσίων
ἐσκόπουν, ὅπως κἀκεῖνοι γυναικῶν εὐπορήσαντες
169 παιδοποιῶνται. γεγενημένων δ' αὐτοῖς ὅρκων
ὥστε μηδενὶ Βενιαμίτῃ συνοικίσαι² θυγατέρα πρὸ
τοῦ πολέμου, οἱ μὲν ὀλιγωρεῖν συνεβούλευον τῶν
ὀμωμοσμένων ὡς ὑπ' ὀργῆς ὀμόσαντες οὐ γνώμῃ
καὶ κρίσει, τῷ δὲ θεῷ μηδὲν ἐναντίον ποιήσειν εἰ

----

¹ Niese: δυνηθείητε codd.   ² edd.: συνοικῆσαι codd.

ᵃ Gr. translation of Heb. Rimmon (=" pomegranate ");
usually identified as modern *Rammun*, a few miles E. of
Bethel, but a more likely site, much nearer to Gibeah, has
been proposed (Burney, *Judges*, p. xxi).

because, in addition to what they had suffered on the woman's account, they had further suffered the slaughter of their men-at-arms.

(12) Howbeit they were smitten with remorse for the Benjamites' calamity and they ordained a fast on their behalf, while yet maintaining that they had justly suffered for their sin against the laws; and they summoned by ambassadors those 600 of them who had escaped and established themselves on a rock called Rhoa *a* in the wilderness. These envoys, deploring a calamity which had struck not the Benjamites only but themselves, in that the victims were their kinsmen, urged them to bear it patiently, to come and join them, and not, so far as in them lay, to pronounce sentence of total extinction upon the tribe of Benjamin. "We grant you," said they, "the territory of the whole tribe and of booty *b* as much as ye can carry off." And the Benjamites, recognizing with contrition that their misfortunes were due to God's decree and to their own iniquity, came down again into the tribe of their fathers, in compliance with this invitation. The Israelites gave them for wives those 400 virgins from Jabesh,*c* and then deliberated concerning the remaining 200 men, how they too might be provided with wives and beget children. Now, whereas they had before the war made oath to give no Benjamite a daughter of theirs in wedlock, some were of opinion that they should disregard those oaths as having been sworn under the sway of passion, without reflexion or judgement; that they would be doing nothing in opposition to God, could they so save a

Reconciliation with the Benjamites: how brides were found for them.
Jd. xxi. 2, 6.
xxi. 13.

xxi. 18.

---

b i.e. cattle.   *c* § 165.

φυλὴν ὅλην κινδυνεύουσαν ἀπολέσθαι σῶσαι δυνηθεῖεν, τάς τε ἐπιορκίας οὐχ ὅταν ὑπὸ ἀνάγκης
γένωνται χαλεπὰς εἶναι καὶ ἐπισφαλεῖς, ἀλλ' ὅταν
170 ἐν κακουργίᾳ τολμηθῶσι. τῆς δὲ γερουσίας πρὸς
τὸ τῆς ἐπιορκίας ὄνομα σχετλιασάσης ἔφη τις
τούτοις τε γυναικῶν εὐπορίαν ἔχειν εἰπεῖν καὶ τήρη-
σιν τῶν ὅρκων. ἐρομένων δὲ τὴν ἐπίνοιαν, " ἡμῖν,"
εἶπεν, " τρὶς τοῦ ἔτους εἰς Σιλὼ συνιοῦσιν ἕπονται
171 κατὰ πανήγυριν αἱ γυναῖκες καὶ αἱ θυγατέρες. τούτων κατὰ ἁρπαγὴν ἐφείσθω γαμεῖν Βενιαμίτας ἃς
ἂν[1] δυνηθεῖεν ἡμῶν οὔτε προτρεπομένων οὔτε
κωλυόντων. πρὸς δὲ τοὺς πατέρας αὐτῶν δυσχεραίνοντας καὶ τιμωρίαν λαμβάνειν ἀξιοῦντας
φήσομεν αὐτοὺς αἰτίους φυλακῆς ἀμελήσαντας
τῶν θυγατέρων, ὅτι δὲ δεῖ τῆς ὀργῆς ἐπὶ Βενιαμίτας ὑφεῖναι[2] χρησαμένους αὐτῇ καὶ θᾶττον ἀμέ-
172 τρως." καὶ οἱ μὲν τούτοις πεισθέντες ψηφίζονται
τὸν διὰ τῆς ἁρπαγῆς γάμον τοῖς Βενιαμίταις.
ἐνστάσης δὲ τῆς ἑορτῆς οἱ μὲν διακόσιοι κατὰ δύο
καὶ τρεῖς πρὸ τῆς πόλεως ἐνήδρευον παρεσομένας
τὰς παρθένους ἔν τε ἀμπελῶσι καὶ χωρίοις ἐν
173 οἷς λήσειν ἔμελλον, αἱ δὲ μετὰ παιδιᾶς οὐδὲν ὑφ-
ορώμεναι τῶν μελλόντων ἀφυλάκτως ᾤδευον· οἱ
δὲ σκεδασθεισῶν εἴχοντο ἐξαναστάντες. καὶ οὗτοι
μὲν οὕτως γαμήσαντες ἐπ' ἔργα τῆς γῆς ἐχώρησαν

---

[1] ἄν secl. Naber. [2] Bekker: ἀφεῖναι RO, ἐφεῖναι rell.

---

[a] Jd. xxi. 19 " Behold there is a (or "the") feast (ḥag) of
the LORD *from year to year* (lit. " from days to days," LXX ἀφ'
ἡμερῶν εἰς ἡμέρας) in Shiloh." The ḥag here alluded to is
the oldest of Jewish festivals, its autumn vintage festival
of *Sukkoth* or " Tabernacles " ; for its annual observance at
Shiloh *cf.* 1 Sam. i. 3. Josephus refers back to those early

whole tribe in danger of extinction ; and that per-
juries were not grave or hazardous when they were
prompted by necessity, but only when rashly committed with malicious intent. When the elders, however, protested at the mere mention of perjury, someone said that he could suggest how to provide wives for
these men and yet to keep their oaths. On being
questioned concerning his plan, " When we meet,"
he replied, " three times a year *a* at Silo, we are accompanied to the festival by our wives and daughters.
Let the Benjamites be permitted to capture as
their brides such of these maidens as they can,
without either encouragement or hindrance on our
part. And if their parents make an ado and demand
punishment, we will tell them that they have but
themselves to blame for neglecting to protect their
daughters, and that we must abate that resentment against the Benjamites, in which already in
the past *b* we had been immoderate." The assembly
assenting thereto decided accordingly to permit the
Benjamites this marriage by capture. So, when the
festival came round, the 200, in twos and threes,
waited in ambush before the city for the coming of
the maidens, in the vineyards and other places where
they would escape their eye. Meanwhile the
damsels, playfully and with no suspicion of what
was on foot, came all unguardedly along ; whereat
the men sprang out upon them and seized them as
they scattered. These Benjamites, thus wedded,
then betook themselves to the labours of the soil

---

days the keeping of the *three* great annual festivals, including
Passover and Pentecost.

b θᾶττον = πρότερον, as elsewhere (with connotation of
precipitancy).

καὶ πρόνοιαν ἐποιήσαντο πάλιν εἰς τὴν προτέραν
174 εὐδαιμονίαν ἐπανελθεῖν. Βενιαμιτῶν μὲν οὖν ἡ
φυλὴ κινδυνεύσασα τελέως ἐκφθαρῆναι τῷ προειρη-
μένῳ τρόπῳ κατὰ τὴν Ἰσραηλιτῶν σοφίαν σώζεται,
ηὔθησέ τε παραχρῆμα καὶ ταχεῖαν εἴς τε πλῆθος
καὶ τὰ ἄλλα πάντα ἐποιήσατο τὴν ἐπίδοσιν. οὗτος
μὲν οὖν ὁ πόλεμος οὕτως παύεται.

175 (iii. 1) Ὅμοια δὲ τούτοις παθεῖν καὶ τὴν Δάνιν[1]
συνέβη φυλὴν ἐξ αἰτίας τοιαύτης εἰς τοῦτο προ-
176 αχθεῖσαν. τῶν Ἰσραηλιτῶν ἐκλελοιπότων ἤδη τὴν
ἐν τοῖς πολέμοις ἄσκησιν καὶ πρὸς τοῖς ἔργοις
ὄντων τῆς γῆς Χαναναῖοι καταφρονήσαντες αὐτῶν
συνεποιήσαντο δύναμιν, οὐδὲν μὲν αὐτοὶ πείσεσθαι
προσδοκῶντες, ὡς δὲ βεβαίαν τὴν τοῦ ποιήσειν
κακῶς τοὺς Ἑβραίους ἐλπίδα λαβόντες ἐπ᾽ ἀδείας
177 τὸ λοιπὸν οἰκεῖν τὰς πόλεις ἠξίουν. ἅρματά τε
οὖν παρεσκευάζοντο καὶ τὸ ὁπλιτικὸν συνεκρότουν
αἵ τε πόλεις αὐτῶν συνεφρόνουν καὶ τῆς Ἰούδα
φυλῆς τὴν Ἀσκάλωνα καὶ Ἀκκαρῶνα παρεσπά-
σαντο ἄλλας τε πολλὰς τῶν ἐν τῷ πεδίῳ καὶ
Δανίτας εἰς τὸ ὄρος ἠνάγκασαν συμφυγεῖν οὐδὲ
ὀλίγον αὐτοῖς ἐπιβατὸν τοῦ πεδίου καταλιπόντες.
178 οἱ δ᾽ οὔτε πολεμεῖν ὄντες ἱκανοὶ γῆν τε οὐκ ἔχοντες
ἀρκοῦσαν πέμπουσιν ἐξ αὐτῶν πέντε ἄνδρας εἰς
τὴν μεσόγειον κατοψομένους γῆν, εἰς ἣν μετοική-
σαιντο. οἱ δ᾽ οὐ πόρρω τοῦ Λιβάνου ὄρους καὶ
ἐλάσσονος Ἰορδάνου τῶν πηγῶν κατὰ τὸ μέγα

---

[1] Niese: Δάνην (Διανὴν) codd.

---

[a] Contrast § 128 (note), where we are told that Akkaron

and devoted their efforts to the recovery of their former prosperity. This, then, was the way in which the tribe of Benjamin, when in danger of complete extinction, was saved through the sagacity of the Israelites; and instantly it flourished and made rapid advance both in numbers and in all beside. And thus ended this war. Jd. fin.

(iii. 1) But like sufferings also befell the tribe of The Danites forced to migrate northwards. Dan, the cause which brought it to this pass being as follows. Now that the Israelites had abandoned the exercise of warfare and were given up to their labours on the land, the Canaanites, holding them in contempt, built up an army, not from expectation of any injury to themselves, but, being now confident of doing mischief to the Hebrews, they counted on henceforth inhabiting their cities in security. So they proceeded to equip chariots and levy troops, their cities unanimously combined, and from the tribe of Judah they wrested Ascalon, Akkarōn *a* and many other cities of the plain, while they forced the Jd. i. 34. Danites to flee in a body to the hills, leaving them not the smallest foothold on the plain. *b*These, in- xviii. 1 f. capable of fighting and not having land to suffice them, sent five of their number into the interior to look for a region whither they could migrate. The 7-11. envoys, having advanced to a spot not far from mount Libanus and the sources of the lesser *c* Jordan, over

had never been conquered; here Josephus conforms to the Hebrew text of Scripture (Jd. i. 18) which names Ekron among the captured cities.

b Here Josephus omits the unedifying story of Micah and his images, which in Scripture is mixed up with this expedition of the Danites (Jd. xvii. f.).

c The course of the Jordan north of the modern lake of Ḥuleh. *Cf. B.J.* iii. 509 f.

JOSEPHUS

πεδίον Σιδῶνος πόλεως ὁδὸν ἡμέρας μιᾶς[1] προελθόντες καὶ κατασκεψάμενοι γῆν ἀγαθὴν καὶ πάμ-
φορον σημαίνουσι τοῖς αὐτῶν· οἱ δ' ὁρμηθέντες
στρατῷ κτίζουσιν αὐτόθι πόλιν Δάνα ὁμώνυμον
τῷ Ἰακώβου παιδὶ φυλῆς δ' ἐπώνυμον τῆς αὐτῶν.

79 (2) Τοῖς δ' Ἰσραηλίταις προύβαινεν ὑπό τε
ἀπειρίας τοῦ πονεῖν τὰ κακὰ καὶ ὑπό[2] τῆς περὶ τὸ
θεῖον ὀλιγωρίας· μετακινηθέντες γὰρ ἅπαξ τοῦ
κόσμου τῆς πολιτείας ἐφέροντο πρὸς τὸ καθ'
ἡδονὴν καὶ βούλησιν ἰδίαν βιοῦν, ὡς καὶ τῶν ἐπι-
χωριαζόντων παρὰ τοῖς Χαναναίοις ἀναπίμπλασθαι
180 κακῶν. ὀργίζεται τοίνυν αὐτοῖς ὁ θεὸς καὶ ἣν
σὺν πόνοις μυρίοις εὐδαιμονίαν ἐκτήσαντο, ταύτην
ἀπέβαλον διὰ τρυφήν. στρατεύσαντος γὰρ ἐπ' αὐτοὺς Χουσαρσάθου[3] τοῦ τῶν Ἀσσυρίων βασιλέως,
πολλούς τε τῶν παραταξαμένων ἀπώλεσαν καὶ
181 πολιορκούμενοι κατὰ κράτος ᾑρέθησαν, εἰσὶ δ' οἳ
διὰ φόβον ἑκουσίως αὐτῷ προσεχώρησαν, φόρους
τε τοῦ δυνατοῦ μείζονας ἐπιταγέντες ἐτέλουν καὶ
ὕβρεις παντοίας ὑπέμενον ἕως ἐτῶν ὀκτώ, μεθ' ἃ
τῶν κακῶν οὕτως ἠλευθερώθησαν.
182 (3) Τῆς Ἰούδα φυλῆς τις Κενίαζος ὄνομα δρα-
στήριος ἀνὴρ καὶ τὸ φρόνημα γενναῖος, χρησθὲν

[1] trium dierum Lat.   [2] SP: ἀπὸ rell.
[3] RO: Chusasartho Lat.: Χουσάρθου rell.: similar *v.ll.* in § 183.

---

[a] So we must translate, carrying on the force of the preceding πόρρω. The translation " advanced *in one day's march*
to . . . over against the great plain of the city of S." is
precluded by distance (upwards of 100 miles); a difficulty
which is scarcely met by the reading of the Latin version,
" *three* days' march."

[b] Bibl. " Cushan-rishathaim (lxx Χουσαρσαθαίμ) king of
242

against the great plain, within a day's march of the
city of Sidon,[a] and having inspected a land good
and wholly fertile, reported this to their brethren ; 29.
and they, setting forth with an army, founded there
a city called Dan(a) after the name of the son of
Jacob, which was also the name of their own tribe.

(2) But the state of the Israelites went from bad
to worse through their loss of aptitude for toil and
their neglect of the Divinity. For, having once parted
from the ordered course of their constitution, they
drifted into living in accordance with their own
pleasure and caprice, and thus became contaminated
with the vices current among the Canaanites. So
God was wroth with them, and all that prosperity
which they had won with myriad labours they now
through idle luxury cast away. For Chusarsathus,
king of the Assyrians,[b] having marched upon them,
they lost multitudes in battle, and were besieged
and carried by storm, whilst some in terror voluntarily surrendered to him, paid tribute beyond
their means at his behest, and underwent indignities
of every kind for eight years, after which they were
delivered from their miseries on this wise.

(3) A man of the tribe of Judah, Keniaz[c] by
name, vigorous and noble-hearted, being warned by

(marginal notes: Israel under the Assyrians. Jd. iii. 5. — iii. 8. — Their deliverance by Keniaz. Jd. iii. 9.)

Aram-naharaim," *i.e.* " of Aram of the two rivers," *alias*
Mesopotamia. The personal name = " Cushan of double-
dyed villainy," a Biblical distortion of some older form.

[c] Bibl. " Othniel the son of Kenaz, Caleb's younger
brother." Josephus has replaced the son by the father ;
similarly in the so-called *Biblical Antiquities of Philo*
(*c.* A.D. 100) Cenez figures as the first judge and a person of
considerable importance (ed. M. R. James, p. 146 note).
The compiler of the Greek summary of the contents of
A. v. mentions Othniel but reverses the relationship (ἡ διὰ
Κενίζου τοῦ Ἀθνιήλου παιδὸς αὐτοῖς ἐλευθερία γενομένη).

αὐτῷ μὴ περιορᾶν ἐν τοιαύτῃ τοὺς Ἰσραηλίτας
ἀνάγκῃ κειμένους ἀλλ᾽ εἰς ἐλευθερίαν αὐτοὺς
ἐξαιρεῖσθαι τολμᾶν, παρακελευσάμενος¹ συλλαμβά-
νεσθαι τῶν κινδύνων αὐτῷ τινάς, ὀλίγοι δ᾽ ἦσαν
οἷς αἰδὼς ἐπὶ τοῖς τότε παροῦσιν ἐτύγχανε καὶ
183 προθυμία μεταβολῆς, πρῶτον μὲν τὴν παρ᾽ αὐτοῖς
οὖσαν φρουρὰν τοῦ Χουσαρσάθου διαφθείρει, προσ-
γενομένων δὲ πλειόνων τῶν συναγωνιζομένων ἐκ
τοῦ μὴ διαμαρτεῖν περὶ τὰ πρῶτα τῆς ἐπιχειρήσεως,
μάχην τοῖς Ἀσσυρίοις συνάπτουσι καὶ πρὸς τὸ
παντελὲς αὐτοὺς ἀπωσάμενοι περαιοῦσθαι τὸν
184 Εὐφράτην ἐβιάζοντο. Κενίαζος δὲ ὡς ἔργῳ πεῖραν
αὐτοῦ δεδωκὼς τῆς ἀνδραγαθίας γέρας ὑπὲρ αὐτῆς
λαμβάνει παρὰ τοῦ πλήθους ἀρχήν, ὥστε κρίνειν
τὸν λαόν. καὶ ἄρξας ἐπ᾽ ἔτη τεσσαράκοντα κατα-
στρέφει τὸν βίον.

185   (iv. 1) Τελευτήσαντος δὲ τούτου πάλιν τὰ τῶν
Ἰσραηλιτῶν ὑπὸ ἀναρχίας ἐνόσει πράγματα, καὶ
τῷ μὴ διὰ τιμῆς ἄγειν τὸν θεὸν μηδὲ τοῖς νόμοις
186 ὑπακούειν ἔτι μᾶλλον ἐκακοῦντο,² ὡς καταφρονή-
σαντα αὐτῶν τῆς ἀκοσμίας τῆς κατὰ τὴν πολιτείαν
Ἐγλῶνα τὸν Μωαβιτῶν βασιλέα πόλεμον πρὸς
αὐτοὺς ἐξενεγκεῖν καὶ πολλαῖς μάχαις αὐτῶν
κρατήσαντα καὶ τοὺς³ φρονήμασι τῶν ἄλλων διαφέροντας ὑποτάξαντα πρὸς τὸ παντελὲς αὐτῶν τὴν
δύναμιν ταπεινῶσαι καὶ φόρους αὐτοῖς ἐπιτάξαι
187 τελεῖν. καθιδρύσας δ᾽ αὐτῷ ἐν Ἱεριχοῦντι βασί-
λειον⁴ οὐδὲν τῆς εἰς τὸ πλῆθος κακώσεως παρέλιπεν
εἴς τε πενίαν αὐτοὺς κατέστησεν ἐπὶ ὀκτωκαίδεκα
ἔτη. λαβὼν δ᾽ οἶκτον ὁ θεὸς τῶν Ἰσραηλιτῶν ἐφ᾽

¹ παρασκευασάμενος ML.
² ἐκακοῦτο RO.   ³ τοῖς codd.

244

an oracle not to leave the Israelites to lie in such
deep distress, but to essay to vindicate their liberty,
after exhorting some others to share his hazards—
and few were they, who were filled with shame at
their present state and longed to alter it—began by
massacring the garrison of Chusarsathus that was
quartered upon them. Then, when larger numbers
rallied to his arms, seeing that he had not miscarried
at this opening of his enterprise, they joined battle
with the Assyrians and, having utterly repulsed
them, forced them to recross the Euphrates. Keniaz,
having thus given practical proof of his prowess,
received as his reward from the people rulership,
to act as judge of the nation. And after ruling for
forty years he ended his days.

(iv. 1) But after his death the affairs of the Israel- Israel under
Eglon, king
of Moab.
Jd. iii. 12.
ites again suffered through lack of government,
while their failure to render homage to God or to
obey the laws aggravated the evil yet more. So,
contemptuous of the disorder prevailing in their
state, Eglon, king of Moab, made war upon them
and, having defeated them in many battles and subjected all who showed more spirit than the rest,
utterly humiliated their strength and imposed tribute
upon them. Then establishing his capital in Jericho,[a]
he ruthlessly molested the people and reduced them
to penury for eighteen years. But God, taking pity
on the Israelites in their afflictions and moved by

---

[a] Jd. iii. 13 " he possessed the city of palm-trees," *i.e.*
Jericho, as the Targum (like Josephus) interprets the phrase.
This implies that Jericho did not remain unbuilt and un-
fortified between the days of Joshua and of Ahab.

---

[4] E Lat. ed. pr.: + ταύτην ἀποδείξας rell.

οἷς ἔπασχον καὶ ταῖς ἱκετείαις αὐτῶν ἐπικλασθεὶς
ἀπήλλαξε τῆς ὑπὸ τοῖς Μωαβίταις ὕβρεως. ἠλευθερώθησαν δὲ τούτῳ τῷ τρόπῳ.

188   (2) Τῆς Βενιαμίτιδος φυλῆς νεανίας Ἰούδης μὲν
τοὔνομα Γήρα δὲ¹¹ πατρός, τολμῆσαί τε ἀνδρειό-
τατος καὶ τῷ σώματι πρὸς τὰ ἔργα χρῆσθαι
δυνατώτατος, τῶν χειρῶν τὴν ἀριστερὰν ἀμείνων
κἀπ᾽ ἐκείνης τὴν ἅπασαν ἰσχὺν ἔχων, κατῴκει
189 μὲν ἐν Ἱεριχοῦντι καὶ αὐτός, συνήθης δὲ γίνεται
τῷ Ἐγλῶνι δωρεαῖς αὐτὸν θεραπεύων καὶ ὑπερχό-
μενος, ὡς διὰ τοῦτο καὶ τοῖς περὶ τὸν βασιλέα
190 προσφιλῆ τυγχάνειν αὐτόν.   καί ποτε σὺν δυσὶν
οἰκέταις δῶρα τῷ βασιλεῖ φέρων ξιφίδιον κρύφα
τῷ δεξιῷ σκέλει περιδησάμενος εἰσῄει πρὸς αὐτόν.
ὥρα δ᾽ ἦν θέρους καὶ τῆς ἡμέρας ἤδη μεσούσης
ἀνεῖντο αἱ φυλακαὶ ὑπό τε τοῦ καύματος καὶ πρὸς
191 ἄριστον τετραμμένων.   δοὺς οὖν τὰ δῶρα τῷ
Ἐγλῶνι ὁ νεανίσκος, διέτριβε δ᾽ ἔν τινι δωματίῳ
δεξιῶς πρὸς θέρος ἔχοντι, πρὸς ὁμιλίαν ἐτράπετο.
μόνοι δ᾽ ἦσαν τοῦ βασιλέως καὶ τοὺς ἐπεισιόντας
τῶν θεραπόντων ἀπιέναι² κελεύσαντος διὰ τὸ πρὸς
192 Ἰούδην ὁμιλεῖν.   καθῆστο δ᾽ ἐπὶ θρόνου καὶ δέος
εἰσῄει τὸν Ἰούδην, μὴ διαμάρτῃ καὶ οὐ³ δῷ
193 καιρίαν πληγήν.   ἀνίστησιν οὖν αὐτόν, ὄναρ εἰπὼν
ἔχειν ἐκ προστάγματος αὐτῷ δηλῶσαι τοῦ θεοῦ.
καὶ ὁ μὲν πρὸς τὴν χαρὰν τοῦ ὀνείρατος ἀνεπή-

¹ τε codd.
² ed. pr. Lat.: ἀπεῖναι codd.   ³ Niese: μὴ codd.

ᵃ Heb. Ehud: lxx Ἀώδ.

their supplications, rid them of this oppression under the Moabites ; and their liberation fell on this wise.

(2) A youth of the tribe of Benjamin, named Judes,[a] son of Gera, of gallant daring and with bodily powers that he was well able to make to serve his ends, being superior with his left hand and therefrom deriving all his strength, was also himself residing in Jericho ;[b] there he became familiar with Eglon, courting and cajoling him with presents, whereby moreover he endeared himself to those in waiting on the king.[b] Now one day, when he with two[c] attendants was bringing gifts to the king, he secretly girt a dagger about his right thigh and so went in to him. It was summer-time and, the day being at noon, the guards had been relaxed both by reason of the heat and because they were gone to lunch. So the young man, having presented his gifts to Eglon, who was lodged in a chamber well-adapted for the summer, fell into conversation. They were alone, the king having ordered even such henchmen as intruded to depart because he was conversing with Judes. He was seated upon a chair, and Judes was beset with fear lest he should strike amiss and not deal a mortal blow. So he made him arise by telling him that he had a dream to disclose to him by commandment of God. The king, for joy at news of this dream, leapt up

Judes (Ehud) slays Eglon.
Jd. iii. 15.

[b] Scripture does not mention Ehud's residence in Jericho nor his attentions to Eglon.

[c] Jd. iii. 18 mentions a retinue, " the people that bare the present," who were dismissed after offering it ; has the number " two " been extracted, through some misreading, out of the description of the dagger, " and it had two edges," *ib.* 16 ?

δησεν ἀπὸ τοῦ θρόνου, πλήξας δ' αὐτὸν ὁ Ἰούδης
εἰς τὴν καρδίαν καὶ τὸ ξιφίδιον ἐγκαταλιπὼν ἔξεισι
προσκλείσας[1] τὴν θύραν. οἵ τε θεράποντες ἠρέμουν,
εἰς ὕπνον τετράφθαι νομίζοντες τὸν βασιλέα.

194   (3) Ὁ δ' Ἰούδης τοῖς Ἱεριχουντίοις ἀποσημαί-
νων κρυπτῶς παρεκάλει τῆς ἐλευθερίας ἀντιλαμ-
βάνεσθαι. οἱ δ' ἀσμένως ἀκούσαντες αὐτοί τε
εἰς τὰ ὅπλα ᾔεσαν καὶ διέπεμπον εἰς τὴν χώραν
τοὺς ἀποσημαίνοντας κέρασιν οἰῶν· τούτοις γὰρ
195 συγκαλεῖν τὸ πλῆθος πάτριον. οἱ δὲ περὶ τὸν
Ἔγλωνα πολὺν μὲν χρόνον ἠγνόουν τὸ συμβεβηκὸς αὐτῷ πάθος, ἐπεὶ δὲ πρὸς ἑσπέραν ἦν,
δείσαντες μή τι νεώτερον εἴη περὶ αὐτὸν γεγονός,
εἰσῆλθον εἰς τὸ δωμάτιον καὶ νεκρὸν εὑρόντες ἐν
ἀμηχανίᾳ καθειστήκεσαν, καὶ πρὶν τὴν φρουρὰν
συστραφῆναι τὸ τῶν Ἰσραηλιτῶν αὐτοῖς ἐπέρχεται
196 πλῆθος. καὶ οἱ μὲν παραχρῆμα ἀναιροῦνται, οἱ
δ' εἰς φυγὴν τρέπονται ὡς ἐπὶ τὴν Μωαβῖτιν σω-
θησόμενοι, ἦσαν δὲ ὑπὲρ μυρίους. καὶ Ἰσραηλῖται
προκατειληφότες τοῦ Ἰορδάνου τὴν διάβασιν διώκοντες ἔκτεινον καὶ κατὰ τὴν διάβασιν πολλοὺς
αὐτῶν ἀναιροῦσι, διέφυγέ τε οὐδὲ εἷς τὰς χεῖρας
197 αὐτῶν. καὶ οἱ μὲν Ἑβραῖοι τούτῳ τῷ τρόπῳ
τῆς ὑπὸ τοῖς Μωαβίταις δουλείας ἀπηλλάγησαν,
Ἰούδης δ' ἐκ[2] τῆς αἰτίας ταύτης τιμηθεὶς τῇ τοῦ
πλήθους παντὸς ἡγεμονίᾳ τελευτᾷ τὴν ἀρχὴν
ἔτεσιν ὀγδοήκοντα κατασχών, ἀνὴρ καὶ δίχα τῆς
προειρημένης πράξεως ἐπαίνου δίκαιος τυγχάνειν.

---

[1] MLE Lat.: προσκλίνας rell.
[2] δ' ἐκ Dindorf ex Lat.: δὲ codd.

from his throne, whereat Judes smote him to the heart and, leaving the dagger in his breast, went forth, locking the door upon him. The henchmen never stirred, supposing that the king had sunk asleep.

(3) Judes meanwhile reported the matter secretly to the men of Jericho *a* and exhorted them to assert their liberty. And they, welcoming his news, themselves rushed to arms and sent heralds throughout the country to give the signal by the sounding of rams' horns, for it was customary to call their people together by these instruments. Eglon's courtiers remained long ignorant of his fate ; but, when evening drew on, fearing that something extraordinary might have befallen him, they entered the chamber and, finding his corpse, stood there in helpless perplexity ; and, before the garrison could be mustered, the host of Israelites was upon them. Some were massacred on the spot ; the rest took flight to seek safety in the land of Moab, in number above ten thousand. But the Israelites, who had betimes occupied the ford of the Jordan, pursued and slew them : at the ford itself multitudes of them were massacred, and not a man escaped their hands. Thus were the Hebrews delivered from their bondage to the Moabites. Judes himself, having for this reason been honoured with the governorship of the whole people, died after holding that office for eighty years *b*—a man, even apart from the aforesaid exploit, deserving of a meed of praise. After

Defeat of Moab and rule of Judes. Jd. iii. 26.

ib. 25.

---

a In Scripture he goes further afield and himself " blew the trumpet in the hill-country of Ephraim."

b Jd. iii. 30 " and the land had rest four-score years," to which the LXX adds " and Aod judged them until he died "; in the Heb. there is no mention of his rulership.

καὶ μετὰ τοῦτον Σανάγαρος ὁ Ἀνάθου παῖς
αἱρεθεὶς ἄρχειν ἐν τῷ πρώτῳ τῆς ἀρχῆς ἔτει
κατέστρεψε τὸν βίον.

198 (v. 1) Ἰσραηλῖται δὲ πάλιν, οὐδὲν γὰρ ἐπὶ διδαχῇ
τοῦ κρείττονος ἐλάμβανον τῶν πρότερον ἠτυχη-
μένων ὑπὸ[1] τοῦ μήτε σέβειν τὸν θεὸν μήθ' ὑπακούειν τοῖς νόμοις, πρὶν ἢ καὶ τῆς ὑπὸ Μωαβίταις
ἀναπνεῦσαι δουλείας πρὸς ὀλίγον, ὑπὸ Ἀβίτου[2]

199 τοῦ Χαναναίων βασιλέως καταδουλοῦνται. οὗτος
γὰρ ἐξ Ἀσώρου πόλεως ὁρμώμενος, αὕτη δ' ὑπέρκειται τῆς Σεμαχωνίτιδος λίμνης, στρατοῦ μὲν
ὁπλιτῶν τριάκοντα ἔτρεφε μυριάδας μυρίους δὲ
ἱππέας, τρισχιλίων δὲ ἁρμάτων ηὐπόρει. ταύτης
οὖν στρατηγῶν τῆς δυνάμεως Σισάρης τιμῆς πρώτης παρὰ τῷ βασιλεῖ τυγχάνων συνελθόντας πρὸς
αὐτὸν τοὺς Ἰσραηλίτας ἐκάκωσε δεινῶς, ὥστε
αὐτοῖς ἐπιτάξαι τελεῖν φόρους.

200 (2) Εἴκοσι μὲν οὖν ἔτη ταῦτα πάσχοντες ἤνυσαν
μήτε αὐτοὶ φρονεῖν ὑπὸ τῆς δυστυχίας ὄντες ἀγαθοὶ
καὶ τοῦ θεοῦ πλέον δαμάσαι[3] θέλοντος αὐτῶν τὴν
ὕβριν διὰ τὴν περὶ αὐτὸν ἀγνωμοσύνην, ἵνα μετα-
θέμενοι τοῦ λοιποῦ σωφρονῶσιν· διδαχθέντες δὲ[4]
τὰς συμφορὰς αὐτοῖς ἐκ τῆς περιφρονήσεως τῶν
νόμων ὑπάρξαι, Δαβώραν τινὰ προφῆτιν, μέλισσαν
δὲ σημαίνει τοὔνομα κατὰ τὴν Ἑβραίων γλῶσσαν,

201 ἱκέτευον δεηθῆναι τοῦ θεοῦ λαβεῖν οἶκτον αὐτῶν

---

[1] + τε codd.   [2] Jabid Lat.: Ἰωαβεῖ Niese.
[3] + ἔτι ROE.   [4] δὲ ins. Niese.

---

[a] Heb. Shamgar : LXX Σαμεγάρ (Σεμεγάρ, etc.).
[b] Amplification.
[c] So Heb. and Josephus below (§ 209) ; here the mss. have
the Latinized form Ἀβίτου (Avitus).

him Sanagar,[a] son of Anath, was elected ruler, but died in the first year of his rule.[b]

(v. 1) Again, however, the Israelites, who had learnt no lesson of wisdom from their previous misfortunes, since they neither worshipped God nor obeyed the laws, ere they had enjoyed a brief respite from their servitude to the Moabites, fell under the yoke of Jabin,[c] king of the Canaanites. For this monarch, issuing from the city of Asor,[d] situate above the lake Semachōnitis,[e] maintained an army of 300,000 foot and 10,000 horse, and was owner of 3000 chariots.[f] Accordingly the general of these forces, Sisares,[g] who held the first rank in the king's favour, so sorely afflicted the Israelites when they joined battle with him, that he forced them to pay tribute.

(2) Twenty years, then, did they pass in this miserable plight, themselves incapable of being schooled by adversity, while God willed to tame their insolence yet more by reason of their ingratitude towards Him, to the end that they might change their ways and thenceforward be wise. But when they had learned [h] that their calamities were due to their contempt of the laws, they besought a certain prophetess named Dabora [i]—the name in the Hebrew tongue means " bee "—to pray God

Sanagar (Shamgar) succeeds him.
ib. 31.
Israel oppressed by Jabin, king of Canaan.
Jd. iv. 1.

Deborah and Barak lead a revolt.
Jd. iv. 3.

[a] Bibl. Hazor ; identified by Garstang with *Tell el-Qedah* about 5 miles S.W. of the southern end of the lake mentioned.

[e] The smaller lake N. of the lake of Galilee, *el Ḥuleh*, sometimes called the " waters of Merom."

[f] Imaginary figures (*cf.* § 64) : Scripture mentions only " 900 chariots of iron."

[g] Bibl. Sisera.

[h] Text and sentence division doubtful.

[i] Bibl. Deborah (="" bee," as correctly stated) ; Scripture adds that " she was judging Israel at that time."

καὶ μὴ περιδεῖν ἀπολλυμένους αὐτοὺς ὑπὸ Χαναναίων. ὁ δὲ θεὸς ἐπένευσε σωτηρίαν αὐτοῖς καὶ
στρατηγὸν αἱρεῖται Βάρακον τῆς Νεφθαλίτιδος
ὄντα φυλῆς· βάρακος δέ ἐστιν ἀστραπὴ κατὰ τὴν
Ἑβραίων γλῶσσαν.

202 (3) Μεταπεμψαμένη δ᾽ ἡ Δαβώρα τὸν Βάρακον
ἐπιλέξαντα τῶν νέων μυρίους ἐκέλευε χωρεῖν ἐπὶ
τοὺς πολεμίους· ἀποχρῆναι γὰρ τοσούτους τοῦ θεοῦ
203 προειρηκότος καὶ νίκην ἀποσημήναντος. Βαράκου
δὲ φαμένου οὐ στρατηγήσειν μὴ κἀκείνης αὐτῷ
συστρατηγούσης ἀγανακτήσασα, "σὺ μέν," εἶπε,
"γυναικὶ παραχωρεῖς ἀξιώματος ὃ σοὶ δέδωκεν ὁ
θεός, ἐγὼ δὲ οὐ παραιτοῦμαι." καὶ συναθροί-
σαντες[1] μυρίους ἐστρατοπέδευσαντο πρὸς Ἰτα-
204 βυρίῳ ὄρει.   ἀπήντα δ᾽ αὐτοῖς ὁ Σισάρης τοῦ
βασιλέως κελεύσαντος καὶ στρατοπεδεύονται τῶν
πολεμίων οὐκ ἄπωθεν. τοὺς δ᾽ Ἰσραηλίτας καὶ
τὸν Βάρακον καταπλαγέντας τὸ πλῆθος τῶν πολεμίων καὶ ἀναχωρεῖν διεγνωκότας ἡ Δαβώρα κατεῖχε
τὴν συμβολὴν ποιεῖσθαι κατ᾽ ἐκείνην κελεύουσα
τὴν ἡμέραν· νικήσειν γὰρ αὐτοὺς καὶ συλλήψεσθαι
τὸν θεόν.

205 (4) Συνῄεσαν οὖν καὶ προσμιγέντων ὄμβρος ἐπιγίνεται μέγας καὶ ὕδωρ πολὺ καὶ χάλαζα, τόν τε
ὑετὸν κατὰ πρόσωπον ἤλαυνε τῶν Χαναναίων
ἄνεμος ταῖς ὄψεσιν αὐτῶν ἐπισκοτῶν, ὡς τὰς
τοξείας ἀχρήστους αὐτοῖς εἶναι καὶ τὰς σφενδόνας·
οἵ τε ὁπλῖται διὰ τὸ κρύος χρῆσθαι τοῖς ξίφεσιν

---

[1] συναριθμήσαντες RO.

---

[a] Tabor.   [b] Amplification.
[c] Not mentioned in the Biblical narrative of the battle,
but derived apparently from the verse in the Song of

to take pity on them and not to suffer them to be destroyed by the Canaanites. God thereupon promised them salvation and chose for general Barak of the tribe of Nephthali ; *barak* denotes " lightning " in the tongue of the Hebrews.

(3) Dabora then summoned Barak and charged him *ib.* 6. to select ten thousand of the youth and to march against the foe : that number would, she said, suffice, God having prescribed it and betokened victory. But Barak declared that he would not take the command unless she shared it with him ; whereto she indignantly replied, " Thou resignest to a woman a rank that God has bestowed on thee ! Howbeit I do not decline it." Then, having mustered ten thousand, they pitched their camp on mount Itabyrion.[a] Sisares thereupon went to meet them at the king's orders and his army encamped not far from their foes. The Israelites and Barak were dismayed at the multitude of the enemy and resolved to retire,[b] but were restrained by Dabora, who ordered them to deliver battle that very day, for they would be victorious and God would lend them aid.

(4) So the forces met, and amidst the clash of arms there came up a great tempest [c] with torrents of rain and hail ; and the wind drove the rain in the faces of the Canaanites, obscuring their vision, so that their bows and their slings were of no service to them, and their infantry by reason of the cold could make no use of their swords. But the Israel- Victory of Israel : death of Sisara and Jabin. Jd. iv. 15.

Deborah, " They fought from heaven ; the stars in their courses fought against Sisera " (Jd. v. 20). To this there are parallels in rabbinic tradition. For a rather similar scene, when the elements aided the enemy of the Jews, *cf. B.J.* vii. 317 ff.

206 οὐκ εἶχον. τοὺς δ' Ἰσραηλίτας ἧττόν τε ἔβλαπτε
κατόπιν γινόμενος ὁ χειμὼν καὶ πρὸς τὴν ἔννοιαν
τῆς βοηθείας τοῦ θεοῦ θάρσος ἐλάμβανον, ὥστε
εἰς μέσους ὠσάμενοι τοὺς πολεμίους πολλοὺς αὐτῶν
ἀπέκτειναν. καὶ οἱ μὲν ὑπὸ τῶν Ἰσραηλιτῶν, οἱ
δ' ὑπὸ τῆς οἰκείας ἵππου ταραχθέντες ἔπεσον, ὡς
ὑπὸ τῶν ἁρμάτων πολλοὺς αὐτῶν ἀποθανεῖν.
207 Σισάρης δὲ καταπηδήσας τοῦ ἅρματος ὡς εἶδε τὴν
τροπὴν γινομένην, φυγὼν ἀφικνεῖται παρά τινα
τῶν Κενελίδων[1] γυναῖκα, Ἰάλην ὄνομα, ἣ κρύψαι
τε ἀξιώσαντα δέχεται καὶ ποτὸν αἰτήσαντι δίδωσι
208 γάλα διεφθορὸς ἤδη. ὁ δὲ πιὼν τοῦ μέτρου
δαψιλέστερον εἰς ὕπνον τρέπεται. ἡ δὲ Ἰάλη
κοιμωμένου σιδήρεον ἧλον ἐλάσασα σφύρῃ κατὰ
τοῦ στόματος καὶ[2] τοῦ χελυνίου διέπειρε τὸ ἔδαφος
καὶ τοῖς περὶ τὸν Βάρακον μικρὸν ὕστερον ἐλθοῦσιν
209 ἐπεδείκνυε τῇ γῇ προσηλωμένον. καὶ οὕτως μὲν
ἡ νίκη αὕτη περιέστη κατὰ τὰ ὑπὸ Δαβώρας
εἰρημένα εἰς γυναῖκα. Βάρακος δὲ στρατεύσας
ἐπ' Ἄσωρον Ἰωαβείν[3] τε ὑπαντιάσαντα κτείνει
καὶ τοῦ στρατηγοῦ πεσόντος καθελὼν εἰς ἔδαφος
τὴν πόλιν στρατηγεῖ τῶν Ἰσραηλιτῶν ἐπ' ἔτη
τεσσαράκοντα.
210 (vi. 1) Τελευτήσαντος δὲ Βαράκου καὶ Δαβώρας
κατὰ τὸν αὐτὸν καιρὸν μετὰ ταῦτα Μαδιανῖται
παρακαλέσαντες Ἀμαληκίτας τε καὶ Ἄραβας
στρατεύουσιν ἐπὶ τοὺς Ἰσραηλίτας καὶ μάχῃ τε
νικῶσι τοὺς συμβαλόντας καὶ τὸν καρπὸν δῃώσαν-

---

[1] Κενετίδων ed. pr.
[2] RO: διὰ τοῦ στόματος κατὰ rell.
[3] Ἰάβ(ε)ινον SP(E): Jabin Lat.

254

ites were less hampered by the storm, which was at their back, and they took courage at the thought of this succour from God ; and so, thrusting into the midst of the foe, they slew multitudes of them. Thus, some beneath the hand of the Israelites, others discomfited by their own cavalry, the enemy fell, many being crushed to death beneath the chariots. But Sisares, having leapt from his chariot when he saw that the rout was come, fled till he reached the abode of a woman of the Kenites [a] named Iale [b] ; she, at his request to conceal him, took him in, and, when he asked for drink, gave him milk that had turned sour. [c] And he, having drunk thereof immoderately, fell asleep. Then, as he slumbered, Iale took an iron nail and drove it with a hammer through his mouth and jaw, piercing the ground ; and when Barak's company [d] arrived soon after she showed him to them nailed to the earth. Thus did this victory redound, as Dabora had foretold, [e] to a woman's glory. But Barak, marching upon Asor, slew Jabin [f] who encountered him and, the general having fallen, razed the city to the ground ; he then held command of the Israelites for forty years. [g] *Cf. v. 31.*

(vi. 1) Barak and Dabora having died simultaneously, thereafter the Madianites, calling the Amalekites and Arabians to their aid, marched against the Israelites, defeated in battle all who opposed them, plundered the crops and carried off the cattle. This *Ravages of the Madianites. Jd. vi. 1.*

[a] Gr. " Kenelides."   [b] Bibl. Jael.
[c] " already corrupt," an amplification of the Biblical text.
[d] Barak himself, in Jd. iv. 22.
[e] Jd. iv. 9.
[f] Or, according to some MSS., Joabin.
[g] Scripture says merely " And the land had rest forty years."

211 τες τὴν λείαν ἐπήγοντο.[1] τοῦτο δὲ ποιούντων ἐπ'
ἔτη ἑπτὰ εἰς τὰ ὄρη τῶν Ἰσραηλιτῶν ἀνεστάλη τὸ
πλῆθος καὶ τῶν πεδίων ἐξεχώρουν, ὑπονόμους τε
καὶ σπήλαια ποιησάμενοι πᾶν ὅ τι τοὺς πολεμίους
212 διέφυγεν ἐν τούτοις εἶχον φυλάττοντες. οἱ γὰρ
Μαδιανῖται κατὰ ὥραν θέρους[2] στρατεύοντες τὸν
χειμῶνα γεωργεῖν τοῖς Ἰσραηλίταις ἐπέτρεπον,
ὅπως ἔχωσι πεπονηκότων αὐτῶν εἰς ἃ βλάπτωσι,
λιμὸς δ' ἦν καὶ σπάνις τροφῆς καὶ τρέπονται πρὸς
ἱκετείαν τοῦ θεοῦ σώζειν αὐτοὺς παρακαλοῦντες.
213 (2) Καὶ Γεδεὼν ὁ Ἰάσου παῖς, Μανασσίτιδος
φυλῆς ἐν ὀλίγοις, δράγματα σταχύων φερόμενος
κρυπτῶς εἰς τὴν ληνὸν ἔκοπτε· τοὺς γὰρ πολεμίους
ἐδεδίει φανερῶς τοῦτο ποιεῖν ἐπὶ τῆς ἅλωος.
φαντάσματος δὲ αὐτῷ παραστάντος νεανίσκου
μορφῇ καὶ φήσαντος εὐδαίμονα καὶ φίλον τῷ
θεῷ, ὑποτυχὼν " τοῦτο γοῦν," ἔφη, " τεκμήριον
τῆς εὐμενείας αὐτοῦ μέγιστον τὸ[3] ληνῷ με νῦν
214 ἀντὶ ἅλωος χρῆσθαι." θαρσεῖν δὲ παρακελευσα-
μένου καὶ πειρᾶσθαι τὴν ἐλευθερίαν ἀνασῴζειν,
ἀδυνάτως ἔχειν ἔλεγε· τήν τε γὰρ φυλὴν ἐξ ἧς
ὑπῆρχε πλήθους ὑστερεῖν καὶ νέον αὐτὸν εἶναι καὶ
τηλικούτων πραγμάτων[4] ἀσθενέστερον. ὁ δὲ θεὸς
αὐτὸς ἀναπληρώσειν τὸ λεῖπον ἐπηγγέλλετο καὶ
νίκην παρέξειν Ἰσραηλίταις αὐτοῦ στρατηγοῦντος.
215 (3) Τοῦτ' οὖν διηγούμενος ὁ Γεδεὼν τισὶ τῶν

---

[1] Niese (cf. xiii. 101): ὑπήγοντο codd.: ἀπήγοντο ed. pr.
[2] ME Lat.: ἔτους rell.
[3] Zonaras: τῇ codd.
[4] πραγμάτων ἐπινοίας MSPL.

---

[a] Bibl. Gideon (lxx Γεδεών) son of Joash (Ἰωάς).
[b] Gr. " one of few " (cf. A. ii. 78, iv. 329, v. 276); here
perhaps with a connotation of the paucity of numbers of the
tribe (§ 214).

being repeated for seven years, the more part of the Israelites withdrew to the hills and forsook the plains ; and, making for themselves underground passages and caverns, they secured therein all that had escaped the enemy. For the Madianites, making their invasions in the height of summer, permitted the Israelites in winter to till the soil, that through their labours they might have somewhat to ravage. So there was famine and dearth of sustenance, and they turned in supplication to God, imploring Him to save them.

(2) Now Gedeon, son of Jas,[a] one of the foremost [b] The call to Gideon. Jd. vi. 11. among the tribe of Manasseh, used to bring his sheaves of corn and beat them out secretly in the winepress ; for, because of the enemy, he feared to do this openly on the threshing-floor. To him there appeared a spectre in the form of a young man, who pronounced him blessed and beloved of God, whereto he made rejoinder: "Indeed, this is a signal proof of his favour that I am now using a winepress instead of a threshing-floor ! " But when his visitor bade him take courage and essay to regain liberty, he replied that this was impossible, seeing that the tribe [c] to which he belonged was lacking in numbers and he himself but young and too feeble for exploits so great. Howbeit God promised Himself to supply what he lacked and to grant victory to the Israelites, should he put himself at their head.[d]

(3) On recounting this matter to some of his Selection of his army

[c] Jd. vi. 15 " Behold, my family (Heb. " thousand ") is the poorest in Manasseh, and I am the least in my father's house."

[d] Josephus omits Jd. vi. 17-40, comprising (1) the reassuring miracles performed for Gideon, (2) his destruction of the altar of Baal, which earned for him the surname of Jerubbaal.

νέων ἐπιστεύετο, καὶ παραχρῆμα πρὸς τοὺς ἀγῶνας
ἕτοιμον ἦν τὸ στρατιωτικὸν¹ μυρίων ἀνδρῶν.
ἐπιστὰς δὲ κατὰ τοὺς ὕπνους ὁ θεὸς τῷ Γεδεῶνι
τὴν ἀνθρωπίνην φύσιν αὐτῷ φίλαυτον οὖσαν ἐδήλου
καὶ πρὸς τοὺς ἀρετῇ διαφέροντας ἀπεχθανομένην,
ὅπως τε τὴν νίκην παρέντες τοῦ θεοῦ δοκεῖν νομί-
σουσιν² ἰδίαν ὡς πολὺς στρατὸς ὄντες καὶ πρὸς
216 τοὺς πολεμίους ἀξιόμαχος. ἵνα μάθωσιν οὖν βοηθείας τῆς αὐτοῦ τὸ ἔργον, συνεβούλευε περὶ
μεσοῦσαν τὴν ἡμέραν, ἐν ἀκμῇ τοῦ καύματος
ὄντος, ἄγειν τὴν στρατιὰν ἐπὶ τὸν ποταμὸν καὶ
τοὺς μὲν κατακλιθέντας καὶ οὕτως πίνοντας εὐ-
ψύχους ὑπολαμβάνειν, ὅσοι δ' ἐσπευσμένως καὶ
μετὰ θορύβου πίνοντες τύχοιεν τούτους³ δειλοὺς
νομίζειν καὶ καταπεπληγότας τοὺς πολεμίους.
217 ποιήσαντος δὲ τοῦ Γεδεῶνος κατὰ τὰς ὑποθήκας
τοῦ θεοῦ, τριακόσιοι ἄνδρες εὑρέθησαν ταῖς χερσὶ
μετὰ φόβου προσενεγκάμενοι τὸ ὕδωρ τεταραγ-
μένως, ἔφησέ τε ὁ θεὸς τούτους ἐπαγομένῳ ἐπιχειρεῖν τοῖς πολεμίοις. ἐστρατοπεδεύοντο δὲ ὑπὲρ
τοῦ Ἰορδάνου μέλλοντες εἰς τὴν ἐπιοῦσαν περαιοῦσθαι.
218 (4) Γεδεῶνος δ' ἐν φόβῳ καθεστῶτος, καὶ γὰρ
νυκτὸς ἐπιχειρεῖν αὐτῷ ὁ θεὸς προειρήκει, τοῦ

---

¹ στρατόπεδον ROE.   ² Niese: νομίζουσιν codd.
³ (after τούτους) δὴ (δὲ M) νομίζειν ὑπὸ δειλίας τοῦτο πάσχειν
MSP Suidas Glycas.

---

[a] In Jd. vii. 3 the army had already been reduced to
10,000, by the dismissal, under divine orders, of 22,000
who were faint-hearted.
[b] Amplification (three words).
[c] Amplification (the hour).   [d] Or " lay."

young friends, Gedeon was trusted ; and instantly Jd. vi. 34;
vii. 2 ff. there was an army of 10,000 [a] men ready for the contest. But God, appearing to Gedeon in his sleep,[b] showed him the proneness of human nature to self-love and the hatred that it bore to those of surpassing merit, and how, far from attributing the victory to God, they would regard it as their own, on the ground that they were a large army and a match for their enemies. In order, therefore, that they might learn that it was His aid that accomplished it, He counselled him towards midday, when the heat was most intense,[c] to march his troops to the river ; and then such of them as knelt [d] down to drink, them he should deem the stalwarts, but all who drank hurriedly and with trepidation, these he should rank as cowards [e] and terrified of the foe. Gedeon having then done in accordance with this counsel of God, there were found 300 men who with fear and trembling raised the water in their hands to their lips ; and these God bade him take with him to attack the enemy.[f] So they pitched their camp above the Jordan,[g] with intent to cross on the morrow.

(4) But Gedeon being terror-struck, having withal Dream of a
Madianite
soldier.
Jd. vii. 9. been divinely ordered to attack by night, God, with

[e] Some MSS. read " should deem that they had acted this way through cowardice."

[f] The correct interpretation of the confused verses, Jd. vii. 5, 6, is probably that the 300 men who lapped the water with their tongues like dogs were those selected for battle, while those who knelt to drink were rejected. Josephus, taking the lapping to mean drinking "with trepidation," implies that the 300 were chosen "lest Israel vaunt themselves " (Jd. vii. 2), *i.e.* God could give victory even to a cowardly army.

[g] At En Harod (Jd. vii. 1), site uncertain.

δέους αὐτὸν ἀπαγαγεῖν βουλόμενος κελεύει προσ-
λαβόντα ἕνα τῶν στρατιωτῶν πλησίον χωρεῖν
ταῖς Μαδιανιτῶν σκηναῖς· παρ' αὐτῶν γὰρ ἐκείνων
219 λήψεσθαι φρόνημα καὶ θάρσος. πεισθεὶς δὲ ᾔει
Φρουρὰν τὸν ἑαυτοῦ θεράποντα παραλαβών, καὶ
πλησιάσας σκηνῇ τινι καταλαμβάνει τοὺς ἐν αὐτῇ
ἐγρηγορότας καὶ τὸν ἕτερον ὄναρ διηγούμενον τῷ
συσκηνοῦντι, ὥστε ἀκούειν τὸν Γεδεῶνα. τὸ δὲ
τοιοῦτον ἦν· μᾶζαν ἐδόκει κριθίνην ὑπ' εὐτελείας
ἀνθρώποις ἄβρωτον διὰ τοῦ στρατοπέδου κυλιο-
μένην τὴν τοῦ βασιλέως σκηνὴν καταβαλεῖν καὶ
220 τὰς τῶν στρατιωτῶν πάντων. ὁ δὲ σημαίνειν
ὄλεθρον τοῦ στρατοῦ τὴν ὄψιν ἔκρινε, λέγων ὅθεν
τοῦτ' αὐτῷ συνιδεῖν ἐπῆλθε, πάντων τῶν σπερμάτων[1]
τὸ καλούμενον κρίθινον εὐτελέστατον ὁμολογεῖσθαι
τυγχάνειν, "τοῦ δ' Ἀσιανοῦ παντὸς τὸ Ἰσραηλιτῶν
ἔστιν ἰδεῖν ἀτιμότερον νῦν γεγενημένον ὅμοιον δὲ
221 τῷ κατὰ κριθὴν γένει. καὶ τὸ παρὰ τοῖς Ἰσραηλίταις νῦν μεγαλοφρονοῦν τοῦτ' ἂν εἴη Γεδεὼν καὶ
τὸ σὺν αὐτῷ στρατιωτικόν. ἐπεὶ οὖν τὴν μᾶζαν
φῂς ἰδεῖν τὰς σκηνὰς ἡμῶν ἀνατρέπουσαν, δέδια
μὴ ὁ θεὸς Γεδεῶνι τὴν καθ' ἡμῶν νίκην ἐπι-
νένευκε."

222 (5) Γεδεῶνα δ' ἀκούσαντα τὸ ὄναρ ἐλπὶς ἀγαθὴ
καὶ θάρσος ἔλαβε, καὶ προσέταξεν ἐν τοῖς ὅπλοις
εἶναι τοὺς οἰκείους διηγησάμενος αὐτοῖς καὶ τὴν
τῶν πολεμίων ὄψιν, οἱ δ' ἕτοιμοι πρὸς τὰ παραγγελλόμενα φρονηματισθέντες ὑπὸ τῶν δεδηλω-

[1] conj.: πᾶν τὸ σπέρμα codd.

intent to banish his fear, bade him take one of his
soldiers and advance close up to the tents of the
Madianites, since from the lips of the very foe he
would derive courage and confidence. Obediently
thereto he went, taking with him his servant Phruras,[a]
and, on approaching one of the tents, found that its
occupants were awake and that one of them was
recounting to his companion a dream, in such fashion
that Gedeon could hear it. Now the dream was on
this wise : it seemed to him that a barley cake, too
vile for man's consumption, came rolling through
the camp and struck down the king's tent and those
of all his soldiers. His comrade interpreted the
vision to betoken the destruction of the army,
stating what led him to understand it so : " Of all
seeds (he said) that called barley is admitted to be
the vilest ; and of all Asiatic races that of the Israelites, as may be seen, has now become the most
ignominious and like to the nature of barley. And
among the Israelites at this moment the high-
spirited party can be none but Gedeon and his
comrades-in-arms. Since, then, thou sayest that
thou sawest that cake overturning our tents, I fear
that God has conceded to Gedeon the victory over
us."

(5) The hearing of this dream inspired Gedeon Defeat
with high hopes and confidence, and he commanded of the
his men to be ready in arms, having also recounted $^{Jd.\ vii.\ 15.}$
to them this vision of the enemy ; and they were
alert to obey his orders, elated by what they had

---

[a] Bibl. Purah, LXX Φαρά (and so the Latin version of
Josephus).

223 μένων ἦσαν. καὶ κατὰ τετάρτην μάλιστα φυλακὴν
προσῆγε τὴν αὑτοῦ στρατιὰν Γεδεὼν εἰς τρία μέρη
διελὼν αὐτήν, ἑκατὸν δὲ ἦσαν ἐν ἑκάστῳ. ἐκόμιζον
δὲ πάντες ἀμφορέας κενοὺς καὶ λαμπάδας ἡμμένας
ἐν αὐταῖς, ὅπως μὴ κατάφωρος τοῖς πολεμίοις ἡ
ἔφοδος αὐτῶν γένηται, καὶ ἐν τῇ δεξιᾷ κριοῦ
224 κέρας· ἐχρῶντο δὲ τούτοις ἀντὶ σάλπιγγος. χωρίον
δὲ πολὺ κατεῖχε τὸ τῶν πολεμίων στράτευμα,[1]
πλείστην γὰρ αὐτοῖς εἶναι συνέβαινε κάμηλον, καὶ
κατὰ τὰ[2] ἔθνη νεμηθέντες ὑφ᾿ ἑνὶ κύκλῳ πάντες
225 ἦσαν.· οἱ δ᾿ Ἑβραῖοι, προειρημένον[3] αὐτοῖς ὁπόταν
γένωνται πλησίον τῶν πολεμίων ἐκ συνθήματος
σάλπιγξί τε ἠχήσαντας καὶ τοὺς ἀμφορέας κατ-
εάξαντας ὁρμῆσαι μετὰ τῶν λαμπάδων ἀλαλάξαντας[4]
καὶ νικᾶν θεοῦ Γεδεῶνι βοηθήσοντος, τοῦτ᾿ ἐποίη-
226 σαν. ταραχὴ δὲ λαμβάνει τοὺς ἀνθρώπους ἔτι
ὑπνοῦντας καὶ δείματα· νὺξ γὰρ ἦν καὶ ὁ θεὸς
τοῦτο ἤθελεν. ἐκτείνοντο δὲ ὀλίγοι μὲν ὑπὸ τῶν
πολεμίων, οἱ δὲ πλείους ὑπὸ τῶν συμμάχων διὰ
τὸ τῇ γλώσσῃ διαφωνεῖν· ἅπαξ δὲ καταστάντες
εἰς ταραχὴν πᾶν τὸ προστυχὸν ἀνῄρουν νομίζοντες
227 εἶναι πολέμιον, φόνος τε πολὺς ἦν. καὶ φήμης
πρὸς τοὺς Ἰσραηλίτας τῆς Γεδεῶνος νίκης ἀφικο-
μένης ἐν τοῖς ὅπλοις ἦσαν, καὶ διώξαντες λαμβάνουσι τοὺς πολεμίους ἐν κοίλῳ τινὶ χαράδρας
περιειλημμένῳ οὐ δυναμέναις διαπερᾶναι χωρίῳ
καὶ περιστάντες κτείνουσιν ἅπαντας καὶ δύο τῶν
228 βασιλέων Ὠρηβόν τε καὶ Ζῆβον. οἱ δὲ λοιποὶ

---

[1] ROE: στρατόπεδον rell.   [2] τὰ om. SP.
[3] Niese: προειρημένου codd.
[4] Niese: ἠχήσαντες . . . κατεάξαντες . . . ἀλαλάξαντες codd.

been told. Then, at about the fourth watch,[a] Gedeon marched forth his army, which he had divided into three sections, each of an hundred men. They all bore empty pitchers with lighted torches inside them, to prevent the enemy from detecting their approach, and in the right hand a ram's horn, which served for a trumpet. Their enemy's camp covered 12. a large area, for they had a vast camel-corps and were divided according to their nationalities, all being enclosed within one ring. The Hebrews had received orders, on approaching the enemy, at a given signal to sound their trumpets, break their pitchers, and rush forward with their torches and with shouts of battle and "Victory, and God will aid Gedeon!" and even so they did. Confusion and panic seized the hapless creatures yet slumbering; for it was night and God willed it so. Thus were they slain, few indeed by their enemies, the more part by the hands of their allies, by reason of their diversity of languages; and, when once confusion reigned, they killed all that they met, taking them for enemies, and there was a great carnage. A rumour of 23. Gedeon's victory reaching the Israelites, they too were up in arms, and pursuing caught the enemy in a valley encompassed with impassable ravines,[b] and, having surrounded them, slew them all with two of their kings, Oreb and Zeb. The other chiefs,

[a] In Jd. vii. 19 they reach the outskirts of the enemy's camp at "the beginning of the middle watch" (of three watches of 4 hours each from 6 P.M. to 6 A.M., *i.e.* at about 10 P.M.); Josephus, following the Roman division of the night into four watches of 3 hours each, represents them as leaving their own camp at about 3 A.M.

[b] This death-trap—the "impassable valley" in which the main body of the enemy is cooped up and annihilated—is a familiar feature of these battle-scenes; *cf.* § 162.

JOSEPHUS

τῶν ἡγεμόνων τοὺς περιλειφθέντας τῶν στρατιωτῶν ἐνάγοντες,[1] ἦσαν δὲ ὡς[2] μύριοι καὶ ὀκτα-
κισχίλιοι, στρατοπεδεύονται πολὺ τῶν Ἰσραηλιτῶν ἄπωθεν. Γεδεὼν δὲ οὐκ ἀπηγορεύκει πονῶν,
ἀλλὰ διώξας μετὰ παντὸς τοῦ στρατοῦ καὶ συμβαλὼν ἅπαντας διέφθειρε τοὺς πολεμίους καὶ τοὺς
λοιποὺς ἡγεμόνας Ζεβὴν καὶ Ζαρμούνην αἰχμα-
229 λώτους λαβὼν ἀνήγαγεν. ἀπέθανον δ᾽ ἐν αὐτῇ τῇ
μάχῃ Μαδιανιτῶν τε καὶ τῶν συστρατευσάντων
αὐτοῖς Ἀράβων περὶ μυριάδας δώδεκα, λεία τε
πολλὴ χρυσὸς καὶ ἄργυρος καὶ ὕφη καὶ κάμηλος
καὶ ὑποζύγια λαμβάνεται τοῖς Ἑβραίοις. Γεδεὼν
δὲ παραγενόμενος εἰς Ἐφρὰν τὴν ἑαυτοῦ πατρίδα
κτείνει τοὺς τῶν Μαδιανιτῶν βασιλέας.

230   (6) Ἡ δ᾽ Ἐφράμιδος φυλὴ τῇ Γεδεῶνος εὐπραγίᾳ
δυσχεραίνουσα στρατεύειν ἐπ᾽ αὐτὸν διεγνώκει, τὸ
μὴ προαγγεῖλαι[3] τὴν ἐπιχείρησιν αὐτοῖς τὴν κατὰ
τῶν πολεμίων ἐγκαλοῦντες. Γεδεὼν δὲ μέτριος
ὢν καὶ πᾶσαν ἀρετὴν ἄκρος, οὐκ αὐτὸς ἔλεγεν
αὐτοκράτορι χρησάμενος λογισμῷ τοῖς ἐχθροῖς
ἐπιθέσθαι χωρὶς αὐτῶν, ἀλλὰ τοῦ θεοῦ κελεύ-
σαντος· τὴν δὲ νίκην οὐχ ἧττον αὐτῶν ἔφασκεν
231 ἰδίαν ἢ τῶν ἐστρατευκότων εἶναι. καὶ τούτοις
παρηγορήσας αὐτῶν τὴν ὀργὴν τοῖς λόγοις μᾶλλον
τοὺς Ἑβραίους ὠφέλησε τῆς ἐπὶ τῶν πολεμίων
εὐπραξίας· ἐμφυλίου γὰρ αὐτοὺς στάσεως ἄρχειν
μέλλοντας ἐρρύσατο. τῆς μέντοιγε ὕβρεως ταύτης
ἡ φυλὴ δίκην ἐξέτισεν, ἣν δηλώσομεν κατὰ καιρὸν
ἴδιον.

---

[1] colligentes (? συνάγοντες) Lat.: ἄγοντες SPE.
[2] MLE Lat.: om. rell.
[3] Dindorf: προσαγγεῖλαι (παρ.) codd.

264

urging on their surviving soldiers, numbering some 18,000,[a] encamped when at a great distance from the Israelites. Gedeon, however, had not renounced the viii. 12. struggle, but, following in pursuit with his whole army, joined battle, annihilated the enemy, and brought back as prisoners the remaining chiefs, Zebes and Zarmunes.[b] In the preceding combat there had fallen of the Madianites and of their 10. Arabian comrades-in-arms about 120,000; and abundant booty—gold, silver, woven stuff, camels and beasts of burden—fell to the Hebrews. Gedeon on 21. his return to Ephra,[c] his native place, put the kings of the Madianites to death.

(6) But the tribe of Ephraim, aggrieved at Gedeon's success, now resolved to march against him, complaining that he had not informed them of his proposed assault on the enemy. Gedeon, however, being a man of moderation and a model of every virtue, replied that it was not of himself by an arbitrary decision [d] that he had attacked the foe without them, but by divine command; while the victory, he declared, belonged no less to them than to those who had taken the field. And by these words, with which he pacified their wrath, he did the Hebrews a greater service than by his military success; for he rescued them from civil strife when they were on the brink of it. Howbeit for its insolent attitude this tribe paid a penalty, which we shall relate in due season.[e]

The aggrieved tribe of Ephraim. Jd. viii. 1.

---

[a] " About 15,000," Jd. viii. 10.

[b] Bibl. Zebah (LXX Ζεβεέ) and Zalmunna (Ζαλμανά). The MSS. of Josephus have various spellings.

[c] Bibl. Ophrah (LXX Ἐφραθά or, in some MSS., Ἐφρά); Jd. vi. 11.

[d] αὐτοκράτορι λογισμῷ after Thuc. iv. 108.   [e] Cf. § 250.

232 (7) Γεδεὼν δὲ τὴν ἀρχὴν ἀποθέσθαι βουλόμενος
βιασθεὶς ἔσχεν αὐτὴν ἐπ' ἔτη τεσσαράκοντα βραβεύων αὐτοῖς τὰ δίκαια καὶ περὶ τῶν διαφορῶν
ἐπ' αὐτὸν βαδιζόντων κύρια[1] πάντα ἦν τὰ ὑπ'
αὐτοῦ λεγόμενα. καὶ ὁ μὲν γηραιὸς τελευτήσας
ἐν Ἐφρὰν τῇ πατρίδι θάπτεται.

233 (vii. 1) Παῖδες δὲ ἦσαν αὐτῷ γνήσιοι μὲν ἑβδομήκοντα, πολλὰς γὰρ ἔγημε γυναῖκας, νόθος δ' εἷς
ἐκ παλλακῆς Δρούμας Ἀβιμέλεχος τοὔνομα, ὃς
μετὰ τὴν τοῦ πατρὸς τελευτὴν ἀναχωρήσας ἐπὶ[2]
Σίκιμα πρὸς τοὺς ἀπὸ μητρὸς συγγενεῖς, ἐντεῦθεν
234 γὰρ ἦν, καὶ λαβὼν ἀργύριον παρ' αὐτῶν * * *[3] οἳ
διὰ πλῆθος ἀδικημάτων ἦσαν ἐπίσημοι, ἀφικνεῖται
σὺν αὐτοῖς εἰς τὸν πατρῷον οἶκον καὶ κτείνει
πάντας τοὺς ἀδελφοὺς πλὴν Ἰωθάμου· σώζεται
γὰρ οὗτος διαφυγεῖν εὐτυχήσας. Ἀβιμέλεχος δὲ
εἰς τυραννίδα τὰ πράγματα μεθίστησι, κύριον αὑτὸν
ὅ τι βούλεται ποιεῖν ἀντὶ τῶν νομίμων ἀποδείξας
καὶ δεινῶς πρὸς τοὺς τοῦ δικαίου προϊσταμένους
ἐκπικραινόμενος.

235 (2) Καί ποτε δημοτελοῦς Σικίμοις οὔσης ἑορτῆς
καὶ τοῦ πλήθους παντὸς ἐκεῖ συνειλεγμένου ὁ
ἀδελφὸς αὐτοῦ Ἰωθάμης, ὃν καὶ διαφυγεῖν ἔφαμεν,
ἀνελθὼν ἐπὶ τὸ ὄρος τὸ Γαριζεῖν, ὑπέρκειται δὲ
τῆς Σικιμίων πόλεως, ἐκβοήσας εἰς ἐπήκοον τοῦ
πλήθους ἡσυχίαν αὐτῷ παρασχόντος[4] ἠξίου μαθεῖν
236 τὰ ὑπ' αὐτοῦ λεγόμενα. γενομένης δὲ σιγῆς

---

[1] Lat.: + τε codd.　　　[2] εἰς RO.
[3] lacuna indicated by Jd. ix. 4.
[4] παρασχόντας Weill.

ᵃ His making of an ephod, which " became a snare to
Gideon and to his house " (Jd. viii. 27), is omitted.

(7) Gedeon then, wishing to resign his command, was constrained to keep it, and continued for forty years to administer justice : men resorted to him concerning their differences, and all his pronouncements had binding weight.[a] He died in ripe old age and was buried at Ephra, his native place.

Gedeon as judge. Jd. viii. 22 28. 32.

(vii. 1) Now he had seventy sons born in wedlock (for he married many wives) and by a concubine, Druma,[b] one bastard named Abimelech. This last, after his father's death, withdrew to the family of his mother at Shechem,[c] her native place, and, having obtained money from them (hired certain miscreants),[d] who were notorious for a multitude of crimes, and with them repaired to his father's house and slew all his brethren, save Jotham : this one had the good fortune to escape alive. Abimelech then transformed the government into a tyranny, setting himself up to do whatsoever he pleased in defiance of the laws and showing bitter animosity against the champions of justice.

Abimelech the tyrant. Jd. viii. 30. ix. 1.

(2) Now one day when there was a public festival [e] at Shechem and the people were all assembled there, his brother Jotham—the one who, as we said, had escaped—ascended Garizin, the mountain which rises above the city of Shechem, and shouting so as to be heard by the crowd if they would but listen to him quietly, begged them to attend to what he had to say. Silence being established, he told them

Jotham's parable to the Shechemites. Jd. ix. 7.

[b] Name not in Scripture. Perhaps it was taken through error from " Arumah," the name of a town where Abimelech dwelt for a time (Jd. ix. 41).

[c] Gr. Sikima (as in most MSS. of LXX).

[d] Lacuna in Greek, to be supplied from Jd. ix. 4 " Abimelech hired vain and light fellows, which followed him."

[e] The public festival is not mentioned in Scripture.

JOSEPHUS

εἶπεν, ὡς τὰ δένδρα φωνὴν ἀνθρώπειον προϊέμενα
συνόδου γενομένης αὐτῶν δεηθείη συκῆς ἄρχειν
αὐτῶν. ἀρνησαμένης δ’ ἐκείνης διὰ τὸ τιμῆς τῆς
ἐπὶ τοῖς καρποῖς οἰκείας οὔσης ἀπολαύειν, οὐχ
ὑπ’ ἄλλων ἔξωθεν προσγινομένης, τὰ δένδρα τῆς
ἐπὶ τῷ ἄρχεσθαι φροντίδος οὐκ ἀπελείπετο, ἐδόκει
237 δ’ αὐτοῖς ἀμπέλῳ τὴν τιμὴν παρασχεῖν. καὶ ἡ
ἄμπελος χειροτονουμένη τοῖς αὐτοῖς τῇ συκῇ
χρησαμένη λόγοις παρῃτεῖτο τὴν ἀρχήν. τὸ δ’
αὐτὸ καὶ τῶν ἐλαιῶν ποιησαμένων ῥάμνος, ἐδεήθη
γὰρ αὐτῆς ὥστε παραλαβεῖν τὴν βασιλείαν τὰ
238 δένδρα, πυρεῖα¹ δὲ ἀγαθὴ παρασχεῖν τῶν ξύλων
ἐστίν, ὑπισχνεῖται τὴν ἀρχὴν ἀναλήψεσθαι καὶ ἀ-
όκνως ἔχειν, δεῖν² μέντοι συνιζάνειν αὐτὰ ὑπὸ τὴν
σκιάν, εἰ δ’ ὄλεθρον ἐπ’ αὐτῇ φρονοῖεν,³ ὑπὸ τοῦ
239 ἐνόντος πυρὸς διαφθαρεῖν. “ ταῦτα δ’ οὐ γέλωτος
ἕνεκα,” φησί, “ λέγω,” ὅτι δὲ πολλῶν ἀγαθῶν ἐκ
Γεδεῶνος πεπειραμένοι περιορῶσιν Ἀβιμέλεχον
ἐπὶ τῶν ὅλων ὄντα πραγμάτων σὺν αὐτῷ τοὺς
ἀδελφοὺς ἀποκτείναντες, ὃν πυρὸς οὐδὲν διοίσειν.
καὶ ὁ μὲν ταῦτα εἰπὼν ὑπεχώρησε καὶ διῃτᾶτο
λανθάνων ἐν τοῖς ὄρεσι δεδιὼς ἐπ’ ἔτη τρία τὸν
Ἀβιμέλεχον.

240 (3) Μετ’ οὐ πολὺ δὲ τῆς ἑορτῆς οἱ⁴ Σικιμῖται,
μετενόησαν γὰρ ἐπὶ τοῖς Γεδεῶνος υἱοῖς πεφονευ-
μένοις, ἐξελαύνουσι τὸν Ἀβιμέλεχον τῆς πόλεως
καὶ τῆς φυλῆς· ὁ δὲ κακοῦν τὴν πόλιν ἐφρόντιζε.
τῆς δ’ ὥρας τῆς τοῦ τρυγᾶν γενομένης ἐδεδίεσαν
συλλέγειν τὸν καρπὸν προϊόντες, μή τι δράσῃ κακὸν

¹ πυρία codd.
² δεῖ codd.   ³ φρονῶεν codd.
⁴ om. RO.

268

how the trees, once gifted with a human voice, held
a meeting and besought a fig-tree [a] to rule over
them. And when she refused, because she enjoyed
the esteem which her fruits brought her, an esteem
that was all her own and not conferred from without
by others, the trees did not renounce their intention
of having a ruler, but thought good to offer this
dignity to the vine. And the vine, when so elected,
on the same grounds as those of the fig-tree, declined
the sovereignty. The olive-trees having done the
like, a bramble—since the trees requested it to accept
the kingship, and it is good in giving wood for
tinder—promised to undertake the office and to
act strenuously. However it behoved them all to
sit down beneath her shadow, and should they plot
her ruin they would be destroyed by the fire within
her. " I tell this fable," said Jotham, " not for your 16.
merriment, but because notwithstanding the mani-
fold benefits that ye have received from Gedeon ye [b]
suffer Abimelech to hold sovereign sway, after aiding
him to slay my brethren. Ye will find him in no
wise different from a fire." Having spoken thus he
absconded and lived in hiding in the hills for three *Cf.* 22.
years from fear of Abimelech.

(3) But not long after the festival [c] the Shechemites, Expulsion of
repenting of the murder of the sons of Gedeon, Jd. ix. 23.
expelled Abimelech from their city and from their
tribe ; and he laid plans for doing the town an
injury. So, when the season of vintage was come,
they were afraid to go out and gather the fruit, for

[a] In Judges the olive-tree is approached first, then the fig-
tree, then the vine.

[b] In the Greek, the Shechemites are not addressed in the
second person.

[c] Not in Scripture.

241 Ἀβιμέλεχος εἰς αὐτούς. ἐπιδημήσαντος δὲ πρὸς
αὐτοὺς τῶν ἀρχόντων τινὸς Γυάλου σὺν ὁπλίταις
καὶ συγγενέσι τοῖς αὐτοῦ, φυλακὴν οἱ Σικιμῖται
δέονται παρασχεῖν αὐτοῖς, ἕως ἂν τρυγήσωσι.
προσδεξαμένου δ' ἐκείνου τὴν ἀξίωσιν προῄεσαν
καὶ Γυάλης σὺν αὐτοῖς τὸ οἰκεῖον ἄγων ὁπλιτικόν.

242 ὅ τε οὖν καρπὸς μετὰ ἀσφαλείας συνάγεται καὶ
δειπνοῦντες κατὰ συμμορίας[1] φανερῶς ἀπετόλμων
ἤδη βλασφημεῖν τὸν Ἀβιμέλεχον, οἵ τε ἄρχοντες
ἐνέδραις καταλαμβανόμενοι τὰ περὶ τὴν πόλιν
πολλοὺς τῶν Ἀβιμελέχου συλλαμβάνοντες ἀνῄρουν.

243 (4) Ζάβουλος δέ τις τῶν Σικιμιτῶν ἄρχων, ξένος
ὢν Ἀβιμελέχου, ὅσα παρώξυνεν Γυάλης τὸν
δῆμον πέμπων ἀγγέλους ἐμήνυεν αὐτῷ καὶ παρῄνει
λοχᾶν πρὸ τῆς πόλεως· πείσειν γὰρ Γυάλην ἐξελθεῖν ἐπ' αὐτόν, καὶ τὸ λοιπὸν ἐπ' ἐκείνῳ τυγχάνειν
ὥστε ἀμύνασθαι· γενομένου γὰρ τούτου διαλλαγὰς

244 αὐτῷ μνηστεύσεσθαι[2] πρὸς τὸν δῆμον. ὅ τε οὖν
Ἀβιμέλεχος ἐκάθισεν ἐνεδρεύων καὶ ὁ Γυάλης
ἀφυλακτοτέρως διέτριβεν ἐπὶ τοῦ προαστείου καὶ
Ζάβουλος σὺν αὐτῷ. ἰδὼν δὲ ὁπλίτας ἐπιφερο-
μένους Γυάλης πρὸς Ζάβουλον ἔλεγεν ἄνδρας

245 αὐτοῖς ἐπιέναι καθωπλισμένους. τοῦ δὲ σκιὰς
εἶναι φαμένου τῶν πετρῶν, πλησίον ἤδη γινομένων
τὸ ἀκριβὲς κατανοῶν οὐ σκιὰς ἔλεγε ταῦτ' εἶναι,
λόχον δ' ἀνδρῶν. καὶ Ζάβουλος " οὐ σὺ μέντοι,"
φησίν, " Ἀβιμέλεχῳ κακίαν ἐπεκάλεις; τί οὖν
οὐκ ἐπιδείκνυσαι τὸ τῆς σῆς ἀρετῆς μέγεθος εἰς

246 μάχην αὐτῷ συμβαλών;" Γυάλης δὲ θορυβού-
μενος συνάπτει τοῖς Ἀβιμελέχου καὶ πίπτουσι μέν

---

[1] ex Lat.: συμμορίαν codd.
[2] Niese: μνηστεύεσθαι codd.

fear that Abimelech would do them some mischief.
But on being visited by Gual,[a] one of their chiefs, 26.
with a retinue of troops and kinsmen, the Shechemites besought him to lend them protection during their
vintage. And when he complied with their request,
they went forth, accompanied by Gual at the head
of his troop. So the fruit was safely gathered in,
and while supping in companies they now ventured
openly to revile Abimelech ; and the chiefs, posting 25.
ambuscades about the town, captured and slew
many of his followers.

(4) But a certain Zabul,[b] a chieftain of the Shechem- The fate of
ites and an old friend of Abimelech, sent messengers Shechem.
to report to him how Gual was stirring up the people, Jd. ix. 30.
and he advised him to lie in wait before the town,
since he would induce Gual to sally out against him
and it would then rest with Abimelech to avenge
himself ; that done, he (Zabul) would procure his
reconciliation with the townsfolk. So Abimelech
sat in ambush, while Gual all too unguardedly
tarried in the suburbs, and Zabul with him. Spying
some men-at-arms hastening up, Gual said to Zabul
that men were upon them in arms. He replied that
they were but shadows of the rocks ; but on their
nearer approach Gual, perceiving them perfectly,
told him that these were no shadows but a company
of men. Said Zabul, " But wert thou not accusing
Abimelech of cowardice ? Why then displayest thou
not that mighty valour of thine by meeting him in
combat ? " Thereat Gual, in confusion, closed with
Abimelech's men, lost some of his own, and himself

---

[a] Greek *Guales*, Bibl. Gaal.
[b] Or, with some MSS., " Zebul " (the Biblical name).

τινες τῶν σὺν αὐτῷ, φεύγει δ' αὐτὸς εἰς τὴν πόλιν
τοὺς ἄλλους ἀγόμενος. καὶ Ζάβουλος πολιτεύεται
Γυάλην ἐκβληθῆναι τῆς πόλεως, κατηγορήσας ὡς
μαλακῶς πρὸς τοὺς Ἀβιμελέχου στρατιώτας ἀγωνί-
247 σαιτο. Ἀβιμέλεχος δὲ πυθόμενος ἐξελευσομένους
αὖθις κατὰ τρύγητον τοὺς Σικιμίους ἐνέδραις
προλοχίζεται τὰ περὶ τὴν πόλιν, καὶ προελθόντων
ἡ μὲν τρίτη μοῖρα τῆς στρατιᾶς καταλαμβάνει
τὰς πύλας ἀφαιρησομένη τὴν εἴσοδον τοὺς πολίτας,
οἱ δ' ἄλλοι σκιδναμένους μεταθέουσι, πανταχοῦ τε
248 φόνος ἦν. καὶ κατασκάψας εἰς ἔδαφος τὴν πόλιν,
οὐ γὰρ ἀντέσχε πρὸς[1] πολιορκίαν, ἅλας κατὰ τῶν
ἐρειπίων σπείρας προῆγε. καὶ Σικιμῖται πάντες
οὕτως ἀπώλοντο· ὅσοι δὲ κατὰ τὴν χώραν σκεδασθέντες διέφυγον τὸν κίνδυνον, οὗτοι συλλεγέντες
ἐπί τινα πέτραν ὀχυρὰν[2] ἐπ' αὐτῆς ἱδρύονται
249 τειχίσαι τε ταύτην παρεσκευάζοντο. ἔφθη τε τὴν
διάνοιαν αὐτῶν Ἀβιμέλεχος μαθὼν ἐλθεῖν ἐπ'
αὐτοὺς μετὰ τῆς δυνάμεως καὶ φακέλους ὕλης
ξηρᾶς περιβαλὼν τῷ χωρίῳ δι' αὐτοῦ φέρων ταῦτα[3]
ποιεῖν τὴν στρατιὰν παρεκελεύσατο. καὶ ταχέως
περιληφθείσης ἐν κύκλῳ τῆς πέτρας, τοῖς ξύλοις
πῦρ ἐμβάλλουσιν ὅσα τε μᾶλλον ἐξάπτειν φύσιν
250 ἔχει καὶ μεγίστην αἴρουσι φλόγα. καὶ διαφεύγει
μὲν ἀπὸ τῆς πέτρας οὐθείς, ἀλλ' ἅμα γυναιξὶ καὶ
τέκνοις ἀπώλοντο, ἄνδρες μὲν περὶ πεντακοσίους
καὶ χιλίους, τὸ δὲ ἄλλο πλῆθος ἱκανόν. καὶ

---

[1] + τὴν RO.
[2] συλλεγέντες ... ὀχυρὰν] πέτραν ὀχυρὰν εὑρόντες RO.
[3] ταὐτὸ MSPL.

272

fled to the town with the rest at his heels. Zabul 41.
now contrived to secure Gual's expulsion from the
town, charging him with feebleness in his encounter
with Abimelech's troops.[a] However Abimelech,
learning that the Shechemites proposed to come out
again for the vintage, posted ambuscades all about
the town ; then, so soon as they emerged, a third of
his force occupied the gates to cut off the citizens
from re-entering, the rest chased them as they
scattered, and there was carnage on all sides. Then,
having razed the city to the ground—for it could not
sustain a siege—he sowed salt over the ruins and
pushed forward. And so perished all the Shechemites.
As for such as had scattered across country and 46.
escaped that peril, these mustering to a strongly
entrenched rock established themselves thereon
and were preparing to fortify it with a wall.[b] But
they were forestalled by Abimelech, who, hearing
of their design, came upon them with his forces and
laid faggots of dry wood round the place, carrying
them with his own hands and bidding his troops to
do the like. The rock being thus quickly encompassed, they set fire to the faggots, flinging in all the
most inflammable materials, and raised an immense
blaze. From that rock not a soul escaped : they
perished with women and children, the men numbering some fifteen hundred,[c] and a great many of the

---

[a] This charge is not mentioned in Scripture.

[b] The Biblical account is different, mentioning a tower,
apparently in an unwalled hamlet of Shechem possessing a
temple : Jd. ix. 46 " And when all the men of the tower of
Shechem heard thereof, they entered into the hold (or
"crypt"—the word is of uncertain meaning) of the temple
of El-berith."

[c] " About a thousand men and women," Jd. ix. 49.

Σικιμίταις μὲν τοιαύτη συμφορὰ συνέπεσε μείζων
καὶ τῆς ἐπ' αὐτῇ λύπης γενομένη, πλὴν ὅτι κατὰ
δίκην ἐπ' ἀνδρὸς εὐεργέτου συνθεῖσι κακὸν τηλι-
κοῦτον.

251   (5) Ἀβιμέλεχος δὲ τοῖς Σικιμιτῶν κακοῖς κατα-
πλήξας τοὺς Ἰσραηλίτας, μειζόνων ἐφιέμενος δῆλος
ἦν καὶ μηδαμοῦ περιγράψων τὴν βίαν, εἰ μὴ πάντας
ἀπολέσειεν. ἤλαυνεν οὖν ἐπὶ Θήβας καὶ τὴν μὲν
πόλιν ἐξ ἐπιδρομῆς αἱρεῖ, πύργου δ' ὄντος ἐν αὐτῇ
μεγάλου, εἰς ὃν πᾶν τὸ πλῆθος συνέφυγε, πολι-
252 ορκεῖν τοῦτον παρεσκευάζετο. καὶ αὐτὸν πλησίον
ὁρμῶντα τῶν πυλῶν γυνὴ θραύσματι μύλης βαλοῦσα
κατὰ τῆς κεφαλῆς τυγχάνει, πεσὼν δὲ Ἀβιμέλεχος
τὸν ὑπασπιστὴν παρεκάλει κτείνειν αὐτόν, μὴ τῆς
γυναικὸς ὁ θάνατος αὐτοῦ δόξειεν ἔργον. καὶ ὁ
253 μὲν τὸ προσταχθὲν ἐποίει. ὁ δὲ τοιαύτην ὑπὲρ
τῆς εἰς τοὺς ἀδελφοὺς παρανομίας ποινὴν ἐξέτισε
καὶ τῶν εἰς Σικιμίους αὐτῷ τετολμημένων· τούτοις
δὲ κατὰ τὴν Ἰωθάμου μαντείαν ἡ συμφορὰ συνέπεσε. τὸ μέντοι σὺν Ἀβιμελέχῳ στράτευμα πεσόντος αὐτοῦ σκεδασθὲν ἀνεχώρησεν ἐπὶ τὰ οἰκεῖα.

254   (6) Τῶν δὲ Ἰσραηλιτῶν τὴν ἡγεμονίαν Ἰαείρης
ὁ Γαλαδηνὸς ἐκ τῆς Μανασσίτιδος φυλῆς παραλαμβάνει, ἀνὴρ τά τε ἄλλα εὐδαίμων καὶ παῖδας
ἀγαθοὺς πεποιημένος τριάκοντα μὲν τὸν ἀριθμὸν
ἱππεύειν δὲ ἀρίστους καὶ τῶν κατὰ τὴν Γα-
λαδηνὴν πόλεων ἀρχὰς ἐγκεχειρισμένους. οὗτος
δύο καὶ εἴκοσι ἔτη τὴν ἀρχὴν κατασχὼν τελευτᾷ

ᵃ Gideon.
ᵇ Bibl. Thebez (ʟxx Θηβής), mod. *Ṭūbās*, some 10 miles
N.E. of Shechem.
ᶜ Gr. " Galadenian." Josephus omits the judge Tola, to
274

rest. Such was the calamity which befell the Shechemites, a calamity too profound for grief, save that it was a righteous doom for the conspirators of so foul a crime against a benefactor.[a]

(5) Abimelech, having terrorized the Israelites by the miserable fate of the Shechemites, let it be seen that he was aspiring higher and would set no bound to his violence until he had exterminated all. So he marched upon Thebes[b] and carried the city with a rush; but finding there a great tower, wherein all the people had taken refuge, he made preparations to besiege it. And then, as he came rushing close beside the gates, a woman hurled a fragment of a millstone and struck him on the head. Prostrated to earth, Abimelech besought his armour-bearer to slay him, lest his death should be deemed the work of this woman; and he obeyed his behest. Such was the penalty paid by Abimelech for the crime that he perpetrated on his brethren and for his outrageous treatment of the Shechemites; and the fate which befell these last fulfilled the prediction of Jotham. Abimelech's army for their part, on the fall of their chief, dispersed and returned to their homes.

(6) The leadership of the Israelites was then taken over by Jair the Gileadite,[c] of the tribe of Manasseh, a man in all ways blessed, and chiefly in his progeny of valiant sons, thirty in number, excellent horsemen, to whom was committed the government of the several cities of Gilead.[d] Their father, after bearing rule for twenty-two years, died in old age

Death of Abimelech.

Jd. ix. 50.

The rule of Jair.
Jd. x. 3.

whom Scripture assigns a 23 years' term of office between Abimelech and Jair, Jd. x. 1 f.

[d] Gr. "Galadene."

275

γηραιὸς καὶ ταφῆς ἐν Καμὼν[1] πόλει τῆς Γαλαδηνῆς
ἀξιοῦται.

255 (7) Πάντα δὲ τὰ τῶν Ἑβραίων εἰς ἀκοσμίαν καὶ
ὕβριν τοῦ θεοῦ καὶ τῶν νόμων ὑπεφέρετο, καὶ
καταφρονήσαντες αὐτῶν Ἀμμανῖται καὶ Παλαιστῖνοι στρατῷ μεγάλῳ διήρπαζον τὴν χώραν καὶ
τὴν Περαίαν ἅπασαν κατασχόντες καὶ ἐπὶ τὴν τῶν
256 λοιπῶν ἤδη κτῆσιν διαβαίνειν ἐτόλμων. Ἑβραῖοι
δὲ σωφρονισθέντες ὑπὸ τῶν κακῶν, εἰς ἱκετείαν
ἐτράποντο τοῦ θεοῦ καὶ θυσίας ἐπέφερον παρακαλοῦντες αὐτὸν μετριάσαντα καὶ πρὸς τὴν δέησιν
αὐτῶν ὑπαχθέντα παύσασθαι τῆς ὀργῆς· ὁ δὲ θεὸς
μεταβαλόμενος εἰς τὸ ἡμερώτερον ἔμελλεν αὐτοῖς
βοηθεῖν.

257 (8) Ἀμμανιτῶν δ' ἐστρατευκότων ἐπὶ τὴν Γαλα-
δηνὴν ὑπήντων οἱ ἐπιχώριοι πρὸς τὸ ὄρος δεόμενοι
τοῦ στρατηγήσοντος. ἦν δέ τις Ἰέφθας ἀνὴρ διὰ
τὴν πατρῴαν ἀρετὴν δυνατὸς καὶ δι' οἰκείαν αὐτοῦ
258 στρατιὰν ἣν ἔτρεφεν αὐτὸς μισθοφόρων. πρὸς
τοῦτον οὖν πέμψαντες ἠξίουν αὐτὸν συμμαχεῖν
ἐπαγγελλόμενοι παρασχεῖν εἰς ἅπαντ' αὐτῷ τὸν
χρόνον τὴν ἰδίαν ἡγεμονίαν. ὁ δ' οὐ προσίεται τὴν
παράκλησιν αὐτῶν, ἐγκαλῶν ὅτι μὴ βοηθήσειαν
259 αὐτῷ ὑπὸ τῶν ἀδελφῶν ἀδικουμένῳ περιφανῶς· οὐ
γὰρ ὄντα ὁμομήτριον αὐτοῖς ἀλλὰ ξένον περὶ τὴν
μητέρα δι' ἐρωτικὴν ἐπιθυμίαν ἐπαχθεῖσαν αὐτοῖς
ὑπὸ τοῦ πατρός, ἐξέβαλον καταφρονήσαντες τῆς
260 αὐτοῦ ἀσθενείας. καὶ ὁ μὲν διέτριβεν ἐν τῇ Γα-

[1] Καλαμὼν RO.

---

[a] Perhaps modern *Kumeim*, some 7 miles S.E. of Gadara.
[b] The introduction of the Philistines as invaders (along
with the Ammonites) *from the east* is strange and has been

276

and received honoured burial at Kamon,[a] a city of Gilead.

(7) But everything with the Hebrews was now drifting towards disorder and contempt of God and of the laws ; so, holding them in disdain, the Ammanites and Philistines [b] with a large army ravaged their country and, after occupying all Peraea,[c] made bold to cross the river for the further conquest of the rest. But the Hebrews, sobered by their afflictions, turned in supplication to God and offered sacrifices, beseeching Him to be considerate and, yielding to their prayers, to desist from wrath. And God, moved to milder action, was now to succour them.

(8) When the Ammanites had invaded Gilead, the people of the country, preparing to meet them, mustered in the hills, lacking a leader to take command. Now there was one Jephthah,[d] a mighty man by reason of the valour of his forefathers as also of his own troop of mercenaries which he maintained himself. To him then they sent, begging him to support them and promising to confer his command upon him for all time. But he declined their request, reproaching them for not having aided him when he was flagrantly wronged by his brethren. For, because he was not their full brother but unconnected on his mother's side, who had been inflicted upon them by their father through his amorous desire, they had cast him out, scorning his helplessness ; and so he was living in the region called Galaditis,[e] receiv-

Israel under the Ammonites and Philistines. Jd. x. 6.

16.

The call to Jephthah. x. 17.

xi. 1.

thought to be due to some confusion in the Biblical text (Jd. x. 7).

[c] Modern Transjordania.

[d] Gr. Jephthas (or Japhthas).

[e] Bibl. (more precisely) "in the land of Tob" (Jd. xi. 3).

λαδίτιδι καλουμένη χώρα πάντας τοὺς ὁποθενοῦν
παραγινομένους πρὸς αὑτὸν ἐπὶ μισθῷ δεχόμενος·
ἐκλιπαρησάντων δ' αὐτῶν καὶ ὀμοσάντων εἰς ἀεὶ
παρέξειν αὐτῷ τὴν ἡγεμονίαν ἐστράτευε.

261 (9) Καὶ ποιησάμενος ὀξεῖαν τὴν τῶν πραγμάτων
ἐπιμέλειαν ἐν πόλει Μασφαθῇ καθίσας τὸν στρατὸν
πρεσβείαν πέμπει παρὰ τὸν Ἀμμανίτην αἰτιώ-
μενος τῆς ἁλώσεως. ὁ δὲ ἀντιπέμψας ᾐτιᾶτο τῶν
Ἰσραηλιτῶν τὴν ἔξοδον τὴν ἀπ' Αἰγύπτου καὶ τῆς
Ἀμοραίας αὐτοὺς ἠξίου παραχωρεῖν ὡς πατρῴας
262 οὔσης ἀρχῆθεν. ἀποκρινάμενος δὲ ὁ Ἰέφθας, ὡς
οὔτε τῆς Ἀμοραίας τοῖς προγόνοις αὐτῶν εὐλόγως
ἐγκαλοῦσι χάριν τε μᾶλλον τῆς Ἀμμανίτιδος αὐτοῖς ἔχειν ὀφείλουσι παρεθείσης, δυνατὸν γὰρ
Μωυσεῖ καὶ ταύτην λαβεῖν[1]· παραχωρεῖν τε ἰδίας
εἰπὼν γῆς, ἣν θεοῦ κατακτησαμένου μετὰ τρια-
κόσια ἔτη νέμονται, μαχεῖσθαι[2] πρὸς αὐτοὺς
ἔφησεν.

263 (10) Καὶ τοὺς μὲν πρέσβεις ταῦτ' εἰπὼν ἀπ-
έλυσεν· αὐτὸς δ' εὐξάμενος νίκην καὶ θυσιάσειν ὑποσχόμενος, ἂν σῶος εἰς τὰ οἰκεῖα ὑποστρέψῃ, καὶ
πᾶν ὅ τι καὶ πρῶτον αὐτῷ συντύχοι ἱερουργήσειν,
συμβαλών τε νικᾷ παρὰ πολὺ καὶ φονεύων ἐδίωκε
μέχρι πόλεως Μανιάθης, καὶ διαβὰς εἰς τὴν
Ἀμμανῖτιν πόλεις τε ἠφάνισε πολλὰς καὶ λείαν
ἤλασε καὶ τοὺς οἰκείους δουλείας ἀπήλλαξεν ἐν
264 ἔτεσιν ὀκτωκαίδεκα ταύτην ὑπομείναντας. ἀνα-

[1] Niese indicates a lacuna.
[2] ex Lat.: μάχεσθαι codd.

[a] Bibl. Mizpah (LXX Μασσηφά) : site uncertain.
[b] "Amoraea" is the country north of the river Arnon.
Cf. A. iv. 85. The Ammonite country is further north

278

ing all who resorted to him from whencesoever and paying them wages. However, when the Hebrews made earnest entreaty and swore to confer the command upon him for ever, he took the field.

(9) Having promptly taken charge of affairs and installed the army in the city of Masphath(e),*a* he sent an embassy to the Ammanite to remonstrate with him on his raid. That monarch sent a counter embassy, reproaching the Israelites for their exodus from Egypt and requiring them to quit Amoraea,*b* as the primeval heritage of his forefathers. Whereto Jephthah replied that the enemy had no just grievance against his people's ancestors on the subject of Amoraea and ought rather to be grateful to them for having left them Ammanitis, which Moses might have taken to boot ; and, bidding him quit that land *c* of theirs which God had won for them and of which three hundred years later they were in possession, he declared that he would battle with them.

Embassies before battle. Jd. xi. 11.

(10) With these words he dismissed the envoys. Then, after praying *d* for victory and promising to sacrifice, should he return to his home unscathed, and to offer up the first creature that should meet him, he closed with the enemy, defeated them outright, and massacring pursued them up to the city of Maniath(e) *e* ; then, crossing into Ammanitis, he destroyed many cities, carried off spoil, and delivered his countrymen from a servitude which they had borne for eighteen years. But on returning

Victory of Jephthah: his daughter's fate. Jd. xi. 30.

x. 8.

with its capital at Rabatha (Bibl. Rabbah) on the river Jabbok. *Cf. A.* iv. 98.

c Text a little uncertain : possibly " saying that he would (not) quit that land " (Weill).

d Or " making vows."

e Bibl. Minnith (Jd. xi. 33) : site unknown.

στρέφων δὲ συμφορᾷ περιπίπτει κατ’ οὐδὲν ὁμοίᾳ
τοῖς κατωρθωμένοις αὐτῷ· ὑπήντησε γὰρ ἡ θυγάτηρ
αὐτῷ, μονογενὴς δ’ ἦν, ἔτι παρθένος. ὁ δὲ ἀνοιμώ-
ξας ἐπὶ τῷ μεγέθει τοῦ πάθους, κατεμέμφετο τῆς
περὶ τὴν ὑπάντησιν σπουδῆς τὴν θυγατέρα· καθ-
265 ιερῶσαι γὰρ αὐτὴν τῷ θεῷ. τῇ δὲ τὸ συμβησόμενον
οὐκ ἀηδῶς προσέπεσεν, ἐπὶ νίκῃ τοῦ πατρὸς καὶ
ἐλευθερίᾳ τῶν πολιτῶν τεθνηξομένη, παρεκάλεσε
δὲ δύο μῆνας αὐτῇ παρασχόντα πρὸς τὸ μετὰ
τῶν πολιτῶν ἀποθρηνῆσαι τὴν νεότητα, τότε ποιεῖν
266 τὰ κατὰ τὴν εὐχήν. συγχωρήσας δὲ τὰ κατὰ τὸν
προειρημένον χρόνον μετὰ τοῦτον διελθόντα θύσας
τὴν παῖδα ὡλοκαύτωσεν, οὔτε νόμιμον οὔτε θεῷ
κεχαρισμένην θυσίαν ἐπιτελῶν, μὴ διαβασανίσας
τῷ λογισμῷ τὸ γενησόμενον οἷόν τε τὸ[1] πραχθὲν
δόξει τοῖς ἀκούσασι.

267 (11) Τῆς δ’ Ἐφράνου[2] φυλῆς ἐπ’ αὐτὸν στρα-
τευσάσης, ὅτι μὴ κοινώσαιτο τὴν ἐπ’ Ἀμμανίτας
ἐλασίαν[3] αὐτοῖς, ἀλλὰ μόνος καὶ τὴν λείαν ἔχοι
καὶ τὴν ἐπὶ τοῖς πεπραγμένοις δόξαν, πρῶτον μὲν
ἔλεγεν, ὡς οὔτε λάθοιεν αὐτοὺς οἱ συγγενεῖς πολε-
μούμενοι καλούμενοί τε πρὸς συμμαχίαν οὐ παρ-
εγένοντο, δέον καὶ πρὸ δεήσεως ἐγνωκότας ἐπειχθῆ-
268 ναι, ἔπειθ’ ὡς ἄδικα πράττειν ἐπιχειροῦσι τοῖς
πολεμίοις οὐ τολμήσαντες εἰς χεῖρας ἐλθεῖν, ἐπὶ
δὲ τοὺς συγγενεῖς ὡρμηκότες· ἠπείλει τε σὺν τῷ
θεῷ λήψεσθαι δίκην παρ’ αὐτῶν, ἂν μὴ σωφρονῶσιν.
269 ὡς δ’ οὐκ ἔπειθεν, ἀλλὰ συνέβαλεν αὐτοῖς ἐλθοῦσι

---

[1] τε τὸ] τε or τὸ codd.
[2] R : Ἐφράμου (-αίμου) rell.　　　[3] ἔλασιν RO.

---

[a] Phraseology based on Thuc. iii. 113. 3.

he fell foul of a calamity far different from these fair ^{xi. 34.} achievements; for it was his daughter who met him, his only daughter, a virgin yet. Wailing in anguish at the greatness of the blow,[a] the father chid his daughter for her haste in meeting him, seeing that he had dedicated her to God. But she without displeasure learnt her destiny, to wit that she must die in return for her father's victory and the liberation of her fellow-citizens; she but asked him to grant her two months wherein to bewail her youth with her fellow-citizens, and thereafter he should do in accordance with his vow. He accorded her the respite aforesaid, and at its close sacrificed his child as a burnt-offering—a sacrifice neither sanctioned by the law nor well-pleasing to God; for he had not by reflection probed what might befall or in what aspect the deed would appear to them that heard of it.[b]

(11) The tribe of Ephraim now took arms against Jephthah's him, because he had not imparted the news of his war with expedition against the Ammanites to them, but had Ephraim. reserved to himself alone the booty and the glory Jd. xii. 1. of the achievement. Thereto he replied first that they were not unaware that their kinsfolk were beset and that when called upon for aid they had not come, whereas they ought, even before being asked, to have learnt of the matter and sped to arms; next that this was an iniquitous enterprise of theirs, after not having dared to face the foe, to rush upon their kinsmen; and he threatened, God helping, to be avenged on them unless they showed themselves reasonable. Failing, however, to influence them, he met them, when they came, with an army

[b] The rash vow is stigmatized in Rabbinical tradition (Weill, quoting *Genesis Rabba*, lx.).

μετὰ στρατιᾶς, ἢ μετάπεμπτος ἐκ τῆς Γαλαδηνῆς
ἐληλύθει, φόνον τε πολὺν αὐτῶν εἰργάσατο καὶ
διώκων τραπέντας προλαβὼν μέρει τινὶ προαπ-
εσταλμένῳ τοῦ Ἰορδάνου τὰς διαβάσεις κτείνει περὶ
δισχιλίους καὶ τετρακισμυρίους γεγονότας.

270   (12) Αὐτὸς δὲ ἄρξας ἓξ ἔτη τελευτᾷ καὶ θάπτεται
ἐν τῇ αὐτοῦ πατρίδι Σεβέῃ· τῆς Γαλαδηνῆς δ'
ἐστὶν αὕτη.

271   (13) Τελευτήσαντος δὲ Ἰάφθα τὴν ἀρχὴν Ἀψάνης
παραλαμβάνει φυλῆς ὢν Ἰουδαϊκῆς Βηθλέμων δὲ
πόλεως. τούτῳ δὲ παῖδες ἦσαν ἑξήκοντα, τριάκοντα μὲν ἄρρενες αἱ λοιπαὶ δὲ θυγατέρες, οὓς καὶ
πάντας ζῶντας κατέλιπε τὰς μὲν ἀνδράσιν ἐκδοὺς
τοῖς δὲ γυναῖκας ἠγμένος. πράξας δ' οὐδὲν ἐν
τῷ ἑπταετεῖ γενομένῳ χρόνῳ λόγου καὶ μνήμης
ἄξιον γηραιὸς ὢν ἀπέθανε καὶ ταφῆς ἐν τῇ πατρίδι
τυγχάνει.

272   (14) Ἀψάνους δ' οὕτως ἀποθανόντος οὐδ' ὁ μετ'
αὐτὸν παραλαβὼν τὴν ἡγεμονίαν Ἤλων[1] ἐπ' ἔτη
δέκα κατασχὼν αὐτὴν φυλῆς ὢν τῆς Ζαβούλης
ἔπραξέ τι σπουδῆς ἄξιον.

273   (15) Ἀβδὼν δὲ Ἤλωνος παῖς φυλῆς μὲν τῆς
Ἐφραμίτιδος πόλεως δὲ τῆς Φαραθωνιτῶν γεγονώς, αὐτοκράτωρ ἡγεμὼν ἀποδειχθεὶς μετ'
Ἤλωνα μόνης ἂν τῆς εὐπαιδίας μνημονευθείη,
μηδὲν ἔργον διὰ τὴν εἰρήνην καὶ τὴν ἄδειαν τῶν
πραγμάτων λαμπρὸν μηδ' αὐτὸς ἐργασάμενος.[2]

274   υἱεῖς δὲ ἦσαν αὐτῷ τεσσαράκοντα καὶ τούτων

---

[1] Hilonis Lat.   [2] ROML: εἰργασμένος SP.

---

[a] Josephus omits the details in Jd. xii. 5-6 on the detection
of the fleeing Ephraimites by their pronunciation of " shib-

which he had recalled from Gilead, worked great havoc among them, and pursuing the fugitives, having sent a party in advance to occupy the fords of the Jordan, slew in all some two and forty thousand.[a]

(12) After ruling for six years he died and was buried at his native place of Sebee,[b] in the land of Gilead.

His death.
Jd. xii. 7.

(13) Upon the death of Jephthah, the rulership passed to Apsanes[c] of the tribe of Judah and the city of Bethlehem. He had sixty children, thirty sons and as many daughters, all of whom he left alive at his death,[d] after bestowing wives and husbands upon all. Having achieved in his seven years of office nothing worthy of record and remembrance, he died in old age and was buried at his native place.

Ibzan. 8.

(14) Apsanes having thus died, his successor, Elon of the tribe of Zabulon, held the leadership for ten years and likewise did nothing of moment.

Elon. 11.

(15) Abdon, son of Elon,[e] of the tribe of Ephraim and the city of Pharathon,[f] who was appointed sovereign leader after Elon, calls for no mention save for his happy paternity, since, thanks to the prevailing peace and security of the state, he too did no brilliant deed. But he had forty sons and, born

Abdon. 13.

boleth " as " sibboleth," probably because the difference in sound could not have been made clear to Greek readers.

[b] The Heb. of Jd. xii. 7 " in the cities of Gilead " is corrupt : read probably " in his city, in Mizpah of Gilead." The loss of the M in Mizpah produced the reading found in some MSS. of the LXX, ἐν Σεφέ (ἐν Σέφ), and through further corruption the name Sebee in Josephus.

[c] Bibl. Ibzan.   [d] Amplification (as in § 274).

[e] Bibl. " son of Hillel."

[f] Heb. " the Pirathonite " : modern *Fer'atha*, 6 miles S.W. of Shechem.

γενεὰς καταλιπόντων[1] τριάκοντα, ἤλαυνέ τε σὺν
αὐτοῖς οὖσιν ἑβδομήκοντα πᾶσιν ἱππάζειν ἀρίστοις
γεγενημένοις, καὶ πάντας ὑπὲρ γῆς ἀπολιπὼν
θνήσκει γηραιὸς καὶ ταφῆς ἐν Φαράθῳ λαμπρᾶς
τυγχάνει.

275 (viii. 1) Μετὰ δὲ τοῦτον Παλαιστῖνοι τελευτήσαντα κρατοῦσι τῶν Ἰσραηλιτῶν καὶ φόρους
παρ' αὐτῶν ἐλάμβανον ἐπ' ἔτη τεσσαράκοντα.
ταύτης δ' ἐλευθεροῦνται τῆς ἀνάγκης τούτῳ τῷ
τρόπῳ·

276 (2) Μανώχης τις Δανιτῶν ἐν ὀλίγοις ἄριστος
καὶ τῆς πατρίδος ὁμολογουμένως[2] πρῶτος εἶχε
γύναιον ἐπ' εὐμορφίᾳ περίβλεπτον καὶ τῶν καθ'
αὐτὸ διαφέρον. παίδων δ' οὐ γινομένων αὐτῷ, δυσ-
φορῶν ἐπὶ τῇ ἀπαιδίᾳ τὸν θεὸν ἱκέτευεν ἐπὶ τὸ
προάστειον συνεχῶς φοιτῶν μετὰ τῆς γυναικὸς
δοῦναι διαδοχὴν αὐτοῖς γνησίαν· μέγα δέ ἐστι
277 τοῦτο τὸ[3] πεδίον. ἦν δὲ καὶ μανιώδης ὑπ' ἔρωτος
ἐπὶ τῇ γυναικὶ καὶ διὰ τοῦτο ζηλότυπος ἀκρατῶς.
μονωθείσῃ δὲ τῇ γυναικὶ φάντασμα ἐπιφαίνεται,
ἄγγελος[4] τοῦ θεοῦ, νεανίᾳ καλῷ παραπλήσιον καὶ
μεγάλῳ, εὐαγγελιζόμενον αὐτῇ παιδὸς γονὴν κατὰ
θεοῦ πρόνοιαν καλοῦ τε καὶ ῥώμην ἐπιφανοῦς, ὑφ'
278 ᾧ πονήσειν Παλαιστίνους ἀνδρουμένῳ. παρήνει τε
τὰς κόμας αὐτῷ μὴ ἀποκείρειν· ἔσται δ' αὐτῷ

---

[1] Text doubtful: et alios ex eorum semine descendentes Lat.
[2] ὁμολογούμενος codd.
[3] conj.: om. codd.
[4] MSPLE: τοῦ θεοῦ ἀστέρος RO.

---

[a] Bibl. " rode on ass colts."
[b] Bibl. " He judged Israel eight years."
[c] Bibl. Manoah (lxx Μανῶε): Josephus indifferently
Manoches and Manochos.

284

of these, thirty grandsons, and was wont to ride with this family of seventy, all excellent horsemen [a] ; he left them all in the land of the living when he died in old age [b] and was buried in state at Pharathon.

(viii. 1) After his death the Philistines conquered the Israelites and exacted tribute from them for forty years. From these straits they were delivered on this wise.

Israel under the Philistines. Jd. xiii. 1.

(2) A certain Manoch,[c] among the most notable of the Danites and without question the first in his native place, had a wife remarkable for her beauty and pre-eminent among the women of her time. But having no children by her and being distressed at the lack of them, he was wont, on his frequent visits with his wife to the outskirts—where there was a great plain [d]—to entreat God to give them off-spring of their wedlock.[e] He was moreover madly enamoured of his wife and hence inordinately jeal-ous.[f] Now once when his wife was alone, a spectre appeared to her from God,[g] in the likeness of a comely and tall youth, bringing her the good news of the approaching birth of a son through God's good providence—a son goodly and illustrious for strength, by whom, on his reaching man's estate, the Philis-tines would be afflicted. He further charged her not to cut the lad's locks, and that he was to renounce

An angel announces the birth of a son to the wife of Manoah. Jd. xiii. 2

---

[d] Unscriptural topographical details.

[e] Gr. " a legitimate succession."

[f] The husband's jealousy and subsequent suspicions are unscriptural. Rabbinical legend attributes his complaints to his wife's barrenness, not to her beauty. For the quarrel between husband and wife cf. Ps.-Philo, *Biblical Anti-quities*, cap. xlii. (tr. M. R. James).

[g] Or (with most mss.) " an angel of God."

πρὸς ἄλλο μὲν πᾶν¹ ποτὸν ἀποστροφὴ τοῦ θεοῦ
τοῦτο προστάσσοντος, πρὸς ὕδωρ δὲ μόνον οἰκειό-
της. καὶ ὁ μὲν ταῦτ᾽ εἰπὼν ᾤχετο, κατὰ βούλησιν
ἐλθὼν τοῦ θεοῦ.

279 (3) Ἡ δὲ τἀνδρὶ παραγενομένῳ τὰ παρὰ τοῦ
ἀγγέλου ἐκδιηγήσατο ἐκθαυμάζουσα τοῦ νεανίσκου
τὸ κάλλος καὶ τὸ μέγεθος, ὡς ἐκεῖνον ἐκ τῶν
ἐπαίνων εἰς ἔκπληξιν κατὰ ζηλοτυπίαν περιστῆναι
καὶ ὑπόνοιαν· τὴν ἐκ τοιούτου πάθους κινουμένην.

280 ἡ δὲ βουλομένη τὴν ἄλογον τἀνδρὸς λύπην σταλῆναι
τὸν θεὸν ἱκέτευε πάλιν πέμψαι τὸν ἄγγελον, ὡς
ἂν καὶ τῷ ἀνδρὶ αὐτῆς ὁραθείη. καὶ παραγίνεται
πάλιν κατὰ χάριν τοῦ θεοῦ ὁ ἄγγελος ὄντων ἐν τῷ
προαστείῳ καὶ τῇ γυναικὶ φαίνεται τοῦ ἀνδρὸς
μεμονωμένῃ. ἡ δ᾽ ἐπιμεῖναι δεηθεῖσα ἕως² ἂν
ἀγάγῃ³ τὸν ἄνδρα συγχωρήσαντος μέτεισι τὸν

281 Μάνωχον. ὁ δὲ θεασάμενος οὐδ᾽ οὕτως ἐπαύετο
τῆς ὑπονοίας ἠξίου τε καὶ αὐτῷ δηλοῦν ὅσα καὶ
τῇ γυναικὶ μηνύσειεν. ἀρκέσειν δὲ φράσαντος
ταύτην μόνην εἰδέναι, τίς εἴη λέγειν ἐκέλευεν, ἵνα
τοῦ παιδὸς γενομένου χάριν αὐτῷ καὶ δωρεὰν παρά-

282 σχωσι. τοῦ δὲ μηδέ τινων⁴ αὐτῷ δεῖσθαι φήσαντος,
οὐδὲ γὰρ κατὰ χρείαν ταῦτα εὐαγγελίσασθαι περὶ
τῆς τοῦ παιδὸς γονῆς, τοῦ δὲ μεῖναι παρακαλοῦντος
καὶ ξενίων μετασχεῖν οὐκ ἐπένευσ᾽, ἐπείσθη⁵ δ᾽
ὅμως λιπαροῦντος ἐπιμεῖναι ὡς ἂν ξένιον αὐτῷ τι

---

¹ πᾶν om. ROE.
² Lat. donec: ὡς codd.
³ L: ἀγάγοι rell.   ⁴ horum Lat.
⁵ Niese ex Lat.: πεισθεὶς codd.

ᵃ In Jd. xiii. 8 it is Manoah who asks for a further vision
of the angel.

286

all other form of drink (so God commanded) and to accustom himself to water only. And having thus spoken the visitor departed, having come but to execute God's will.

(3) The woman, when her husband arrived, re- ported what she had heard from the angel, extolling the young man's comeliness and stature in such wise that he in his jealousy was driven by these praises to distraction and to conceive the suspicions that such passion arouses. But she,[a] wishing to allay her husband's unreasonable distress, entreated God to send the angel again that her husband also might see him. And again by the grace of God the angel came, while they were in the suburb,[b] and appeared to the woman when parted from her husband. She besought him to stay until she could fetch her husband and, obtaining his assent, went in pursuit of Manoch. But the husband, on beholding the angel, even then did not desist from his suspicion, and he requested him to repeat to him too all that he had revealed to his wife. The angel having de- clared that it would suffice that it should be made known to her alone, Manoch bade him say who he was, in order that on the birth of the child they might tender him their thanks and make him a present. He replied that he had need of naught, for it was not from want that he had announced this good news of the birth of a child; and though Manoch invited him to stay and partake of hospi- tality, he consented not. Howbeit, at his earnest entreaty, he was persuaded to remain that some token of hospitality might be brought to him. So,

The angel's second visit. Jd. xiii. 6.

17.

---

[b] Bibl. " as she sat in the field."

283 κομίσῃ. καὶ θύσαντος ἔριφον τοῦ Μανώχου καὶ
τοῦτον ὀπτᾶν τῇ γυναικὶ κελεύσαντος, ἐπεὶ πάντ'
ἦν εὐτρεπῆ, προσέταξεν ἐπὶ τῆς πέτρας ἀποθέσθαι
τούς τε ἄρτους καὶ τὰ κρέα χωρὶς τῶν ἀγγείων.
284 καὶ ποιησάντων ἅπτεται τῇ ῥάβδῳ ᾗ εἶχε τῶν
κρεῶν, τὰ δὲ λάμψαντος πυρὸς ἅμα τοῖς ἄρτοις
ἐκαίετο καὶ ὁ ἄγγελος διὰ τοῦ καπνοῦ ὥσπερ
ὀχήματος ἀνιὼν εἰς οὐρανὸν αὐτοῖς φανερὸς ἦν.
Μανώχην δὲ φοβούμενον, μή τι σφαλερὸν αὐτοῖς
ἐκ τῆς ὄψεως τοῦ θεοῦ γενήσοιτο, θαρσεῖν ἡ γυνὴ
παρεκελεύετο· ἐπὶ γὰρ συμφέροντι τῷ αὐτῶν τὸν
θεὸν αὐτοῖς ὁραθῆναι.

285 (4) Καὶ κύει τε ἐκείνη καὶ φυλακὴν εἶχε τῶν
ἐντολῶν καὶ γενόμενον τὸ παιδίον Σαμψῶνα κα-
λοῦσιν, ἰσχυρὸν δ' ἀποσημαίνει τὸ ὄνομα. ηὔξετο
δ' ὁ παῖς ῥᾳδίως καὶ δῆλος ἦν προφητεύσων ὑπὸ
τῆς περὶ τὴν δίαιταν σωφροσύνης καὶ τῆς τῶν
τριχῶν ἀνέσεως.

286 (5) Ἀφικόμενος δὲ μετὰ τῶν γονέων εἰς Θάμνα[1]
πόλιν τῶν Παλαιστίνων πανηγύρεως ἀγομένης
ἐρᾷ παρθένου τῶν ἐπιχωρίων παρακαλεῖ τε τοὺς
γονεῖς ἄγεσθαι πρὸς γάμον αὐτῷ τὴν κόρην. τῶν
δὲ ἀρνουμένων διὰ τὸ μὴ ὁμόφυλον εἶναι, τοῦ θεοῦ
κατὰ τὸ Ἑβραίων σύμφορον ἐπινοοῦντος τὸν γάμον,

[1] v.l. Θαμναθὰ (as also in § 296).

---

[a] The angel's directions are unscriptural; "apart from
(χωρίς) the vessels" possibly has some connexion with the
strange reading in some LXX mss. καὶ διεχώρισεν ποιῆσαι
(Jd. xiii. 19).
[b] So Ps.-Philo, Biblical Antiquities, xlii. (tr. M. R. James)
"the angel put forth (his hand) and touched it with the end
of his sceptre."

Manoch having killed a kid and bidden his wife to
cook it, when all was ready, the angel ordered them
to set out the loaves and the meat upon the rock,
without the vessels.[a] That done, he with the rod
which he held touched the meat [b] and, a fire blazing
out, it was consumed along with the bread, while
the angel, borne on the smoke as on a chariot, was
plainly seen by them ascending into heaven. Manoch
thereat fearing that some mischief might befall
them from this vision of God, his wife bade him take
heart, since it was for their good that it had been
given them to see God.

(4) And the woman conceived and paid good Birth of
heed to the injunctions laid upon her ; and when Samson.
the infant was born they called him Samson, a name
which means ".strong.[c]" And the child grew apace
and it was plain from the frugality of his diet and
his loosely flowing locks that he was to be a prophet.

(5) Now the lad having gone with his parents to His court-
Thamna,[d] a town of the Philistines, during the cele- ship and
bration of a festival, became enamoured of a maiden with a lion.
of the country and begged his parents to get the Jd. xiv. 1.
damsel for him to wife. They were for refusing
because she was not of their race : God, however,
was designing this marriage in the interests of the

[c] One of the author's loose etymological statements. The
connexion of the name (Heb. Shimshon : Gr. Σαμψών) with
the Hebrew *shemesh* (="sun ") " may be considered certain "
(Burney). But Josephus may have had in mind biblical
passages in which the sun symbolizes strength. The Bab.
Talmud (Soṭah 10a) says, " Samson received a name applied
to God, for Scripture says (Ps. lxxxiv. 12) ' A sun and shield
is the Lord God.'"

[d] Heb. Timnah, LXX Θαμναθά, modern *Tibneh* ; a border
town in the Shephelah held at various times by Dan, Judah
and the Philistines.

289

287 ἐκνικᾷ μνηστεύσασθαι τὴν παρθένον. συνεχῶς δ'
ἀπερχόμενος πρὸς τοὺς γονεῖς αὐτῆς συντυγχάνει
λέοντι καὶ γυμνὸς ὢν ἐκδεξάμενος αὐτὸν ἄγχει ταῖς
χερσὶ καὶ εἰς τὸ χωρίον τὸ[1] ὑλῶδες ἐνδοτέρω τῆς
ὁδοῦ ῥίπτει τὸ θηρίον.

288 (6) Πάλιν τε ἀπιὼν πρὸς τὴν κόρην ἐπιτυγχάνει
σμήνει μελιττῶν ἐν τῷ στήθει τοῦ λέοντος ἐκείνου
νενοσσευκότων, καὶ ἀνελόμενος τρία μέλιτος κηρία
σὺν τοῖς λοιποῖς δώροις οἷς ἐκόμιζε δίδωσι τῇ
289 παιδί. τῶν δὲ Θαμνιτῶν παρὰ τὴν εὐωχίαν τὴν
τῶν γάμων, εἱστία γὰρ αὐτοὺς ἅπαντας, διὰ δέος
τῆς ἰσχύος τοῦ νεανίσκου τριάκοντα δόντων αὐτῷ
τοὺς ἀκμαιοτάτους λόγῳ μὲν ἑταίρους ἐσομένους
ἔργῳ δὲ φύλακας, μή τι παρακινεῖν ἐθελήσειεν, τοῦ
πότου προβάντος καὶ παιδιᾶς οὔσης, οἷα φιλεῖ
παρὰ τοὺς τοιούτους καιρούς, ὁ Σαμψὼν εἶπεν,
290 " ἀλλὰ προβάλλοντος ἐμοῦ λόγον εἰ λύσετε τοῦτον
ἐφ' ἡμέρας ἑπτὰ ποιούμενοι τὴν ζήτησιν, ὀθόνας
τε καὶ στολὰς γέρας τῆς συνέσεως κατ' ἄνδρα
ἕκαστον φέρεσθε παρ' ἐμοῦ." φιλοτιμουμένων δὲ
ὁμοῦ τε συνετῶν δόξαν καὶ κέρδος εὕρασθαι καὶ
λέγειν ἀξιούντων, φησὶν ὅτι τὸ πάμβορον γεγεννήκοι
βορὰν ἡδεῖαν ἐξ αὐτοῦ καὶ πάνυ ἀηδοῦς ὄντος.
291 τῶν δ' ἐπὶ τρεῖς ἡμέρας[2] οὐ δυναμένων ἐξευρεῖν τὸ
νοούμενον παρακαλούντων δὲ τὴν κόρην μαθοῦσαν
παρὰ τοῦ ἀνδρὸς αὐτοῖς μηνῦσαι, καὶ γὰρ ἠπείλουν
πιμπρήσειν αὐτὴν τοῦτο μὴ παρασχοῦσαν, ὁ Σαμψὼν δεομένης τῆς κόρης εἰπεῖν αὐτῇ τὸ μὲν πρῶτον

---

[1] εἴς τι χωρίον SPL.
[2] ἐπὶ τρισὶν ἡμέραις RO.

---

[a] Gr. " within " or " on the inner side of."
[b] Amplification, like other details in this narrative.

Hebrews, and so he won his way to woo the maid.
In the course of his constant visits to her parents he
encountered a lion and, unarmed as he was, grappled
with it, strangled it with his hands, and flung the
beast into the coppice on the border of [a] the road.

(6) On another of his journeys to the damsel he His riddle.
Jd. xiv. 5.
came upon a swarm of bees that had hived in that
lion's breast, and, taking three [b] honeycombs, he
gave them, along with the rest of the gifts which he
bore, to the maiden. Now the Thamnites, on the
occasion of the wedding feast—for he entertained
them all—from fear of this young man's strength,
presented him with thirty of their chief stalwarts,
ostensibly as companions, in reality as his guardians,
lest he should be minded to create any disturbance ;
and, when the drinking was far gone and joviality
prevailed, as is customary on such occasions, Samson
said, " Come, I will propound a riddle, and if ye
solve it after seven days' search, ye shall receive
every man from me fine linen and apparel as a
reward for your sagacity." Ambitious to win at once
a renown for sagacity and a prize, they begged him
to state it, whereupon he said : " The omnivorous
eater produced pleasant meat from himself though
grossly unpleasant." [c] When the Philistines at the
end of three days were unable to discover what it
meant, they urged the damsel to find out from her
husband and report to them : nay, they threatened
to burn her should she fail to do so. Samson,
upon the damsel's entreating him to tell her, at

[c] Bibl. " Out of the eater came forth meat, and out of the
strong came forth sweetness," Jd. xiv. 14. The Peshitto
Syriac version, rendering the word " strong " by "bitter,"
presents, like Josephus, a double antithesis.

292 ἀντεῖχεν,[1] ἐγκειμένης δ' αὐτῆς καὶ εἰς δάκρυα προ-
πιπτούσης καὶ τεκμήριον τιθεμένης τῆς πρὸς
αὐτὴν δυσνοίας τὸ μὴ λέγειν αὐτῇ, μηνύει τὰ περὶ
τὴν ἀναίρεσιν αὐτῇ τοῦ λέοντος καὶ ὡς τὰ τρία
βαστάσας ἐξ αὐτοῦ κηρία μέλιτος γεγονότα κομί-
293 σειεν αὐτῇ. καὶ ὁ μὲν οὐδὲν ὑφορώμενος δολερὸν
σημαίνει τὸ πᾶν, ἡ δ' ἐκφέρει τὸν λόγον τοῖς δεη-
θεῖσι. κατὰ οὖν τὴν ἑβδόμην ἡμέραν, καθ' ἣν ἔδει
τὸν προβληθέντα λόγον αὐτῷ διασαφεῖν, πρὶν ἢ
δῦναι τὸν ἥλιον συνελθόντες φασίν '' οὔτε λέοντος
ἀηδέστερόν τι τοῖς ἐντυγχάνουσιν οὔτε ἥδιον
294 μέλιτος χρωμένοις.'' καὶ ὁ Σαμψὼν εἶπεν οὐδὲ
γυναικὸς εἶναί τι δολερώτερον, '' ἥτις ὑμῖν ἐκφέρει
τὸν ἡμέτερον λόγον.'' κἀκείνοις μὲν δίδωσιν ἃ
ὑπέσχετο λείαν ποιησάμενος Ἀσκαλωνιτῶν τοὺς
κατὰ τὴν ὁδὸν αὐτῷ συντυχόντας, Παλαιστῖνοι δ'
εἰσὶ καὶ οὗτοι, τὸν δὲ γάμον ἐκεῖνον παραιτεῖται·
καὶ ἡ παῖς ἐκφαυλίσασα τῆς ὀργῆς αὐτὸν συνῆν
αὐτοῦ φίλῳ νυμφοστόλῳ γεγονότι.
295
(7) Πρὸς δὲ τὴν ὕβριν ταύτην Σαμψὼν παροξυνθεὶς ἅπαντας ἔγνω σὺν αὐτῇ Παλαιστίνους
μετέρχεσθαι. θέρους δ' ὄντος καὶ πρὸς ἄμητον
ἤδη τῶν καρπῶν ἀκμαζόντων συλλαβὼν τριακοσίας
ἀλώπεκας καὶ τῶν οὐρῶν ἐξάψας λαμπάδας ἡμμένας ἐξαφίησιν[2] εἰς τὰς ἀρούρας τῶν Παλαιστίνων.
296 καὶ φθείρεται μὲν οὕτως αὐτοῖς ὁ καρπός, Παλαιστῖνοι δὲ γνόντες Σαμψῶνος εἶναι τὸ ἔργον καὶ τὴν
αἰτίαν δι' ἣν ἔπραξε, πέμψαντες τοὺς ἄρχοντας εἰς

[1] ἀντέχειν ἐπειρᾶτο RO.
[2] ἐπαφίησιν E: ἀφίησιν RO.

---

[a] Bibl. '' If ye had not plowed with my heifer, ye had not
found out my riddle,'' Jd. xiv. 18.

first resisted, but, when she pressed him and burst into tears and protested that his refusal to tell her proved his want of affection for her, he revealed the story of the slaying of the lion and how he had carried off the three honeycombs sprung from its carcase and brought them to her. Suspecting no fraud he recounted all, but she betrayed his story to her questioners. So on the seventh day, whereon they were required to give him the answer to the riddle, assembling before sunset they announced, " Nothing is more unpleasant to meet than a lion nor more pleasant to taste than honey." And Samson added, " Nor is ought more deceitful than a woman who betrays our speech to you." [a] And he gave them what he had promised, after despoiling certain Ascalonites who encountered him on the road (these too being Philistines) ; but he renounced those nuptials, and the girl, scorning him for his wrath, was united to that friend of his who had given her away.[b]

(7) Furious at this affront,[c] Samson resolved to visit it upon all the Philistines along with her. So, summer being come and the crops already ripening for harvest, he caught three hundred foxes and, fastening lighted torches to their tails, let them loose in the fields of the Philistines ; and thus their crop was ruined. But the Philistines, on discovering that this was Samson's deed and for what cause he had done it, sent their magistrates to Thamna and burnt

He destroys the crops of the Philistines. Jd. xv. 3.

[b] Or " who had been his best man." The Biblical narrative refers to " the friend of the bridegroom " (John iii. 29).
[c] Josephus omits Samson's interview with his former father-in-law which provoked this outbreak, Jd. xv. 1 f.

Θάμνα, τὴν γενομένην αὐτοῦ γυναῖκα καὶ τοὺς
συγγενεῖς ζῶντας κατέπρησαν ὡς αἰτίους τῶν
κακῶν γεγονότας.

297 (8) Σαμψὼν δὲ πολλοὺς ἐν τῷ πεδίῳ τῶν Παλαιστίνων ἀποκτείνας Αἰτὰν κατῴκει, πέτρα δ' ἐστὶν
ὀχυρὰ τῆς Ἰούδα φυλῆς. Παλαιστῖνοι δ' ἐστρά-
τευον ἐπὶ τὴν φυλήν. τῶν δ' οὐ δικαίως λεγόν-
των τιμωρίαν αὐτοὺς εἰσπράττεσθαι περὶ τῶν
Σαμψῶνος ἁμαρτημάτων φόρους αὐτοῖς[1] τελοῦντας,
εἰ βούλονται μὴ ἔχειν αἰτίαν ἔφασαν αὐτοῖς
298 ὑποχείριον Σαμψῶνα δοῦναι. οἱ δὲ ἀνεπίκλητοι
βουλόμενοι τυγχάνειν παρῆσαν ἐπὶ τὴν πέτραν
τρισχιλίοις ὁπλίταις[2] καὶ καταμεμψάμενοι τῶν εἰς
Παλαιστίνους αὐτῷ τετολμημένων ἄνδρας ἅπαντι
τῷ γένει τῶν Ἑβραίων συμφορὰν ἐπενεγκεῖν
δυναμένους, ἥκειν τε λέγοντες ὅπως αὐτὸν λαβόντες
ὑποχείριον δῶσιν αὐτοῖς, ἠξίουν ἑκόντι τοῦθ'
299 ὑπομένειν. ὁ δὲ λαβὼν ὅρκους παρ' αὐτῶν μηδὲν
τούτων ποιήσειν περισσότερον ἀλλὰ τοῖς ἐχθροῖς
ἐγχειριεῖν[3] μόνον, καταβὰς ἐκ τῆς πέτρας αὐτὸν
ἐν τῇ τῶν φυλετῶν τίθησιν ἐξουσίᾳ, κἀκεῖνοι
δήσαντες αὐτὸν δυσὶ καλωδίοις ἦγον παραδοῦναι
300 τοῖς Παλαιστίνοις. καὶ γενομένων κατά τι χωρίον,
ὃ Σιαγὼν καλεῖται νῦν διὰ τὴν Σαμψῶνος ἀνδρα-
γαθίαν ἐπ' αὐτῷ γενομένην, πάλαι δ' ἦν ἀνώνυμον,
οὐκ ἄπωθεν ἐστρατοπεδευκότων τῶν Παλαιστίνων,
ἀλλ' ὑπαντώντων μετὰ χαρᾶς καὶ βοῆς ὡς ἐπὶ
κατωρθωμένοις οἷς ἐβούλοντο, διαρρήξας τὰ δεσμὰ
Σαμψὼν ἁρπασάμενος ὄνου σιαγόνα παρὰ ποσὶν

---

[1] Niese: αὐτοὺς codd.   [2] τρισχίλιοι ὁπλῖται RO.
[3] Bekker: ἐγχειρεῖν codd.

[a] Bibl. Etam.

her that had been his wife and her kinsfolk alive,
as having been the cause of their disasters.

(8) Samson, after slaying multitudes of the His exploit
Philistines in the plain, then settled at Aeta,^a a with the
rocky stronghold within the tribe of Judah ; where- jawbone.
upon the Philistines took the field against that tribe. Jd. xv. 8.
These pleading that it was unjust to exact punishment
for Samson's misdeeds from them that paid them
tribute, the Philistines retorted that if they would
keep clear of blame they must deliver Samson into
their hands. And they, wishing to be above reproach,
visited the rock with three thousand men-at-arms, and
after roundly rebuking him for his outrageous treatment of the Philistines, people powerful enough to
bring ruin upon the whole race of the Hebrews, and
telling him that they were come to take and deliver
him into their hands, they besought him to submit to
this of his own free will. And he, after receiving an
oath from them that they would do no more than
merely commit him to the hands of the foe, descended from the rock and put himself at the mercy
of these representatives of the tribe ; and they,
having bound him with two cords, led him off to
deliver him to the Philistines. Then, when they
were come to a spot which to-day is called Jawbone ^b
by reason of the exploit there performed by Samson
but which of old was nameless, the Philistines being
encamped not far off and coming to meet them with
exultant cries, thinking to have achieved their end,
Samson, bursting his bonds asunder and seizing the

^b Bibl. Lehi = " Jawbone," as translated here and in the
LXX (Σιαγών). " Probably the name was originally given
to some hill or ridge on account of its resemblance to a
jawbone " (Burney, adducing the similar name Ὄνου γνάθος
given to a promontory in Laconia).

οὖσαν εἰς τοὺς πολεμίους ὤσατο καὶ παίων αὐτοὺς
τῇ σιαγόνι¹ κτείνει εἰς χιλίους, τοὺς δὲ ἄλλους
τρέπεται ταραχθέντας.

301 (9) Σαμψὼν δὲ μεῖζον ἢ χρὴ ἐπὶ τούτῳ φρονῶν
οὐ κατὰ θεοῦ συνεργίαν ἔλεγε τοῦτο συμβῆναι, τὴν
δ᾽ ἰδίαν ἀρετὴν ἐπέγραψε τῷ γεγονότι, σιαγόνι²
τῶν πολεμίων τοὺς μὲν πεσεῖν τοὺς δ᾽ εἰς φυγὴν
302 τραπῆναι διὰ τοῦ παρ᾽ αὐτοῦ δέους αὐχῶν. δίψους
δ᾽ αὐτὸν ἰσχυροῦ κατασχόντος κατανοῶν ὡς οὐδέν
ἐστιν ἀνθρώπειος ἀρετή, τῷ θεῷ πάντα προσεμαρ-
τύρει καὶ καθικέτευε μηδὲν τῶν εἰρημένων πρὸς
ὀργὴν λαβόντα τοῖς πολεμίοις αὐτὸν ἐγχειρίσαι,
παρασχεῖν δὲ βοήθειαν πρὸς τὸ δεινὸν καὶ ῥύσασθαι
303 τοῦ κακοῦ. καὶ πρὸς τὰς ἱκετείας ἐπικλασθεὶς
ὁ θεὸς πηγὴν κατά τινος πέτρας ἀνίησιν ἡδεῖαν
καὶ πολλήν, ὅθεν καὶ Σαμψὼν ἐκάλει τὸ χωρίον
Σιαγόνα καὶ μέχρι τοῦ δεῦρο τοῦτο λέγεται.

304 (10) Μετὰ δὲ ταύτην τὴν μάχην Σαμψὼν καταφρονῶν τῶν Παλαιστίνων εἰς Γάζαν ἀφικνεῖται
καὶ ἔν τινι τῶν καταγωγίων διέτριβε. μαθόντες
δὲ τῶν Γαζαίων οἱ ἄρχοντες τὴν αὐτόθι παρουσίαν
αὐτοῦ τὰ πρὸ τῶν πυλῶν ἐνέδραις καταλαμβάνου-
305 σιν, ὅπως ἐξιὼν μὴ λάθῃ. Σαμψὼν δέ, οὐ γὰρ
λανθάνουσιν αὐτὸν ταῦτα μηχανησάμενοι, περὶ
μεσοῦσαν ἤδη τὴν νύκτα ἀναστὰς ἐνράσσει ταῖς
πύλαις, αὐταῖς τε φλιαῖς καὶ μοχλοῖς ὅση τε ἄλλη
περὶ αὐταῖς ἦν ξύλωσις ἀράμενος κατωμαδὸν εἰς
τὸ ὑπὲρ Ἑβρῶνος ὄρος φέρων κατατίθησι.

¹ τῇ σιαγόνι om. MSP.　　　² om. ROE.

<hr/>

ᵃ In Judges (xv. 19) En-hakkore (" the spring of him that
called "), while Ramath-lehi (" hill of the jawbone ") is the

296

jawbone of an ass that lay at his feet, rushed upon his enemies and smiting them with this weapon slew a thousand of them, routing the rest in dire dismay.

(9) Yet Samson, unduly proud of this feat, did not say that it was God's assistance that had brought it to pass, but ascribed the issue to his own valour, boasting of having with a jawbone prostrated some of his enemies and put the rest to rout through the terror that he inspired. But, being seized with a mighty thirst and recognizing that human valour is a thing of naught, he acknowledged that all was attributable to God and implored Him not, in anger at any words of his, to deliver him into his enemies' hands, but to lend him aid in his dire need and to rescue him from his distress. And God, moved by his supplications, caused a spring of water to well out of a rock, sweet and abundant ; whence it was ·that Samson called that place Jawbone, a name which it bears to this day.[a]

The miraculous spring. Jd. xv. 16.

(10) After this combat Samson, scorning the Philistines, came to Gaza and lodged at one of the inns.[b] Thereupon the chiefs of the Gazites, informed of his presence in the town, posted ambuscades before the gates to prevent his leaving it without their knowledge. But Samson, not unaware of these schemes, when midnight was come arose, flung himself against the gates, hoisted them—posts, bolts, woodwork and all—upon his shoulders, bore them to the mountain above Hebron[c] and there deposited them.

Samson's escape from Gaza by night. Jd. xvi. 1.

name given to the place where he cast his weapon away (17).

[b] Jd. "and saw there an harlot and went in unto her." For the interchange of " harlot " and " innkeeper " see § 8 note.　　　　　[c] Nearly 40 miles away !

306 (11) Παρέβαινε δ' ἤδη τὰ πάτρια καὶ τὴν οἰκείαν
δίαιταν παρεχάρασσεν ξενικῶν μιμήσει ἐθισμῶν,
καὶ τοῦτ' ἀρχὴ αὐτῷ κακοῦ γίνεται· γυναικὸς γὰρ
ἑταιριζομένης παρὰ τοῖς Παλαιστίνοις ἐρασθεὶς
307 Δαλάλης¹ τοὔνομα συνῆν αὐτῇ. καὶ τῶν Παλαιστίνων οἱ τοῦ κοινοῦ προεστῶτες ἐλθόντες πρὸς αὐτὴν
πείθουσιν ἐπαγγελίαις μαθεῖν παρὰ τοῦ Σαμψῶνος
τὴν αἰτίαν τῆς ἰσχύος, ὑφ' ἧς ἄληπτός ἐστι τοῖς
ἐχθροῖς. ἡ δὲ παρὰ πότον καὶ τοιαύτην συνουσίαν
θαυμάζουσα τὰς πράξεις αὐτοῦ ἐτεχνίτευε μαθεῖν,
308 τίνι τρόπῳ τοσοῦτον² προύχει κατ' ἀρετήν. ὁ
δὲ Σαμψῶν, ἔτι γὰρ φρονεῖν ἰσχυρὸς ἦν, ἀντ-
ηπάτα τὴν Δαλάλην φάμενος,³ εἰ κλήμασιν ἑπτὰ
δεθείη ἀμπελίνοις ἔτι καὶ περιειλεῖσθαι δυναμένοις,
309 ἀσθενέστερος ἂν πάντων ἔσοιτο. ἡ δὲ τότε μὲν
ἡσύχασεν, ἀποσημήνασα δὲ τοῖς ἄρχουσι τῶν Παλαιστίνων ἐνήδρευσε τῶν στρατιωτῶν ἔνδον τινὰς
καὶ μεθύοντα⁴ κατέδει τοῖς κλήμασι κατὰ τὸ
310 ἰσχυρότατον, ἔπειτ' ἀνεγείρασα ἐδήλου παρεῖναί
τινας ἐπ' αὐτόν. ὁ δὲ ῥήξας τὰ κλήματα βοηθεῖν
ὡς ἐπερχομένων αὐτῷ τινων ἐπειρᾶτο. καὶ ἡ γυνὴ
συνεχῶς ὁμιλοῦντος αὐτῇ τοῦ Σαμψῶνος δεινῶς
ἔχειν ἔλεγεν, εἰ κατ' ἀπιστίαν εὐνοίας τῆς πρὸς
αὐτὸν μὴ λέγει ταῦθ' ἅπερ δεῖται, ὡς οὐ σιγησο-
μένης ὅσα μὴ γινώσκεσθαι συμφέρειν οἶδεν αὐτῷ.
311 τοῦ δὲ πάλιν ἀπατῶντος αὐτὴν καὶ φήσαντος ἑπτὰ

---

¹ v.ll. δαδάλης, δαληδῆς, etc.
² M: τοσούτων ROSPE.   ³ + ὅτι Dindorf.
⁴ dormientem Lat.: pr. καθεύδοντα MSPL.

ᵃ Bibl. Delilah, lxx Δαλειδά.
ᵇ Heb. " with seven fresh bowstrings (or sinews) which
have not been dried " (v. 7).

(11) Howbeit he was already transgressing the laws of his forefathers and debasing his own rule of life by the imitation of foreign usages ; and this proved the beginning of his disaster. For, being enamoured of a woman who was a harlot among the Philistines, Dalala [a] by name, he consorted with her ; and the presidents of the Philistine confederacy came and induced her by large promises to discover from Samson the secret of that strength which rendered him invulnerable to his foes. So she, over their cups and in like intercourse, by admiration of his exploits would craftily seek to discover by what means he had come by such extraordinary valour. But Samson, whose wits were yet robust, countered Dalala's ruse by another, telling her that were he bound with seven vine-shoots still flexible,[b] he would be the weakest of men. At the moment she held her peace, but, after reporting this to the lords of the Philistines, she posted some soldiers in ambush within and while Samson was drunken [c] bound him with the shoots as firmly as possible, and then awoke him with the announcement that men were upon him. But he burst the shoots asunder and made ready for defence as though his assailants were coming. And then this woman, with whom Samson was continually consorting, would say that she took it ill that he had not confidence enough in her affection for him to tell her just what she desired, as though she would not conceal what she knew must in his interests not be divulged. But again he deluded her, telling her that were he bound with seven [d]

11.

[c] Or, according to another reading, " asleep." Drunkenness, not mentioned in Scripture, indicates violation of his Nazirite vow (*cf.* § 306).

[d] So lxx (many mss.) : the Heb. mentions no number.

κάλοις δεθέντα τὴν ἰσχὺν ἀπολέσειν, ἐπεὶ καὶ τοῦτο
ποιήσασα οὐδὲν ἤνυσεν, τρίτον ἐνυφῆναι[1] τὰς κόμας
312 αὐτοῦ ἐμήνυσεν. ὡς δ᾽ οὐδὲ τούτου γενομένου
τἀληθὲς[2] ηὑρίσκετο, δεομένης τελευταῖον ὁ Σαμψῶν, ἔδει γὰρ αὐτὸν συμφορᾷ περιπεσεῖν, χαρίζεσθαι βουλόμενος τῇ Δαλάλῃ " ἐμοῦ," φησίν, " ὁ
θεὸς κήδεται καὶ κατὰ τὴν ἐκείνου πρόνοιαν
γεννηθεὶς κόμην ταύτην τρέφω παρεγγυήσαντος
μὴ ἀποκείρειν τοῦ θεοῦ· τὴν γὰρ ἰσχὺν εἶναί μοι
313 κατὰ τὴν ταύτης αὔξησιν καὶ παραμονήν." ταῦτα
μαθοῦσα καὶ στερήσασα τῆς κόμης αὐτὸν παρα-
δίδοι τοῖς πολεμίοις οὐκέτ᾽ ὄντα ἰσχυρὸν ἀμύνασθαι
τὴν ἔφοδον αὐτῶν. οἱ δ᾽ ἐκκόψαντες αὐτοῦ τοὺς
ὀφθαλμοὺς δεδεμένον ἄγειν παρέδοσαν.
314 (12) Προϊόντος δὲ τοῦ χρόνου ηὔξετο ἡ κόμη τῷ
Σαμψῶνι, καὶ ἑορτῆς οὔσης τοῖς Παλαιστίνοις
δημοτελοῦς καὶ τῶν ἀρχόντων καὶ γνωριμωτάτων
ἐν ταὐτῷ εὐωχουμένων, οἶκος δ᾽ ἦν δύο κιόνων
στεγόντων αὐτοῦ τὸν ὄροφον, ἄγεται μεταπεμ-
ψαμένων ὁ Σαμψῶν εἰς τὸ συμπόσιον, ὅπως ἐν-
315 υβρίσωσιν αὐτῷ παρὰ τὸν πότον. ὁ δὲ δεινότερον
τῶν κακῶν ὑπολαμβάνων τὸ μὴ δύνασθαι ὑβριζό-
μενος ἀμύνασθαι, τὸν χειραγωγοῦντα παῖδα πείθει,
προσαναπαύσασθαι χρῄζειν εἰπὼν ὑπὸ κόπου, τοῖς
316 κίοσιν αὐτὸν ἐγγὺς ἀγαγεῖν. ὡς δὲ ἧκεν, ἐνσει-
σθεὶς αὐτοῖς ἐπικαταβάλλει τὸν οἶκον ἀνατραπέντων
τῶν κιόνων τρισχιλίοις ἀνδράσιν, οἳ πάντες ἀπέθανον, ἐν αὐτοῖς δὲ καὶ Σαμψῶν. καὶ τὸν μὲν

---

[1] συνυφῆναι RO.
[2] ἀληθὲς codd.: ἀληθὴς (ex Lat. verax) Niese.

---

[a] Scripture says that " there were upon the roof [apparently
overlooking an open courtyard] three thousand men and
300

cords he would lose his strength ; and when she had
tried this too with no success, a third time he advised
her to weave his locks into a web. But when even
by this experiment the truth was not discovered, at
last, at her petitions, Samson—since he must needs
fall a victim to calamity—wishing to humour Dalala
said : " I am under God's care : and under His 17.
providence since birth, I nurse these locks, God
having enjoined upon me not to cut them, for that
my strength is measured by their growth and preservation." The secret learnt, she reft him of his
locks and delivered him to his enemies, being now
powerless to repulse their assault ; and they, having
put out his eyes, delivered him over to be led away
in chains.

(12) But in course of time Samson's locks grew ; Samson's
and once when the Philistines were keeping a public Jd. xvi. 22.
festival and their lords and chief notables were feasting together in one place—a hall with two columns
supporting its roof—Samson at their summons was
led to the banquet, that they might mock at him
over their cups. And he, deeming it direr than all
his ills to be unable to be avenged of such insults,
induced the boy who led him by the hand—telling
him that from weariness he needed a stay whereon
to rest—to conduct him close to the columns. And
when he was come thither, flinging all his weight
upon them, he brought down the hall, overturning
the columns, upon three thousand men,[a] who all
perished and among them Samson. Such was his

women," in addition to all the lords of the Philistines below,
Jd. xvi. 27. Some commentators suspect that these three
thousand on the roof " are an addition to the original
narrative, exaggerating the catastrophe " (G. F. Moore).

τοιοῦτον κατέσχε τέλος ἄρξαντα τῶν Ἰσραηλιτῶν
317 εἴκοσιν ἔτη. θαυμάζειν δὲ ἄξιον τῆς ἀρετῆς καὶ
τῆς ἰσχύος καὶ τοῦ περὶ τὴν τελευτὴν μεγαλόφρονος
τὸν ἄνδρα καὶ τῆς ὀργῆς τῆς μέχρι τοῦ τελευτᾶν
πρὸς τοὺς πολεμίους. καὶ τὸ μὲν ὑπὸ γυναικὸς
ἁλῶναι δεῖ τῇ φύσει τῶν ἀνθρώπων προσάπτειν
ἥττονι ἁμαρτημάτων οὔσῃ, μαρτυρεῖν δὲ ἐκείνῳ
τὴν εἰς τὰ ἄλλα πάντα τῆς ἀρετῆς περιουσίαν. οἱ
δὲ συγγενεῖς ἀράμενοι τὸ σῶμα αὐτοῦ θάπτουσιν
ἐν Σαρασᾷ τῇ πατρίδι μετὰ τῶν συγγενῶν.

318 (ix. 1) Μετὰ δὲ τὴν Σαμψῶνος τελευτὴν προέστη
τῶν Ἰσραηλιτῶν Ἠλεὶς ὁ ἀρχιερεύς. ἐπὶ τούτου
λιμῷ τῆς χώρας κακοπαθούσης αὐτῶν Ἀβιμέλεχος[1]
ἐκ Βηθλέμων, ἔστι δὲ ἡ πόλις αὕτη τῆς Ἰούδα
φυλῆς, ἀντέχειν τῷ δεινῷ μὴ δυνάμενος τήν τε
γυναῖκα Ναάμιν καὶ τοὺς παῖδας τοὺς ἐξ αὐτῆς
αὐτῷ γεγεννημένους Χελλίωνα καὶ Μαλαῶνα ἐπ-
319 αγόμενος εἰς τὴν Μωαβῖτιν μετοικίζεται. καὶ προ-
χωρούντων αὐτῷ κατὰ νοῦν τῶν πραγμάτων
ἄγεται τοῖς υἱοῖς γυναῖκας Μωαβίτιδας Χελλίωνι
μὲν Ὀρφᾶν Ῥούθην δὲ Μαλαῶνι. διελθόντων δὲ
δέκα[2] ἐτῶν ὅ τε Ἀβιμέλεχος καὶ μετ' αὐτὸν οἱ
320 παῖδες δι' ὀλίγου τελευτῶσι, καὶ ἡ Ναάμις πικρῶς
ἐπὶ τοῖς συμβεβηκόσι φέρουσα καὶ τὴν ὑπ' ὄψιν[3]
τῶν φιλτάτων ἐρημίαν οὐχ ὑπομένουσα, δι' οὓς[4]

[1] Ἐλιμέλεχος L Lat. (et infra).
[2] decem et octo Lat.   [3] om. Lat.
[4] ed. pr. Lat.: ἦν codd.

---

[a] Jd. xvi. 31 " between Zorah (lxx Σαραά or in one
minuscule, as in Josephus, Σαρασά) and Eshtaol, in the
burying-place of Manoah his father " ; Zorah is the modern
Ṣurah, some 14 miles due W. of Jerusalem.

[b] Bibl. simply " in the days when the judges judged ";

end, after governing Israel for twenty years. And it is but right to admire the man for his valour, his strength, and the grandeur of his end, as also for the wrath which he cherished to the last against his enemies. That he let himself be ensnared by a woman must be imputed to human nature which succumbs to sins; but testimony is due to him for his surpassing excellence in all the rest. His kinsfolk then took up his body and buried him at Sarasa,[a] his native place, with his forefathers.

(ix. 1) After the death of Samson, the leader of the Israelites was Eli the high priest. In his days,[b] their country was afflicted by a famine, and Abimelech[c] of Bethlehem, a city of the tribe of Judah, being unable to withstand this scourge, took with him his wife Naamis[d] and the sons whom he had begotten by her, Chellion[e] and Malaon,[f] and migrated to the land of Moab. His affairs there prospering to his heart's content, he took for his sons[g] wives of the women of Moab, for Chellion Orpha[h] and for Malaon Ruth. Ten years having passed, Abimelech died, and his sons not long after him; and Naamis, sorely disheartened at her misfortunes and unable to bear that bereavement, ever before her eyes, in the loss of her dearest ones, for whose sakes she had

The widow Naomi returns to Bethlehem with Ruth. Ruth i. 1.

Josephus infers the date of this episode from the number of generations between Boaz and David (Reinach). One rabbinic tradition identifies Boaz with the judge Ibzan, others make him a contemporary of Deborah.

[c] Bibl. Elimelech : the name Abimelech appears also in many mss. of the lxx.

[d] Bibl. Naomi (or Noomi). [e] Bibl. Chilion.

[f] Bibl. Mahlon (lxx Μααλών).

[g] In Ruth i. 3 f. the father's death precedes the sons' marriages.

[h] Bibl. Orpah (lxx Ὀρφά).

καὶ τῆς πατρίδος ἐξεληλύθει, πάλιν εἰς αὐτὴν
ἀπηλλάττετο· καὶ γὰρ ἤδη καλῶς τὰ κατ' αὐτὴν
321 ἐπυνθάνετο χωρεῖν. οὐκ ἐκαρτέρουν δὲ διαζευγνύ-
μεναι αὐτῆς αἱ νύμφαι, οὐδὲ παραιτουμένη βου-
λομένας συνεξορμᾶν πείθειν ἐδύνατο, ἀλλ' ἐγκειμένων εὐξαμένη γάμον εὐτυχέστερον αὐταῖς οὗ
διημαρτήκεσαν παισὶ τοῖς αὐτῆς γαμηθεῖσαι καὶ
322 τῶν ἄλλων ἀγαθῶν κτῆσιν, ὅτε τὰ¹ πρὸς αὐτὴν
οὕτως ἐστί, μένειν αὐτόθι παρεκάλει καὶ μὴ συμ-
μεταλαμβάνειν αὐτῇ βούλεσθαι πραγμάτων ἀδήλων
τὴν πάτριον γῆν καταλιπούσας. ἡ μὲν οὖν Ὀρφὰ
μένει, τὴν δὲ Ῥούθην μὴ πεισθεῖσαν ἀπήγαγε
κοινωνὸν παντὸς τοῦ προστυχόντος γενησομένην.
323 (2) Ἐλθοῦσαν δὲ Ῥούθην μετὰ τῆς πενθερᾶς εἰς
τὴν Βηθλεέμων Βόαζος² Ἀβιμελέχου συγγενὴς ὢν
δέχεται ξενίᾳ. καὶ ἡ Ναάμις, προσαγορευόντων
αὐτὴν ὀνομαστί,³ "δικαιότερον" εἶπε "Μαρὰν
ἂν καλοίητε⁴ με"· σημαίνει δὲ καθ' Ἑβραίων
γλῶτταν νάαμις μὲν εὐτυχίαν, μαρὰ δὲ ὀδύνην.
324 ἀμήτου δὲ γενομένου⁵ ἐξῄει καλαμησομένη κατὰ
συγχώρησιν τῆς πενθερᾶς ἡ Ῥούθη, ὅπως τροφῆς
εὐποροῖεν, καὶ εἰς τὸ Βοώζου τυχαίως ἀφικνεῖται
χωρίον. παραγενόμενος δὲ Βόαζος μετ' ὀλίγον καὶ
θεασάμενος τὴν κόρην ἀνέκρινε τὸν ἀγροκόμον
περὶ τῆς παιδός. ὁ δὲ μικρὸν ἔμπροσθεν παρ' αὐτῆς ἅπαντα προπεπυσμένος ἐδήλου τῷ δεσπότῃ.

¹ ὅτε (om. τὰ) RO : ὅτι τε τὰ rell.
² Ἀλεξῆς M : Ἄλεξις Βόοζος L.
³ + τῶν πολιτῶν MLE.
⁴ ἂν καλοίητε Bekker : καλεῖσθαι RO : vocate Lat. : καλώ(ι)ητε
rell.   ⁵ RO : ὄντος rell.

ᵃ In Ruth i. 7 both daughters-in-law actually start with
her.

304

left her country, thought to repair thither again, for
she had learnt that all was now going well with it.
But her daughters-in-law had not the heart to be
parted from her, nor for all her pleading when they
were fain to set out with her *a* could she prevail with
them ; then, as they urged her yet, she prayed that
they might find happier wedlock than that whereof
they had been disappointed in marrying her sons,
and obtain all blessings beside, but, seeing the case
in which she lay, she implored them to remain where
they were and not to crave to share her uncertain
fortunes in quitting their native land. So Orpha
stayed, but, since Ruth would not be persuaded,
Naamis took her with her, to be her partner in all
that should befall.

(2) Now when Ruth was come with her mother- Reception
in-law to the town of Bethlehem, Boaz, being a kins- by Boaz.
man of Abimelech, hospitably received them.*b* And Ruth ii. 1.
Naamis, when folk addressed her by that name, i. 19.
said, " More rightly would ye call me Mara "—
Naamis in the Hebrew tongue signifying " felicity "
and Mara " grief." *c* It being now harvest-time, ii. 2.
Ruth by permission of her mother-in-law went out
to glean, to provide for their sustenance, and by
chance came to the ground of Boaz. Boaz arriving a
little later and seeing the young woman, questioned
the steward of his estate concerning this child; and he,
having just learnt all her story from herself, informed

---

b This statement, which appears inconsistent with the
sequel, and is absent from other Biblical texts, recurs in the
Armenian version, which appends to Ruth ii. 1 " et dedit
Noomin domum viduitatis habitare in ea." We must suppose
that Boaz provided a lodging but did not meet his guests.

c Naomi = " my delight " : Mara = " bitter."

325 ὁ δὲ τῆς περὶ τὴν πενθερὰν εὐνοίας ἅμα καὶ
μνήμης τοῦ παιδὸς αὐτῆς ᾧ συνῴκησεν ἀσπασάμενος καὶ εὐξάμενος αὐτῇ πεῖραν ἀγαθῶν, καλαμᾶσθαι μὲν αὐτὴν οὐκ ἠξίωσεν θερίζειν δὲ πᾶν ὅ
τι καὶ δύναιτο καὶ λαμβάνειν ἐπιτρέπει προστάξας
τῷ ἀγροκόμῳ μηδὲν αὐτὴν διακωλύειν[1] ἄριστόν
τε παρέχειν αὐτῇ καὶ ποτόν, ὁπότε σιτίζοι τοὺς
326 θερίζοντας. Ῥούθη δὲ ἄλφιτα λαβοῦσα παρ'
αὐτοῦ ἐφύλαξε τῇ ἑκυρᾷ καὶ παρῆν ὀψὲ κομίζουσα
μετὰ τῶν σταχύων· ἐτετηρήκει δ' αὐτῇ καὶ ἡ
Ναάμις ἀπομοίρας βρωμάτων τινῶν, οἷς αὐτὴν
ἐπολυώρουν οἱ γειτονεύοντες· διηγεῖται δὲ αὐτῇ
καὶ τὰ παρὰ τοῦ Βοάζου πρὸς αὐτὴν εἰρημένα.
327 δηλωσάσης δ' ἐκείνης ὡς συγγενής ἐστι καὶ τάχα
ἂν δι' εὐσέβειαν[2] προνοήσειεν αὐτῶν, ἐξῄει πάλιν
ταῖς ἐχομέναις ἡμέραις ἐπὶ καλάμης συλλογὴν σὺν
ταῖς Βοάζου θεραπαινίσιν.

328 (3) Ἐλθών τε μετ' οὐ πολλὰς ἡμέρας καὶ Βόαζος ἤδη τῆς κριθῆς λελικμημένης, ἐπὶ τῆς ἅλωος
ἐκάθευδε. τοῦτο πυθομένη ἡ Ναάμις τεχνᾶται
παρακατακλῖναι τὴν Ῥούθην αὐτῷ· καὶ γὰρ ἔσεσθαι χρηστὸν αὐταῖς ὁμιλήσαντα τῇ παιδί· καὶ
πέμπει τὴν κόρην ὑπνωσομένην αὐτοῦ παρὰ τοῖς
329 ποσίν. ἡ δέ, πρὸς οὐδὲν γὰρ ἀντιλέγειν τῶν ὑπὸ
τῆς ἑκυρᾶς κελευομένων ὅσιον ἡγεῖτο, παραγίνεται καὶ παραυτίκα μὲν λανθάνει τὸν Βόαζον
βαθέως καθυπνωκότα, περιεγερθεὶς δὲ περὶ μέσην
νύκτα καὶ αἰσθόμενος τῆς ἀνθρώπου παρακατακει-
330 μένης ἀνέκρινε τίς εἴη. τῆς δ' εἰπούσης τοὔνομα
καὶ φαμένης ὡς αὐτῆς[3] δεσπότην συγχωρεῖν, τότε

---

[1] +λαμβάνειν ROMSP.

[2] εὐλάβειαν ROSP.   [3] ROE: αὐτὸν rell.

his master. And Boaz, alike for her loyalty to her
mother-in-law and for her[a] remembrance of that
son of hers to whom she had been united, bade her
welcome and wished her enjoyment of blessings : he
would not have her glean but permitted her to reap
and carry away all that she could ; while he charged
his steward in no wise to hinder her and to provide
her with lunch and drink when he fed the reapers.
But Ruth, having received of him barley-meal, kept ii. 14, 18.
thereof for her mother-in-law and brought it to her,
on her return at even, along with her sheaves ;
while Naamis on her side had reserved for her portions of some food with which attentive neighbours
had provided her.[b] Ruth also recounted to her
mother-in-law what Boaz had said to her. And
Naamis having told her that he was a kinsman and
might haply for piety's sake take care of them, she
went out again on the following days to glean with
the handmaids of Boaz.

(3) Not many days later Boaz himself came and, Boaz and
when the winnowing of the barley was done, slept Ruth in the
threshing-
on the threshing-floor. On learning of this, Naamis floor.
schemed to bring Ruth to his side, deeming that he Ruth iii. 1.
would be gracious to them after consorting with the
child ; so she sent the damsel to sleep at his feet.
And she, regarding it as a pious duty in nothing to
gainsay the behests of her mother-in-law, repaired
thither, and at the moment escaped the eye of Boaz,
who was fast asleep ; but, awaking towards midnight
and becoming aware of the woman lying beside him,
he inquired who she was. And she having mentioned
her name and prayed him, as her master, to pardon

[a] Or perhaps " his "; Naomi's son was Boaz's kinsman
as well as Ruth's husband.   [b] Amplification.

307

μὲν ἡσυχίαν ἄγει, ὄρθριος δὲ πρὶν ἢ τοὺς οἰκέτας
ἄρξασθαι κινεῖσθαι πρὸς τὸ ἔργον, περιεγείρας
αὐτὴν κελεύει τῶν κριθῶν λαβοῦσαν ὅ τι καὶ
δύναιτο πορεύεσθαι πρὸς τὴν ἑκυρὰν πρὶν ὀφθῆναί
τισιν αὐτόθι κεκοιμημένην, φυλάττεσθαι[1] σῶφρον
ὂν[2] τὴν ἐπὶ τοιούτοις διαβολὴν καὶ μάλιστ' ἐπὶ
331 μὴ γεγονόσι. " περὶ μέντοι τοῦ παντὸς οὕτω,"
φησίν, " ἔσται, ἐρωτᾶν[3] τὸν ἔγγιστά μου τῷ
γένει τυγχάνοντα, εἴ σου χρεία γαμετῆς ἐστιν
αὐτῷ, καὶ λέγοντι μὲν ἀκολουθήσεις ἐκείνῳ, παρ-
αιτουμένου δὲ νόμῳ σε συνοικήσουσαν ἄξομαι."
332 (4) Ταῦτα τῇ ἑκυρᾷ δηλωσάσης εὐθυμία κατεῖχεν
αὐτὰς ἐν ἐλπίδι τοῦ πρόνοιαν ἕξειν αὐτῶν Βόαζον
γενομένας. κἀκεῖνος ἤδη μεσούσης τῆς ἡμέρας
κατελθὼν εἰς τὴν πόλιν τήν τε γερουσίαν συνῆγε
καὶ μεταπεμψάμενος Ῥούθην ἐκάλει καὶ τὸν συγ-
333 γενῆ, καὶ παραγενομένου φησίν· " ' Αβιμελέχου
καὶ τῶν υἱῶν αὐτοῦ κλήρων κρατεῖς;" ὁμολογή-
σαντος δὲ συγχωρούντων τῶν νόμων κατὰ ἀγχι-
στείαν, " οὐκοῦν," φησὶν ὁ Βόαζος, " οὐκ ἐξ ἡμισείας δεῖ μεμνῆσθαι τῶν νόμων, ἀλλὰ πάντα ποιεῖν
κατ' αὐτούς. Μαάλου[4] γὰρ δεῦρ' ἥκει γύναιον,
ὅπερ εἰ θέλεις τῶν ἀγρῶν κρατεῖν γαμεῖν σε δεῖ
334 κατὰ τοὺς νόμους." ὁ δὲ Βοάζῳ καὶ τοῦ κλήρου
καὶ τῆς γυναικὸς παρεχώρει συγγενεῖ μὲν ὄντι καὶ
αὐτῷ τῶν τετελευτηκότων, εἶναι δὲ καὶ γυναῖκα

---

[1] + γὰρ MSPL. [2] ὂν conj.
[3] om. RO Lat.
[4] v.ll. Μαλλίωνος, Μαλῶνος.

---

[a] Niese's conjecture, σου for μου, is needless : the superlative in τὸν ἔγγιστά μου includes the comparative.

her, he for the time held his peace ; but at day-break, ere his servants began to move to their work, he roused her and bade her take as much of the barley as she could carry and be off to her mother-in-law, before anyone should see that she had slept there, since it was wise to guard against scandal of that kind, and the more so when nothing had passed. " But as concerning the whole matter," said he, " thus shall it be. He that is nearer of kin (to thee) than I,[a] must be asked whether he would have thee to wife : if he says yea, thou shalt follow him ; if he declines, I will take thee for my lawful bride."

(4) Ruth having reported this to her mother-in-law, they were well content, in the expectation that Boaz would take them under his care. And he, having towards midday [b] gone down into the city, assembled the elders,[b] sent for Ruth and summoned the kinsman also, upon whose coming he said to him, " Art thou the possessor of the heritage of Abimelech and his sons ? " " Yes," he admitted, " the laws cede it to me in virtue of nearness of kin." " Then," said Boaz, " thou oughtest not to remember but one half of those laws, but to do all that they require. Maalon's young wife is come hither : if thou wouldest retain those lands, thou must marry her in accordance with the laws." He, however, renounced both the heritage and the woman to Boaz, who was himself likewise a kinsman of the dead, on the plea that he had a wife and

[b] Amplification, like the question addressed to the kinsman below and other details in this narrative. The reference to the γερουσία, " council of elders " or " senate," has a parallel in the Targum which says that Boaz came before the court of the Sanhedrin. Scripture says merely " he took ten men of the elders of the city " (iv. 2).

335 λέγων αὐτῷ καὶ παῖδας ἤδη. μαρτυράμενος οὖν
ὁ Βόαζος τὴν γερουσίαν ἐκέλευε τῇ γυναικὶ
ὑπολῦσαι αὐτὸν προσελθοῦσαν κατὰ τὸν νόμον καὶ
πτύειν εἰς τὸ πρόσωπον. γενομένου δὲ τούτου
Βόαζος γαμεῖ τὴν 'Ρούθην καὶ γίνεται παιδίον
336 αὐτοῖς μετ' ἐνιαυτὸν ἄρρεν. τοῦτο ἡ Ναάμις
τιτθευομένη κατὰ συμβουλίαν τῶν γυναικῶν 'Ωβή-
δην ἐκάλεσεν ἐπὶ γηροκομίᾳ τῇ αὑτῆς τραφησό-
μενον· ὠβήδης γὰρ κατὰ διάλεκτον τὴν 'Εβραίων
ἀποσημαίνει δουλεύων. 'Ωβήδου δὲ γίνεται[1]
'Ιεσσαῖος, τούτου Δαυίδης ὁ βασιλεύσας καὶ παισὶ
τοῖς αὑτοῦ καταλιπὼν τὴν ἡγεμονίαν ἐπὶ μίαν καὶ
337 εἴκοσι γενεὰς ἀνδρῶν. τὰ μὲν οὖν κατὰ 'Ρούθην
ἀναγκαίως διηγησάμην, ἐπιδεῖξαι βουλόμενος τὴν
τοῦ θεοῦ δύναμιν, ὅτι τούτῳ παράγειν ἐφικτόν
ἐστιν εἰς ἀξίωμα λαμπρὸν καὶ τοὺς ἐπιτυχόντας,
εἰς οἷον ἀνήγαγε καὶ Δαυίδην ἐκ τοιούτων γενόμενον.

338 (x. 1) 'Εβραῖοι δὲ τῶν πραγμάτων αὐτοῖς ὑπ-
ενεχθέντων πάλιν πόλεμον ἐκφέρουσι Παλαιστίνοις
διὰ τοιαύτην αἰτίαν. 'Ηλεῖ τῷ ἀρχιερεῖ δύο παῖδες
339 ἦσαν 'Οφνίης τε καὶ Φινεέσης. οὗτοι καὶ πρὸς
ἀνθρώπους ὑβρισταὶ γενόμενοι καὶ πρὸς τὸ θεῖον
ἀσεβεῖς οὐδενὸς ἀπείχοντο παρανομήματος, καὶ
τὰ μὲν ἐφέροντο τῶν γερῶν κατὰ τιμήν, ἃ δ'
ἐλάμβανον αὐτοῖς[2] ἁρπαγῆς τρόπῳ, γυναῖκάς τε
τὰς ἐπὶ θρησκείᾳ παραγινομένας ὕβριζον φθοραῖς,
ταῖς μὲν βίαν προσφέροντες τὰς δὲ δώροις ὑπαγό-

---

[1] +παῖς RO.   [2] αὑτοῖς codd.

[a] Amplification: there is no mention in Scripture of a
previous marriage.

310

children already.[a] Boaz therefore, having taken the elders to witness, bade the woman loose the man's shoe, approaching him as the law ordained, and to spit in his face.[b] That done, Boaz married Ruth, and a year after a boy was born to them. This infant was nursed by Naamis, who on the counsel of the women called him Obed, because he was to be brought up to be the stay of her old age ; for *obed* in the Hebrew tongue signifies " one who serves." Of Obed was born Jesse, and of him David, who became king and bequeathed his dominion to his posterity for one and twenty generations. This story of Ruth I have been constrained to relate, being desirous to show the power of God and how easy it is for Him to promote even ordinary folk to rank so illustrious as that to which he raised David, sprung from such ancestors.

(x. 1) The Hebrews, whose affairs had declined, again made war upon the Philistines, the occasion being on this wise. Eli the high priest had two sons, Hophnies[c] and Phinees.[c] These, grown both insolent to men and impious to the Divinity, abstained from no iniquity : of the offerings some they carried off as the prizes of office, others they seized in robber fashion ; they dishonoured the women who came for worship, doing violence to some and seducing

[b] This last detail is taken from the law (Deut. xxv. 9 ; *A.* iv. 256), but is not mentioned in Ruth, which describes a different ceremony, the giving of his shoe by the purchaser to the seller, as a symbol of exchange. In this case the kinsman should presumably not have been subjected to the humiliating ceremony prescribed by the law of levirate marriage in Deuteronomy, inasmuch as he was not a brother of Ruth's dead husband.

[c] Bibl. Hophni, and Phinehas.

μενοι· τυραννίδος δ' οὐθὲν ἀπέλειπεν ὁ βίος αὐτῶν.
340 ὅ τε οὖν πατὴρ αὐτὸς¹ ἐπὶ τούτοις χαλεπῶς εἶχεν
ὅσον οὐδέπω προσδοκῶν ἥξειν ἐκ θεοῦ τιμωρίαν
αὐτοῖς ἐπὶ τοῖς πραττομένοις, τό τε πλῆθος ἐδυσ-
φόρει, κἀπειδὴ φράζει τὴν ἐσομένην συμφορὰν ὁ
θεὸς τοῖς παισὶν αὐτοῦ τῷ τε Ἠλεῖ καὶ Σαμουήλῳ
τῷ προφήτῃ παιδὶ τότε² ὄντι, τότε φανερὸν ἐπὶ τοῖς
υἱοῖς πένθος ἦγε.

341   (2) Βούλομαι δὲ τὰ περὶ τοῦ προφήτου πρότερον
διεξελθὼν ἔπειθ' οὕτως τὰ περὶ τοὺς Ἠλεῖ παῖδας
εἰπεῖν καὶ τὴν δυστυχίαν τὴν τῷ παντὶ λαῷ
342 Ἑβραίων γενομένην. Ἀλκάνης Λευίτης ἀνὴρ τῶν
ἐν μέσῳ πολιτῶν τῆς Ἐφράμου κληρουχίας Ἀρμα-
θὰν³ πόλιν κατοικῶν ἐγάμει δύο γυναῖκας Ἄνναν
τε καὶ Φενάνναν. ἐκ δὴ ταύτης καὶ παῖδες αὐτῷ
γίνονται, τὴν δ' ἑτέραν ἄτεκνον οὖσαν ἀγαπῶν
343 διετέλει. ἀφικομένου δὲ μετὰ τῶν γυναικῶν τοῦ
Ἀλκάνου εἰς Σιλὼ πόλιν θῦσαι, ἐνταῦθα γὰρ ἡ
σκηνὴ τοῦ θεοῦ ἐπεπήγει καθὼς προειρήκαμεν,
καὶ πάλιν κατὰ τὴν εὐωχίαν νέμοντος μοίρας
κρεῶν ταῖς τε γυναιξὶ καὶ τοῖς τέκνοις, ἡ Ἄννα
θεασαμένη τοὺς τῆς ἑτέρας παῖδας τῇ μητρὶ περι-
καθισαμένους, εἰς δάκρυά τε προὔπεσε καὶ τῆς
ἀπαιδίας αὐτὴν ὠλοφύρετο καὶ τῆς μονώσεως.

---

¹ αὐτοῖς M: αὐτῶν LE (quorum Lat.).
² MLE: τε rell.: ἔτι Dindorf.
³ Ῥαμαθὰν ROM: Aramath Lat.: forte l. Ἀραμαθὰν.

ᵃ The order of words is peculiar: the Greek might be
rendered " when God announced to his servants, Eli and
Samuel . . . the fate that was in store."
   ᵇ For this phrase with regard to the arrangement of the
narrative cf. iv. 196.   ᶜ Bibl. Elkanah.
   ᵈ 1 Chron. vi. 27 (not stated in Samuel).

others by presents; in short, their manner of life differed in no whit from a tyranny. And so their father was himself in sore distress thereat, hourly expecting to see them visited by chastisement from God for their misdeeds, and the people were chafing; and when God announced both to Eli and to Samuel the prophet, then but a child, the fate that was in store for his sons,[a] then did Eli openly make mourning over his sons.

(2) But here I would first recount the story of the prophet and then proceed[b] to speak of the fate of Eli's sons and the disaster that befell the whole people of the Hebrews. Alkanes,[c] a Levite[d] of the middle classes, of the tribe of Ephraim and an inhabitant of the city of Armatha,[e] married two wives, Anna and Phenanna.[f] By the latter he had children, but the other, though childless, remained beloved of her husband. Now when Alkanes was come with his wives to the city of Silo to sacrifice—for it was there that the tabernacle of God had been pitched, as we have said before[g]—and when thereafter[h] at the banquet he was distributing portions of meat to his wives and children, Anna, beholding the children of the other wife seated around their mother, burst into tears and bewailed her barrenness and lonesome

Eli announces to Hannah the birth of a son.
1 Sam. i. 1.

[e] Bibl. Ramathaim-zophim (LXX Ἁρμαθαὶμ Σειφά), another name for Ramah and possibly identical with the N.T. Arimathaea : site disputed.

[f] Bibl. Hannah and Peninnah (LXX, like Josephus, Φενάννα).

[g] A. v. 68.

[h] πάλιν, probably an Aramaism; Wellhausen notes that in Mark's Gospel "πάλιν, like Aramaic tub, means not only 'again,' but also 'further,' 'thereupon'" (Einleitung in die drei ersten Evangelien, ed. 2, pp. 21 f.). There are other indications that this Josephan narrative of the birth of Samuel is drawn from an Aramaic source.

344 καὶ τῆς τἀνδρὸς παραμυθίας τῇ λύπῃ κρατήσασα
εἰς τὴν σκηνὴν ᾤχετο τὸν θεὸν ἱκετεύουσα δοῦναι
γονὴν αὐτῇ καὶ ποιῆσαι μητέρα, ἐπαγγελλομένη
τὸ πρῶτον αὐτῇ γενησόμενον καθιερώσειν ἐπὶ
διακονίᾳ τοῦ θεοῦ, δίαιταν οὐχ ὁμοίαν τοῖς ἰδιώταις

345 ποιησόμενον.   διατριβούσης δ᾽ ἐπὶ ταῖς εὐχαῖς
πολὺν χρόνον Ἡλεὶς ὁ ἀρχιερεύς, ἐκαθέζετο γὰρ
πρὸ τῆς σκηνῆς, ὡς παροινοῦσαν ἐκέλευεν ἀπιέναι.
τῆς δὲ πιεῖν ὕδωρ φαμένης, λυπουμένης δ᾽ ἐπὶ
παίδων ἀπορίᾳ τὸν θεὸν ἱκετεύειν, θαρσεῖν παρεκελεύετο, παρέξειν αὐτῇ παῖδας τὸν θεὸν κατ-
αγγέλλων.

346 (3) Παραγενομένη δ᾽ εὔελπις πρὸς τὸν ἄνδρα
τροφὴν χαίρουσα προσηνέγκατο, καὶ ἀναστρε-
ψάντων εἰς τὴν πατρίδα κύειν ἤρξατο·καὶ γίνεται
παιδίον αὐτοῖς, ὃν Σαμούηλον προσαγορεύουσι·
θεαίτητον ἄν τις εἴποι.   παρῆσαν οὖν ὑπὲρ τῆς
τοῦ παιδὸς θύσοντες γενέσεως δεκάτας τ᾽ ἔφερον.

347 ἀναμνησθεῖσα δ᾽ ἡ γυνὴ τῆς εὐχῆς τῆς ἐπὶ τῷ
παιδὶ γεγενημένης παρεδίδου τῷ Ἡλεῖ ἀνατιθεῖσα
τῷ θεῷ προφήτην γενησόμενον· κόμη τε οὖν αὐτῷ
ἀνεῖτο καὶ ποτὸν ἦν ὕδωρ. καὶ Σαμούηλος μὲν
ἐν τῷ ἱερῷ διῆγε τρεφόμενος, Ἀλκάνῃ δ᾽ ἐκ τῆς
Ἄννας υἱεῖς τε ἄλλοι[1] γίνονται καὶ τρεῖς θυγατέρες.

---

[1] ἄλλοι om. ROM.

---

[a] A close parallel from a Targum is supplied by Mr.
(now Archdeacon) Hunkin, " a woman who begins to
bear a first-born," *Journal of Theol. Studies*, xxv. (1924),
p. 398, n. 2.

lot. And, her grief proving stronger than her husband's consolation, she went off to the tabernacle, to beseech God to grant her offspring and to make her a mother, promising that her first-born should be consecrated to the service of God and that his manner of life should be unlike that of ordinary men. And as she lingered a long time over her prayers, Eli the high priest, who was seated at the entrance of the tabernacle, taking her for a drunkard, bade her begone. But, on her replying that she had drunk but water and that it was for grief at the lack of children that she was making supplication to God, he exhorted her to be of good cheer, announcing that God would grant her children.

(3) Repairing thus in good hope to her husband, she took her food with gladness, and on their return to their native place she began to conceive ^{a}; and an infant was born to them, whom they called Samuel, as one might say " asked of God." ^{b} They came therefore again to offer sacrifices for the birth of the child and brought their tithes also. ^{c} And the woman, mindful of the vow which she had made concerning the child, delivered him to Eli, dedicating him to God to become a prophet; so his locks were left to grow and his drink was water. Thus Samuel lived and was brought up in the sanctuary, but Alkanes had by Anna yet other sons and three daughters. ^{d}

9.

12.

Birth and
dedication
of Samuel.
1 Sam. i. 18

ii. 21

^{b} This biblical etymology (1 Sam. i. 20) is now abandoned: " Name of God " is the probable meaning.

^{c} The offerings are specified in 1 Sam. i. 24 : for the tithes *cf.* the addition in LXX to v. 21, καὶ πάσας τὰς δεκάτας τῆς γῆς αὐτοῦ.

^{d} Bibl. " three sons and two daughters ": possibly a figure γ´ (=3) has fallen out of the text of Josephus before γίνονται.

348 (4) Σαμούηλος δὲ πεπληρωκὼς ἔτος ἤδη δωδέ-
κατον προεφήτευε. καί ποτε κοιμώμενον ὀνομαστὶ
ἐκάλεσεν ὁ θεός· ὁ δὲ νομίσας ὑπὸ τοῦ ἀρχιερέως
πεφωνῆσθαι παραγίνεται πρὸς αὐτόν. οὐ φαμένου
δὲ καλέσαι τοῦ ἀρχιερέως ὁ θεὸς εἰς τρὶς τοῦτο
349 ποιεῖ. καὶ Ἡλεὶς διαυγασθείς[1] φησι πρὸς αὐτόν,
" ἀλλ' ἐγὼ μέν, Σαμούηλε, σιγὴν ὡς καὶ τὸ πρὶν
ἦγον, θεὸς δ' ἐστὶν ὁ καλῶν, σήμαινέ τε[2] πρὸς
αὐτόν, ὅτι παρατυγχάνω." καὶ τοῦ θεοῦ φθεγ-
ξαμένου πάλιν ἀκούσας ἠξίου λαλεῖν ἐπὶ τοῖς
χρωμένοις· οὐ γὰρ ὑστερήσειν αὐτὸν ἐφ' οἷς ἂν
350 θελήσειε διακονίας. καὶ ὁ θεὸς " ἐπεί," φησί,
" παρατυγχάνεις, μάνθανε συμφορὰν Ἰσραηλίταις
ἐσομένην λόγου μείζονα καὶ πίστεως τοῖς παρα-
τυγχάνουσι, καὶ τοὺς Ἡλεῖ δὲ παῖδας ἡμέρᾳ μιᾷ
τεθνηξομένους καὶ τὴν ἱερωσύνην μετελευσομένην
εἰς τὴν Ἐλεαζάρου οἰκίαν· Ἡλεὶς γὰρ τῆς ἐμῆς
θεραπείας μᾶλλον τοὺς υἱοὺς καὶ παρὰ τὸ συμ-
351 φέρον αὐτοῖς ἠγάπησε." ταῦτα βιασάμενος ὅρκοις
εἰπεῖν αὐτῷ τὸν προφήτην Ἡλείς, οὐ γὰρ ἐβούλετο λυπεῖν αὐτὸν λέγων, ἔτι μᾶλλον βεβαιοτέραν
εἶχε τὴν προσδοκίαν τῆς τῶν τέκνων ἀπωλείας.
Σαμουήλου δὲ ηὔξετο ἐπὶ πλέον ἡ δόξα πάντων ὧν
προεφήτευσεν ἀληθινῶν βλεπομένων.
352 (xi. 1) Κατὰ τοῦτον δὴ τὸν καιρὸν[3] Παλαιστῖνοι

[1] διυπνισθεὶς SPL.
[2] Niese (ex RO ἐσήμαινέ τε): ἀλλὰ σήμαινε rell.
[3] + καὶ ROM.

---

[a] Age not mentioned in Scripture.
[b] Greek " speak upon (*i.e.* " concerning ") His oracles,"
again suggesting a Semitic original ; the Hebrew use of
dibber 'al is exactly parallel.

(4) Samuel had now completed his twelfth year *a* God's revelation to Samuel.
when he began to act as a prophet. And one night
as he slept God called him by name ; but he, supposing that he had been summoned by the high
priest, went off to him. But the high priest replied 1 Sam. iii. 3.
that he had not called him, and God did this thing
thrice. Then Eli, enlightened, said to him, " Nay,
Samuel, *I* held my peace even as before : it is God
that calleth thee. Say then to Him, Here am I."
So, when God spake again, Samuel hearing Him
besought Him to speak *b* His oracles, for he would
not fail to serve Him in whatsoever He might desire.
And God said, " Since thou art there, learn that a
calamity will befall the Israelites passing the speech
or belief of them that witness it,*c* aye and that the
sons of Eli shall die on the selfsame day and that the
priesthood shall pass to the house of Eleazar.*d* For ii. 29.
Eli hath loved his sons more dearly than my worship,
and not to their welfare." All this Eli constrained iii. 15.
the prophet by oath to reveal to him—for Samuel
was loth to grieve him by telling it—and he now
awaited with yet more certainty than before the loss
of his children. But the renown of Samuel increased
more and more, since all that he prophesied was
seen to come true.

(xi. 1) This then was the time when the Philis- Victory of the

c " Those on the spot " is the usual sense of the verb in
Josephus and it has been so used twice just above (" Here
am I," " thou art there ") ; others here render " anyone "
(" any chance persons ").

d *Cf.* 1 Sam. ii. 30 ff.: the prophecy there made to Eli
himself was, according to Scripture, fulfilled under king
Solomon, when Abiathar of the house of Ithamar was replaced by Zadok of the house of Eleazar (1 Kings ii. 27, 35 ;
A. viii. 11).

στρατεύσαντες ἐπὶ τοὺς Ἰσραηλίτας στρατοπεδεύονται κατὰ πόλιν Ἀμφεκᾶν, δεξαμένων δ' ἐξ ὀλίγου τῶν Ἰσραηλιτῶν συνήεσαν εἰς τὴν ἐχομένην
καὶ νικῶσιν οἱ Παλαιστῖνοι καὶ κτείνουσι μὲν τῶν
Ἑβραίων εἰς τετρακισχιλίους, τὸ δὲ λοιπὸν πλῆθος
συνδιώκουσιν εἰς τὸ στρατόπεδον.

353 (2) Δείσαντες δὲ περὶ τῶν ὅλων Ἑβραῖοι¹ πέμπουσιν ὡς τὴν γερουσίαν καὶ τὸν ἀρχιερέα, τὴν
κιβωτὸν τοῦ θεοῦ κελεύοντες κομίζειν, ἵνα παρούσης
αὐτῆς παρατασσόμενοι κρατῶσι τῶν πολεμίων,
ἀγνοοῦντες ὅτι μείζων ἐστὶν ὁ καταψηφισάμενος
αὐτῶν τὴν συμφορὰν τῆς κιβωτοῦ, δι' ὃν καὶ ταύ-
354 την² συνέβαινεν εἶναι. παρῆν τε οὖν ἡ κιβωτὸς
καὶ οἱ τοῦ ἀρχιερέως υἱεῖς τοῦ πατρὸς αὐτοῖς
ἐπιστείλαντος, εἰ ληφθείσης τῆς κιβωτοῦ ζῆν
ἐθέλουσιν,³ εἰς ὄψιν αὐτῷ μὴ παραγίνεσθαι.
Φινεέσης δὲ ἤδη καὶ ἱερᾶτο, τοῦ πατρὸς αὐτῷ
355 παρακεχωρηκότος διὰ τὸ γῆρας. θάρσος οὖν
ἐπιγίνεται πολὺ τοῖς Ἑβραίοις ὡς διὰ τὴν ἄφιξιν
τῆς κιβωτοῦ περιεσομένοις τῶν πολεμίων, κατ-
επλήττοντο δὲ οἱ πολέμιοι δεδιότες τὴν παρουσίαν
τῆς κιβωτοῦ τοῖς Ἰσραηλίταις. ταῖς μέντοι γε
ἑκατέρων προσδοκίαις οὐχ ὅμοιον ἀπήντησε τὸ
356 ἔργον, ἀλλὰ συμβολῆς γενομένης ἣν μὲν ἤλπιζον

___

¹ RO: pr. οἱ rell. ² + ἐν τιμῇ SP.
³ ἐθελήσουσιν SP.

___

ᵃ Bibl. Aphek : in the plain of Sharon, perhaps the
modern *el Mejdel*.
318

tines, taking the field against the Israelites, pitched their camp over against the city of Amphekas.[a] The Israelites having hastily confronted them, the armies met on the following day, and the Philistines were victorious, slaying some four thousand of the Hebrews and pursuing the remainder of the host to their camp.

Philistines. 1 Sam. iv. 1

(2) Fearing a complete disaster, the Hebrews sent word to the council of elders[b] and to the high priest to bring the ark of God, in order that, through its presence in their ranks, they might overcome their enemies, ignorant that He who had decreed their discomfiture was mightier than the ark, seeing that it was to Him indeed that it owed its being.[c] And so the ark arrived, and with it the sons of the high priest, having received injunctions from their father, if they wished to survive the capture of the ark, not to venture into his sight. Phinees was already acting as high priest, his father having made way for him by reason of old age.[d] Confidence then mightily revived among the Hebrews, who hoped through the coming of the ark to get the better of their enemies, while the enemy were in consternation, dreading that presence of the ark among the Israelites. Howbeit, the event did not answer to the expectations of either of them, but when the clash

Further defeat of the Hebrews and capture of the ark. 1 Sam. iv. 3.

[b] In scripture the elders at the camp suggest that the ark be brought from Shiloh.

[c] Or, according to another reading, " for His sake that it was held in veneration."

[d] Amplification (along with the father's injunctions to his sons). Rabbinic tradition also states that Phinehas officiated as High Priest in the lifetime of Eli. The latter's blindness (1 Sam. iii. 3) would have disqualified him from office according to Jewish law (Lev. xxi. 18, Josephus, B.J. i. 270).

νίκην Ἑβραῖοι τῶν Παλαιστίνων αὕτη γίνεται,
ἣν δ᾽ ἐφοβοῦντο ἧτταν οὗτοι, ταύτην Ἑβραῖοι
παθόντες ἔγνωσαν αὑτοὺς μάτην ἐπὶ τῇ κιβωτῷ
τεθαρσηκότας· ἐτράπησάν τε γὰρ εὐθὺς εἰς χεῖρας
ἐλθόντες τῶν πολεμίων καὶ ἀπέβαλον εἰς τρισμυρίους, ἐν οἷς ἔπεσον καὶ οἱ τοῦ ἀρχιερέως υἱεῖς,
ἥ τε κιβωτὸς ἤγετο πρὸς τῶν πολεμίων.

357   (3) Ἀπαγγελθείσης δὲ τῆς ἥττης εἰς τὴν Σιλὼ
καὶ τῆς αἰχμαλωσίας τῆς κιβωτοῦ, Βενιαμίτης
γάρ τις αὐτοῖς ἄγγελος ἀφικνεῖται νεανίας παρα-
τετευχὼς τῷ γεγονότι, πένθους ἀνεπλήσθη πᾶσα
358 ἡ πόλις. καὶ Ἡλεὶς ὁ ἀρχιερεύς, ἐκαθέζετο γὰρ
καθ᾽ ἑτέρας τῶν πυλῶν ἐφ᾽ ὑψηλοῦ θρόνου, ἀκούσας
οἰμωγῆς καὶ νομίσας νεώτερόν τι πεπρᾶχθαι περὶ
τοὺς οἰκείους καὶ μεταπεμψάμενος τὸν νεανίαν,
ὡς ἔγνω τὰ κατὰ τὴν μάχην, ῥᾷων ἦν ἐπί τε
τοῖς παισὶ καὶ τοῖς συνενηνεγμένοις[1] περὶ τὸ στρατόπεδον ὡς ἂν προεγνωκὼς παρὰ τοῦ θεοῦ τὸ
συμβησόμενον καὶ προαπηγγελκώς· συνέχει[2] γὰρ
ἱκανῶς[3] τὰ παρὰ τὴν[4] προσδοκίαν συντυχόντα τῶν
359 δεινῶν. ὡς δὲ καὶ τὴν κιβωτὸν ἤκουσεν ἠχμα-
λωτίσθαι πρὸς τῶν πολεμίων, ὑπὸ τοῦ παρ᾽
ἐλπίδας αὐτῷ τοῦτο προσπεσεῖν περιαλγήσας
ἀποκυλισθεὶς ἀπὸ τοῦ θρόνου τελευτᾷ, ὀκτὼ καὶ
ἐνενήκοντα βιώσας ἔτη τὰ πάντα καὶ τούτων τὰ[5]
τεσσαράκοντα κατασχὼν τὴν ἀρχήν.

360   (4) Θνῄσκει δὲ κατ᾽ ἐκείνην τὴν ἡμέραν καὶ ἡ
Φινεέσου τοῦ παιδὸς γυνὴ μὴ καρτερήσασα ζῆν
ἐπὶ τῇ τἀνδρὸς δυστυχίᾳ. κυούσῃ μὲν αὐτῇ

---

[1] Text doubtful: ἐπὶ τῷ τοῖς παισὶ τοῖς αὐτοῦ συνενηνεγμένῳ
Niese.   [2] confundunt Lat.: συγχεῖ Naber.
[3] ἀκριβῶς ROE.   [4] τὰ κατὰ OE: τὰ R.   [5] τὰ om. ROE.

came, that victory for which the Hebrews hoped went to the Philistines, and that defeat which these feared was sustained by the Hebrews, who learnt that their trust in the ark had been in vain. For soon as ever they closed with the enemy they were routed and lost some thirty thousand men, among the fallen being the sons of the high priest; and the ark was carried off by the enemy.

(3) When the defeat and the capture of the ark were reported in Silo—the news was brought by a young Benjamite who had been present at the action —the whole city was filled with lamentation. And Eli the high priest, who was sitting at one of the two gates on a lofty seat, hearing the wails and surmising that some grave disaster had befallen his offspring, sent for the young man; and when he learnt the issue of the battle, he bore with moderate composure the fate of his sons and that which had happened to the army, seeing that he had known beforehand from God and had forewarned them of that which was to come, for men are affected most by those shocks that fall unexpectedly. But when he heard moreover that the ark had been captured by the enemy, in an agony of grief at this unlooked for tidings, he tumbled from his seat and expired, having lived ninety and eight years in all and for forty [a] of them held supreme power.

(4) That same day died also the wife of his son Phinees, having not the strength to survive her husband's misfortune. She was indeed with child

Death of Eli.
1 Sam. iv. 12.

15.
18.

Death of
the wife of
Phinehas.
1 Sam. iv. 19.

---

[a] So Heb. and some MSS. of LXX: the majority of the MSS. of the Greek Bible read "twenty."

προσηγγέλη τὸ περὶ τὸν ἄνδρα πάθος, τίκτει δ'
ἑπταμηνιαῖον παῖδα, ὃν καὶ ζήσαντα Ἰωχάβην[1]
προσηγόρευσαν, σημαίνει δὲ ἀδοξίαν τὸ ὄνομα, διὰ
τὴν προσπεσοῦσαν δύσκλειαν τότε τῷ στρατῷ.

361 (5) Ἦρξε δὲ πρῶτος Ἠλεὶς Ἰθαμάρου τῆς
ἑτέρου τῶν Ἀαρῶνος υἱῶν οἰκίας· ἡ γὰρ Ἐλεαζάρου οἰκία τὸ πρῶτον ἱερᾶτο παῖς παρὰ πατρὸς
ἐπιδεχόμενοι τὴν τιμήν, ἐκεῖνός τε Φινεέσῃ τῷ
362 παιδὶ αὐτοῦ παραδίδωσι, μεθ' ὃν Ἀβιεζέρης υἱὸς
ὢν αὐτοῦ τὴν τιμὴν παραλαβὼν παιδὶ αὐτοῦ Βόκκι
τοὔνομα αὐτὴν κατέλιπε, παρ' οὗ διεδέξατο Ὄζις
υἱὸς ὤν, μεθ' ὃν Ἠλεὶς ἔσχε τὴν ἱερωσύνην, περὶ
οὗ νῦν ὁ λόγος, καὶ τὸ γένος τὸ ἀπ' ἐκείνου μέχρι
τῶν κατὰ τὴν τοῦ[2] Σολόμωνος βασιλείαν καιρῶν.
τότε δὲ οἱ Ἐλεαζάρου πάλιν αὐτὴν ἀπέλαβον.

---

[1] v.ll. Ἰωαχάβην, Ἰαχώβην etc.
[2] τοῦ om. MSPLE.

---

[a] Unscriptural detail. Rabbinic tradition includes Samuel
but not Ichabod, among seven months' children.
[b] Bibl. I-chabod (= " no glory ").

when she was told of his fate, and she gave birth to a seven months'[a] son; and him, since he lived, they called Jochabes[b] (a name signifying "ingloriousness") because of the ignominy that then befell the army.

(5) Eli was the first to bear rule of the house of Ithamar,[c] the second[d] of Aaron's sons; for the house of Eleazar held the high priesthood at the first, the dignity descending from father to son. Eleazar transmitted it to Phinees his son, after whom Abiezer[e] his son received it, leaving it to his son, named Bokki,[f] from whom Ozis[g] his son inherited it; it was after him that Eli, of whom we have been speaking, held the priesthood, as also his posterity down to the times of the reign of Solomon. Then the descendants of Eleazar once more recovered it.

Succession of the high priests.

1 Chron. vi. 4 f.

Cf. 1 Kings ii. 27, 35.

[c] Based not on Scripture, but on tradition (see M. Weill's note).

[d] Gr. "one of two." Of the four sons of Aaron—Nadab, Abihu, Eleazar and Ithamar—the first two died young (1 Chron. xxiv. 1 f.).

[e] Bibl. Abishua (1 Chron. vi. 4).

[f] Bibl. Bukki.

[g] Bibl. Uzzi.

ΒΙΒΛΙΟΝ ϛ

(i. 1) Λαβόντες δ' οἱ Παλαιστῖνοι τὴν τῶν
πολεμίων κιβωτὸν αἰχμάλωτον, ὡς προειρήκαμεν
μικρὸν ἔμπροσθεν, εἰς Ἄζωτον ἐκόμισαν πόλιν καὶ
παρὰ τὸν αὐτῶν θεὸν ὥσπερ τι λάφυρον, Δαγὼν
2 δ' οὗτος ἐκαλεῖτο, τιθέασι. τῇ δ' ἐπιούσῃ πάντες
ὑπὸ τὴν τῆς ἡμέρας ἀρχὴν εἰσιόντες εἰς τὸν ναὸν
προσκυνῆσαι τὸν θεὸν ἐπιτυγχάνουσιν αὐτῷ τοῦτο
ποιοῦντι τὴν κιβωτόν· ἔκειτο γὰρ[1] ἀποπεπτωκὼς
τῆς βάσεως, ἐφ' ἧς ἑστὼς διετέλει· καὶ βαστά-
σαντες πάλιν ἐφιστᾶσιν αὐτὸν ἐπὶ ταύτης, δυσφορή-
σαντες ἐπὶ τῷ γεγενημένῳ. πολλάκις δὲ φοιτῶντες παρὰ τὸν Δαγὼν καὶ καταλαμβάνοντες
ὁμοίως ἐπὶ τοῦ προσκυνοῦντος τὴν κιβωτὸν
σχήματος κείμενον, ἐν ἀπορίᾳ δεινῇ καὶ συγχύσει
3 καθίσταντο. καὶ τελευταῖον ἀπέσκηψεν εἰς τὴν
τῶν Ἀζωτίων πόλιν καὶ τὴν χώραν αὐτῶν φθορὰν
τὸ θεῖον καὶ νόσον· ἀπέθνησκον γὰρ ὑπὸ δυσεντε-
ρίας, πάθους χαλεποῦ καὶ τὴν ἀναίρεσιν ὀξυτάτην
ἐπιφέροντος πρὶν ἢ τὴν ψυχὴν αὐτοῖς εὐθανάτως
ἀπολυθῆναι τοῦ σώματος, τὰ ἐντὸς ἀναφέροντες[2]
διαβεβρωμένα καὶ παντοίως ὑπὸ τῆς νόσου δι-
εφθαρμένα· τὰ δ' ἐπὶ τῆς χώρας μυῶν πλῆθος

---

[1] Ε: + ἀπ' αὐτῆς SP: + ἐπ' αὐτῆς rell.
[2] + ἐξεμοῦντες codd. (gloss).

324

BOOK VI

(i. 1) THE Philistines, having captured their enemies' ark, as we have said a while ago, carried it to the city of Azotus *a* and placed it as a trophy beside their own god, who was called Dagon. But on the morrow, when all at break of day entered the temple to adore their god, they found him doing the like to the ark ; for he lay prostrate, having fallen from the pedestal whereon he had always stood. So they lifted him and set him again thereon, sore distressed at what had passed. But when oft-times *b* visiting Dagon they ever found him in a like posture of prostration before the ark, they were plunged into dire perplexity and dismay. And in the end the Deity launched upon the city of the Azotians and upon their country destruction and disease. For they died of dysentery,*c* a grievous malady and inflicting most rapid dissolution, or ever their soul by blessed death was parted from the body, for they brought up their entrails all consumed and in every way corrupted by the disease. As for what was on the land, a swarm of

The ark in Philistia and the plagues arising therefrom.
1 Sam. v. 1.

v. 6 LXX.

---

a The Greek (LXX) name for the Heb. Ashdod.
b The Bible mentions only a second visit, adding details on the shattering of the image.
c The word used in Scripture probably means "plague boils."

325

ἀνελθὼν[1] κατέβλαψε μήτε φυτῶν μήτε καρπῶν
4 ἀποσχόμενον. ἐν δὴ τούτοις ὄντες τοῖς κακοῖς
οἱ Ἀζώτιοι καὶ πρὸς τὰς συμφορὰς ἀντέχειν οὐ
δυνάμενοι συνῆκαν ἐκ τῆς κιβωτοῦ ταύτας αὐτοῖς
ἀνασχεῖν, καὶ τὴν νίκην καὶ τὴν ταύτης αἰχμαλω-
σίαν οὐκ ἐπ᾽ ἀγαθῷ γεγενημένην. πέμπουσιν οὖν
πρὸς τοὺς Ἀσκαλωνίτας ἀξιοῦντες τὴν κιβωτὸν
5 αὐτοὺς παρὰ σφᾶς δέχεσθαι. τοῖς δὲ οὐκ ἀηδὴς
ἡ τῶν Ἀζωτίων δέησις προσέπεσεν, ἀλλ᾽ ἐπι-
νεύουσι μὲν αὐτοῖς τὴν χάριν, λαβόντες δὲ τὴν
κιβωτὸν ἐν τοῖς ὁμοίοις δεινοῖς κατέστησαν· συνεξ-
εκόμισε γὰρ αὐτῇ τὰ τῶν Ἀζωτίων ἡ κιβωτὸς
πάθη πρὸς τοὺς ἀπ᾽ ἐκείνων αὐτὴν δεχομένους· καὶ
πρὸς ἄλλους παρ᾽ αὐτῶν ἀποπέμπουσιν Ἀσκαλω-
6 νῖται. μένει δ᾽ οὐδὲ παρ᾽ ἐκείνοις· ὑπὸ γὰρ τῶν
αὐτῶν παθῶν ἐλαυνόμενοι πρὸς τὰς ἐχομένας
ἀπολύουσι πόλεις. καὶ τοῦτον ἐκπεριέρχεται τὸν
τρόπον τὰς πέντε τῶν Παλαιστίνων πόλεις ἡ
κιβωτὸς ὥσπερ δασμὸν ἀπαιτοῦσα παρ᾽ ἑκάστης
τοῦ πρὸς αὐτὰς ἐλθεῖν ἃ δι᾽ αὐτὴν ἔπασχον.
7 (2) Ἀπειρηκότες δὲ τοῖς κακοῖς οἱ πεπειραμένοι καὶ τοῖς ἀκούουσιν αὐτὰ διδασκαλία γινό-
μενοι τοῦ μὴ προσδέξασθαι τὴν κιβωτόν ποτε πρὸς
αὐτοὺς ἐπὶ τοιούτῳ μισθῷ καὶ τέλει, τὸ λοιπὸν
ἐζήτουν μηχανὴν καὶ πόρον ἀπαλλαγῆς αὐτῆς.
8 καὶ συνελθόντες οἱ ἐκ τῶν πέντε πόλεων ἄρχοντες,
Γίττης καὶ Ἀκκάρων καὶ Ἀσκάλωνος ἔτι δὲ

[1] Lat.: + ἐπὶ (τὰ ἐπὶ M, ἀπὸ E, ἐκ SP) τῆς γῆς codd.

mice,[a] coming up from beneath, ravaged it all, sparing neither plant nor fruit. Being, then, in this evil plight and powerless to withstand their calamities, the Azotians understood that it was from the ark that they arose and that their victory and the capture of this trophy had not been for their welfare. They therefore sent to the men of Ascalon[b] and begged them to receive the ark into their keeping. And these, listening not unwillingly to the request of the Azotians, consented to do them this service; but no sooner had they taken the ark than they found themselves in the like woes, for the ark carried along with it the plagues of the Azotians to those who received it from their hands. So the Ascalonites rid themselves of it, sending it off to others. But neither did it abide with these, for, being beset by the same sufferings, they dismissed it to the neighbouring cities. And on this wise the ark went the round of the five cities of the Philistines, exacting from each, as it were toll for its visit to them, the ills which it caused them to suffer.

(2) Exhausted by these miseries, the victims, whose fate was becoming a lesson to all who heard of it never to receive this ark among them at such a meed and price, henceforth sought ways and means to get rid of it. So the lords of the five cities—Gitta, Akkaron, Ascalon, along with Gaza and Azotus— *Delibera-tion and decision of the Philistines. Cf. 1 Sam. vi. 1.*

---

[a] Josephus agrees with the LXX in mentioning the mice at this point: the Hebrew text only alludes to them later (vi. 4 f.).

[b] In Scripture, after a meeting of the lords of the Philistines, the ark is sent first to Gath and then to Ekron (LXX Ascalon).

Γάζης καὶ Ἀζώτου, ἐσκόπουν τί δεῖ ποιεῖν. καὶ
τὸ μὲν πρῶτον ἐδόκει τὴν κιβωτὸν ἀποπέμπειν
τοῖς οἰκείοις, ὡς ὑπερεκδικοῦντος αὐτὴν τοῦ θεοῦ
καὶ συνεπιδημησάντων αὐτῇ τῶν δεινῶν διὰ τοῦτο
καὶ συνεισβαλόντων μετ' ἐκείνης εἰς τὰς πόλεις
9 αὐτῶν· ἦσαν δὲ οἱ λέγοντες τοῦτο μὲν μὴ ποιεῖν
μηδ' ἐξαπατᾶσθαι τὴν αἰτίαν τῶν κακῶν εἰς
ἐκείνην ἀναφέροντας· οὐ γὰρ ταύτην εἶναι τὴν
δύναμιν αὐτῇ[1] καὶ τὴν ἰσχύν· οὐ γὰρ ἄν ποτ'
αὐτῆς κηδομένου τοῦ θεοῦ ὑποχείριον ἀνθρώποις
γενέσθαι. ἡσυχάζειν δὲ καὶ πρᾴως ἔχειν ἐπὶ τοῖς
συμβεβηκόσι παρῄνουν, αἰτίαν τούτων οὐκ ἄλλην
ἢ μόνην λογιζομένους τὴν φύσιν, ἣ καὶ σώμασι καὶ
γῇ καὶ φυτοῖς καὶ πᾶσι τοῖς ἐξ αὐτῆς συνεστῶσι
κατὰ χρόνων περιόδους τίκτει τοιαύτας μεταβολάς.
10 νικᾷ δὲ τὰς προειρημένας γνώμας ἀνδρῶν ἔν τε
τοῖς ἐπάνω χρόνοις συνέσει καὶ φρονήσει διαφέρειν[2] πεπιστευμένων συμβουλία καὶ τότε μάλιστα
δοξάντων ἁρμοζόντως λέγειν τοῖς παροῦσιν, οἳ
μήτ' ἀποπέμπειν ἔφασαν τὴν κιβωτὸν μήτε κατασχεῖν, ἀλλὰ πέντε μὲν ἀνδριάντας ὑπὲρ ἑκάστης
πόλεως χρυσοῦς ἀναθεῖναι τῷ θεῷ χαριστήριον,
ὅτι προενόησεν αὐτῶν τῆς σωτηρίας καὶ κατέσχεν ἐν τῷ βίῳ διωκομένους ἐξ αὐτοῦ παθήμα-
σιν, οἷς οὐκέτι ἦν ἀντιβλέψαι, τοσούτους δὲ τὸν
ἀριθμὸν μύας χρυσοῦς τοῖς κατανεμηθεῖσιν αὐτῶν

---

[1] ex Lat. Hudson: ὑγιῆ codd.   [2] om. ROM.

---

[a] In Scripture (vi. 2) the Philistines summon " the priests
and the diviners," who propose the course which is followed.
The meeting described in Josephus, with the views of the
three parties, is an invention of the " Sophoclean " assistant:
for a similar conflict of opinions cf. A. iii. 96 ff., where, as

met to deliberate what they ought to do.[a] Their first resolution was to send the ark back to its own people, inasmuch as God was championing its cause and that was why these horrors had accompanied it and burst along with it into their cities. But there were others who said that they should not do thus nor be deluded into attributing the cause of their misfortunes to the ark : it possessed no such power and might, for, were it under the care of God, it would never have fallen into the hands of men. Their advice was to sit still and to bear these accidents with equanimity, accounting their cause to be no other than nature herself, who periodically produces such changes in men's bodies, in earth, and in plants and all the products of earth. However, both these proposals were defeated by the counsel of men who in times past had obtained credit for superior intelligence and sagacity, and who now above all seemed to say just what befitted the occasion. Their verdict was neither to send back the ark nor to detain it, but to dedicate to God five images[b] of gold, 4. one on behalf of each city, as a thank-offering[c] to Him for His care for their salvation and for having kept them in the land of the living when they were like to be harried out of it by plagues which they could no longer face, and withal as many golden mice like to those that had overrun and ruined their

here (§ 9), one party is for retaining composure ($\pi\rho\dot{\alpha}\omega s$ $\check{\epsilon}\chi\epsilon\iota\nu$). This assistant's love of trichotomy extends to details, e.g. the $\tau\rho\iota o\delta os$ (§ 11) and the division of the 5 cities into $3+2$ by the insertion of $\check{\epsilon}\tau\iota$ $\delta\dot{\epsilon}$ (§ 8).

[b] Statuettes in human form : bibl. " tumours " or rather " boils," LXX $\check{\epsilon}\delta\rho\alpha s$ (models of the *anus*, as symbols of the plague).

[c] In Scripture as a " guilt-offering " (vi. 3), in compensation for the wrong done to the ark.

11 καὶ διαφθείρασι τὴν χώραν ἐμφερεῖς· ἔπειτα
βαλόντας εἰς γλωσσόκομον αὐτοὺς καὶ θέντας
ἐπὶ τὴν κιβωτόν, ἅμαξαν αὐτῇ καινὴν κατασκευάσαι, καὶ βόας ὑποζεύξαντας ἀρτιτόκους τὰς
μὲν πόρτις ἐγκλεῖσαι καὶ κατασχεῖν, μὴ ταῖς
μητράσιν ἐμποδὼν ἑπόμεναι γένωνται, πόθῳ δ'
αὐτῶν ὀξυτέραν ποιῶνται τὴν πορείαν· ἐκείνας δ'
ἐξελάσαντας τὴν κιβωτὸν φερούσας ἐπὶ τριόδου
καταλιπεῖν αὐταῖς ἐπιτρέψαντας ἣν βούλονται τῶν
12 ὁδῶν ἀπελθεῖν· κἂν μὲν τὴν Ἑβραίων ἀπίωσι καὶ
τὴν τούτων χώραν ἀναβαίνωσιν, ὑπολαμβάνειν τὴν
κιβωτὸν αἰτίαν τῶν κακῶν, "ἂν δὲ ἄλλην τρά-
πωνται, μεταδιώξωμεν αὐτήν," ἔφασαν, "μαθόντες
ὅτι μηδεμίαν ἰσχὺν τοιαύτην ἔχει."
13 (3) Ἔκριναν δ' αὐτὰ καλῶς εἰρῆσθαι καὶ τοῖς
ἔργοις εὐθὺς τὴν γνώμην ἐκύρωσαν. καὶ ποιήσαντες μὲν τὰ προειρημένα προάγουσι τὴν ἅμαξαν
ἐπὶ τὴν τρίοδον καὶ καταλιπόντες ἀνεχώρησαν, τῶν
δὲ βοῶν τὴν ὀρθὴν ὁδὸν ὥσπερ ἡγουμένου τινὸς
αὐταῖς ἀπιουσῶν, ἠκολούθουν οἱ τῶν Παλαιστίνων
ἄρχοντες, ποῦ ποτε στήσονται καὶ πρὸς τίνας
14 ἥξουσι βουλόμενοι μαθεῖν. κώμη δέ τίς ἐστι τῆς
Ἰούδα φυλῆς Βήθης[1] ὄνομα· εἰς ταύτην ἀφικνοῦνται
αἱ βόες, καὶ πεδίου μεγάλου καὶ καλοῦ τὴν
πορείαν αὐτῶν ἐκδεξαμένου παύονται προσωτέρω
χωρεῖν, στήσασαι τὴν ἅμαξαν αὐτόθι. θέα δὲ ἦν
τοῖς ἐν τῇ κώμῃ καὶ περιχαρεῖς ἐγένοντο· θέρους
γὰρ ὥρᾳ πάντες ἐπὶ τὴν συγκομιδὴν τῶν καρπῶν

---

[1] Βηθσάμη SP, Bethsamis Lat.

---

[a] Bibl. Beth-shemesh (LXX Βαιθσάμυς), modern 'Ain
Shems, on the border of Judah about 12 miles S.E. of Ekron.
330

country. Then, having placed these in a coffer and
set it upon the ark, they should make for this a new
wain, and should yoke thereto kine that had freshly
calved, and should shut up and retain the calves, in
order that these might not retard their mothers by
following them, and they, through yearning for their
young, might make the more speed upon their way.
Then having driven them, drawing the ark, out to a
place where three roads met, they should there leave
them, suffering them to take which of the roads they
would. Should the kine take the route to the Hebrews 9.
and mount into their country, they must regard the
ark as the cause of all these ills ; but should they
turn elsewhere, " then," said they, " let us pursue
after it, having learnt that it possesses no such
power."

(3) Judging this to have been well spoken, they Return of
straightway ratified the counsel by acting thereon. the ark to
Having made the objects aforesaid, they conducted shemesh.
the wain to the cross-roads, where they left it and 1 Sam.
retired. Then, seeing the kine go straight on, as vi. 10.
though someone were leading them, the lords of the
Philistines followed, fain to find out where they would
halt and to whom they would betake themselves.
Now there is a village of the tribe of Judah by name
Bethes [a] : thither it was that the kine came : a
great and beauteous plain awaited their footsteps [b]—
they would proceed no further but stayed the wagon
there. A sight was this for the villagers and they
were overcome with joy ; for it being the summer
season when all were out in the cornfields to gather

[b] " The cart came into the field of Joshua the Beth-
shemite," 1 Sam. vi. 14.

331

ἐν ταῖς ἀρούραις ὑπάρχοντες, ὡς εἶδον τὴν κιβωτόν, ὑφ᾽ ἡδονῆς ἁρπαγέντες καὶ τὸ ἔργον ἐκ τῶν
χειρῶν ἀφέντες ἔδραμον εὐθὺς ἐπὶ τὴν ἅμαξαν.
15 καὶ καθελόντες τὴν κιβωτὸν καὶ τὸ ἄγγος, ὃ τοὺς
ἀνδριάντας εἶχε καὶ τοὺς μύας, τιθέασιν ἐπί τινος
πέτρας, ἥτις ἦν ἐν τῷ πεδίῳ, καὶ θύσαντες λαμπρῶς
τῷ θεῷ καὶ κατευωχηθέντες τήν τε ἅμαξαν καὶ
τοὺς βόας ὡλοκαύτωσαν. καὶ ταῦτ᾽ ἰδόντες οἱ τῶν
Παλαιστίνων ἄρχοντες ἀνέστρεψαν ὀπίσω.

16   (4) Ὀργὴ δὲ καὶ χόλος τοῦ θεοῦ μέτεισιν ἑβδομήκοντα τῶν ἐκ τῆς Βήθης κώμης, οὓς[1] οὐκ
ὄντας ἀξίους ἅψασθαι τῆς κιβωτοῦ, ἱερεῖς γὰρ οὐκ
ἦσαν, καὶ προσελθόντας αὐτῇ βαλὼν ἀπέκτεινεν.
ἔκλαυσαν δὲ ταῦτα παθόντας αὐτοὺς οἱ κωμῆται,
καὶ πένθος ἐπ᾽ αὐτοῖς[2] ἤγειραν οἷον εἰκὸς ἐπὶ
θεοπέμπτῳ κακῷ καὶ τὸν ἴδιον ἕκαστος ἀπεθρήνει·
17 τοῦ τε μένειν τὴν κιβωτὸν παρ᾽ αὐτοῖς ἀναξίους
ἀποφαίνοντες αὐτοὺς καὶ πρὸς τὸ κοινὸν τῶν
Ἑβραίων πέμψαντες ἐδήλουν ἀποδεδόσθαι τὴν
κιβωτὸν ὑπὸ τῶν Παλαιστίνων. κἀκεῖνοι γνόντες
τοῦτο ἀποκομίζουσιν αὐτὴν εἰς Καριαθιαρεὶμ
18 γείτονα πόλιν τῆς Βήθης κώμης.[3] ἔνθα τινὸς
Λευίτου τὸ γένος Ἀμιναδάβου δόξαν ἔχοντος ἐπὶ
δικαιοσύνῃ καὶ θρησκείᾳ καταβιοῦντος εἰς οἰκίαν

---

[1] Niese: ὡς codd.   [2] edd.: αὐτοὺς codd.
[3] τῆς Β. κώμης] τοῖς Βηθσαμίταις M (Lat.): τοῖς Βηθάμης SP.

---

[a] " To Ekron," *ib.* 16.
[b] Bibl. " seventy men (and) fifty thousand men " (similarly
LXX); an impossible reading. The larger figure is commonly rejected as a gloss, from which, it appears, the Biblical
text of Josephus was free.
[c] Not in Scripture, which merely says that " they had
looked into (or rather " gazed upon ") the ark." For the

in the crops, so soon as they saw the ark, they were transported with delight and, dropping their work from their hands, ran straight for the wain. Then, having taken down the ark and the vessel containing the images and the mice, they set them upon a rock which stood in the plain, and, after offering splendid sacrifice to God and keeping merry feast, consumed wagon and kine as a burnt-offering. And, having seen all this, the lords of the Philistines turned back again.[a]

(4) Howbeit, the wrath and indignation of God visited seventy[b] of them of the village of Bethes, whom He smote and slew for approaching the ark, which, not being priests,[c] they were not privileged to touch. The villagers bewailed these victims, raising over them lamentation such as was fitting over a God-sent evil, and each man mourned for his own. Then, pronouncing themselves unworthy of retaining the ark among them, they sent word to the general assembly[d] of the Hebrews that the ark had been restored by the Philistines. And these, on hearing thereof, conveyed it away to Kariathiareim,[e] a neighbouring city of the village of Bethes; and since there lived there a man of the stock of Levi, Aminadab,[f] reputed for his righteousness and piety,

The penalty for touching the ark : its removal to the house of Aminadab.
1 Sam. vi.19.

vii. 1.

Rabbinical opinions concerning the nature of their crime see M. Weill's note.

[d] In Scripture (1 Sam. vi. 21) word is sent, not to all the Hebrews, but only to the inhabitants of Kiriath-jearim.

[e] So LXX: Heb. Kiriath-jearim, perhaps the modern *Kuryet el 'Enab*, some 9 miles N.E. of Beth-shemesh. Shiloh, the original home of the ark, was possibly now in Philistine hands.

[f] So LXX: Heb. Abinadab. Scripture does not say that he was a Levite. A Levite Aminadab, contemporary with David, is mentioned in 1 Chr. xv. 11.

τὴν κιβωτὸν ἤγαγον, ὥσπερ εἰς πρέποντα τῷ θεῷ
τόπον ἐν ᾧ κατῴκει δίκαιος ἄνθρωπος. ἐθεράπευον
δὲ τὴν κιβωτὸν οἱ τούτου παῖδες, καὶ τῆς ἐπιμελείας
ταύτης ἕως ἐτῶν εἴκοσι προέστησαν· τοσαῦτα
γὰρ ἔμεινεν ἐν τῇ Καριαθιαρεὶμ ποιήσασα παρὰ
τοῖς Παλαιστίνοις μῆνας τέσσαρας.

19 (ii. 1) Τοῦ δὲ λαοῦ παντὸς ἐκείνῳ τῷ χρόνῳ,
καθ' ὃν εἶχεν ἡ τῶν Καριαθιαριμιτῶν πόλις τὴν
κιβωτόν, ἐπ' εὐχὰς καὶ θυσίας τραπέντος τοῦ
θεοῦ καὶ πολλὴν ἐμφανίζοντος τὴν περὶ αὐτὸν
θρησκείαν καὶ φιλοτιμίαν, ὁ προφήτης Σαμουῆλος
ἰδὼν αὐτῶν τὴν προθυμίαν, ὡς εὔκαιρον ὂν[1] πρὸς
οὕτως ἔχοντας εἰπεῖν περὶ ἐλευθερίας καὶ τῶν
ἀγαθῶν τῶν ἐν αὐτῇ, χρῆται λόγοις οἷς ᾤετο
μάλιστα τὴν διάνοιαν αὐτῶν προσάξεσθαι καὶ
20 πείσειν. "ἄνδρες," γὰρ εἶπεν, "οἷς ἔτι νῦν βαρεῖς
μὲν πολέμιοι Παλαιστίνοι, θεὸς δ' εὐμενὴς ἄρχεται
γίνεσθαι καὶ φίλος, οὐκ ἐπιθυμεῖν ἐλευθερίας δεῖ
μόνον, ἀλλὰ καὶ ποιεῖν δι' ὧν ἂν ἔλθοι πρὸς
ὑμᾶς, οὐδὲ βούλεσθαι μὲν ἀπηλλάχθαι δεσποτῶν
ἐπιμένειν δὲ πράττοντας ἐξ ὧν οὗτοι διαμενοῦσιν.
21 ἀλλὰ γίνεσθε δίκαιοι, καὶ τὴν πονηρίαν ἐκ-
βαλόντες τῶν ψυχῶν καὶ θεραπεύοντες αὐτάς,[2]
ὅλαις ταῖς διανοίαις προστρέπεσθε[3] τὸ θεῖον καὶ
τιμῶντες διατελεῖτε· ταῦτα γὰρ ὑμῖν ποιοῦσιν
ἥξει τὰ ἀγαθά, δουλείας ἀπαλλαγὴ καὶ νίκη
πολεμίων, ἃ λαβεῖν οὔθ' ὅπλοις οὔτε σωμάτων

---

[1] conj. Niese.
[2] ex Lat. easque purgantes: καὶ θεραπεύοντες (-σαντες RO)
αὐτὴν codd.: καὶ θ. ἀρετὴν Weill.
[3] Hudson: προτρέπεσθε codd.

---

[a] Bibl. " Eleazar his son."

they brought the ark into his house, as to a place beseeming God, being the abode of a righteous man. This man's sons [a] tended the ark and had the charge of it for twenty years; for it remained all that time at Kariathiareim, after spending four months [b] among the Philistines.

(ii. 1) Now throughout the time when the city of Kariathiareim had the ark in its keeping, the whole people betook themselves to prayer and the offering of sacrifices to God, and displayed great zeal in serving Him. So the prophet Samuel, seeing their ardour and reckoning the occasion meet, while they were of this mind, to speak to them of liberty and the blessings that it brings, addressed them in words which he deemed most apt to win and to persuade their hearts. " Sirs," said he, " ye who yet to-day have grievous enemies in the Philistines, albeit God is beginning to be gracious to you and a friend, ye ought not to be content to yearn for liberty, but should do also the deeds whereby ye may attain it, nor merely long to be rid of your masters, while continuing so to act that they shall remain so. Nay, be ye righteous and, casting out wickedness [c] from your souls and purging them,[d] turn with all your hearts to the Deity and persevere in honouring Him. Do ye but so and there will come prosperity, deliverance from bondage and victory over your foes, blessings which are to be won neither by arms nor

Samuel exhorts the Hebrews and musters them to Mizpah.
1 Sam. vii. 2.

---

[b] Bibl. " seven months " (1 Sam. vi. 1).

[c] Bibl. " put away the strange gods and the Ashtaroth from among you " (vii. 3).

[d] Text a little doubtful : it has been proposed, by a slight change, to read " and cultivating virtue " ($\dot{\alpha}\rho\epsilon\tau\dot{\eta}\nu$ in place of $\alpha\dot{\upsilon}\tau\dot{\alpha}s$).

ἀλκαῖς οὔτε πλήθει συμμάχων δυνατόν ἐστιν· οὐ
γὰρ τούτοις ὁ θεὸς ὑπισχνεῖται παρέξειν αὐτά,
τῷ δ' ἀγαθοὺς εἶναι καὶ δικαίους· ἐγγυητὴς δὲ
22 αὐτοῦ τῶν ὑποσχέσεων ἐγὼ γίνομαι." ταῦτ' εἰπόντος ἐπευφήμησε τὸ πλῆθος ἡσθὲν τῇ παραινέσει
καὶ κατένευσεν αὐτὸ παρέξειν κεχαρισμένον τῷ
θεῷ. συνάγει δ' αὐτοὺς ὁ Σαμουῆλος εἴς τινα
πόλιν λεγομένην Μασφάτην· κατοπτευόμενον τοῦτο
σημαίνει κατὰ τὴν τῶν Ἑβραίων γλῶτταν· ἐντεῦθεν ὑδρευσάμενοί τε σπένδουσι τῷ θεῷ καὶ δια-
νηστεύσαντες ὅλην τὴν ἡμέραν ἐπ' εὐχὰς τρέπονται.
23 (2) Οὐ λανθάνουσι δὲ τοὺς Παλαιστίνους ἐκεῖ
συναχθέντες, ἀλλὰ μαθόντες οὗτοι τὴν ἄθροισιν
αὐτῶν, μεγάλῃ στρατιᾷ καὶ δυνάμει κατ' ἐλπίδα
τοῦ μὴ προσδοκῶσι μηδὲ παρεσκευασμένοις ἐπι-
24 πεσεῖσθαι τοῖς Ἑβραίοις ἐπέρχονται. καταπλήττει
δ' αὐτοὺς τοῦτο καὶ εἰς ταραχὴν ἄγει καὶ δέος,
καὶ δραμόντες πρὸς Σαμουῆλον, ἀναπεπτωκέναι
τὰς ψυχὰς αὐτῶν ὑπὸ φόβου καὶ τῆς προτέρας
ἥττης ἔφασκον καὶ διὰ τοῦτ' ἠρεμεῖν, "ἵνα μὴ
κινήσωμεν τὴν τῶν πολεμίων δύναμιν, σοῦ δ'
ἀναγαγόντος ἡμᾶς ἐπ' εὐχὰς καὶ θυσίας καὶ
ὅρκους γυμνοῖς καὶ ἀόπλοις ἐπεστράτευσαν οἱ
πολέμιοι· ἐλπὶς οὖν ἡμῖν οὐκ ἄλλη σωτηρίας, ἢ
μόνη ἡ παρὰ σοῦ καὶ τοῦ θεοῦ ἱκετευθέντος ὑπὸ

ᵃ Bibl. Mizpah (= " watch-tower," " outlook-point "),
LXX Μασ(σ)ηφάθ: identified by some scholars with modern
Neby Samwil, 5 miles N.W. of Jerusalem, by others with
Tell-en-Naṣbeh, about 8 miles due N. of Jerusalem.
ᵇ Or " a conspicuous (place)."
ᶜ Gr. " with a great army and strength," an instance
of hendiadys or the use of two words for one, which from

by personal prowess nor by a host of combatants ; for it is not for these that God promises to bestow those blessings, but for lives of virtue and righteousness. And as surety for His promises, here I take my stand." These words were acclaimed by the people, who were delighted with the exhortation and vowed to render themselves acceptable unto God. Samuel then vii. 5. gathered them to a city called Masphate,[a] which in the Hebrew tongue signifies "espied." [b] There, having drawn water, they made libations to God and, fasting throughout the day, gave themselves unto prayer.

(2) However their gathering at this spot did not Hebrew pass unperceived by the Philistines, who, having victory learnt of their mustering, advanced upon the Hebrews over the with an army mighty in strength,[c] hoping to sur- Philistines. prise them while off their guard and unprepared. 1 Sam. vii. 7. Dismayed by this attack and plunged into confusion and alarm, the Hebrews, hastening to Samuel, declared that their courage had flagged through fear and the memory of their former defeat. "That," said they, "was why we sat still, in order not to stir up the enemy's forces. But, when thou hadst brought us up hither for prayers, sacrifices and oaths, now the enemy are upon us while we are naked and unarmed. Other hope of salvation therefore have we none, save from thee alone and from God, should He be entreated

this point onward characterizes this book : cf. § 24 ταραχὴ καὶ δέος, γυμνοῖς καὶ ἀόπλοις, § 25 νίκη καὶ κράτος etc. The preference for the double word distinguishes the writer of this portion—whether Josephus himself or another assistant —from the " Sophoclean " assistant who has a partiality for grouping in threes (e.g. § 21 τὰ ἀγαθά, δουλείας ἀπαλλαγὴ καὶ νίκη . . . οὔθ' ὅπλοις οὔτε σωμάτων ἀλκαῖς οὔτε πλήθει). See Vol. IV. Introduction.

25 σοῦ παρασχεῖν ἡμῖν διαφυγεῖν Παλαιστίνους.'' ὁ
δὲ θαρρεῖν τε προτρέπεται καὶ βοηθήσειν αὐτοῖς
τὸν θεὸν ἐπαγγέλλεται, καὶ λαβὼν ἄρνα γαλαθηνὸν
ὑπὲρ τῶν ὄχλων θύει καὶ παρακαλεῖ τὸν θεὸν
ὑπερσχεῖν αὐτῶν τὴν δεξιὰν ἐν τῇ πρὸς Παλαιστίνους μάχῃ καὶ μὴ περιϊδεῖν αὐτοὺς δεύτερον δυσ-
τυχήσαντας. ἐπήκοος δὲ γίνεται τῶν εὐχῶν ὁ
θεὸς καὶ προσδεξάμενος εὐμενεῖ καὶ συμμάχῳ τῇ
διανοίᾳ τὴν θυσίαν ἐπινεύει νίκην αὐτοῖς καὶ
26 κράτος. ἔτι δ' ἐπὶ τοῦ βωμοῦ τὴν θυσίαν ἔχοντος
τοῦ θεοῦ καὶ μήπω πᾶσαν διὰ τῆς ἱερᾶς φλογὸς
ἀπειληφότος, προῆλθεν ἐκ τοῦ στρατοπέδου ἡ τῶν
πολεμίων δύναμις καὶ παρατάσσεται εἰς μάχην,
ἐπ' ἐλπίδι μὲν νίκης, ὡς ἀπειλημμένων ἐν ἀπορίᾳ
τῶν Ἰουδαίων μήτε ὅπλα ἐχόντων μήτε ὡς ἐπὶ
μάχῃ ἐκεῖσε ἀπηντηκότων, περιπίπτουσι δὲ οἷς
27 οὐδ' εἰ προύλεγέ τις ῥᾳδίως ἐπείσθησαν. πρῶτον
μὲν γὰρ αὐτοὺς ὁ θεὸς κλονεῖ σεισμῷ καὶ τὴν
γῆν αὐτοῖς ὑπότρομον καὶ σφαλερὰν κινήσας τίθησιν, ὡς σαλευομένης τε τὰς βάσεις ὑποφέρεσθαι
καὶ διϊσταμένης εἰς ἔνια τῶν χασμάτων καταφέρε-
σθαι, ἔπειτα βρονταῖς καταψοφήσας καὶ διαπύροις
ἀστραπαῖς ὡς καταφλέξων αὐτῶν τὰς ὄψεις
περιλάμψας καὶ τῶν χειρῶν ἐκκροτήσας τὰ ὅπλα,
28 γυμνοὺς εἰς φυγὴν ἀπέστρεψεν. ἐπεξέρχεται δὲ
Σαμουῆλος μετὰ τῆς πληθύος καὶ πολλοὺς κατα-
σφάξας κατακολουθεῖ μέχρι Κορραίων τόπου τινὸς
οὕτω λεγομένου, καὶ καταπήξας ἐκεῖ λίθον ὥσπερ

---

[a] Gr. " God still had the sacrifice upon the altar " etc. ;
a Semitic form of expression (sacrifice being conceived as
the food of the Deity) here imported into the Biblical text,
which has merely " And as Samuel was offering up the
burnt-offering."

by thee to afford us escape from the Philistines."
But Samuel bade them be of good cheer and promised
that God would succour them. Then, taking a sucking lamb, he sacrificed it on behalf of the throng and
besought God to extend His right hand over them in
the battle with the Philistines and not suffer them to
undergo a second reverse. And God hearkened to
his prayers and, accepting the sacrifice in gracious
and befriending spirit, gave them assurance of victory
and triumph. God's victim was still upon the altar vii. 10.
and He had not yet wholly consumed it through the
sacred flame,[a] when the enemy's forces issued from
their camp and drew up for battle, expectant of
victory, thinking to have caught the Jews [b] in a hopeless plight, seeing that they were without arms and
had assembled there with no intention of battle. But
the Philistines encountered what, had one foretold
it, they would scarcely have believed. For, first,
God vexed them with earthquake,[c] rocking and making tremulous and treacherous the ground beneath
them, so that from its reeling their footsteps staggered
and at its parting they were engulfed in sundry of
its chasms. Next He deafened them with thunder-
claps, made fiery lightning to flash around them as
it were to burn out their eyes, struck the arms from
their hands, and so turned them weaponless to flight.
But Samuel now rushed upon them with his people
and, having massacred many, pursued them to a
certain place called Korraea[d]; and there he set up

---

[b] A recurrent anachronism for " Hebrews " or " Israelites " (§§ 30, 40 etc.).
[c] Scripture mentions only " a great thunder."
[d] Bibl. Beth-car, lxx Βαιθχόρ : possibly modern '*Ain
Karim*, some 5 miles S. of Mizpah, and due W. of Jerusalem.

ὅρον τῆς νίκης καὶ τῆς φυγῆς τῶν πολεμίων,
ἰσχυρὸν αὐτὸν προσαγορεύει, σύμβολον τῆς παρὰ
τοῦ θεοῦ γενομένης αὐτοῖς κατὰ τῶν ἐχθρῶν
ἰσχύος.

29 (3) Οἱ δὲ μετ' ἐκείνην τὴν πληγὴν οὐκέτ' ἐστράτευσαν[1] ἐπὶ τοὺς Ἰσραηλίτας, ἀλλ' ὑπὸ δέους καὶ
μνήμης τῶν συμβεβηκότων ἡσύχαζον· ὃ δ' ἦν
πάλαι θάρσος τοῖς Παλαιστίνοις ἐπὶ τοὺς Ἑβραί-
30 ους, τοῦτ' ἐκείνων μετὰ τὴν νίκην ἐγένετο. καὶ
Σαμουῆλος στρατεύσας ἐπ' αὐτοὺς ἀναιρεῖ πολλοὺς
καὶ τὰ φρονήματ' αὐτῶν εἰς τὸ παντελὲς ταπεινοῖ
καὶ τὴν χώραν ἀφαιρεῖται, ἣν τῶν Ἰουδαίων
ἀπετέμοντο πρότερον κρατήσαντες τῇ μάχῃ· αὕτη
δ' ἦν μέχρι πόλεως Ἀκκάρων ἀπὸ τῶν τῆς Γίττης
ὅρων ἐκτεταμένη. ἦν δὲ κατ' ἐκεῖνον τὸν καιρὸν
φίλια τοῖς Ἰσραηλίταις τὰ ὑπολειπόμενα τῶν
Χαναναίων.

31 (iii. 1) Ὁ δὲ προφήτης Σαμουῆλος διακοσμήσας
τὸν λαὸν καὶ πόλιν ἑκάστοις[2] ἀποδοὺς εἰς ταύτην
ἐκέλευσε συνερχομένοις περὶ τῶν πρὸς ἀλλήλους
κρίνεσθαι διαφορῶν, αὐτὸς δὲ δι' ἔτους[3] ἐπ-
ερχόμενος τὰς πόλεις ἐδίκαζεν αὐτοῖς καὶ πολλὴν
32 ἐβράβευεν εὐνομίαν ἐπὶ χρόνον πολύν. (2) ἔπειθ'
ὑπὸ γήρως βαρυνόμενος καὶ τὰ συνήθη πράττειν
ἐμποδιζόμενος, τοῖς υἱοῖς τὴν ἀρχὴν καὶ τὴν προ-

---

[1] οὐκέτ' ἐστράτ. Niese: οὐκ ἐπεστράτευσαν codd.
[2] conj.: αὐτοῖς codd.
[3] δι' ἔτους RO: δὶς τοῦ ἔτους rell., Lat., E (vid.).

---

[a] Bibl. Eben-'ezer (="stone of help"), LXX Ἀβενέζερ
(adding the translation λίθος τοῦ βοηθοῦ, "stone of the
helper"); in place of 'ezer Josephus probably read 'oz
("strength").

340

a stone as landmark of the victory and of the flight of the foe, and called it " Strong (stone)," [a] in token of the strength which God had lent them against their enemies.

(3) Those enemies, after that discomfiture, invaded the Israelites no more, but through fear and a remembrance of what had befallen them remained still ; and that confidence which of old had animated the Philistines against the Hebrews passed after this victory to their opponents. And so Samuel, taking the field against them, slew multitudes, utterly humbled their pride, and took from them the country which they had erstwhile torn from the Jews after their victory in battle, to wit the region extending from the borders of Gitta to the city of Akkaron.[b] And at that time there was amity between the Israelites and the remnant of the Canaanites.[c]

(iii. 1) Moreover, the prophet Samuel, having re-divided the people and assigned a city to each group,[d] bade them resort thither for trial of the differences that arose between them. He himself going annually [e] on circuit to these cities judged their causes and so continued for long to administer perfect justice.

(2) Thereafter, oppressed with age and impeded from following his wonted course, he consigned the

Samuel recovers territory. Sam. vii. 13.

Samuel as judge. 1 Sam. vii. 15.

Degeneracy of Samuel's sons.

[b] *i.e.* " from Ekron even unto Gath " (1 Sam. vii. 14).

[c] Bibl. " And there was peace between Israel and the Amorites."

[d] With slight emendation of the Greek, which reads " a city to them." Scripture mentions three cities—Bethel, Gilgal, Mizpah—which Samuel annually visited from his home at Ramah.

[e] Another reading is " *twice* a year." M. Weill, adopting this text, suggests that it is " a Haggadic deduction from the repetition of the word *shanah* (year) in the Hebrew (LXX κατ᾽ ἐνιαυτὸν ἐνιαυτόν)."

στασίαν τοῦ ἔθνους[1] παραδίδωσιν, ὧν ὁ μὲν
πρεσβύτερος Ἰοῦλος[2] προσηγορεύετο, τῷ δὲ νεω-
τέρῳ Ἀβίρα[3] ὄνομα ἦν. προσέταξε δὲ τὸν μὲν ἐν
Βεθήλῳ πόλει καθεζόμενον κρίνειν, τὸν δ' ἕτερον
ἐν Βερσουβεὶ[4] μερίσας τὸν ὑπακουσόμενον ἑκατέρῳ
33 λαόν. ἐγένοντο δὲ σαφὲς οὗτοι παράδειγμα καὶ
τεκμήριον τοῦ μὴ τὸν τρόπον ὁμοίους τοῖς φύσασι
γίνεσθαί τινας, ἀλλὰ τάχα μὲν χρηστοὺς καὶ
μετρίους ἐκ πονηρῶν, τότε μέν γε φαύλους ἐξ
34 ἀγαθῶν παρέσχον αὐτοὺς γενομένους· τῶν γὰρ τοῦ
πατρὸς ἐπιτηδευμάτων ἐκτραπόμενοι καὶ τὴν
ἐναντίαν ὁδὸν ἀπελθόντες δώρων καὶ λημμάτων
αἰσχρῶν καθυφίεντο τὸ δίκαιον, καὶ τὰς κρίσεις οὐ
πρὸς τὴν ἀλήθειαν ἀλλὰ πρὸς τὸ κέρδος ποιούμενοι καὶ πρὸς τρυφὴν καὶ πρὸς διαίτας πολυτελεῖς
ἀπονενευκότες, πρῶτον μὲν ὑπεναντία ταῦτα ἔπρασ-
σον τῷ θεῷ, δεύτερον δὲ τῷ προφήτῃ πατρὶ δ'
ἑαυτῶν, ὃς πολλὴν καὶ τοῦ τὸ πλῆθος εἶναι δίκαιον
σπουδὴν εἰσεφέρετο καὶ πρόνοιαν.
35 (3) Ὁ δὲ λαὸς ἐξυβριζόντων εἰς τὴν προτέραν
κατάστασιν καὶ πολιτείαν τῶν τοῦ προφήτου
παίδων, χαλεπῶς τε τοῖς πραττομένοις ἔφερε καὶ
πρὸς αὐτὸν συντρέχουσι, διέτριβε δ' ἐν Ἀρμαθᾷ
πόλει, καὶ τάς τε τῶν υἱῶν παρανομίας ἔλεγον καὶ
ὅτι γηραιὸς ὢν αὐτὸς ἤδη καὶ παρειμένος ὑπὸ τοῦ
χρόνου τῶν πραγμάτων οὐκέτι τὸν αὐτὸν προ-
36 εστάναι δύναται τρόπον· ἐδέοντό τε καὶ ἱκέτευον
ἀποδεῖξαί τινα αὐτῶν βασιλέα, ὃς ἄρξει τοῦ ἔθνους
καὶ τιμωρήσεται Παλαιστίνους ὀφείλοντας ἔτ' αὐ-

---

[1] RO: πλήθους rell.   [2] RO: Οὔηλος vel Ἰώηλος (Ἰωήλ) rell.
[3] M(SP): Ἐβία RO: Ἀβίας E Lat.: Ἀβία Zon.
[4] Βαρσουβαὶ MSP: Bersabe Lat.

government and direction of the nation to his sons, 1 Sam.
of whom the elder was called Iulus *a* and the younger viii. 1.
bore the name of Abira *b* ; and he charged the one
to sit in judgement at the city of Bethel and the
other at Bersubei,*c* apportioning the people that
should come under the jurisdiction of each. Howbeit
these youths furnished a signal illustration and proof
that sons need not be like in character to their sires,
nay, that maybe good, honest folk are sprung from
knaves, while the offspring of virtuous parents have
proved depraved.   For they, turning from their
father's ways and taking the contrary road, betrayed
justice for bribes and filthy lucre, pronounced judgement with regard not to the truth but to their own
profit, and abandoned themselves to luxury and
sumptuous fare, thereby acting in defiance first of
God and secondly of the prophet, their own father,
who was devoting much zeal and care to instilling
even into the multitude the idea of righteousness.

(3) But the people,*d* seeing these outrages upon The people's
their former constitution and government committed demand for
by the prophet's sons, brooked their proceedings ill 1 Sam.
and together sped to Samuel, then living in the city viii. 4.
of Armatha.*e* They told him of his sons' iniquities
and added that, old as he now was and enfeebled
by age, he could no longer himself direct affairs as
aforetime ; they therefore begged and implored him
to appoint from among them a king, to rule the
nation and to wreak vengeance on the Philistines,

a Bibl. Joel.
b Bibl. Abijah (lxx 'Aβιά, with *v.l.* 'Aβειρά as in Josephus).
c Bibl. "They were judges in Beer-sheba" (Bethel not
being mentioned).
d Bibl. " all the elders of Israel."
e Ramah.

τοῖς δίκας τῶν προτέρων ἀδικημάτων. ἐλύπησαν
δὲ σφόδρα τὸν Σαμουῆλον οἱ λόγοι διὰ τὴν σύμ-
φυτον δικαιοσύνην καὶ τὸ πρὸς τοὺς βασιλέας μῖσος·
ἥττητο γὰρ δεινῶς τῆς ἀριστοκρατίας ὡς θείας καὶ
μακαρίους ποιούσης τοὺς χρωμένους αὐτῆς τῇ
37 πολιτείᾳ. ὑπὸ δὲ φροντίδος καὶ βασάνου τῆς ἐπὶ
τοῖς εἰρημένοις οὔτε τροφῆς ἐμνημόνευσεν οὔτε
ὕπνου, δι' ὅλης δὲ τῆς νυκτὸς στρέφων τὰς περὶ
τῶν πραγμάτων ἐννοίας διεκαρτέρει.

38 (4) Ἔχοντι δὲ οὕτως ἐμφανίζεται τὸ θεῖον καὶ
παραμυθεῖται μὴ δυσφορεῖν ἐφ' οἷς ἠξίωσε τὸ
πλῆθος, ὡς οὐκ ἐκεῖνον ὑπερηφανήσαντας ἀλλ'
ἑαυτόν,[1] ἵνα[2] μὴ βασιλεύσῃ[3] μόνος· ταῦτα δὲ ἀφ' ἧς
ἡμέρας ἐξήγαγεν αὐτοὺς ἀπ' Αἰγύπτου μηχανᾶσθαι
τὰ ἔργα· λήψεσθαι μέντοι γε οὐκ εἰς μακρὰν
μετάνοιαν αὐτοὺς ἐπίπονον, "ὑφ' ἧς οὐδὲν μὲν
ἀγένητον ἔσται τῶν ἐσομένων, ἐλεγχθήσονται δὲ
καταφρονήσαντες καὶ βουλὰς οὐκ εὐχαρίστους πρὸς
39 ἐμὲ καὶ τὴν σὴν προφητείαν λαβόντες. κελεύω δή
σε[4] χειροτονεῖν αὐτοῖς ὃν ἂν ἐγὼ[5] προείπω βασιλέα
προδηλώσαντα ποταπῶν τε πειραθήσονται βασι-
λευόμενοι κακῶν καὶ διαμαρτυράμενον ἐφ' οἵαν
σπεύδουσι μεταβολήν."

40 (5) Ταῦτ' ἀκούσας Σαμουῆλος ἅμα ἔῳ συγκαλέσας τοὺς Ἰουδαίους ἀποδείξειν αὐτοῖς βασιλέα
ὡμολόγησεν, ἔφη δὲ δεῖν πρῶτον μὲν αὐτοῖς
ἐκδιηγήσασθαι τὰ παρὰ τῶν βασιλέων ἐσόμενα καὶ
ὅσοις συνενεχθήσονται κακοῖς· "γινώσκετε γὰρ

---

[1] ἢ αὐτόν SP: εἰς αὐτόν E: αὐτόν M.   [2] εἰ RO.
[3] βασιλεύσει R: βασιλεὺς ᾖ SP.
[4] σοι SE.   [5] +σοι SPE.

who yet owed them an accounting for past injuries. These words sorely grieved Samuel by reason of his innate righteousness and his hatred of kings; for he was keenly enamoured of aristocratic government, accounting it divine and productive of bliss to those who adopted it. So, from the anxiety and the torment which these speeches caused him, he had no thought for food or sleep, but passed the whole night turning over these matters in his mind.[a]

(4) Such was his state when the Deity appeared and consoled him, telling him not to take these demands of the multitude amiss, since it was not him whom they had spurned, but God Himself, not wishing Him to reign alone; these deeds, moreover, they had (He said) been devising from the day when He had brought them forth from Egypt; howbeit they would ere long be seized with painful remorse, "a remorse by which nought will be undone of that which is to be, but which will convict them of contempt and of adopting a course ungrateful toward Me and to thy prophetic office. I therefore now charge thee to elect for them whomsoever I shall name as king, after forewarning them what ills they will suffer under kingly rule and solemnly testifying into what a change they are rushing."

God charges Samuel to elect a king. 1 Sam. viii. 7.

(5) Having heard these words, Samuel at daybreak called the Jews[b] together and consented to appoint them a king, but he said that he must first set forth to them what would befall them at the hands of their kings and how many ills they would encounter. "For ye must know," said he, "that first they will

Samuel warns the people of the evils of monarchy. 1 Sam. viii. 10.

---

[a] Amplification (cf. A. ii. 171): Scripture says merely "And Samuel prayed unto the Lord" (1 Sam. viii. 6).
[b] See § 26 note.

ὅτι πρῶτον μὲν ὑμῶν ἀποσπάσουσι τὰ τέκνα καὶ
τὰ μὲν αὐτῶν ἁρματηλάτας εἶναι κελεύσουσι, τοὺς
δ᾽ ἱππεῖς καὶ σωματοφύλακας, δρομεῖς δὲ ἄλλους
καὶ χιλιάρχους καὶ ἑκατοντάρχους, ποιήσουσι δὲ
καὶ τεχνίτας ὁπλοποιοὺς καὶ ἁρματοποιοὺς καὶ
ὀργάνων τέκτονας γεωργούς τε καὶ τῶν ἰδίων
41 ἀγρῶν ἐπιμελητὰς καὶ σκαπανεῖς ἀμπέλων, καὶ
οὐδέν ἐστιν ὃ μὴ κελευόμενοι ποιήσουσιν ἀνδρα-
πόδων ἀργυρωνήτων τρόπον· καὶ τὰς θυγατέρας δ᾽
ὑμῶν μυρεψοὺς ἀποφανοῦσι καὶ ὀψοποιοὺς καὶ
σιτοποιούς, καὶ πᾶν ἔργον ὃ θεραπαινίδες ἐξ
ἀνάγκης πληγὰς φοβούμεναι καὶ βασάνους ὑπ-
ηρετήσουσι. κτῆσιν δὲ τὴν ὑμετέραν ἀφαιρήσονται
καὶ ταύτην εὐνούχοις καὶ σωματοφύλαξι δωρήσονται
καὶ βοσκημάτων ἀγέλας τοῖς αὐτῶν προσνεμοῦσι.
42 συνελόντι δ᾽ εἰπεῖν, δουλεύσετε μετὰ πάντων τῶν
ὑμετέρων τῷ βασιλεῖ σὺν[1] τοῖς αὐτῶν οἰκέταις·
ὃς γενόμενος[2] μνήμην ὑμῖν τῶνδε τῶν λόγων
γεννήσει καὶ τῷ[3] πάσχειν αὐτὰ μεταγινώσκοντας
ἱκετεῦσαι τὸν θεὸν ἐλεῆσαί τε ὑμᾶς καὶ δωρή-
σασθαι ταχεῖαν ἀπαλλαγὴν τῶν βασιλέων· ὁ δ᾽ οὐ
προσδέξεται τὰς δεήσεις, ἀλλὰ παραπέμψας ἐάσει
δίκην ὑποσχεῖν ὑμᾶς τῆς αὐτῶν κακοβουλίας.''
43 (6) Ἦν δ᾽ ἄρα καὶ πρὸς τὰς προρρήσεις τῶν
συμβησομένων ἀνόητον τὸ πλῆθος καὶ δύσκολον
ἐξελεῖν τῆς διανοίας κρίσιν ἤδη παρὰ τῷ λογισμῷ
καθιδρυμένην· οὐδὲ γὰρ ἐπεστράφησαν οὐδ᾽ ἐμέλη-

---

[1] καὶ MSP: om. Lat.
[2] ὃς γενόμενος] ἴσοι γενόμενοι M Lat. (+ καὶ Lat. ut vid.).
[3] τὸ ROSP.

---

[a] "Hundreds" as in lxx (1 Sam. viii. 12), whereas the
Heb. has "fifties."

carry off your children and will order some of them
to be charioteers, others horsemen and bodyguards,
others runners or captains of thousands or of hundreds [a]; they will make of them craftsmen also,
makers of armour, of chariots and of instruments;
husbandmen, too, tillers of their estates, diggers of
their vineyards; nay, there is nothing which your
sons will not do at their behest, after the manner of
slaves bought at a price. Of your daughters also
they will make perfumers, cooks and bakers, and
subject them to every menial task which handmaids
must perforce perform from fear of stripes and
tortures. They will moreover rob you of your
possessions and bestow them upon eunuchs and
bodyguards, and confer your herds of cattle upon their
retainers. In a word, ye with all yours will be bond-
servants to the king along with your own domestics;
and he, when he is come,[b] will beget in you a memory
of these words of mine and (cause you) through these
sufferings to repent and to implore God to take pity
on you and to grant you speedy deliverance from
your kings. Howbeit He will not hearken to your
prayers, but will disregard them and suffer you to
pay the penalty for your own perversity."

(6) Yet even to these predictions of what was to
come the multitude was deaf and obstinately refused [c]
to eradicate from their minds a resolution now deep-
seated in their calculations. Nay, they would not be
turned, nor recked they aught of the words of Samuel,

He yields
to their
insistence.
1 Sam.
viii. 19.

[b] Text doubtful. According to another reading, " . . . to
the king, being made equal to your own domestics; and
your suffering will beget, etc., . . . and (cause you) to
repent, etc."
[c] Or " and it was difficult."

σεν αὐτοῖς τῶν Σαμουήλου λόγων, ἀλλ' ἐνέκειντο
λιπαρῶς καὶ χειροτονεῖν ἠξίουν ἤδη τὸν βασιλέα
44 καὶ μὴ φροντίζειν τῶν ἐσομένων· ἐπὶ γὰρ τιμωρίᾳ
τῶν ἐχθρῶν ἀνάγκη τὸν πολεμήσοντα σὺν αὐτοῖς
ἔχειν, καὶ οὐδὲν ἄτοπον εἶναι τῶν πλησιοχώρων
βασιλευομένων τὴν αὐτὴν ἔχειν αὐτοὺς πολιτείαν.
ὁρῶν δ' αὐτοὺς μηδ' ὑπὸ τῶν προειρημένων
ἀπεστραμμένους ὁ Σαμουῆλος, ἀλλ' ἐπιμένοντας
"νῦν μέν," εἶπεν, "ἄπιτε πρὸς αὐτοὺς ἕκαστος,
μεταπέμψομαι δὲ ὑμᾶς εἰς δέον, ὅταν μάθω παρὰ
τοῦ θεοῦ τίνα δίδωσιν ὑμῖν βασιλέα."
45 (iv. 1) Ἦν δέ τις ἐκ τῆς Βενιαμίτιδος φυλῆς
ἀνὴρ εὖ γεγονὼς καὶ ἀγαθὸς τὸ ἦθος, Κεὶς ὄνομα·
τούτῳ παῖς ὑπῆρχεν, ἦν δὲ νεανίας τὴν μορφὴν
ἄριστος καὶ τὸ σῶμα μέγας, τό τε φρόνημα καὶ τὴν
46 διάνοιαν ἀμείνων τῶν βλεπομένων· Σαοῦλον αὐτὸν
ἐκάλουν. οὗτος ὁ Κεὶς, ὄνων αὐτῷ ἐκ τῆς νομῆς
καλῶν ἀποπλανηθεισῶν, ἥδετο γὰρ αὐταῖς ὡς
οὐκ ἄλλῳ τινὶ τῶν κτημάτων, τὸν υἱὸν μεθ' ἑνὸς
θεράποντος ἐπὶ ζήτησιν τῶν κτηνῶν ἐξέπεμψεν·
ὁ δ' ἐπεὶ τὴν πάτριον περιῆλθε φυλὴν ἐξερευνῶν
τὰς ὄνους¹ εἰς τὰς ἄλλας ἀφίκετο, οὐδ' ἐν ταύταις
δ' ἐπιτυχὼν ἀπιέναι² διεγνώκει, μὴ ποιήσῃ περὶ
47 αὐτοῦ τῷ πατρὶ λοιπὸν φροντίδα. τοῦ δ' ἑπομένου
θεράποντος ὡς ἐγένοντο κατὰ τὴν Ἀρμαθὰ πόλιν
εἶναι προφήτην ἐν αὐτῇ φήσαντος ἀληθῆ καὶ πρὸς
αὐτὸν βαδίζειν συμβουλεύσαντος, γνώσεσθαι γὰρ
παρ' αὐτοῦ τὸ περὶ τῶν ὄνων τέλος, οὐθὲν ἔχειν

¹ ἐξερ. τ. ὄνους om. RO.   ² ἀνιέναι conj. Boysen.

but pressed him importunately and insisted that he should elect their king forthwith, and take no thought for the future ; since for the punishment of their foes they must needs have one to fight their battles with them, and there could be nothing strange, when their neighbours were ruled by kings, in their having the same form of government. So Samuel, seeing that even by his predictions they were not turned from their intent but persisted therein, said, " For the present, depart ye each to his home : I will summon you at need, when I shall have learnt from God whom He gives you for your king."

(iv. 1) Now there was a man of the tribe of Benjamin of good birth and virtuous character, named Kis.[a] He had a son, a youth of a noble presence and tall of stature, and withal gifted with a spirit and mind surpassing these outward advantages ; they called him Saul. This Kis, one day when some fine asses of his had strayed from the pastures, in which he took more delight than in all that he possessed, sent off his son with one servant in search of the beasts. And he, after going all over his father's tribe in quest of the asses, passed to the other tribes and failing there also to find them, resolved to return, lest he should now cause his father anxiety concerning himself. But when they were come over against the city of Armatha,[b] the servant who accompanied him told him that there was there a true prophet, and counselled that they should go to him, since they would learn from him what had become of the asses. Whereto

SAUL, in
quest of his
father's
asses,
encounters
Samuel.
1 Sam. ix. 1.

---

[b] Ramah (v. 342 note, vi. 35): bibl. " when they were come to the land of Zuph " (1 Sam. ix. 5), naming the district in Ephraim wherein Ramah lay, cf. 1 Sam. i. 1 " a certain man of Ramathaim-zophim."

πορευθέντας εἶπεν ἀντὶ τῆς προφητείας ὃ παρά-
σχωσιν αὐτῷ· κεκενῶσθαι γὰρ ἤδη τῶν ἐφοδίων.
48 τοῦ δ' οἰκέτου τέταρτον αὐτῷ παρεῖναι σίκλου
φήσαντος καὶ τοῦτο δώσειν, ὑπὸ γὰρ ἀγνοίας τοῦ
μὴ λαμβάνειν τὸν προφήτην μισθὸν ἐπλανῶντο,
παραγίνονται καὶ πρὸς ταῖς πύλαις παρατυγχά-
νοντες παρθένοις ἐφ' ὕδωρ βαδιζούσαις ἐρωτῶσιν
αὐτὰς τοῦ προφήτου τὴν οἰκίαν. αἱ δὲ σημαίνουσι
καὶ σπεύδειν παρεκελεύσαντο πρὶν αὐτὸν εἰς τὸ
δεῖπνον κατακλιθῆναι· πολλοὺς γὰρ ἑστιᾶν καὶ
49 προκατακλίνεσθαι τῶν κεκλημένων. ὁ δὲ Σαμουῆλος διὰ τοῦτο πολλοὺς ἐπὶ τὴν ἑστίαν τότε
συνήγαγε· δεομένῳ γὰρ κατὰ πᾶσαν ἡμέραν αὐτῷ
τοῦ θεοῦ προειπεῖν τίνα ποιήσει βασιλέα τῇ
παρελθούσῃ τοῦτον μηνύσαντος, πέμψειν γὰρ
αὐτός τινα νεανίσκον ἐκ τῆς Βενιαμίτιδος φυλῆς
κατὰ τήνδε τὴν ὥραν, αὐτὸς μὲν ἐπὶ τοῦ δώ-
ματος καθεζόμενος ἐξεδέχετο τὸν καιρὸν γενέσθαι,
πληρωθέντος δ' αὐτοῦ καταβὰς ἐπὶ τὸ δεῖπνον
50 ἐπορεύετο. συναντᾷ δὲ τῷ Σαούλῳ καὶ ὁ θεὸς
αὐτῷ σημαίνει τοῦτον εἶναι τὸν ἄρξειν μέλλοντα.
Σαοῦλος δὲ πρόσεισι τῷ Σαμουήλῳ καὶ προσ-
αγορεύσας ἐδεῖτο μηνύειν τὴν οἰκίαν τοῦ προφήτου·
51 ξένος γὰρ ὢν ἀγνοεῖν ἔφασκε. τοῦ δὲ Σαμουήλου
αὐτὸν εἶναι φράσαντος καὶ ἄγοντος ἐπὶ τὸ δεῖπνον,
ὡς τῶν ὄνων ἐφ' ὧν τὴν ζήτησιν ἐκπεμφθείη
σεσωσμένων τά τε πάντα ἀγαθὰ ἔχειν αὐτῷ
κεκυρωμένα, ὑποτυχών[1] "ἀλλ' ἥττων," εἶπεν,
"ἐγώ, δέσποτα, ταύτης τῆς ἐλπίδος καὶ φυλῆς

---

[1] Holwerda: προστυχών codd.

---

[a] Scripture does not say that Samuel accepted no reward.

Saul replied that, if they went to the prophet, they had nothing to offer him in return for his oracle, since their supplies were by now exhausted. However, the servant said that he had a quarter of a shekel and would present that—for their ignorance that the prophet accepted no reward misled them [a]—and so they went and, meeting at the gates maidens going to draw water, they asked them which was the prophet's house. And these pointed it out and bade them make speed ere he sat down to supper, for he was entertaining many and would take his seat before his invited guests.[b] Now the reason why Samuel had at that hour assembled so many to the feast was this : he had been praying daily to God to reveal to him whom He would make king and, on the day before, God had announced him, saying that He would Himself send him a young man of the tribe of Benjamin at that selfsame hour. So, seated upon the housetop, Samuel was awaiting the coming of the time, and when the hour was ripe he descended to go to the supper. And he met Saul, and God revealed to him that this was he that was to rule. But Saul approached Samuel and greeting him prayed him to show him the prophet's house, for he said that as a stranger he was ignorant of it. Samuel then told him that he was the prophet and led him to the supper, assuring him that the asses in quest of which he had been sent were safe and that for him (Saul) were destined all good things[c]; whereat Saul broke in, " Nay, master, I am too lowly to hope for this, I come of a

[b] According to Scripture, Samuel was not the host, but attended the feast as one in charge of public sacrifice.

[c] The text is a little awkward. but the meaning is clear. *Cf.* 1 Sam. ix. 20, " To whom belong all the desirable things of Israel, if not to thee (Saul) and thy father's house ? "

μικροτέρας ἢ βασιλέας ποιεῖν καὶ πατριᾶς ταπει-
νοτέρας τῶν ἄλλων πατριῶν. σὺ δὲ παίζεις καὶ
γέλωτά με τίθεσαι περὶ μειζόνων ἢ κατὰ τὴν
52 ἐμὴν χώραν¹ διαλεγόμενος.'' ὁ δὲ προφήτης ἀγαγὼν αὐτὸν ἐπὶ τὴν ἑστίασιν κατακλίνει καὶ τὸν
ἀκόλουθον ἐπάνω τῶν κεκλημένων· οὗτοι δ' ἦσαν
ἑβδομήκοντα τὸν ἀριθμόν· προστάσσει δὲ τοῖς
διακόνοις παραθεῖναι τῷ Σαούλῳ μερίδα βασιλικήν.
ἐπεὶ δὲ κοίτης ὥρα προσῆγεν, οἱ μὲν ἀναστάντες
ἀνέλυον πρὸς αὑτοὺς ἕκαστοι, ὁ δὲ Σαοῦλος παρὰ
τῷ προφήτῃ σὺν τῷ θεράποντι κατεκοιμήθη.
53 (2) Ἅμα δὲ ἡμέρα Σαμουῆλος ἀναστήσας αὐτὸν
ἐκ τῆς κοίτης προύπεμπε καὶ γενόμενος ἔξω τῆς
πόλεως ἐκέλευσε τὸν μὲν θεράποντα ποιῆσαι
προελθεῖν, ὑπολείπεσθαι δὲ αὐτόν· ἔχειν γὰρ αὐτῷ
54 τι φράσαι μηδενὸς ἄλλου παρόντος.² καὶ ὁ μὲν
Σαοῦλος ἀποπέμπεται τὸν ἀκόλουθον, λαβὼν δ' ὁ
προφήτης τὸ ἀγγεῖον,³ ἔλαιον καταχεῖ τῆς τοῦ
νεανίσκου κεφαλῆς καὶ κατασπασάμενος ''ἴσθι,''
φησί, ''βασιλεὺς ὑπὸ τοῦ θεοῦ κεχειροτονημένος
ἐπί τε Παλαιστίνους καὶ τὴν ὑπὲρ Ἑβραίων
ἄμυναν. τούτων δὲ ἔσται σοι σημεῖον ὅ σε
55 βούλομαι προγινώσκειν· ὅταν ἀπέλθῃς ἐντεῦθεν
καταλήψῃ τρεῖς ἀνθρώπους ἐν τῇ ὁδῷ προσκυνῆσαι
τῷ θεῷ πορευομένους εἰς Βέθηλα, ὧν τὸν μὲν
πρῶτον τρεῖς ἄρτους ὄψει κομίζοντα, τὸν δὲ
δεύτερον ἔριφον, ὁ τρίτος δὲ ἀσκὸν οἴνου φέρων

---

¹ χρείαν MSP. ² μηδενὸς παρόντος om. RO.
³ ROE Lat. (cf. 1 Sam. x. 1, LXX τὸν φακὸν τοῦ ἐλαίου):
ἅγιον rell.

352

tribe too little to create kings, and of a family of humbler sort than all others. Thou but mockest and makest sport of me in speaking of matters too high for my station." Howbeit the prophet led him to the banquet-chamber, gave him and his attendant places above the invited guests, who were seventy [a] in number, and charged his henchmen to set a royal portion before Saul. Then, when bedtime came, the rest arose and departed each to his own home, but Saul and his servant slept at the prophet's house.[b]

(2) At break of day Samuel roused him from his bed, escorted him on his way, and, when outside the town, bade him cause his servant to go on before and to remain behind himself, for he had somewhat to tell him privately. So Saul dismissed his companion, and the prophet, taking his vial, poured oil upon the young man's head and kissed him and said : " Know that thou art king, elected of God to combat the Philistines and to defend the Hebrews. And of this there shall be unto thee a sign which I would have thee learn beforehand. When thou art departed hence, thou shalt find on thy road three men [c] going to worship God at Bethel ; the first thou shalt see carrying three loaves, the second a kid,[d] and the third

Samuel
anoints
Saul.
1 Sam.
ix. 26.

x. 1.

[a] So LXX : Heb. " about thirty," 1 Sam. ix. 22.

[b] After LXX, which here preserves the true text, καὶ διέστρωσαν τῷ Σαοὺλ ἐπὶ τῷ δώματι καὶ ἐκοιμήθη, Heb. " he communed with S. upon the housetop," 1 Sam. ix. 25. In the Biblical narrative the sacrifice and subsequent feast are held at " the high place," whence Samuel and Saul descend to the city to the prophet's house.

[c] Josephus reverses the Biblical order of the first two incidents : there the meeting with the messenger at Rachel's tomb comes first.

[d] " One carrying three kids and another carrying three loaves," 1 Sam.

ἀκολουθήσει. ἀσπάσονται δέ σε οὗτοι καὶ φιλο-
φρονήσονται καὶ δώσουσί σοι ἄρτους δύο, σὺ δὲ
56 λήψῃ. κἀκεῖθεν ἥξεις εἰς τὸ Ῥαχήλας καλούμενον μνημεῖον, ὅπου συμβαλεῖς τῷ σεσῶσθαί
σου τὰς ὄνους εὐαγγελιουμένῳ· ἔπειτ' ἐκεῖθεν
ἐλθὼν εἰς Γαβαθὰ¹ προφήταις ἐκκλησιάζουσιν
ἐπιτεύξῃ καὶ γενόμενος ἔνθεος προφητεύσεις σὺν
αὐτοῖς, ὡς πάνθ' ὄντιν'² ὁρῶντα ἐκπλήττεσθαί
τε καὶ θαυμάζειν λέγοντα "πόθεν εἰς τοῦτο εὐ-
57 δαιμονίας ὁ Κεισαίου παῖς παρῆλθεν;" ὅταν δέ
σοι ταῦτα γένηται τὰ σημεῖα, τὸν θεὸν ἴσθι μετὰ
σοῦ τυγχάνοντα, ἄσπασαί τε τὸν πατέρα σου καὶ
τοὺς συγγενεῖς. ἥξεις δὲ μετάπεμπτος εἰς Γάλγαλα
ὑπ'³ ἐμοῦ, ἵνα χαριστήρια τούτων θύσωμεν τῷ
θεῷ." φράσας ταῦτα καὶ προειπὼν ἀποπέμπει
τὸν νεανίσκον· τῷ Σαούλῳ δὲ πάντα κατὰ τὴν
Σαμουήλου προφητείαν ἀπήντησεν.

58   (3) Ὡς δ' ἦλθεν εἰς τὴν οἰκίαν, τοῦ συγγενοῦς
αὐτοῦ Ἀβηνάρου, καὶ γὰρ ἐκεῖνον τῶν ἄλλων
οἰκείων μᾶλλον ἔστεργεν, ἀνερωτῶντος περὶ τῆς
ἀποδημίας καὶ τῶν κατ' αὐτὴν⁴ γεγονότων, τῶν
μὲν ἄλλων οὐδὲν ἀπεκρύψατο οὐδ' ὡς ἀφίκοιτο
παρὰ Σαμουῆλον τὸν προφήτην οὐδ' ὡς ἐκεῖνος
αὐτῷ σεσῶσθαι τὰς ὄνους ἔφρασε, περὶ δὲ τῆς
59 βασιλείας καὶ τῶν κατ' αὐτήν, ἃ⁵ φθόνον ἀκού-

---

¹ Γεβαθὰ RO: Γαιβαθὰ SP.   ² +οὖν MSP.
³ ἐξ OE.   ⁴ αὐτὸν ROE.
⁵ ἃ καὶ MSP Lat.

ᵃ Bibl. "two men."
ᵇ Bibl. "to Gibeah (or "the hill," LXX τὸν βουνόν) of
God." Cf. on § 95.
ᶜ These last words are amplification. Scripture has "do
what thy hand shall find."

will follow bearing a wine-skin. These men will
salute thee, show thee kindness and give thee two
loaves; and thou shalt accept them. And thence 2.
thou shalt come to the place called 'Rachel's tomb,'
where thou shalt meet one *a* who will bring thee
news that thy asses are safe. Thereafter, on coming
thence to Gabatha,*b* thou shalt light upon an assembly 5.
of prophets and, divinely inspired, thou shalt prophesy
with them, insomuch that whosoever beholdeth thee *Cf.* 11 f.
shall be amazed and marvel, saying, 'How hath the
son of Kis come to this pitch of felicity?' And when 7.
these signs are come unto thee, know thou that God
is with thee; and go to salute thy father and thy
kinsfolk.*c* But thou shalt come, when summoned by
me, to Galgala, that we may offer thank-offerings to
God for these mercies." After these declarations and
predictions he let the young man go; and everything
befell Saul as Samuel had foretold.

(3) But when he entered his *d* house and his kins- Saul's
man Abēnar *e*—for he was of all his relatives the one silence.
whom he loved the best—questioned him concerning 1 Sam.
his journey and the events thereof, Saul concealed x. 13.
from him nothing of all the rest, how he had visited
Samuel the prophet and how he had told him that
the asses were safe. But concerning the kingdom
and all relating thereto, deeming that the recital

d Gr. "the"; perhaps render "the house of his kinsman A. . . . and he questioned him." Josephus appears
to have read in 1 Sam. x. 13 "he came to the house" (a
reading preferred by modern critics) instead of "he came
to the high place."

e Scripture mentions his "uncle," here unnamed but elsewhere called Ner. Josephus speaks of his cousin Abner,
the son of Ner and afterwards captain of Saul's host, 1 Sam.
xiv. 50. *Cf.* § 130.

μενα καὶ ἀπιστίαν ἔχειν ᾤετο, σιωπᾷ πρὸς αὐτοὶ
καὶ οὐδὲ πρὸς εὔνουν σφόδρα δοκοῦντα εἶναι
καὶ περισσότερον τῶν ἀφ' αἵματος ὑπ' αὐτοῦ
στεργόμενον ἀσφαλὲς ἢ σῶφρον ἔδοξε μηνύειν
λογισάμενος, οἶμαι, τὴν ἀνθρωπίνην φύσιν οἵα ταῖς
ἀληθείαις ἐστίν, ὅτι βεβαίως οὐδεὶς εὔνους[1] οὔτε
φίλων οὔτε συγγενῶν οὐδ' ἄχρι τῶν παρὰ τοῦ θεοῦ
λαμπρῶν ἀποσώζει τὴν διάθεσιν, ἀλλὰ πρὸς τὰς
ὑπεροχὰς κακοήθεις τυγχάνουσιν ἤδη καὶ βάσκανοι.

60   (4) Σαμουῆλος δὲ συγκαλεῖ[2] τὸν λαὸν εἰς
Μασφαθὰ πόλιν καὶ πρὸς αὐτὸν διατίθεται λόγους,
οὓς κατ' ἐντολὴν φράζειν ἔλεγε τοῦ θεοῦ, ὅτι τὴν
ἐλευθερίαν αὐτοῖς ἐκείνου παρασχόντος καὶ τοὺς
πολεμίους δουλώσαντος ἀμνημονήσειαν τῶν εὐεργεσιῶν, καὶ τὸν μὲν θεὸν ἀποχειροτονοῦσι τῆς
βασιλείας οὐκ εἰδότες ὡς συμφορώτατον ὑπὸ τοῦ
61 πάντων ἀρίστου προστατεῖσθαι, θεὸς δὲ πάντων
ἄριστος, αἱροῦνται δ' ἔχειν ἄνθρωπον βασιλέα, ὃς
ὡς κτήματι[3] τοῖς ὑποτεταγμένοις κατὰ βούλησιν
καὶ ἐπιθυμίαν καὶ τῶν ἄλλων παθῶν ὁρμὴν
χρήσεται τῆς ἐξουσίας ἀφειδῶς ἐμφορούμενος, ἀλλ'
οὐχ ὡς ἴδιον ἔργον καὶ κατασκεύασμα τὸ τῶν
ἀνθρώπων γένος οὕτως διατηρῆσαι σπουδάσει, ὁ
θεὸς δὲ κατὰ ταύτην τὴν αἰτίαν ἂν[4] κήδοιτο.
"ἀλλ' ἐπεὶ δέδοκται ταῦτα ὑμῖν καὶ κεκράτηκεν ἡ
πρὸς τὸν θεὸν ὕβρις, τάχθητε πάντες κατὰ φυλάς
τε καὶ σκῆπτρα καὶ κλήρους βάλετε."

----

[1] εὔνους om. ROE.   [2] καλεῖ RO : ἐκάλει E.
[3] κτήμασι ed. pr. : jumentis Lat.   [4] ἂν om. codd.

----

[a] The renewed strictures of Samuel are an amplification of
Scripture. His earlier warning (1 Sam. viii. 10) is given
above in § 40.

thereof would excite jealousy and distrust, he held his peace; nay, even to one who seemed most loyal of friends and whom he loved more affectionately than all those of his blood, he judged it neither safe nor prudent to disclose this secret—reflecting, I ween, on what human nature in truth is, and how no one, be he friend or kinsman, shows unwavering loyalty or preserves his affection when brilliant distinctions are bestowed by God, but all men straightway regard these eminences with malice and envy.

(4) Samuel now called the people together to the city of Masphatha and made them an address, which he delivered, as he told them, at the commandment of God. He said that, albeit God had granted them liberty and enslaved their enemies, they had been unmindful of His benefits and rejected His sovereignty, unaware that it was to their highest interest to have the best of all rulers at their head and that the best of all was God; nay, they chose to have a man for their king, who would treat his subjects as chattels at his will and pleasure and at the impulse of his other passions, indulging his power to the full; one who, not being the author and creator of the human race, would not lovingly study to preserve it, while God for that very reason would cherish it with care.[a] "Howbeit," he added, "since it pleases you thus, and this intent to outrage God has prevailed, range yourselves all of you by tribes and families[b] and cast lots."

---

[b] The Gr. σκῆπτρον, lit. "staff," is the usual LXX rendering of Heb. shēbeṭ which means both "staff" and "tribe." Josephus here reverses the order of words in the LXX, 1 Sam. x. 19, where σκῆπτρον = "tribe" and φυλή = "family"; φυλή in the LXX usually = "tribe," less often = "family."

62 (5) Ποιησάντων δὲ τοῦτο τῶν Ἑβραίων ὁ τῆς
Βενιαμίτιδος κλῆρος ἐξέπεσε, ταύτης δὲ κληρωθείσης ἔλαχεν ἡ Ματρὶς καλουμένη πατριά, ἧς
κατ' ἄνδρα κληρωθείσης λαγχάνει ὁ Κεισαίου
63 βασιλεύειν παῖς Σάουλος. γνοὺς δὲ τοῦθ' ὁ νεανίσκος φθάσας ἐκποδὼν αὑτὸν ποιεῖ μὴ βουλόμενος,
οἶμαι, δοκεῖν τὴν ἀρχὴν ἑκὼν λαμβάνειν, ἀλλὰ
τοσαύτην ἐνεδείξατο ἐγκράτειαν καὶ σωφροσύνην,
ὥστε τῶν πλείστων οὐδ' ἐπὶ μικραῖς εὐπραγίαις
τὴν χαρὰν κατασχεῖν δυναμένων, ἀλλ' εἰς τὸ πᾶσι
γενέσθαι φανεροὺς προπιπτόντων,[1] ὁ δ' οὐ μόνον
οὐδὲν ἐνέφηνε τοιοῦτον ἐπὶ βασιλείᾳ καὶ τῷ
τοσούτων καὶ τηλικούτων ἐθνῶν ἀποδεδεῖχθαι
δεσπότης, ἀλλὰ καὶ τῆς ὄψεως αὑτὸν τῆς τῶν βασι-
λευθησομένων ἐξέκλειψεν καὶ ζητεῖν αὐτὸν καὶ περὶ
64 τοῦτο πονεῖν παρεσκεύασεν. ὧν ἀμηχανούντων
καὶ φροντιζόντων ὅ τι καὶ[2] γένοιτο ἀφανὴς ὁ
Σάουλος, ὁ προφήτης ἱκέτευε τὸν θεὸν δεῖξαι ποῦ
ποτ' εἴη καὶ παρασχεῖν εἰς ἐμφανὲς τὸν νεανίσκον.
65 μαθὼν δὲ παρὰ τοῦ θεοῦ τὸν τόπον ἔνθα κέκρυπται[3]
ὁ Σάουλος πέμπει τοὺς ἄξοντας αὐτὸν καὶ παρα-
γενόμενον ἵστησι μέσον τοῦ πλήθους. ἐξεῖχε δὲ
ἁπάντων καὶ τὸ ὕψος ἦν βασιλικώτατος.
66 (6) Λέγει δὲ ὁ προφήτης· "τοῦτον ὑμῖν ὁ θεὸς
ἔδωκε βασιλέα· ὁρᾶτε δὲ ὡς καὶ κρείττων ἐστὶ
πάντων καὶ τῆς ἀρχῆς ἄξιος." ὡς δ' ἐπευφήμησε
τῷ βασιλεῖ σωτηρίαν ὁ λαός, τὰ μέλλοντα συμβήσεσθαι καταγράψας αὐτοῖς ὁ προφήτης ἀνέγνω
τοῦ βασιλέως ἀκροωμένου καὶ τὸ βιβλίον τίθησιν

---

[1] RE: προσπιπτόντων rell.
[2] καὶ om. MSP: ἔτι μὴ conj. Schmidt.
[3] κρύπτεται ROE.

(5) The Hebrews having so done, the lot fell to the tribe of Benjamin, and when lots had been cast for it the family called Matris[a] was successful; and lots being cast for the individuals of that family Saul son of Kis obtained the kingdom. Learning thereof, the young man promptly took himself away, not wishing, I imagine, to appear eager to take the sovereignty. Nay, such was the restraint and modesty[b] displayed by him that, whereas most persons are unable to contain their joy over the slightest success but rush to display themselves before all the world, he, far from showing any such pride on obtaining a kingdom and being appointed lord of all those mighty peoples, actually stole away from the view of his future subjects and forced them to search for him, not without trouble. These being baffled and perplexed at Saul's disappearance, the prophet besought God to show where the young man was and to bring him before their eyes. And having learnt from God the place where Saul lay in hiding, he sent to fetch him and, when he was come, set him in the midst of the throng. And he overtopped them all and in stature was indeed most kingly.

(6) Then said the prophet, " This is he whom God hath given you for king; see how he both excels all and is worthy of sovereignty ! " But after the acclamations of the people, " Long live the king ! " the prophet, having put in writing for them all that should come to pass, read it in the hearing of the king[c] and then laid up the book in the tabernacle of

---

[a] Bibl. Matri, LXX Ματταρεί, etc.

[b] Rabbinic tradition (cf. Ginzberg, vi. 231) also emphasizes Saul's modesty.

[c] 1 Sam. x. 25 " Then Samuel told the people the manner of the kingdom and wrote it in a book."

ἐν τῇ τοῦ θεοῦ σκηνῇ ταῖς μετέπειτα γενεαῖς
67 μαρτύριον ὧν προείρηκε. ταῦτ᾽ ἐπιτελέσας ὁ
Σαμουῆλος ἀπολύει τὴν πληθύν· καὶ αὐτὸς δὲ εἰς
᾽Αρμαθὰ παραγίνεται πόλιν, πατρὶς γὰρ ἦν αὐτῷ,
Σαούλῳ δὲ ἀπερχομένῳ εἰς Γαβαθήν, ἐξ ἧς
ὑπῆρχε, συνήρχοντο πολλοὶ μὲν ἀγαθοὶ τὴν
προσήκουσαν βασιλεῖ τιμὴν νέμοντες, πονηροὶ δὲ
πλείους, οἳ καταφρονοῦντες αὐτοῦ καὶ τοὺς
ἄλλους¹ ἐχλεύαζον καὶ οὔτε δῶρα προσέφερον
οὔτ᾽ ἐν σπουδῇ καὶ λόγῳ τὸ ἀρέσκεσθαι τὸν
Σαοῦλον ἐτίθεντο.

68 (v. 1) Μηνὶ δ᾽ ὕστερον ἄρχει² τῆς παρὰ πάντων
αὐτῷ τιμῆς ὁ πρὸς Ναάσην πόλεμος τὸν τῶν
᾽Αμμανιτῶν βασιλέα· οὗτος γὰρ πολλὰ κακὰ τοὺς
πέραν τοῦ ᾽Ιορδάνου ποταμοῦ κατῳκημένους τῶν
᾽Ιουδαίων διατίθησι, μετὰ πολλοῦ καὶ μαχίμου
69 στρατεύματος διαβὰς ἐπ᾽ αὐτούς· καὶ τὰς πόλεις
αὐτῶν εἰς δουλείαν ὑπάγεται, ἰσχύι μὲν καὶ
βίᾳ πρὸς τὸ παρὸν αὐτοὺς χειρωσάμενος, σοφίᾳ
δὲ καὶ ἐπινοίᾳ πρὸς τὸ μηδ᾽ αὖθις ἀποστάντας
δυνηθῆναι τὴν ὑπ᾽ αὐτῷ δουλείαν διαφυγεῖν ἀσθενεῖς ποιῶν· τῶν γὰρ ἢ κατὰ πίστιν ὡς αὐτὸν
ἀφικνουμένων ἢ λαμβανομένων πολέμου νόμῳ τοὺς
70 δεξιοὺς ὀφθαλμοὺς ἐξέκοπτεν. ἐποίει δὲ τοῦθ᾽,
ὅπως τῆς ἀριστερᾶς αὐτοῖς ὄψεως ὑπὸ τῶν θυρεῶν
71 καλυπτομένης ἄχρηστοι παντελῶς εἶεν. καὶ ὁ μὲν
τῶν ᾽Αμμανιτῶν βασιλεὺς ταῦτ᾽ ἐργασάμενος τοὺς
πέραν τοῦ ᾽Ιορδάνου, ἐπὶ τοὺς Γαλαδηνοὺς λεγο-

----

¹ πολλούς ROE. ² SP: ἀρχὴ rell.

ᵃ Josephus follows the LXX, which begins a new chapter
(1 Sam. xi.) with the words μετὰ μῆνα, probably reading
mi-ḥōdesh " after a month," whereas the Heb. (x. 27 = end of

God, as a testimony to after generations of what he had foretold. That task accomplished, Samuel dismissed the multitude and betook himself to the city of Armatha, his native place. Saul, for his part, departed for Gabatha, whence he was sprung; he was accompanied by many honest folk, tendering him the homage due to a king, but by knaves yet more, who, holding him in contempt, derided the rest and neither offered him presents nor took any pains or care to gain the favour of Saul.

(v. 1) However, a month later,[a] he began to win the esteem of all by the war with Naas,[b] king of the Ammanites. For this monarch had done much harm to the Jews who had settled beyond the river Jordan, having invaded their territory with a large and warlike army. Reducing their cities to servitude, he not only by force and violence secured their subjection in the present, but by cunning and ingenuity weakened them in order that they might never again be able to revolt and escape from servitude to him; for he cut out the right eyes of all who either surrendered to him under oath or were captured by right of war. This he did with intent— since the left eye was covered by the buckler—to render them utterly unserviceable. Having then so dealt with the people beyond Jordan,[c] the Ammanite king carried his arms against those called Galadenians.[d]

War with Nahash the Ammonite.

1 Sam. xi. 1.

preceding chapter) has *maharîsh* "was silent," referring to Saul's attitude toward the disaffected elements.

[b] Bibl. Nahash, LXX Ναάς.

[c] These earlier conquests of Nahash are not mentioned in Scripture.

[d] Bibl. Jabesh Gilead, that is the city Jabesh (perhaps modern *Wady Yābis*) in Gilead, the country east of the Jordan, extending north and south of the river Jabbok.

μένους ἐπεστράτευσε καὶ στρατοπεδευσάμενος πρὸς
τῇ μητροπόλει τῶν πολεμίων, Ἰαβὶς δ' ἐστὶν αὕτη,
πέμπει πρὸς αὐτοὺς πρέσβεις κελεύων ἤδη[1] παραδοῦναι σφᾶς αὐτοὺς ἐπὶ τῷ τοὺς δεξιοὺς αὐτῶν
ὀφθαλμοὺς ἐξορύξαι, ἢ πολιορκήσειν[2] ἠπείλει καὶ
τὰς πόλεις αὐτῶν ἀναστήσειν· τὴν δ' αἵρεσιν ἐπ'
αὐτοῖς εἶναι, πότερόν ποτε βραχύ τι τοῦ σώματος
ἀποτεμεῖν θέλουσιν ἢ παντάπασιν[3] ἀπολωλέναι.
72 οἱ δὲ Γαλαδηνοὶ καταπλαγέντες πρὸς οὐδέτερον
μὲν ἐτόλμησαν οὐδὲν εἰπεῖν, οὔτ' εἰ παραδιδόασιν
αὐτοὺς οὔτ' εἰ πολεμοῦσιν, ἀνοχὴν δ' ἡμερῶν ἑπτὰ
λαβεῖν ἠξίωσαν, ἵνα πρεσβευσάμενοι πρὸς τοὺς
ὁμοφύλους παρακαλέσωσι συμμαχεῖν αὐτοῖς καὶ εἰ
μὲν ἔλθοι βοήθεια πολεμῶσιν, εἰ δ' ἄπορα εἴη τὰ
παρ' ἐκείνων, παραδώσειν αὐτοὺς ἔφασκον ἐπὶ τῷ
παθεῖν ὅ τι ἂν αὐτῷ δοκῇ.
73   (2) Ὁ δὲ Ναάσης καταφρονήσας τοῦ τῶν Γαλαδηνῶν πλήθους καὶ τῆς ἀποκρίσεως αὐτῶν, δίδωσί
τε αὐτοῖς τὴν ἀνοχὴν καὶ πέμπειν πρὸς οὓς ἂν
θέλωσι συμμάχους ἐπιτρέπει. πέμψαντες[4] οὖν εὐθὺς
κατὰ πόλιν τοῖς Ἰσραηλίταις διήγγελον[5] τὰ παρὰ
τοῦ Ναάσου καὶ τὴν ἀμηχανίαν ἐν ᾗ καθειστή-
74 κεσαν. οἱ δ' εἰς δάκρυα καὶ λύπην ὑπὸ τῆς ἀκοῆς
τῶν περὶ τοὺς Ἰαβισηνοὺς προήχθησαν καὶ πέρα
τούτων οὐδὲν αὐτοῖς ἄλλο πράττειν συνεχώρει τὸ
δέος· γενομένων δὲ τῶν ἀγγέλων καὶ ἐν τῇ Σαούλου
τοῦ βασιλέως πόλει καὶ τοὺς κινδύνους ἐν οἷς εἶναι
συνέβαινε τοὺς Ἰαβισηνοὺς φρασάντων, ὁ μὲν
λαὸς ταὐτὰ τοῖς πρώτοις ἔπασχεν· ὠδύρετο γὰρ

[1] RO: ἡ rell.   [2] conj. Niese: πολιορκῆσαι codd.
[3] πάντες MSP Lat.   [4] πέμπουσιν ROE.
[5] οἱ ἤγγελον RO.

Pitching his camp near the capital of his enemies, to 1 Sam. xi. 2
wit Jabis, he sent envoys to them, bidding them
instantly to surrender on the understanding that
their right eyes would be put out : if not, he
threatened to besiege and overthrow their cities : it
was for them to choose, whether they preferred the
cutting out a small portion of the body or to perish
utterly. The Galadenians, terror-struck, durst not
reply at all to either proposal, whether they would
surrender or whether they would fight ; but they
asked for a seven days' respite, in order to send
envoys to their countrymen and solicit their support :
if assistance were forthcoming they would fight, but
if there should be no hope from that quarter, they
undertook to deliver themselves up to suffer whatsoever should seem good to him.

(2) Naas, contemptuous of these Galadenian people Saul learns
of the
Gileadites
plight.
and their answer, gave them their respite and permission to send to whatever allies they would. They 1 Sam. xi. 4.
therefore straightway sent messengers to each city
of the Israelites to report the menaces of Naas and
the desperate straits whereto they were reduced.
These, on hearing of the plight of the men of Jabis,
were moved to tears and grief, but, beyond that,
fear permitted them to do no more. When, however,
the messengers reached the city of king Saul and
recounted the peril wherein they of Jabis lay, the
people here too were moved even as were those others,

363

75 τὴν συμφορὰν τὴν τῶν συγγενῶν· ὁ δὲ Σαοῦλος
ἀπὸ τῶν περὶ τὴν γεωργίαν παραγενόμενος ἔργων
εἰς τὴν πόλιν ἐπιτυγχάνει κλαίουσι τοῖς αὐτοῦ
πολίταις, καὶ πυθόμενος τὴν αἰτίαν τῆς συγχύσεως
καὶ κατηφείας αὐτῶν μανθάνει τὰ παρὰ τῶν
76 ἀγγέλων. καὶ ἔνθεος γενόμενος ἀποπέμπει μὲν
τοὺς Ἰαβισηνούς, ὑποσχόμενος αὐτοῖς ἥξειν βοηθὸς
τῇ τρίτῃ τῶν ἡμερῶν καὶ πρὶν ἥλιον ἀνασχεῖν
κρατήσειν τῶν πολεμίων, ἵνα καὶ νενικηκότας ἤδη
καὶ τῶν φόβων ἀπηλλαγμένους ὁ ἥλιος ἐπιτείλας
ἴδῃ· ὑπομεῖναι δ᾽ ἐκέλευσέ τινας αὐτῶν ἡγησομέ-
νους τῆς ὁδοῦ.

77 (3) Βουλόμενος δὲ φόβῳ ζημίας τὸν λαὸν ἐπὶ
τὸν πρὸς Ἀμμανίτας ἐπιστρέψαι πόλεμον καὶ
συνελθεῖν αὐτοὺς ὀξύτερον, ὑποτεμὼν τῶν αὐτοῦ
βοῶν τὰ νεῦρα ταυτὰ¹ διαθήσειν ἠπείλησε τοὺς
ἁπάντων, εἰ μὴ πρὸς τὸν Ἰόρδανον ὡπλισμένοι κατὰ
τὴν ἐπιοῦσαν ἀπαντήσουσιν ἡμέραν καὶ ἀκολου-
θήσουσιν αὐτῷ καὶ Σαμουήλῳ τῷ προφήτῃ, ὅπου
78 ποτ᾽ ἂν αὐτοὺς ἀγάγωσι. τῶν δὲ δι᾽ εὐλάβειαν
τῆς κατεπηγγελμένης ζημίας εἰς τὸν ὡρισμένον
καιρὸν συνελθόντων ἐξαριθμεῖται ἐν Βαλᾶ τῇ
πόλει τὸ πλῆθος· εὑρίσκει δὲ τὸν ἀριθμὸν χωρὶς
τῆς Ἰούδα φυλῆς εἰς ἑβδομήκοντα μυριάδας
συνειλεγμένους, τῆς δὲ φυλῆς ἐκείνης ἦσαν μυ-
79 ριάδες ἑπτά. διαβὰς δὲ τὸν Ἰόρδανον καὶ σχοίνων

¹ Niese: ταῦτα RO Lat.: ταὐτὸ SPE: τοῦτο M.

for they bewailed the calamity of their brethren ; but Saul, entering the city from his labours in husbandry, encountered his fellow-citizens in tears and, on asking the reason for their distress and dejection, learnt the messengers' report. Thereon, divinely inspired, he dismissed the men from Jabis with a promise to come to their aid on the third day [a] and ere sunrise to defeat the foe, so that the ascending sun should see them already victors and freed from their fears. Some, however, among them he bade remain with him so that they might guide him on his march.

(3) Then wishing to urge the people, through fear of the penalty, to the war against the Ammanites and that they might come together more quickly he cut the sinews [b] of his own oxen and threatened to do the like to the beasts of all who should fail to appear at the Jordan in arms on the following day and follow him and Samuel the prophet whithersoever they should lead them. But when they, through fear of the threatened penalty, mustered at the appointed hour, he had the host numbered at the city of Bala [c] and found them to have gathered together to the number of 700,000,[d] apart from the tribe of Judah : of that tribe there were 70,000.[e] Then crossing the Jordan and accomplishing in an all-

1 Sam **xi. 8**

[a] In Scripture (1 Sam. xi. 9) Saul (or, in the Heb., the Israelites) promises that deliverance will come on the morrow; moreover, the promise is made after the tribes are summoned.

[b] In Scripture (1 Sam. xi. 7) Saul dismembers a team of oxen and sends the pieces throughout the borders of Israel.

[c] Bibl. Bezek, LXX Βέζεκ ('Αβιέζεκ etc.) ἐν Βαμά, perhaps the modern *Khirbet Ibzīq*, about twelve miles N.E. of Shechem and a little W. of the Jordan, opposite Jabesh Gilead.

[d] Heb. 300,000, LXX 600,000.

[e] Heb. 30,000, LXX 70,000.

δέκα δι' ὅλης τῆς νυκτὸς ἀνύσας ὁδὸν φθάνει μὲν
ἥλιον ἀνίσχοντα, τριχῇ δὲ τὸ στράτευμα διελὼν
ἐπιπίπτει πανταχόθεν αἰφνιδίως οὐ προσδοκῶσι
τοῖς ἐχθροῖς, καὶ συμβαλὼν εἰς μάχην ἄλλους τε
πολλοὺς ἀποκτείνει τῶν Ἀμμανιτῶν καὶ Ναάσην
80 τὸν βασιλέα. τοῦτο λαμπρὸν ἐπράχθη τῷ Σαούλῳ
τὸ ἔργον καὶ πρὸς πάντας αὐτὸν διήγγειλε τοὺς
Ἑβραίους ἐπαινούμενον καὶ θαυμαστῆς ἀπολαύοντα
δόξης ἐπ' ἀνδρείᾳ· καὶ γὰρ εἴ τινες ἦσαν οἳ
πρότερον αὐτοῦ κατεφρόνουν, τότε μετέστησαν ἐπὶ
τὸ τιμᾶν καὶ πάντων ἄριστον νομίζειν· οὐ γὰρ
ἤρκεσεν αὐτῷ τοὺς Ἰαβισηνοὺς σεσωκέναι μόνον,
ἀλλὰ καὶ τῇ τῶν Ἀμμανιτῶν ἐπιστρατεύσας χώρᾳ
πᾶσαν αὐτὴν καταστρέφεται καὶ πολλὴν λαβὼν
81 λείαν λαμπρὸς[1] εἰς τὴν οἰκείαν ὑπέστρεψεν. ὁ δὲ
λαὸς ὑφ' ἡδονῆς τῶν Σαούλῳ κατωρθωμένων
ἔχαιρε μὲν ὅτι τοιοῦτον ἐχειροτόνησε βασιλέα,
πρὸς δὲ τοὺς οὐδὲν ὄφελος αὐτὸν ἔσεσθαι τοῖς
πράγμασι λέγοντας ἐβόων "ποῦ νῦν εἰσιν οὗτοι"
καὶ "δότωσαν δίκην" καὶ πάνθ' ὅσα φιλεῖ λέγειν
ὄχλος ἐπ' εὐπραγίαις ἠρμένος πρὸς τοὺς ἐξευτε-
82 λίζοντας ἔναγχος τοὺς τούτων αἰτίους. Σαοῦλος
δὲ τούτων μὲν ἠσπάζετο τὴν εὔνοιαν καὶ τὴν περὶ
αὐτὸν προθυμίαν, ὤμοσε δὲ μήτινα περιόψεσθαι
τῶν ὁμοφύλων ἀναιρούμενον ἐπ' ἐκείνης τῆς
ἡμέρας· ἄτοπον γὰρ εἶναι τὴν ὑπὸ τοῦ θεοῦ δε-
δομένην νίκην αἵματι φῦραι καὶ φόνῳ τῶν ἐκ

[1] λαμπρῶς ROME.

night march a distance of ten *schoenoi*,[a] he arrived before the sun was up and, dividing his army into three, fell suddenly from all sides upon the foe, who looked for no such thing, and having joined battle he slew multitudes of the Ammanites and king Naas himself.[b] This brilliant exploit achieved by Saul spread his praises throughout all the Hebrews and procured him a marvellous renown for valiance ; for if there were some who before despised him, they were now brought round to honour him and to deem him the noblest of all men. For, not content with having rescued the inhabitants of Jabis, he invaded the country of the Ammanites, subdued it all, and, having taken much booty, returned in glory to his own land.[c] The people, in their delight at Saul's achievements, exulted at having elected such a king, and, turning upon those who had declared that he would bring no profit to the state, they cried, " Where now are those men ? ", " Let them pay for it ! "— in short all that a crowd, elated by success, is wont to utter against those who were of late disparaging the authors of it. But Saul, while welcoming their good-will and devotion to himself, yet swore that he would not suffer one of his countrymen to be put to death that day, for it were monstrous to defile that God-given victory with bloodshed and murder of men of

Saul's victory over Nahash the Ammonite.
1 Sam. xi. 12.

[a] The *schoenos* varied in length between thirty and forty stades, that is, roughly between four and five miles. The length of Saul's march, not given in Scripture, was, therefore, between forty and fifty miles. The distance between the supposed sites of Bezek and Jabesh Gilead is less than twenty miles.

[b] 1 Sam. xi. 1 " not two men were left together."

[c] This conquest of Ammonite territory is not mentioned in Scripture.

ταὐτοῦ γένους αὐτοῖς, πρέπειν δὲ μᾶλλον πρὸς
ἀλλήλους εὐμενῶς διακειμένους[1] ἑορτάζειν.

83 (4) Σαμουήλου δὲ φήσαντος καὶ δευτέρᾳ δεῖν
χειροτονίᾳ Σαούλῳ τὴν βασιλείαν ἐπικυρῶσαι
συνίασι πάντες εἰς Γάλγαλα πόλιν· ἐκεῖ γὰρ
αὐτοὺς ἐκέλευσεν ἐλθεῖν. καὶ πάλιν ὁρῶντος τοῦ
πλήθους ὁ προφήτης χρίει τὸν Σαούλον τῷ ἁγίῳ
ἐλαίῳ καὶ δεύτερον ἀναγορεύει βασιλέα. καὶ
οὕτως ἡ τῶν Ἑβραίων πολιτεία εἰς βασιλείαν
84 μετέπεσεν. ἐπὶ γὰρ Μωυσέος καὶ τοῦ μαθητοῦ
αὐτοῦ Ἰησοῦ, ὃς ἦν στρατηγός, ἀριστοκρατού-
μενοι διετέλουν· μετὰ δὲ τὴν ἐκείνου[2] τελευτὴν
ἔτεσι τοῖς πᾶσι δέκα καὶ πρὸς τούτοις ὀκτὼ τὸ
85 πλῆθος αὐτῶν ἀναρχία κατέσχε. μετὰ ταῦτα δ᾽
εἰς τὴν προτέραν ἐπανῆλθον πολιτείαν τῷ κατὰ
πόλεμον ἀρίστῳ δόξαντι γεγενῆσθαι καὶ κατ᾽
ἀνδρείαν περὶ τῶν ὅλων δικάζειν ἐπιτρέποντες·
καὶ διὰ τοῦτο τὸν χρόνον τοῦτον τῆς πολιτείας
κριτῶν ἐκάλεσαν.

86 (5) Ἐκκλησίαν δὲ Σαμουῆλος ποιήσας ὁ προφήτης τῶν Ἑβραίων "ἐπόμνυμαι,"[3] φησίν, "ὑμῖν τὸν
μέγιστον θεόν, ὃς τοὺς ἀδελφοὺς τοὺς ἀγαθοὺς[4] ἐκείνους, λέγω δὴ Μωυσῆν καὶ Ἀαρῶνα, παρήγαγεν εἰς
τὸν βίον καὶ τοὺς πατέρας ἡμῶν ἐξήρπασεν Αἰγυπτίων καὶ τῆς ὑπ᾽ αὐτοῖς δουλείας, μηδὲν μήτ᾽ αἰδοῖ
χαρισαμένους μήτε ὑποστειλαμένους φόβῳ μήτε
ἄλλῳ τινὶ πάθει παραχωρήσαντας εἰπεῖν, εἴ[5] τί μοι
πέπρακται σκαιὸν καὶ ἄδικον ἢ κέρδους ἕνεκα ἢ
87 πλεονεξίας ἢ χάριτος τῆς πρὸς ἄλλους· ἐλέγξαι δὲ

---

[1] τῶν ἐκ ταὐτοῦ . . . διακειμένους SP: τῶν πρὸς ἀλλήλους
συγγενῶν RO.   [2] ἐκείνων SP Lat.   [3] ἐπόμνυμι SPE.
[4] τοὺς ἀγαθοὺς om. RO.   [5] εἰ om. ROME.

their own race, and it better beseemed them to keep feast in a spirit of mutual goodwill.[a]

(4) Samuel having now declared it necessary to confirm the kingdom to Saul by a second election, all assembled at the city of Galgala,[b] for thither had he bade them come. So yet again, in the sight of all the people, the prophet anointed Saul with the holy oil, and for the second time proclaimed him king. And thus was the government of the Hebrews transformed into a monarchy. For under Moses and his disciple Joshua, who was commander-in-chief, they remained under aristocratic rule : after Joshua's death for full eighteen years[c] the people continued in a state of anarchy : whereafter they returned to their former polity, entrusting supreme judicial authority to him who in battle and in bravery had proved himself the best ; and that is why they called this period of their political life the age of Judges.

Samuel a second time proclaims Saul king. 1 Sam. xi. 14.

(5) Samuel the prophet now called an assembly of the Hebrews and said : " I adjure you by the most High God, who brought those excellent brothers, I mean Moses and Aaron, into this world, and rescued our fathers from the Egyptians and bondage beneath their yoke, that without showing favour through respect, without suppressing aught through fear, without giving room to any other feeling, ye tell me if I have done anything sinister and unjust through love of lucre or cupidity or out of favour to others.

Samuel's address to the people. 1 Sam. xii. 1

---

[a] Variant reading (after " bloodshed "): " and to celebrate it (the victory) with the murder of their kinsmen."

[b] Bibl. Gilgal. Probably the city near Jericho is meant. Cf. A. v. 20.

[c] The only basis for this number seems to be the interval of Moabite oppression after the death of Kenaz, the first judge (according to Josephus). Cf. A. v. 187.

εἰ καὶ τῶν τοιούτων τι προσηκάμην, μόσχον ἢ
πρόβατον, ἃ πρὸς τροφὴν ἀνεμέσητον δοκεῖ
λαμβάνειν, ἢ εἴ τινος ὑποζύγιον εἰς ἐμὴν ἀπο-
σπάσας χρείαν ἐλύπησα, τούτων ἔν τι κατειπεῖν
παρόντος ὑμῶν τοῦ βασιλέως.'' οἱ δὲ ἀνέκραγον
τούτων οὐδὲν ὑπ' αὐτοῦ γεγονέναι, προστῆναι δὲ
ὁσίως αὐτὸν καὶ δικαίως τοῦ ἔθνους.

88 (6) Σαμουῆλος δὲ ταύτης ἐξ ἁπάντων τῆς
μαρτυρίας αὐτῷ γενομένης ''ἐπεὶ δεδώκατέ μοι,''
φησί, ''τὸ μηδὲν ἄτοπον ἔθ' ὑμᾶς περὶ ἐμοῦ
δύνασθαι λέγειν, φέρε νῦν μετὰ παρρησίας ἀκού-
σατέ μου λέγοντος, ὅτι μεγάλα ἠσεβήσατε εἰς
89 τὸν θεόν, αἰτησάμενοι βασιλέα. διαμνημονεύειν δὲ
ὑμᾶς προσῆκεν, ὅτι σὺν ἑβδομήκοντα μόνοις ἐκ
τοῦ γένους ἡμῶν ὁ πάππος Ἰάκωβος διὰ λιμὸν
εἰς Αἴγυπτον ἦλθε, κἀκεῖ πολλῶν μυριάδων ἐπι-
τεκνωθεισῶν, ἃς εἰς δουλείας καὶ χαλεπὰς ὕβρεις
ἤγαγον οἱ Αἰγύπτιοι, ὁ θεὸς εὐξαμένων τῶν
πατέρων χωρὶς βασιλέως παρέσχεν αὐτοῖς ῥύσασθαι τῆς ἀνάγκης τὸ πλῆθος, Μωυσῆν αὐτοῖς
καὶ Ἀαρῶνα πέμψας ἀδελφούς, οἳ ἤγαγον ὑμᾶς
90 εἰς τήνδε τὴν γῆν, ἣν νῦν ἔχετε. καὶ τούτων
ἀπολαύσαντες ἐκ τοῦ θεοῦ προδεδώκατε τὴν
θρησκείαν καὶ τὴν εὐσέβειαν. οὐ μὴν ἀλλὰ καὶ
τοῖς πολεμίοις ὑποχειρίους γενομένους ἠλευθέρωσε
πρῶτον μὲν Ἀσσυρίων καὶ τῆς ἐκείνων ἰσχύος
ὑπερτέρους ἀπεργασάμενος, ἔπειτα Ἀμμανιτῶν
κρατῆσαι παρασχὼν καὶ Μωαβιτῶν καὶ τελευ-
ταίων[1] Παλαιστίνων. καὶ ταῦτ' οὐ βασιλέως
ἡγουμένου διεπράξασθε, ἀλλ' Ἰεφθάου καὶ Γε-

[1] τελευταῖον MSP.

Convict me if I have accepted aught of such things, heifer or sheep, the acceptance of which for food is yet deemed void of offence ; or if I have aggrieved any man by purloining his beast of burden for my own use, convict me of any one such crime here in the presence of your king." Thereat all cried out that he had done none of these things, but had governed the nation with holiness and justice.

(6) Then Samuel, having received this testimony from them all, said : " Seeing that ye grant me that ye can lay no crime to my charge to this day, come now and hearken while I tell you with all boldness what great impiety ye have shown towards God in asking for a king. Nay, it behoved you to remember how that with but seventy souls of our race our grandsire Jacob, through stress of famine, came into Egypt ; and how there, when his posterity, increased by many myriads, had been subjected to bondage and grievous outrage by the Egyptians, God, at the prayer of our fathers, without any king, brought deliverance to the multitude from their distress by sending to them the brothers Moses and Aaron, who brought you into this land which ye now possess. And yet after enjoying these things from God, ye have been traitors to His worship and His religion. Yet for all that, when ye were fallen under the hand of your enemies, He delivered you, first by causing you to triumph over the Assyrians[a] and their might, then by granting you victory over the Ammanites and Moabites, and last over the Philistines. And all this ye accomplished, not under the leadership of a king, but with Jephthah

Samuel protests against election of a king.
1 Sam. xii.7.

---

[a] A reference to the victory over King Cushan of Aram-Naharaim (Jd. iii. 8), whom Josephus, A. v. 180, calls " king of the Assyrians."

91 δεῶνος στρατηγούντων. τίς οὖν ἔσχεν ὑμᾶς ἄνοια
φυγεῖν μὲν τὸν θεόν, ὑπὸ βασιλέα δὲ εἶναι θέλειν;
ἀλλ᾽ ἐγὼ μὲν ἀπέδειξα τοῦτον ὃν αὐτὸς ἐπελέξατο.
ἵνα μέντοι γε φανερὸν ὑμῖν¹ ποιήσω τὸν θεὸν
ὀργιζόμενον καὶ δυσχεραίνοντα τῇ τῆς βασιλείας
ὑμῶν αἱρέσει, δηλῶσαι τοῦθ᾽ ὑμῖν τὸν θεὸν² παρα-
σκευάσω διὰ σημείων ἐναργῶς· ὃ γὰρ οὐδέπω
πρότερον εἶδεν³ ὑμῶν οὐδεὶς ἐνταῦθα γεγενημένον,
θέρους ἀκμῇ χειμῶνα, αἰτησάμενος τὸν θεὸν
92 παρέξω τοῦτο νῦν ὑμῖν ἐπιγνῶναι." καὶ ταῦτα
εἰπόντος πρὸς τὸ πλῆθος τοῦ Σαμουήλου, βρονταῖς
σημαίνει τὸ θεῖον καὶ ἀστραπαῖς καὶ χαλάζης
καταφορᾷ τὴν τοῦ προφήτου περὶ πάντων ἀλήθειαν,
ὡς τεθαμβηκότας αὐτοὺς καὶ περιδεεῖς γινομένους ἁμαρτεῖν τε ὁμολογεῖν καὶ κατ᾽ ἄγνοιαν
εἰς τοῦτο προπεσεῖν, καὶ ἱκετεύειν τὸν προφήτην
ὡς πατέρα χρηστὸν καὶ ἐπιεικῆ, τὸν θεὸν αὐτοῖς
εὐμενῆ καταστῆσαι καὶ ταύτην ἀφεῖναι τὴν
ἁμαρτίαν, ἣν πρὸς οἷς ἐξύβρισαν ἄλλοις καὶ παρ-
93 ηνόμησαν προσεξειργάσαντο. ὁ δὲ ὑπισχνεῖται
καὶ παρακαλέσειν τὸν θεὸν συγγνῶναι περὶ τούτων
αὐτοῖς καὶ πείσειν, συνεβούλευε μέντοι δικαίους
εἶναι καὶ ἀγαθοὺς καὶ μνημονεύειν ἀεὶ τῶν
διὰ τὴν παράβασιν τῆς ἀρετῆς αὐτοῖς κακῶν
συμπεσόντων καὶ τῶν σημείων τοῦ θεοῦ καὶ τῆς
Μωυσέος νομοθεσίας, εἰ σωτηρίας αὐτοῖς καὶ
τῆς μετὰ τοῦ βασιλέως εὐδαιμονίας ἐστὶν ἐπιθυμία.
94 εἰ δὲ τούτων ἀμελήσουσιν, ἔλεγεν ἥξειν αὐτοῖς τε
καὶ τῷ βασιλεῖ μεγάλην ἐκ θεοῦ πληγήν. καὶ
ὅ⁴ Σαμοῦηλος μὲν ταῦτα τοῖς Ἑβραίοις προφη-

---

¹ ὑμῖν om. RO.   ² τὸν θεὸν om. RO.
³ οἶδεν conj. Niese.   ⁴ ὁ om. RO.

and Gedeon for generals. What madness then possessed you to flee your God and to wish to be under a king ? Nay, I have appointed him whom He Himself hath chosen. Howbeit, to manifest to you that God is wroth and ill-content at your choice of kingly rule, I will prevail with Him to reveal this to you by signs clearly. For that which not one of you ever saw befall here before—a tempest at midsummer—that through prayer to God I shall cause you now to witness." Scarce had Samuel spoken these words to the people, when the Deity by thunderings, lightning, and a torrent of hail, attested the truth of all that the prophet had said ; whereat astounded and terrified they confessed their sin, into which, they said, they had fallen through ignorance, and implored the prophet, as a kind and gentle father, to render God gracious to them that He might forgive this sin which they had committed in addition to all their other insolences and transgressions. And he promised that he would beseech God to pardon them in this thing and would withal move Him thereto ; howbeit, he exhorted them to be righteous and good, and ever to remember the ills that their transgression of virtue had brought upon them, the miracles of God and the legislation of Moses, if they had any desire for continued salvation and continued felicity under their king. But should they neglect these things, there would come, said he, both on them and on their king a great visitation from God. And after thus prophesying to the Hebrews, Samuel dismissed them to their

The storm attests God's displeasure. 1 Sam. xii. 18.

373

τεύσας ἀπέλυσεν αὐτοὺς ἐπὶ τὰ οἰκεῖα βεβαιώσας
ἐκ δευτέρου τῷ Σαούλῳ τὴν βασιλείαν.

95 (vi. 1) Οὗτος δ᾽ ἐπιλέξας ἐκ τοῦ πλήθους ὡς
περὶ¹ τρισχιλίους, τοὺς μὲν δισχιλίους ὥστε
σωματοφυλακεῖν αὐτὸν² λαβὼν αὐτὸς διέτριβεν
ἐν πόλει Βεθήβῳ,³ Ἰωνάθῃ δὲ τῷ παιδὶ τοὺς
λοιποὺς δοὺς ὥστε σωματοφυλακεῖν αὐτὸν εἰς
Γέβαλ᾽⁴ ἔπεμψεν. ὁ δ᾽ ἐκπολιορκεῖ τι φρούριον
96 τῶν Παλαιστίνων οὐ πόρρω Γεβάλων. οἱ γὰρ⁵
Παλαιστῖνοι καταστρεφόμενοι τοὺς Ἰουδαίους τά
τε ὅπλα αὐτοὺς ἀφῃροῦντο καὶ τοὺς ὀχυρωτάτους
τῆς χώρας τόπους φρουραῖς κατελαμβάνοντο καὶ
σιδηροφορεῖν χρῆσθαί⁶ τε καθάπαξ ἀπηγόρευον
σιδήρῳ, καὶ διὰ ταύτην τὴν ἀπόρρησιν⁷ οἱ γεωργοί,
εἴποτε δεήσει᾽ αὐτοὺς ἐπισκευάσαι τι τῶν ἐργα-
λείων, ἢ ὕνιν ἢ δίκελλαν⁸ ἢ ἄλλο τι τῶν εἰς γεωργίαν
χρησίμων, φοιτῶντες εἰς τοὺς Παλαιστίνους ταῦτα
97 ἔπραττον. ὡς δὲ ἠκούσθη τοῖς Παλαιστίνοις ἡ
τῆς φρουρᾶς ἀναίρεσις ἀγανακτήσαντες καὶ δεινὴν
ὕβριν τὴν καταφρόνησιν ἡγησάμενοι στρατεύουσιν
ἐπὶ τοὺς Ἰουδαίους πεζῶν μὲν τριάκοντα μυριάσιν
ἅρμασι δὲ τρισμυρίοις, ἵππον δὲ ἑξακισχιλίαν
98 ἐπήγοντο· καὶ στρατοπεδευσαμένων⁹ πρὸς πόλει
Μαχμά, τοῦτο Σαῦλος ὁ τῶν Ἑβραίων βασιλεὺς

---

¹ περὶ om. RO. ² ὥστε . . . αὐτὸν om. Lat.
³ Bethleem Lat. ⁴ Γαβὰς MSP: Gabatha Lat.
⁵ + τῆς Γαβὰς MSP: Lat.
⁶ κεχρῆσθαι Schmidt cum RO.
⁷ πρόρρησιν RO: causam Lat.
⁸ RO: μάκελλαν (-ην) rell.
⁹ στρατοπεδεύονται MSP Lat.

ᵃ Gr. Bethēbos, bibl. Bethel.
ᵇ The repetition of the Greek phrase " to guard his body "
indicates a text corruption.

homes, having for the second time confirmed the kingdom to Saul.

(vi. 1) But Saul chose out of the multitude some three thousand men, and taking two thousand for his bodyguard abode for his part in the city of Bethēl(os)[a]; the rest he gave as guards[b] to his son Jonathan and sent him to Gebala.[c] And Jonathan besieged and took a fortress of the Philistines not far from Gebala. For the Philistines, in their subjugation of the Jews, had deprived them of their arms and occupied the strongest positions in the country with garrisons, further forbidding the vanquished to carry any weapon of iron or to make any use at all of iron. In consequence of this interdict, whenever the peasantry needed to repair any of their tools, ploughshare or mattock or other agricultural instrument, they would go to the Philistines to do this. So when the Philistines heard of the destruction of their garrison, infuriated and deeming such scorn of them a monstrous affront, they marched against the Jews with 300,000 footmen,[d] 30,000 chariots, and 6000 horse to support them, and pitched their camp beside the city of Machma.[e] On learning of this, Saul, king of

Saul prepares for war with the Philistines.
1 Sam. xiii. 2.

19.

5.

3.

---

[c] Bibl. Gibeath Benjamin, LXX Γαβεὲ (Γαβαὰ etc.) τοῦ Βενιαμείν, perhaps a different site from the Gaba (bibl. Gibeah) mentioned in *A.* v. 140. Gibeah (of which Gibeath is a construct form in Hebrew) and Gaba or Geba are related words meaning "hill," *cf.* LXX βουνός. The relation of various sites by these names in the same territory is uncertain because of their confusion in Scripture.

[d] Scripture gives no number for the foot-soldiers. *Cf.* 1 Sam. xiii. 5 "and people like the sand on the seashore in multitude."

[e] Bibl. Michmash, LXX Μαχεμάς, Μαχμάς, etc., modern *Mukhmās*, about two miles N.W. of the supposed site of Geba, and eight miles N.W. of Jerusalem.

μαθὼν εἰς Γάλγαλα καταβαίνει πόλιν καὶ διὰ πάσης
κηρύσσει τῆς χώρας, ἐπ' ἐλευθερίᾳ καλῶν τὸν
λαὸν ἐπὶ τὸν πόλεμον τὸν πρὸς Παλαιστίνους, τὴν
δύναμιν ἐκφαυλίζων αὐτῶν καὶ διασύρων ὡς οὐκ
ἀξιόλογον οὐδ' ὥστε φοβεῖσθαι διακινδυνεύειν πρὸς
99 αὐτούς. κατανοήσαντες δὲ τὸ πλῆθος τῶν Παλαιστίνων οἱ τοῦ Σαούλου κατεπλάγησαν, καὶ οἱ μὲν
εἰς τὰ σπήλαια καὶ τοὺς ὑπονόμους ἔκρυψαν
αὑτούς, οἱ πλείους δὲ εἰς τὴν πέραν τοῦ Ἰορδάνου
γῆν ἔφυγον· αὕτη δ' ἦν Γάδου καὶ Ῥουβήλου.
100 (2) Πέμψας δὲ Σαοῦλος πρὸς τὸν προφήτην
ἐκάλει πρὸς αὐτὸν συνδιασκεψόμενον περὶ τοῦ
πολέμου καὶ τῶν πραγμάτων. ὁ δὲ περιμένειν
αὐτὸν ἐκέλευσεν αὐτόθι καὶ παρασκευάζειν θύματα·
μετὰ γὰρ ἡμέρας ἕξ[1] πρὸς αὐτὸν ἥξειν, ὅπως
θύσωσι τῇ ἑβδόμῃ τῶν ἡμερῶν, ἔπειθ' οὕτως
101 συμβάλωσι τοῖς πολεμίοις. καὶ περιμένει μὲν ὡς
ὁ προφήτης ἐπέστειλεν, οὐκέτι μέντοι γε διατηρεῖ
τὴν ἐντολήν, ἀλλ' ὡς ἑώρα βραδύνοντα μὲν τὸν
προφήτην, αὐτὸν δὲ ὑπὸ τῶν στρατιωτῶν κατα-
λειπόμενον, λαβὼν τὰ θύματα τὴν θυσίαν ἐπετέλει[2]·
ἐπεὶ δὲ τὸν Σαμούηλον ἤκουσε προσιόντα ὑπ-
102 αντησόμενος ἐξῆλθεν. ὁ δ' οὐκ ὀρθῶς αὐτὸν ἔφη
πεποιηκέναι παρακούσαντα ὧν ἐπέστειλεν αὐτὸς
καὶ φθάσαντα τὴν παρουσίαν, ἣν κατὰ βούλησιν
γινομένην τοῦ θείου πρὸς τὰς εὐχὰς καὶ τὰς
θυσίας τὰς ὑπὲρ τοῦ πλήθους προλάβοι, κακῶς
103 ἱερουργήσας καὶ προπετὴς γενόμενος. ἀπολογου-
μένου δὲ τοῦ Σαούλου καὶ περιμεῖναι μὲν τὰς

---

[1] om. RO: septem Lat.   [2] προσήγαγεν MSP.

the Hebrews, came down to the city of Galgala and
sent heralds throughout all the country to call up the
people in the name of liberty to the war against the
Philistines, belittling and disparaging their strength
as inconsiderable and not such that they need fear
to hazard battle with them.[a] But, on perceiving that 6.
host of Philistines, Saul's recruits were in consternation ; and while some hid themselves in the caverns
and cavities, the more part fled beyond the Jordan
into the territory of Gad and Rubel.[b]

(2) Saul then sent word to the prophet, summoning Saul's
him to his presence to confer with him concerning premature sacrifice.
the war and the situation. Samuel bade him wait 1 Sam. xiii.
where he was and make ready victims for sacrifice, 8.
for after six days he would come to him, that so they x. 8.
might sacrifice on the seventh day and, that done,
join battle with the enemy. So Saul waited awhile
as the prophet had enjoined upon him ; then, however,
he would observe his command no longer, but when
he saw that the prophet tarried and that his own
soldiers were deserting him, he took the victims and xiii. 9.
performed the sacrifice himself. Then, hearing that
Samuel was approaching, he went out to meet him.
But the prophet told him that he had not done rightly
in disobeying his injunctions and anticipating his
advent : he was paying that visit in accordance with
the will of the Deity to preside at the prayers and
the sacrifices on behalf of the people, and now he had
forestalled him by having offered sacrifice wrongly
and by his precipitate haste. Thereat Saul excused
himself, saying that he had waited during those

---

[a] Saul's disparaging remarks about the Philistines are an
addition to Scripture.
[b] 1 Sam. xiii. 7 " and the land of Gad and Gilead."

ἡμέρας ἃς ὥρισε λέγοντος, ὑπὸ δὲ ἀνάγκης καὶ
ἀναχωρήσεως μὲν τῶν αὑτοῦ στρατιωτῶν διὰ φόβον, στρατοπεδείας δὲ τῶν ἐχθρῶν ἐν Μαχμᾶ καὶ
ἀκοῆς τῆς ἐπ᾽ αὐτὸν εἰς Γάλγαλα καταβάσεως
ἐπειχθῆναι πρὸς τὴν θυσίαν, ὑπολαβὼν δὲ ὁ
104 Σαμουῆλος "ἀλλὰ σύγε," φησίν, "εἰ δίκαιος ἦσθα
καὶ μὴ παρήκουσας ἐμοῦ μηδ᾽ ὧν ὑπέθετό μοι
περὶ τῶν παρόντων ὁ θεὸς ὠλιγώρησας ταχύ-
τερος ἢ συνέφερε τοῖς πράγμασι γεγονώς, σοί
τ᾽ αὐτῷ πλεῖστον ἂν βασιλεῦσαι χρόνον ἐξεγένετο
105 καὶ τοῖς σοῖς ἐγγόνοις.[1]" καὶ Σαμουῆλος μὲν
ἀχθόμενος ἐπὶ τοῖς γεγενημένοις ἀνεχώρησε
παρ᾽ αὐτόν, Σαοῦλος δὲ εἰς Γαβαὼν πόλιν ἔχων
ἑξακοσίους[2] μεθ᾽ ἑαυτοῦ μόνον ἧκε σὺν Ἰωνάθῃ
τῷ παιδί. τούτων δὲ οἱ πλείους οὐκ εἶχον ὅπλα,
τῆς χώρας σπανιζούσης σιδήρου καὶ τῶν ὅπλα
χαλκεύειν δυναμένων· οὐ γὰρ εἴων οἱ Παλαιστῖνοι ταῦτα εἶναι, καθὼς[3] μικρὸν ἔμπροσθεν δεδη-
106 λώκαμεν. διελόντες δ᾽ εἰς τρία μέρη τὴν στρατιὰν
οἱ Παλαιστῖνοι καὶ κατὰ τοσαύτας ὁδοὺς ἐπερ-
χόμενοι τὴν τῶν Ἑβραίων χώραν ἐπόρθουν, βλεπόντων τε Σαούλου τοῦ βασιλέως αὐτῶν καὶ τοῦ
παιδὸς Ἰωνάθου ἀμῦναί τε τῇ γῇ, μεθ᾽ ἑξακο-
107 σίων γὰρ μόνων ἦσαν, οὐ δυναμένων. καθεζόμενοι
δ᾽ αὐτός τε καὶ ὁ παῖς αὐτοῦ καὶ ὁ ἀρχιερεὺς
Ἀχίας,[4] ἀπόγονος ὢν Ἠλὶ τοῦ ἀρχιερέως, ἐπὶ
βουνοῦ ὑψηλοῦ καὶ τὴν γῆν λεηλατουμένην ὁρῶντες
ἐν ἀγωνίᾳ δεινῇ καθεστήκεσαν. συντίθεται δὲ ὁ
Σαούλου παῖς τῷ ὁπλοφόρῳ, κρύφα πορευθέντες
αὐτοὶ εἰς τὴν τῶν πολεμίων παρεμβολὴν ἐκδρα-

---

[1] ἐκγόνοις MSP.
[2] διακοσίους E.
[3] + καὶ SP: καθὰ καὶ M.
[4] Ἀχίας RO.

days which Samuel had appointed, but that necessity, the desertion of his terrified troops, the enemy's encampment at Machma and a report of their intended descent upon him at Galgala, had impelled him to speed the sacrifice. Then Samuel rejoining, " Nay, but for thy part," said he, " hadst thou been righteous and not disobeyed me nor lightly regarded the counsels which God has given me touching the present matter, by acting more hastily than befitted the matter, then would it have been given thee to reign exceeding long, and to thy posterity as well." So Samuel, vexed at what had befallen, returned to his home, while Saul, with but six hundred followers, came with his son Jonathan to the city of Gabaon.[a] Most of his men had no arms, the country being destitute of iron and of men capable of forging arms ; for the Philistines had prohibited this, as we said just now.[b] And now, dividing their army into three companies and advancing by as many routes,[c] the Philistines proceeded to ravage the country of the Hebrews under the eyes of Saul, their king, and of his son Jonathan, who, with but six hundred followers, were powerless to defend their land. Seated on a lofty hill, Saul and his son and the high priest Achias,[d] a descendant of Eli the high priest, as they watched the devastation of the land, were in a state of deepest anguish. Saul's son then proposed to his armour-bearer that they should secretly sally out alone into the enemy's

Saul and
Jonathan
encamp at
Gibeah.
1 Sam. xiii.
16.

Jonathan's
exploit.
1 Sam. xiv. 1.

---

[a] Bibl. Gibeath Benjamin. *Cf.* on § 95.

[b] § 96.

[c] 1 Sam. xiii. 17 specifies the roads to Ophrah, Beth Horon and "the way of the border looking toward the valley of Zeboim"—all in the territory N. of Jerusalem.

[d] Bibl. Ahiah. His genealogy is given in 1 Sam. xiv. 3. *Cf.* on § 122.

μεῖν καὶ ταραχὴν ἐμποιῆσαι καὶ θόρυβον αὐτοῖς.[1]

108 τοῦ δὲ ὁπλοφόρου προθύμως ἐφέψεσθαι[2] φήσαντος
ὅποι ποτ᾽ ἂν ἡγῆται, κἂν ἀποθανεῖν δέῃ, προσ-
λαβὼν τὴν τοῦ νεανίσκου συνεργίαν καὶ καταβὰς
ἀπὸ τοῦ βουνοῦ πρὸς τοὺς πολεμίους ἐπορεύετο.
ἦν δὲ τὸ τῶν πολεμίων στρατόπεδον ἐπὶ κρημνοῦ,[3]
τρισὶν ἄκραις εἰς λεπτὸν ἀπηκονημέναις μῆκος
πέτρας ἐν κύκλῳ περιστεφανούσης ὥσπερ προ-
109 βόλοις τὰς ἐπιχειρήσεις ἀπομαχόμενον. ἔνθεν συνέβαινεν ἠμελῆσθαι τὰς φυλακὰς τοῦ στρατοπέδου
διὰ τὸ φύσει περιεῖναι τῷ χωρίῳ τὴν ἀσφάλειαν
καὶ παντὶ[4] νομίζειν ἀμήχανον εἶναι κατ᾽ ἐκείνας
110 οὐκ ἀναβῆναι μόνον ἀλλὰ καὶ προσελθεῖν. ὡς
οὖν ἧκον εἰς τὴν παρεμβολὴν ὁ Ἰωνάθης παρ-
εθάρσυνε τὸν ὁπλοφόρον καὶ "προσβάλωμεν τοῖς
πολεμίοις," ἔλεγε, "κἂν μὲν ἀναβῆναι κελεύσωσι
πρὸς αὐτοὺς ἡμᾶς ἰδόντες, σημεῖον τοῦτο νίκης
ὑπολάμβανε,[5] ἐὰν δὲ φθέγξωνται μηδὲν ὡς οὐ
111 καλοῦντες ἡμᾶς, ὑποστρέψωμεν.[6]" προσιόντων δὲ
αὐτῶν τῷ στρατοπέδῳ τῶν πολεμίων ὑποφαι-
νούσης ἤδη τῆς ἡμέρας ἰδόντες οἱ Παλαιστῖνοι,
πρὸς ἀλλήλους ἔλεγον ἐκ τῶν ὑπονόμων καὶ τῶν[7]
σπηλαίων προϊέναι τοὺς Ἑβραίους, καὶ πρὸς
Ἰωνάθην καὶ τὸν ὁπλοφόρον αὐτοῦ "δεῦτ᾽," ἔφασαν,
"ἀνέλθετε πρὸς ἡμᾶς, ἵνα ὑμᾶς τιμωρησώμεθα
112 τῶν τετολμημένων ἀξίως." ἀσπασάμενος δὲ τὴν
φωνὴν ὁ τοῦ Σαούλου παῖς ὡς νίκην αὐτῷ ση-
μαίνουσαν, παραυτίκα μὲν ἀνεχώρησαν ἐξ οὗπερ

---

[1] αὐτοῖς om. RO.
[2] SP: ἕπεσθαι rell.
[3] S: κρημνῷ rell.
[4] πάντη M: valde Lat.
[5] M: ὑπολαμβάνειν SP.
[6] ὑποστρέψωμεν RO.
[7] τῶν om. RO.

camp and create confusion and panic among them. When the armour-bearer replied that he would gladly follow whithersoever he led, though it were to his death, Jonathan, having gained the young man's support, descended from the hill and set off towards the enemy. Now the enemy's camp lay on a cliff, enclosed in a ring of rocks, with three[a] peaks tapering to a long narrow ridge and serving as a bulwark to beat off all attacks. Consequently it came about that no care had been taken to guard the camp, because nature had given the place security and it was believed to be absolutely impossible for any man not merely to scale those crags but even to approach them. When therefore they were nearing the encampment, Jonathan encouraged his armour-bearer, saying : " Now let us attack the enemy ; and if, on seeing us, they bid us mount up to them, take that for a presage of victory, but if they utter not a word, as though they invited us not, let us then return." But, as they drew nigh to the enemy's camp, just at the dawn of day,[b] the Philistines espied them and said one to another, " Here are the Hebrews coming out of their holes and caverns," and then to Jonathan and his armour-bearer, " Come on," they cried, " come up to us, to receive the due punishment for your audacity."[c] But Saul's son welcoming that shout as a token of victory, they straightway withdrew from the spot where they

Jonathan and his armour-bearer rout the

---

[a] Scripture mentions only two peaks, Bozez and Seneb.
[b] The time of the attack is not given in Scripture.
[c] 1 Sam. xiv. 12, " come up and we will show you a thing."

ὤφθησαν τόπου τοῖς πολεμίοις, παραμειψάμενοι[1]
δὲ τοῦτον ἐπὶ τὴν πέτραν ἧκον[2] ἔρημον οὖσαν τῶν
113 φυλαττόντων διὰ τὴν ὀχυρότητα. κἀκεῖθεν ἀν-
ερπύσαντες μετὰ πολλῆς ταλαιπωρίας ἐβιάσαντο
τὴν τοῦ χωρίου φύσιν ὡς[3] ἀνελθεῖν ἐπὶ τοὺς
πολεμίους, ἐπιπεσόντες δ' αὐτοῖς κοιμωμένοις ἀπο-
κτείνουσι μὲν ὡς εἴκοσι, ταραχῆς δὲ καὶ ἐκπλήξεως
αὐτοὺς ἐγέμισαν, ὡς τινὰς μὲν φυγεῖν τὰς παν-
114 οπλίας ἀπορρίψαντας, οἱ δὲ πολλοὶ μὴ γνωρίζοντες
ἑαυτοὺς διὰ τὸ ἐκ πολλῶν ἐθνῶν εἶναι, πολεμίους
ὑπονοοῦντες ἀλλήλους, καὶ γὰρ[4] εἴκαζον ἀναβῆναι
πρὸς αὐτοὺς τῶν Ἑβραίων οὐ[5] δύο μόνους, εἰς
μάχην ἐτράποντο. καὶ οἱ μὲν αὐτῶν ἀπέθνησκον
κτεινόμενοι, τινὲς δὲ φεύγοντες κατὰ τῶν πετρῶν
ὠθούμενοι κατεκρημνίζοντο.
115 (3) Τῶν δὲ τοῦ Σαούλου κατασκόπων τετα-
ράχθαι τὸ στρατόπεδον τῶν Παλαιστίνων φρασάντων τῷ βασιλεῖ, Σαοῦλος ἠρώτα μή τις εἴη τῶν
αὐτοῦ κεχωρισμένος. ἀκούσας δὲ τὸν υἱὸν καὶ
σὺν αὐτῷ τὸν ὁπλοφόρον ἀπεῖναι, κελεύει τὸν
ἀρχιερέα λαβόντα τὴν ἀρχιερατικὴν στολὴν προφητεύειν αὐτῷ περὶ τῶν μελλόντων. τοῦ δὲ νίκην
ἔσεσθαι καὶ κράτος κατὰ τῶν πολεμίων φράσαντος
ἐπεξέρχεται τοῖς Παλαιστίνοις καὶ τεταραγμένοις

---

[1] παραμειψάμενος MSP.
[2] conj. Niese: ἧκεν codd. Lat.　　　[3] ὡς om. R.O.
[4] + οὐκ SP.　　　[5] οὐ om. SP.

---

[a] Details of the fight are an amplification, in harmony
with Josephus's rationalizing tendency.

[b] The unscriptural details about the rocks are perhaps
suggested by the LXX rendering, in some mss. (ἐν πετροβόλοις),
of the obscure Hebrew text of 1 Sam. xiv. 14.

had been sighted by the enemy and, turning aside ^{Philistines.} from it, reached the rock which by reason of its strength had been left destitute of guards. Thence, creeping up with great labour, they forced their way over the difficulties of the ground and mounted up to the enemy ; falling upon these as they slept, they slew some twenty of them and filled the host with such tumult and alarm, that some flung off all their arms and fled, while the more part, not recognizing their comrades, because of the many nationalities of which their army was composed, and taking each other for enemies—for they did not suppose that there had come up against them two only of the Hebrews—they turned to fight one another.^a And some of them perished by the sword, others as they fled were driven over the rocks and hurled headlong.^b

Philistines.
1 Sam. xiv.
12.

(3) Saul's spies having now reported to the king ^{Saul's} that there was a commotion in the camp of the Philistines, Saul inquired whether any of his men had gone from him. Then, on hearing that his son and, with him, his armour-bearer were absent, he ordered the high priest to don his high-priestly robes ^c and to prophesy to him what would befall. The high priest having declared that it would be victory and triumph over his enemies, the king set off against the Philistines and fell upon them while they were yet panic-

Saul's
oath of
allegiance.
1 Sam. xiv.
16.

^c In agreement with the LXX which reads " ephod " against the Heb. which has " ark," although the ark was presumably still at Kirjath Jearim. Josephus may, however, have read *'ephod* for *'aron* (ark) in his Heb. text, in which some scholars suspect a deliberate alteration to obviate the inference that there was more than one ark. (*Cf.* W. R. Arnold, *Ephod and Ark.*) The rabbinic commentaries on this passage explain that the ephod with the Urim and Thummin was in the ark.

383

JOSEPHUS

116 προσβάλλει καὶ φονεύουσιν ἀλλήλους. προσρέουσι
δ᾽ αὐτῷ καὶ οἱ πρότερον εἴς τε τοὺς ὑπονόμους καὶ
εἰς τὰ σπήλαια συμφυγόντες, ἀκούσαντες ὅτι νικᾷ
Σαοῦλος· γενομένων δὲ ὡς μυρίων ἤδη τῶν
Ἑβραίων διώκει τοὺς πολεμίους κατὰ πᾶσαν
ἐσκορπισμένους τὴν χώραν. εἴτε δὲ ὑπὸ τῆς ἐπὶ
τῇ νίκῃ χαρᾶς οὕτω παραλόγως γενομένη (συμβαίνει γὰρ μὴ κρατεῖν τοῦ λογισμοῦ τοὺς οὕτως
εὐτυχήσαντας) εἴθ᾽ ὑπὸ ἀγνοίας, εἰς δεινὸν προ-
117 πίπτει[1] καὶ πολλὴν ἔχον κατάμεμψιν ἔργον· βουλόμενος γὰρ αὐτῷ τε τιμωρῆσαι καὶ δίκην ἀπολαβεῖν
παρὰ τῶν Παλαιστίνων ἐπαρᾶται τοῖς Ἑβραίοις,
ἵν᾽ εἴ τις ἀποσχόμενος τοῦ φονεύειν τοὺς ἐχθροὺς
φάγοι[2] μέχρι[3] νὺξ ἐπελθοῦσα τῆς ἀναιρέσεως
καὶ τῆς διώξεως αὐτοὺς παύσει τῶν πολεμίων,
118 οὗτος ἐπάρατος ᾖ. τοῦ δὲ Σαούλου τοῦτο φήσαντος, ἐπεὶ κατά τινα δρυμὸν ἐγένοντο βαθὺν καὶ
μελισσῶν γέμοντα τῆς Ἐφράμου κληρουχίας, ὁ
τοῦ Σαούλου παῖς οὐκ ἐπακηκοὼς τῆς τοῦ πατρὸς
ἀρᾶς οὐδὲ τῆς ἐπ᾽ αὐτῇ τοῦ πλήθους ὁμολογίας,
119 ἀποθλίψας τι κηρίον τοῦ μέλιτος ἤσθιε. μεταξὺ
δὲ γνοὺς ὅτι μετὰ δεινῆς ἀρᾶς ὁ πατὴρ ἀπεῖπε
μὴ γεύσασθαί τινα πρὸ ἡλίου δυσμῶν, ἐσθίων
μὲν ἐπαύσατο, ἔφη δὲ οὐκ ὀρθῶς[4] κωλῦσαι τὸν
πατέρα· μετὰ μείζονος γὰρ ἰσχύος ἂν καὶ προ-

[1] προσπίπτει MSP.
[2] + καὶ μὴ codd. Glycas: an leg. καὶ δὴ ?
[3] μέχρις οὗ MSP Glycas: ἕως οὗ E: antequam Lat.
[4] + τοῦτο MSP

384

stricken and massacring one another. Moreover those
who earlier had taken refuge in the tunnels and caves,
on hearing that Saul was victorious, came streaming
toward him; and with now some ten thousand[a]
Hebrews at his back, he pursued the enemy scattered
over the whole countryside. But, whether through
exultation at a victory so unexpected—for men are
apt to lose control of reason when thus blest by
fortune—or through ignorance,[b] he rushed into a
dreadful and very blameworthy deed. For, in his
desire to avenge himself and to exact punishment
from the Philistines, he invoked a curse upon the
Hebrews, that should any man desist from slaughtering the foe and take food, before oncoming night
should stay them from carnage and the pursuit of
the enemy, he should be accursed. Now after that
Saul had so spoken, when they were come to a dense
oak-coppice[c] swarming with bees in the portion of
Ephraim,[d] Saul's son, not having heard his father's
curse nor the people's approbation thereof, broke off[e]
a piece of a honeycomb and began to eat it. But
learning, as he did so, how his father under a dire curse
had forbidden any man to taste aught before sun-
down, he ceased to eat,[f] but said that his father's
interdict was not right, for they would have had
more strength and ardour for the pursuit, had they

Jonathan's breach of the oath.
1 Sam. xiv. 25.

[a] So in the LXX; Heb. omits the number.

[b] Cf. LXX, 1 Sam. xiv. 24 Σαοὺλ ἠγνόησεν ἄγνοιαν μεγάλην:
Heb. has nothing corresponding.

[c] The "oak-coppice" is taken from the LXX; Heb. has
ya‘ar which may mean either forest (so the Targum here) or
honeycomb.

[d] So the LXX, 1 Sam. xiv. 23; not mentioned in Heb.

[e] 1 Sam. xiv. 27, "put forth the end of the staff that was
in his hand and dipped it in the honeycomb."

[f] Scripture does not say that he ceased to eat.

θυμίας διώκοντας, εἰ τροφῆς μετελάμβανον, πολλῷ
πλείονας καὶ λαβεῖν τῶν ἐχθρῶν καὶ φονεῦσαι.

120 (4) Πολλὰς γοῦν¹ κατακόψαντες μυριάδας τῶν
Παλαιστίνων, δείλης ὀψίας ἐπὶ διαρπαγὴν τοῦ
στρατοπέδου τῶν Παλαιστίνων τρέπονται, καὶ
λείαν πολλὴν καὶ βοσκήματα λαβόντες κατασφά-
ζουσι καὶ ταῦτ' ἔναιμα² κατήσθιον. ἀπαγγέλλεται
δὲ τῷ βασιλεῖ ὑπὸ τῶν γραμματέων ὅτι τὸ πλῆθος εἰς τὸν θεὸν ἐξαμαρτάνει θῦσαν καὶ πρὶν ἢ τὸ
αἷμα καλῶς ἀποπλῦναι καὶ τὰς σάρκας ποιῆσαι
121 καθαρὰς ἐσθίον. καὶ ὁ Σαοῦλος κελεύει κυλι-
σθῆναι λίθον μέγαν εἰς μέσον καὶ κηρύσσει θύειν
ἐπ' αὐτοῦ τὸν ὄχλον τὰ ἱερεῖα, καὶ τὰ κρέα μὴ σὺν
τῷ αἵματι δαίνυσθαι· τοῦτο γὰρ οὐκ εἶναι τῷ
θεῷ κεχαρισμένον. τοῦτο δὲ πάντων κατὰ τὴν
πρόσταξιν τοῦ βασιλέως ποιησάντων ἵστησιν ἐκεῖ
βωμὸν ὁ Σαοῦλος καὶ ὡλοκαύτωσεν ἐπ' αὐτοῦ
ἐκεῖ³ τῷ θεῷ. τοῦτον πρῶτον βωμὸν κατεσκεύασεν.

122 (5) Ἄγειν δ' εὐθὺς τὴν στρατιὰν ἐπὶ τὴν
παρεμβολὴν τῶν πολεμίων ἐπὶ τὴν διαρπαγὴν
τῶν ἐν αὐτῇ βουλόμενος πρὶν ἡμέρας, καὶ τῶν
στρατιωτῶν οὐκ ὀκνούντων ἕπεσθαι, πολλὴν δ' εἰς
ἃ προστάττει προθυμίαν ἐνδεικνυμένων, καλέσας
ὁ βασιλεὺς Ἀχίτωβον τὸν ἀρχιερέα κελεύει⁴
αὐτὸν γνῶναι εἰ δίδωσιν αὐτοῖς ὁ θεὸς καὶ συγχωρεῖ βαδίσασιν ἐπὶ τὸ στρατόπεδον τῶν ἐχθρῶν

---

¹ RO: δ' οὖν MSP: οὖν E.
² SPE: ἐν αἵματι rell.
³ ἐκεῖ secl. edd.; cf. lxx, 1 Sam. xiv. 34.
⁴ ἐκέλευσεν MSP.

partaken of food, and would thus have captured and slain many more of the foe.

(4) Many, for all that, were the myriads of Philistines whom they cut down ere at dusk they turned to the pillage of the enemy's camp ; where, having taken much booty and cattle, they slaughtered and set to devouring them all reeking with blood. Thereupon it was reported to the king by the scribes,[a] that the host were sinning against God in that, having sacrificed, they were now eating, before they had duly washed away the blood and made the flesh clean.[b] Then Saul ordered a great stone to be rolled into the midst and made proclamation to the throng to sacrifice their victims thereon and not to feast upon the flesh with the blood, since that was not well-pleasing to God. And when all had so done in obedience to the king's command, Saul set up an altar there and offered burnt-offerings[c] thereon to God. This was the first altar that he built.

Plundering of the Philistines' camp. 1 Sam. xiv. 31.

(5) Being now desirous to lead his army forthwith to the enemy's encampment to plunder everything therein before daybreak, and seeing that his soldiers, far from hesitating to follow him, showed great alacrity to obey his orders, the king summoned Achitob[d] the high priest and bade him ascertain whether God would grant and permit them to proceed to the camp of the foe and destroy such as were

Saul's discovery of Jonathan's error. 1 Sam. xiv. 36.

---

[a] Not mentioned in Scripture.

[b] Cf. A. iii. 260 on Lev. xix. 26, Deut. xii. 16.

[c] Scripture does not specify that the sacrifices were burnt-offerings, as do Josephus and the rabbis in their discussion of this passage, Bab. Talmud, Zebaḥim 120 a.

[d] Priest's name not mentioned in Scripture ; according to § 107, the high priest at this time was Achias (bibl. Ahiah), the son of Achitob (bibl. Ahitub).

123 διαφθεῖραι τοὺς ἐν αὐτῷ τυγχάνοντας. εἰπόντος
δὲ τοῦ ἱερέως μὴ ἀποκρίνεσθαι τὸν θεόν "ἀλλ' οὐ
δίχα αἰτίας,[1]" εἶπεν ὁ Σαοῦλος, "πυνθανομένοις
ἡμῖν φωνὴν οὐ δίδωσιν ὁ θεός, ὃς πρότερον αὐτὸς
προεμήνυσε πάντα καὶ μηδ' ἐπερωτῶσιν ἔφθασε[2]
λέγων, ἀλλ' ἔστι τι λανθάνον ἐξ ἡμῶν ἁμάρτημα
124 πρὸς αὐτὸν αἴτιον τῆς σιωπῆς. καὶ ὄμνυμί γε
τοῦτον αὐτόν, ἦ μὴν κἂν ὁ παῖς ὁ ἐμὸς Ἰωνάθης ᾖ
τὸ ἁμάρτημα τοῦτο ἐργασάμενος ἀποκτείνειν[3]
αὐτὸν καὶ τὸν θεὸν οὕτως ἱλάσασθαι,[4] ὡς ἂν εἰ καὶ
παρ' ἀλλοτρίου καὶ μηδὲν ἐμοὶ προσήκοντος τὴν
125 ὑπὲρ αὐτοῦ δίκην ἀπελάμβανον." τοῦ δὲ πλήθους
τοῦτο ποιεῖν ἐπιβοήσαντος, παραχρῆμα πάντας
ἵστησιν εἰς ἕνα τόπον, ἵσταται δὲ καὶ αὐτὸς σὺν
τῷ παιδὶ κατ' ἄλλο μέρος καὶ κλήρῳ τὸν ἡμαρτη-
κότα μαθεῖν ἐπεζήτει· καὶ λαγχάνει δοκεῖν οὗτος
126 εἶναι Ἰωνάθης. ἐπερωτώμενος δὲ ὑπὸ τοῦ πατρὸς
τί πεπλημμέληκε καὶ τί[5] παρὰ τὸν βίον οὐκ
ὀρθῶς οὐδὲ ὁσίως αὐτῷ διαπραξαμένῳ συνέγνωκε
"πάτερ," εἶπεν, "ἄλλο μὲν οὐδέν," ὅτι δὲ χθὲς
ἀγνοῶν τὴν ἀρὰν αὐτοῦ καὶ τὸν ὅρκον μεταξὺ
διώκων τοὺς πολεμίους ἐγεύσατο κηρίων. Σαοῦλος
δ' ἀποκτείνειν αὐτὸν ὄμνυσι καὶ τῆς γενέσεως καὶ
127 τῆς φύσεως τῶν φίλτρων ἐτίμησε[6] τὸν ὅρκον. ὁ
δ' οὐ καταπλήττεται τὴν ἀπειλὴν τοῦ θανάτου,
παραστησάμενος δ' εὐγενῶς καὶ μεγαλοφρόνως
"οὐδ' ἐγώ σε," φησίν, "ἱκετεύσω φείσασθαί μου,
πάτερ, ἥδιστος δέ μοι ὁ θάνατος ὑπέρ τε τῆς σῆς

---

[1] +τινός SP.
[2] edd.: ἔφθανε MSP: φθάσαι RO.
[3] codd.: ἀποκτενεῖν Hudson.   [4] ἱλάσεσθαι Naber.
[5] τί περ RO: τί πεποίηκε καὶ τί SP Glycas.
[6] προτιμήσας ed. pr.: praeponeret Lat.

found therein. The priest having reported that there was no response from God, " Nay, but it is not without cause," said Saul, " that God gives no answer to our inquiry, He who ere now forewarned us of all Himself and spoke to us even before we inquired of Him. Nay, it is some secret sin against Him on our part that is the cause of this silence.[a] Aye and I swear by God Himself that verily, be it my own son Jonathan who hath committed this sin, I will slay him and thus propitiate God, even as though it were from a stranger without kinship with me that I was taking vengeance on His behalf." The multitude thereon calling upon him so to do, he forthwith caused them all to stand in one place, and stood himself with his son in another, and sought by the lot to discover the sinner ; and the lot indicated Jonathan. Being asked by his father wherein he had gone astray and of what wrong or unholy act in all his life he was conscious, " Of nothing, father," said he, " save that yesterday, all ignorant of that imprecation and oath of thine,[b] while in pursuit of the enemy, I tasted a honeycomb." Saul thereat swore to slay him, respecting his oath more than the tender ties of fatherhood and of nature. Yet Jonathan quailed not before this menace of death, but surrendering himself nobly and magnanimously, " Neither will I," said he, " entreat thee to spare me, father. Very sweet to me were death undergone for thy

---

[a] First part of Saul's speech is an addition to Scripture.
[b] Here the Gr. changes to indirect speech.

εὐσεβείας γινόμενος καὶ ἐπὶ νίκῃ λαμπρᾷ· μέγιστον
γὰρ παραμύθιον τὸ καταλιπεῖν Ἑβραίους Παλαι-
128 στίνων κεκρατηκότας." ἐπὶ τούτοις ὁ λαὸς πᾶς
ἤλγησε καὶ συνέπαθεν, ὤμοσέ τε μὴ περιόψεσθαι
τὸν αἴτιον τῆς νίκης Ἰωνάθην ἀποθανόντα. καὶ τὸν
μὲν οὕτως ἐξαρπάζουσι τῆς τοῦ πατρὸς ἀρᾶς, αὐτοὶ
δὲ εὐχὰς ὑπὲρ τοῦ νεανίσκου ποιοῦνται τῷ θεῷ
ὥστ᾽ αὐτὸν ἀπολῦσαι τοῦ ἁμαρτήματος.

129   (6) Καὶ ὁ Σαοῦλος εἰς τὴν ἑαυτοῦ πόλιν ὑπέστρεψε διαφθείρας ὡσεὶ μυριάδας ἓξ τῶν πολεμίων. βασιλεύει δὲ εὐτυχῶς, καὶ τὰ πλησιόχωρα
τῶν ἐθνῶν πολεμήσας χειροῦται τό τε Ἀμμανιτῶν
καὶ Μωαβιτῶν καὶ[1] Παλαιστίνους, Ἰδουμαίους τε
καὶ[2] Ἀμαληκίτας[3] καὶ τὸν βασιλέα τῆς Σωβᾶς.[4]
ἦσαν δὲ παῖδες αὐτῷ τρεῖς μὲν ἄρσενες Ἰωνάθης
καὶ Ἰησοῦς καὶ Μέλχισος, θυγατέρες δὲ Μερόβη
καὶ Μιχαάλ.[5] στρατηγὸν δὲ εἶχε τὸν τοῦ θείου
130 παῖδα Ἀβήναρον· Νῆρος δ᾽ ἐκεῖνος ἐκαλεῖτο,
Νῆρος δὲ καὶ Κεὶς ὁ Σαούλου πατὴρ ἀδελφοὶ
ἦσαν, υἱοὶ δ᾽ Ἀβελίου.[6] ἦν δὲ καὶ πλῆθος ἁρμάτων Σαούλῳ καὶ ἱππέων, οἷς[7] δὲ[8] πολεμήσειε
νικήσας ἀπηλλάσσετο, καὶ τοὺς Ἑβραίους εἰς
εὐπραγίας καὶ μέγεθος εὐδαιμονίας προηγάγετο
καὶ τῶν ἄλλων ἀπέδειξεν ἐθνῶν δυνατωτέρους,[9]
καὶ τῶν[10] νέων τοὺς δὴ καὶ μεγέθει καὶ κάλλει
διαφέροντας φύλακας τοῦ σώματος ἐποιεῖτο.

    [1] καὶ om. RO.   [2] τε καὶ SP: om. rell.
           [3] om. Lat.: +τε ROME.
    [4] Bosius ex Lat.: ὠβᾶς codd. E: σουβᾶ Zon.
        [5] M: μελχαᾶ SP: χθαάλ RO.
[6] Abihel Lat.: Ἀβιήλου conj. Hudson ex lxx.   [7] οὖς SE.
    [8] RO: δ᾽ ἂν rell.   [9] ROE: δυνατωτάτους rell. Lat.
        [10] καὶ τῶν RO: τῶν δὲ MSP.

piety's sake and after brilliant victory ; for highest consolation were it to leave Hebrews triumphant over Philistines." [a]   Thereupon all the people were moved to grief and sympathy and they swore that they would not suffer Jonathan, the author of that victory, to die. Thus then did they snatch him from his father's curse, and themselves offered prayers [b] for the young man to God, that He would grant him absolution from his sin.

(6) So Saul returned to his own city after destroying some sixty thousand of the enemy. He then reigned happily and, having made war on the neighbouring nations, subdued those of the Ammonites and Moabites, besides Philistines, Idumaeans and Amalekites, and the king of Sōba. He had three sons, Jonathan, Jesus [c] and Melchis, [d] and his daughters were Merobe [e] and Michaal. [f]   For commander of his army he had Abēnar, [g] his uncle's son ; that uncle was named Ner, and Ner and Kis, the father of Saul, were brothers, sons of Abelios. [h] Saul had, moreover, abundance of chariots and horsemen, and with whomsoever he fought he returned victorious ; and he brought the Hebrews to greatness of success and prosperity and rendered them more powerful than the other nations, and of the young men such as excelled in stature and beauty he took for his bodyguards.

Saul's victories. 1 Sam. xiv. 46.

---

[a] Jonathan's speech is unscriptural.

[b] "snatch" and "offered prayers" combine the Heb. "redeemed" (or "rescued") and the LXX "prayed for" of 1 Sam. xiv. 45.

[c] Bibl. Ishui, Heb. *Yishwi*, LXX Ἰεσσιούλ (*v.l.* Ἰσουεί).

[d] Bibl. Melchishua, LXX Μελχεισά.

[e] Bibl. Merab, LXX Μερόβ.

[f] Bibl. Michal, LXX Μελχόλ.

[g] Bibl. Abner, Heb. *Abīner*, LXX Ἀβεννήρ. *Cf.* § 58.

[h] Bibl. Abiel.

391

131 (vii. 1) Σαμουῆλος δὲ παραγενόμενος πρὸς τὸν
Σαοῦλον πεμφθῆναι πρὸς αὐτὸν ἔφασκεν ὑπὸ τοῦ
θεοῦ, ὅπως αὐτὸν ὑπομνήσῃ ὅτι βασιλέα προ-
κρίνας αὐτὸν ἁπάντων ὁ θεὸς ἀπέδειξε, καὶ διὰ
τοῦτο πείθεσθαι καὶ κατήκοον αὐτῷ γενέσθαι, ὡς
αὐτοῦ μὲν ἔχοντος τὴν τῶν ἐθνῶν ἡγεμονίαν, τοῦ
δὲ θεοῦ τὴν καὶ[1] ἐκείνου καὶ τῶν ὅλων πραγμά-

132 των. λέγειν τοίνυν ἔφασκε τὸν θεόν· "ἐπεὶ
πολλὰ κακὰ τοὺς Ἑβραίους Ἀμαληκῖται διέθηκαν
κατὰ τὴν ἔρημον, ὅτε ἐξελθόντες ἀπ' Αἰγύπτου εἰς
τὴν νῦν ὑπάρχουσαν αὐτοῖς ἐστέλλοντο χώραν,
κελεύω πολέμῳ τιμωρησάμενον τοὺς Ἀμαληκίτας

133 καὶ κρατήσαντα μηδέν[2] αὐτῶν ὑπολιπεῖν, ἀλλὰ πάσης διεξελθεῖν ἡλικίας, ἀρξαμένους ἀπὸ γυναικῶν
κτείνειν καὶ νηπίων καὶ τοιαύτην ὑπὲρ ὧν τοὺς
προγόνους ὑμῶν εἰργάσαντο τιμωρίαν ἀπολαβεῖν,
φείσασθαι δὲ μήτε ὑποζυγίων μήτε τῶν ἄλλων
βοσκημάτων εἰς ὠφέλειαν καὶ κτῆσιν ἰδίαν, ἅπαντα
δ' ἀναθεῖναι τῷ θεῷ καὶ τὸ Ἀμαλήκου ὄνομα ταῖς
Μωυσέος κατακολουθήσαντ' ἐντολαῖς ἐξαλεῖψαι."

134 (2) Ὁμολογεῖ δὲ ποιήσειν Σαοῦλος τὰ προστασ-
σόμενα, τὴν δὲ πειθαρχίαν τὴν πρὸς τὸν θεὸν οὐκ
ἐν τῷ ποιήσασθαι τὴν πρὸς τοὺς Ἀμαληκίτας
στρατείαν λογιζόμενος εἶναι μόνον, ἀλλὰ καὶ τῷ
τὴν ἑτοιμότητα καὶ τὸ τάχος ἀναβολῆς οὐ προσ-
ούσης ἔτι μᾶλλον ἐμφανίζειν,[3] ἀθροίζει τε πᾶσαν
τὴν δύναμιν καὶ ταύτην ἐξαριθμήσας ἐν Γαλγάλοις
εὑρίσκει τῶν Ἰσραηλιτῶν ἔξω τῆς Ἰούδα φυλῆς
περὶ τεσσαράκοντα μυριάδας· ἤδε γὰρ ἡ φυλὴ καθ'

---

[1] τὴν καί conj. Niese: καὶ τὴν κατ' codd.
[2] S: μηδὲν rell.
[3] τῷ τὴν ... ἐμφανίζειν ex Lat.: τὴν ... ἐμφανίζει codd.

392

(vii. 1) Samuel now came to Saul and said that he had been sent to him by God to recall to him that God had preferred him above all others and created him king, and that he ought therefore to obey and give ear to Him, for, while he had dominion over the nations, God had dominion both over him and over the universe. He thereupon announced that God had spoken thus: " Forasmuch as the Amalekites did much evil to the Hebrews in the wilderness, when they were come out of Egypt and on their way to the land that now is theirs, I command thee to take vengeance on the Amalekites in war and, when victorious, to leave not one of them remaining; but you shall deal death to all of every age, beginning with the women and infants, and in this wise take vengeance for what they did to your forefathers; thou art to spare neither beasts of burden nor any cattle at all for private profit or possession, but to devote all to God and, in compliance with the behests of Moses,[a] to blot out the name of Amalek."

(2) These injunctions Saul promised to fulfil; and reflecting that obedience to God lay not merely in making this campaign against the Amalekites, but would be displayed yet more by an alacrity and haste that brooked no delay, he mustered all his forces and, having numbered them at Galgala,[b] found that the Israelites, apart from the tribe of Judah, were some 400,000 men; that tribe by itself furnished 30,000

Samuel sends Saul to exterminate the Amalekites.
1 Sam. xv. 1.

Saul musters his troops at Gilgal.
1 Sam. xv. 4.

---

[a] Cf. A. iii. 60 on Ex. xvii. 14, and A. iv. 304 on Deut. xxv. 17. Moses is not mentioned in Scripture at this point.

[b] So the LXX; Heb. has Telaim, a city in southern Judah.

135 αὐτήν ἐστι στρατιῶται τρισμύριοι. Σαοῦλος δ'
ἐμβαλὼν εἰς τὴν τῶν Ἀμαληκιτῶν χώραν ἐνέδρας
πολλὰς καὶ λόχους περὶ τὸν χειμάρρουν τίθησιν, ὡς
μὴ μόνον ἐκ τοῦ φανεροῦ μαχόμενος[1] αὐτοὺς
κακῶς ποιεῖν, ἀλλὰ καὶ μὴ προσδοκῶσι κατὰ τὰς
ὁδοὺς ἐπιπίπτων καὶ κυκλούμενος[2] ἀναιρεῖν· καὶ
δὴ συμβαλὼν αὐτοῖς εἰς μάχην τρέπεται τοὺς
πολεμίους καὶ διαφθείρει πάντας, φεύγουσιν ἐπ-
136 ακολουθῶν. ὡς δ' ἐκεῖνο τὸ ἔργον αὐτῷ κατὰ
τὴν τοῦ θεοῦ προφητείαν ἐχώρησε, ταῖς πόλεσι
τῶν Ἀμαληκιτῶν προσέβαλε καὶ τὰς μὲν μηχα-
νήμασι, τὰς δὲ ὀρύγμασιν ὑπονόμοις καὶ τείχεσιν
ἔξωθεν ἀντῳκοδομημένοις, τὰς δὲ λιμῷ καὶ δίψει,
τὰς δὲ ἄλλοις τρόποις ἐκπολιορκήσας καὶ λαβὼν
κατὰ κράτος, ἐπὶ σφαγὴν γυναικῶν καὶ νηπίων
ἐχώρησεν, οὐδὲν ὠμὸν οὐδ' ἀνθρωπίνης σκληρό-
τερον διαπράσσεσθαι φύσεως ἡγούμενος, πρῶτον μὲν
πολεμίους ταῦτα δρῶν, ἔπειτα προστάγματι θεοῦ, ᾧ
137 τὸ μὴ πείθεσθαι κίνδυνον ἔφερε. λαμβάνει δὲ καὶ
τὸν βασιλέα τῶν ἐχθρῶν Ἄγαγον αἰχμάλωτον,
οὗ θαυμάσας τὸ κάλλος καὶ τὸ μέγεθος τοῦ
σώματος σωτηρίας ἄξιον ἔκρινεν, οὐκέτι τοῦτο
ποιῶν κατὰ βούλησιν τοῦ θεοῦ, πάθει δὲ νικώμενος
ἰδίῳ καὶ χαριζόμενος ἀκαίρως περὶ ὧν οὐκ εἶχεν
138 ἀκίνδυνον ἐξουσίαν οἴκτῳ. ὁ μὲν[3] γὰρ θεὸς οὕτως
ἐμίσησε τὸ τῶν Ἀμαληκιτῶν ἔθνος, ὡς μηδὲ

---

[1] conj. Niese ex Lat.: μαχομένους codd.
[2] conj. Niese: ἐπιπίπτειν καὶ κυκλουμένους codd.
[3] μὲν om. MSP.

---

[a] Both numbers in agreement with most mss. of the lxx;
Heb. has 200,000 and 10,000 respectively.
[b] Josephus here omits Saul's invitation to the Kenites to
separate themselves from Amalek (1 Sam. xv. 6), before his

combatants.[a] Having then invaded the country of
the Amalekites,[b] Saul posted numerous pickets and
ambuscades around the ravine,[c] with intent not only
to molest them in open warfare, but also to fall
upon them unexpectedly on the roads and envelop
and destroy them ; and in fact, on joining battle
with them he routed the enemy on, pursuing the
fugitives, destroyed them all. That task having, in
accordance with God's prediction, been successfully
achieved, he attacked the cities of the Amalekites ;
and when, some by engines of war, others by mining
operations and exterior opposing walls, others by
hunger and thirst, and yet others by other means,[d] he
had carried and stormed them all, he then proceeded
to the slaughter of women and infants, deeming
naught therein cruel or too savage for human nature
to perform, first because they were enemies whom
he was treating thus, and then because of the commandment of God, whom it was dangerous to disobey.
But he also took prisoner the enemy's king, Agag,
whom out of admiration for his beauty and his stature[e]
he accounted worthy to be saved ; herein he was no
longer acting in accordance with the will of God, but
giving way to feelings of his own, and yielding inop-
portunely to compassion where it was not permitted
to him without peril. For God so hated the race of
the Amalekites that He had ordered him to spare not

Saul
captures
Agag.
1 Sam. xv 8.

attack upon the latter. In § 140 he alludes to this scriptural
passage in mentioning the Sikimites. *Cf.* note *ad loc.*

[c] Scripture does not tell us what ravine (Heb. *naḥal*, " bed
of a stream," *cf.* Arabic *wady*) is meant; the geographical
details are vague throughout this account.

[d] Details of the invasion and sieges are an amplification.

[e] Saul's aesthetic motive for sparing Agag is an invention
of Josephus.

νηπίων φείσασθαι κελεῦσαι πρὸς ἃ μᾶλλον ἔλεος
γίνεσθαι πέφυκε, Σαοῦλος δὲ αὐτῶν¹ τὸν βασιλέα
καὶ τὸν ἡγεμόνα τῶν εἰς Ἑβραίους κακῶν ἔσωσε,
τῆς μνήμης ὧν ἐπέστειλεν ὁ θεὸς τὸ τοῦ πολεμίου
139 κάλλος ἐπίπροσθεν ποιησάμενος. συνεξήμαρτε δ'
αὐτῷ καὶ τὸ πλῆθος· καὶ γὰρ ἐκεῖνοι τῶν ὑποζυγίων καὶ τῶν βοσκημάτων ἐφείσαντο καὶ διήρπασαν, μὴ τηρεῖν αὐτὰ τοῦ θεοῦ κελεύσαντος, τά τε
ἄλλα χρήματα καὶ τὸν πλοῦτον ἐξεφόρησαν, εἰ δέ τι
μὴ σπουδῆς ἦν ἄξιον ὥστε κεκτῆσθαι διέφθειραν.
140 (3) Νικήσας δὲ Σαοῦλος ἅπαντας τοὺς ἀπὸ Πη-
λουσίου τῆς Αἰγύπτου καθήκοντας ἕως τῆς Ἐρυθρᾶς
θαλάσσης διέφθειρε πολεμίους,² παραλιπὼν τὸ τῶν
Σικιμιτῶν ἔθνος· οὗτοι γὰρ ἐν τῇ Μαδιηνῇ χώρα
μέσοι κατῴκηνται. πρὸ δὲ τῆς μάχης πέμψας
παρήγγειλεν αὐτοῖς ἀναχωρεῖν, μὴ τοῖς Ἀμαληκίταις κοινωνήσωσι συμφορᾶς· συγγενεῖς γὰρ αὐτοὺς
ὄντας Ῥαγουήλου τοῦ Μωυσέος πενθεροῦ σώζειν
αἰτίαν ἔχειν.
141 (4) Καὶ Σαοῦλος μὲν ὡς μηδενὸς παρακούσας
ὧν ὁ προφήτης ἐπέστειλε μέλλοντι τὸν πρὸς
Ἀμαληκίτας ἐκφέρειν πόλεμον, ἀλλ' ὡς ἐπὶ πᾶσιν
ἐκείνοις ἀκριβῶς πεφυλαγμένοις νενικηκὼς τοὺς
πολεμίους οἴκαδε πρὸς αὐτὸν ὑπέστρεψε χαίρων

¹ αὐτὸν R¹S: regem Agag Lat.
² RO Lat.: τὴν τῶν πολεμίων M (+ χώραν E): τὰ τῶν πολεμίων SP.

ᵃ 1 Sam. xv. 7 " from Havilah until thou comest to Shur
over against Egypt"; Josephus reverses the directions, assum-
ing that Shur corresponds to Pelusium and that Havilah
is somewhere near the Red Sea.
ᵇ 1 Sam. xv. 6 " Kenites." " Sikimites," which is geo-
graphically impossible (= inhabitants of Shechem), may

even the infants, to whom it is more natural that pity should be shown; but Saul saved their king, the author of all the injuries to the Hebrews, having had more regard for the beauty of his enemy than for memory of what God enjoined. The people too were his partners in sin; for they spared the beasts and the cattle and took for their prey what God had forbidden to be preserved, and carried off all the chattels and riches beside; but whatever was not worth coveting as a possession that did they destroy.

(3) Conquering the whole district extending from Pelusium in Egypt to the Red Sea,[a] Saul destroyed the inhabitants as enemies, saving only the race of the Sikimites,[b] who had settled in the heart of the country of Madian. To these he had, before the combat, sent messengers admonishing them to withdraw, lest they should share the fate of the Amalekites; for, being kinsmen of Raguel, the father-in-law of Moses, he had, as he said, good reason to spare them.[c]

Saul's further conquests.
1 Sam. xv. 6, 7.

(4) So Saul, as though he had neglected none of the injunctions which he had received from the prophet when embarking on his campaign against the Amalekites, but had strictly observed them all in having conquered his enemies, returned homeward

God's anger at Saul's transgression.
1 Sam. xv. 10.

be due to corruption in Josephus's text. Rappaport makes the interesting suggestion that either Josephus wrote " Silimites," the Greek form of the Targum's name " Shalma'ah " for the Kenites, and that this was corrupted to "Sikimites," or that he connected Shalma'ah with Shechem on the basis of Gen. xxxiii. 18 " Shalem a city of Shechem."

[c] Cf. A. v. 127. The reference to the kinship with Moses is paralleled in rabbinic tradition. Scripture ascribes Saul's consideration to the Israelites' memory of services rendered them by the Kenites in the Exodus.

142 ἐπὶ τοῖς κατωρθωμένοις. ὁ δὲ θεὸς ἄχθεται τῇ
τε¹ τοῦ βασιλέως τῶν Ἀμαληκιτῶν σωτηρίᾳ καὶ
τῇ τῶν βοσκημάτων διαρπαγῇ τοῦ πλήθους, ὅτι
μὴ συγχωρήσαντος αὐτοῦ ταῦτ᾽ ἐπράχθη· δεινὸν
γὰρ ἡγεῖτο νικᾶν μὲν καὶ περιγίνεσθαι τῶν ἐχθρῶν
ἐκείνου τὴν ἰσχὺν διδόντος αὐτοῖς, καταφρονεῖσθαι
δὲ καὶ παρακούεσθαι μηδὲ ὡς ἄνθρωπον βασιλέα.
143 μετανοεῖν οὖν ἔλεγε πρὸς τὸν προφήτην Σαμοῦηλον
ἐπὶ τῷ χειροτονῆσαι βασιλέα τὸν Σαοῦλον, μηδὲν
ὧν αὐτὸς κελεύει πράττοντα, τῇ δ᾽ οἰκείᾳ βουλήσει
χρώμενον. σφόδρα ταῦτ᾽ ἀκούσας ὁ Σαμοῦηλος
συνεχύθη² καὶ δι᾽ ὅλης τῆς νυκτὸς παρακαλεῖν
ἤρξατο τὸν θεὸν καταλλάττεσθαι τῷ Σαούλῳ καὶ
144 μὴ χαλεπαίνειν. ὁ δὲ τὴν συγγνώμην οὐκ ἐπένευσεν εἰς τὸν Σαοῦλον αἰτουμένῳ τῷ προφήτῃ,
λογισάμενος οὐκ εἶναι δίκαιον ἁμαρτήματα³ χαρίζεσθαι παραιτήσει⁴· οὐ γὰρ ἐξ ἄλλου τινὸς φύεσθαι
μᾶλλον ἢ τοῦ καταμαλακίζεσθαι⁵ τοὺς ἀδικου-
μένους· θηρωμένους γὰρ δόξαν ἐπιεικείας καὶ
χρηστότητος λανθάνειν αὐτοὺς⁶ ταῦτα γεννῶντας.
145 ὡς οὖν ἀπεῖπεν ὁ θεὸς τῇ τοῦ προφήτου δεήσει
καὶ δῆλος ἦν⁷ μεταμελόμενος, ἅμ᾽ ἡμέρᾳ Σαμοῦηλος
εἰς Γάλγαλα παραγίνεται πρὸς Σαοῦλον· θεασάμενος δ᾽ αὐτὸν ὁ βασιλεὺς προστρέχει καὶ κατασπασάμενος "τῷ θεῷ," φησίν, "εὐχαριστῶ δόντι
μοι τὴν νίκην, ἅπαντα μέντοι γε τὰ κελευσθέντα
146 ὑπ᾽ αὐτοῦ πέπρακται.⁸" Σαμοῦηλος δὲ πρὸς τοῦθ᾽
ὑπολαβὼν "πόθεν οὖν ἀκούω θρεμμάτων," εἶπε,

¹ M Suidas: τῇ ROE: ἐπί τε τῇ SP.
² διεχύθη RO.   ³ ed. pr.: ἁμαρτήμασι codd.
⁴ Niese: παραίτησιν codd. (-τήσεων ed. pr.).
⁵ μαλακίζεσθαι O.   ⁶ P²: αὐτοὺς rell.
⁷ +μὴ MSP Lat.ᵛⁱᵈ·   ⁸ O: πεπρᾶχθαι rell.

exultant at his success. But God was ill pleased at his sparing the life of the king of Amalek and at the people's making plunder of the cattle, because these things had not been permitted by Him ; for He deemed it an outrage that when they had conquered and defeated the foe through the might which He had given them, He should meet with such contempt and disobedience as they would show to no human king. He therefore told the prophet Samuel that He repented of having elected Saul as king, since he was in no wise executing His commands, but doing according to his own pleasure. On hearing this Samuel was sore troubled, and all night long set himself to entreat God to be reconciled to Saul and not wroth with him. But God would grant no pardon to Saul at the prophet's request, accounting it not just to condone sins at the intercession of another ; for nothing more favoured their growth than laxity on the part of the wronged, who in seeking a reputation for mildness and kindness are unwittingly the begetters of crime. When therefore God had refused the prophet's prayer and showed that He repented Himself,[a] Samuel at break of day repaired to Galgala to meet Saul. At sight of him, the king ran to him and embraced him. " I render thanks," said he, " to God who has given me victory ; and moreover, all His commands have been performed." Whereto Samuel replied, " Whence comes it then

Samuel at Gilgal prophesies Saul's doom. 1 Sam. xv. 12.

---

[a] *i.e.* of having made Saul king, *cf.* 1 Sam. xv. 35. The variant text δῆλος ἦν μὴ μεταμελόμενος " and showed no change of mind " is probably due to scribes who thought that Josephus was referring to God's decision to punish Saul in spite of Samuel's intercession.

JOSEPHUS

" καὶ ὑποζυγίων βοῆς ἐν τῷ στρατοπέδῳ; " ὁ δὲ
τὸν λαὸν ταῦτ᾽ εἰς θυσίας ἀπεκρίνατο τετηρηκέναι·
τὸ μέντοι γε τῶν Ἀμαληκιτῶν γένος ἅπαν ἐξη-
φανίσθαι κατὰ τὴν ἐντολὴν καὶ περιλείπεσθαι ἄλλον
μηδένα, πρὸς δ᾽ αὐτὸν ἀγαγεῖν μόνον τηρήσαντα
αὐτῶν τὸν βασιλέα, περὶ οὗ τί δεῖ ποιεῖν βουλεύσε-
147 σθαι¹ πρὸς ἀλλήλους ἔφασκεν. ὁ δὲ προφήτης
οὐχὶ θυσίαις ἔλεγεν ἥδεσθαι τὸ θεῖον, ἀλλὰ τοῖς
ἀγαθοῖς καὶ δικαίοις· οὗτοι δέ εἰσιν οἱ τῇ βουλήσει
καὶ ταῖς ἐντολαῖς αὐτοῦ κατακολουθοῦντες καὶ
μηδὲν ἄλλο πραχθήσεσθαι καλῶς ὑφ᾽ ἑαυτῶν νομίζοντες ἢ ὅ τι ἂν ποιήσωσι τοῦ θεοῦ κεκελευκότος·
καταφρονεῖσθαι γὰρ οὐχ ὅταν αὐτῷ μὴ θύῃ τις,
148 ἀλλ᾽ ὅταν ἀπειθεῖν δοκῇ. " παρὰ δὲ τῶν οὐχ
ὑποτασσομένων οὐδ᾽ ἀληθῆ καὶ μόνην τῷ θεῷ
κεχαρισμένην θρησκευόντων θρησκείαν, οὔτ᾽ ἂν
πολλὰ καὶ πιμελῆ καταθύσωσιν ἱερεῖα, οὔτ᾽ ἂν
κόσμον ἀναθημάτων ἐξ ἀργύρου καὶ χρυσοῦ πεποιημένων προσφέρωσι, δέχεται ταῦτ᾽ εὐμενῶς,
ἀλλ᾽ ἀποστρέφεται καὶ δείγματα τῆς πονηρίας οὐκ
149 εὐσέβειαν ἡγεῖται. τοῖς δ᾽ ἓν καὶ μόνον τοῦθ᾽ ὅ τι
περ ἂν φθέγξηται καὶ κελεύσῃ ὁ θεὸς διὰ μνήμης
ἔχουσι καὶ τεθνάναι μᾶλλον ἢ παραβῆναί τι τούτων
αἱρουμένοις ἐπιτέρπεται, καὶ οὔτε θυσίαν ἐπιζητεῖ
παρ᾽ αὐτῶν καὶ παρὰ θυόντων δέ, κἂν ᾖ λιτά, τῆς
πενίας ἥδιον τὴν τιμὴν ἢ παρὰ τῶν πλουσιωτάτων
150 δεξιοῦται. σὺ τοίνυν ἴσθι σαυτὸν δι᾽ ὀργῆς ὄντα
τῷ θεῷ· κατεφρόνησας γὰρ καὶ κατημέλησας ὧν
ἐπέστειλε. πῶς οὖν οἴει τὴν θυσίαν ἂν αὐτὸν
προσβλέπειν ἐξ ὧν κατέκρινεν ἀπολέσθαι γινο-

---

¹ Ernesti ex Lat.: βουλεύεσθαι codd.

400

that I hear sounds of cattle and beasts of burden in the camp?" The king answered that the people had reserved these for sacrifice, but that the race of the Amalekites had been utterly exterminated in accordance with the divine command, and that not one had been left alive, save only their king, whom he had preserved and brought to Samuel, and concerning whose fate they would, he said, take counsel together. But the prophet answered that the Deity took not delight in sacrifices, but in good and righteous men, namely such as follow His will and His commandments and deem that no act of theirs will have been rightly done save what they do at God's bidding ; for contempt of God, he said, is shown not in withholding sacrifice but in appearing to disobey Him. " And from such as submit not nor offer the true worship that alone is acceptable to God, even though they sacrifice many fat victims, even though they present to Him sumptuous offerings wrought of silver and gold, yet does He not receive these gifts graciously, but rejects them and regards them as tokens of iniquity rather than as piety. But they who are mindful of this one thing alone, to wit what God has spoken and commanded, and who choose rather to die than to transgress aught thereof, in them does He rejoice ; from them He requires no sacrifice, or, should they offer any, however modest, more gladly does He welcome this homage from poverty than that of the wealthiest. Know, then, that thou thyself hast incurred the wrath of God, for thou hast held lightly and neglected His commandments. How thinkest thou that He could look upon a sacrifice offered from those things which He doomed

μένην; πλὴν εἰ μὴ νομίζεις ὅμοιον ὀλέθρῳ[1] τὸ
θύεσθαι ταῦτα τῷ θεῷ. προσδόκα τοίνυν τὴν
βασιλείαν ἀφαιρεθησόμενος καὶ τὴν ἐξουσίαν, ἀφ'
ἧς ὁρμώμενος τοῦ παρασχόντος σοι θεοῦ ταύτην
151 ἠμέλησας.'' Σαοῦλος δὲ ἀδικεῖν ὡμολόγει καὶ τὴν
ἁμαρτίαν οὐκ ἠρνεῖτο· παραβῆναι γὰρ τὰς ἐντολὰς
τοῦ προφήτου· κατὰ μέντοι γε δέος καὶ τὸν ἀπὸ
τῶν στρατιωτῶν φόβον μὴ κωλῦσαι διαρπάζοντας
αὐτοὺς τὴν λείαν μηδ' ἐπισχεῖν. '' ἀλλὰ συγ-
γίνωσκε καὶ πρᾶος ἴσθι·'' φυλάξεσθαι γὰρ εἰς
τοὐπιὸν ἁμαρτεῖν, παρεκάλει δὲ τὸν προφήτην
ὑποστρέψαντα θυσίας χαριστηρίους ἐπιτελέσαι τῷ
θεῷ· ὁ δέ, οὐ γὰρ ἑώρα τὸν θεὸν διαλλαττόμενον,
ἀπῄει πρὸς ἑαυτόν.
152 (5) Σαοῦλος δὲ κατασχεῖν βουλόμενος τὸν Σαμουῆλον ἐλλαμβάνεται[2] τῆς διπλοΐδος, καὶ βιαίας
τῆς ὁλκῆς διὰ τὸ μεθ' ὁρμῆς ἀπιέναι[3] τὸν Σαμου-
153 ῆλον γενομένης διασχίζει τὸ ἱμάτιον. τοῦ δὲ προφήτου τὴν βασιλείαν οὕτως αὐτοῦ διασχισθῆναι
φήσαντος καὶ λήψεσθαι ταύτην ἀγαθὸν καὶ δίκαιον,
ἐμμένειν γὰρ τὸν θεὸν τοῖς περὶ αὐτοῦ κεκριμένοις,
ὡς τοῦ μεταβάλλεσθαι καὶ στρέφειν τὴν γνώμην
154 ἀνθρωπίνου πάθους ὄντος οὐχὶ θείας ἰσχύος, ὅ[4]
Σαοῦλος ἀσεβῆσαι μὲν ἔλεγεν, ἀγένητα δὲ ποιῆσαι
τὰ πεπραγμένα μὴ δύνασθαι· τιμῆσαί γε μὴν αὐτὸν
παρεκάλει, τοῦ πλήθους ὁρῶντος, σὺν αὐτῷ παρα-
γενόμενον τὸν θεὸν προσκυνῆσαι. δίδωσι δὲ τοῦτο
Σαμουῆλος αὐτῷ καὶ συνελθὼν προσκυνεῖ τῷ θεῷ.

---

[1] SPM[1]: ὀλέθρου M[2]: ὄλεθρον O.
[2] ἐπιλαμβάνεται S[2] Zon (cf. lxx codd.).
[3] Dindorf: ἀπεῖναι codd.
[4] + δὲ codd.

to destruction ? Unless it be that thou regardest the sacrificing of them to God as equivalent to destroying them ! Expect, therefore, that thou wilt be deprived of thy kingship and of the power upon which thou hast presumed in neglecting the God who gave it thee." Saul admitted that he had done wrong and did not deny his sin ; yes, he said, he had transgressed the prophet's commands ; yet indeed it was from fear and dread of his soldiers that he had not prevented them from plundering the spoils nor restrained them. " But," said he, " pardon me and be merciful," and promised to beware of offending in future. Then he besought the prophet to return (with him) and sacrifice thank-offerings [a] to God. But Samuel, seeing that God was not to be reconciled, departed to his home.

(5) Then Saul, seeking to detain Samuel, laid hold upon his mantle and, since Samuel was hastening to be gone, pulled it so violently that he rent the garment in twain. Whereat the prophet said that even so had his kingdom been rent from him, and that one would succeed to it who was virtuous and just, for God would abide by what He had decreed concerning him, as change and reversal of judgement were the part of human frailty and not of divine power. Saul replied that, impious though he had been, he could not undo what had been done ; howbeit he besought him at least to do him honour in the eyes of the multitude by coming with him to worship God.[b] Samuel granted him this request and went with him and worshipped God. Then too was

Samuel has Agag put to death.
1 Sam. xv. 26.

---

[a] 1 Sam. xv. 25 " that I may worship the Lord."

[b] Josephus infers that Samuel also worshipped. Scripture says that Samuel returned with Saul and " Saul worshipped the Lord."

155 ἄγεται δὲ καὶ ὁ τῶν Ἀμαληκιτῶν βασιλεὺς Ἄγαγος
πρὸς αὐτόν· καὶ πυνθανομένου πῶς εἴη πικρὸς ὁ
θάνατος, εἶπεν " ὡς σὺ πολλὰς μητέρας Ἑβραίων
ἐπὶ τέκνοις ὀδύρεσθαι καὶ πένθος ἄγειν ἐποίησας,
οὕτως ὀδυνήσεις ἐπὶ σαυτῷ διαφθαρέντι τὴν μητέρα." καὶ κελεύει παραχρῆμα αὐτὸν ἐν Γαλγάλοις ἀποθανεῖν. καὶ αὐτὸς δὲ εἰς Ἀρμαθὰν πόλιν
ἀπαλλάσσεται.

156 (viii. 1) Σαοῦλος δὲ ὁ βασιλεὺς αἰσθόμενος ὧν
ἂν[1] πειραθείη κακῶν ἐχθρὸν αὐτῷ τὸν θεὸν
κατασκευάσας, εἰς τὸ βασίλειον ἀναβαίνει Γαβᾶ,
σημαίνει[2] βουνὸν ἑρμηνευόμενον τὸ ὄνομα, καὶ μετ᾽
ἐκείνην οὐκέτι τὴν ἡμέραν εἰς ὄψιν ἔρχεται τῷ
157 προφήτῃ. Σαμουήλῳ δὲ λυπουμένῳ περὶ αὐτοῦ
παύσασθαι μὲν τῆς φροντίδος ἐκέλευσεν ὁ θεός,
λαβόντι δὲ τὸ ἅγιον ἔλαιον[3] εἰς Βηθλέμην ἀπελθεῖν
πόλιν πρὸς Ἰεσσαῖον παῖδα Ὠβήδου καὶ χρῖσαι
τῶν υἱῶν αὐτοῦ ὃν ἂν αὐτὸς ἐπιδείξῃ βασιλέα
γενησόμενον. ὁ δὲ εὐλαβεῖσθαι φήσας, μὴ τοῦτο
μαθὼν Σαοῦλος ἀνέλῃ λοχήσας αὐτὸν ἢ καὶ
φανερῶς, ὑποθεμένου τοῦ θεοῦ καὶ δόντος ἀσφα-
158 λείας ὁδὸν ἧκεν εἰς τὴν προειρημένην πόλιν. καὶ
πάντες αὐτὸν ἠσπάζοντό τε καὶ τὴν αἰτίαν τῆς
ἀφίξεως ἀνηρώτων, ἔλεγε δὲ ἥκειν ἵνα θύσῃ τῷ
θεῷ. ποιήσας οὖν τὴν θυσίαν καλεῖ τὸν Ἰεσσαῖον
μετὰ τῶν τέκνων ἐπὶ τὰ ἱερὰ[4] καὶ θεασάμενος

---

[1] ἂν ins. Niese. [2] + δὲ MSP.
[3] ἅγιον ἔλαιον] ἀγγεῖον τοῦ ἐλαίου E Lat.
[4] ἱερεῖα MSP.

---

[a] So, apparently, the LXX and Targum of 1 Sam. xv. 32.
The Hebrew is obscure and is variously explained by Jewish
interpreters.

brought to him Agag, king of the Amalekites ; and
when the prisoner asked what manner of bitter death
his would be,*a* Samuel said, " As thou hast made many
mothers of Hebrews to lament and mourn for their
children, so shalt thou cause thy mother to grieve
over thine own destruction." He then ordered him
instantly to be put to death *b* in Galgala, and he himself departed to the city of Armatha.

(viii. 1) But King Saul, perceiving what ills he had
incurred in making God his enemy, went up to his
palace at Gaba *c* (a name which is interpreted to
mean " hill ") and from that day onward came no
more into the prophet's sight. As Samuel, however,
yet grieved for him, God bade him banish his care
and, taking the holy oil, to repair to the city of
Bethlehem to Jesse son of Obed,*d* and to anoint
from among his sons him whom He Himself should
point out as the future king. Samuel replied that
he was fearful lest Saul on learning of this should slay
him by ambush or even openly ; but, God having
advised him *e* and provided him a way of safety, he
came to the city aforesaid. Here all greeted him
and questioned him concerning the cause of his
coming, and he said that he was come to sacrifice to
God. Having then performed the sacrifice, he called
Jesse with his children to the sacred feast, and when

Samuel goes
to Beth-
lehem to
anoint a
son of Jesse
as king.
1 Sam. xv.
34.

---

b Josephus discreetly passes over the details ; 1 Sam. xv.
33 " and Samuel hewed Agag in pieces before the Lord."
Rabbinic tradition states that the execution was not in accordance with Jewish forms of justice.

c So LXX ; Heb. Gibeah of Saul. *Cf.* § 95 note.

d 1 Sam. xvi. 1 " Jesse the Bethlehemite." His father's
name is given earlier, *A.* v. 336 (Ruth iv. 22).

e Scripture explains more fully by mentioning, at this
point, the pretext of sacrificing.

αὐτοῦ τὸν πρεσβύτατον τῶν υἱῶν εὐμεγέθη καὶ
καλόν, εἴκασεν ἐκ τῆς εὐμορφίας τοῦτον εἶναι τὸν
159 μέλλοντα βασιλεύειν. διαμαρτάνει δὲ τῆς τοῦ θεοῦ
προνοίας· ἐπερωτήσαντι γὰρ αὐτὸν εἰ χρίσει τῷ
ἐλαίῳ τὸν νεανίσκον ὃν αὐτὸς ἐτεθαυμάκει[1] καὶ τῆς
βασιλείας ἄξιον ἔκρινεν, οὐ τὰ αὐτὰ βλέπειν
160 ἀνθρώπους εἶπε καὶ θεόν· '' ἀλλὰ σὺ μὲν εἰς τὸ
κάλλος ἀπιδὼν τοῦ νεανίσκου καὶ δὴ τοῦτον ἡγῇ
ἄξιον τοῦ βασιλεύειν εἶναι, ἐγὼ δ' οὐ σωμάτων
εὐμορφίας ἔπαθλον ποιοῦμαι τὴν βασιλείαν ἀλλὰ
ψυχῶν ἀρετῆς, καὶ ζητῶ ὅστις ταύτης[2] ἐστὶ τελέως
εὐπρεπής, εὐσεβείᾳ καὶ δικαιοσύνῃ καὶ ἀνδρείᾳ καὶ
πειθοῖ, ἐξ ὧν τὸ τῆς ψυχῆς συνίσταται κάλλος,
161 κατακεκοσμημένος.'' ταῦτα φράσαντος τοῦ θεοῦ
πάντας ἐκέλευσεν αὐτῷ τὸν Ἰεσσαῖον τοὺς υἱοὺς
ἐπιδεῖξαι Σαμουῆλος· ὁ δὲ πέντε ἄλλους ἐποίησεν
ἐλθεῖν, ὧν ὁ μὲν πρεσβύτερος Ἐλίαβος,[3] ὁ δεύ-
τερος Ἀμινάδαβος, Σάμαλος ὁ τρίτος, ὁ τέταρτος
Ναθαναῆλος, καὶ Ῥάηλος ὁ πέμπτος ἐκαλεῖτο, ὁ δὲ
162 ἕκτος Ἄσαμος. ἰδὼν δὲ καὶ τούτους ὁ προφήτης
μηδὲν χείρους τοῦ πρεσβυτέρου[4] ταῖς μορφαῖς ἐπ-
ηρώτησε τὸν θεὸν τίνα τούτων αἱρεῖται βασιλέα.
εἰπόντος δ' οὐδένα, πυνθάνεται τοῦ Ἰεσσαίου, μὴ
163 πρὸς τούτοις αὐτῷ καὶ ἄλλοι παῖδές εἰσι. φήσαντος
δὲ εἶναι Δαυίδην[5] τοὔνομα, ποιμαίνειν δὲ καὶ τῆς

---

[1] αὐτός τε θαυμάζει RO.
[2] ταύτῃ Cocceji: ταύτην Ernesti.
[3] Ταλίαβος RO.
[4] πρεσβυτάτου Niese.
[5] Δαβίδην RO et sic infra.

---

[a] His name, Eliab, is given below, § 161.
[b] These virtues, perhaps intended to correspond to the

he beheld his eldest son,[a] well-grown and fair, he
surmised from his comeliness that this was the
destined king. But he mistook God's design ; for,
when he asked Him whether he should anoint with
the oil this young man whom he himself had admired
and accounted worthy of the kingship, He replied
that men and God see not the same things. " Nay,
thou, looking upon this young man's beauty, thinkest
none other than him worthy to be king ; but I make
not of the kingdom a prize for comeliness of body,
but for virtue of soul, and I seek one who in full
measure is distinguished by this, one adorned with
piety, justice, fortitude and obedience, qualities [b]
whereof beauty of soul consists." When God had
thus spoken, Samuel bade Jesse bring all his sons
before him, and he caused five [c] others to appear.
The eldest was called Eliab, the second Aminadab,[d]
the third Samal,[e] the fourth Nathanael, the fifth
Rael,[f] and the sixth Asam.[g] The prophet, seeing
these to be in no way inferior to the eldest in appearance, asked God which among them He chose for
king. When God answered, " None," he inquired
of Jesse whether he had yet other children. He said
that he had one named David, but that he was a

Platonic-Stoic cardinal virtues, are, of course, not specified
in Scripture.

[c] 1 Sam. xvi. 10 (*cf.* xvii. 12) mentions seven sons excluding
David, and the chapter gives the names of only the three
eldest ; the others' names are supplied from 1 Chron. ii. 13 ff.
which tells us that there were seven sons altogether.

[d] So LXX ; Heb. Abinadab.

[e] Bibl. Shammah (Chron. *Shim'a*), LXX Σαμά (*v.l.* Σαμαά
κτλ.).

[f] Bibl. Raddai, LXX Ζαδδαί (*v.l.* Ζαβδαί, 'Ραδδαί), Luc.
Ρεηλαί.

[g] Bibl. Ozem (Heb. *'Osem*), LXX Ἄσομ, Luc. Ἄσαμ.

τῶν βοσκημάτων φυλακῆς ἐπιμελεῖσθαι, κελεύει
καλεῖν αὐτὸν ἐν τάχει· κατακλιθῆναι γὰρ εἰς
εὐωχίαν οὐκ εἶναι δυνατὸν αὐτοῖς ἐκείνου μὴ
164 παρόντος. ὡς δ᾿ ἧκεν ὁ Δαυίδης μεταπεμφθεὶς
ὑπὸ τοῦ πατρός, παῖς ξανθὸς μὲν τὴν χρόαν γοργὸς
δὲ τὰς ὄψεις καὶ καλὸς ἄλλως " οὗτός ἐστιν,"
εἰπὼν ἡσυχῇ πρὸς αὐτὸν Σαμουῆλος, " ὁ βασιλεύειν
ἀρέσας τῷ θεῷ," κατακλίνεται μὲν αὐτός, κατακλίνει δ᾿ ὑφ᾿ αὑτὸν τὸν νεανίσκον καὶ τὸν Ἰεσσαῖον
165 μετὰ καὶ τῶν παίδων. ἔπειτα λαβὼν ὁρῶντος τοῦ
Δαυίδου τὸ ἔλαιον ἀλείφει τ᾿ αὐτὸν καὶ πρὸς τὸ
οὖς ἠρέμα λαλεῖ καὶ σημαίνει τοῦθ᾿, ὅτι βασιλεύειν
αὐτὸν ὁ θεὸς ᾔρηται. παρῄνει δ᾿ εἶναι δίκαιον καὶ
κατήκοον αὐτοῦ τῶν προσταγμάτων· οὕτως γὰρ
αὐτῷ παραμενεῖν τὴν βασιλείαν εἰς πολὺν χρόνον
καὶ τὸν οἶκον λαμπρὸν καὶ περιβόητον γενήσεσθαι,[1]
καταστρέψεσθαι[2] δὲ καὶ Παλαιστίνους, καὶ οἷς ἂν
ἔθνεσι πολεμῇ νικῶντα καὶ περιόντα τῇ μάχῃ
κλέος ἀοίδιμον ζῶντά τε ἕξειν καὶ τοῖς μετ᾿ αὐτὸν
ἀπολείψειν.

166 (2) Καὶ Σαμουῆλος μὲν ἀπαλλάσσεται ταῦτα
παραινέσας, πρὸς δὲ τὸν Δαυίδην μεταβαίνει τὸ
θεῖον καταλιπὸν Σαοῦλον. καὶ ὁ μὲν προφητεύειν
ἤρξατο τοῦ θείου πνεύματος εἰς αὐτὸν μετοικισα-
μένου· τὸν Σαοῦλον δὲ περιήρχετο πάθη τινὰ καὶ
δαιμόνια πνιγμοὺς αὐτῷ καὶ στραγγάλας ἐπι-
φέροντα, ὡς τοὺς ἰατροὺς ἄλλην μὲν αὐτῷ θερα-
πείαν μὴ ἐπινοεῖν, εἰ δέ τίς ἐστιν ἐξᾴδειν δυνάμενος
καὶ ψάλλειν ἐπὶ κινύρα τοῦτον ἐκέλευσαν ζητή-

---

[1] Dindorf: παραμένειν . . . γενέσθαι codd.
[2] ed. pr.: καταστρέψασθαι MSP.

[a] 1 Sam. xvi. 12 " with beautiful eyes."

shepherd and busied with keeping the flocks; whereat
Samuel bade him call him in haste, for it was not
possible for them to sit down to the feast without
him. Now so soon as David appeared at his father's
summons,—a lad of ruddy colour, with piercing *a* eyes
and in other ways handsome,—"This," said Samuel
softly to himself,*b* "is he whom it has pleased God
to make king"; and he sat himself down and made
the youth sit beside him, and then Jesse with his
other sons. Then, in the sight of David, he took the
oil and anointed him and spoke low into his ear, ex-
plaining that God had chosen him to be king. He
also exhorted *c* him to be righteous and obedient to
His commandments, for so would the kingship long
continue to be his, and his house would become
splendid and renowned; he would subdue the Philistines and, victorious and triumphant over all nations
with whom he might wage war, he would in his lifetime attain glorious fame and bequeath it to his
posterity.

(2) So, after these exhortations, Samuel went his
way,*d* and the Deity abandoned Saul and passed over
to David, who, when the divine spirit had removed
to him, began to prophesy.*e* But as for Saul, he was
beset by strange disorders and evil spirits which
caused him such suffocation *f* and strangling that the
physicians *g* could devise no other remedy save to
order search to be made for one with power to charm
away spirits and to play upon the harp, and, whenso-

Samuel anoints David.
1 Sam. xvi. 12.

Saul takes David as his musician and armour-bearer.
1 Sam. xvi. 13.

---

b In Scripture, God prompts Samuel to recognize David.
c The exhortation is unscriptural.   *d* To Ramah.
e Scripture does not say that David prophesied.
f After the LXX of 1 Sam. xvi. 14 ἔπνιγεν; Heb. has
simply "troubled."
g Bibl. "the servants of Saul."

409

σαντας, ὁπόταν αὐτῷ προσίῃ¹ τὰ δαιμόνια καὶ
ταράττῃ,² ποιεῖν ὑπὲρ κεφαλῆς στάντα ψάλλειν τε
167 καὶ τοὺς ὕμνους ἐπιλέγειν. ὁ δὲ οὐκ ἠμέλησεν,
ἀλλὰ ζητεῖσθαι προσέταξε τοιοῦτον ἄνθρωπον·
φήσαντος δέ τινος αὐτῷ τῶν παρόντων ἐν Βηθ-
λεέμῃ πόλει τεθεᾶσθαι Ἰεσσαίου μὲν υἱὸν ἔτι
παῖδα τὴν ἡλικίαν, εὐπρεπῆ δὲ καὶ καλὸν τά τε
ἄλλα σπουδῆς ἄξιον καὶ δὴ καὶ ψάλλειν εἰδότα
καὶ ᾄδειν ὕμνους καὶ πολεμιστὴν ἄκρον, πέμψας
πρὸς τὸν Ἰεσσαῖον ἐκέλευσεν ἀποστέλλειν αὐτῷ
τὸν Δαυίδην τῶν ποιμνίων ἀποσπάσαντα· βούλεσθαι γὰρ αὐτὸν ἰδεῖν, περὶ τῆς εὐμορφίας καὶ
168 τῆς ἀνδρείας ἀκούσας τοῦ νεανίσκου. ὁ δὲ
Ἰεσσαῖος πέμπει τὸν υἱὸν καὶ ξένια δοὺς κομίσαι
τῷ Σαούλῳ. ἐλθόντι δὲ ἥσθη καὶ ποιήσας ὁπλοφόρον διὰ πάσης ἦγε³ τιμῆς· ἐξῄδετο γὰρ ὑπ'
αὐτοῦ καὶ πρὸς τὴν ἀπὸ τῶν δαιμονίων ταραχήν,
ὁπότε αὐτῷ ταῦτα προσέλθοι, μόνος ἰατρὸς ἦν
λέγων τε τοὺς ὕμνους καὶ ψάλλων ἐν τῇ κινύρα
169 καὶ ποιῶν ἑαυτοῦ γίνεσθαι τὸν Σαούλον. πέμπει
τοίνυν πρὸς τὸν πατέρα τοῦ παιδὸς Ἰεσσαῖον ἐᾶσαι
παρ' αὐτῷ τὸν Δαυίδην κελεύων· ἥδεσθαι γὰρ αὐτῷ
βλεπομένῳ καὶ παρόντι· τὸν δ' οὐκ ἀντειπεῖν⁴ τῷ
Σαούλῳ, συγχωρῆσαι⁵ δὲ κατέχειν.
170 (ix. 1) Χρόνοις δ' ὕστερον οὐ πολλοῖς οἱ Παλαιστῖνοι πάλιν συνελθόντες καὶ δύναμιν ἀθροίσαντες
μεγάλην ἐπίασι τοῖς Ἰσραηλίταις καὶ μεταξὺ
Σωχοῦς καὶ Ἀζηκοῦς⁶ καταλαμβανόμενοι στρατο-

¹ προσίοι SPE.　　² ταράττοι codd. E.
³ εἶχε MSP.
⁴ τὸν δ' οὐκ ἀντ.] ὁ δὲ οὐκ ὂν ἀντειπεῖν Holwerda.
⁵ RO: συνεχώρησε MSP (+ δὴ Holwerda).
⁶ Azeca Lat.

ever the evil spirits should assail and torment Saul, to have him stand over the king and strike the strings and chant his songs. Saul did not neglect this advice, but ordered search to be made for such a man. And when one of those present said that he had seen in the city of Bethlehem a son of Jesse, a mere boy in years, but of pleasing and fair appearance and in other ways worthy of regard, who was, moreover, skilled in playing on the harp and in the singing of songs, and an excellent soldier, Saul sent to Jesse and ordered him to take David from the flocks and send him to him ; he wished, he said, to see the young man, having heard of his comeliness and valour. So Jesse sent his son, also giving him presents to carry to Saul. When he came, Saul was delighted with him, made him his armour-bearer and held him in the highest honour, for his illness was charmed away by him ; and against that trouble caused by the evil spirits, whensoever they assailed him, he had no other physician than David, who, by singing his songs and playing upon the harp, restored Saul to himself. He accordingly sent to Jesse, the lad's father, desiring him to leave David with him, since the sight of the boy and his presence gave him pleasure. Jesse would not gainsay Saul, but permitted him to keep David.

(ix. 1) Not long afterwards the Philistines again assembled and mustered a great force, and marched against the Israelites ; occupying the ground between Sochūs *a* and Azēkūs *b* they established their

Goliath challenges the Hebrews to combat. 1 Sam. xvii. 1.

---

a Bibl. Sochoh (A.V. Shochoh), lxx Σοκχώθ.
b Bibl. Azekah. Both places are in the valley of Elah (1 Sam. xvii. 2) on the border of Judah and Philistia, about 15 miles due W. of Bethlehem.

πεδεύονται. ἀντεπεξάγει δ᾽ αὐτοῖς τὴν στρατιὰν
καὶ Σαοῦλος καὶ ἐπί τινος ὄρους στρατοπεδευσάμενος ἀναγκάζει τοὺς Παλαιστίνους τὸ μὲν πρῶτον
στρατόπεδον καταλιπεῖν, ὁμοίως δ᾽ ἐπί τινος[1] ὄρους
ἀντικρὺ τοῦ καταληφθέντος ὑπὸ τοῦ Σαούλου
171 στρατοπεδεύσασθαι. διέστησε[2] δ᾽ ἀπ᾽ ἀλλήλων τὰ
στρατόπεδα μέσος αὐλὼν τῶν ὀρῶν ἐφ᾽ ὧν ἦν.
καταβὰς οὖν τις τῶν ἐκ τοῦ Παλαιστίνων στρατοπέδου, Γολίαθος[3] ὄνομα πόλεως δὲ Γίττης, ἀνὴρ
παμμεγεθέστατος· ἦν γὰρ πηχῶν τεσσάρων καὶ
σπιθαμῆς, ὅπλα τῇ φύσει τοῦ σώματος ἀναλογοῦντα
περικείμενος· θώρακα μὲν γὰρ ἐνεδέδυτο σταθμὸν
ἄγοντα πέντε χιλιάδας σίκλων, κόρυθα δὲ καὶ
κνημῖδας χαλκέας ὁποίας εἰκὸς ἦν ἀνδρὸς οὕτω
παραδόξου τὸ μέγεθος σκεπάσαι μέλη,[4] δόρυ δὲ
ἦν οὐ κοῦφον βάσταγμα δεξιᾶς, ἀλλ᾽ ἐπὶ τῶν ὤμων
αὐτὸ αἴρων ἔφερεν, εἶχε δὲ καὶ λόγχην ἑξακοσίων
σίκλων, εἵποντο δὲ πολλοὶ βαστάζοντες τὰ ὅπλα·
172 στὰς τοίνυν ὁ Γολίαθος οὗτος μεταξὺ τῶν παρα-
τάξεων βοήν τε ἀφίησι μεγάλην καὶ πρὸς τὸν
Σαοῦλον καὶ τοὺς Ἑβραίους λέγει· " μάχης μὲν
ὑμᾶς καὶ κινδύνων ἀπαλλάττω· τίς γὰρ ἀνάγκη
τὴν στρατιὰν ὑμῶν[5] συμπεσοῦσαν κακοπαθεῖν;
173 δότε δ᾽ ὅστις ἐμοὶ μαχεῖται τῶν ὑμετέρων, καὶ
βραβευθήσεται τὰ τοῦ πολέμου[6] ἑνὶ[7] τῷ νενικηκότι·

---

[1] δ᾽ ἐπί τινος Niese: δέ τινος RO: ἐπὶ ὁμοίου δέ τινος MSP.
[2] διέστη ROE: δίεστη Niese.
[3] Γολιάθης codd., sed infra Γολίαθος codd. plur.
[4] Niese ex Lat.: μέρη codd.   [5] SP: ἡμῶν rell.
[6] τὸ τοῦ πολέμου τέλος MSP.
[7] ἑνὶ ex Lat.: ἐν codd.

---

[a] Josephus infers from 1 Sam. xvii. 3, mentioning a moun-

camp there. Saul, on his side, led out his army against them, and, having pitched his camp on a certain mountain, forced the Philistines to abandon their first camp *a* and to take up a similar position on another mountain over against that which he had occupied himself. The two camps were separated by a valley between the hills on which they lay. And now there came down from the camp of the Philistines one by name Goliath, of the city of Gitta, a man of gigantic stature. For he measured four *b* cubits and a span, and was clad in armour proportioned to his frame. He wore a breastplate weighing 5000 shekels, with a helmet and greaves of bronze such as were meet to protect the limbs of a man of such prodigious size. His spear was not light enough to be borne in the right hand, but he carried it elevated on his shoulders ; he had also a spear weighing 600 shekels,*c* and many followed him, carrying his armour.*d* Standing, then, between the opposing forces, this Goliath gave a mighty shout and said to Saul and the Hebrews, " I hereby deliver you from battle and its perils. For what need is there for your *e* troops to join arms and to suffer heavy losses ? Give me one of your men to fight with me, and the issue of the war shall be decided by the single victor, and to

tain for the first time, that the Philistines had changed their camp.

b So most mss. of the LXX ; Heb. and LXX A have " six." The figures here given equal about 6 ft. 8 in.

c Or " and it had a head weighing 600 shekels " ; whether the whole spear or the spearhead alone weighed 600 shekels is not clear either from the Heb. or LXX of 1 Sam. xvii. 7. The latter, like Josephus, has λόγχη, which means either " spear " or " spearhead."

d Bibl. " and his shield-bearer went before him."

e Variant " our."

δουλεύσουσι γὰρ ἐκεῖνοι τοῖς ἑτέροις, ὧν ἂν ὁ
νικήσας γένηται· πολὺ δὲ κρεῖττον οἶμαι[1] καὶ
σωφρονέστατον ἑνὸς κινδύνῳ λαβεῖν ὃ βούλεσθε
174 ἢ τῷ ἁπάντων.[2]'' ταῦτ' εἰπὼν ἀνεχώρησεν εἰς τὸ
τῶν οἰκείων στρατόπεδον. τῇ δ' ἐχομένῃ πάλιν
ἐλθὼν τοὺς αὐτοὺς ἐποιήσατο λόγους καὶ μέχρι
τεσσαράκοντα ἡμερῶν οὐ διέλειπε προκαλούμενος
ἐπὶ τοῖς προειρημένοις τοὺς πολεμίους, ὡς καταπλαγῆναι αὐτόν τε τὸν Σαοῦλον καὶ τὴν στρατιάν.
καὶ παρετάσσοντο μὲν ὡς εἰς μάχην, οὐκ ἤρχοντο
δὲ εἰς χεῖρας.

175 (2) Τοῦ δὲ πολέμου συνεστηκότος τοῖς Ἑβραίοις
καὶ τοῖς Παλαιστίνοις Σαοῦλος ἀπέλυσε τὸν
Δαυίδην πρὸς τὸν πατέρα Ἰεσσαῖον ἀρκούμενος
αὐτοῦ τοῖς τρισὶν υἱοῖς, οὓς ἐπὶ συμμαχίαν καὶ
176 τοὺς κινδύνους ἔπεμψεν. ὁ δὲ τὸ μὲν πρῶτον ἐπὶ
τὰ ποίμνια πάλιν καὶ τὰς νομὰς τῶν βοσκημάτων
παραγίνεται, μετ' οὐ πολὺ δὲ ἔρχεται εἰς τὸ στρατόπεδον τῶν Ἑβραίων πεμφθεὶς ὑπὸ τοῦ πατρὸς
κομίσαι τε τοῖς ἀδελφοῖς ἐφόδια καὶ γνῶναι τί
177 πράττουσι. τοῦ δὲ Γολιάθου πάλιν ἐλθόντος καὶ
προκαλουμένου καὶ ὀνειδίζοντος ὅτι μηδείς ἐστιν
ἀνδρεῖος ἐν αὐτοῖς, ὃς εἰς μάχην αὐτῷ τολμᾷ κατα-
βῆναι, μεταξὺ τοῖς ἀδελφοῖς ὁμιλῶν Δαυίδης περὶ
ὧν ἐπέστειλεν ὁ πατήρ, ἀκούσας βλασφημοῦντος
τὴν στρατιὰν καὶ κακίζοντος τοῦ Παλαιστίνου
ἠγανάκτησε καὶ πρὸς τοὺς ἀδελφοὺς αὐτοῦ εἶπεν
178 ἑτοίμως ἔχειν μονομαχῆσαι τῷ πολεμίῳ. πρὸς
τοῦθ' ὁ πρεσβύτατος τῶν ἀδελφῶν Ἐλίαβος[3] ἐπ-
έπληξεν αὐτῷ, τολμηρότερον παρ' ἡλικίαν καὶ
ἀμαθῆ τοῦ προσήκοντος εἰπών, ἐκέλευσέ τε πρὸς
τὰ ποίμνια καὶ τὸν πατέρα βαδίζειν. κατ-

414

the people of the victor the other side shall be slaves. It is far better, I think, and more prudent to attain your end by the hazard of one man's life rather than of all." Having so spoken he retired to his own camp. On the morrow he came again and delivered the same speech, and so, for forty days, he did not cease to challenge his enemies in these same terms, to the utter dismay both of Saul and his army. And though they remained drawn up as for battle, they never came to close quarters.

xvii. 16.

(2) Now, on the outbreak of the war between the Hebrews and the Philistines, Saul had sent David away to his father Jesse, being content with the latter's three sons whom he had sent to share the dangers of the campaign. David then returned at first to his flocks and cattle-pastures, but before long visited the camp of the Hebrews, being sent by his father to carry provisions to his brothers and to learn how they fared. Now when Goliath came again, challenging and taunting the Hebrews with not having among them a man brave enough to venture down to fight with him, David was talking with his brothers about the matters wherewith his father had charged him, and hearing the Philistine reviling and abusing their army, he became indignant and said to his brothers that he was ready to meet this adversary in single combat. Thereat the eldest of his brothers, Eliab, rebuked him, telling him that he was bolder than became his years and ignorant of what was fitting, and bade him be off to the flocks and to his

David asks
Saul for
permission
to fight
Goliath.
1 Sam. xvii.
13.

---

1 Bekker: εἶναι codd.
2 Niese: τῶν ἁπάντων RO: τῷ πάντων SP.
3 MSP: Ἰάναβος RO: Aminadab Lat.

αἰδεσθεὶς δὲ τὸν ἀδελφὸν ὑπεχώρησε καὶ πρός
τινας τῶν στρατιωτῶν ἀπελάλησεν ὅτι θέλοι μάχε-
179 σθαι τῷ προκαλουμένῳ. δηλωσάντων δ' εὐθὺς τῷ
Σαούλῳ τὴν τοῦ νεανίσκου προαίρεσιν μεταπέμ-
πεται αὐτὸν ὁ βασιλεύς, καὶ πυθομένου τί βούλεται λέγει¹ " μὴ ταπεινὸν ἔστω τὸ φρόνημα μηδ'
εὐλαβές,² ὦ βασιλεῦ· καθαιρήσω γὰρ ἐγὼ τὴν
ἀλαζονείαν τοῦ πολεμίου χωρήσας αὐτῷ διὰ μάχης
καὶ τὸν ὑψηλὸν καὶ μέγαν ὑπ' ἐμαυτῷ βαλών.
180 γένοιτο μὲν ἂν αὐτὸς οὕτως καταγέλαστος, ἔνδοξον
δὲ τὸ σὸν στράτευμα, εἰ μηδ' ὑπ' ἀνδρὸς πολεμεῖν
ἤδη δυναμένου καὶ πιστευομένου παράταξιν καὶ
μάχας, ἀλλ' ὑπὸ παιδὸς ἔτι δοκοῦντος καὶ ταύτην
ἔχοντος τὴν ἡλικίαν ἀποθάνοι."
181 (3) Τοῦ δὲ Σαούλου τὸ μὲν τολμηρὸν αὐτοῦ καὶ
τὴν εὐψυχίαν θαυμάζοντος, οὐ θαρροῦντος δὲ ἐπ'
αὐτῷ διὰ τὴν ἡλικίαν, ἀλλ' ἀσθενέστερον εἶναι διὰ
ταύτην πρὸς εἰδότα πολεμεῖν μάχεσθαι λέγοντος,
" ταῦτ'," εἶπε Δαυίδης, " ἐπαγγέλλομαι τῷ θεῷ
θαρρῶν ὄντι μετ' ἐμοῦ· πεπείραμαι γὰρ αὐτοῦ τῆς
182 βοηθείας. λέοντα γὰρ ἐπελθόντα μού ποτε τοῖς
ποιμνίοις καὶ ἁρπάσαντα ἄρνα διώξας καταλαμ-
βάνω καὶ τὸν μὲν ἄρνα τοῦ³ στόματος ἐξαρπάζω
τοῦ θηρός, αὐτὸν δ' ὁρμήσαντα ἐπ' ἐμὲ τῆς οὐρᾶς
183 βαστάσας καὶ προσρήξας τῇ γῇ διαφθείρω. ταὐτὸ
δὲ καὶ ἄρκτον ἀμυνόμενος διατίθεμαι. νομιζέσθω
δὴ καὶ ὁ πολέμιος ἐκείνων εἶναι τῶν θηρίων,
ὀνειδίζων ἐκ πολλοῦ τὴν στρατιὰν καὶ βλασφημῶν
ἡμῶν τὸν θεόν, ὃς αὐτὸν ὑποχείριον ἐμοὶ θήσει."

¹ Niese: (καὶ) λέγειν codd.   ² +εἶπεν SP.
³ ἐκ τοῦ MSPE.
416

father. Out of respect for his brother David withdrew, but gave out to some of the soldiers that he wished to fight with the challenger. As they straightway reported the lad's resolve to Saul, the king sent for him ; and David, when asked by him what he wished, said, " Let not thy spirit be downcast nor fearful, O King, for I will bring down the presumption of the foe by joining battle with him and throwing this mighty *a* giant down before me. Thus would he be made a laughing-stock, and thine army have the more glory, should he be slain, not by a grown man fit for war and entrusted with the command of battles, but by one to all appearance and in truth no older than a boy." *b*

(3) Saul admired the lad's daring and courage, but could not place full confidence in him by reason of his years, because of which, he said, he was too feeble to fight with a skilled warrior. " These promises," replied David, " I make in the assurance that God is with me ; for I have already had proof of His aid. Once when a lion attacked my flocks and carried off a lamb, I pursued and caught him and snatched the lamb from the beast's jaws, and, when he sprang upon me, lifted him by the tail and killed him by dashing him upon the ground.*c* And I did the very same thing in battle with a bear. Let this enemy then be reckoned even as one of those wild beasts, so long has he insulted our army and blasphemed our God, who will deliver him into my hands."

David answers Saul's doubts. 1 Sam. xvii. 33.

---

a Or "lofty-vaunting," as Professor Capps suggests.

b The last part of David's speech is an amplification of Scripture.

c 1 Sam. xvii. 35 " I seized him by the beard (LXX and Targum " throat " or " jaws ") and struck him and killed him."

417

184 (4) Τῇ προθυμίᾳ τοιγαροῦν καὶ τῇ τόλμῃ τοῦ
παιδὸς ὅμοιον γενέσθαι τέλος παρὰ τοῦ θεοῦ
Σαοῦλος εὐξάμενος " ἄπιθι," φησί, " πρὸς τὴν
μάχην." καὶ περιθεὶς αὐτῷ τὸν αὐτοῦ θώρακα
καὶ περιζώσας τὸ ξίφος καὶ περικεφαλαίαν ἁρ-
185 μόσας ἐξέπεμψεν.[1] ὁ δὲ Δαυίδης βαρυνόμενος ὑπὸ
τῶν ὅπλων, οὐκ ἐγεγύμναστο γὰρ οὐδ' ἐμεμαθήκει
φέρειν ὅπλα, " ταῦτα μέν," εἶπεν, " ὦ βασιλεῦ,
σὸς ἔστω κόσμος τοῦ καὶ βαστάζειν δυναμένου,
συγχώρησον δὲ ὡς δούλῳ σου καὶ ὡς ἐγὼ βούλομαι
μαχεσθῆναι." τίθησιν οὖν τὰ ὅπλα καὶ τὴν βακτη-
ρίαν ἀράμενος καὶ πέντε λίθους ἐκ τοῦ χειμάρρου βαλὼν εἰς τὴν πήραν τὴν ποιμενικὴν καὶ
σφενδόνην ἐν τῇ δεξιᾷ χειρὶ φέρων ἐπὶ τὸν Γολίαθον
186 ἐπορεύετο. καταφρονεῖ δὲ οὕτως ἰδὼν αὐτὸν ὁ
πολέμιος ἐρχόμενον καὶ προσέσκωψεν, ὡς οὐχ οἷα
πρὸς ἄνθρωπον[2] ὅπλα νενόμισται ταῦτ' ἔχων μέλλοι
μάχεσθαι, οἷς δὲ κύνας ἀπελαύνομεν καὶ φυλασ-
σόμεθα. μὴ αὐτὸν ἀντὶ ἀνθρώπου κύνα εἶναι
δοκεῖ; ὁ δ' οὐχὶ τοιοῦτον ἀλλὰ καὶ χείρω κυνὸς
αὐτὸν νομίζειν ἀπεκρίνατο. κινεῖ δὲ πρὸς ὀργὴν
τὸν Γολίαθον, καὶ ἀρὰς αὐτῷ τίθεται ἐκ τῆς
προσηγορίας τοῦ θεοῦ καὶ δώσειν ἠπείλησε τὰς
σάρκας αὐτοῦ τοῖς ἐπιγείοις καὶ τοῖς μεταρσίοις
187 διασπάσασθαι· ἀμείβεται δ' αὐτὸν ὁ Δαυίδης· " σὺ
μὲν ἐπέρχῃ μοι ἐν ῥομφαίᾳ καὶ δόρατι καὶ θώρακι,
ἐγὼ δὲ χωρῶν ἐπὶ σὲ τὸν θεὸν ὥπλισμαι, ὃς σέ τε
καὶ τὴν πᾶσαν ὑμῶν στρατιὰν χερσὶ ταῖς ἡμετέραις
διολέσει. καρατομήσω μὲν γάρ σε σήμερον καὶ τὸ

---

[1] SP: ἐξέπεμπεν ME: ἔπεμψεν RO.
[2] ἀνθρώπων Niese (ex Lat. hominum).

(4) So then Saul, praying that the lad's zeal and hardihood might be rewarded by God with a like success, said, " Go forth to battle." [a] And he clad him in his own breastplate, girt his sword about him, fitted a helmet upon his head and so sent him out. But David was weighed down by this armour, for he had not been trained nor taught to wear armour, and said, " Let this fine apparel be for thee, O King, for thou indeed art able to wear it,[b] but suffer me, as thy servant, to fight just as I will." Accordingly he laid down the armour and, taking up his staff, he put five stones from the brook into his shepherd's wallet, and with a sling in his right hand advanced against Goliath. The enemy, seeing him approaching in this manner, showed his scorn, and derided him for coming to fight, not with such weapons as men are accustomed to use against other men, but with those wherewith we drive away and keep off dogs. Or did he perhaps take him for a dog, and not a man ? " No," replied David, " not even for a dog, but something still worse." [c] This roused Goliath's anger, and he called down curses upon him in his god's name and threatened to give his flesh to the beasts of earth and the birds of heaven to rend asunder. But David answered him, " Thou comest against me with sword, spear and breastplate, but I, in coming against thee, have God for my armour, who will destroy both thee and all your host by our hands. For I will this day

[a] 1 Sam. xvii. 37 " Go forth and may the Lord be with thee." Weill's note, " in the Bible this prayer is put in David's mouth," overlooks the fact that David's brief prayer for deliverance is given by Josephus in the preceding sentence. Here he is amplifying Saul's blessing just quoted.

[b] Amplification.

[c] So the LXX ; this reply is not found in the Hebrew.

ἄλλο σῶμα τοῖς ὁμοφύλοις κυσὶ παραβαλῶ, μαθή-
σονται δὲ πάντες ὅτι προέστηκεν Ἑβραίων τὸ θεῖον
καὶ ὅπλα ἡμῖν καὶ ἰσχὺς τοῦτ᾿ ἔστι κηδόμενον,
ἡ δ᾿ ἄλλη παρασκευὴ καὶ δύναμις ἀνωφελὴς
188 θεοῦ μὴ παρόντος.᾿᾿ ὁ δὲ Παλαιστῖνος ὑπὸ βάρους
τῶν ὅπλων εἰς ὠκύτητα καὶ δρόμον ἐμποδιζόμενος
βάδην ἐπὶ τὸν Δαυίδην παραγίνεται καταφρονῶν
καὶ πεποιθὼς γυμνὸν ὁμοῦ καὶ παῖδα ἔτι τὴν
ἡλικίαν ἀπόνως ἀναιρήσειν.
189   (5) Ἀπαντᾷ δὲ ὁ νεανίσκος μετὰ συμμάχου μὴ
βλεπομένου τῷ πολεμίῳ· θεὸς δ᾿ ἦν οὗτος.   καὶ
ἀνελόμενος ἐκ τῆς πήρας ὧν εἰς αὐτὴν κατέθηκεν
ἐκ τοῦ χειμάρρου λίθον ἕνα καὶ ἁρμόσας τῇ σφεν-
δόνῃ βάλλει ἐπὶ τὸν Γολίαθον εἰς τὸ μέτωπον·
καὶ διῆλθεν ἕως τοῦ ἐγκεφάλου τὸ βληθέν, ὡς
εὐθὺς καρωθέντα πεσεῖν τὸν Γολίαθον ἐπὶ τὴν
190 ὄψιν. δραμὼν δ᾿ ἐφίσταται τῷ πολεμίῳ κειμένῳ
καὶ τῇ ῥομφαίᾳ τῇ ἐκείνου, μάχαιραν οὐκ ἔχων
191 αὐτός, ἀποτέμνει τὴν κεφαλὴν αὐτοῦ. πεσὼν δ᾿
ὁ Γολίαθος ἧττα καὶ φυγὴ γίνεται Παλαιστίνοις·
τὸν γὰρ δοκιμώτατον ἰδόντες ἐρριμμένον καὶ περὶ
τῶν ὅλων δείσαντες οὐκέτι μένειν διέγνωσαν, ἀλλ᾿
αἰσχρᾷ καὶ ἀκόσμῳ φυγῇ παραδόντες ἑαυτοὺς
ἐξαρπάζειν τῶν κινδύνων ἐπειρῶντο. Σαοῦλος δὲ
καὶ πᾶς ὁ τῶν Ἑβραίων στρατὸς ἀλαλάξαντες ἐκ-
πηδῶσιν εἰς αὐτοὺς καὶ πολλοὺς ἀποσφάττοντες
διώκουσιν ἄχρι τῶν Γίττης ὁρίων καὶ τῶν πυλῶν

* 1 Sam. xvii. 46 " I will give the carcase of the camp

cut off thine head and fling thy carcase to the dogs, thy fellows,[a] and all men shall learn that Hebrews have the Deity for their protection, and that He in His care for us is our armour and strength, and that all other armament and force are unavailing where God is not." And now the Philistine, impeded by the weight of his armour from running more swiftly, came on toward David at a slow pace,[b] contemptuous and confident of slaying without any trouble an adversary at once unarmed and of an age so youthful.

(5) But the youth advanced to the encounter, accompanied by an ally invisible to the foe, and this was God. Drawing from his wallet one of the stones from the brook which he had put therein, and fitting it to his sling, he shot it at Goliath, catching him in the forehead, and the missile penetrated to the brain, so that Goliath was instantly stunned and fell upon his face. Then, running forward, David stood over his prostrate foe and with the other's broadsword, having no sword of his own, he cut off his head. Goliath's fall caused the defeat and rout of the Philistines; for, seeing their best warrior laid low and fearing a complete disaster, they resolved to remain no longer, but sought to save themselves from danger by ignominious and disorderly flight. But Saul and the whole Hebrew army, with shouts of battle, sprang upon them and with great carnage pursued them to the borders of Gitta [c] and to the gates of Ascalon.[d]

David slays Goliath; the Philistines are routed. 1 Sam. xvii. 49.

of the Philistines to the birds of heaven, etc." Josephus evidently read " thy carcase to the camp, etc."

[b] Unscriptural details.

[c] Bibl. Gath. *Cf. A.* v. 87.

[d] So the LXX in the first occurrence of the name in 1 Sam. xvii. 52 ; in the second part of the verse it agrees with the Hebrew in reading Ekron.

192 τῶν Ἀσκάλωνος. καὶ θνήσκουσι μὲν τῶν Παλαιστίνων εἰς τρισμυρίους, δὶς δὲ τοσοῦτοι τραυματίαι
γίνονται. Σαοῦλος δὲ ὑποστρέψας εἰς τὸ στρατόπεδον αὐτῶν διαρπάζει τὸ χαράκωμα καὶ ἐνέπρησε·
τὴν κεφαλὴν δὲ Γολιάθου¹ Δαυίδης εἰς τὴν ἰδίαν
σκηνὴν ἐκόμισε καὶ τὴν ῥομφαίαν ἀνέθηκε τῷ θεῷ.

193 (x. 1) Φθόνον δὲ καὶ μῖσος τοῦ Σαούλου πρὸς
αὐτὸν αἱ γυναῖκες ἐρεθίζουσιν· ὑπαντῶσαι γὰρ τῇ
στρατιᾷ νικηφόρῳ μετὰ κυμβάλων καὶ τυμπάνων
καὶ παντοίας χαρᾶς ᾖδον αἱ μὲν γυναῖκες, ὡς
πολλὰς Σαοῦλος ἀπώλεσε Παλαιστίνων χιλιάδας,
αἱ παρθένοι δέ, ὡς μυριάδας Δαυίδης ἀφανίσειε.

194 τούτων δὲ ἀκούων ὁ βασιλεύς, ὡς τὸ μὲν ἔλαττον
τῆς μαρτυρίας αὐτὸς λάβοι, τὸ δὲ τῶν μυριάδων
πλῆθος ἀνατεθείη τῷ νεανίσκῳ, καὶ λογισάμενος
μηδὲν οὕτω μετὰ λαμπρὰν εὐφημίαν ἢ τὴν βασιλείαν ὑστερεῖν αὐτῷ, φοβεῖσθαι καὶ ὑποπτεύειν

195 ἤρξατο τὸν Δαυίδην. καὶ τῆς μὲν πρώτης τάξεως,
ἐπεὶ τῷ δέει πλησίον αὐτοῦ καὶ λίαν ἐγγὺς ἐδόκει,
ἐποίησε γὰρ αὐτὸν ὁπλοφόρον, μεταστήσας ἀπο-
δείκνυσι χιλίαρχον δοὺς αὐτῷ χώραν ἀμείνονα μὲν
ἀσφαλεστέραν² δὲ ὡς ἐνόμιζεν αὐτῷ³· ἐβούλετο

---

¹ RO: τὴν δὲ κεφαλὴν τοῦ Γ. rell.
² σφαλερὰν SP.   ³ Niese: αὐτῷ codd.

ᵃ Unscriptural numbers.

ᵇ 1 Sam. xvii. 53 " The Israelites returned from pursuing
the Philistines and plundered (LXX κατεπάτουν " trampled
down ") their camp." Perhaps Josephus took the Heb. root
dlq, " pursue," in its other sense " burn " (cf. Latin version
of Scripture, comburentes), or possibly read κατέκαιον instead
of κατεπάτουν.

ᶜ The reverse of Scripture, 1 Sam. xvii. 54 which reads
" And David took the head of the Philistine and brought it
to Jerusalem, but his armour he put in his tent." Later, in

Of the Philistines 30,000 [a] were slain and twice as many wounded. Saul then returning to their camp destroyed the palisade and set fire to it [b]; while David carried the head of Goliath to his own tent and dedicated his sword to God.[c]

(x. 1) [d] But envy and hatred of David were now aroused in Saul by the women. For they, coming to meet the victorious army with cymbals, timbrels and every sign of rejoicing, sang, the elder women how Saul had slain many thousands of the Philistines, but the maidens [e] how David had destroyed tens of thousands. The king on hearing this, and how he was given the lesser portion of the credit, while the larger number, the myriads, was ascribed to the youth, thought within himself that after so splendid an acclamation nothing more was lacking to David save the kingship, and now began to fear him and to regard him with suspicion. So he removed him from his former station—for he had made him his armour-bearer—since in his alarm he thought this far too close to his person, and appointed him captain of a thousand,[f] thus giving him a better post, but one, as he thought, safer for himself.[g] For

§ 244, Josephus tells us, in accordance with Scripture, 1 Sam. xxi. 9 (10), that David had dedicated Goliath's sword to God in the temple at Nob.

[d] Josephus, with many MSS. of the LXX, omits the presentation of David by Abner and the covenant with Jonathan which follow immediately upon the close of the battle, 1 Sam. xviii. 1-4.

[e] Scripture does not distinguish the women by age.

[f] Gr. "chiliarch." In the Hebrew this change is made after Saul's attack on David while playing the harp, 1 Sam. xviii. 10-11. Josephus omits the incident, as do many MSS. of the LXX.

[g] Variant "more treacherous for him (David)."

γὰρ εἰς τοὺς πολεμίους αὐτὸν ἐκπέμπειν καὶ τὰς
μάχας ὡς ἐν τοῖς κινδύνοις τεθνηξόμενον.

196 (2) Δαυίδης δὲ πανταχοῦ τὸν θεὸν ἐπαγόμενος
ὅποι ποτ' ἀφίκοιτο κατώρθου καὶ διευπραγῶν
ἐδείκνυτο,[1] ὡς δι' ὑπερβολὴν τῆς ἀνδρείας τόν τε
λαὸν αὐτοῦ[2] καὶ τὴν Σαούλου θυγατέρα παρθένον
ἔτι οὖσαν λαβεῖν ἔρωτα καὶ τοῦ πάθους ὑπερ-
κρατοῦντος γενέσθαι φανερὰν καὶ διαβληθῆναι πρὸς
197 τὸν πατέρα. ὁ δ' ὡς ἀφορμῇ χρησόμενος[3] τῆς
ἐπὶ Δαυίδην ἐπιβουλῆς ἡδέως ἤκουσε καὶ δώσειν
προθύμως αὐτῷ τὴν παρθένον πρὸς τοὺς τὸν ἔρωτα
μηνύσαντας αὐτῆς ἔφη, γενησόμενον ἀπωλείας καὶ
κινδύνων αἴτιον αὐτῷ ληψομένῳ· '' κατεγγυῶ γάρ,''
εἶπεν, '' αὐτῷ τὸν τῆς θυγατρός μου γάμον, ἂν
198 ἑξακοσίας μοι κομίσῃ κεφαλὰς τῶν πολεμίων. ὁ
δὲ καὶ γέρως οὕτω λαμπροῦ προτεθέντος καὶ
βουλόμενος ἐπ' ἔργῳ παραβόλῳ καὶ ἀπίστῳ λαβεῖν
κλέος, ὁρμήσει μὲν ἐπὶ τὴν πρᾶξιν, διαφθαρήσεται
δὲ ὑπὸ τῶν Παλαιστίνων καὶ χωρήσει μοι τὰ κατ'
αὐτὸν εὐπρεπῶς· ἀπαλλαγήσομαι γὰρ αὐτοῦ, δι'
ἄλλων αὐτόν, ἀλλ' οὐχὶ δι' ἐμαυτοῦ κτείνας.''
199 διάπειραν δὴ τῆς τοῦ Δαυίδου διανοίας κελεύει
τοὺς οἰκέτας λαμβάνειν, πῶς ἔχει πρὸς τὸ γῆμαι
τὴν κόρην. οἱ δ' ἤρξαντο διαλέγεσθαι πρὸς αὐτόν,
ὅτι στέργει μὲν αὐτὸν ὁ βασιλεὺς Σαοῦλος καὶ
ὁ λαὸς ἅπας, βούλεται δ' αὐτῷ κηδεῦσαι τὴν
200 θυγατέρα. ὁ δέ '' μικρὸν ἄρ' ὑμῖν,'' εἶπε, '' δοκεῖ
γαμβρὸν γενέσθαι βασιλέως; ἐμοὶ δ' οὐχὶ τοιοῦτον

---

[1] RO: ἐβλέπετο rell. (Lat.).
[2] + ἐρᾶν M.   [3] M : χρησάμενος rell.

---

[a] His younger daughter, Michal, cf. § 204 note.   Josephus
424

he proposed to send him out against the enemy and into battle, in the hope that amidst these dangers he would meet his death.

(2) But David, being everywhere attended by God whithersoever he went, achieved success and showed himself so fortunate in all things that by his extraordinary valour he won the heart not only of the people but of Saul's daughter,[a] who was still a virgin ; and so overmastering was her passion that it betrayed her and was reported to her father. He, thinking to seize this occasion for plotting against David, welcomed the news and told those who had informed him of his daughter's love that he would gladly give David the maiden, since the match, should he accept it, would prove the cause of danger and destruction to him. " For," said he, " I pledge him my daughter in marriage, if he will but bring me the heads of six hundred [b] of the foe. Now, at the offer of a prize so splendid and in his desire to win renown for a hazardous and incredible exploit, he will rush to perform it and be killed by the Philistines ; so will my designs against him succeed admirably, for I shall be rid of him, yet cause his death at the hands of others and not my own." He accordingly ordered his men to sound the mind of David touching marriage with the maid ; and they began to speak with him, telling him that King Saul felt affection for him, as did all the people, and wished to unite his daughter with him in marriage. Whereto David replied, " Does it then seem to you a small thing to become a king's son-in-law ? To me it does not appear so,

Saul's daughter Michal (Melcha) falls in love with David.
1 Sam. xviii. 20.

Saul treacherously lays down conditions for the marriage.
1 Sam. xviii. 22.

omits the Scriptural reference, 1 Sam. xviii. 17, to Saul's offer of his elder daughter, Merab.

[b] Bibl. " a hundred foreskins of the Philistines."

φαίνεται καὶ μάλιστα ὄντι ταπεινῷ καὶ δόξης καὶ
τιμῆς ἀμοίρῳ.'' Σαοῦλος δὲ ἀγγειλάντων αὐτῷ
τῶν οἰκετῶν τὰς τοῦ Δαυίδου ἀποκρίσεις '' οὐ
χρημάτων,'' ἔφη, '' δεῖσθαί με φράζετε αὐτῷ οὐδὲ
ἕδνων, ἀπεμπολᾶν γὰρ ἔστιν οὕτως¹ τὴν θυγατέρα
μᾶλλον ἢ συνοικίζειν, γαμβροῦ δὲ ἀνδρείαν ἔχοντος
καὶ τὴν ἄλλην ἀρετὴν ἅπασαν, ἣν ὁρᾶν ὑπάρχουσαν
201 αὐτῷ. βούλεσθαι δή με παρ' αὐτοῦ λαβεῖν ἀντὶ
τοῦ γάμου τῆς θυγατρὸς οὐ χρυσὸν οὐδ' ἄργυρον
οὐδ' ὅπως ταῦτα ἐκ τῶν τοῦ πατρὸς οἰκιῶν²
κομίσῃ, Παλαιστίνων δὲ τιμωρίαν καὶ κεφαλὰς
202 αὐτῶν ἑξακοσίας. αὐτῷ τε γὰρ ἐμοὶ τούτων οὐδὲν
ἂν οὔτε ποθεινότερον οὔτε λαμπρότερον³ δῶρον
γένοιτο, τῇ τε παιδί μου πολὺ τῶν νενομισμένων
ἕδνων ζηλωτότερον τὸ συνοικεῖν ἀνδρὶ τοιούτῳ καὶ
μαρτυρουμένῳ τὴν τῶν πολεμίων ἧτταν.''
203 (3) Κομισθέντων δὲ τούτων πρὸς τὸν Δαυίδην
τῶν λόγων ἡσθεὶς τὸν Σαοῦλον ἐσπουδακέναι νομίζων αὐτοῦ περὶ τὴν συγγένειαν, οὐδὲ βουλεύσασθαι
περιμείνας οὐδ' εἰ δυνατὸν ἢ δύσκολόν ἐστι τὸ προκείμενον ἔργον τῷ λογισμῷ περινοήσας ὥρμησεν
εὐθὺς μετὰ τῆς ἑταιρίας ἐπὶ τοὺς πολεμίους καὶ
τὴν ὑπὲρ τοῦ γάμου κατηγγελμένην πρᾶξιν καὶ
(θεὸς γὰρ ἦν ὁ πάντα ποιῶν εὐμαρῆ καὶ δυνατὰ
τῷ Δαυίδῃ) κτείνας πολλοὺς καὶ κεφαλὰς ἑξακοσίων ἀποτεμὼν ἧκε πρὸς τὸν βασιλέα διὰ τῆς
τούτων ἐπιδείξεως τὸν ἀντὶ τούτων γάμον ἀπαιτῶν.
204 Σαοῦλος δὲ οὐκ ἔχων ἀναφυγεῖν⁴ ἐκ τῶν ὑπ-
εσχημένων, αἰσχρὸν γὰρ ὑπελάμβανεν ἢ ψεύσασθαι

---

¹ τοῦτο Ernesti.   ² ΜΕ: οἰκείων rell.
³ +οὔτε προτιμότερον SPE.
⁴ ἀναφυγὴν Naber.

especially as I am of such humble rank and with no portion of glory or honour." When Saul was informed by his men of David's response, "Tell him," he said, " that I desire no money nor wedding gifts —that would be to sell my daughter, not to give her in marriage—but a son-in-law possessed of fortitude and all other virtues, such as I see in him. I wish, therefore, to receive of him, in return for his marriage with my daughter, neither gold nor silver—not these would I have him bring from his father's house—but the punishment of the Philistines and six hundred of their heads. For to myself no gift could be more desirable or magnificent [a] than that, and to my child it would be far more pleasing than the customary wedding presents to be united to such a husband who has the credit for defeating our enemies." [b]

(3) When these words were reported to David, he was delighted at the thought that Saul was eager to be related to him, and without waiting to deliberate, without reasonably considering whether the proposed enterprise was possible or difficult, he straightway, with his companions, set upon the foe to accomplish the task that was appointed him as the condition of the marriage ; and, thanks to God, who rendered all things possible and easy to David, he slew many men, cut off the heads of six hundred [c] and returned to the king, displaying these and claiming the bride as his recompense. So Saul, finding no way to evade his promises—since he saw that it would be disgraceful for him either to appear to have lied or to have held

David wins Michal by slaying six hundred Philistines. 1 Sam. xviii. 26.

---

[a] Some MSS. add " nor more precious."
[b] Saul's speech is an amplification of 1 Sam. xviii. 25.
[c] 1 Sam. xviii. 27 " he and his men . . slew of the Philistines two hundred (LXX " one hundred ") and David brought their foreskins."

δοκεῖν ἢ δι' ἐπιβουλὴν ἵν'[1] ἀδυνάτοις ἐπιχειρῶν ὁ
Δαυίδης ἀποθάνῃ τὸν γάμον ἐπηγγέλθαι, δίδωσιν
αὐτῷ τὴν θυγατέρα Μελχὰν[2] ὀνόματι.

205 (xi. 1) Ἔμελλε δὲ οὐκ ἐπὶ πολὺ τοῖς γεγενημένοις
ἐμμένειν Σαοῦλος ἄρα· ὁρῶν γὰρ τὸν Δαυίδην παρὰ
τῷ θεῷ καὶ παρὰ τοῖς ὄχλοις εὐδοκιμοῦντα κατέδεισε, καὶ τὸν φόβον οὐκ ἔχων ἀποκρύψασθαι περὶ
μεγάλων ὄντα, βασιλείας τε καὶ ζωῆς, ὧν καὶ
θατέρου στερηθῆναι συμφορὰ δεινή, κτείνειν τὸν
Δαυίδην διεγνώκει καὶ προστάσσει τὴν ἀναίρεσιν
αὐτοῦ Ἰωνάθῃ τε τῷ παιδὶ καὶ τοῖς πιστοτάτοις
206 τῶν οἰκετῶν. ὁ δὲ τὸν πατέρα τῆς ἐπὶ τῷ Δαυίδῃ
μεταβολῆς θαυμάσας οὐκ ἐπὶ μετρίοις ἀπὸ τῆς
πολλῆς εὐνοίας ἀλλ' ἐπὶ θανάτῳ γενομένης, καὶ
τὸν νεανίσκον ἀγαπῶν καὶ τὴν ἀρετὴν αὐτοῦ
καταιδούμενος λέγει πρὸς αὐτὸν τὸ τοῦ πατρὸς
207 ἀπόρρητον καὶ τὴν προαίρεσιν. συμβουλεύει μέντοι φυλάσσεσθαι γενόμενον ἐκποδὼν τὴν ἐπιοῦσαν
ἡμέραν· αὐτὸς γὰρ ἀσπάσεσθαι[3] τὸν πατέρα· καὶ
καιροῦ παραφανέντος αὐτῷ διαλεχθήσεσθαι περὶ
αὐτοῦ καὶ τὴν αἰτίαν μαθήσεσθαι καὶ ταύτην
208 ἐκφαυλίσειν, ὡς οὐ δεῖν ἐπ' αὐτῇ κτείνειν τοσαῦτα
μὲν ἀγαθὰ τὸ πλῆθος ἐργασάμενον εὐεργέτην δ'
αὐτοῦ γεγενημένον, δι' ἃ καὶ συγγνώμην ἂν ἐπὶ
τοῖς μεγίστοις ἁμαρτήμασιν εἰκότως εὕρατο. "δη-
λώσω δέ σοι τὴν τοῦ πατρὸς γνώμην." Δαυίδης
δὲ πεισθεὶς συμβουλίᾳ χρηστῇ ὑπεξίσταται τῆς
τοῦ βασιλέως ὄψεως.

209 (2) Τῇ δ' ἐπιούσῃ πρὸς τὸν Σαοῦλον Ἰωνάθης

---

[1] + ὡς codd.
[2] Μελχώνην SP: Μελχὼ Glycas: Melchon Lat.
[3] ed. pr., Lat.: ἀσπάσασθαι codd.

out this marriage merely in order to bring about David's death on an impossible enterprise [a]—gave him his daughter, Melcha [b] by name.

(xi. 1) However Saul was not for long to acquiesce in this state of things; for, seeing David in favour both with God and with the multitude, he took alarm and, being unable to conceal his fears—concerning, as they did, such great interests as his kingdom and his life, the loss of either of which would be a dreadful calamity—he resolved to slay David and charged Jonathan his son and the most trusted of his men to make away with him. Jonathan was amazed at this change in his father's feelings toward David from great benevolence to not merely moderate dislike but to the compassing of his death; and, loving the lad and reverencing him for his virtue, he told him of his father's secret plan and intent. He counselled him, moreover, to take heed to himself and to keep out of sight on the morrow, saying that he would himself go to greet his father and, when the opportunity presented itself, would converse with him about David, and discover the reason (of his dislike); he would then make light of this, representing that he ought not on such ground to put to death one who had rendered so many services to the people and proved a benefactor to Saul himself, on account of which he might well have secured pardon for even the gravest crimes. " And I will inform thee," he added, " what is my father's mind." David, in compliance with this excellent counsel, withdrew himself from the king's sight.

(2) The next day Jonathan went to Saul and, find-

Jonathan warns David of Saul's plot; David flees. 1 Sam. xix. 1.

---

[a] No such thoughts are attributed to Saul in Scripture.

[b] Bibl. Michal. LXX Μελχόλ.

JOSEPHUS

ἐλθὼν ὡς ἱλαρόν τε καὶ χαίροντα κατέλαβεν ἤρξατο
λόγους αὐτῷ περὶ τοῦ Δαυίδου προσφέρειν· "τί
καταγνοὺς αὐτοῦ μικρὸν ἢ μεῖζον ἀδίκημα, πάτερ,[1]
προσέταξας ἀνελεῖν ἄνδρα μέγα μὲν αὐτῷ πρὸς
σωτηρίαν ὄφελος γεγενημένον, μεῖζον δὲ πρὸς τὴν
210 Παλαιστίνων τιμωρίαν, ὕβρεως δὲ καὶ χλεύης ἀπ-
αλλάξαντα τὸν Ἑβραίων λαὸν ἣν ἐπὶ τεσσαράκοντα
ἡμέρας ὑπέμεινεν οὐδενὸς τολμῶντος[2] ὑποστῆναι
τὴν τοῦ πολεμίου πρόκλησιν, καὶ μετὰ ταῦτα κομί-
σαντα μὲν ὅσας ἐπετάχθη κεφαλὰς τῶν ἐχθρῶν,
λαβόντα δ' ἐπὶ τούτῳ γέρας τὴν ἐμὴν ἀδελφὴν
πρὸς γάμον, ὡς ἂν ἀλγεινὸς[3] αὐτοῦ γένοιθ' ἡμῖν ὁ
θάνατος οὐ διὰ τὴν ἀρετὴν μόνον, ἀλλὰ καὶ διὰ
τὴν συγγένειαν· συναδικεῖται γὰρ αὐτοῦ τῷ θανάτῳ
καὶ ἡ σὴ θυγάτηρ χηρείαν πρὶν ἢ τῆς συμβιώσεως
211 εἰς ὄνησιν ἐλθεῖν μέλλουσα πειράζειν. ταῦτα λογισάμενος μεταβαλοῦ πρὸς τὸ ἡμερώτερον καὶ μηδὲν
ποιήσῃς κακὸν ἄνδρα πρῶτον μὲν ἡμᾶς[4] εὐεργεσίαν
μεγάλην εὐεργετήσαντα τὴν σὴν σωτηρίαν, ὅτε σοι
τοῦ πονηροῦ πνεύματος καὶ τῶν δαιμονίων ἐγκαθ-
εζομένων τὰ μὲν ἐξέβαλεν, εἰρήνην δὲ ἀπ' αὐτῶν
τῇ ψυχῇ σου παρέσχεν, δεύτερον δὲ τὴν ἀπὸ τῶν
πολεμίων ἐκδικίαν· αἰσχρὸν γὰρ τούτων ἐπιλελῆ-
212 σθαι." τούτοις παρηγορεῖται τοῖς λόγοις Σάουλος
καὶ μηδὲν ἀδικήσειν τὸν Δαυίδην ὄμνυσι τῷ παιδί·
κρείττων γὰρ ὀργῆς καὶ φόβου δίκαιος λόγος.
Ἰωνάθης δὲ μεταπεμψάμενος τὸν Δαυίδην σημαίνει
τε αὐτῷ χρηστὰ καὶ σωτήρια τὰ παρὰ τοῦ πατρός,

¹ ὦ πάτερ MSP.

430

ing him cheerful and gay,[a] began to address him
concerning David. " What wrongdoing small or
great, father, canst thou have found in him that thou
hast ordered us to put to death one who has done
so much in aiding thine own welfare and yet more
in punishing the Philistines, and so has delivered
the Hebrew people from the contumely and derision
which for forty days they had endured when no one
else dared face the enemy's challenge, and who thereafter brought thee the appointed number of enemy
heads and received as his recompense my sister in
marriage ? Thus his death would be grievous to us,
not only by reason of his merits, but also of the ties of
kinship ; for thy daughter will likewise be wronged by
his death, destined to experience widowhood before
even entering on the joy of wedded life. Let these
reflections move thee to greater mildness ; do no
injury to one who first rendered us that great service
of restoring thee to health, when he drove out the
evil spirit and the demons that beset thee and brought
peace from them to thy soul, and then avenged us
upon our enemies. Shameful would it be to forget
these things." [b] By these words Saul was won over
and he swore to his son that he would do David
no wrong ; so does a just cause prevail over anger
and fear. Jonathan then sent for David and not only
informed him of the kindly and reassuring attitude

Jonathan
persuades
Saul to take
David back.
1 Sam. xix. 4.

---

[a] Unscriptural detail.
[b] The references to Michal and to the healing of Saul are
unscriptural.

---

[2] οὐδενὸς τολμῶντος ex Lat. Niese : μόνος τολμῶν codd. : μόνον
τολμῶντα Naber.
[3] ἀλγεινότερος MSP Lat.
[4] ἡμᾶς om. RO.

ἄγει τε πρὸς αὐτόν, καὶ παρέμενε τῷ βασιλεῖ
Δαυίδης ὥσπερ ἔμπροσθεν.

213 (3) Κατὰ δὲ τοῦτον τὸν καιρὸν τῶν Παλαιστίνων
στρατευσαμένων πάλιν ἐπὶ τοὺς Ἑβραίους πέμπει
μετὰ στρατιᾶς τὸν Δαυίδην πολεμήσοντα τοῖς
Παλαιστίνοις, καὶ συμβαλὼν πολλοὺς αὐτῶν ἀπ-
έκτεινε καὶ νικήσας ἐπάνεισι πρὸς τὸν βασιλέα.
προσδέχεται δ᾽ αὐτὸν ὁ Σαοῦλος οὐχ ὡς ἤλπισεν
ἀπὸ τοῦ κατορθώματος, ἀλλ᾽ ὑπὸ τῆς εὐπραγίας
αὐτοῦ λυπηθεὶς ὡς ἐπισφαλέστερος αὐτὸς ἐκ τῶν
214 ἐκείνου πράξεων γενόμενος. ἐπεὶ δὲ πάλιν αὐτὸν
προσελθὸν τὸ δαιμόνιον ἐθορύβει πνεῦμα καὶ συν-
ετάραττε, καλέσας εἰς τὸ δωμάτιον ἐν ᾧ κατέκειτο,
κατέχων τὸ δόρυ προσέταξε τῷ ψαλμῷ καὶ τοῖς
ὕμνοις ἐξᾴδειν αὐτόν. ἐκείνου δὲ τὰ κελευσθέντα
ποιοῦντος διατεινάμενος ἀκοντίζει τὸ δόρυ· καὶ τὸ
μὲν προϊδόμενος ὁ Δαυίδης ἐξέκλινε, φεύγει δὲ εἰς
τὸν οἶκον τὸν αὑτοῦ καὶ δι᾽ ὅλης ἔμεινεν ἡμέρας
αὐτόθι.

215 (4) Νυκτὸς δὲ πέμψας ὁ βασιλεὺς ἐκέλευσεν
αὐτὸν ἄχρι τῆς ἕω φυλάττεσθαι μὴ καὶ λάθῃ παντελῶς ἀφανὴς γενόμενος, ἵνα παραγενόμενος[1] εἰς
τὸ δικαστήριον καὶ κρίσει παραδοὺς ἀποκτείνῃ.
Μελχὰ δὲ ἡ γυνὴ Δαυίδου θυγάτηρ δὲ τοῦ βασιλέως
τὴν τοῦ πατρὸς μαθοῦσα διάνοιαν τῷ ἀνδρὶ παρ-
ίσταται δειλὰς ἔχουσα τὰς περὶ αὐτοῦ ἐλπίδας καὶ
περὶ τῆς ἰδίας ψυχῆς ἀγωνιῶσα· οὐδὲ γὰρ αὐτὴν
216 ζῆν ὑπομενεῖν[2] ἐκείνου στερηθεῖσαν. καὶ " μή
σε," φησίν, " ὁ ἥλιος ἐνταυθοῖ καταλάβῃ[3]· οὐ γὰρ

[1] παραγόμενος conj. Thackeray.
[2] Dindorf: ὑπομένειν codd.
[3] E: καταλάβοι codd.

of his father, but brought him into his presence ; and David stayed with the king as before.

(3) About this time the Philistines again took the field against the Hebrews, and Saul sent David with an army to fight against them, and he, having joined battle with them, slew many and returned victorious to the king. Saul, however, did not give him the reception which he expected after that achievement, but was aggrieved by his success, believing that David had become more dangerous to him by reason of his exploits. And when the evil spirit again came upon him to trouble and confuse him, he called David to the chamber wherein he lay, and, holding his spear in his hand, bade him charm away the spell with his harp and songs. Then, when David did as he had been commanded, Saul hurled his spear at him with all his might. David, seeing it coming, got out of its way ; then he fled to his own house and remained there all that day.

(4) But at night the king sent officers with orders to guard him till dawn lest he escape and disappear altogether ; Saul's intent was to come before the court and deliver him to justice to be put to death.[a] But when Melcha, the wife of David and daughter of the king, learned of her father's intent, she came to aid her husband, having faint hope for him and also feeling dreadful anxiety about her own life, for she could not endure to live if bereft of him.[b] " Let not the sun," she said, " find thee here ; else it will never

Saul attacks David on his return from battle with the Philistines.
1 Sam. xix.

Michal's stratagem saves David from arrest.
1 Sam. xix. 11.

---

[a] Scripture says nothing of Saul's intention to have David put on trial ; 1 Sam. xix. 11 " Saul also sent messengers to David's house to watch him and to slay him in the morning."

[b] This motive is supplied by Josephus.

ἔτ' ὄψεταί σε. φεῦγε δ' ἕως¹ τοῦτό σοι δύναται
παρασχεῖν ἡ παροῦσα νύξ· καὶ ποιήσειε² δέ σοι
ταύτην ὁ θεὸς μακροτέραν· ἴσθι γὰρ σαυτὸν ἂν
217 εὑρεθῇς ὑπὸ τοῦ πατρὸς ἀπολούμενον." καὶ καθ-
ιμήσασα διὰ θυρίδος αὐτὸν ἐξέσωσεν· ἔπειτα σκευ-
άσασα τὴν κλίνην ὡς ἐπὶ νοσοῦντι καὶ ὑποθεῖσα
τοῖς ἐπιβολαίοις ἧπαρ αἰγός, ἅμ' ἡμέρᾳ τοῦ πατρὸς
ὡς αὐτὴν³ πέμψαντος ἐπὶ τὸν Δαυίδην ὠχλῆσθαι
διὰ τῆς νυκτὸς εἶπε τοῖς παροῦσιν, ἐπιδείξασα
τὴν κλίνην κατακεκαλυμμένην καὶ τῷ πηδήματι
τοῦ ἥπατος σαλεύοντι τὴν ἐπιβολὴν πιστωσαμένη
218 τὸ κατακείμενον τὸν Δαυίδην ἀσθμαίνειν.⁴ ἀπ-
αγγειλάντων δὲ τῶν πεμφθέντων ὅτι γένοιτο διὰ
τῆς νυκτὸς ἀσθενέστερος, ἐκέλευσεν οὕτως ἔχοντα
κομισθῆναι· βούλεσθαι γὰρ αὐτὸν ἀνελεῖν. ἐλθόντες δὲ καὶ ἀνακαλύψαντες τὴν κλίνην καὶ τὸ
σόφισμα τῆς γυναικὸς εὑρόντες ἀπήγγειλαν τῷ
219 βασιλεῖ. μεμφομένου δὲ τοῦ πατρὸς αὐτὴν ὅτι
σώσειε μὲν τὸν ἐχθρὸν αὐτοῦ κατασοφίσαιτο δ'⁵
αὐτόν, ἀπολογίαν σκήπτεται πιθανήν· ἀπειλήσαντα
γὰρ αὐτὴν ἀποκτείνειν ἔφησε τυχεῖν ἐκ τοῦ δέους
τῆς πρὸς τὸ σωθῆναι συνεργίας· ὑπὲρ ἧς συγγνῶναι καλῶς ἔχειν αὐτῇ, κατ' ἀνάγκην ἀλλὰ μὴ
κατὰ προαίρεσιν γενομένης· "οὐ γὰρ οὕτως,"
ἔλεγεν, "οἶμαι τὸν ἐχθρὸν ἐζήτεις ἀποθανεῖν, ὡς

¹ ex Lat. Niese: δὲ ὡς codd.
² ποιήσει RO: ποιήσοι MSP: faciat Lat.
³ ὡς αὐτὴν] αὐτῆς MSP.
⁴ M: ἀσθενεῖν rell.: dormire Lat.
⁵ ed. pr.: τ' codd.: vero Lat.

ᵃ 1 Sam. xix. 13 " And Michal took the teraphim (A.V.
" an image ") and laid them in the bed and placed a goat's
skin (?) at its head " (A.V " put a pillow of goats' *hair* for his

look on thee again. Flee while the night which is still upon us permits, and may God prolong its hours for thee ; for know that if thou art found by my father, thou art a lost man." And she let him down through a window and got him safely away. Next she made up the bed as for a sick person and put a goat's liver[a] beneath the covers ; and when at daybreak her father sent to fetch David, she told those who came for him that he had been attacked by illness during the night, and she showed them the bed all covered up, and by the quivering of the liver which shook the bedclothes convinced them that what lay there was David gasping for breath.[b] When the messengers reported to Saul that David had fallen ill during the night, he ordered him to be brought just as he was, for he wished to kill him. And when they came and uncovered the bed, they discovered the woman's trick, which they reported to the king. But when her father rebuked her for having saved his enemy and tricked himself, she resorted to a plausible defence ; her husband, she declared, had threatened to kill her and so, by terrifying her, had secured her aid in his escape, for which she deserved pardon, seeing that she had acted under constraint and not of her own free will. " For," said she, " I cannot think that thou wert as desirous for thy enemy's death as for the safety of my life."

Michal excuses her conduct to Saul. 1 Sam. xix. 17.

bolster "). The teraphim were probably household images in human form. The Heb. *kebîr*, here rendered " skin," is of doubtful meaning, and was read as *kebēd*," liver," by the LXX, followed by Josephus. The context shows that it must have been something round and hairy to give the appearance of a human head, and so it was understood by the rabbis.

[b] The details of Michal's stratagem are invented by Josephus.

ἐμὲ σώζεσθαι." καὶ συγγινώσκει δὲ τῇ κόρῃ
220 Σαοῦλος. ὁ δὲ Δαυίδης ἐκφυγὼν τὸν κίνδυνον ἧκε
πρὸς τὸν προφήτην Σαμουῆλον εἰς Ἀρμαθὰ καὶ
τὴν ἐπιβουλὴν αὐτῷ τὴν τοῦ βασιλέως ἐδήλωσε
καὶ ὡς παρὰ μικρὸν ὑπ' αὐτοῦ τῷ δόρατι βληθεὶς
ἀποθάνοι, μήτ' ἐν τοῖς πρὸς αὐτὸν κακὸς γενόμενος
μήτ' ἐν τοῖς πρὸς τοὺς πολεμίους ἀγῶσιν ἄνανδρος,
ἀλλ' ἐν ἅπασι μετὰ τοῦ θεοῦ[1] καὶ ἐπιτυχής.
τοῦτο δ' ἦν αἴτιον Σαούλῳ τῆς πρὸς Δαυίδην
ἀπεχθείας.

221 (5) Μαθὼν δ' ὁ προφήτης τὴν τοῦ βασιλέως
ἀδικίαν καταλείπει μὲν τὴν πόλιν Ἀρμαθάν,
ἀγαγὼν δὲ τὸν Δαυίδην ἐπί τινα τόπον Γαλβουὰθ[2]
ὄνομα ἐκεῖ διέτριβε σὺν αὐτῷ. ὡς δ' ἀπηγγέλη
τῷ Σαούλῳ παρὰ τῷ προφήτῃ τυγχάνων ὁ Δαυίδης,
πέμψας ὁπλίτας πρὸς αὐτὸν ἄγειν προσέταξε συλ-
222 λαμβάνοντας.[3] οἱ δ' ἐλθόντες πρὸς τὸν Σαμουῆλον
καὶ καταλαβόντες προφητῶν ἐκκλησίαν, τοῦ θείου
μεταλαμβάνουσι πνεύματος καὶ προφητεύειν ἤρ-
ξαντο· Σαοῦλος δ' ἀκούσας ἄλλους ἔπεμψεν ἐπὶ
τὸν Δαυίδην· κἀκείνων ταὐτὸ τοῖς πρώτοις παθόντων πάλιν ἀπέστειλεν ἑτέρους· προφητευόντων δὲ
καὶ τῶν τρίτων τελευταῖον ὀργισθεὶς αὐτὸς ἐξ-
223 ώρμησεν. ἐπεὶ δ' ἐγγὺς ἦν ἤδη, Σαμουῆλος πρὶν
ἰδεῖν αὐτὸν προφητεύειν ἐποίησεν. ἐλθὼν δὲ πρὸς
αὐτὸν Σαοῦλος ὑπὸ τοῦ πολλοῦ πνεύματος ἐλαυ-
νόμενος ἔκφρων γίνεται καὶ τὴν ἐσθῆτα περιδύσας
ἑαυτὸν καταπεσὼν ἔκειτο δι' ὅλης ἡμέρας τε καὶ
νυκτὸς Σαμουήλου τε καὶ Δαυίδου βλεπόντων.

224 (6) Ἰωνάθης δὲ ὁ Σαούλου παῖς, ἀφικομένου πρὸς

---

[1] (τοῦ) θυμοῦ RO: et pronus Lat.
[2] Βαλγουὰθ SP: Γελβούαθον E.   [3] συλλαβόντας SP.

So Saul pardoned the girl. Meanwhile David, having escaped from danger, repaired to the prophet Samuel at Armatha, and recounted to him the king's plot against him, and how he had wellnigh been struck by his spear and killed, though he had never dealt ill with him nor been cowardly in combating his foes, but had ever with God's aid been indeed fortunate. Now that was the reason for Saul's hatred of David.

David finds refuge with Samuel at Ramah (Armatha). 1 Sam. xix. 18.

(5) On learning of the king's iniquity, the prophet left the city of Armatha and brought David to a place named Galbouath [a] and there abode with him. Now when it was told Saul that David was staying with the prophet, he sent armed men with orders to arrest him and bring him to him. But they, on coming to Samuel and finding there an assembly of prophets, were themselves possessed by the spirit of God and began to prophesy. Saul, hearing thereof, sent others after David, and when these met with the same experience as the first, he dispatched yet more ; but this third company prophesied likewise, and finally in a rage he set out himself. But so soon as he came near them, Samuel, even before seeing him, caused him too to prophesy.[b] On reaching him, Saul, losing his reason under the impulse of that mighty spirit, stripped off his clothes and lay prostrate on the ground for a whole day and night in the sight of Samuel and David.

Saul and his men, pursuing David, are possessed and prophesy. Ib.

(6) Thence David betook himself to Jonathan, son

---

[a] Bibl. Naioth (Heb. *Nawath* or *Nayōth*), LXX Αὐὰθ (*v.l.* Ναυιώθ κτλ.) ἐν ʿΡαμά ; these forms appear to be corrupt. The Targum renders it *Beth 'ulphānā* " house of instruction." The source of Josephus's form is unknown.

[b] Josephus omits to state, as does Scripture, 1 Sam. xix. 24, that this incident explains the saying " Is Saul also among the prophets ? "

αὐτὸν ἐκεῖθεν Δαυίδου καὶ περὶ τῆς τοῦ πατρὸς
ἀποδυρομένου ἐπιβουλῆς καὶ λέγοντος ὡς οὐδὲν
ἀδικήσας οὐδ'[1] ἐξαμαρτὼν σπουδάζοιτο ὑπὸ τοῦ
πατρὸς αὐτοῦ φονευθῆναι, μήθ' ἑαυτῷ τοῦθ' ὑπο-
νοοῦντι πιστεύειν παρεκάλει μήτε τοῖς διαβάλ-
λουσιν, εἴ τινες ἄρα εἰσὶν οἱ τοῦτο πράττοντες,
ἀλλ' αὐτῷ προσέχειν καὶ θαρρεῖν· μηδὲν γὰρ τοιοῦτον ἐπ' αὐτῷ φρονεῖν τὸν πατέρα· φράσαι γὰρ
ἂν αὐτῷ περὶ τούτου καὶ σύμβουλον παραλαβεῖν,
225 τῇ κοινῇ γνώμῃ καὶ τἆλλα πράττοντα. ὁ δὲ
Δαυίδης ὤμνυεν ἦ μὴν οὕτως ἔχειν, καὶ πιστεύοντ'
ἠξίου προνοεῖν αὐτοῦ μᾶλλον ἢ καταφρονοῦντ' ἐπ'
ἀληθέσι τοῖς λόγοις τότε ἀληθὲς ὑπολαβεῖν, ὅταν
ἢ θεάσηται πεφονευμένον αὐτὸν[2] ἢ πύθηται· μηδὲν
λέγειν δ' αὐτῷ τὸν πατέρα περὶ τούτων ἔφασκεν
εἰδότα τὴν πρὸς αὐτὸν φιλίαν καὶ διάθεσιν.

226 (7) Λυπηθεὶς δ' ἐφ' ὅτῳ πιστωσάμενος τὴν τοῦ
Σαούλου προαίρεσιν Ἰωνάθης οὐκ ἔπεισεν, ἐπηρώτα
τίνος ἐξ αὐτοῦ βούλεται τυχεῖν. ὁ δέ " οἶδα γάρ,"
ἔφη, " πάντα σε χαρίζεσθαί μοι καὶ παρέχειν
ἐθέλοντα· νουμηνία μὲν εἰς τὴν ἐπιοῦσάν ἐστιν, ἔθος
227 δ' ἔχω δειπνεῖν σὺν τῷ βασιλεῖ καθήμενος· εἰ δή
σοι δοκεῖ, πορευθεὶς ἔξω τῆς πόλεως ἐν τῷ πεδίῳ
λανθάνων διαμενῶ, σὺ δ' ἐπιζητήσαντος αὐτοῦ λέγε
πορευθῆναί με εἰς τὴν πατρίδα Βηθλεέμην ἑορτήν
μου τῆς φυλῆς ἀγούσης, προστιθεὶς ὅτι σύ μοι
συγκεχώρηκας. κἂν μέν, οἷον εἰκὸς καὶ σύνηθές
ἐστι λέγειν ἐπὶ φίλοις ἀποδημοῦσιν, ' ἐπ' ἀγαθῷ

[1] Dindorf: οὔτ' codd.
[2] πεφονευμένον αὐτὸν om. RO Lat.

of Saul, and complained to him of his father's designs, David complains to Jonathan of Saul's enmity. 1 Sam. xx. 1.
saying that though he had been guilty of no iniquity
or crime, his father was making every effort to have
him murdered. Jonathan entreated him to put no
faith either in his own suspicions or in slanderers,
if indeed there were any such, but to pay heed
to him and take courage ; for, he said, his father
was meditating nothing of the sort, else he would
have told him of it and taken him into his counsel,
since in all else he acted in concert with him. But
David swore [a] that it was truly so, and he asked
Jonathan to believe him and look out for his safety
instead of contemptuously questioning the truth of
his words and waiting to recognize their truth until
he should actually behold or learn of his assassination.
His father, he declared, had told him nothing of all
this because he knew of his son's friendship and affection for himself.

(7) Grieved that his assurance of Saul's disposition Jonathan agrees to inform David secretly of Saul's intention. 1 Sam. xx. 4.
failed to convince David, Jonathan asked him what
he would have him do. " I know," he replied, " that
thou art ready to grant me any favour or do any thing.
Now to-morrow is the new moon, when my custom
is to dine with the king. If, then, it please thee, I
will go forth from the city and remain concealed in
the plain ; but do thou, if he ask for me, say that
I am gone to my native Bethlehem, where my tribe [b]
is keeping a feast, adding that thou didst give
me leave. Should he then say, as is proper and
customary to say about friends going away, ' A good

[a] So the Hebrew ; LXX " answered."
[b] Or " clan "; cf. Heb. mishpāḥāh (A.V. " family "),
which the LXX here renders, like Josephus, by φυλή, but the
latter can mean " clan " (subdivision of a tribe) as well as
" tribe," cf. § 62 note.

βεβάδικεν᾽ εἴπῃ, ἴσθι μηδὲν ὕπουλον παρ᾽ αὐτοῦ
εἶναι μηδ᾽ ἐχθρόν· ἂν δ᾽ ὡς ἄλλως ἀποκρίνηται
τοῦτ᾽ ἔσται τεκμήριον τῶν κατ᾽ ἐμοῦ βεβουλευ-
228 μένων. μηνύσεις δέ μοι τὴν διάνοιαν τὴν τοῦ
πατρός, οὕτω τε νέμων τοῦτο καὶ φιλίᾳ, δι᾽ ἣν
πίστεις τε παρ᾽ ἐμοῦ λαβεῖν ἠξίωκας αὐτός τε
ἐμοὶ δοῦναι δεσπότης ὢν οἰκέτῃ σῷ.¹ εἰ δ᾽
εὑρίσκεις τι ἐν ἐμοὶ πονηρόν, αὐτὸς ἄνελε καὶ
φθάσον τὸν πατέρα.''

229   (8) Πρὸς δὲ τὸ τελευταῖον δυσχεράνας τῶν λόγων Ἰωνάθης ποιήσειν ταῦτ᾽ ἐπηγγείλατο κἄν
τι σκυθρωπὸν ὁ πατὴρ αὐτοῦ καὶ τὴν ἀπέχθειαν
ἐμφανίζον² ἀποκρίνηται μηνύσειν.³ ἵνα δ᾽ αὐτῷ
θαρρῇ μᾶλλον, ἐξαγαγὼν αὐτὸν εἰς ὕπαιθρον καὶ
καθαρὸν ἀέρα οὐδὲν παρήσειν ὑπὲρ τῆς Δαυίδου
230 σωτηρίας ὤμνυε· '' τὸν γὰρ θεόν,'' εἶπε, '' τοῦτον
ὃν πολὺν ὁρᾷς καὶ πανταχοῦ κεχυμένον, καὶ πρὶν
ἑρμηνεῦσαί με τοῖς λόγοις τὴν διάνοιαν ἤδη μου
ταύτην εἰδότα, μάρτυρα ποιοῦμαι τῶν πρὸς σὲ
συνθηκῶν, ὡς οὐκ ἀνήσω τὸν πατέρα πολλάκις
αὐτοῦ τῆς προαιρέσεως διάπειραν λαμβάνων, πρὶν
ἢ καταμαθεῖν ἥτις ἐστὶ καὶ παρὰ τοῖς ἀπορρήτοις
231 αὐτοῦ τῆς ψυχῆς γενέσθαι. καταμαθὼν δ᾽ οὐκ
ἀποκρύψομαι, καταμηνύσω δὲ πρὸς σὲ καὶ πρᾷον
ὄντα καὶ δυσμενῶς διακείμενον. οἶδε δὲ οὗτος⁴ ὁ
θεὸς πῶς αὐτὸν εἶναι μετὰ σοῦ διὰ παντὸς εὔχομαι·
ἔστι μὲν γὰρ νῦν καὶ οὐκ ἀπολείψει σε, ποιήσει δὲ
τῶν ἐχθρῶν ἄντε ὁ πατὴρ ὁ ἐμὸς ᾖ⁵ ἄντ᾽ ἐγὼ
232 κρείττονα. σὺ μόνον μνημόνευε τούτων, κἂν ἀπο-

---

¹ οἰκέτῃ σῷ om. RO.   ² ἐμφανίζων ROMS.
        ³ Niese: μηνύειν codd.   ⁴ αὐτὸς Naber.
            ⁵ Niese: εἴη RO: om. MSP: est Lat.

journey to him,'[a] know that he bears no hidden malice nor enmity ; but should he answer otherwise, that will be a sign of his designs against me. And thou shalt inform me of thy father's state of mind in token of thy pity and of that friendship for which thou hast seen fit to receive pledges from me and to grant me the like thyself, though thou art the master, and I thy servant. But if thou findest any wickedness in me, slay me thyself and so anticipate thy father."

(8) Although displeased by these last words, Jonathan promised to do this and said that if his father gave some sullen answer indicative of hate, he would inform David thereof. And, that he might have the more confidence in him, he brought him out into the open and pure air and swore to leave nothing undone for his safety. "This God," said he, "whom thou seest to be so great and everywhere extended, and who, before I have expressed my thought in words, already knows what it is,[b]—Him do I take as witness of my covenant with thee, to wit, that I will not give up my constant endeavour to discover my father's purpose until I have clearly learnt it and come close to the secrets of his soul. And having learnt it, I will not hide it, but will disclose to thee whether he be graciously or evilly disposed. This God of ours knows how I pray that He may always be with thee. Indeed, He is with thee now and will not forsake thee, but will make thee stronger than thy foes, be it my father or be it myself. Do thou but remember this,

Jonathan
swears an
oath of
friendship
to David.
1 Sam. xx. 9.

[a] A free rendering of 1 Sam. xx. 7 "It is well," perhaps suggested by the customary Hebrew salutation, "Go in peace."

[b] These divine attributes are an amplification of the Scriptural "Lord God of Israel."

θανεῖν μοι γένηται τὰ τέκνα μου σῶζε, καὶ τὴν
ὑπὲρ τῶν παρόντων μοι ἀμοιβὴν εἰς ἐκεῖνα κατά-
θου." ταῦτ' ἐπομόσας ἀπολύει τὸν Δαυίδην εἴς
τινα τόπον ἀπελθεῖν τοῦ πεδίου φράσας, ἐν ᾧ
γυμναζόμενος διετέλει· γνοὺς γὰρ τὰ παρὰ τοῦ
πατρὸς ἥξειν πρὸς αὐτὸν ἔφησεν ἐκεῖ μόνον ἐπ-
233 αγόμενος παῖδα. "κἂν[1] τρία ἀκόντια δὲ βαλὼν
ἐπὶ τὸν σκοπὸν κομίσαι τῷ παιδὶ προστάσσω τὰ
ἀκόντια (κεῖσθαι γὰρ ἔμπροσθεν αὐτοῦ[2]), γίνωσκε
μηδὲν εἶναι φαῦλον παρὰ τοῦ πατρός· ἂν δὲ τὰ
ἐναντία τούτων ἀκούσῃς μου λέγοντος, καὶ τὰ
234 ἐναντία παρὰ τοῦ βασιλέως προσδόκα. τῆς μέντοι
γε ἀσφαλείας τεύξῃ παρ' ἐμοῦ καὶ οὐδὲν μὴ πάθῃς
ἄτοπον· ὅπως δὲ μνησθῇς τούτων παρὰ τὸν τῆς
εὐπραγίας καιρὸν σκόπει καὶ τοῖς υἱοῖς μου γενοῦ
χρήσιμος." Δαυίδης μὲν οὖν ταύτας λαβὼν παρὰ
Ἰωνάθου τὰς πίστεις εἰς τὸ συγκείμενον ἀπηλλάγη
χωρίον.

235 (9) Τῇ δ' ἐχομένῃ, νουμηνία δ' ἦν,[3] ἁγνεύσας,
ὡς ἔθος εἶχεν, ὁ βασιλεὺς ἧκεν ἐπὶ τὸ δεῖπνον, καὶ
παρακαθεσθέντων αὐτῷ τοῦ μὲν παιδὸς Ἰωνάθου
ἐκ δεξιῶν Ἀβενήρου δὲ τοῦ ἀρχιστρατήγου ἐκ τῶν
ἑτέρων, ἰδὼν τὴν τοῦ Δαυίδου καθέδραν κενὴν
ἡσύχασεν ὑπονοήσας οὐ καθαρεύσαντα αὐτὸν ἀπὸ
236 συνουσίας ὑστερεῖν. ὡς δὲ καὶ τῇ δευτέρᾳ τῆς
νουμηνίας οὐ παρῆν ἐπυνθάνετο παρὰ τοῦ παιδὸς
Ἰωνάθου ὅτι καὶ τῇ παρελθούσῃ καὶ ταύτῃ τοῦ

---

[1] S: καὶ rell.　　　[2] + καὶ ἂν ταῦτα φησὶν ἀκούσῃς RO.
[3] δ' ἦν ed. pr.: δ' ἦν δι' ἣν codd.

---

[a] Unscriptural detail.
[b] So, apparently, the lxx (σχίζαις ἀκοντίζων); Heb.
"arrows."

and, should death befall me, preserve my children's
lives and make over to them the recompense that
is due me for my present services." After he had
taken these oaths, he dismissed David, telling him
to go to a certain place in the plain where he (Jonathan) was wont to exercise himself [a]; there, he said,
when he had learnt his father's mind, he would re-
join him, accompanied only by a lad. " And if, after
throwing three darts [b] at the mark, I order the lad
to bring them to me, for they will be found lying in
front of it,[c] know that no mischief is to be feared
from my father ; but if thou hearest me say the contrary, then look thou also for the contrary from the
king. Howbeit thou wilt find safety at my hands and
thou shalt suffer no harm. But see that thou re-
memberest this in the time of thy prosperity, and
deal kindly with my children." Then David, having
received these pledges from Jonathan, departed to
the appointed place.

(9) The next day, which was the new moon, the
king, after purifying himself as the custom was, came
to the feast ; and when his son Jonathan had seated
himself on his right side and Abener, the commander
of the army, on his left, he marked that David's seat
was empty, but held his peace, surmising that he had
been delayed by not having finished his purification
after sexual intercourse.[d] But when, on the second
day of the feast of the new moon, David again did not
appear, he asked his son Jonathan why, both on the

Jonathan excuses David's absence at the feast.
1 Sam. xx. 24.

---

[c] *i.e.* the mark, or perhaps " him," *i.e.* the lad ; 1 Sam.
xx. 21 " the arrows are this side of thee."
[d] This interpretation of 1 Sam. xx. 26 " it is an accident "
(A.V. " something hath befallen him ") is similar to that of
the rabbis, who took *miqreh,* lit. " happening," in its physio-
logical sense of nocturnal emission.

δείπνου καὶ τῆς ἑστιάσεως ὁ τοῦ Ἰεσσαίου παῖς
ἀπολέλειπται. ὁ δὲ πεπορεῦσθαι κατὰ τὰς συνθήκας ἔφησεν αὐτὸν εἰς τὴν ἑαυτοῦ πατρίδα, τῆς
φυλῆς ἑορτὴν ἀγούσης, ἐπιτρέψαντος αὐτοῦ· παρα-
καλέσαι μέντοι καὶ αὐτὸν ἐλθεῖν ἐπὶ τὴν θυσίαν
καὶ εἰ συγχωρηθείη φησὶν ἀπέρχεσθαι[1]· " τὴν γὰρ
237 εὔνοιάν μου τὴν πρὸς αὐτὸν ἐπίστασαι." τότε τὴν
πρὸς Δαυίδην τοῦ πατρὸς Ἰωνάθης ἐπέγνω δυσ-
μένειαν καὶ τρανῶς τὴν ὅλην αὐτοῦ βούλησιν εἶδεν·
οὐ γὰρ κατέσχε Σαοῦλος τῆς ὀργῆς, ἀλλὰ βλασφημῶν ἐξ αὐτομόλων γεγενημένον καὶ πολέμιον
ἀπεκάλει καὶ κοινωνὸν τοῦ Δαυίδου καὶ συνεργὸν
ἔλεγεν καὶ μήτ᾿[2] αὐτὸν αἰδεῖσθαι μήτε τὴν μητέρα
αὐτοῦ ταῦτα φρονοῦντα καὶ μηδὲ βουλόμενον πει-
σθῆναι τοῦθ᾿, ὅτι μέχρις οὗ περίεστι Δαυίδης
ἐπισφαλῶς αὐτοῖς τὰ τῆς βασιλείας ἔχει· " μετά-
πεμψαι τοιγαροῦν αὐτόν," ἔφησεν, " ἵνα δῷ δίκην."
238 ὑποτυχόντος δ᾿ Ἰωνάθου, " τί δ᾿ ἀδικοῦντα κολάσαι
θέλεις;" οὐκέτ᾿ εἰς λόγους καὶ βλασφημίας τὴν
ὀργὴν ὁ Σαοῦλος ἐξήνεγκεν, ἀλλ᾿ ἁρπάσας τὸ δόρυ
ἀνεπήδησεν ἐπ᾿ αὐτὸν ἀποκτεῖναι θέλων. καὶ τὸ
μὲν ἔργον οὐκ ἔδρασε διακωλυθεὶς ὑπὸ τῶν φίλων,
φανερὸς δ᾿ ἐγένετο τῷ παιδὶ μισῶν τὸν Δαυίδην
καὶ διαχρήσασθαι ποθῶν, ὡς παρὰ μικρὸν δι᾿
ἐκεῖνον αὐτόχειρ καὶ τοῦ παιδὸς γεγονέναι.
239 (10) Καὶ τότε μὲν ὁ τοῦ βασιλέως παῖς ἐκπηδήσας
ἀπὸ τοῦ δείπνου καὶ μηδὲν ὑπὸ λύπης προσενέγκα-
σθαι δυνηθείς, κλαίων αὐτὸν μὲν τοῦ παρὰ μικρὸν
ἀπολέσθαι τοῦ κατακεκρίσθαι δ᾿ ἀποθανεῖν Δαυίδην

---

[1] κἂν συγχωρῇς ἀπέρχομαι MSP (Lat. E).
[2] Dindorf: μηδ᾿ codd.

444

past day and on this, the son of Jesse had been absent from the festive meal. Jonathan replied, as had been agreed, that he had gone to his native place where his tribe was keeping festival, and with his (Jonathan's) permission. "What is more," he added, "he even invited me to attend that sacrifice, and, if leave be given me, I shall go; for thou knowest the affection that I bear to him." [a] Then did Jonathan discover all his father's malevolence toward David and plainly perceive his whole intent. For Saul did not restrain his wrath, but with curses denounced him as the offspring of renegades and an enemy, and accused him of being in league with David and his accomplice, and as having respect neither for himself nor for his mother in taking that attitude and in refusing to believe that, so long as David lived, their hold upon the kingdom was insecure. "Now then, send for him," said he, "that he may be punished." "But," Jonathan objected, "for what crime wouldst thou punish him?" Whereupon the wrath of Saul found vent no more in words and abuse, but, seizing his spear, he leapt toward him with intent to slay him. And although his friends prevented him [b] from perpetrating the deed, he had now made plain to his son how he hated David and craved to make away with him, seeing that on his account he had wellnigh become the slayer even of his own son.

(10) The king's son instantly rushed from the feast and, prevented by grief from tasting a morsel, passed the night in tears at the thought that he himself had narrowly escaped death and that David was doomed

Saul attacks Jonathan as David's accomplice. 1 Sam. xx. 30.

Jonathan secretly meets David in the fields to say farewell.

---

[a] David's invitation to Jonathan is unscriptural.

[b] Unscriptural detail.

διενυκτέρευσεν. ἅμα δὲ ἡμέρᾳ πρὸ τῆς πόλεως
εἰς τὸ πεδίον ὡς γυμνασόμενος μὲν δηλώσων δὲ
τῷ φίλῳ τὴν τοῦ πατρὸς διάθεσιν, ὡς συνέθετο,
240 πρόεισι. ποιήσας δὲ ὁ Ἰωνάθης τὰ συγκείμενα
τὸν μὲν ἑπόμενον ἀπολύει εἰς τὴν πόλιν παῖδα, ἣν
δ' ἠρεμία¹ τῷ Δαυίδῃ παρελθεῖν² εἰς ὄψιν αὐτῷ
καὶ λόγους. ἀναφανεὶς δ' οὗτος πίπτει πρὸ τῶν
Ἰωνάθου ποδῶν καὶ προσκυνῶν σωτῆρα αὐτοῦ τῆς
241 ψυχῆς ἀπεκάλει. ἀνίστησι δ' ἀπὸ τῆς γῆς αὐτόν,
καὶ περιπλακέντες ἀλλήλοις μακρά τε ἠσπάζοντο
καὶ δεδακρυμένα, τήν τε ἡλικίαν ἀποθρηνοῦντες
αὐτῶν καὶ τὴν ἐφθονημένην ἑταιρίαν καὶ τὸν μέλλοντα διαχωρισμόν, ὃς οὐδὲν αὐτοῖς ἐδόκει θανάτου
διαφέρειν. μόλις δ' ἐκ τῶν θρήνων ἀνανήψαντες
καὶ μεμνῆσθαι τῶν ὅρκων ἀλλήλοις παρακελευσά-
μενοι διελύθησαν.
242 (xii. 1) Δαυίδης δὲ φεύγων τὸν βασιλέα καὶ τὸν
ἐξ αὐτοῦ θάνατον εἰς Ναβὰν παραγίνεται πόλιν
πρὸς Ἀβιμέλεχον³ τὸν ἀρχιερέα,⁴ ὃς ἐπὶ τῷ μόνον
ἥκοντα ἰδεῖν καὶ μήτε φίλον σὺν αὐτῷ μήτ' οἰκέτην
παρόντα ἐθαύμασε καὶ τὴν αἰτίαν τοῦ μηδένα εἶναι
243 σὺν αὐτῷ μαθεῖν ἤθελεν. ὁ δὲ πρᾶξιν ἀπόρρητον
ἐπιταγῆναι παρὰ τοῦ βασιλέως ἔφησεν, εἰς ἣν
συνοδίας αὐτῷ βουλομένῳ λαθεῖν οὐκ ἔδει· "τοὺς
μέντοι θεράποντας εἰς τόνδε μοι τὸν τόπον ἀπαντᾶν

---

¹ ὁ δ' ἐν ἐρημίᾳ MSP (Lat.).
² παρῆλθεν MSP : ἦλθεν E.
³ ROE Zonaras : Ἀχιμέλεχον MSP (Lat.).
⁴ ἱερέα MSP Lat.

ᵃ Unscriptural detail.
ᵇ Josephus omits the account, 1 Sam. xx. 36-37, of Jona-

to die. But at daybreak he went out into the plain ^{1 Sam. xx.} before the city, seemingly for exercise,^a in reality ^{34.} to make known to his friend, in accordance with their agreement, the temper of his father. Then, after doing what had been prearranged, Jonathan sent back the boy who attended him to the city,^b and David was undisturbed in coming out to meet him and to speak with him. Appearing in the open, he fell at Jonathan's feet and did him homage, calling him the preserver of his life. But Jonathan raised him from the ground, and, putting their arms about each other, they took a long and tearful farewell, bewailing their youth, the companionship which was begrudged them and their coming separation,^c which seemed to them nothing less than death. Then, hardly recovering from their lamentation and exhorting each other to remember their oaths, they parted.

(xii. 1) But David, fleeing from the king and death at his hands, now came to the city of Naba ^d to Abimelech ^e the high priest, who was astonished to see him arrive alone with neither friend nor servant in attendance, and desired to know the reason why no man accompanied him. He replied that he had been charged by the king with a secret matter for which he required no escort since he wished to remain unknown. " Howbeit," he added, " I have ordered my servants to join me at this place.^f " He also re-

David receives help from the high priest Ahimelech (Abimelech) at Nob (Naba).
1 Sam. xxi. I (2 Heb.).

than's shooting the arrows beyond the lad to indicate Saul's displeasure.

^c These details of their parting are an amplification.

^d Bibl. Nob, LXX Νόμβα. The exact site is uncertain, but it was probably a little north of Jerusalem, in the territory of Benjamin, cf. Neh. xi. 32.

^e Variant Achimelech, as in Scripture ; the LXX MSS. also vary between the two forms.

^f Bibl. " at such and such a place."

προσέταξα." ἠξίου δὲ λαβεῖν ἐφόδια· φίλου γὰρ
αὐτὸν ποιήσειν ἔργον παρασχόντα καὶ πρὸς τὸ
244 προκείμενον συλλαμβανομένου. τυχὼν δὲ τούτων
ἤτει καὶ ὅπλον τι μετὰ χεῖρας ῥομφαίαν ἢ δοράτιον[1]
παρῆν δὲ καὶ Σαούλου δοῦλος γένει μὲν Σύρος
Δώηγος[2] δὲ ὄνομα τὰς τοῦ βασιλέως ἡμιόνους
νέμων· ὁ δ᾽ ἀρχιερεὺς ἔχειν μὲν αὐτὸς οὐδέν τι
εἶπε τοιοῦτον, εἶναι δὲ τὴν Γολιάθου ῥομφαίαν, ἣν
ἀποκτείνας τὸν Παλαιστῖνον αὐτὸς ἀναθείη τῷ θεῷ.

245 (2) Λαβὼν δὲ ταύτην ὁ Δαυίδης ἔξω τῆς τῶν
Ἑβραίων χώρας εἰς Γίτταν διέφυγε τὴν Παλαιστίνων, ἧς Ἄγχους ἐβασίλευεν.[3] ἐπιγνωσθεὶς δὲ
ὑπὸ τῶν τοῦ βασιλέως οἰκετῶν καὶ φανερὸς αὐτῷ
γενόμενος, μηνυόντων ἐκείνων ὅτι Δαυίδης ὁ πολλὰς
ἀποκτείνας Παλαιστίνων μυριάδας εἴη, δείσας μὴ
πρὸς αὐτοῦ θάνῃ καὶ τὸν κίνδυνον ὃν ἐξέφυγε παρὰ
Σαούλου παρ᾽ ἐκείνου πειράσῃ προσποιεῖται μανίαν
καὶ λύσσαν, ὡς ἀφρὸν κατὰ τοῦ στόματος αὐτοῦ
φερόμενον καὶ τὰ ἄλλα[4] ὅσα συνίστησι μανίαν[5]
πίστιν παρὰ τῷ Γίττης βασιλεῖ γενέσθαι[6] τῆς νόσου.
246 καὶ τοῖς οἰκέταις ὁ βασιλεὺς προσδυσχεράνας ὡς
ἔκφρονα πρὸς αὐτὸν ἀγάγοιεν ἄνθρωπον ἐκέλευσε
τὸν Δαυίδην ὡς τάχος ἐκβάλλειν.

247 (3) Διασωθεὶς δὲ οὕτως[7] ἐκ τῆς Γίττης εἰς τὴν
Ἰούδα παραγίνεται φυλὴν καὶ ἐν τῷ πρὸς Ἀδουλ-

[1] ῥομφ. ἢ δορ. om. Lat. E. [2] Δώηκος SPE.
[3] SP : ἐβασίλευσεν rell.
[4] + δὲ MSP. [5] μανίας MSP.
[6] Niese: γενήσεσθαι ROM : γεγενῆσθαι SP.
[7] οὗτος ROME.

quested him to furnish him with provisions for a journey ; in so doing, he would, he said, be acting like a friend and assisting the cause in hand. Having obtained these,[a] he further asked for any weapon in his keeping, sword or spear. Now there was present also a certain slave of Saul, of Syrian [b] race, by name Doeg, keeper of the king's mules.[c] The high priest replied that he himself possessed no such thing, but that he had there that sword of Goliath which David himself, after slaying the Philistine, had dedicated to God.[d]

(2) Taking this weapon, David fled beyond Hebrew territory to Gitta, a city of the Philistines, of which Anchūs [e] was king. Here he was recognized by the king's servants who then made his presence known to the king, reporting that this was that David who had slain many myriads of Philistines. Thereat David, fearing that he would be put to death by him and, after escaping that peril at the hands of Saul, meet the like fate at his hands, feigned raging madness, foaming at the mouth and displaying all the other symptoms of madness, so as to convince the king of Gitta of his malady. The king was exceedingly angry with his servants for having brought him a madman and gave orders for David's instant expulsion.

(3) Having thus escaped with his life from Gitta, he betook himself to the tribe of Judah [f] and, taking

David flees to Gath (Gitta); feigning madness he is expelled. 1 Sam. xxi. 10 (11 Heb.

---

[a] Josephus omits the Scriptural details about the hallowed bread which was the only food at the priest's disposal.
[b] So the LXX ; Heb. " an Edomite."
[e] So the LXX ; Heb. " chief of the shepherds " (A.V. " herdsmen ").
[d] Cf. § 192.
[e] So the LXX (Luc. 'Ακχούς) ; bibl. Achish.
[f] The reference to Judah is an added detail.

λάμη[1] πόλει σπηλαίῳ διατρίβων πέμπει πρὸς τοὺς
ἀδελφοὺς δηλῶν αὐτοῖς ἔνθα εἴη. οἱ δὲ μετὰ πάσης
συγγενείας ἧκον πρὸς αὐτόν· καὶ τῶν ἄλλων δὲ
ὅσοις ἢ χρεία ἦν ἢ φόβος ἐκ Σαούλου τοῦ βασιλέως συνερρύησαν πρὸς αὐτὸν καὶ ποιεῖν τὰ ἐκείνῳ
δοκοῦντα ἑτοίμως ἔχειν ἔλεγον. ἐγένοντο δὲ οἱ
248 πάντες ὡσεὶ τετρακόσιοι. θαρρήσας δὲ ὡς καὶ
χειρὸς αὐτῷ καὶ συνεργίας ἤδη προσγεγενημένης
ἀπάρας ἐκεῖθεν ἀφικνεῖται πρὸς τὸν τῶν Μωαβιτῶν
βασιλέα, καὶ τοὺς γονεῖς αὐτοῦ εἰς τὴν ἑαυτοῦ
χώραν προσδεξάμενον ἕως ἂν ἐπιγνῷ[2] τὸ καθ' αὑτὸν
τέλος ἔχειν παρεκάλει· κατανεύσαντος δ' αὐτοῦ τὴν
χάριν καὶ πάσης τοὺς γονεῖς τοῦ Δαυίδου τιμῆς
παρ' ὃν ἐτύγχανον παρ' αὐτῷ χρόνον ἀξιώσαντος.
249 (4) Αὐτὸς τοῦ προφήτου κελεύσαντος αὐτὸν τὴν
μὲν ἐρημίαν ἐκλιπεῖν, πορευθέντα δ' εἰς τὴν κλη-
ρουχίαν τῆς Ἰούδα φυλῆς ἐν αὐτῇ διάγειν πεί-
θεται καὶ παραγενόμενος εἰς Σάριν[3] πόλιν ἐν αὐτῇ
250 κατέμενε. Σαοῦλος δ' ἀκούσας ὅτι μετὰ πλήθους
ὀφθείη ὁ Δαυίδης, οὐκ εἰς τυχόντα θόρυβον καὶ
ταραχὴν ἐνέπεσεν, ἀλλ' εἰδὼς τὸ φρόνημα τοῦ
ἀνδρὸς καὶ τὴν εὐτολμίαν οὐδὲν ἐξ αὐτοῦ μικρὸν
ἀνακύψειν ἔργον, ὑφ' οὗ κλαύσεσθαι πάντως καὶ
251 πονήσειν, ὑπενόησε. καὶ συγκαλέσας τοὺς φίλους
καὶ τοὺς ἡγεμόνας καὶ τὴν φυλὴν ἐξ ἧς αὐτὸς ἦν

---

[1] M : Ἀδολλαάμη RO : Ἀδυλλάμη SP.
[2] ἕως οὗ ἐπὶ RO : ἕως ἂν ἀπογνῷ rell. Lat.
[3] Σάρην SP.

---

[a] Called Odollam (as in the LXX) in A. viii. 246 ; bibl.
"cave of Adullam." It has been identified by some with
the modern *Khirbet 'Aid el-Ma*, 12 miles S.W. of Bethlehem,
by others with *Khirbet esh-Sheikh Madhkūr* close by. Both

up his abode in a cave close to the city of Adullam,^a sent word to his brothers where he was to be found. They, with all his kinsfolk, came to him ; and besides them, all who were in want or in fear of King Saul streamed to him and declared themselves ready to obey his orders. They were in all about four hundred. Encouraged at now finding himself with a force to assist him, David departed thence and made his way to the Moabite king and besought him to receive his parents into his country and to keep them until he himself should know what was finally to become of him. This favour the king accorded him and showed all honour to David's parents so long as they were with him.

David's rebel camp in the cave of Adullam. 1 Sam. xxii. 1.

(4) David himself was bidden by the prophet ^b to quit the desert and repair to the territory of the tribe of Judah and remain there ; so, obedient to this counsel, he came to the city of Saris ^c and there abode. But Saul, on hearing that David had been seen with a large following, was thrown into no ordinary confusion and dismay ; for, knowing the mettle and hardihood of the man, he surmised that it would be no small labour that would arise from David's acts, but one that would surely cause him regret and suffering. So summoning to him his friends and chieftains and the tribe from which he himself came, to the hill^d where

David in Judah ; Saul urges his friends to remain loyal. 1 Sam. xxii. 5.

places, incidentally, are at the southern end of the Valley of Elah, *cf.* § 170 note.

^b The prophet Gad, according to Scripture.

^c So, nearly, the LXX ; Heb. " forest of Hareth " ; the site is uncertain but is identified by some with the modern *Kharas*, 7 miles N.W. of Hebron, and a little S.E. of the supposed sites of Adullam.

^d Josephus, like the LXX, takes Gibeah (" hill ") as a common noun.

451

πρὸς αὐτὸν ἐπὶ τὸν βουνόν, οὗ τὸ βασίλειον εἶχε,
καὶ καθίσας ἐπ' Ἀρούρης, τόπος δ' ἦν τις οὕτω
προσαγορευόμενος,[1] τιμῆς πολιτικῆς περὶ αὐτὸν
οὔσης καὶ[2] τάξεως σωματοφυλάκων λέγει πρὸς
αὐτούς· " ἄνδρες ὁμόφυλοι, μέμνησθε μὲν οἶδ' ὅτι
τῶν ἐμῶν εὐεργεσιῶν, ὅτι καὶ ἀγρῶν τινας ἐποίησα
δεσπότας καὶ τιμῶν τῶν ἐν τῷ πλήθει καὶ τάξεων
252 ἠξίωσα. πυνθάνομαι τοιγαροῦν εἰ μείζονας τούτων δωρεὰς καὶ πλείονας παρὰ τοῦ Ἰεσσαίου
παιδὸς προσδοκᾶτε· οἶδα γὰρ ὅτι πάντες ἐκείνῳ
προστέθεισθε[3] τοὐμοῦ παιδὸς Ἰωνάθου αὐτοῦ τε
253 οὕτως φρονήσαντος καὶ ὑμᾶς ταῦτα[4] πείσαντος· οὐ
γὰρ ἀγνοῶ τοὺς ὅρκους καὶ τὰς συνθήκας τὰς πρὸς
Δαυίδην αὐτῷ γεγενημένας, οὐδ' ὅτι σύμβουλος
μὲν καὶ συνεργὸς Ἰωνάθης ἐστὶ τῶν κατ' ἐμοῦ
συντεταγμένων, μέλει δὲ ὑμῶν οὐδενὶ περὶ τούτων,
ἀλλὰ τὸ ἀποβησόμενον ἡσυχάζοντες σκοπεῖτε."
254 σιωπήσαντος δὲ τοῦ βασιλέως ἄλλος μὲν οὐδεὶς
ἀπεκρίνατο τῶν παρόντων, Δώηγος δ' ὁ Σύρος ὁ
τὰς ἡμιόνους αὐτοῦ βόσκων εἶπεν ὡς ἴδοι τὸν
Δαυίδην εἰς Ναβὰν πόλιν πρὸς Ἀβιμέλεχον ἐλθόντα
τὸν ἀρχιερέα τά τε μέλλοντα παρ' αὐτοῦ προφητεύσαντος μαθεῖν, καὶ λαβόντα ἐφόδια καὶ τὴν
ῥομφαίαν τοῦ Γολιάθου πρὸς οὓς ἐβούλετο μετὰ
ἀσφαλείας προπεμφθῆναι.
255 (5) Μεταπεμψάμενος οὖν τὸν ἀρχιερέα καὶ πᾶσαν
αὐτοῦ τὴν γενεὰν Σαοῦλος " τί παθὼν ἐξ ἐμοῦ,"
εἶπε, " δεινὸν καὶ ἄχαρι τὸν Ἰεσσαίου παῖδα προσ-
εδέξω καὶ σιτίων μὲν αὐτῷ μετέδωκας καὶ ὅπλων

---

[1] οὕτω προσ. om. RO.   [2] καὶ om. codd.
[3] (R)ME: προστεθήσεσθε O: προστίθεσθε SP Lat.
[4] Ernesti: ταῦτα codd.

he had his palace, and seating himself at a certain spot called Arūra,[a] with his officers of state [b] and his company of bodyguards [b] around him, he addressed them thus : " Fellow tribesmen, you remember, I doubt not, my benefactions, how I have made some of you owners of estates and to others have granted honours and high positions among the people. I ask you, therefore, if you look for larger and more bounties than these from the son of Jesse ? I know very well that you have all gone over to him, because my own son Jonathan himself has taken this stand and has persuaded you to do the like. Nor am I ignorant of those oaths and covenants that he has made with David, nor that Jonathan is the counsellor and accomplice of those who are arrayed against me ; and not one of you is concerned about these things, but you are quietly waiting to see what will happen." When the king was silent, no other of those present made reply ; only Doeg the Syrian, the keeper of his mules, said that he had seen David when he came to the city of Naba to Abimelech the high priest, where through the priest's prophecies David had learnt what was to come, and, having received provisions and the sword of Goliath, he had safely been sent on his way to those whom he was seeking.

Doeg the informer.
1 Sam. xxii. 9.

(5) Saul, therefore, sent for the high priest and all his family, and said : " What wrong have I done thee or what injury that thou didst receive the son of Jesse and gavest food and arms to him who is a

Saul rebukes Ahimelech, who excuses himself.
1 Sam. xxii. 11.

---

[a] " Plowland " ; so the lxx translates Heb. 'ēshel, a kind of tree (A.V. " tamarisk "). Cf. § 377.
[b] Bibl. "servants."

453

JOSEPHUS

ὄντι τῆς ἐμῆς βασιλείας ἐπιβούλῳ, τί δὲ δὴ περὶ
τῶν μελλόντων ἐχρημάτιζες; οὐ γὰρ δή σε φεύγων
256 ἐμὲ καὶ μισῶν τὸν ἐμὸν οἶκον ἐλάνθανεν." ὁ δ'
ἀρχιερεὺς οὐκ ἐπ' ἄρνησιν ἐτράπη τῶν γεγονότων,
ἀλλὰ μετὰ παρρησίας ταῦτα παρασχεῖν ὡμολόγει
οὐχὶ Δαυίδῃ χαριζόμενος, ἀλλ' αὑτῷ· πολέμιον γὰρ
σὸν οὐκ εἰδέναι ἔφασκε, πιστὸν δὲ ἐν τοῖς μάλιστα
δοῦλον καὶ χιλίαρχον καὶ τὸ τούτων μεῖζον γαμ-
257 βρόν τε ἤδη καὶ συγγενῆ. ταῦτα δ' οὐκ ἐχθροῖς
παρέχειν τοὺς ἀνθρώπους, ἀλλὰ τοῖς εὐνοίᾳ καὶ
τιμῇ τῇ πρὸς αὐτοὺς ἀρίστοις. προφητεῦσαι δὲ
οὐ νῦν πρῶτον αὐτῷ, πολλάκις δὲ καὶ ἄλλοτε
τοῦτο πεποιηκέναι· "φήσαντι δὲ ὑπὸ σοῦ πεμφθῆναι κατὰ πολλὴν σπουδὴν ἐπὶ πρᾶξιν, τὸ[1] μηδὲν
παρασχεῖν ὧν ἐπεζήτει, σοὶ μᾶλλον ἀντιλέγειν ἢ
258 ἐκείνῳ περὶ αὐτῶν ἐλογιζόμην. διὸ μηδὲν πονηρὸν
κατ' ἐμοῦ φρονήσῃς μηδὲ πρὸς ἃ νῦν ἀκούεις
Δαυίδην ἐγχειρεῖν πρὸς ταῦτα τὴν τότε μου
δοκοῦσαν φιλανθρωπίαν ὑποπτεύσῃς· φίλῳ γὰρ καὶ
γαμβρῷ σῷ καὶ χιλιάρχῳ παρέσχον, οὐ πολεμίῳ."
259 (6) Ταῦτα λέγων ὁ ἀρχιερεὺς οὐκ ἔπεισε τὸν
Σαοῦλον (δεινὸς γὰρ ὁ φόβος μηδ' ἀληθεῖ πιστεύειν
ἀπολογίᾳ), κελεύει δὲ τοῖς ὁπλίταις περιστᾶσιν[2]
αὐτὸν μετὰ τὰς γενεᾶς[3] ἀποκτεῖναι. μὴ θαρρούν-
των δ' ἐκείνων ἅψασθαι τοῦ ἀρχιερέως, ἀλλὰ τὸ
θεῖον εὐλαβουμένων μᾶλλον ἢ τὸ παρακοῦσαι τοῦ
βασιλέως, τῷ Σύρῳ Δωήγῳ προστάσσει τὸν φόνον.
260 καὶ παραλαβὼν ὁμοίως αὐτῷ[4] πονηροὺς ἐκεῖνος
ἀποκτείνει τὸν Ἀβιμέλεχον καὶ τὴν γενεὰν αὐτοῦ·

[1] τῷ ex Lat. Niese.   [2] περισταθεῖσιν ROME.
[3] μετὰ τ. γεν. om. RO.
[4] Niese: ὁμοίους αὐτῷ codd.

454

plotter against my realm ? And why, pray, didst thou deliver oracles concerning the future ? For assuredly thou wert not ignorant that he was fleeing from me and that he hated my house." The high priest did not resort to a denial of what had taken place, but frankly confessed that he had rendered those services, yet not to gratify David, but Saul. " I knew him not," said he, " for thine enemy, but as one of thy most faithful servants and thy captain, and, what is more, as thy son-in-law now and kinsman. Men bestow such dignities not on their enemies, but on those who show them the greatest goodwill and esteem. Nor was this the first time that I prophesied for him ; often have I done so on other occasions as well. And when he told me that he had been sent by thee in great haste on a certain matter, had I refused any of his desires, I should have thought this to be gain-saying thee rather than him.[a] Therefore, think not ill of me, nor, from what thou now hearest of David's designs, regard with suspicion what I then deemed an act of humanity ; for it was to thy friend and to thy son-in-law and captain that I rendered it, not to thine enemy."

(6) These words of the high priest did not persuade Saul, for fear is strong enough to disbelieve even a truthful plea ; and he ordered his soldiers to surround him and his kin, and slay them. But as they dared not lay hands on the high priest, dreading more to offend the Deity than to disobey the king, he charged Doeg the Syrian to carry out the murder. This fellow, taking to help him others as wicked as him-self,[b] slew Abimelech and his kin, who were in all

At Saul's order, Doeg slays Ahimelech and his kin; Nob is destroyed. 1 Sam. xxii. 16.

---

[a] This last sentence is an addition to Scripture.
[b] In Scripture, Doeg alone slays the priests.

ἦσαν δὲ πάντες ὡσεὶ πέντε καὶ τριακόσιοι.[1] πέμψας δὲ Σαοῦλος καὶ εἰς τὴν πόλιν τῶν ἱερέων
Ναβὰν πάντας τε αὐτοὺς ἀπέκτεινεν, οὐ γυναικῶν
οὐ νηπίων οὐδ' ἄλλης ἡλικίας φεισάμενος, αὐτὴν
261 δὲ ἐνέπρησε. διασώζεται δὲ παῖς εἷς Ἀβιμελέχου
Ἀβιάθαρος ὄνομα. ταῦτα μέντοι γε συνέβη, καθὼς
προεφήτευσεν ὁ θεὸς τῷ ἀρχιερεῖ Ἠλί, διὰ τὰς
τῶν υἱῶν αὐτοῦ δύο παρανομίας εἰπὼν διαφθαρή-
σεσθαι τοὺς ἐγγόνους.

262 (7) Σαοῦλος δὲ ὁ βασιλεὺς ὠμὸν οὕτως ἔργον
διαπραξάμενος καὶ γενεὰν ὅλην ἀρχιερατικῆς ἀπο-
σφάξας τιμῆς καὶ μήτ' ἐπὶ νηπίοις λαβὼν οἶκτον
μήτ' ἐπὶ γέρουσιν αἰδῶ, καταβαλὼν δὲ καὶ τὴν
πόλιν, ἣν πατρίδα καὶ τροφὸν τῶν ἱερέων καὶ
προφητῶν αὐτὸ[2] τὸ θεῖον ἐπελέξατο καὶ μόνην εἰς
τὸ τοιούτους φέρειν ἄνδρας ἀπέδειξε, μαθεῖν ἅπασι
παρέσχε καὶ κατανοῆσαι τὸν ἀνθρώπινον τρόπον,
263 ὅτι μέχρις οὗ μέν εἰσιν ἰδιῶταί τινες καὶ ταπεινοί,
τῷ μὴ δύνασθαι χρῆσθαι τῇ φύσει μηδὲ τολμᾶν
ὅσα θέλουσιν, ἐπιεικεῖς εἰσι καὶ μέτριοι καὶ μόνον
διώκουσι τὸ δίκαιον, καὶ πρὸς αὐτὸ[3] τὴν πᾶσαν
εὔνοιάν[4] τε καὶ σπουδὴν ἔχουσι, τότε δὲ καὶ περὶ
τοῦ θείου πεπιστεύκασιν ὅτι πᾶσι τοῖς γινομένοις
ἐν τῷ βίῳ πάρεστι καὶ οὐ τὰ ἔργα μόνον ὁρᾷ
τὰ πραττόμενα, ἀλλὰ καὶ τὰς διανοίας ἤδη σαφῶς
264 οἶδεν, ἀφ' ὧν μέλλει ταῦτ' ἔσεσθαι· ὅταν δὲ εἰς
ἐξουσίαν παρέλθωσι καὶ δυναστείαν, τότε πάντ'
ἐκεῖνα μετεκδυσάμενοι καὶ ὥσπερ ἐπὶ σκηνῆς

---

[1] ex Lat. Niese (cf. lxx) : πέντε καὶ ὀγδοήκοντα RO : πέντε
καὶ ὀγδοήκοντα καὶ τριακόσιοι MSP : πεντακόσιοι καὶ τριάκοντα E.
[2] conj. edd. : αὐτόθι codd. : om. Lat.
[3] αὐτῷ Niese.   [4] ἔννοιαν Dindorf.

some three hundred and five.[a]   Moreover Saul sent
men to Naba, the city of the priests, and slew all
therein, sparing neither women nor infants nor those
of any age, and burnt the town.   One son of Abimelech alone escaped, Abiathar [b] by name.   Now all
these things came to pass in full accordance with
what God had foretold to Eli the high priest, when
He declared that by reason of the iniquities of his two
sons his posterity should be destroyed.[c]

(7) [d] But as for King Saul, by perpetrating a deed
so cruel as slaughtering a whole family of high-
priestly rank, feeling neither pity for infants nor
reverence for age, and then proceeding to demolish
the city which the Deity Himself had chosen as the
home and nurse of priests and prophets and set apart
as the sole place to produce such men—Saul thereby
gave all to know and understand the character of
men, namely that so long as they are of private and
humble station, through inability to indulge their
instincts or to dare all that they desire, they are
kindly and moderate and pursue only what is right,
and turn thereto their every thought and endeavour;
then too, concerning the Deity, they are persuaded
that He is present in all that happens in life and that
He not only sees the acts that are done, but clearly
knows even the thoughts whence those acts are to
come.   But when once they attain to power and
sovereignty, then, stripping off all those qualities and
laying aside their habits and ways as if they were

Reflections
on the
changes in
character
caused by
accession to
power.

[a] Emended text, agreeing with the LXX, 1 Sam. xxii. 18,
where the Heb. has 85 ; the MSS. vary between 85 and 385,
while the Epitome has 530.   Below, § 268, Josephus has 300.
[b] Heb. *Ebyāthār*.   [c] *Cf. A.* v. 350.
[d] With this digression in criticism of Saul contrast the
eulogy below, §§ 343 ff.

457

προσωπεῖα τὰ ἤθη καὶ τοὺς τρόπους ἀποθέμενοι
μεταλαμβάνουσι τόλμαν ἀπόνοιαν καταφρόνησιν ἀν-
265 θρωπίνων τε καὶ θείων, καὶ ὅτε μάλιστα δεῖ τῆς
εὐσεβείας αὐτοῖς καὶ τῆς δικαιοσύνης, ἔγγιστα τοῦ
φθονεῖσθαι γεγενημένοις καὶ πᾶσι φανεροῖς ἐφ'
οἷς ἂν νοήσωσιν ἢ πράξωσι καθεστῶσι, τόθ' ὡς
οὐκέτι βλέποντος αὐτοὺς τοῦ θεοῦ ἢ διὰ τὴν
ἐξουσίαν δεδιότος οὕτως ἐμπαροινοῦσι τοῖς πράγ-
266 μασιν. ἃ δ' ἂν ἢ φοβηθῶσιν ἀκούσαντες[1] ἢ
μισήσωσι * * θελήσαντες[2] ἢ στέρξωσιν ἀλόγως,
ταῦτα κύρια καὶ βέβαια καὶ ἀληθῆ καὶ ἀνθρώποις
ἀρεστὰ καὶ θεῷ δοκοῦσι, τῶν δὲ μελλόντων λόγος
267 αὐτοῖς οὐδὲ εἷς· ἀλλὰ τιμῶσι μὲν τοὺς πολλὰ
ταλαιπωρήσαντας, τιμήσαντες δὲ φθονοῦσι, καὶ
παραγαγόντες εἰς ἐπιφάνειαν οὐ ταύτης ἀφαιροῦνται
μόνον τοὺς τετυχηκότας, ἀλλὰ διὰ ταύτην καὶ τοῦ
ζῆν ἐπὶ πονηραῖς αἰτίαις καὶ δι' ὑπερβολὴν αὐτῶν
ἀπιθάνοις· κολάζουσι δ' οὐκ ἐπ' ἔργοις δίκης
ἀξίοις, ἀλλ' ἐπὶ διαβολαῖς καὶ κατηγορίαις ἀ-
βασανίστοις, οὐδ' ὅσους[3] ἔδει τοῦτο παθεῖν, ἀλλ'
268 ὅσους ἀποκτεῖναι δύνανται. τοῦτο Σαοῦλος ἡμῖν
ὁ Κείσου παῖς, ὁ πρῶτος μετὰ τὴν ἀριστοκρατίαν
καὶ[4] τὴν ἐπὶ τοῖς κριταῖς πολιτείαν Ἑβραίων βασιλεύσας, φανερὸν πεποίηκε τριακοσίους ἀποκτείνας
ἱερέας καὶ προφήτας ἐκ τῆς πρὸς Ἀβιμέλεχον
ὑποψίας, ἐπικαταβαλὼν δὲ αὐτοῖς καὶ τὴν πόλιν,
καὶ τὸν[5] τρόπῳ τινὶ ναὸν σπουδάσας ἱερέων καὶ
προφητῶν ἔρημον καταστῆσαι, τοσούτους μὲν ἀν-

---

[1] ἀκούσιοι conj. Thackeray.
[2] ἐθελήσαντες SP : ἐθελοκακήσαντες Naber.
[3] οὖς Niese.   [4] καὶ om. RO.
[5] + ἐν codd.

458

stage masks, they assume in their place audacity, recklessness, contempt for things human and divine ; and at the moment when they most need piety and righteousness, being now within closest reach of envy, with all their thoughts and acts exposed to all men, then, as though God no longer saw them or were over-awed by their power, they break out into these riotous acts. Their fear of rumours, their wilful hates,[a] their irrational loves—these they regard as valid, sure and true, acceptable to man and God, but of the future they take not the least account. They first honour those who have toiled in their service, and then envy them the honours which they have conferred ; and, after promoting men to high distinction, they deprive them not only of this, but, on its very account, of life itself, on malicious charges which their extravagance renders incredible. Their punishments are inflicted not for acts deserving of chastisement, but on the faith of calumnies and unsifted accusations, nor do they fall on those who ought so to suffer, but on whomsoever they can put to death. Of this we have a signal example in the conduct of Saul, son of Kis, the first to become king of the Hebrews after the period of aristocracy and the government under the judges, for he slew three hundred priests and prophets from suspicion of Abimelech, and further demolished their city and strove to leave what was virtually their temple [b] destitute of priests and prophets,[c] by first slaying so many of

---

[a] Text uncertain.
[b] The first real temple was, of course, to be built later in Jerusalem by Solomon.
[c] The reference to prophets is unscriptural.

ἐλών, μεῖναι δ' ἐάσας οὐδὲ τὴν πατρίδα αὐτῶν πρὸς
τὸ καὶ μετ' ἐκείνους ἄλλους γενέσθαι.

269 (8) Ὁ δ' Ἀβιάθαρος ὁ τοῦ Ἀβιμελέχου παῖς ὁ
μόνος διασωθῆναι[1] δυνηθεὶς ἐκ τοῦ γένους τῶν ὑπὸ
Σαούλου φονευθέντων ἱερέων φυγὼν πρὸς Δαυίδην
τὴν τῶν οἰκείων αὐτοῦ συμφορὰν ἐδήλωσε καὶ τὴν
270 τοῦ πατρὸς ἀναίρεσιν. ὁ δ' οὐκ ἀγνοεῖν ἔφη ταῦτα
περὶ αὐτοὺς ἐσόμενα ἰδὼν τὸν Δώηγον· ὑπονοῆσαι
γὰρ διαβληθήσεσθαι πρὸς αὐτοῦ τὸν ἀρχιερέα τῷ
βασιλεῖ, καὶ τῆς ἀτυχίας ταύτης αὐτοῖς αὐτὸν
ᾐτιᾶτο. μένειν[2] δ' αὐτόθι καὶ σὺν αὐτῷ διατρίβειν
ὡς οὐκ ἐν ἄλλῳ τόπῳ λησόμενον οὕτως ἠξίου.

271 (xiii. 1) Κατὰ δὲ τοῦτον τὸν καιρὸν ἀκούσας ὁ
Δαυίδης τοὺς Παλαιστίνους ἐμβεβληκότας εἰς τὴν
Κιλλανῶν χώραν καὶ ταύτην διαρπάζοντας δίδωσιν
ἑαυτὸν στρατεύειν ἐπ' αὐτούς, τοῦ θεοῦ διὰ τοῦ
προφήτου πυθόμενος εἰ ἐπιτρέπει νίκην. τοῦ δὲ
σημαίνειν φήσαντος ἐξώρμησεν ἐπὶ τοὺς Παλαιστίνους μετὰ τῶν ἑταίρων καὶ φόνον τε αὐτῶν
272 πολὺν ἐξέχεε καὶ λείαν ἤλασεν. καὶ παραμείνας
τοῖς Κιλλανοῖς, ἕως οὗ τὰς ἅλως[3] καὶ τὸν καρπὸν
συνεῖλον ἀδεῶς, Σαούλῳ τῷ βασιλεῖ μηνύεται παρ'
αὐτοῖς ὤν· τὸ γὰρ ἔργον καὶ τὸ κατόρθωμα οὐκ
ἔμεινε παρ' οἷς ἐγένετο, φήμη[4] δ' ἐπίπαν εἴς τε τὰς
τῶν ἄλλων ἀκοὰς καὶ πρὸς τὰς τοῦ βασιλέως
διεκομίσθη αὐτό[5] τε συνιστάνον καὶ τὸν πεποιη-
273 κότα. χαίρει δὲ Σαοῦλος ἀκούσας ἐν Κίλλᾳ τὸν

---

[1] διασωθ. om. RO.
[2] τὸ μένειν codd.　　　　[3] ἅλῳ codd.: ἀλώνας ed. pr.
[4] φήμη Ernesti.　　　　[5] αὐτό Dindorf.

---

[a] Cf. below on § 273.
[b] In Scripture no mention is made at this point of a prophet,

them and then not suffering even their native place
to remain, that others might come after them.

(8) Now Abiathar, the son of Abimelech, who alone
of the family of priests slaughtered by Saul had been
able to escape, fled to David and told him of the
tragedy of his kin and the slaying of his father. David
replied that he had known that this fate would befall
them, when he saw Doeg ; he had, he said, suspected
that the high priest would be denounced to the king
by this man, and he blamed himself as the cause
of this misfortune to them. Howbeit he besought
Abiathar to abide there and to live with him, since
nowhere else would he be so safely hidden.

Abiathar, the high priest's son, flees to David. 1 Sam. xxii. 20.

(xiii. 1) At this same time David, hearing that the
Philistines had invaded the country of the Killanians *a*
and were ravaging it, offered to take the field against
them, after inquiring of God through the prophet *b*
whether He would grant him victory. And when
the prophet reported that God had so signified, he
threw himself upon the Philistines with his companions, made a great slaughter of them and carried
off their spoils. As he then remained with the Killanians until they had secured their threshing-floors
and safely got in their crops,*c* his presence there was
reported to King Saul. For this exploit and its
success did not remain confined to those who had wit-
nessed them, but the fame of it was carried abroad
to the ears of all, the king's included, with praise of
the deed and the doer of it. Saul rejoiced to hear

David saves Keilah (Killa) from the Philistines. 1 Sam. xxiii 1.

but in 1 Sam. xxiii. 9 we read that David consulted God about
leaving Keilah, through the priest Abimelech by means of
the ephod—a detail omitted in Josephus's account below,
§ 274.

c The safeguarding of the crops is an amplification of
Scripture.

Δαυίδην, καί '' θεὸς ἤδη χερσὶ ταῖς ἐμαῖς ὑπέθετο
αὐτόν,'' εἰπών, '' ἐπεὶ καὶ συνηνάγκασεν ἐλθεῖν
εἰς πόλιν τείχη καὶ πύλας καὶ μοχλοὺς ἔχουσαν,''
τῷ λαῷ παντὶ προσέταξεν ἐπὶ τὴν Κίλλαν ἐξορ-
μῆσαι καὶ πολιορκήσαντι καὶ ἑλόντι τὸν Δαυίδην
274 ἀποκτεῖναι. ταῦτα δὲ αἰσθόμενος ὁ Δαυίδης καὶ
μαθὼν παρὰ τοῦ θεοῦ ὅτι μείναντα παρ' αὐτοῖς
οἱ Κιλλῖται ἐκδώσουσι τῷ Σαούλῳ, παραλαβὼν
τοὺς τετρακοσίους ἀπῆρεν ἀπὸ τῆς πόλεως εἰς
τὴν ἔρημον ἐπάνω τῆς Ἐνγεδὼν¹ λεγομένης. καὶ ὁ
μὲν βασιλεὺς ἀκούσας αὐτὸν πεφευγότα παρὰ τῶν
Κιλλιτῶν ἐπαύσατο τῆς ἐπ' αὐτὸν στρατείας.

275 (2) Δαυίδης δὲ ἐκεῖθεν ἄρας εἴς τινα τόπον
Καινὴν² καλουμένην τῆς Ζιφηνῆς παραγίνεται, εἰς
ὃν Ἰωνάθης ὁ τοῦ Σαούλου παῖς συμβαλὼν αὐτῷ
καὶ κατασπασάμενος θαρρεῖν τε καὶ χρηστὰς περὶ
τῶν μελλόντων ἔχειν ἐλπίδας παρεκάλει καὶ μὴ
κάμνειν τοῖς παροῦσι· βασιλεύσειν γὰρ αὐτὸν καὶ
πᾶσαν τὴν Ἑβραίων δύναμιν ἕξειν ὑφ' ἑαυτῷ,
φιλεῖν δὲ τὰ τοιαῦτα σὺν μεγάλοις ἀπαντᾶν πόνοις.
276 πάλιν δ' ὅρκους ποιησάμενος τῆς εἰς ἅπαντα τὸν
βίον πρὸς ἀλλήλους εὐνοίας καὶ πίστεως καὶ τὸν
θεὸν μάρτυρα καλέσας, ὧν ἐπηράσατο αὑτῷ παρα-

¹ Ἐνγελαὶν MS: Ἐνγαλαὶν P: Ἐνγεδαὶν Naber.
² M Lat.: Κενὴν ROSPE.

that David was in Killa.[a] " At last," said he, " God
has delivered him into my hands, since He has forced
him to enter a city with walls, gates and bars," and
he ordered the whole people to march against Killa
and, when they had besieged and taken it,[b] to kill
David.   But when David discovered this and learned
from God that if he remained in Killa the inhabitants
would give him up to Saul, he took his four hundred [c]
men and withdrew from the city into the desert lying
above a place called Engedōn.[d]   Thereupon the king,
hearing that he had fled from the people of Killa,
abandoned his campaign against him.

(2) David, departing thence, came to a place called
Kainē [e] (" New ") in the region of Ziphēnē.[f]   Here
he was met by Jonathan, son of Saul, who, after em-
bracing him, bade him take courage, hope well for
the future and not be crushed by his present state,
for (he assured him) he would yet be king and would
have all the forces of the Hebrews under him, but
such things were wont to demand great toil for their
attainment.   Then, having renewed his oaths of
life-long, mutual affection and fidelity, and having
called God to witness the curses which he invoked

Jonathan renews his pledge to David at Ziph. 1 Sam. xxiii. 16.

---

[a] Bibl. Keilah, LXX Κεειλά, perhaps the modern *Khirbet
Qila*, about 2 miles S. of the supposed site of Adullam
(*cf.* § 247 note).

[b] Or " besieged it and taken him."

[c] So the LXX; Heb. 600.

[d] Bibl. Engedi; mentioned below, § 282.   1 Sam. xxiii. 13
" and went whithersoever they could go."

[e] So the LXX, reading Heb. *ḥadāshāh* " new " for *ḥōreshāh*
" thicket " in 1 Sam. xxiii. 15 ; the latter is perhaps to be
taken as a proper name, and may be the modern *Khirbet
Khoreisa.*

[f] Bibl. Ziph, LXX Ζείφ, probably the modern *Tell Zif*,
4 miles S.E. of Hebron.

βάντι τὰ συγκείμενα καὶ μεταβαλλομένῳ[1] πρὸς
τἀναντία, τὸν μὲν αὐτόθι καταλείπει μικρὰ τῶν
φροντίδων καὶ τοῦ δέους ἐπικουφίσας, αὐτὸς δὲ
277 πρὸς αὐτὸν ἐπανέρχεται. οἱ δὲ Ζιφηνοὶ χαριζό-
μενοι τῷ Σαούλῳ μηνύουσιν αὐτῷ παρ' αὐτοῖς
διατρίβειν τὸν Δαυίδην καὶ παραδώσειν ἔφασαν ἐπ'
αὐτὸν ἐλθόντι· καταληφθέντων γὰρ τῶν τῆς Ζιφηνῆς
278 στενῶν οὐκ εἶναι φυγεῖν αὐτὸν[2] πρὸς ἄλλους. ὁ δὲ
βασιλεὺς ἐπῄνεσεν αὐτούς, χάριν ἔχειν ὁμολογήσας
τὸν ἐχθρὸν αὐτῷ μεμηνυκόσι, καὶ οὐκ εἰς μακρὰν
ἀμείψεσθαι[3] τῆς εὐνοίας ὑποσχόμενος αὐτούς, ἔπεμψε τοὺς ζητήσοντας τὸν Δαυίδην καὶ τὴν ἐρημίαν ἐξ-
ερευνήσοντας, αὐτὸς δ' ἀκολουθήσειν ἀπεκρίνατο.
279 καὶ οἱ μὲν ἐπὶ τὴν θήραν καὶ τὴν σύλληψιν τοῦ
Δαυίδου προῆγον τὸν βασιλέα σπουδάζοντες μὴ
μόνον αὐτῷ[4] μηνῦσαι τὸν ἐχθρόν, ἀλλὰ καὶ τῷ
παρασχεῖν αὐτὸν εἰς ἐξουσίαν φανερωτέραν καταστῆσαι αὐτῷ τὴν εὔνοιαν[5]· διήμαρτον δὲ τῆς ἀδίκου
καὶ πονηρᾶς ἐπιθυμίας, οἳ μηδὲν κινδυνεύειν ἔμελ-
280 λον ἐκ τοῦ μὴ ταῦτ' ἐμφανίσαι τῷ Σαούλῳ, διὰ
δὲ κολακείαν καὶ κέρδους προσδοκίαν παρὰ τοῦ
βασιλέως ἄνδρα θεοφιλῆ καὶ παρὰ δίκην ζητού-
μενον ἐπὶ θανάτῳ καὶ λανθάνειν δυνάμενον διέβαλον
καὶ παραδώσειν ὑπέσχοντο· γνοὺς γὰρ ὁ Δαυίδης
τὴν τῶν Ζιφηνῶν κακοήθειαν καὶ τὴν τοῦ βασιλέως
ἔφοδον ἐκλείπει μὲν τὰ στενὰ τῆς ἐκείνων χώρας,

---

[1] μεταβαλομένῳ Bekker.
[2] φυγὴν αὐτῷ SP : φυγεῖν αὐτῷ M.
[3] Niese : ἀμείψασθαι codd. (Lat. vid.).
[4] αὐτῷ τῷ MSP.
[5] αὐτῷ τὴν εὔνοιαν om. RO : post ἐχθρὸν (supra) rell.

---

[a] At Gibeah (lxx " the hill," cf. § 251 note), 1 Sam. xxiii. 19.

upon himself should he violate their covenant and change to the contrary, he left him there, having a little lightened his cares and fear, and returned to his own home. But the men of Ziph, to win favour with Saul, reported to him ^a that David was sojourning among them, and promised, if he would come after him, to deliver him up ; for, if the passes into their country were occupied, it would be impossible for him to escape elsewhere. The king commended them and expressed his thanks for their having given him information of his enemy, and promised that their loyalty should not long await its reward ^b ; he then sent a party to search for David and to scour the desert, assuring them that he would himself follow. Thus they spurred the king on to the pursuit and capture of David, because they were anxious not merely to denounce his enemy to him, but to give more palpable proof of their loyalty to him by actually delivering David into his hands. They failed, however, in their iniquitous and base desire, which was the more so in that they would have incurred no risk by not informing Saul of these things ; yet, from obsequiousness and in the expectation of receiving gain from the king, they calumniated and promised to deliver up a God-favoured man whose death was being unjustly sought, and who might have remained concealed.^c For David, learning of the evil designs of the Ziphites and the king's approach, quitted the

The men of Ziph betray David to Saul. 1 Sam. xxiii. 19.

^b This promise is not mentioned in Scripture.
^c These reflections on the conduct of the Ziphites are an addition to Scripture.

φεύγει δὲ ἐπὶ τὴν μεγάλην πέτραν τὴν οὖσαν ἐν τῇ
Σίμωνος ἐρήμῳ.

281　(3) Ὥρμησεν δὲ ἐπ᾽ ἐκείνην διώκειν Σαοῦλος·
κατὰ γὰρ τὴν ὁδὸν ἀναχωρήσαντα ἐκ τῶν στενῶν
μαθὼν τὸν Δαυίδην, ἐπὶ τὸ ἕτερον μέρος τῆς πέτρας
ἀπῆρεν. ἀντιπεριέσπασαν δὲ τὸν Σαοῦλον ἀπὸ τῆς
διώξεως τοῦ Δαυίδου μέλλοντος ἤδη συλλαμβάνε-
σθαι Παλαιστῖνοι πάλιν ἐπὶ τὴν Ἑβραίων ἐστρα-
τευκέναι χώραν ἀκουσθέντες· ἐπὶ γὰρ τούτους ἀν-
έστρεψε φύσει πολεμίους ὄντας, αὐτοὺς ἀμύνασθαι
κρίνας ἀναγκαιότερον ἢ τὸν ἴδιον σπουδάζοντα
λαβεῖν ἐχθρὸν ὑπεριδεῖν τὴν γῆν κακωθεῖσαν.

282　(4) Καὶ Δαυίδης μὲν οὕτως ἐκ παραλόγου τὸν
κίνδυνον διαφυγὼν εἰς τὰ στενὰ τῆς Ἐγγεδηνῆς
ἀφικνεῖται· Σαούλῳ δὲ ἐκβαλόντι τοὺς Παλαιστίνους ἧκον ἀπαγγέλλοντές τινες τὸν Δαυίδην ἐν
283　τοῖς Ἐγγεδηνῆς διατρίβειν ὅροις. λαβὼν δὲ τρισχιλίους ἐπιλέκτους[1] ὁπλίτας ἐπ᾽ αὐτὸν ἠπείγετο,
καὶ γενόμενος οὐ πόρρω τῶν τόπων ὁρᾷ παρὰ τὴν
ὁδὸν σπήλαιον βαθὺ καὶ κοῖλον, εἰς πολὺ καὶ μῆκος
ἀνεῳγὸς καὶ πλάτος, ἔνθα συνέβαινε τὸν Δαυίδην
μετὰ τῶν τετρακοσίων κεκρύφθαι· ἐπειγόμενος οὖν
ὑπὸ τῶν κατὰ φύσιν εἴσεισιν εἰς αὐτὸ μόνος θεαθεὶς
284 δ᾽ ὑπό τινος τῶν μετὰ Δαυίδου· καὶ φράσαντος

---

[1] ἐπιλέκτους post ὁπλίτας MSP: om. E Lat.

---

[a] 1 Sam. xxiii. 24 " in the wilderness of Maon, in the plain
on the south (lit. " right ") of Jeshimon," lxx ἐν τῇ ἐρήμῳ
τῇ Μαὰν (v.l. Μαὼν, Luc. ἐν τῇ ἐπηκόῳ) καθ᾽ ἑσπέραν ἐκ
δεξιῶν τοῦ Ἰεσσαιμοῦ. Thackeray, Josephus the Man, etc.,
p. 88, writes " both in Josephus and in Lucian an intrusive
initial shin has converted the proper name [Maon] into
Shim'on . . . Lucian translates it by ἐπήκοος ' into the

defiles of their country and fled to the great rock
which is in the wilderness of Simon.[a]

(3) Thither Saul hastened to pursue him ; for he
had learnt on the way that David had withdrawn
from the defiles, and so he set off for the other side of
the rock. But, just as David was about to be caught,
Saul was diverted from the pursuit by the news that
the Philistines had made a fresh invasion into Hebrew
territory. He accordingly returned to face them as
his natural enemies, judging it more imperative to
fight against them than, through his zeal to capture
his personal enemy, to leave the land to be ravaged.[b]

(4) David, after this unexpected escape from
danger, repaired to the narrow passes of Engedēnē [c] ;
but, after Saul had expelled the Philistines, word
was brought to him that David was sojourning within
the borders of Engedēnē. So, with three thousand
picked soldiers, he pressed on after him. And, when
he was not far from the region, he saw by the wayside
a deep and hollow cave, extending to a great distance
both in length and breadth, where, as it chanced,
David with his four hundred men lay concealed.
Urged then by the needs of nature, Saul entered it
alone, and was espied by one of David's companions.

A Philistine invasion diverts Saul from pursuit of David.
1 Sam. xxiii. 26.

David spares Saul's life at En-gedi (Engedene).
1 Sam. xxiii 29 (xxiv. 1 Heb., LXX).

listening wilderness,' as in fact Josephus does elsewhere,"
and refers to *A.* i. 304 "the name Σεμέων signifies that
God listened (ἐπήκοον γεγονέναι)." I think, however, that
Josephus's *Simōn* represents the bibl. Jeshimon (Heb.
Yeshīmōn), which it might easily have done if Josephus had
read it in a form like that of the Targum where, with the
preposition *lᵉ*, it is *liyshīmōn* (by a phonetic law, the consonant *y* is assimilated to the preceding vowel), from an
apparent root *Shīmōn* = Gr. *Simōn*.

   [b] The last sentence is an amplification of Scripture.

   [c] Bibl. En-gedi, LXX Ἐνγάδδει, modern ʿĀin Jidy, a
rocky height half-way down the west shore of the Dead Sea.

τοῦ θεασαμένου πρὸς τὸν ἐχθρὸν αὐτοῦ παρὰ τοῦ
θεοῦ καιρὸν ἔχειν ἀμύνης καὶ συμβουλεύοντος τοῦ
Σαούλου ἀποτεμεῖν τὴν κεφαλὴν καὶ τῆς πολλῆς
ἄλης αὐτὸν ἀπαλλάξαι καὶ ταλαιπωρίας, ἀναστὰς
ἀναιρεῖ μὲν τὴν κροκύδα¹ τοῦ ἱματίου μόνον οὗ
Σαοῦλος ἀμπείχετο, μετανοήσας δ᾽ εὐθύς " οὐ
δίκαιον," εἶπε, " φονεύειν τὸν αὐτοῦ δεσπότην,
οὐδὲ τὸν ὑπὸ τοῦ θεοῦ βασιλείας ἀξιωθέντα· καὶ
γὰρ εἰ πονηρὸς οὗτος εἰς ἡμᾶς, ἀλλ᾽ οὐκ ἐμὲ
285 δεῖ τοιοῦτον εἶναι πρὸς αὐτόν." τοῦ δὲ Σαούλου
τὸ σπήλαιον ἐκλιπόντος προελθὼν² ὁ Δαυίδης ἔκρα-
γεν, ἀκοῦσαι τὸν Σαοῦλον ἀξιῶν. ἐπιστραφέντος
δὲ τοῦ βασιλέως προσκυνεῖ τε αὐτὸν πεσὼν ἐπὶ
πρόσωπον, ὡς ἔθος, καί φησιν· " οὐ πονηροῖς, ὦ
βασιλεῦ, καὶ ψευδεῖς πλάττουσι διαβολὰς παρ-
έχοντα δεῖ τὰς ἀκοὰς χαρίζεσθαι μὲν ἐκείνοις τὸ
πιστεύειν αὐτοῖς, τοὺς δὲ φιλτάτους δι᾽ ὑπονοίας
ἔχειν, ἀλλὰ τοῖς ἔργοις σκοπεῖν τὴν ἁπάντων διά-
286 θεσιν. διαβολὴ μὲν γὰρ ἀπατᾷ, σαφὴς δ᾽ ἀπό-
δειξις εὐνοίας τὰ πραττόμενα· καὶ λόγος μὲν ἐπ᾽
ἀμφότερα πέφυκεν ἀληθής τε καὶ ψευδής, τὰ δὲ
287 ἔργα γυμνὴν ὑπ᾽ ὄψει τὴν διάνοιαν τίθησιν. ἴσθι
τοίνυν ἐκ τούτων καλῶς ἔχειν με πρὸς σὲ καὶ τὸν
σὸν οἶκον κἀμοὶ³ πιστεῦσαι δεῖ, καὶ μὴ τοῖς κατ-
ηγοροῦσιν ἃ μήτε εἰς νοῦν ἐβαλόμην μήτε δύναται
γενέσθαι προσθέμενον μεταδιώκειν τὴν ἐμὴν ψυχήν,
καὶ μηδὲν μήθ᾽ ἡμέρας μήτε νυκτὸς ἔχειν διὰ
φροντίδος ἢ τὴν ἐμὴν ἀναίρεσιν, ἣν ἀδίκως μετα-

---

¹ ἀναιρεῖ . . . κροκύδα] ἀποτέμνει . . . πτέρυγα SPE (Lat.).
² E: προσελθὼν codd. Lat.
³ ex Lat. conj. Thackeray: ἐμοὶ codd.

468

The man who saw him said to David that here was his God-sent opportunity for vengeance on his enemy and counselled him to cut off Saul's head [a] and so deliver himself from his long wandering and misery, whereupon David arose and only pulled off some of the woollen nap [b] of the mantle that Saul was wearing ; but, repenting forthwith, said, " It is not right to murder one's own master or one whom God has accounted worthy of kingship. And even though he treats me ill, yet I must not do the like to him." Then, when Saul had left the cave, David came forth and cried aloud, beseeching Saul to hear him. And, as the king turned, he prostrated himself before him with his face to the ground, as the custom was, and said, " Thou oughtest not, O King, to give ear to miscreants and fabricators of lying charges and do them the honour of believing their lies, while holding thy best friends in suspicion ; no, but by their actions shouldest thou judge the character of all men. For calumny only deceives, while actions clearly reveal the honest friend ; words are of two-fold nature, either true or false, but deeds lay bare to sight the intention. [c] Know then by these tokens that I wish well to thee and to thy house, and thou shouldst trust in me instead of putting faith in those who accuse me of things which I never took into my head to do and which could never even have been done, and constantly seeking my life, with no thought day or night except for my destruction, for which thou

David reproaches Saul.
1 Sam. xxiv. 9 (10).

---

[a] Bibl. " do to him as it shall seem good unto thee."

[b] Variant (as in Scripture) " cut off the skirt " ($\pi\tau\epsilon\rho\nu\gamma\alpha$) ; this latter text is found below, § 289.

[c] The last remark, like some of the other moral reflections in David's speech, is an amplification of Scripture.

288 πορεύῃ· πῶς γὰρ οὐχὶ[1] ψευδῆ περὶ ἐμοῦ δόξαν
εἴληφας ὡς ἀποκτεῖναί σε θέλοντος; ἢ πῶς οὐκ
ἀσεβεῖς εἰς τὸν θεόν, ἄνθρωπον τήμερον αὐτῷ τιμωρῆσαι δυνάμενον καὶ παρὰ σοῦ λαβεῖν δίκην καὶ
μὴ θελήσαντα μηδὲ τῷ καιρῷ χρησάμενον, ὃν εἰ
σοὶ κατ' ἐμοῦ περιέπεσεν οὐκ ἂν αὐτὸς[2] παρῆκας,
289 διαχρήσασθαι ποθῶν καὶ νομίζων πολέμιον; ὅτε
γάρ σου τὴν πτέρυγα τοῦ ἱματίου ἀπέτεμον, τότε
σου καὶ τὴν κεφαλὴν ἠδυνάμην." ἐπιδείξας δὲ τὸ
ῥάκος ἰδεῖν πιστεύειν παρεῖχεν. " ἀλλ' ἐγὼ μὲν
ἀπεσχόμην δικαίας ἀμύνης," φησί, " σὺ δὲ μῖσος
ἄδικον οὐκ αἰδῇ κατ' ἐμοῦ τρέφων.[3] ὁ θεὸς ταῦτα
δικάσειε καὶ τὸν ἑκατέρου τρόπον ἡμῶν ἐλέγξειε."
290 Σαοῦλος δὲ ἐπὶ τῷ παραδόξῳ τῆς σωτηρίας θαυμάσας καὶ τὴν τοῦ νεανίσκου μετριότητα καὶ φύσιν
ἐκπλαγεὶς ἀνῴμωξε· τὸ δ' αὐτὸ κἀκείνου ποιήσαντος αὐτὸν εἶναι δίκαιον στένειν ἀπεκρίνατο·
" σὺ μὲν γάρ," φησίν, " ἀγαθῶν αἴτιος ἐμοὶ
γέγονας, ἐγὼ δὲ σοὶ συμφορῶν. ἐπεδείξω δὲ σήμερον τὴν ἀρχαίων ἔχοντα σαυτὸν δικαιοσύνην, οἳ
τοὺς ἐχθροὺς ἐν ἐρημίᾳ λαβόντας[4] σώζειν παρ-
291 ήγγελλον. πέπεισμαι δὴ νῦν ὅτι σοὶ τὴν βασιλείαν
ὁ θεὸς φυλάττει καὶ περιμένει σε τὸ πάντων τῶν
Ἑβραίων κράτος. δὸς δή μοι πίστεις ἐνόρκους μή
μου τὸ γένος ἐξαφανίσαι μηδ' ἐμοὶ μνησικακοῦντα
τοὺς ἐμοὺς ἐγγόνους ἀπολέσαι, τηρῆσαι δέ μοι καὶ
σῶσαι τὸν οἶκον." ὀμόσας δὲ καθὼς ἠξίωκε[5] Δαυίδης Σαοῦλον μὲν εἰς τὴν ἰδίαν ἀπέλυσε βασιλείαν,

---

[1] οὐχὶ om. MSP.
[2] αὐτὸν RO: οὕτως ex Lat. conj. Naber.
[3] E: φέρων rell.   [4] Hudson: λαβόντες codd.
[5] ἠξίωσε conj. Niese.

strivest so unjustly. How indeed could the opinion
not be false which thou didst hold of me, namely that
I wished to kill thee, or how canst thou be other than
impious toward God when thou art eager to destroy,
and accountest as an enemy, a man who this day had
it in his power to avenge himself and to punish thee,
and yet refused to do so or to avail himself of an
opportunity, which, had it been given to thee to use
against me, thou wouldst never have let slip ? For
when I cut off the skirt of thy mantle, I might at the
same time have cut off thy head." And here he
produced the piece of cloth in token of the truth of
his words. " But yet," he continued, " I refrained
from righteous vengeance, while thou art not ashamed
to nurse unjust hatred against me. May God be judge
thereof and examine the motives of us both." Thereupon Saul, in wonder at his extraordinary escape and
amazed at the youth's forbearance and nature, wailed
aloud. And when David did the like, he replied,
" It is for me to moan,[a] since thou hast brought me
only good, while I have brought thee affliction. Thou
hast shown thyself this day to have the righteousness
of the ancients, who bade those who captured their
enemies in a lonely place to spare their lives.[b] Now,
therefore, I fully believe that God is reserving the
kingdom for thee and that dominion over all the
Hebrews awaits thee. Give me then assurance on
oath that thou wilt not exterminate my race nor, from
rancour against me, destroy my posterity, but wilt
save and preserve my house." David gave the
desired oath and let Saul depart to his kingdom,

Saul is
reconciled
to David.
1 Sam. xxiv.
16 (17).

[a] Unscriptural detail.
[b] An amplification of 1 Sam. xxiv. 19 (20) (of which, however, the text seems to be defective), " If a man find his enemy
will he let him go well away ? "

αὐτὸς δὲ μετὰ τῶν σὺν αὐτῷ εἰς τὴν Μασθηρῶν ἀνέβη στενήν.

292 (5) Ἀποθνήσκει δὲ κατὰ τοῦτον τὸν καιρὸν καὶ Σαμουῆλος ὁ προφήτης, ἀνὴρ οὐ τῆς τυχούσης ἀπολαύσας[1] παρὰ τοῖς Ἑβραίοις τιμῆς· ἐνεφάνισε γὰρ τὴν ἀρετὴν αὐτοῦ καὶ τὴν τοῦ πλήθους πρὸς αὐτὸν εὔνοιαν τὸ πένθος, ὃ ἐπὶ πολὺν χρόνον ὁ λαὸς ἤγετο, καὶ ἡ περὶ τὴν ταφὴν αὐτοῦ καὶ τὴν τῶν νομιζομένων ἀναπλήρωσιν φιλοτιμία τε
293 καὶ σπουδή. θάπτουσι γὰρ αὐτὸν ἐν τῇ πατρίδι Ἀρμαθᾷ καὶ ἐπὶ πολλὰς πάνυ ἡμέρας ἔκλαυσαν, οὐ κοινὸν τοῦτο πάσχοντες ὡς ἐπ' ἀλλοτρίου τελευτῇ,
294 ὡς[2] οἰκεῖον δ' ἕκαστος ἴδιον ποθῶν. ἐγένετο δ' ἀνὴρ δίκαιος καὶ χρηστὸς τὴν φύσιν καὶ διὰ τοῦτο μάλιστα φίλος τῷ θεῷ. ἦρξε δὲ καὶ προέστη τοῦ λαοῦ μετὰ τὴν Ἠλεὶ τοῦ ἀρχιερέως τελευτὴν μόνος μὲν ἔτη δώδεκα, μετὰ δὲ Σαούλου τοῦ βασιλέως δέκα πρὸς τοῖς ὀκτώ. καὶ τὰ μὲν περὶ Σαμουῆλον οὕτω πέρας ἔσχεν.

295 (6) Ἦν δέ τις τῶν Ζιφηνῶν ἐκ πόλεως Ἐμμᾶν[3] πλούσιος καὶ πολυθρέμματος· τρισχιλίων μὲν γὰρ αὐτῷ[4] ποίμνη προβάτων ἐνέμετο, χιλίων δ' αἰγῶν. ταῦτα Δαυίδης ἀσινῆ τηρεῖν τε καὶ ἀβλαβῆ παρήγγελλε τοῖς σὺν αὐτῷ καὶ μήτε ὑπὸ ἐπιθυμίας μήτε ὑπὸ ἐνδείας μήτε ὑπὸ τῆς ἐρημίας καὶ τοῦ δύνασθαι

---

[1] SP: ἀπολάβων RO: ἀπολαύων Niese cum Hudson.
[2] +εἰς MSP.
[3] Ἐμμᾶ MSP Exc.: Ammon Lat.
[4] Cocceji: αὐτοῦ codd. E.

---

[a] Heb. 'al ha-meṣûdāh " up to the stronghold " ; Josephus follows the lxx which takes this as a proper name and, in a duplicate rendering, translates it as εἰς τὴν Μεσσαρὰ στενήν.

while he with his men went up to the pass of Masthera.[a]

(5) About this time the prophet Samuel died, a man who had enjoyed no common esteem among the Hebrews. His virtue and the affection of the multitude for him were manifested by the prolonged mourning which the people made, and by the display and zeal given to his burial and to the observance of the customary rites. For they buried him in his native Armatha and wept for him very many days, with no mere public mourning as for the death of a stranger, but each privately grieving as for his own.[b] He was a man of just and kindly nature and for that reason very dear to God. He was ruler and leader of the people after the death of the high priest Eli, for twelve years alone, and together with King Saul for eighteen more.[c] Such then was the end of Samuel.

Death and burial of Samuel.
1 Sam. xxv. 1.

(6) Now there was a certain Ziphite of the city of Emman,[d] who was wealthy and had much cattle; indeed he maintained a flock of three thousand sheep and a thousand goats. Now David had charged his men to see that these flocks should be safe and unharmed, and that neither through greed nor want nor because they were in the wilderness and could escape detection, should they do them any injury,

The wealthy Nabal churlishly refuses presents to David.
1 Sam. xxv. 2.

[b] The details of the burial and mourning are additions to Scripture.

[c] No figures are given in Scripture; the common rabbinic tradition fixes Samuel's term as prophet at 12 years, another, also found in Julius Africanus, makes it 40 years. Ginzberg plausibly suggests that the latter figure was reached by combining Josephus's statement that Samuel began to prophesy at 12 years, *A.* v. 348, with the rabbinic tradition that Samuel was 52 years old when he died.

[d] Bibl. "A man of Maon"; his possessions were in Carmel, just south of Ziph.

λανθάνειν καταβλάπτειν, τούτων δ' ἁπάντων ἐπάνω
τίθεσθαι τὸ μηδέν"¹ ἀδικεῖν καὶ τὸ τῶν ἀλλοτρίων
ἅπτεσθαι δεινὸν ἡγεῖσθαι καὶ πρόσαντες τῷ θεῷ.
296 ταῦτα δ' ἐδίδασκεν αὐτοὺς οἰόμενος ἀνθρώπῳ χαρίζεσθαι ἀγαθῷ καὶ ταύτης τυγχάνειν ἀξίῳ τῆς
προνοίας· ἦν δὲ Νάβαλος, τοῦτο γὰρ εἶχεν ὄνομα,
σκληρὸς καὶ πονηρὸς τοῖς ἐπιτηδεύμασιν ἐκ κυνικῆς
ἀσκήσεως πεποιημένος τὸν βίον, γυναικὸς δ' ἀγαθῆς
καὶ σώφρονος καὶ τὸ εἶδος σπουδαίας λελογχώς.²
297 πρὸς οὖν τὸν Νάβαλον τοῦτον καθ' ὃν ἔκειρε τὰ
πρόβατα καιρὸν πέμψας ὁ Δαυίδης ἄνδρας δέκα
τῶν σὺν αὐτῷ διὰ τούτων αὐτὸν ἀσπάζεται καὶ
συνεύχεται τοῦτο ποιεῖν ἐπ' ἔτη πολλά· παρασχεῖν
δὲ ἐξ ὧν δυνατός ἐστιν αὐτῷ παρεκάλει μαθόντα³
παρὰ τῶν ποιμένων ὅτι μηδὲν αὐτοὺς ἠδίκησαν,⁴
ἀλλὰ φύλακες αὐτῶν τε καὶ τῶν ποιμνίων γεγόνασι⁴
πολὺν ἐν τῇ ἐρήμῳ διατρίβοντες ἤδη χρόνον· μετα-
298 νοήσει δ' οὐδὲν Δαυίδῃ παρασχόμενος. ταῦτα δὲ
τῶν πεμφθέντων διακονησάντων πρὸς τὸν Νάβαλον
ἀπανθρώπως σφόδρα καὶ σκληρῶς ἀπήντησεν·
ἐρωτήσας γὰρ αὐτούς, τίς ἐστι Δαυίδης, ὡς τὸν
υἱὸν ἤκουσεν Ἰεσσαίου, " νῦν ἄρα," εἶπε, " μέγα
φρονοῦσιν ἐφ' αὑτοῖς οἱ δραπέται καὶ σεμνύνον-
299 ται τοὺς δεσπότας καταλιπόντες." ὀργίζεται δ'
αὐτῶν φρασάντων ὁ Δαυίδης καὶ τετρακοσίους
μὲν ὡπλισμένους αὐτῷ κελεύσας ἕπεσθαι, διακοσίους δὲ φύλακας τῶν σκευῶν καταλιπών, ἤδη γὰρ
εἶχεν ἑξακοσίους, ἐπὶ τὸν Νάβαλον ἐβάδιζεν ὀμόσας

---

¹ μηδένα Exc.: μηδὲν codd. Lat.
² ὡραίας λελαχώς RO.
³ Exc., edd.: μαθόντι codd.
⁴ RO Lat.: ἠδικήσαμεν . . . γεγόναμεν rell.

474

but should hold it more important than all these
things to wrong no man and should reckon it a crime
and an offence against God to touch what belonged to
another. These instructions he gave to his men in the
belief that he was obliging a good man and one worthy
of such consideration.[a] But Nabal—such was his
name—was a hard man and of bad character, who lived
according to the practices of the cynics.[b] He had,
however, been blessed with a wife who was virtuous,
discreet and good to look upon. At the time, then,
when this Nabal was shearing his sheep, David sent
ten of his men by whom he greeted him and joined
him in praying that he might be so employed for
many years to come. He then besought him to grant
him somewhat from his abundant means ; he would
have learnt from his shepherds that David and his
men had done them no wrong, but had been the
guardians of their persons and of their flocks throughout their long sojourn in the wilderness, nor would he
ever repent of having given anything to David. The
messengers acquitted themselves of this mission to
Nabal, but he gave them a very uncivil and harsh
reception. He first asked them who this David was,
and, on being told that he was the son of Jesse,
said, " So then nowadays fugitives think much of
themselves and boast about deserting their masters."
These words being reported to David aroused his
indignation, and bidding four hundred of his men to
follow him in arms and leaving two hundred to guard
the baggage—for he had by now six hundred men—
he marched against Nabal, having sworn utterly to

[a] David's instructions are an amplification of Scripture.
[b] Bibl. " and he was a Calebite " ; lxx, reading Heb.
keleb " dog," καὶ ὁ ἄνθρωπος κυνικός, which Josephus takes
in its technical philosophical sense.

ἐκείνῃ τῇ νυκτὶ τὸν οἶκον αὐτοῦ καὶ τὴν κτῆσιν
ὅλην ἀφανίσειν· οὐ γὰρ ἄχθεσθαι μόνον ὅτι γέγονεν
ἀχάριστος εἰς αὐτούς, μηδὲν ἐπιδοὺς πολλῇ φιλ-
ανθρωπίᾳ πρὸς αὐτὸν χρησαμένοις, ἀλλ' ὅτι καὶ
προσεβλασφήμησε καὶ κακῶς εἶπε μηδὲν ὑπ' αὐτῶν
λελυπημένος.

300   (7) Δούλου δέ τινος τῶν τὰ ποίμνια φυλασσόντων
τὰ τοῦ Ναβάλου πρὸς τὴν δέσποιναν μὲν ἑαυτοῦ
γυναῖκα δ' ἐκείνου κατειπόντος ὅτι πέμψας ὁ
Δαυίδης αὐτῆς πρὸς τὸν ἄνδρα μηδενὸς τύχοι τῶν
μετρίων, ἀλλὰ καὶ προσυβρισθείη βλασφημίαις
δειναῖς πάσῃ περὶ αὐτοὺς προνοίᾳ καὶ φυλακῇ τῶν
ποιμνίων χρησάμενος, γέγονε[1] δὲ τοῦτο ἐπὶ κακῷ
301 τῷ τοῦ δεσπότου καὶ αὐτῆς[2]· ταῦτ' ἐκείνου φήσαντος Ἀβιγαία, προσηγορεύετο γὰρ οὕτως, ἐπι-
σάξασα[3] τοὺς ὄνους καὶ πληρώσασα παντοίων ξενίων
καὶ μηδὲν εἰποῦσα τἀνδρί, ὑπὸ γὰρ μέθης ἀναίσ-
θητος ἦν, ἐπορεύετο πρὸς Δαυίδην· καταβαινούσῃ
δὲ τὰ στενὰ τοῦ ὄρους ἀπήντησε Δαυίδης μετὰ τῶν
302 τετρακοσίων ἐπὶ Νάβαλον ἐρχόμενος. θεασαμένη
δ' αὐτὸν ἡ γυνὴ κατεπήδησε καὶ πεσοῦσα ἐπὶ
πρόσωπον προσεκύνει[4] καὶ τῶν μὲν Ναβάλου λόγων
ἐδεῖτο μὴ μνημονεύειν, οὐ γὰρ ἀγνοεῖν[5] αὐτὸν
ὅμοιον ὄντα τῷ ὀνόματι, Νάβαλος γὰρ κατὰ τὴν
Ἑβραίων γλῶτταν ἀφροσύνην δηλοῖ, αὐτὴ δ' ἀπ-
ελογεῖτο μὴ θεάσασθαι τοὺς πεμφθέντας ὑπ' αὐτοῦ
303 " διὸ συγγίνωσκέ μοι," φησί, " καὶ τῷ θεῷ χάριν

---

[1] RO: γεγονέναι rell.   [2] αὐτῆς ex Lat. ins. Niese.
[3] εὐθέως ἐπισ. SP.   [4] προσεκύνησε ROE.
[5] οὐ γὰρ ἀγν. om. ROE Lat.

---

[a] The latter motive is not found in Scripture.

destroy his house and all his possessions that selfsame night ; for he was angry not merely at his ingratitude in making no return to those who had shown
him such great kindness, but also because he had
further insulted and abused those from whom he had
received no injury.[a]

(7) But one of the slaves [b] that kept the flocks of
Nabal brought word to his mistress, Nabal's wife,
that David had sent a message to her husband and
not only had failed to receive a fair answer but had
been further insulted with shocking abuse, although
he had shown all consideration to the shepherds
and had protected their flocks. Such action, he
added, would result in mischief for his master and
for herself. At the servant's story, Abigaia[c]—such
was her name—saddled her asses, loaded them with
all manner of presents [d] and, without a word to her
husband, who was insensible from drink,[e] set off to
find David. And as she was descending the defiles
of the mountain, she was met by David coming
against Nabal with his four hundred men. At sight
of him the woman leapt to the ground, and falling
on her face bowed down before him ; she entreated
him not to mind the words of Nabal, for he could not
be ignorant that the man was like his name (*Nabal*
in the Hebrew tongue signifies " folly "),[f] while for
herself she pleaded that she had not seen David's
messengers. " Wherefore pardon me," she said,
" and render thanks to God who has prevented thee

Abigail
(Abigaia),
Nabal's wife,
appeases
David by
presents.
1 Sam. xxv.
14.

---

[b] Bibl. " young men."
[c] Bibl. Abigail, LXX 'Αβειγαία.
[d] In the form of provisions, according to Scripture.
[e] Unscriptural detail, anticipating 1 Sam. xxv. 36, *cf.* § 306.
[f] So also the LXX translates.

ἔχε κωλύοντί σε μιανθῆναι ἀνθρωπίνῳ αἵματι·
μένοντα γάρ σε καθαρὸν ἐκεῖνος αὐτὸς ἐκδικήσει
παρὰ τῶν πονηρῶν· ἃ γὰρ ἐκδέχεται κακὰ Νάβαλον
ταῦτα καὶ ταῖς τῶν ἐχθρῶν σου κεφαλαῖς ἐμπέσοι.

304 γενοῦ δὲ εὐμενής μοι κρίνας ἀξίαν τοῦ παρ' ἐμοῦ
ταῦτα δέξασθαι, καὶ τὸν θυμὸν καὶ τὴν ὀργὴν τὴν
ἐπὶ τὸν ἄνδρα μου καὶ τὸν οἶκον αὐτοῦ εἰς τὴν
ἐμὴν τιμὴν ἄφες· πρέπει γὰρ ἡμέρῳ σοι καὶ φιλαν-
θρώπῳ τυγχάνειν, καὶ ταῦτα μέλλοντι βασιλεύειν."

305 ὁ δὲ τὰ δῶρα δεξάμενος "ἀλλά σε," φησίν, "ὦ
γύναι, θεὸς εὐμενὴς ἤγαγε πρὸς ἡμᾶς τήμερον· οὐ
γὰρ ἂν τὴν ἐπερχομένην ἡμέραν εἶδες, ἐμοῦ τὸν
οἶκον τὸν Ναβάλου διὰ τῆσδε τῆς νυκτὸς ὀμόσαντος
ἀπολέσειν[1] καὶ μηδένα ὑμῶν ἀπολείψειν ἀπὸ ἀνδρὸς[2]
πονηροῦ καὶ ἀχαρίστου πρὸς ἐμὲ καὶ τοὺς ἐμοὺς
ἑταίρους γενομένου. νῦν δὲ φθάσασα προέλαβες
καταμειλίξασθαί μου τὸν θυμὸν κηδομένου σου
τοῦ θεοῦ. ἀλλὰ Νάβαλος μὲν κἂν ἀφεθῇ διὰ σὲ
νῦν τῆς τιμωρίας οὐ φεύξεται τὴν δίκην, ἀλλ' ὁ
τρόπος αὐτὸν ἀπολεῖ λαβὼν αἰτίαν ἄλλην."

306 (8) Ταῦτ' εἰπὼν ἀπολύει τὴν γυναῖκα· ἡ δ' εἰς
τὸν οἶκον ἐλθοῦσα καὶ καταλαβοῦσα τὸν ἄνδρα μετὰ
πολλῶν εὐωχούμενον καὶ κεκαρωμένον ἤδη, τότε
μὲν οὐδὲν τῶν γεγενημένων διεσάφει, τῇ δὲ ἐπιούσῃ νήφοντι ἅπαντα δηλώσασα παρεθῆναι καὶ πᾶν
αὐτῷ νεκρωθῆναι τὸ σῶμα ὑπὸ τῶν λόγων καὶ
τῆς ἐπ' αὐτοῖς λύπης ἐποίησε· καὶ δέκα οὐ πλείους
ἐπιζήσας ἡμέρας τὸν βίον κατέστρεψεν ὁ Νάβαλος

307 ἀκούσας δ' αὐτοῦ τὴν τελευτὴν ὁ Δαυίδης ἐκδική-
θῆναι μὲν αὐτὸν ὑπὸ τοῦ θεοῦ καλῶς ἔλεγεν· ἀπο-

---

[1] Niese: ἀπολέσαι codd.   [2] + ἕως τετραπόδου RO.

478

from soiling thy hands with human blood. For if thou remainest clean, He Himself will avenge thee on the wicked ; and may the evil that awaits Nabal fall likewise on the heads of thy foes. But be gracious to me in deigning to receive these presents from me, and, out of regard for me, dismiss thy indignation and wrath against my husband and against his house. For it becomes thee to show mildness and humanity, especially as thou art destined to be king." And David accepted the presents and said, " In truth, lady, it was gracious God who led thee to us this day ; else thou wouldst not have seen the coming day, for I had sworn to destroy the house of Nabal this very night and to leave not one of you, belonging as you do to a man who has been so mean and ungrateful to me and to my comrades. But now thou hast forestalled me and mollified my wrath, since thou art in God's care. But as for Nabal, though for thy sake to-day he be spared chastisement, yet will he not escape retribution, but his conduct will find another occasion to prove his ruin." [a]

(8) Having so spoken, he dismissed the woman. And she, returning to her home, found her husband carousing with a large company and already heavy with drink, and so, at the moment, she revealed nothing of what had passed ; but on the morrow, when he was sober, she told him all, causing him to collapse and his whole body to become dead through her words and the pain they produced. Ten days and no more did Nabal remain alive and then departed this life. And when David heard of his death, he said that he had been well avenged by God, for Nabal

Death of Nabal ; David marries Abigail. 1 Sam. xxv. 36.

_____

[a] This prediction is unscriptural.

θανεῖν γὰρ Νάβαλον ὑπὸ τῆς ἰδίας πονηρίας καὶ
δοῦναι δίκην αὐτῷ καθαρὰν ἔχοντι τὴν δεξιάν·
ἔγνω δὲ καὶ τότε τοὺς πονηροὺς ἐλαυνομένους ὑπὸ
τοῦ θεοῦ,[1] μηδενὸς τῶν ἐν ἀνθρώποις ὑπερορῶντος,
διδόντος δὲ τοῖς μὲν ἀγαθοῖς τὰ ὅμοια, τοῖς δὲ
308 πονηροῖς ὀξεῖαν[2] ἐπιφέροντος τὴν ποινήν. πέμψας
δ' αὐτοῦ πρὸς τὴν γυναῖκα συνοικήσουσαν καὶ
γαμηθησομένην ἐκάλει πρὸς αὐτόν· ἡ δὲ ἀναξία
μὲν εἶναι καὶ ποδῶν ἅψασθαι τῶν ἐκείνου πρὸς
τοὺς παρόντας ἔλεγεν, ὅμως δὲ μετὰ πάσης τῆς[3]
θεραπείας ἧκε. καὶ συνῴκησε μὲν αὐτῷ ταύτην
λαβοῦσα τὴν τιμὴν καὶ διὰ τὸ τὸν τρόπον σώφρονα
εἶναι καὶ δίκαιον, τυχοῦσα δ' αὐτῆς καὶ διὰ τὸ
309 κάλλος. εἶχε δὲ Δαυίδης γυναῖκα πρότερον, ἣν ἐξ
'Αβισάρου πόλεως ἔγημε· Μελχὰν δὲ τὴν Σαούλου
τοῦ βασιλέως θυγατέρα τὴν γενομένην τοῦ Δαυίδου
γυναῖκα ὁ πατὴρ τῷ Φελτίῳ υἱῷ Λίσου συνέζευξεν
ἐκ πόλεως ὄντι Γεθλᾶς.[4]
310   (9) Μετὰ ταῦτά τινες ἐλθόντες τῶν Ζιφηνῶν
ἀπήγγειλαν τῷ Σαούλῳ, ὡς εἴη πάλιν ὁ Δαυίδης
ἐν τῇ χώρᾳ αὐτῶν καὶ δύνανται συλλαβεῖν αὐτὸν
βουλομένῳ συνεργῆσαι. ὁ δὲ μετὰ τρισχιλίων
ὁπλιτῶν ἐβάδιζεν ἐπ' αὐτὸν καὶ νυκτὸς ἐπελθούσης
ἐστρατοπέδευσεν ἐπί τινι τόπῳ Σικέλλα[5] λεγο-

---

[1] + καὶ codd.   [2] ROP: ἀξίαν MS Exc. Lat.
[3] + ἰδίας E Lat.
[4] Goliath Lat. (cf. lxx[L]).
[5] Σεκέλλα M: Σεκελλὰ (Σεκελᾶ infra) SP: Sicela Lat.

---

[a] Variant "condign."
[b] 1 Sam. xxv. 41 "let thine handmaid be a servant to wash
the feet of the servants of my lord."
[c] Called Achima below, §320; Bibl. Ahinoam, lxx 'Αχεινάαι
(v.l. 'Αχινάαμ).

480

had died through his own wickedness and had given
him revenge, while he himself still had clean hands. At
the same time he learnt that the wicked are pursued
by God who overlooks no act of man but repays the
good in kind, while He inflicts swift[a] punishment
upon the wicked. David then sent to the woman,
inviting her to live with him and become his wife.
She replied to the messengers that she was unworthy
so much as to touch his feet,[b] but came nevertheless
with all her servants. And so she lived with him,
having attained that honour because of her modest
and upright character and also because of her beauty.
David already had a wife,[c] whom he had taken from
the city of Abisar[d]; as for Melcha, the daughter of
Saul and once the wife of David, her father had given
her in marriage to Pheltias[e] son of Lisos[f] of the city
of Gethla.[g]

(9) [h] After this certain of the Ziphites came and
informed Saul that David was again in their country
and that they could catch him, if Saul would lend
them aid. So with three thousand soldiers he
marched against him and, on the approach of night,
encamped at a place called Sikella.[i] David, hearing

David spares
Saul's life a
second time.
1 Sam.
xxvi. 1.

---

[d] Bibl. Jezreel, LXX Ἰεζραέλ (*v.l.* Ἰσραήλ κτλ.).

[e] Bibl. Phalti, LXX Φαλτεί (Φελτεί).

[f] Bibl. Laish, LXX Ἀμείς, Luc. Ἰωάς.

[g] Bibl. Gallim, LXX Ῥομμά, Luc. Γολιάθ.

[h] The following account of David's second encounter with
Saul (1 Sam. xxvi.) is obviously a variant of that found in
1 Sam. xxiv., *cf.* §§ 282 ff.

[i] In 1 Sam. xxvi. 1 Heb. has Hachilah, LXX Χελμάθ (*v.l.*
Ἀχιλά), Luc. Ἐχελά ; in vs. 4 Heb. has " Saul came in
readiness " (A.V. " in very deed "), LXX ἕτοιμος εἰς Κεειλά,
Luc. Σεκελάγ. Josephus either followed a LXX reading
similar to Lucian's, or confused the name here with Σεκέλλα
=bibl. Ziklag mentioned below, § 322.

311 μένῳ. Δαυίδης δὲ ἀκούσας τὸν Σαοῦλον ἐπ' αὐτὸν
ἥκοντα πέμψας κατασκόπους ἐκέλευσε δηλοῦν αὐτῷ,
ποῦ τῆς χώρας Σαοῦλος ἤδη προεληλύθοι.[1] τῶν
δ' ἐν Σικέλλᾳ φρασάντων διανυκτερεύειν διαλαθὼν
τοὺς ἰδίους εἰς τὸ τοῦ Σαούλου στρατόπεδον παραγίνεται ἐπαγόμενος τὸν ἐκ τῆς ἀδελφῆς αὐτοῦ
Σαρουίας Ἀβισαῖον[a] καὶ Ἀβιμέλεχον[2] τὸν Χετ-
312 ταῖον. τοῦ δὲ Σαούλου κοιμωμένου καὶ περὶ αὐτὸν ἐν κύκλῳ τῶν ὁπλιτῶν καὶ τοῦ στρατηγοῦ
Ἀβεννήρου κειμένων, ὁ Δαυίδης εἰσελθὼν εἰς τὸ
στρατόπεδον τὸ τοῦ βασιλέως οὔτ' αὐτὸς ἀναιρεῖ
τὸν Σαοῦλον, ἐπιγνοὺς αὐτοῦ τὴν κοίτην ἐκ τοῦ
δόρατος, τοῦτο γὰρ αὐτῷ παρεπεπήγει, οὔτε τὸν
Ἀβισαῖον βουλόμενον φονεῦσαι καὶ πρὸς τοῦτο
ὡρμηκότα εἴασεν, ἀλλὰ τὸν ὑπὸ τοῦ θεοῦ κεχειρο-
τονημένον βασιλέα φήσας εἶναι δεινὸν ἀποκτεῖναι
κἂν ᾖ πονηρός, ἥξειν γὰρ αὐτῷ παρὰ τοῦ δόντος
τὴν ἀρχὴν σὺν χρόνῳ τὴν δίκην, ἐπέσχε τῆς ὁρμῆς.
313 σύμβολον δὲ τοῦ κτεῖναι δυνηθεὶς ἀποσχέσθαι
λαβὼν αὐτοῦ τὸ δόρυ καὶ τὸν φακὸν τοῦ ὕδατος,
ὃς ἦν παρ' αὐτῷ κείμενος[3] τῷ Σαούλῳ, μηδενὸς
αἰσθομένου τῶν ἐν τῷ στρατοπέδῳ πάντων δὲ
κατακοιμωμένων ἐξῆλθεν, ἀδεῶς πάντ' ἐργασάμενος ὅσα καὶ τοῦ καιροῦ δόντος αὐτῷ καὶ τῆς
314 τόλμης διέθηκε τοὺς τοῦ βασιλέως. διαβὰς δὲ τὸν
χείμαρρον καὶ ἐπὶ τὴν κορυφὴν ἀνελθὼν τοῦ ὄρους,

---

[1] Niese: προσεληλύθοι, -ει codd.
[2] Ἀχιμέλεχον MSP Lat.
[3] ὃς . . . κειμ.] + κοιμωμένῳ P(S): ὃς κοιμωμένῳ παρέκειτο
M: appositum dormienti Saul Lat.

---

[a] Bibl. Abishai, lxx Ἀβεσσά (v.l. Ἀβεισά κτλ.).

that Saul was coming against him, sent out scouts
with orders to report what part of the country Saul
had now reached ; and when they told him that he
was passing the night at Sikella, he set off, without
the knowledge of his men, for Saul's camp, taking
with him Abisai,[a] son of his sister Saruia,[b] and
Abimelech[c] the Hittite. Saul was sleeping, with
his soldiers and their commander Abenner lying in
a circle around him, when David penetrated to the
king's camp ; yet he would not himself slay Saul,
whose sleeping-place he recognized from the spear
fixed in the ground at his side, nor would he permit
Abisai, who wished to kill him and darted forward
with that intent, to do so. He objected that it was
monstrous to slay the king elected of God, even if
he was a wicked man, saying that from Him who had
given him the sovereignty punishment would come
in due time ; and so he stayed Abisai from his purpose. However, in token that he might have slain
him and yet had refrained, he took the spear and the
flask of water that was placed just beside Saul and,
unseen by any in the camp where all lay fast asleep,
he passed out, having safely accomplished all the
things that the favourable opportunity and his daring
had enabled him to inflict on the king's men. Then, David re-
after crossing a stream[d] and climbing to the top of bukes Abner

[b] Bibl. Zeruiah (Heb. *Ṣerúyāh*), LXX = Josephus. That she
was David's sister is stated in 1 Chron. ii. 16.

[c] Variant (as in Scripture) Achimelech ; the LXX MSS. also
vary between the two forms. According to Scripture, however, only Abishai accompanied David.

[d] 1 Sam. xxvi. 13 " Then David went over to the other side
and stood on the top of a hill afar off ; a great space being
between them." Josephus naturally thought of the space
as being a *wady*, the bed of a winter stream (χειμάρρους),
such as are common in Palestine.

ὅθεν ἔμελλεν ἐξάκουστος εἶναι, ἐμβοήσας τοῖς στρατιώταις τοῦ Σαούλου καὶ τῷ στρατηγῷ Ἀβεν-
νήρῳ διανίστησιν αὐτοὺς ἐκ τοῦ ὕπνου τοῦτόν τε
ἐφώνει καὶ τὸν λαόν. ἐπακούσαντος δὲ τοῦ στρατηγοῦ καὶ τίς ὁ καλέσας αὐτόν ἐστιν ἐρομένου
315 Δαυίδης εἶπεν· '' ἐγώ, παῖς μὲν Ἰεσσαίου, φυγὰς
δὲ ὑμέτερος. ἀλλὰ τί δήποτε μέγας τε ὢν καὶ
τὴν πρώτην ἔχων παρὰ τῷ βασιλεῖ τιμήν, οὕτως
ἀμελῶς τὸ τοῦ δεσπότου φυλάσσεις σῶμα, καὶ
ὕπνος ἡδίων ἐστί σοι τῆς τούτου σωτηρίας καὶ
προνοίας; θανάτου γὰρ ἄξια ταῦτα καὶ τιμωρίας,
οἵ γε μικρὸν ἔμπροσθεν εἰσελθόντας τινὰς ὑμῶν
εἰς τὸ στρατόπεδον ἐπὶ τὸν βασιλέα καὶ πάντας
τοὺς ἄλλους[1] οὐκ ἐνοήσατε. ζήτησον οὖν τὸ δόρυ
τοῦ βασιλέως καὶ τὸν φακὸν τοῦ ὕδατος καὶ
μαθήσῃ πηλίκον ὑμᾶς ἔλαθε κακὸν ἐντὸς γενό-
316 μενον.'' Σαοῦλος δὲ γνωρίσας τὴν τοῦ Δαυίδου
φωνὴν καὶ μαθὼν ὅτι λαβὼν αὐτὸν ἔκδοτον ὑπὸ
τοῦ ὕπνου καὶ τῆς τῶν φυλασσόντων ἀμελείας οὐκ
ἀπέκτεινεν, ἀλλ' ἐφείσατο δικαίως ἂν αὐτὸν ἀνελών,
χάριν ἔχειν αὐτῷ τῆς σωτηρίας ἔλεγε καὶ παρεκάλει θαρροῦντα καὶ μηδὲν ἔτι πείσεσθαι δεινὸν
ἐξ αὐτοῦ φοβούμενον ἀναχωρεῖν ἐπὶ τὰ οἰκεῖα·
317 πεπεῖσθαι γὰρ ὅτι μηδ' αὐτὸν[2] οὕτως ἀγαπήσειεν,
ὡς ὑπ' ἐκείνου στέργεται, ὃς[3] τὸν μὲν φυλάττειν
αὐτὸν δυνάμενον καὶ πολλὰ δείγματα τῆς εὐνοίας
παρεσχημένον ἐλαύνοι καὶ τοσοῦτον ἐν φυγῇ χρόνον
καὶ ταῖς περὶ τὴν ψυχὴν ἀγωνίαις ἠνάγκασε ζῆσαι
φίλων καὶ συγγενῶν ἔρημον· αὐτὸς δ' οὐ παύεται

---

[1] ἐπὶ . . . ἄλλους om. RO: καὶ . . . ἄλλους om. E.
[2] ex Lat. Bekker: αὐτὸν codd.
[3] ὡς RO.

a hill from which his voice could be heard, he shouted to the troops of Saul and to their commander Abenner, and, awaking them from their sleep, addressed him and his people. When the commander heard this and asked who was calling him, David replied, " I, son of Jesse, the fugitive from you.[a] But how comes it that one so great as thou, holding the first rank in the king's service, art so negligent in guarding the person of thy master, and that sleep is more to thy liking than his safety and protection ? This conduct indeed merits the punishment of death, for à little while since some men penetrated right through your camp to the king's person and to all the others, and you did not even perceive it. Look now for the king's spear and his flask of water and thou wilt learn what mischief has befallen in your midst without your knowing of it." Then Saul, when he recognized the voice of David and learned that though he had had him at his mercy, being asleep and neglected by his guards, he had yet not slain him but spared the life which he might justly have taken, gave him thanks for his preservation and exhorted him to be of good courage and, without fear of suffering further injury from himself, to return to his home.[b] For, he said, he was now persuaded that he did not love his own self so well as he was loved by David, seeing that he had pursued this man who might have been his safeguard and who had given many proofs of his loyalty, and that he had forced him to live so long in exile, in terror of his life, bereft of friends and of kindred, while he himself had been repeatedly spared by him

for his neglect of Saul.

1 Sam. xxvi. 13.

Saul is again reconciled to David.

1 Sam. xxvi. 17.

[a] This phrase is unscriptural. There is also some amplification in the rest of David's speech.

[b] Josephus omits David's protest against Saul's treatment of him, 1 Sam. xxvi. 18-20.

πολλάκις[1] ὑπ' αὐτοῦ σωζόμενος, οὐδὲ τὴν ψυχὴν
318 φανερῶς ἀπολλυμένην λαμβάνων. ὁ δὲ Δαυίδης
πέμψαντα ἀπολαβεῖν ἐκέλευσε τὸ δόρυ καὶ τὸν
φακὸν τοῦ ὕδατος, ἐπειπὼν ὡς " ὁ θεὸς ἑκατέρῳ
τῆς ἰδίας φύσεως καὶ τῶν κατ' αὐτὴν πεπραγμένων ἔσται δικαστής, ὃς ὅτι καὶ κατὰ τὴν παροῦσαν
ἡμέραν ἀποκτεῖναί σε δυνηθεὶς ἀπεσχόμην οἶδε."
319 (10) Καὶ Σαοῦλος μὲν δεύτερον διαφυγὼν τὰς
Δαυίδου χεῖρας εἰς τὰ βασίλεια καὶ τὴν οἰκείαν
ἀπηλλάσσετο, φοβηθεὶς δὲ Δαυίδης μὴ μένων
αὐτόθι συλληφθῇ ὑπὸ τοῦ Σαούλου, συμφέρειν
ἔκρινεν εἰς τὴν Παλαιστίνην καταβὰς[2] διατρίβειν
ἐν αὐτῇ, καὶ μετὰ τῶν ἑξακοσίων, οἳ περὶ αὐτὸν
ἦσαν, παραγίνεται πρὸς Ἀγχοῦν τὸν Γίττης βασι-
320 λέα· μία δ' ἦν αὕτη τῶν πέντε πόλεων. δεξαμένου
δ' αὐτὸν τοῦ βασιλέως σὺν τοῖς ἀνδράσι καὶ δόντος
οἰκητήριον, ἔχων ἅμα καὶ τὰς δύο γυναῖκας Ἀχι-
μὰν καὶ Ἀβιγαίαν διῆγεν ἐν τῇ Γίττῃ. Σαούλῳ
δὲ ταῦτ' ἀκούσαντι λόγος οὐκέτ' ἦν πέμπειν ἐπ'
αὐτὸν ἢ βαδίζειν· δὶς γὰρ ἤδη κινδυνεῦσαι παρὰ
μικρὸν ἐπ' ἐκείνῳ γενόμενον, συλλαβεῖν αὐτὸν σπου-
321 δάσαντα. Δαυίδῃ δ' οὐκ ἔδοξεν ἐν τῇ πόλει τῶν
Γιττῶν μένειν, ἀλλ' ἐδεήθη τοῦ βασιλέως αὐτῶν,
ἵν' ἐπειδὴ φιλανθρώπως αὐτὸν ὑπεδέξατο καὶ τοῦτο
χαρίσηται, τόπον τινὰ τῆς χώρας δοὺς αὐτῷ πρὸς
κατοίκησιν· αἰδεῖσθαι γὰρ διατρίβων ἐν τῇ πόλει
322 βαρὺς αὐτῷ καὶ φορτικὸς εἶναι. δίδωσι δὲ Ἀγχοῦς

---

[1] πολλάκις om. RO.
[2] ex Lat. Niese: ἀναβὰς codd.

---

[a] Saul's speech is greatly amplified by Josephus.

and had received at his hands a life clearly marked
for destruction.[a] David then bade him send someone to fetch the spear and the flask of water,[b] adding,
" God shall be judge of the character of either of us
and of the actions arising therefrom. He knows that
when this day I had power to slay thee I refrained."

(10) So Saul, having for the second time escaped
from David's hands, returned to his palace and his
country ; but David, fearful of being captured by
Saul if he remained where he was, deemed it wise to
go down to the land of the Philistines and abide there.
With his band of six hundred followers he betook himself to Anchūs,[c] king of Gitta, which was one of their
five cities.[d] The king welcomed him and his men and
gave them a habitation ; and so, along with his two
wives, Achima[e] and Abigaia, he settled in Gitta.
Saul, on hearing of this, thought no more of sending
or marching against him, for twice already he had
been in imminent danger of falling into his hands
while striving to catch him.[f] David, however, was
not minded to remain in the city of Gitta, but besought its king, since he had given him kindly welcome, to grant one favour more and give him some
place in his country to dwell in ; he had scruples, he
said, about being a burden and encumbrance to him
by continuing to live in that city.[g] So Anchūs gave

David is
welcomed
by Achish
(Anchus),
king of
Gath, and
settles in
Philistia.
1 Sam
xxvii. 1.

[b] The return of the flask of water is not mentioned in
Scripture.
[c] Bibl. Achish, *cf.* § 245 note.
[d] The five Philistine cities were Gath (Gitta), Ekron
(Akkaron), Ascalon, Gaza, Ashdod (Azotus), *cf.* *A.* v. 128,
vi. 8.
[e] Bibl. Ahinoam, *cf.* § 309 note.
[f] This reason is not mentioned in Scripture.
[g] David's scrupulous request is an amplification of 1 Sam.
xxvii. 5.

αὐτῷ κώμην τινὰ Σέκελλαν καλουμένην, ἣν βασιλεύσας ὁ Δαυίδης ἀγαπῶν ἴδιον κτῆμα ἐτίμησεν
εἶναι καὶ οἱ παῖδες αὐτοῦ. ἀλλὰ περὶ μὲν τούτων
ἐν ἄλλοις δηλώσομεν· ὁ δὲ χρόνος ὃν κατῴκησε
Δαυίδης ἐν Σεκέλλᾳ τῆς Παλαιστίνης ἐγένετο
323 μῆνες τέσσαρες πρὸς ταῖς εἴκοσιν ἡμέραις. ἐπ-
ερχόμενος δὲ λάθρα τοῖς πλησιοχώροις τῶν Παλαιστίνων Σερρίταις καὶ Ἀμαληκίταις διήρπαζεν
αὐτῶν τὴν χώραν καὶ λείαν πολλὴν κτηνῶν καὶ
καμήλων λαμβάνων ὑπέστρεφεν· ἀνθρώπων γὰρ
ἀπείχετο δεδιὼς μὴ καταμηνύσωσιν αὐτὸν πρὸς
Ἀγχοῦν τὸν βασιλέα, τὸ μέντοι γε τῆς λείας μέρος
324 αὐτῷ δωρεὰν ἔπεμπε. τοῦ δὲ βασιλέως πυθομένου τίσιν ἐπιθέμενος τὴν λείαν ἀπήλασε; τοῖς
πρὸς τὸν νότον τῶν Ἰουδαίων τετραμμένοις καὶ
ἐν τῇ πεδιάδι κατοικοῦσιν εἰπὼν πείθει τὸν Ἀγχοῦν
φρονῆσαι οὕτως· ἤλπισε γὰρ οὗτος ὅτι Δαυίδης
ἐμίσησε τὸ ἴδιον ἔθνος, καὶ δοῦλον ἕξειν παρ' ὃν
ζῇ χρόνον ἐν τοῖς αὐτοῦ καταμένοντα.
325 (xiv. 1) Κατὰ δὲ τὸν αὐτὸν καιρὸν τῶν Παλαιστίνων ἐπὶ τοὺς Ἰσραηλίτας στρατεύειν διεγνω-
κότων καὶ περιπεμψάντων πρὸς τοὺς συμμάχους
ἅπαντας, ἵνα παρῶσιν[1] αὐτοῖς εἰς τὸν πόλεμον εἰς

---

[1] συμπαρῶσιν MSP.

---

[a] Bibl. Ziklag (Heb. Ṣiqlag), LXX Σεκελάκ. The site is
uncertain; it may be the modern *Khirbet Zuḥeiliqah*, about
10 miles S.E. of Gaza.
[b] 1 Sam. xxvii. 6 " Wherefore Ziklag pertaineth to the
kings of Judah unto this day."
[c] The only other reference to Ziklag is in §§ 356 ff. where
its sack by the Amalekites is described.
[d] Heb. " a year (lit. " days ") and four months," LXX " four
months."

him a certain village called Sekella,^{a} which David so
well liked after becoming king that he regarded it
as his private domain, as did his sons after him.^{b} But
of that we shall speak elsewhere.^{c} Now the time
during which David dwelt in Sekella in Philistia was
four months and twenty days.^{d} He made clandestine raids on the neighbours of the Philistines, the
Serrites ^{e} and Amalekites, ravaging their country and
returning with abundant booty of cattle and camels ;
he refrained from (taking captive) ^{f} any men, for fear
that they would denounce him to King Anchūs, to
whom, however, he sent a present of a portion of the
spoils.^{g} And when the king inquired whom he had
attacked to have carried off all this booty, he said it was
the people lying southward of the Judaeans, inhabiting
the plain,^{h} and succeeded in making Anchūs believe
this. For the king had hopes that David had come
to hate ^{i} his own nation and that he would have him
for his servant so long as he lived, settled among his
own people.

(xiv. 1) About the same time the Philistines resolved to take the field against the Israelites and
sent word around to all their allies to join them at

David
makes raids
from Ziklag
(Sekella) on
neighbour-
ing tribes.
1 Sam.
xxvii. 8.

Achish en-
lists David
in Philistine

^{e} Bibl. the Geshurite and Girzite (Targum Gizrite, A.V.
Gezrite), LXX τὸν Γεσειρί, Luc. τὸν Γεσουραῖον καὶ τὸν Ἰεζραῖον.
^{f} A euphemism for " killed," cf. 1 Sam. xxvii. 9, 11 " and
left neither man nor woman alive." Other translators take
ἀπείχετο in its usual sense of " spared " and note the contra-
diction to Scripture.
^{g} Scripture does not say that David sent Achish a portion
of the spoils.
^{h} 1 Sam. xxvii. 10 specifies the peoples involved.
^{i} So the Targum of 1 Sam. xxvii. 12 ; Heb. " is in bad
odour among his people " (A.V. " made his people Israel
utterly to abhor him "), LXX " is put to shame among his
people."

Ῥεγάν,[1] ἔνθεν ἔμελλον ἀθροισθέντες ἐξορμᾶν ἐπὶ
τοὺς Ἑβραίους, ὁ τῶν Γιττῶν βασιλεὺς Ἀγχοῦς
συμμαχῆσαι τὸν Δαυίδην αὐτῷ μετὰ τῶν ἰδίων
326 ὁπλιτῶν ἐκέλευσε.[2] τοῦ δὲ προθύμως ὑποσχομένου
καὶ φήσαντος παραστῆναι καιρόν, ἐν ᾧ τὴν ἀμοιβὴν
αὐτῷ τῆς εὐεργεσίας καὶ τῆς ξενίας ἀποδώσει,
ποιήσειν αὐτὸν καὶ[3] φύλακα τοῦ σώματος μετὰ τὴν
νίκην καὶ τοὺς ἀγῶνας τοὺς πρὸς τοὺς πολεμίους
κατὰ νοῦν χωρήσαντας αὐτοῖς ἐπηγγείλατο, τῆς
τιμῆς καὶ πίστεως ὑποσχέσει τὸ πρόθυμον αὐτοῦ
μᾶλλον αὔξων.

327   (2) Ἔτυχε δὲ Σαοῦλος ὁ τῶν Ἑβραίων βασιλεὺς
τοὺς μάντεις καὶ τοὺς ἐγγαστριμύθους καὶ πᾶσαν
τὴν τοιαύτην τέχνην ἐκ τῆς χώρας ἐκβεβληκὼς
ἔξω τῶν προφητῶν. ἀκούσας δὲ τοὺς Παλαιστίνους ἤδη παρόντας καὶ ἔγγιστα Σούνης πόλεως
ἐν τῷ πεδίῳ[4] ἐστρατοπεδευκότας ἐξώρμησεν ἐπ᾽
328 αὐτοὺς μετὰ τῆς δυνάμεως. καὶ παραγενόμενος
πρὸς ὄρει τινὶ Γελβουὲ καλουμένῳ βάλλεται στρατόπεδον ἀντικρὺ τῶν πολεμίων. ταράττει δ᾽ αὐτὸν

---

[1] Ῥεγγᾶν MS : Ῥέγγαν P : Ῥιγὰν O : Rella Lat. : φάραγγα(ν)
conj. Mez.
[2] ἐκέλευε E : ἐπὶ τοὺς Ἑβραίους ἠξίου MSP Lat.
[3] ἀποδώσει . . . καὶ] ex Lat. Niese : ἀποδώσειν αὐτὸν καὶ
RO : ἀποδώσειν καὶ ποιήσειν αὐτὸν M : αὐτὸν ἀποδώσειν καὶ
ποιήσειν αὐτὸν SP.
[4] +κειμένης SP Exc. Lat. (-ῃ M).

---

[a] No such place is mentioned in Scripture ; it is explained
by Mez *ap.* Thackeray, *op. cit.* p. 88 n. 39, as a corruption
of φάραγγα(ν) " valley," which was, in turn, a mistranslation
of the Targum ḥêlā meaning both " valley," and " warfare "

Rega[a] whence they would make a combined assault army. upon the Hebrews. Accordingly Anchūs, king of Gitta, bade David aid him with his own soldiers. David promptly promised to do so, declaring that here was an opportunity for him to repay Anchūs for his good offices and hospitality, whereupon the king undertook to make him his bodyguard[b] after the victory, if the outcome of the struggle against the enemy should be favourable to them.[c] By this promise of honour and confidence he hoped to increase David's ardour still more.

1 Sam.
xxviii. 1.

(2) Now Saul, the king of the Hebrews, had, as it happened, banished from the country the diviners, ventriloquists[d] and all practitioners of such arts, except the prophets.[e] Hearing now that the Philistines were upon him and had encamped quite close to the city of Sūnē[f] in the plain, he went out against them at the head of his forces, and, on reaching a mountain called Gelboue,[g] pitched his camp over against the enemy. But here he was greatly dis-

Saul and
the witch
of Endor.
1 Sam.
xxviii. 3.

or " host "—the latter rendering being called for by the Heb. *ṣābā'* " warfare " in 1 Sam. xxviii. 1.

[b] Bibl. " keeper of my head," LXX ἀρχισωματοφύλακα " chief of the bodyguard."

[c] In Scripture, Achish does not make the conferring of the title conditional upon victory in battle.

[d] So the LXX translates Heb. *'ōb* (A.V. " one that had familiar spirits "); the exact meaning is unknown, but its Biblical use and Jewish tradition show that a talisman as an instrument of divination is meant, rather than a person— the latter being called in Hebrew *ba'al 'ōb* " possessor of the *'ōb*."

[e] The prophets are not expressly excepted in Scripture.

[f] Bibl. Shunem, LXX Σωμάν (*v.l.* Σωνάμ); the modern *Solam* in the Plain of Esdraelon, about half-way between Nazareth and Mt. Gilboa in a N.W.–S.E. line.

[g] So the LXX; bibl. Gilboa, modern *Jebel Fuḳu'a.*

οὐχ ὡς ἔτυχεν ἰδόντα[1] ἡ τῶν ἐχθρῶν δύναμις
πολλή τε οὖσα καὶ τῆς οἰκείας κρείττων ὑπονοου-
μένη, καὶ τὸν θεὸν διὰ τῶν προφητῶν ἠρώτα περὶ
τῆς μάχης καὶ τοῦ περὶ ταύτην ἐσομένου τέλους
329 προειπεῖν. οὐκ ἀποκρινομένου δὲ τοῦ θεοῦ ἔτι
μᾶλλον ὁ Σαοῦλος κατέδεισε καὶ τὴν ψυχὴν ἀν-
έπεσε, τὸ κακὸν οἷον εἰκὸς οὐ παρόντος αὐτῷ κατὰ
χεῖρα τοῦ θείου προορώμενος. ζητηθῆναι δ' αὐτῷ
κελεύει γύναιόν τι τῶν ἐγγαστριμύθων καὶ τὰς
τῶν τεθνηκότων ψυχὰς ἐκκαλουμένων ὡς οὕτως
γνωσομένῳ ποῖ χωρεῖν αὐτῷ μέλλει τὰ πράγματα·
330 τὸ γὰρ τῶν ἐγγαστριμύθων γένος ἀνάγον τὰς τῶν
νεκρῶν ψυχὰς δι' αὐτῶν προλέγει τοῖς δεομένοις τὰ
ἀποβησόμενα. μηνυθέντος δ' αὐτῷ παρά τινος τῶν
οἰκετῶν εἶναί τι γύναιον τοιοῦτον ἐν πόλει Δώρῳ,[2]
λαθὼν πάντας τοὺς ἐν τῷ στρατοπέδῳ καὶ μετεκδὺς
τὴν βασιλικὴν ἐσθῆτα δύο παραλαβὼν οἰκέτας, οὓς
ᾔδει πιστοτάτους ὄντας,[3] ἧκεν εἰς τὴν Δῶρον πρὸς
τὴν γυναῖκα καὶ παρεκάλει μαντεύεσθαι καὶ ἀνάγειν
331 αὐτῷ ψυχὴν οὗπερ ἂν αὐτὸς εἴπῃ. τῆς δὲ γυναικὸς
ἀπομαχομένης καὶ λεγούσης οὐ καταφρονήσειν τοῦ
βασιλέως, ὃς τοῦτο τὸ γένος τῶν μάντεων ἐξήλασεν,
οὐδ' αὐτὸν δὲ ποιεῖν καλῶς ἀδικηθέντα μηδὲν ὑπ'
αὐτῆς, ἐνεδρεύοντα δὲ εἰς τὰ κεκωλυμένα λαβεῖν
αὐτὴν ἵνα δῷ δίκην, ὤμοσε μηδένα γνώσεσθαι μηδὲ
παρ' ἄλλον ἄγειν αὐτῆς τὴν μαντείαν, ἔσεσθαι δ'
332 ἀκίνδυνον. ὡς δὲ τοῖς ὅρκοις αὐτὴν ἔπεισε μὴ
δεδιέναι, κελεύει τὴν Σαμουήλου ψυχὴν ἀναγαγεῖν
αὐτῷ. ἡ δ' ἀγνοοῦσα τὸν Σαμουῆλον ὅστις ἦν
καλεῖ τοῦτον ἐξ ᾅδου· φανέντος δ' αὐτοῦ θεα-

---

[1] ἰδόντα om. ROE.

[2] Ἀενδώρῳ MSP : Endor Lat.   [3] ἄνδρας RO : om. Lat.

mayed at sight of the hostile force which was very large and, as he surmised, superior to his own ; and he asked through the prophets for an oracle from God concerning the battle and its issue. But, as no response came from God, Saul was yet more afraid and his heart failed him, foreseeing inevitable disaster since the Deity was no longer at his side. However, he gave orders to search out for him a woman among the ventriloquists and those who call up the spirits of the dead, that so he might learn how matters would turn out for him. For this sort of ventriloquist raises up the spirits of the dead and through them foretells the future to those who inquire of them. Being informed by one of his servants that there was such a woman in the city of Dor,[a] Saul, without the knowledge of any in the camp, stripped off his royal robes and, accompanied by two servants whom he knew to be quite trustworthy, came to Dor to this woman and besought her to bring up for him by divination the soul of whomever he should name. The woman, however, objected, saying that she would not defy the king, who had expelled that class of diviners ; nor was it fair on his part, who had suffered no wrong from her, to lay this snare to catch her in forbidden acts and cause her to be punished. Thereupon Saul swore that none should know of it, that he would tell no one else of her divination and that she should be in no danger. Having by these oaths persuaded her to forget her fears, he bade her bring up for him the soul of Samuel. The woman, ignorant who Samuel was, summoned him from Hades. And when he

The witch raises the spirit of

---

[a] Bibl. Endor, LXX Ἀελδώρ (v.l. Ἀενδώρ, cf. v.l. in Josephus) ; modern 'Endor, about 3 miles N.E. of Shunem, on the slopes of Jebel Dūhy.

σάμενον τὸ γύναιον ἄνδρα σεμνὸν καὶ θεοπρεπῆ
ταράττεται, καὶ πρὸς τὴν ὄψιν ἐκπλαγέν, " οὐ σύ,"
φησίν, " ὁ βασιλεὺς εἶ Σαοῦλος; " ἐδήλωσε γὰρ
333 αὐτὸν Σαμουῆλος. ἐπινεύσαντος δ᾽ ἐκείνου καὶ
τὴν ταραχὴν αὐτῆς ἐρομένου πόθεν γένοιτο, βλέπειν εἶπεν ἀνελθόντα τῷ θεῷ τινα τὴν μορφὴν
ὅμοιον. τοῦ δὲ τὴν εἰκόνα φράζειν[1] καὶ τὸ σχῆμα
τοῦ θεαθέντος καὶ τὴν ἡλικίαν κελεύσαντος,[2] γέ-
ροντα μὲν ἤδη καὶ ἔνδοξον ἐσήμαινεν, ἱερατικὴν
334 δὲ περικείμενον διπλοΐδα. ἐγνώρισεν ἐκ τούτων ὁ
βασιλεὺς τὸν Σαμουῆλον ὄντα καὶ πεσὼν ἐπὶ τὴν
γῆν ἠσπάζετο καὶ προσεκύνησε· τῆς δὲ Σαμουήλου
ψυχῆς πυθομένης διὰ τί κινήσειεν αὐτὴν καὶ ἀν-
αχθῆναι ποιήσειεν, τὴν[3] ἀνάγκην ἀπωδύρετο· τοὺς
πολεμίους γὰρ[4] ἐπικεῖσθαι βαρεῖς αὐτῷ, αὐτὸν δὲ
ἀμηχανεῖν τοῖς παροῦσιν ἐγκαταλελειμμένον ὑπὸ
τοῦ θεοῦ καὶ μηδὲ[5] προρρήσεως τυγχάνοντα μήτε
διὰ προφητῶν μήτε δι᾽ ὀνειράτων, " καὶ διὰ τοῦτο
ἐπὶ σὲ τὸν[6] ἐμοῦ προνοησόμενον[7] κατέφυγον."
335 Σαμουῆλος δὲ τέλος αὐτὸν ἔχοντα ἤδη τῆς μεταβολῆς ὁρῶν " περισσὸν μέν," εἶπεν, " ἔτι καὶ παρ᾽
ἐμοῦ βούλεσθαι μαθεῖν τοῦ θεοῦ καταλελοιπότος
αὐτόν· ἄκουέ γε μὴν ὅτι βασιλεῦσαι δεῖ Δαυίδην
336 καὶ κατορθῶσαι τὸν πόλεμον, σὲ δὲ καὶ τὴν ἀρχὴν

---

[1] + εἰπόντος SPE.
[2] κελεύσαντος om. ROE.   [3] τὴν om. ROE.
[4] γὰρ Hudson cum cod. Vat.: om. rell.
[5] Dindorf: μήτε codd.   [6] + ἀεὶ M Lat.
[7] προνοησάμενον ed. pr. Lat.

---

[a] Scripture does not tell us how the witch recognized Saul;
1 Sam. xxviii. 12 " Why hast thou deceived me? for thou
art Saul." Rabbinic tradition accounts for it by the legend

appeared, the woman, beholding a venerable and Samuel, who foretells Saul's doom 1 Sam. xxviii. 11.
godlike man, was overcome and, in her terror at the
apparition, cried, " Art thou not King Saul ? " for
Samuel revealed who he was.[a]   When Saul indicated
that it was so and asked whence came her alarm, she
replied that she saw someone arise in form like God.
Saul then bade her describe the appearance, the
dress and the age of the man she saw, and she repre-
sented him as of advanced age, of distinguished
aspect and clad in a priestly mantle.[b]   By these
tokens the king recognized him to be Samuel and,
falling to the ground, saluted him and made obeisance.
Being asked by the shade of Samuel wherefore he
had disturbed him and caused him to be brought up,
Saul bewailed his necessity ; the enemy, he said, was
pressing heavily upon him and he was helpless in his
present plight, being abandoned by God and failing
to obtain an oracle whether through prophets or
through dreams. " That is why I have betaken
myself to thee, for thou wilt provide for me."   But
Samuel, seeing that Saul was now approaching a final
change of fortune,[c] said, " It is idle to seek to learn
any more from me, since God has abandoned thee.
But this much thou mayest hear, that David is
destined to be king and to achieve success in this war,
while thou must lose both thy sovereignty and thy

that spirits appear head downward unless summoned by a
king.

[b] Heb. *meʿîl* " upper garment " (A.V. " mantle "), LXX
διπλοίς. Josephus adds the word " priestly " because *meʿîl*
is the word used regularly in later Hebrew of the priest's
robe.   Tradition states that this garment worn by Samuel's
spirit was the same as that made for him by his mother when
he was a child (1 Sam. ii. 19) and that he had been buried in.

[c] Lit. " having already an end of change."

καὶ τὴν ζωὴν ἀπολέσαι, τοῦ θεοῦ παρακούσαντα
ἐν τῷ πρὸς Ἀμαληκίτας πολέμῳ καὶ τὰς ἐντολὰς
αὐτοῦ μὴ φυλάξαντα, καθὼς προεφήτευσά σοι καὶ
ζῶν. ἴσθι τοίνυν καὶ τὸν λαὸν ὑποχείριον τοῖς
ἐχθροῖς γενησόμενον καὶ σαυτὸν μετὰ τῶν τέκνων
αὔριον πεσόντα ἐπὶ τῆς μάχης μετ' ἐμοῦ γενησόμενον."

337 (3) Ταῦτ' ἀκούσας ὁ Σαοῦλος ἄφωνος ὑπὸ λύπης
ἐγένετο καὶ κατενεχθεὶς εἰς τοὔδαφος, εἴτε διὰ τὴν
προσπεσοῦσαν ἐκ τῶν δεδηλωμένων ὀδύνην, εἴτε
διὰ τὴν ἔνδειαν, οὐ γὰρ προσενήνεκτο τροφὴν τῇ
παρελθούσῃ ἡμέρᾳ τε καὶ νυκτί, ῥᾳδίως ἔκειτο
338 νέκυς ὥς τις.[1] μόλις δὲ ἑαυτοῦ γενόμενον συνηνάγκασεν ἡ γυνὴ γεύσασθαι, ταύτην αἰτουμένη
παρ' αὐτοῦ τὴν χάριν ἀντὶ τῆς παραβόλου μαντείας, ἣν οὐκ ἐξὸν αὐτῇ ποιήσασθαι διὰ τὸν ἐξ
αὐτοῦ φόβον ἀγνοουμένου τίς ἦν, ὅμως ὑπέστη
καὶ παρέσχεν. ἀνθ' ὧν παρεκάλει τράπεζάν τε
αὐτῷ παραθεῖναι καὶ τροφήν, ὡς ἂν τὴν ἰσχὺν
συλλεξάμενος εἰς τὸ τῶν οἰκείων ἀποσωθῇ στρα-
τόπεδον· ἀντέχοντα δὲ καὶ τελέως ἀπεστραμμένον
339 ὑπὸ ἀθυμίας ἐβιάσατο καὶ συνέπεισεν. ἔχουσα δὲ
μόσχον ἕνα συνήθη καὶ τῆς κατ' οἶκον ἐπιμελείας
καὶ τροφῆς ἀξιούμενον ὑπ' αὐτῆς, ὡς γυνὴ χερνῆτις
καὶ τούτῳ μόνῳ προσαναπαυομένη τῷ κτήματι,

---

[1] Niese: ἔκειτο νέκυς ὅστις RO: κατενήνεκτο MSP (Exc.):
non facile valebat exurgere Lat.

---

[a] Text uncertain.
[b] Or "joined (his servants) in constraining"; cf. 1 Sam.
xxviii. 23 "But his servants, together with the woman, com-
pelled him."
496

life, because thou disobeyedst God in the war with the Amalekites and didst not observe His commandments, even as I foretold to thee while I was alive. Know then that thy people shall be delivered into the hands of their foes and that thou thyself with thy sons shalt fall to-morrow in the battle, and thou shalt be with me."

(3) On hearing these words, Saul was made speechless by grief and, falling to the ground, whether from the shock inflicted by these revelations or through exhaustion—for he had taken no food during the past day and night—lay inert[a] as a corpse. Then, when with difficulty he had come to himself, the woman constrained[b] him to partake of food, asking this favour of him in return for that hazardous act of divination, which though not lawful for her to perform through fear of him so long as she had not recognized him,[c] she had nevertheless undertaken to carry out. Wherefore she entreated him to let her set a table with food before him, that so having collected his strength he might return safely to his own camp ; and, when in his despondency he refused and resolutely turned away, she insisted and helped to persuade him. Though she owned but one calf, which she had brought up[d] and had taken trouble to care for and feed beneath her roof, for she was a labouring woman and had to be content with this as her sole

The witch of Endor succours Saul.
1 Sam. xxviii. 20.

---

[c] The language of Josephus is ambiguous. It may mean that the witch feared to defy the king, whom she did not recognize in the person of Saul, or that she had been afraid to do Saul's bidding so long as she was ignorant of his identity.

[d] Lit. " familiar " or " tame " ; Heb. *marbeq* " tied up " (A.V. " fat," *cf.* Targum " fatted "), LXX δαμαλὶς νομάς " grazing heifer " (Luc. μοσχάριον γαλαθηνόν " sucking calf ").

κατασφάξασα τοῦτον καὶ τὰ κρέα παρασκευάσασα
τοῖς οἰκέταις αὐτοῦ καὶ αὐτῷ παρατίθησι. καὶ
Σαοῦλος μὲν διὰ τῆς νυκτὸς ἦλθεν εἰς τὸ στρατόπεδον.

340 (4) Δίκαιον δὲ ἀποδέξασθαι τῆς φιλοτιμίας τὴν
γυναῖκα, ὅτι καίπερ τῇ τέχνῃ κεκωλυμένη χρήσασθαι ὑπὸ τοῦ βασιλέως, παρ' ἧς ἂν αὐτῇ τὰ
κατὰ τὸν οἶκον ἦν ἀμείνω καὶ διαρκέστερα, καὶ
μηδέποτε αὐτὸν πρότερον τεθεαμένη οὐκ ἐμνησι-
κάκησε τῆς ἐπιστήμης ὑπ' αὐτοῦ καταγνωσθείσης,
οὐκ ἀπεστράφη δὲ ὡς ξένον καὶ μηδέποτε ἐν
341 συνηθείᾳ γεγενημένον, ἀλλὰ συνεπάθησέ τε καὶ
παρεμυθήσατο καὶ πρὸς ἃ διέκειτο λίαν ἀηδῶς
προετρέψατο, καὶ τὸ μόνον αὐτῇ παρὸν ὡς ἐν
πενίᾳ τοῦτο παρέσχεν ἐκτενῶς καὶ φιλοφρόνως,
οὔθ' ὑπὲρ εὐεργεσίας ἀμειβομένη τινὸς γεγενημένης οὔτε χάριν μέλλουσαν θηρωμένη, τελευτή-
σοντα γὰρ αὐτὸν ἠπίστατο, φύσει τῶν ἀνθρώπων
ἢ πρὸς τοὺς ἀγαθόν τι παρεσχημένους φιλοτιμουμένων, ἢ παρ' ὧν ἄν τι δύνωνται λαβεῖν ὄφελος
342 τούτους προθεραπευόντων. καλὸν οὖν ἐστι μιμεῖ-
σθαι τὴν γυναῖκα καὶ ποιεῖν εὖ πάντας τοὺς ἐν χρείᾳ
γενομένους, καὶ μηδὲν ὑπολαμβάνειν ἄμεινον μηδὲ
μᾶλλόν τι προσήκειν τῷ τῶν ἀνθρώπων γένει τούτου μηδ' ἐφ' ᾧ[1] τὸν θεὸν εὐμενῆ καὶ χορηγὸν τῶν
ἀγαθῶν ἕξομεν.[2] καὶ τὰ μὲν περὶ τῆς γυναικὸς
343 ἐν τοσούτοις ἀρκεῖ δεδηλῶσθαι· τὸν δὲ πόλεσι καὶ
δήμοις καὶ ἔθνεσι συμφέροντα λόγον καὶ προσ-

---

[1] ὅτῳ S[2] Vat. ap. Hudson.
[2] μᾶλλον ἕξομεν conj. Naber.

---

[a] The following eulogy of the witch of Endor is, of course,
an addition to Scripture.

498

possession, she slaughtered it, prepared the meat and set it before his servants and himself. And Saul that night returned to his camp.

(4) ^a Here it is but right to commend the generosity Eulogy of the witch of Endor. of this woman who, though she had been prevented by the king from practising an art which would have made it easier and more comfortable for her at home, and though she had never seen Saul before, yet bore him no resentment for having condemned her profession nor turned him away as a stranger and as one with whom she had never been acquainted ; but instead she gave him sympathy and consolation, exhorted him to do that which he regarded with great unwillingness,^b and offered him with open friendliness the one thing which in her poverty she possessed. And this she did, not in return for any benefit received, nor in quest of any favour to come—for she knew that he was about to die—, whereas men are by nature wont either to emulate those who have bestowed some kindness upon them or to be beforehand in flattering those from whom they may possibly receive some benefit. It is well, then, to take this woman for an example and show kindness to all who are in need, and to regard nothing as nobler than this or more befitting the human race or more likely to make God gracious and ready to bestow upon us His blessings. Concerning this woman, then, let these words suffice. ^c But now I shall touch on a subject Reflections on the heroism of Saul. profitable to states, peoples and nations, and of

---

^b That is, to partake of food.

^c Contrast the eulogy of Saul which follows (and is an addition to Scripture) with the characterization above, §§ 262 ff. So also rabbinic tradition is divided between blame of Saul's pride and praise of his heroism.

ήκοντα τοῖς ἀγαθοῖς, ὑφ᾽ οὗ προαχθήσονται πάντες
ἀρετὴν διώκειν[1] καὶ ζηλοῦν τὰ[2] δόξαν καὶ μνήμην
αἰώνιον παρασχεῖν δυνησόμενα,[3] ποιήσομαι, πολλὴν
καὶ βασιλεῦσιν ἐθνῶν καὶ ἄρχουσι πόλεων ἐπιθυμίαν καὶ σπουδὴν τῶν καλῶν ἐνθήσοντα, καὶ
πρός τε κινδύνους καὶ τὸν ὑπὲρ τῶν πατρίδων
θάνατον προτρεψόμενον, καὶ πάντων καταφρονεῖν
344 διδάξοντα τῶν δεινῶν. ἔχω δ᾽ αἰτίαν τοῦ λόγου
τούτου Σαοῦλον τὸν τῶν Ἑβραίων βασιλέα· οὗτος
γὰρ καίπερ εἰδὼς τὰ συμβησόμενα καὶ τὸν ἐπι-
κείμενον θάνατον τοῦ προφήτου προειρηκότος οὐκ
ἔγνω φυγεῖν αὐτὸν οὐδὲ φιλοψυχήσας προδοῦναι
μὲν τοὺς οἰκείους τοῖς πολεμίοις καθυβρίσαι δὲ
345 τὸ τῆς βασιλείας ἀξίωμα, ἀλλὰ παραδοὺς αὑτὸν
πανοικὶ μετὰ τῶν τέκνων τοῖς κινδύνοις καλὸν
ἡγήσατο εἶναι πεσεῖν μετὰ τούτων ὑπὲρ τῶν
βασιλευομένων μαχόμενος, καὶ τοὺς παῖδας ἀποθανεῖν μᾶλλον ἀγαθοὺς ὄντας ἢ καταλιπεῖν ἐπ᾽
ἀδήλῳ τῷ ποδαποὶ γενήσονται τὸν τρόπον· διάδοχον[4] γὰρ καὶ γένος τὸν ἔπαινον καὶ τὴν ἀγήρω
346 μνήμην ἕξειν. οὗτος οὖν δίκαιος καὶ ἀνδρεῖος καὶ
σώφρων ἔμοι γε δοκεῖ μόνος καὶ[5] εἴ τις γέγονε
τοιοῦτος ἢ γενήσεται τὴν μαρτυρίαν ἐπ᾽ ἀρετῇ καρ-
πποῦσθαι παρὰ πάντων ἄξιος· τοὺς γὰρ μετ᾽ ἐλπίδων
ἐπὶ πόλεμον ἐξελθόντας ὡς καὶ κρατήσοντας καὶ
σῶς[6] ὑποστρέψαντας,[7] ἐπειδάν τι διαπράξωνται
λαμπρόν, οὔ μοι δοκοῦσι καλῶς ποιεῖν ἀνδρείους

---

[1] Dindorf: διώξειν codd.
[2] ζηλοῦν τὰ] Bekker: ζηλοῦντα vel δηλοῦντα codd.: ζηλοῦν
τὸ Niese. [3] δυνησόμενον ROS[2] Exc.
[4] διαδοχὴν MSP Exc. [5] δοκεῖν καὶ μόνος conj. Niese.
[6] ἴσως RO: σώους MSP Exc.
[7] Bekker: ἐπιστρέψοντας codd.

interest to all good men—one whereby all should be
induced to pursue virtue and to aspire to those things
which may procure them glory and eternal renown,
one, moreover, that should instil into the hearts of
kings of nations and rulers of cities a great desire and
zeal for noble deeds, should stimulate them to face
dangers and death for their country's sake, and teach
them to despise all terrors. The occasion for this
discourse I find in the person of Saul, king of the
Hebrews. For he, although he knew of what was
to come and his impending death, which the prophet
had foretold, yet determined not to flee from it or,
by clinging to life, to betray his people to the enemy
and dishonour the dignity of kingship ; instead, he
thought it noble to expose himself, his house and his
children to these perils and, along with them, to fall
fighting for his subjects.[a] He preferred to have his
sons meet death as brave men rather than leave them
behind, while still uncertain what kind of men they
might prove to be ; for thus, as successors and
posterity, he would obtain glory and an ageless name.[b]
Such a man alone, in my opinion, is just, valiant and
wise, and he, if any has been or shall be such, deserves
to have all men acknowledge his virtue. For men who
have gone forth to war with high hopes, thinking to
conquer and return in safety, and have accomplished
some brilliant feat are, to my mind, mistakenly de-

[a] The rabbis also emphasize Saul's heroism in exposing
himself and his sons to danger in battle.

[b] That is, glory etc. would take the place of physical
posterity. The last phrase is perhaps a conscious echo of
ἀγήρων ἔπαινον in Pericles' funeral oration, Thucydides ii. 43.

ἀποκαλοῦντες, ὅσοι περὶ τῶν τοιούτων ἐν ταῖς
ἱστορίαις καὶ τοῖς ἄλλοις συγγράμμασιν εἰρήκασιν·
347 ἀλλὰ δίκαιοι μέν εἰσι κἀκεῖνοι τυγχάνειν ἀποδοχῆς,
εὔψυχοι δὲ καὶ μεγαλότολμοι καὶ τῶν δεινῶν κατα-
φρονηταὶ μόνοι δικαίως ἂν λέγοιντο πάντες οἱ
Σαοῦλον μιμησάμενοι. τὸ μὲν γὰρ οὐκ εἰδότας τί
μέλλει συμβήσεσθαι κατὰ τὸν πόλεμον αὐτοῖς μὴ
μαλακισθῆναι περὶ αὐτόν, ἀλλ' ἀδήλῳ τῷ μέλλοντι
παραδόντας αὐτοὺς ἐπ' αὐτοῦ σαλεύειν οὔπω[1] γεν-
348 ναῖον, κἂν ἔργα πολλὰ διαπραξάμενοι τύχωσι· τὸ
δὲ μηδὲν τῇ διανοίᾳ χρηστὸν προσδοκῶντας, ἀλλὰ
προειδότας ὡς δεῖ θανεῖν καὶ τοῦτο παθεῖν μαχομένους, εἶτα μὴ φοβηθῆναι μηδὲ καταπλαγῆναι τὸ
δεινόν, ἀλλ' ἐπ' αὐτὸ χωρῆσαι προγινωσκόμενον,
τοῦτ' ἀνδρείου ἀληθῶς τεκμήριον ἐγὼ κρίνω.
349 Σαοῦλος τοίνυν τοῦτο ἐποίησεν ἐπιδείξας ὅτι πάντας μὲν προσήκει τῆς μετὰ τὸν θάνατον εὐφημίας
γλιχομένους ταῦτα ποιεῖν, ἐξ ὧν ἂν αὐτοῖς ταύτην
καταλείποιεν,[2] μάλιστα δὲ τοὺς βασιλέας, ὡς οὐκ
ἐξὸν αὐτοῖς διὰ τὸ μέγεθος τῆς ἀρχῆς οὐ μόνον
οὐ κακοῖς εἶναι περὶ τοὺς ἀρχομένους, ἀλλ' οὐδὲ
350 μετρίως χρηστοῖς. ἔτι τούτων πλείω περὶ Σαούλου
καὶ τῆς εὐψυχίας λέγειν ἠδυνάμην, ὕλην ἡμῖν χορη-
γησάσης τῆς ὑποθέσεως, ἀλλ' ἵνα μὴ φανῶμεν
ἀπειροκάλως αὐτοῦ χρῆσθαι τοῖς ἐπαίνοις, ἐπάνειμι
πάλιν ἀφ' ὧν εἰς τούτους ἐξέβην.
351 (5) Κατεστρατοπεδευκότων γὰρ τῶν Παλαιστίνων, ὡς προεῖπον, καὶ κατὰ ἔθνη καὶ βασιλείας
καὶ σατραπείας ἐξαριθμούντων τὴν δύναμιν, τελευ-

---

[1] οὐδ' οὕτω(ς) M Exc.: οὐχ οὕτως SP: non valde Lat.
[2] καταλίποιεν SP: -λίποιε M.

scribed as valiant by the historians and other writers who have spoken of such persons. Certainly it is just that these too receive approbation ; but the terms " stout-hearted," " greatly daring," " contemptuous of danger " can justly be applied only to such as have emulated Saul. That men, not knowing what is to happen to them in war, should not flinch from it, but should commit themselves to an uncertain future and ride the stormy seas of chance—all this still falls short of magnanimity,[a] however many the exploits they may accomplish. On the other hand, to harbour in one's heart no hope of success, but to know beforehand that one must die and die fighting, and then not to fear nor be appalled at this terrible fate, but to meet it with full knowledge of what is coming—that, in my judgement, is proof of true valour. And this Saul did, thereby showing that it behoves all men who aspire to fame after death so to act as to leave such a name after them ; especially should kings do so, since the greatness of their power forbids them not merely to be bad to their subjects, but even to be less than wholly good. I might say still more than this about Saul and his courage, for they are subjects which afford us ample material ; but, lest we should appear to lack good taste in delivering this panegyric, I will return again to the point from which I made this digression.

(5) The Philistines had pitched their camp, as I said before, and were reviewing their forces by nations, kingdoms and satrapies,[b] when last of all

The Philistines compel Achish

---

[a] Variant " is not so magnanimous."

[b] Suggested by the LXX σατράπαι τῶν ἀλλοφύλων = Heb. *sarne Pelishtīm* (A.V. " lords of the Philistines ") ; cf. 1 Sam. xxix. 2 " And the lords of the Philistines passed on by hundreds and by thousands."

ταῖος βασιλεὺς παρῆλθεν Ἀγχοῦς μετὰ τῆς ἰδίας
στρατιᾶς καὶ[1] Δαυίδης μετὰ τῶν ἑξακοσίων ὁπλιτῶν
352 εἵπετο. θεασάμενοι δὲ αὐτὸν οἱ στρατηγοὶ τῶν
Παλαιστίνων, πόθεν εἴησαν ἥκοντες οἱ Ἑβραῖοι
καὶ τίνων καλεσάντων ἠρώτων τὸν βασιλέα. ὁ δὲ
Δαυίδην ἔλεγεν εἶναι, ὃν[2] φυγόντα Σαοῦλον τὸν
ἑαυτοῦ δεσπότην καὶ πρὸς αὐτὸν ἐλθόντα δέξασθαι,
καὶ νῦν τῆς χάριτος ἀμοιβὴν ἐκτῖσαι βουλόμενον
καὶ τιμωρήσασθαι τὸν Σαοῦλον συμμαχεῖν αὐτοῖς.
353 ἐμέμφθη δὲ ὑπὸ τῶν στρατηγῶν ἄνδρα παρειληφὼς
ἐπὶ συμμαχίᾳ πολέμιον, καὶ ἀποπέμπειν συνεβούλευον, μὴ καὶ λάθῃ μέγα δι' αὐτὸν κακὸν τοὺς
φίλους ἐργασάμενος· καιρὸν[3] γὰρ αὐτῷ[4] παρέξειν
τοῦ καταλλαγῆναι[5] πρὸς τὸν δεσπότην κακώσαντι[6]
354 τὴν ἡμετέραν δύναμιν. ὃ δὴ καὶ προορώμενον εἰς
τὸν τόπον ὃν ἔδωκεν αὐτῷ κατοικεῖν ἐκέλευον
ἀποπέμπειν σὺν τοῖς ἑξακοσίοις ὁπλίταις· τοῦτον
γὰρ εἶναι τὸν[7] Δαυίδην, ὃν ᾄδουσιν αἱ παρθένοι
πολλὰς μυριάδας Παλαιστίνων ἀπολέσαντα. ταῦτ'
ἀκούσας ὁ τῶν Γιττῶν βασιλεὺς καὶ καλῶς εἰρῆσθαι
λογισάμενος καλέσας τὸν Δαυίδην "ἐγὼ μέν,"
355 εἶπε, "μαρτυρῶ σοι πολλὴν περὶ ἐμὲ σπουδὴν καὶ
εὔνοιαν καὶ διὰ τοῦτό σε σύμμαχον ἐπηγόμην· οὐ
δοκεῖ δὲ ταὐτὸ τοῖς στρατηγοῖς. ἀλλ' ἄπιθι μεθ'
ἡμέραν εἰς ὃν ἔδωκά σοι τόπον μηδὲν ὑπονοῶν
ἄτοπον, κἀκεῖ φύλασσέ μοι τὴν χώραν, μή τινες
εἰς αὐτὴν τῶν πολεμίων ἐμβάλωσιν. ἔστι δὲ καὶ

---

1 + μετὰ τοῦτον (αὐτὸν) δ' (δὲ) ὁ MSPE: et post eum Lat.
    2 Niese: τὸν codd.   3 M Lat.: καὶ rell.
        4 οὕτω RO.   5 + πρόφασιν SP.
            6 Naber: κακώσαντα vel κακώσοντα codd.
                7 τὸν om. MSPE.

appeared King Anchūs with his own troops, followed by David with his six hundred soldiers. On seeing him, the Philistine generals asked the king whence these Hebrews [a] had come and who had summoned them. The king replied that this was David who had fled from Saul, his master, and had come to him ; he had received him, and now David, wishing to repay that favour and to be avenged on Saul, was fighting in their ranks.[b] The generals, however, reproached him for having taken as an ally one that was their enemy, and they advised him to dismiss him lest on David's account he should unwittingly do grave mischief to his friends ; for he would be affording David an opportunity of becoming reconciled to his master by injuring their army. Accordingly they bade him with this in mind to send David with his six hundred soldiers back to the place which he had given him for his habitation ; for this was that same David of whom the virgins sang that he had slain many myriads of the Philistines. Having listened to these words and considering them well spoken, the king of Gitta called David and said, " For myself, I can testify to the great zeal and friendliness which thou hast shown to me, and it was for that reason that I brought thee as an ally ; but such is not the view of our chiefs. Now then, go within a day's time to the place which I have given thee, and suspect nothing untoward. There keep guard for me over the country, lest any of the enemy invade it. That too

---

[a] So the Hebrew, *'Ibrîm* ; lxx, reading *'ôbrîm* " passersby," has διαπορευόμενοι.

[b] This explanation of David's motives is added by Josephus.

356 τοῦτο συμμαχίας μέρος.'' καὶ Δαυίδης μέν, ὡς
ἐκέλευσεν ὁ τῶν Γιττῶν βασιλεύς, ἧκεν εἰς Σέκελλαν. καθ' ὃν δὲ καιρὸν ἐξ αὐτῆς συμμαχήσων τοῖς
Παλαιστίνοις ἀπῆλθε τὸ τῶν Ἀμαληκιτῶν ἔθνος
ἐπελθὸν αἱρεῖ τὴν Σέκελλαν κατὰ κράτος, καὶ
ἐμπρήσαντες καὶ πολλὴν λείαν[1] ἔκ τ' αὐτῆς ἐκείνης
καὶ τῆς ἄλλης τῶν Παλαιστίνων χώρας λαβόντες
ἀνεχώρησαν.

357 (6) Ἐκπεπορθημένην δὲ τὴν Σέκελλαν καταλαβὼν ὁ Δαυίδης καὶ διηρπαγμένα πάντα καὶ τὰς
γυναῖκας τὰς ἑαυτοῦ, δύο γὰρ ἦσαν, καὶ τὰς
γυναῖκας τῶν ἑταίρων σὺν τοῖς τέκνοις ἠχμαλω-
358 τισμένας, περιρρήγνυται εὐθὺς τὴν ἐσθῆτα. κλαίων
δὲ καὶ ὀδυρόμενος μετὰ τῶν φίλων ἐπὶ τοσοῦτον
παρείθη τοῖς κακοῖς, ὥστε αὐτὸν ἐπιλιπεῖν ἤδη
καὶ τὰ δάκρυα· ἐκινδύνευσε[2] δὲ καὶ βληθεὶς ὑπὸ
τῶν ἑταίρων ἀλγούντων ἐπὶ ταῖς αἰχμαλωσίαις τῶν
γυναικῶν καὶ τῶν τέκνων ἀποθανεῖν· αὐτὸν γὰρ
359 τῶν γεγονότων ᾐτιῶντο. ἀνασχὼν δ' ἐκ τῆς λύπης
καὶ τὴν διάνοιαν πρὸς τὸν θεὸν ἀναστήσας παρεκάλεσε τὸν ἀρχιερέα Ἀβιάθαρον ἐνδύσασθαι τὴν
ἱερατικὴν στολὴν καὶ ἐπερωτῆσαι τὸν θεὸν καὶ
προφητεῦσαι εἰ διώξαντι τοὺς Ἀμαληκίτας δίδωσι
καταλαβεῖν καὶ σῶσαι μὲν τὰς γυναῖκας καὶ τὰ
360 τέκνα, τιμωρήσασθαι δὲ τοὺς ἐχθρούς. τοῦ δ'
ἀρχιερέως διώκειν κελεύσαντος ἐκπηδήσας μετὰ
τῶν ἑξακοσίων ὁπλιτῶν εἵπετο τοῖς πολεμίοις· παραγενόμενος δ' ἐπί τινα χειμάρρουν Βάσελον λεγό-

---

[1] λείαν ἄλλην codd.: ἄλλην om. Lat.
[2] κινδυνεῦσαι RO.

---

[a] This last instruction to guard Philistine territory is an
amplification of the LXX addition to 1 Sam. xxix. 11, φν-

is the part of an ally." [a] So David, as the king of David finds
Ziklag
Gitta ordered, went to Sekella. But at the very sacked
time when he had left there to lend aid to the Phi- by the
Amalekites.
listines, the Amalekite nation had made an invasion 1 Sam.
and taken Sekella by storm, and, after setting fire xxx. 1.
to it and capturing much booty both from that town
and from the rest of the Philistine territory, had
retired.

(6) Now when David found that Sekella had been The
sacked and everything therein pillaged and that his Israelites
mourn for
two wives and the wives of his comrades along with their
their children had been taken captive, he straightway captured
wives and
rent his clothes,[b] and, wailing and lamenting with children.
his friends, he was so utterly undone by this calamity 1 Sam.
xxx. 4.
that at length even tears failed him. Moreover he
was not far from being stoned to death by his comrades, who were deeply grieved by the capture of
their wives and children, and held him responsible
for what had happened. Recovering from his grief,
however, and lifting his thoughts to God, he besought
the high priest Abiathar to put on his priestly robe [c]
and to inquire of God and predict to him whether, if
he pursued the Amalekites, He would grant him
to overtake them, and to rescue the women and
children and avenge himself on his foes. And when God
the high priest bade him pursue, he rushed off with commands
David to
his six hundred soldiers on the track of the enemy. pursue the
On reaching a stream called Baselos,[d] he came upon Amalekites
1 Sam.
xxx. 8.

λάσσειν τὴν γῆν ; the Hebrew says merely " And David and
his men rose early in the morning to return to the land of the
Philistines."

[b] The rending of the clothes is an unscriptural detail.

[c] 1 Sam. xxx. 7 " bring me hither the ephod."

[d] Bibl. Besor, lxx Βοσόρ ; site unknown.

μενον καὶ πλανωμένῳ τινὶ περιπεσὼν Αἰγυπτίῳ
μὲν τὸ γένος ὑπ' ἐνδείας δὲ καὶ λιμοῦ παρει-
μένῳ, τρισὶ γὰρ ἡμέραις ἐν τῇ ἐρημίᾳ πλανώμενος
ἄσιτος διεκαρτέρησε, πρῶτον αὐτὸν ποτῷ καὶ
τροφῇ παραστησάμενος καὶ ἀναλαβὼν ἐπύθετο
361 τίς¹ τε εἴη καὶ πόθεν. ὁ δὲ γένος μὲν ἐσήμαινεν
Αἰγύπτιος ὤν, καταλειφθῆναι δὲ ὑπὸ τοῦ δεσπότου
κατ' ἀρρωστίαν ἔπεσθαι μὴ δυνάμενον· ἐδήλου δ'
αὐτὸν² τῶν καταπρησάντων καὶ διηρπακότων ἄλλα
362 τε τῆς Ἰουδαίας καὶ τὴν Σέκελλαν εἶναι. χρησάμενος οὖν ὁ Δαυίδης τούτῳ ἐπὶ τοὺς Ἀμαληκίτας
ὁδηγῷ καὶ καταλαβὼν αὐτοὺς³ ἐπὶ γῆς ἐρριμ-
μένους, καὶ τοὺς μὲν ἀριστῶντας, τοὺς δὲ καὶ
μεθύοντας ἤδη καὶ λελυμένους ὑπὸ τοῦ οἴνου καὶ
τῶν λαφύρων καὶ τῆς λείας ἀπολαύοντας, ἐπιπεσὼν
αἰφνιδίως πολὺν αὐτῶν φόνον εἰργάσατο· γυμνοὶ
γὰρ ὄντες καὶ μηδὲν προσδοκῶντες τοιοῦτον, ἀλλὰ
πρὸς τὸ πιεῖν καὶ εὐωχεῖσθαι τετραμμένοι πάντες
363 ἦσαν εὐκατέργαστοι. καὶ οἱ μὲν αὐτῶν ἔτι τῶν
τραπεζῶν παρακειμένων ἐπικαταλαμβανόμενοι παρ'
αὐταῖς ἀνῃροῦντο καὶ παρέσυρεν αὐτοῖς τὰ σιτία
καὶ τὴν τροφὴν τὸ αἷμα, τοὺς δὲ δεξιουμένους
ἀλλήλους ταῖς προπόσεσι διέφθειρεν, ἐνίους δὲ καὶ
πρὸς ὕπνον ὑπὸ τοῦ ἀκράτου κατενηνεγμένους.
ὁπόσοι δ' ἔφθασαν περιθέμενοι τὰς πανοπλίας ἐξ
ἐναντίας αὐτῷ⁴ στῆναι, τούτους οὐδὲν ἧττον εὐχερῶς
364 τῶν γυμνῶν κατακειμένων ἀπέσφαττε.⁵ διέμειναν
δὲ οἱ σὺν τῷ Δαυίδῃ καὶ αὐτοὶ⁶ ἀναιροῦντες ἀπὸ

---

¹ τίνος MSP Lat. (cf. lxx).
² Edd.: αὐτὸν ROM: αὐτῷ SP.   ³ αὐτοὺς om. RO.
⁴ ed. pr.: τε (τ') αὐτῷ codd.   ⁵ ἀπέσφαττον RO.
⁶ αὐτὸς conj. Niese.

a straggler, an Egyptian by race, who was exhausted from want and hunger, having endured three days' wandering in the wilderness without food. After he had first revived him and restored him with food and drink, David asked him who he was [a] and whence he came. He revealed that he was of Egyptian race and had been left behind by his master, being unable to follow because of sickness ; he further made known that he was one of those who had burnt and ravaged Sekella as well as parts of Judaea. So David made use of the man to guide him to the Amalekites, and came upon them lying around on the ground, some at their morning meal, others already drunken and relaxed with wine, regaling themselves with their spoils and booty. Falling suddenly upon them, he made a great slaughter of them, for, being unarmed and expecting no such thing but intent upon drinking and revelry, they were all an easy prey. Some, being surprised at the outspread tables, were massacred beside them, and their streaming blood swept victuals and food away ; others were drinking each other's health when he slew them ; still others, under the influence of strong drink, were plunged in sleep ; while those who had been quick enough to put on their armour and make a stand against him—these too he cut to pieces with no less ease than those who lay defenceless on the ground.[b] David's companions too continued the slaughter from the first

David's men surprise the Amalekites and massacre them.

1 Sam. xxx. 15.

---

[a] Variant (as in Scripture) "to whom he belonged."
[b] The details of the massacre are an amplification of Scripture.

πρώτης ὥρας ἕως ἑσπέρας, ὡς μὴ περιλειφθῆναι
τῶν Ἀμαληκιτῶν πλείονας ἢ τετρακοσίους· καὶ
οὗτοι δὲ δρομάσι καμήλοις ἐπιβάντες διέφυγον.
ἀνέσωσε δὲ τά τ᾽ ἄλλα¹ πάντα ἃ διήρπασαν αὐτῶν
οἱ πολέμιοι καὶ τάς τε αὑτοῦ γυναῖκας καὶ τὰς
365 τῶν ἑταίρων. ὡς δὲ ἀναστρέφοντες ἧκον ἐπὶ τὸν
τόπον, ἔνθα διακοσίους μὴ δυναμένους αὐτοῖς
ἕπεσθαι καταλελοίπεσαν ἐπὶ τῶν σκευῶν, οἱ μὲν
τετρακόσιοι τῆς μὲν ἄλλης ὠφελείας τε καὶ λείας
οὐκ ἠξίουν αὐτοῖς ἀπομερίζειν· οὐ συνακολουθή-
σαντας γὰρ ἀλλὰ μαλακισθέντας περὶ τὴν δίωξιν
ἀγαπήσειν ἀνασεσωσμένας τὰς γυναῖκας ἀπολαμ-
366 βάνοντας ἔλεγον· Δαυίδης δὲ πονηρὰν καὶ ἄδικον
αὐτῶν ταύτην ἀπέφηνε τὴν γνώμην· εἶναι γὰρ
ἀξίους, τοῦ θεοῦ παρασχόντος αὐτοῖς ἀμύνασθαι
μὲν τοὺς πολεμίους, κομίσασθαι δὲ πάντα τὰ
αὐτῶν, πᾶσιν ἐξ ἴσου τοῖς συστρατευσαμένοις μερί-
ζεσθαι τὴν ὠφέλειαν, καὶ ταῦτ᾽ ἐπὶ φυλακῇ τῶν
367 σκευῶν μεμενηκότων. καὶ ἐξ ἐκείνου νόμος οὗτος
ἐκράτησε παρ᾽ αὐτοῖς ἵνα ταὐτὰ τοῖς μαχομένοις
λαμβάνωσιν οἱ τὰ σκεύη φυλάσσοντες. γενόμενος
δ᾽ ἐν Σεκέλλᾳ Δαυίδης διέπεμψε πᾶσι τοῖς ἐν τῇ
Ἰούδα φυλῇ συνήθεσι καὶ φίλοις ἀπομοίρας τῶν
λαφύρων. καὶ τὰ μὲν περὶ τὴν Σεκέλλων πόρθησιν
καὶ Ἀμαληκιτῶν ἀναίρεσιν οὕτως ἐγένετο.

368   (7) Τῶν δὲ Παλαιστίνων συμβαλόντων καὶ καρ-
τερᾶς μάχης γενομένης νικῶσιν² οἱ Παλαιστῖνοι καὶ
πολλοὺς ἀναιροῦσι τῶν ἐναντίων, Σαοῦλος δὲ ὁ

---

¹ Niese: τὰ ἄλλα vel τἆλλα codd.
² νικῶσι μὲν SP Lat.

hour until evening, so that there were left of the
Amalekites no more than four hundred; these, by
mounting swift camels, had escaped. So David recovered not only the booty which the enemy had
carried off, but also his wives and those of his companions. When, on their return, they arrived at the
spot where they had left in charge of the baggage
two hundred men who were unable to follow, the
other four hundred were unwilling to share with them
in their gains and booty, saying that, as they had not
gone along but had been unequal to the pursuit, they
ought to be content with getting back their wives
who had been rescued. But David pronounced this
view of theirs wicked and unjust; for, he said, seeing
that God had enabled them to avenge themselves
on their enemies and to recover all their possessions,
they were bound to give an equal share of their gains
to all who had taken part in the expedition, especially
as they had remained to guard the baggage. And
thenceforward this law has prevailed among them,
that those who guard the baggage receive the same
share as those who do the fighting. Moreover, on
his return to Sekella, David sent around portions
of the spoils to all his acquaintances and friends in
the tribe of Judah.[a] Such, then, was the affair of
the sacking of Sekella and the slaughter of the
Amalekites.

(7) Meanwhile[b] the Philistines had joined battle
with the Israelites and, after a sharp contest, the
Philistines were victorious and slew multitudes of

*A dispute
about spoils
is equitably
decided by
David.
1 Sam. xxx.
21.*

*The
Philistines
defeat the
Israelites at*

---

[a] Bibl. "to the elders of Judah, to his friends" (LXX
"kinsmen"). Josephus omits the names of the favoured
cities, 1 Sam. xxx. 27-30.

[b] Continuing the account of the battle near Mt. Gilboa
from §§ 327 ff.

τῶν Ἰσραηλιτῶν βασιλεὺς καὶ οἱ παῖδες αὐτοῦ γενναίως ἀγωνιζόμενοι καὶ πάσῃ προθυμίᾳ χρώμενοι,
ὡς ἐν μόνῳ τῷ καλῶς ἀποθανεῖν καὶ παραβόλως
διακινδυνεῦσαι τοῖς πολεμίοις τῆς ὅλης αὐτοῖς δόξης
ἀποκειμένης, οὐδὲν γὰρ τούτου περισσότερον εἶχον,
369 ἐπιστρέφουσι πᾶσαν εἰς αὐτοὺς τὴν τῶν ἐχθρῶν
φάλαγγα καὶ περικυκλωθέντες ἀποθνήσκουσι πολλοὺς τῶν Παλαιστίνων καταβαλόντες. ἦσαν δὲ οἱ
παῖδες[1] Ἰωνάθης καὶ Ἀμινάδαβος[a] καὶ Μέλχισος.[b]
τούτων πεσόντων τρέπεται τὸ τῶν Ἑβραίων πλῆθος
καὶ ἀκοσμία καὶ σύγχυσις γίνεται καὶ φόνος ἐπι-
370 κειμένων τῶν πολεμίων. Σαοῦλος δὲ φεύγει τὸ
καρτερὸν ἔχων[2] περὶ αὐτόν· καὶ τῶν Παλαιστίνων
ἐπιπεμψάντων ἀκοντιστὰς καὶ τοξότας πάντας μὲν
ἀποβάλλει πλὴν ὀλίγων, αὐτὸς δὲ λαμπρῶς ἀγωνισά-
μενος καὶ πολλὰ τραύματα λαβών, ὡς μηκέτι δια-
καρτερεῖν μηδ᾽ ἀντέχειν ταῖς πληγαῖς, ἀποκτεῖναι
μὲν αὐτὸν ἠσθένει, κελεύει δὲ τὸν ὁπλοφόρον σπα-
σάμενον τὴν ῥομφαίαν ταύτην αὐτοῦ διελάσαι, πρὶν
371 ζῶντα συλλαβεῖν αὐτὸν τοὺς πολεμίους. μὴ τολμῶντος δὲ τοῦ ὁπλοφόρου κτεῖναι τὸν δεσπότην,
αὐτὸς τὴν ἰδίαν σπασάμενος[3] καὶ στήσας ἐπὶ τὴν
ἀκμὴν ῥίπτει κατ᾽ αὐτῆς ἑαυτόν· ἀδυνατῶν δὲ[4]
μήτ᾽[5] ὤσασθαι[6] μήτ᾽ ἐπερείσας διαβαλεῖν αὐτοῦ
τὸν σίδηρον ἐπιστρέφεται, καὶ νεανίσκου τινὸς
ἑστῶτος πυθόμενος τίς εἴη καὶ μαθὼν ὡς Ἀμαλη-

---

[1] Σαούλου παῖδες MSP Lat.
[2] καρτερὸν στῖφος ἔχων M : καρτερὸν ἔχων στῖφος SP.
[3] + μάχαιραν SP Lat. Glycas.
‘δὲ ins. Niese: ἀδυνατῶν RO : καὶ μὴ δυνάμενος MSPE.
[5] μηδ᾽ codd.   [6] ἵστασθαι RO.

---

[a] So most mss. of the lxx (v.l. Ἰωναδάβ) ; bibl. Abinadab.
[b] Bibl. Melchishua (Heb. Malki-shu'a), lxx Μελχεισά.

their adversaries. Saul, king of Israel, and his sons struggled valiantly and threw all their ardour into the fight, as though their entire glory rested solely on their dying nobly and desperately hazarding all against the enemy, for nothing else was left them. Thus they drew upon themselves the whole line of the foe and, so surrounded, perished, after laying many of the Philistines low. Now his sons were Jonathan, Aminadab [a] and Melchis.[b] When these fell, the Hebrew host took flight, disorder and confusion ensued, and there was a massacre as the enemy fell upon them. But Saul fled, having the ablest men around him ; of these, when the Philistines sent javelin-throwers and archers after him, he lost all but a few. He himself, after fighting magnificently and receiving numerous wounds,[c] until he could no longer hold out nor endure under these blows, was too weak to kill himself and bade his armour-bearer draw his sword and thrust it through him before the enemy should take him alive. But, as the armour-bearer did not dare to slay his master, Saul drew his own sword himself and, fixing it with its point toward him, sought to fling himself upon it, but was unable either to push it in or, by leaning upon it, to drive the weapon home. Then he turned [d] and, seeing a youth standing there, asked him who he was, and, on learning that he was an Amalekite,

Marginal notes:

Mt. Gilboa. Saul's sons are slain. 1 Sam. xxxi. 1.

Saul, too weak to kill himself, bids an Amalekite slay him. 1 Sam. xxxi. 4 ; 2 Sam. i. 6.

---

[c] So the LXX ἐτραυματίσθη, 1 Sam. xxxi. 3, translating Heb. *wayyāḥel*, which the Targum and Jewish interpreters render "was afraid." The details of the rout are unscriptural.

[d] Josephus has combined the contradictory accounts of Saul's death given by Scripture in 1 Sam. xxxi. and 2 Sam. i. In the earlier account Saul kills himself after his armour-bearer declines to do so through fear ; in the later chapter he is slain, at his own request, by the Amalekite. Josephus repeats the second account below, *A*. vii. 1 ff.

κίτης ἐστὶ παρεκάλεσεν ἐπερείσαντα τὴν ῥομφαίαν,
διὰ τὸ μὴ ταῖς χερσὶν αὐτὸν τοῦτο δύνασθαι
ποιῆσαι,[1] παρασχεῖν αὐτῷ τελευτὴν ὁποίαν αὐτὸς
372 βούλεται. ποιήσας δὲ τοῦτο καὶ περιελόμενος τὸν
περὶ τὸν βραχίονα αὐτοῦ χρυσὸν καὶ τὸν βασιλικὸν
στέφανον ἐκποδὼν ἐγένετο. θεασάμενος δ' ὁ ὁπλο-
φόρος Σαοῦλον ἀνῃρημένον ἀπέκτεινεν ἑαυτόν· δι-
εσώθη δ' οὐδεὶς τῶν σωματοφυλάκων τοῦ βασιλέως,
ἀλλὰ πάντες ἔπεσον περὶ τὸ καλούμενον Γελβουὲ
373 ὄρος. ἀκούσαντες δὲ τῶν Ἑβραίων οἱ τὴν κοιλάδα
πέραν τοῦ Ἰορδάνου κατοικοῦντες καὶ οἱ ἐν τῷ
πεδίῳ τὰς πόλεις ἔχοντες, ὅτι Σαοῦλος πέπτωκε
καὶ οἱ παῖδες αὐτοῦ, καὶ τὸ σὺν αὐτῷ πλῆθος ἀπό-
λωλε, καταλιπόντες τὰς ἑαυτῶν πόλεις εἰς ὀχυ-
ρότητας[2] ἔφυγον. οἱ δὲ Παλαιστῖνοι τὰς κατα-
λελειμμένας ἐρήμους εὑρόντες κατῴκησαν.
374   (8) Τῇ δ' ἐπιούσῃ σκυλεύοντες οἱ Παλαιστῖνοι
τοὺς τῶν πολεμίων νεκροὺς ἐπιτυγχάνουσι τοῖς
τοῦ Σαούλου καὶ τῶν παίδων αὐτοῦ σώμασι καὶ
σκυλεύσαντες ἀποτέμνουσιν αὐτῶν τὰς κεφαλάς,
καὶ κατὰ πᾶσαν περιήγγειλαν τὴν χώραν πέμψαντες ὅτι πεπτώκασιν οἱ πολέμιοι· καὶ τὰς μὲν
πανοπλίας αὐτῶν ἀνέθηκαν εἰς τὸ Ἀσταρτεῖον
ἱερόν, τὰ δὲ σώματα ἀνεσταύρωσαν πρὸς τὰ τείχη
τῆς Βηθσὰν[3] πόλεως, ἢ νῦν Σκυθόπολις καλεῖται.
375 ἐπεὶ δὲ ἤκουσαν οἱ ἐν Ἰαβεῖ[4] πόλει τῆς Γαλαδίτιδος
κατοικοῦντες, ὅτι λελώβηνται τὸν Σαούλου νεκρὸν

---

[1] τοῦτο . . . ποιῆσαι MSP: δύνασθαι RO: διὰ τὸ . . .
ποιῆσαι om. E Lat.
[2] Cocceii: ὀχυροτάτας (-ωτάτας) codd.
[3] RO: Βηθσιὼν rell.: Bessam Lat.
[4] E: Ναβεῖ RO: Ἰαβ(ε)ισσῷ SP: Iabes Lat.

begged him to force the sword in, since he could not
do this with his own hands, and so procure him such
a death as he desired. This he did, and, after stripping off the bracelet of gold on Saul's arm and his
royal crown, disappeared. Then the armour-bearer,
seeing that Saul was dead, killed himself ; and of
the king's bodyguard not a man escaped, but all fell
on that mountain called Gelboue. And when the
Hebrews who inhabited the valley across the Jordan
and those who had their cities in the plain *a* heard
that Saul and his sons had fallen and that all his host
had perished, they forsook their cities and fled to the
strongholds *b* ; and the Philistines, finding these cities
deserted, settled therein.

1 Sam. xxxi. 7.

(8) On the morrow the Philistines, while stripping
the corpses of their enemies, came upon the bodies
of Saul and his sons ; these they stripped and cut off
their heads, and then sent tidings throughout all the
country round about that their enemies had fallen.
Their armour they set up as an offering in the temple
of Astarte,*c* and impaled their bodies to the walls of
the city of Bethsan,*d* which is now called Scythopolis.
But when the inhabitants of Jabis *e* in the region of
Galaditis heard that they had mutilated the corpses

The men of Jabesh-Gilead bury the mutilated bodies of Saul and his sons.
1 Sam. xxxi. 11.

---

a Of Esdraelon.

b Emended text ; mss. " to the strongest (cities)." Scripture says simply " they fled."

c 1 Sam. xxxi. 10 does not make clear where the temple
was ; 1 Chron. x. 10 reads " And they put his armour in the
house of their gods, and fastened his head in the temple of
Dagon," that is, in Philistia. Recent excavations have uncovered a Canaanite temple of the fifteenth century B.C.
and figures of Astarte (bibl. Ashtoreth) in Beth Shan.

d Bibl. Beth-Shan, LXX Βαιθσάν (*v.l.* Βαιθέμ), modern
Beisan, cf. A. v. 83 note.

e Bibl. Jabesh-Gilead, *cf.* § 71 note.

JOSEPHUS

καὶ τοὺς τῶν παίδων αὐτοῦ, δεινὸν ἡγησάμενοι
περιιδεῖν ἀκηδεύτους, ἐξελθόντες οἱ ἀνδρειότατοι
καὶ τόλμῃ διαφέροντες (ἡ δὲ πόλις αὕτη καὶ σώμασιν ἀλκίμους καὶ ψυχαῖς φέρει) καὶ δι᾽ ὅλης τῆς
376 νυκτὸς ὁδεύσαντες ἦλθον εἰς Βηθσάν· καὶ προσ-
ελθόντες τῷ τείχει τῶν πολεμίων καὶ καθελόντες
τὸ σῶμα Σαούλου καὶ τὰ τῶν παίδων αὐτοῦ κομίζουσιν εἰς Ἰάβησαν μηδὲ τῶν πολεμίων αὐτοὺς
κωλῦσαι δυνηθέντων ἢ¹ τολμησάντων διὰ τὴν ἀν-
377 δρείαν. οἱ δὲ Ἰαβησηνοὶ πανδημεὶ κλαύσαντες²
θάπτουσι τὰ σώματα ἐν τῷ καλλίστῳ τῆς χώρας
τόπῳ Ἀρούρης λεγομένῳ, καὶ πένθος ἐφ᾽ ἡμέρας
ἑπτὰ σὺν γυναιξὶ καὶ τέκνοις ἐπ᾽ αὐτοῖς ἦγον
κοπτόμενοι καὶ θρηνοῦντες τὸν βασιλέα καὶ τοὺς
παῖδας αὐτοῦ μήτε τροφῆς μήτε ποτοῦ γευσάμενοι.
378 (9) Τοῦτο Σαοῦλος τὸ τέλος ἔσχε προφητεύσαντος
Σαμουήλου διὰ τὸ παρακοῦσαι τοῦ θεοῦ τῶν ἐπ᾽
Ἀμαληκίταις ἐντολῶν, καὶ ὅτι τὴν Ἀβιμελέχου
τοῦ ἀρχιερέως γενεὰν καὶ Ἀβιμέλεχον αὐτὸν καὶ
τὴν τῶν ἀρχιερέων πόλιν ἀνεῖλεν. ἐβασίλευσε δὲ
Σαμουήλου ζῶντος ἔτη ὀκτὼ πρὸς τοῖς δέκα, τελευτήσαντος δὲ δύο καὶ εἴκοσι.³ καὶ Σαοῦλος μὲν
οὕτω κατέστρεψε τὸν βίον.

¹ δυν. ἢ om. ROE.   ² καύσαντες conj. Niese (cf. lxx).
³ δ. καὶ εἴκοσι] duos Lat.

ᵃ Unscriptural detail.
ᵇ So the mss., κλαύσαντες; Niese conjectures καύσαντες
"having burnt," to make Josephus agree with Scripture,
1 Sam. xxxi. 12.
ᶜ So the lxx; Heb. ᾽ēshel, a kind of tree; cf. § 251 note.
ᵈ Cf. § 336.
ᵉ Josephus agrees with rabbinic tradition in making the

516

of Saul and his sons, they were horrified at the thought
of leaving them unburied, and so the most valiant
and hardy among them—and this city breeds men
stalwart of body and soul—set forth and, having
marched all night, reached Bethsan. Then, having
advanced to the enemy's ramparts and taken down
the bodies of Saul and his sons, they bore them to
Jabēsa, and the enemy was neither able nor dared to
hinder them, because of their prowess.ᵃ The Jabē-
sēnians with public mourning ᵇ buried the bodies in
the fairest spot in their country, called Aroura ᶜ
(" Plowland "), and, with their wives and children,
continued for seven days to mourn for them, beating
the breast and bewailing the king and his sons, without touching either meat or drink.

(9) To such an end did Saul come, as Samuel had
predicted, because he had disobeyed God's commandments touching the Amalekites,ᵈ and because he had
destroyed the family of Abimelech the high priest
and Abimelech himself and the city of the high
priests.ᵉ He reigned eighteen years during the lifetime of Samuel and for twenty-two ᶠ years more after
the latter's death. Thus then did Saul depart this life.

Brief
summary of
Saul's reign.
Cf. 1 Chron.
c. 13.

slaughter of the priests of Nob one of the reasons for Saul's
doom, but omits reference to the sin of consulting the witch,
cf. 1 Chron. x. 13.

ᶠ Or (with Lat.) " two," *i.e.* 20 years in all, instead of 40.
This would agree with *A.* x. 143 and with later Jewish
tradition (*Sepher Yuḥasin*) citing this passage. No figures
are given in Scripture, but *cf.* the LXX addition to 1 Sam.
xiii. 1 stating that Saul reigned 2 years (Luc. 30 years). On
the other hand the tradition in Acts xiii. 21 gives 40 years.
Rappaport suggests that a Christian scribe has changed the
text of Josephus here to " twenty-two " to make it conform
to the New Testament, and that the author of *Sepher Yuḥasin*
is indirectly combating this view.

AN ANCIENT TABLE OF CONTENTS

ΒΙΒΛΙΟΝ Δ

α΄. Ἑβραίων δίχα τῆς Μωυσέος γνώμης μάχη πρὸς Χαναναίους καὶ ἧττα.

β΄. Στάσις Κορέου καὶ τοῦ πλήθους πρὸς Μωυσῆν καὶ τὸν ἀδελφὸν αὐτοῦ περὶ τῆς ἱερωσύνης.

γ΄. Τὰ συμβάντα τοῖς Ἑβραίοις ἐν τῇ ἐρήμῳ ἔτεσιν ὀκτὼ καὶ τριάκοντα.[1]

δ΄. Ὡς Σηχῶνα καὶ Ὤγην τοὺς Ἀμορραίων βασιλεῖς νικήσας Μωυσῆς καὶ τὴν στρατιὰν [ἅπασαν][2] αὐτῶν διαφθείρας κατεκλήρωσεν αὐτῶν τὴν χώραν δυσὶ φυλαῖς καὶ ἡμισείᾳ τῶν Ἑβραίων.[3]

ε΄. Μωυσέος πολιτεία καὶ πῶς ἐξ ἀνθρώπων ἠφανίσθη.

Περιέχει ἡ βίβλος αὕτη[4] χρόνον ἐτῶν τριάκοντα καὶ ὀκτώ.

---

[1] + δ΄ (om. P) ὡς οἱ μὲν τῆς στάσεως κατάρξαντες διεφθάρησαν κατὰ βούλησιν τοῦ θεοῦ, τὴν δ' ἱερωσύνην Ἀαρὼν ὁ Μωϋσέως ἀδελφὸς κάτεσχε καὶ οἱ ἔγγονοι (ἔκγ. P) αὐτοῦ: L inserts this section between (ii) and (iii).

[2] om. Lat.: trs. αὐτῶν ἅπασαν SP.

[3] + ς΄ (om. PL) περὶ Βαλάμου τοῦ μάντεως καὶ ποταπὸς (ποταπὸν S) ἦν τὸ εἶδος. ὡς ἐπὶ Μαδιανίτας Ἑβραῖοι στρατεύσαντες ἐκράτησαν αὐτῶν SPL.   [4] R Lat.: om. rell.

518

AN ANCIENT TABLE OF CONTENTS

BOOK IV

This books covers a period of thirty-eight years.

[a] Gr. Sēchon and Ogēs; the latter is more precisely described in the text (*A.* iv. 96) as " king of Galadene and Gaulanitis."

519

ΒΙΒΛΙΟΝ Ε

α΄.[1] Ὡς Ἰησοῦς ὁ στρατηγὸς τῶν Ἑβραίων πολεμήσας πρὸς Χαναναίους καὶ κρατήσας αὐτῶν τοὺς μὲν διέφθειρε τὴν δὲ γῆν κατακληρουχήσας διένειμε ταῖς φυλαῖς.

β΄. Ὡς ἀποθανόντος τοῦ στρατηγοῦ παραβαίνοντες οἱ Ἰσραηλῖται τοὺς πατρίους νόμους μεγάλων ἐπειράθησαν συμφορῶν, καὶ στασιασάντων ἡ Βενιαμὶς διεφθάρη φυλὴ χωρὶς ἀνδρῶν ἑξακοσίων.

γ΄. Πῶς μετὰ ταύτην τὴν κακοπραγίαν ἀσεβήσαντας αὐτοὺς ὁ θεὸς Ἀσσυρίοις ἐδούλωσεν.

δ΄. Ἡ διὰ Κενίζου τοῦ Ἀθνιήλου[2] παιδὸς αὐτοῖς ἐλευθερία γενομένη ἄρξαντος ἔτη τεσσαράκοντα λεγομένου δὲ παρά τε Ἕλλησι καὶ Φοίνιξι κριτοῦ.

ε΄. Ὅτι πάλιν ὁ λαὸς ἡμῶν ἐδούλευσε Μωαβίταις ὀκτωκαίδεκα ἔτη καὶ ὑπό τινος Ἰούδου[3] τῆς

---

[1] Numeros om. MSPL.
[2] Bernard : Ἀενιήλου ROML : Ναθαναήλου S : Ναθαήλου P.
[3] Niese : Ἰουδοῦς ROL : Ἠουδοῦς MS : Ἰουδοῦ, ι ex ἡ corr. P : Aod Lat.

---

[a] Bibl. Othniel, the son of Kenaz ; cf. A. v. 182 note.

520

ANCIENT TABLE OF CONTENTS

BOOK V

δουλείας ἀπηλλάγη τὴν ἀρχὴν ἐπ' ἔτη κατασχόντος ὀγδοήκοντα.

ϛ'. Ὡς Χαναναίων αὐτοὺς καταδουλωσαμένων ἐπ' ἔτη εἴκοσιν ἠλευθερώθησαν ὑπὸ Βαράκου καὶ Δεβώρας, οἳ ἦρξαν αὐτῶν ἐπ' ἔτη τεσσαράκοντα.

ζ'. Ὅτι πολεμήσαντες Ἀμαληκῖται τοῖς Ἰσραηλίταις ἐνίκησάν τε καὶ τὴν χώραν ἐκάκωσαν ἔτη ἑπτά.

η'. Ὡς Γεδεὼν αὐτοὺς ἠλευθέρωσεν ἀπὸ Ἀμαληκιτῶν καὶ ἦρξε τοῦ πλήθους ἐπὶ ἔτη τεσσαράκοντα.

θ'. Ὅτι μετ' αὐτὸν πολλοὶ γενόμενοι διάδοχοι τοῖς πέριξ ἔθνεσιν ἐπολέμησαν ἱκανῷ χρόνῳ.

ι'. Περὶ τῆς Σαμψῶνος ἀνδρείας καὶ ὅσων κακῶν αἴτιος Παλαιστίνοις ἐγένετο.

ια'. Ὡς οἱ υἱοὶ Ἠλὶ τοῦ ἱερέως ἐσφάγησαν ἐν τῇ πρὸς Παλαιστίνους μάχῃ.

ιβ'. Ὡς ὁ πατὴρ αὐτῶν ἀκούσας τὴν συμφορὰν βαλὼν ἑαυτὸν ἀπὸ τοῦ θρόνου ἀπέθανεν.

ιγ'. Ὡς νικήσαντες ἐν τούτῳ τῷ πολέμῳ τοὺς Ἑβραίους οἱ Παλαιστῖνοι καὶ τὴν κιβωτὸν αὐτῶν αἰχμάλωτον ἔλαβον.

ιδ'. Ὡς οἱ ἀπὸ Κενίζου[1] ἄρξαντες πάντες κριταὶ ἐκλήθησαν.[2]

[1] Κενέζου SP.
[2] Caput XIV om. Lat.

---

[a] The Amalekites are mentioned only incidentally as allies of the Midianites in A. v. 210 ff.

[b] These were Abimelech, Jair, Jephthah, Ibzan, Elon and Abdon.

[c] This table omits special mention of the stories of Ruth, §§ 318-337; and Samuel, §§ 341-351.

[d] "Tumbled" in A. v. 359.

ANCIENT TABLE OF CONTENTS

[e] Section xiii properly belongs before section xii.
[f] Section xiv is obviously out of place; originally it must
have belonged to section iv.

523

Περιέχει ἡ βίβλος χρόνον ἐτῶν τετρακοσίων ἑβδομήκοντα.[1]

ΒΙΒΛΙΟΝ ϛ

α΄.[2] Φθορὰ Παλαιστίνων καὶ τῆς γῆς αὐτῶν ἐξ ὀργῆς τοῦ θεοῦ διὰ τὴν αἰχμαλωτευθεῖσαν ὑπ᾽ αὐτῶν κιβωτόν, καὶ τίνα τρόπον ἀπέπεμψαν αὐτὴν τοῖς Ἑβραίοις.

β΄. Στρατεία Παλαιστίνων ἐπ᾽ αὐτοὺς καὶ νίκη Ἑβραίων Σαμουήλου στρατηγοῦντος αὐτῶν τοῦ προφήτου.

γ΄. Ὡς Σαμουῆλος διὰ τὸ γῆρας ἀσθενὴς ὢν τὰ πράγματα διοικεῖν τοῖς παισὶν αὐτοῦ ἐνεχείρισεν.

δ΄. Ὡς οὐ καλῶς προϊσταμένων ἐκείνων τῆς ἀρχῆς, τὸ πλῆθος ὑπ᾽ ὀργῆς ᾐτήσατο βασιλεύεσθαι.

ε΄. Σαμουήλου πρὸς τοῦτο ἀγανάκτησις καὶ βασιλέως αὐτοῖς ἀνάδειξις Σαούλου τοὔνομα, κελεύσαντος τοῦ θεοῦ.

ϛ΄. Σαούλου στρατεία ἐπὶ τὸ Ἀμμανιτῶν ἔθνος καὶ νίκη καὶ διαρπαγὴ τῶν πολεμίων.[3]

ζ΄. Ὡς στρατευσάμενοι πάλιν ἐπὶ τοὺς Ἑβραίους οἱ Παλαιστῖνοι ἡττήθησαν.

η΄. Σαούλου πρὸς Ἀμαληκίτας πόλεμος καὶ νίκη.

---

[1] + ἑξ (οϛ΄ P) SPEL Lat.
[2] Numeros om. SP.
[3] πολεμίων ἤ (καὶ P) τῶν πόλεων SP.

ANCIENT TABLE OF CONTENTS

This book covers a period of four hundred and seventy [a] years.

BOOK VI

[a] Variant " seventy-six."

θ΄. Ὅτι παραβαίνοντος Σαούλου τὰς ἐντολὰς τοῦ προφήτου Σαμουῆλος ἄλλον ἀπέδειξε βασιλέα κρύφα Δαυίδην¹ ὄνομα κατ᾽ ἐπιτροπὴν τοῦ θεοῦ.

ι΄. Ὡς καὶ πάλιν ἐπεστράτευσαν τοῖς Ἑβραίοις οἱ Παλαιστῖνοι ἔτι Σαούλου βασιλεύοντος.²

ια΄.³ Μονομαχία Δαυίδου τότε⁴ πρὸς Γολίαθον τὸν ἄριστον τῶν Παλαιστίνων καὶ ἀναίρεσις τοῦ Γολιάθου καὶ ἧττα τῶν Παλαιστίνων.⁵

ιβ΄. Ὡς θαυμάσας Σαοῦλος⁶ τὸν Δαυίδην τῆς ἀνδρείας συνῴκισεν αὐτῷ τὴν θυγατέρα.

ιγ΄. Ὅτι μετὰ ταῦτα ὕποπτον αὐτῷ τὸν Δαυίδην γενόμενον ὁ βασιλεὺς ἐσπούδασεν ἀποκτεῖναι.

ιδ΄. Ὡς πολλάκις καὶ Δαυίδης κινδυνεύσας ἀποθανεῖν ὑπὸ τοῦ Σαούλου διέφυγε καὶ Σαοῦλον δὶς ἐπ᾽ αὐτῷ γενόμενον ὥστε ἀνελεῖν οὐ διεχρήσατο.

ιε΄. Ὡς στρατευσαμένων Παλαιστίνων πάλιν ἐπὶ τοὺς Ἑβραίους ἡττήθησαν οἱ Ἑβραῖοι τῇ μάχῃ καὶ ὁ βασιλεὺς αὐτῶν Σαοῦλος ἀπέθανε μετὰ τῶν παίδων μαχόμενος.

Περιέχει ἡ βίβλος χρόνον ἐτῶν λβ΄.

---

¹ Δανείδην M : Δαβίδην RO : Dauid Lat.
² Σαούλου βασιλεύοντος] Σαμουήλου προφητεύοντος P.
³ Caput XI decimo adiungunt SP.
⁴ τότε om. SP.   ⁵ + κρατερά SP.
⁶ Σαοῦλος (Σαούλου RO) post θυγατέρα tr. ROM.

ANCIENT TABLE OF CONTENTS

This book covers a period of thirty-two years.

[a] This table omits special mention of the relations of David and Jonathan, the sojourn of David among the Philistines, and Saul's visit to the witch of Endor.